Uncertain Risks Regulated

Uncertain Risks Regulated compares various models of risk regulation in order to understand how these systems shape the relationship between law and science, and how they attempt to overcome public distrust in science-based decision making. The book contributes to the ongoing debate relating to uncertainty and risks – and the difficulties faced by the European Union in particular – in regulating these issues, taking account of both national and international constraints.

The term 'uncertain risk' is comparable with notions of hazard and indeterminate risk, as deployed within the social sciences; but it also aims to capture the modern regulatory reality that a non-quantifiable hazard must still be addressed by society, law and its regulators. Decisions must be taken in the face of uncertainty. And, while it is not possible to provide clear cut models of risk regulation, in focusing on regulatory practices at a national, EU and international level, the contributors to this volume aim to use fact finding as a core instrument of learning for risk regulation.

Michelle Everson is Professor of European Union Law at Birkbeck College, University of London. She has researched widely in the field of European Law and has particular interests in the areas of European regulatory law, European administrative and constitutional law and European citizenship.

Ellen Vos is Professor of European Union Law at the Law Faculty of Maastricht University. She has published extensively in the field of EU law, institutional law (comitology and agencies), market integration and risk regulation (precautionary principle; food safety).

Law, Science and Society

Law's role has often been understood as one of implementing political decisions concerning the relationship between science and society. Increasingly, however, as our understanding of the complex dynamic between law, science and society deepens, this instrumental characterisation is seen to be inadequate, but as yet we have only a limited conception of what might take its place. If progress is to be made in our legal and scientific understanding of the problems society faces, then there needs to be space for innovative and radical thinking about law and science. *Law, Science and Society* is intended to provide that space.

The overarching aim of the series is to support the publication of new and groundbreaking empirical or theoretical contributions that will advance understanding between the disciplines of law, and the social, pure and applied sciences. General topics relevant to the series include studies of:

- law and the international trade in science and technology;
- risk and the regulation of science and technology;
- law, science and the environment;
- the reception of scientific discourses by law and the legal process;
- law, chaos and complexity;
- law and the brain.

Uncertain Risks Regulated

Edited by
Michelle Everson and Ellen Vos

Routledge
Taylor & Francis Group
LONDON AND NEW YORK

First published 2009 by Routledge-Cavendish

Published 2019 by Routledge
2 Park Square, Milton Park, Abingdon, Oxon OX14 4RN
52 Vanderbilt Avenue, New York, NY 10017

First issued in paperback 2012

Routledge is an imprint of the Taylor & Francis Group, an informa business

British Library Cataloguing in Publication Data
A catalogue record for this book is available from the British Library

Library of Congress Cataloging-in-Publication Data
A catalogue record for this book has been requested

Typeset in Baskerville by RefineCatch Limited, Bungay, Suffolk

ISBN13: 978–0–41554–252–4 (pbk)
ISBN13: 978–1–84472–162–7 (hbk)

Contents

Foreword and acknowledgements

This book aims to compare various models of risk regulation in order to better understand how these systems shape the relationship established between law and science, and how they seek to overcome a public lack of trust in science-based decision making. Building upon the potential of existing systems to act as a productive learning process, the book seeks to provide a positive contribution to the ongoing debate about uncertainty and risk, and, in particular, to suggest various ways in which the European Union might overcome the specific obstacles that it faces attempting to regulate these issues.

The book deploys a notion of 'uncertain risk'. This term is comparable with concepts of hazard and indeterminate risk used within the social sciences, but seeks also to capture the specific modern regulatory reality that non-quantifiable hazard must still be addressed by society, law and its regulators. Decisions must be taken in the face of uncertainty. As such, the book does not present us with clear models of risk regulation. Rather, the book focuses on regulatory practices at national, EU and international level, with the aim of using fact finding as a core instrument of learning for risk regulation.

The book therefore begins with a critical analysis of the principles that currently act to orient risk regulation and, in particular, investigates the limits to the precautionary principle as a regulative legal norm in cases of 'uncertain' or incalculable risk. Subsequently, national, EU and international (WTO) models on foodstuffs and biotechnology are examined (Parts II and III). The study of the regulatory framework of foodstuffs deals with food safety, while the study of biotechnology discusses non-food issues, in particular the framework regulating the environmental aspects and the commercialisation of GMOs. It examines the different schemes of institutional organisation that are currently applied, seeking to highlight learning processes around issues of procedure, participation and deliberation. In particular, this section highlights the pragmatic efforts made at national, European and international level to integrate scientific expertise within public decision-making structures. It is a feature of real-world risk regulation that the learning processes that cluster around it necessitate the constant re-assessment and re-evaluation of regulatory structures. Accordingly individual contributions also highlight ongoing processes of institutional reform, addressing, in particular, the crisis in public confidence.

Drawing on these findings, the book then moves on to highlight and examine general problems of legitimacy and the potential loss of credibility within the regulation of uncertain risks. Notions of participation, procedural requirements and deliberative initiatives characterise national, European and international learning processes about risk regulation, albeit to differing degrees. Accordingly, Part IV focuses on each issue in turn, seeking both at the theoretical and pragmatic level to sketch out and explore solutions to the intractable problem of the regulating of uncertain risk.

We would like to thank a few colleagues without whom this book would not have been possible. First and foremost, thanks go to Marina Jodogne, who provided invaluable assistance through her able and patient work in the formatting and editing of this book. Marina is not only a true professional but also a lovely person to work with. We would like to thank Tanja Ehnert, Valerie Kelley and Babette Vos, all of whom helped us with proofreading and checking all the footnotes. We would also like to thank Kate Murphy, Holly Davis and Colin Perrin of Routledge-Cavendish, Julian Bates, copy editor, and Bob Banbury of RefineCatch Ltd for all their skilful assistance and support in the publishing of this book. Last but not least, we would like to thank the Netherlands Organisation of Scientific Research (NWO) for having supported us financially under the Innovational Research Scheme.

Michelle Everson and Ellen Vos

List of abbreviations

AB	Appellate Body
ACAF	Advisory Committee on Animal Feedingstuffs
ACNFP	Advisory Committee on Novel Foods and Processes
ACRE	Advisory Committee on Releases into the Environment
AEBC	Agriculture and Environment Biotechnology Commission
AFFSA	Agence Française de Sécurité Sanitaire des Aliments (French Food Safety Agency)
AFNOR	Association Française de Normalisation (French standards association)
AHPA	Animal Health Protection Act
AOC	Appellation d'Origine Contrôlée (Controlled Term of Origin)
APHIS	Animal and Plant Health Inspection Service
ARiMR	Agencja Restrukuryzacji i Modernizacji Rolnictwa (Polish Agency for the Restructuring and Modernisation of Agriculture)
ARR	Agencja Rynku Rolnego (Polish Agricultural Market Agency)
ATSDR	Agency for Toxic Substances and Disease Registry
BEUC	Bureau Européen des Unions de Consommateurs (European Consumers' Organisation)
BNA	Bureau of National Affairs
BSE	Bovine Spongiform Encephalopathy
CAD	Canadian Dollar
CAP	Common Agricultural Policy
CBF	Commission for Biotechnology and Food
CBOS	Centrum Badania Opinii Społecznej (Polish Public Opinion Research Centre)
CCMAS	Codex Committee on Methods of Analysis and Sampling
CCRVDF	Codex Committee for Residues of Veterinary Drugs in Foods
CEN	Comité Européen de Normalisation (European Committee for Standardization)
CENLEC	Comité Européen de Normalisation Electrotechnique (European Committee for Electronical Standardization)
CEQ	Council on Environmental Quality
CFI	Court of First Instance
CFR	Code of Federal Regulations
CGEM	Commission du Genie Biomoléculaire (Biomolecular Engineering Commission)

CNA	Conseil National de l'Alimentation (French National Food Council)
CNRS	Centre National de la Recherche Scientifique (National Center for Scientific Research)
CO_2	Carbon dioxide
COGEM	Commission on Genetic Manipulation
COKZ	Centraal Orgaan voor Kwaliteitsaangelegenheden in de Zuivel (Netherlands Controlling Authority for Milk and Milk Products)
COM	Commission
CTG	College ter Beoordeling van Geneesmiddelen (Medicines Evaluation Board)
CVD	Chief Veterinary Doctor
DEFRA	Department of the Environment, Food and Rural Affairs
DG	Directorate General
DG SANCO	DG Santé et Protection des Consommateurs (Directorate General for Health and Consumer Affairs)
DGAL	Direction Générale de l'Alimentation (Department of the French Ministry of Agriculture)
DNA	Deoxyribonucleic Acid
DNV	Det Norske Veritas
DSU	Dispute Settlement Understanding
EA	Environmental Assessment
EC	European Community
ECJ	European Court of Justice
ECR	European Court Report
ECT	European Community Treaty
EEC	European Economic Community
EFSA	European Food Safety Authority
EIS	Environmental Impact Statement
EP	European Parliament
EPA	US Environmental Protection Agency
EPLA	Environmental Protection Law Act
EPSPs	Excitatory Post-Synaptic Potentials
EU	European Union
EZ	Ministrie van Economische Zaken (Dutch Ministry of Economic Affairs)
FACA	Federal Advisory Committee Act
FAO	Food and Agriculture Organization
FDA	Food and Drug Administration
FFDCA	Federal Food, Drug and Cosmetic Act
FIFRA	Federal Insecticide, Fungicide and Rodenticide Act
FNSEA	Fédération Nationale des Syndicats d'Exploitants Agricoles (French Farmers' Union)
FOIA	Freedom of Information Act
FQPA	Food Quality Protection Act
FSA	Food Standards Agency
FSCs	Foreign Sales Corporations
FSEs	Farm Scale Evaluations
FVO	Food and Veterinary Office

GALA	General Administrative Law Act
GATS	General Agreement on Trade in Services
GATT	General Agreement on Tariffs and Trade
GE	Genetically Engineered
GFL	General Food Law
GM	Genetically Modified
GMHT	Genetically Modified Herbicide Tolerant
GMO	Genetically Modified Organism
GMP	Good Manufacturing Practices
GRAS	Generally Recognised As Safe
GSP	Generalised System of Preferences
HACCP	Hazard Analysis Critical Control Point
HHS	Health and Human Services
ICNIRP	International Commission on Non-Ionising Radiation Protection
IDF	International Dairy Federation
IJC	International Joint Commission
INAO	Institut National des Appellations d'Origine
INGO	International Non-Governmental Organisation
INRA	Inland Northwest Research Alliance
InVS	Institut de Veille Sanitaire (French Sanitary Surveillance Institute)
IPCC	Intergovernmental Panel on Climate Change
IPPC	International Plant Protection Convention
ISEEF	Integrated Socio-Ethical Evaluation Framework
ISO	International Standards Organization
JECFA	Joint FAO/WHO Expert Committee on Food Additives
JEMRA	Joint FAO/WHO Expert Meetings on Microbiological Risk Assessment
JMPR	Joint FAO/WHO Meeting on Pesticide Residues
KvW	Keuringsdienst van Waren (Inspectorate for Health Protection and Veterinary Public Health)
LEI	Landbouw Economisch Institute (Agricultural Economic Research Institute)
LNV	Ministerie van Landbouw, Natuurbeheer en Voedselkwaliteit (Dutch Ministry of Agriculture)
LOAEL	Lowest Observed Adverse Effect Level
MAFF	Ministry of Agriculture, Fisheries and Food (UK)
MB	Management Board
MDW	Marktwerking, Deregulering en Wetgevingskwalieit (Market mechanisms, Deregulation and other Quality Measures)
MEB	Medicines Evaluation Board
MLs	Maximum Levels
MLC	Meat and Livestock Commission
MRLs	Maximum Residue Levels
NAS	National Academies
NEPA	National Environmental Policy Act
NGO	Non-governmental Organisation
NIABA	Nederlandse Biotechnologie Associatie (Dutch Biotechnology Association)

NOAEL	No Observed Adverse Effect Level
NRC	National Research Council
NRDC	Natural Resources Defense Council
OECD	Organisation for Economic Co-operation and Development
OGM	Organisme Génétiquement Modifié (Genetically Modified Organism)
OIE	Office International des Epizooties (World Organisation for Animal Health)
OJ	Official Journal
OSTP	Office of Science and Technology Policy
PACs	Polycyclic Aromatic Carbonates
PAHs	Polycyclic Aromatic Hydrocarbons
PCBs	Polychlorinated Biphenyls
PCS	Polish Committee for Standardisation
PIFB	Pew Initiative on Food and Biotechnology
PIPs	Plant-Incorporated Protectants
R&D	Research and Development
RASFF	Rapid Alert System for Food and Feed
rBST	Recombinant Bovine Somatotropin
REACH	Registration, Evaluation, Authorisation of Chemicals
RfC	Reference Concentration
RfD	Reference Dose
RIKILT	Rijks- en Kwaliteitsinstituut voor Land- en Tuinbouwproducten (Dutch Institute of Food Safety)
RIVM	Rijksinstituut voor Volksgezondheid en Milieu (Dutch National Institute for Public Health and the Environment)
RMNO	Raad voor Ruimtelijk, Milieu en Natuuronderzoek (Dutch Advisory Council for Research on Spatial Planning, Nature and the Environment)
RVV	Rijksdienst voor de keuring van Vee en Vlees (Dutch National Inspection Service for Livestock and Meat)
SARS	Severe Acute Respiratory Syndrome
SCAN	Scientific Committee on Animal Nutrition
SCFCAH	Standing Committee on the Food Chain and Animal Health
SCIMAC	Supply Chain Initiative on Modified Agricultural Crops
SCOOP	Scientific Cooperation
SEAC	Spongiform Encephalopathy Advisory Committee
SPS	Sanitary and PhytoSanitary
SSC	Scientific Steering Committee
SSI	State Sanitary Inspectorate
StCFe	Standing Committee on Feeding-stuffs
STS	Science and Technology Studies
TBT	Technical Barriers to Trade
TNO	Nederlands Instituut voor Toegepast Natuurwetenschappelijk Onderzoek (Dutch Institute for Applied Natural Science)
TRIPs	Trade-Related Aspects of Intellectual Property Rights
TSCA	Toxic Substances Control Act
UK	United Kingdom

UKIE	Urząd Komitetu Integracji Europejskiej (Polish Office of the Committee for European Integration)
UNECE	United Nations Economic Commission for Europe
UP	University Press
US	United States
USA	United States of America
USC	United States Code
USD	United States Dollar
USDA	United States Department of Agriculture
USTR	United States Trade Representative
vCJD	variant Creutzfeldt-Jakob Disease
VOC	Volatile Organic Compound
VROM	Volkshuisvesting, Ruimtelijke Ordening en Milieubeheer (Dutch Ministry of Housing, Spatial Planning and the Environment)
VWA	Voedsel en Waren Autoriteit (Food and Consumer Product Safety Authority)
VWS	Ministerie van Volksgezondheid, Welzijn en Sport (Ministry of Public Health, Welfare and Sports)
WBGU	Wissenschaftliche Beirat der Bundesregierung Globale Umweltveränderungen (German Advisory Council on Global Change)
WHO	World Health Organization
WTO	World Trade Organization
WUR	Wageningen University and Research Centre
ZBOs	Zelfstandige Bestuursorganen (Autonomous Administrative Bodies)

List of contributors

Marjolein B.A. van Asselt holds the Risk Governance chair at the Department of Technology and Science Studies at Maastricht University. Her research interests are focused on uncertainty, risk, knowledge-expertise-and-society, as well as on interdisciplinary methodology.

Julien Besançon is a Ph.D. candidate at the Centre de Sociologie des Organisations (CNRS) of Sciences-PO, Paris. He works on the transformations of the French food safety regulation system and on the development of health safety agencies in France.

Olivier Borraz is a senior fellow researcher at the Centre de Sociologie des Organisations (CNRS) and he teaches at Sciences-PO, Paris. His research and teaching are on risk governance and the politics of risk.

Patrycja Dąbrowska is a lecturer in EU law at the Centre for Europe, University of Warsaw. Her research and teaching interests include EU governance and risk regulation (biotechnology and GMOs, food safety and the environment) as well as EU institutional and administrative law. Her recent publications include articles on GMO regulations and governance in the EU.

Michelle Everson is Professor of European Union Law at the School of Law, Birkbeck College, University of London, UK. She has researched widely in the field of European law and has particular interests in the areas of European regulatory law, European administrative and constitutional law, and European citizenship.

Elizabeth Fisher is a Tutorial Fellow in Law at Corpus Christi College and CUF lecturer in the Faculty of Law at the University of Oxford. She has written widely on the precautionary principle and technological risk regulation.

Christian Joerges is Professor at the University of Bremen as well as fellow and member of the advisory council of the Centre for European Law and Politics (ZERP). His recent publications deal with the Europeanisation of Economic and Private Law, transnational risk regulation, compliance and legitimacy problems of transnational governance arrangement. A further long-term project deals with anti-liberal traditions of legal thought in Germany and other European countries.

Andreas Klinke is head of the research group 'Governance of Infrastructures' at the Social Science Department at the Aquatic Research Institute in Dübendorf, Switzerland. He published widely on risk evaluation, risk management, international governance, and public deliberation.

Harry Kuiper is co-ordinator of the SAFE FOODS project and was senior researcher at the Institute of Food Safety, RIKILT, Wageningen University Research Centre, The Netherlands. He is also a member of the GMO Panel of the European Food Safety Authority. He has published extensively in the area of GMOs.

Maria Lee is Professor in Law at University College London. She has published widely in environmental law, and recently completed a book on the regulation of agricultural biotechnology in the EU, published by Edward Elgar in 2008.

Marielle Matthee is researcher in International and European Law associated with the University of Maastricht. Her research is concerned with the role of the Codex Alimentarius Commission and its standards.

Bernd van der Meulen is Professor of Law and Governance at Wageningen University. He is also Chairman of the Dutch Food Law Association and Director of the European Institute for Food Law. The Law and Governance Group focuses its research and teaching on the legal and socio-legal aspects of natural resources and the agro-food-chain (see www.law.wur.nl).

Christine Noiville is working as a CNRS (National Centre for Scientific Research) senior researcher in Pantheon-Sorbonne Faculty of Law (Université Paris 1, UMR CNRS 8103). She is directing the research centre 'Droit, sciences et techniques'. Most of her publications focus on the precautionary principle, international trade, health, medical, environmental or biotechnology law, and industrial property.

Bram Rooijackers is a Master's student at the Department of Technology and Science Studies of Maastricht University.

Mark A. Pollack is Associate Professor of Political Science at Temple University. His research agenda focuses on the role of international institutions in the regional and global governance, with specific projects examining the delegation of powers to the supranational organisations in the European Union, the creation of new mechanisms for the governance of the transatlantic relationship, and the 'mainstreaming' of gender issues in international organisations.

Michael Rodemeyer is an Instructor in the Department of Science, Technology and Society at the University of Virginia. He was the founding Executive Director of the Pew Initiative on Food and Biotechnology, a non-profit research and education project of the University of Richmond. He is presently a part-time senior consultant to the Initiative.

Henry Rothstein is Deputy Director of the King's Centre for Risk Management, King's College London. His publications include the co-authored *The Government of Risk* (OUP, 2001) and numerous articles on risk regulation and its reform in journals such as *Public Administration, Economy and Society* and *Science, Technology and Human Values.*

Joanne Scott is Professor of European Union Law, Director of the Centre for Law and Governance in Europe, and Vice-Dean for International Links, at University College London. Her main areas of research are in EU Law, WTO Law, and the interface between the two. She is particularly interested in law and new approaches to governance, with a specific interest in environment and public health.

Gregory Shaffer is Melvin C. Steen Professor of Law at University of Minnesota Law School. He teaches courses in a number of subject areas, including international trade law, international law, European Union law, international business transactions, and a variety of research seminars.

Han Somsen is Professor of Law, Technology and Science at the Tilburg Institute for Law, Technology and Society of the Tilburg University. Professor Somsen specialises in issues of international, European and domestic biotechnology law, as well as EC law, with a particular interest in EC environmental law.

Aleksander Surdej is Associate Professor at the Department of European Studies of the Krakow University of Economics. His research interests focus on the policies of social regulations and on the political economy of post-communist transformations in Central Europe.

Ellen Vos is Professor of European Union Law at the Law Faculty of Maastricht University. She has published extensively in the field of EU law, institutional law (comitology and agencies), governance, market integration and risk regulation.

Vern R. Walker is Professor of Law at the Hofstra University School of Law in New York, where he teaches courses in scientific evidence, torts, products liability, administrative law, and European Union law.

Karolina Żurek is a researcher and Ph.D. candidate at the Department of Law, European University Institute, Florence. Her research concerns the social implications of Europeanisation of risk regulation in the area of food safety.

Chapter 1

The scientification of politics and the politicisation of science

Michelle Everson and Ellen Vos

1 THE CRISIS IN CONFIDENCE: A TALE OF RISK, SCIENCE AND GOVERNANCE

The ramifications of the BSE crisis of the 1990s have stretched far into the 21st century. The collapse of consumer confidence caused by shortcomings in the institutionalisation of scientific knowledge within both the EU Member States and within the Union itself prompted wholesale re-evaluation of the prevailing structures of science-based decision making. However, the loss in consumer confidence was not the only catalyst for the change in the manner in which we view the legitimate use of science within government. In addition to the undeniable need for a review of the quality of scientific advice used to verify agricultural production methods, the extraordinary degree of public political disquiet about the authorised use of genetically modified organisms within agriculture and industry has raised new questions about science-based governance. Today, the issue is not merely one of assuring that the science used in governance is sound. Instead, thought must also be given to the balancing of scientific opinion against wider ethical and social values.

Images of burning cows in English fields, slaughterhouses, cattle-blood and cattle-brains not only led to a fall in beef consumption, but also resulted in a reduction of the belief of citizens in the credibility of government. How could citizens ever again trust governance that had placed the protection of agricultural interests over the need to secure public health?[1] Governmental responses included institutional and procedural reform to ensure the quality and transparency of science-based decision making and an invitation to citizens to participate throughout the process. A very similar political outcry greeted the issue of the authorisation of GMOs and only intensified the need for governmental reform of the institutions of risk governance. In addition to exposing failings in the quality of scientific advice used within decision making, the BSE crisis also highlighted problems of scientific uncertainty. It became common knowledge among the public that scientists would not always have answers to problems of risk. To what degree would infected beef within the food chain result in full scale infection of the human population with the new

1 See as regards the UK, the BSE Inquiry Report, 2000, <http://www.bseinquiry.gov.uk/report/index.htm> and as regards the EU, Medina Ortega Report, Inquiry Committee set up by the European Parliament, 1997, A4–0020/97/A, PE 220.544/fin/A.

Creutzfeldt-Jakob disease? The debate around GMOs was not only marked by an even greater degree of conflict about scientific uncertainty, but also began to raise issues of whether, under conditions of scientific uncertainty, it would be legitimate to demand that scientific rationalities could ever be overruled by ethical or social values.

New approaches to risk analysis introduced in the wake of BSE and in the face of a growing controversy about the authorised use of GMOs sought to combat the 'organised irresponsibility' (see Beck 1986, 2005) which had marked much risk policy at both Member State and EU level in the previous years. Reform was carried through at an institutional level, with a clearer separation made between risk assessment and risk management; a reform which consolidated executive management of risk, making clear which portions of risk policy would be attributed to scientists and bureaucracies, as well as the rules under which scientific advice was to be collated and adopted.[2] Further, reform also saw an increase in procedural standards of risk oversight, above all with regard to the strengthening of the principles of openness and participation as well as the introduction of the precautionary principle, a seemingly 'neutral' standard allowing pre-emptive regulatory intervention to combat uncertain risks.[3]

One side-effect of the effort to regain public trust in the credibility of risk regulators and regulation was the strengthening of the bureaucracy and executive centred on risk regulation; the newly consolidated executive, with its newly apportioned responsibilities within the process of risk analysis was to be the main vehicle through which public trust might be retained. Equally, the consolidation of executive powers within the risk constellation was only augmented by virtue of the globalisation of markets and the consequent internationalisation of risks and the institutions designed to deal with them. Even though the Commission and other Member States were keen to portray BSE as a purely British problem, consolidated food markets within the EU determined that the Commission and national regulatory authorities were inevitably confronted with the management of the BSE risk. By the same token, GMOs are not geographically confined, such that a consolidated EU GMO policy will still require coordination with national and international policies and institutions of market management. Within an increasingly globalised trade context, normative, practical and legal pressures tend to encourage networking of executives and of bureaucratic/legal rationales. For example, the technical standards generated within the framework of the Codex Alimentarius Commission have gained in significance as an evidential aid within the science-based WTO framework and thus now inevitably function as magnet for the executive agenda-setting preoccupations of national and supranational bureaucracies such as the European Commission (see Masson-Matthee 2007).

In this ever more global world of risk management, the EU executive has an increasingly complex risk management function. As the most powerful supranational bureaucracy, the European Commission has unparalleled importance, acting as a nodal management structure between national and international

2 See contributions by H. Rothstein, J. Besançon and O. Borraz, A. Surdej and K. Zurek, B. van der Meulen, and E. Vos, in this volume.

3 See in particular E. Fisher and V. Walker, in this volume.

frameworks of risks. This book aims to investigate the dynamics of European risk governance and its embeddedness within an increasingly global context of risk regulation.

2 RISK ASSESSMENT: SCIENTIFIC UNCERTAINTY AND THE DANGERS OF EXECUTIVE ACTION

In the light of evident shortcomings within the bureaucratic response to the BSE crisis, one important line of reform involved the separation of risk assessment and risk management at the EU and national level. Science and the responsibility for scientific advice were displaced from the traditional executive framework into independent bodies. Regulatory provision was made to ensure that risk assessment and management would be institutionally independent from one another both at European and at Member State level, thus reproducing the international concept of risk analysis pursued within the Codex Alimentarius Commission.[4] This new regulatory philosophy whereby, wherever it is possible, hazard potential is formulated as a quantifiable risk with reference to technical and scientific criteria alone, has found immediate institutional approval in the creation of independent scientific/technical bodies such as the European Food Safety Authority (EFSA) at European level and the British Food Standards Agency (FSA), the French *Agence Française de Sécurité Sanitaire des Aliments* (AFFSA) and the Dutch *Voedsel- en Warenautoriteit* (VWA) at national level. By the same token, clear responsibility for the risk management function, or the final decision on the acceptability of risk, was given to traditional executive bodies such as the European Commission at European level and national administrations within the Member States.

Within this emergent regulatory philosophy of the rationalisation of risk assessment and management functions, growing reliance on technical and scientific criteria for the framing of the risk problem and the mode of combating risk interestingly also extends to constellations of scientific uncertainty and to the overcoming of uncertain risk. In other words, even in cases where science cannot adequately quantify risk, or situations in which there are scientifically unverified suspicions about the existence of hazard, rationalising regulatory strategies may yet prevail. Typically, 'uncertain risks' concern particular instances of suspected possible hazards, which are usually associated with complex causalities, large-scale, long-term and trans-border processes, and which are usually difficult to control.[5] Equally typically, these uncertain risks not only reveal the limits of science but also unveil their political character as a wider public perceives that such hazards could impact negatively upon society and therefore demand that some action be taken by political actors.

Nonetheless, with a notion of 'precaution', now constitutionalised within the European Union as the precautionary principle, uncertain risk may yet be treated within a rational framework of decision making devoid of direct interaction, whether deliberative or otherwise, between social and technical values. Alternatively,

4 *Working Principles for Risk Analysis*, Codex Alimentarius Commission – 14th Procedural Manual.

5 See M. van Asselt, E. Vos and B. Rooijackers, in this volume.

in one analysis, precautionary action – or the notion that restrictive interventions are justified where hazard may not be verified in a quantifiable manner, but qualitative analysis suggests that potential damage is large-scale, irreversible and impacts significantly upon large sectors of society – is still founded in rational-technical science.[6]

Science and rationality as a panacea: as an introductory chapter to this volume demonstrates,[7] executives – whether made up of traditional bureaucratic bodies such as the European Commission or now found in independent bodies dedicated solely to technical analysis and the promulgation of science – can restore and secure public faith in the credibility of risk regulation through application of a rational instrumentalist model of administrative decision making. Risk may pose great threats to the joint enjoyment of the social environment. Equally, hazard and uncertain risk remain a constant source of social anxiety. Nonetheless, the distinction made between risk assessment and risk management, clear rules that guarantee the quality of scientific advice and the independence of experts, together with a rationalist constitutional reading of the precautionary principle, seemingly combine together to provide us with a rational framework that obviates irrational fears. It thus ensures that decision making takes place in a context free from interest politics and the 'value irrationalism' that otherwise marks unstructured public political debate.[8]

Offering us a tool to combat the negative externalities of the global risk society which has developed in tandem with global, liberal patterns of trade and development, rational instrumentalist philosophies both help to structure executive action and further facilitate interaction between executives within the global complex of national, supra-national and international executives. One language is spoken by all; a language, furthermore, which, with its Weberian claim to establish common truths out of diversity, is perfectly suited to the management of risk between diverse societies.

However, the 'panacea' of science and instrumental rationality is, perhaps, not all it would seem to be, especially where – most paradoxically – resort to science is taken in situations of scientific uncertainty (see Weingart 1999). It is by definition in these situations of uncertainty that science reveals its true limits and that other factors, such as social and ethical concerns, are bound to play a role. Thus, for example, European Commission application of the precautionary principle recognises that factors other than science should be taken into account in the decision-making process.[9] Inevitably, this has led to much controversy, with some arguing that the principle of precaution gives *carte blanche* to arbitrary decision making, and others, taking a more positive line, stating that the principle allows for a more reflexive and pluralistic decision-making process.[10] Interestingly, it is increasingly argued that there cannot be a single definition of the principle, equally applicable to the European Union, national and global levels, since the principle depends

6 See Ch. Joerges, in this volume.
7 See E. Fisher, in this volume.
8 See M. Everson, in this volume.
9 Communication of the Commission on the Precautionary Principle, COM(2000) 1 final.
10 See E. Fisher, in this volume.

largely upon its context of application and the legal culture within which it is embedded (see Fisher 2007).

We have already noted that failings within the historical scheme of 'organised irresponsibility' for risk regulation led to an immediate crisis of public confidence and a governance response, which stressed the need to re-establish credibility through the 'scientification' of knowledge production on risk and a clear apportionment of assessment and management responsibilities. This governance response, privileging technical rationalities and leading to a consolidation of the executive, was also well suited to the complexities of a global trade regime and the need to find decisional criteria that could overcome cultural sensitivities and confrontation between economic and non-economic values. However, the expanded and consolidated executive function which this evolution has entailed, together with the technically rational philosophy within which it is founded, is itself a new governance threat: executives thrive on consolidation and conformity. Thus, for example, notwithstanding its recognition that socio-economic values impact upon the precautionary decisional equation, the European Commission nonetheless seeks to promote a monolithic conception of precaution, viewed in some sections of society as an arbitrary yardstick, which fails to take account either of science or of the very series of diverse social and cultural interests it was designed to protect.[11]

At one level, the monolithic nature of the principle of precautionary action, which the Commission promotes, raises a very old spectre indeed. Although he argued in favour of formal bureaucratic rationalities, Max Weber expressed concern that rationalising tendencies within modernity would also give new life to the danger of inhuman behaviour (Weber 1969). A rational administration would also be deaf to human concerns that are not readily recognisable within rationally structured discourse. Within the expanded and consolidated executive function, spanning national, supranational and international entities, we might accordingly be concerned that the emphasis laid on the use of science to define and frame the problems which risk regulation must address, together with the instrumental rationality that marks processes of interlinked risk management across the global institutions of trade regulation, might lead to a fatal disregard for ethical and social sensibilities (Everson and Eisner 2007).

Equally, however, the spread of the executive function across local boundaries to embrace a global world can also be argued to obscure the real rationales that underlie decision making. As empirical analysis of the case of *Pfizer* – a European refusal to authorise the use of particular antibiotics as growth promoters within European pork markets – demonstrates (Van Asselt and Vos 2006), executive decision makers may be tempted to hide behind ambiguous scientific findings in order to pursue their own agendas. In this case, the European Commission did not listen to the relevant European scientific body saying that there was no immediate risk to human health and preferred, instead, to refer to other scientific bodies (Dutch Health Council, WHO, UK House of Lords), who had noted the existence of scientific uncertainty. Thus, the Commission was able to claim that a notion of scientific uncertainty underpinned its ban of the relevant antibiotics on the European market, and failed openly to acknowledge that the ban was, in fact, an

11 Fisher, in this volume.

outcome of its desire/policy to combat resistance to antibiotics, a major human health concern within the Community. On the other hand, empirical analysis also makes it clear that the Commission is in desperate need of scientific advice in this highly technical and complex area; advice which guides it in its decision making, and whose importance led one Commission official to picture the relationship between the Commission and EFSA as being one of a blind driver (Commission) with a passenger giving directions (EFSA) (Vos and Wendler 2006: 122).

Seen in this light, the executive nature of global risk governance raises a dual and interconnected problem of too great an emphasis on the decisional legitimacy of scientific and technical criteria, together with a refusal to make the true social and economic values that guide decision makers transparent. The problem is one of de-politicisation, or, better stated, a politicisation of the scientific executive function, which might and can lead to obscure and insensitive decision making at the level of the simple application of science to complex social relations, and one which might, furthermore, deny its own normative underpinnings or commitment to positive values such as human health.

In a final analysis, then, the tension between the functionalist necessity for science-based decision making and the wider demand for a form of public participation within risk governance continues to be the primary characteristic of modern risk governance regimes. The potential 'inhumanity'[12] and obscurity of a science-based rationally instrumentalist executive must be balanced by public participation, which is more transparently dedicated to the re-introduction of ethical and social criteria within the bureaucratic discourse. At the same time, however, explicitly political debate must be subject to the limits of science, and more particularly must continue to be disciplined in the light of neutral, technical-scientific criteria.

3 RISK MANAGEMENT: PRECAUTION AND THE PROBLEMS OF POLITICAL PLURALISM

If modern schemes of risk governance might be said to be characterised by ongoing tension between scientific/technical rationalities and the demand for appropriate consideration of the ethical, social and economic values that may also be affected by global trade regimes; then, by the same token, the primary function of risk governance might also be argued to be the effort to bring scientific rationales and social/ethical values into a lasting equilibrium within stable institutional structures of governance. As a consequence, the process of risk management, which, as we have seen, is sometimes simply conceived of as a bureaucratic exercise of the adaptation of regulatory intervention in the light of technocratic/scientific analysis, might be viewed in a wholly different manner. Where the task is one of balancing rationales and values, risk management is a political exercise, a discursive process of the establishment and implementation of a policy about risk and its regulation.

As the case studies reveal, both in practice as well as in theory, the precautionary principle is coming to be regarded less as a neutral procedural standard to be

12 See M. Everson, in this volume.

applied in the exceptional context of uncertain risk and more as an institution in its own right, within which risk policy is drawn up. As Rothstein notes in relation to the activities of the UK Food Standards Agency, recent regulatory debates within the UK reveal 'how scientific, normative and institutional uncertainties provide significant scope for conflict on what constitutes precautionary action'.[13] The core of this contention is provided by the insight that, even in relation to simple (quantifiable) risks, 'scientific knowledge does not provide an uncontested universal evidential basis for decision making'. Instead, a proposed UK ban on sausage skins teaches us that where a country has no economic and societal interest in maintaining a product on its market, it is not difficult to address uncertain risks within a precautionary action, which is then considered to be proportional. This was not the case within the whole of the EU, and more particularly in Germany, where natural sausage skins are used on a very large scale. The notion of proportional precautionary action allowed the Scientific Steering Committee at EU level to shift its evidential basis and reject a precautionary ban on sausage skins on the basis of the relative lack of risk posed by them in comparison to normal carcass meat.[14]

The perception that precaution is a policy and not a simple neutral cost-benefit criterion, since costs and benefits may vary in relation to the overall socio-economic context within which risk is posed, is further confirmed by the legal reasoning structures adopted by US courts in their oversight of food regulation. Here precaution does not have a meta-legal status as an independent criterion that may be applied to all cases regardless of their factual constellation. Instead, it is argued to be a 'high-level policy', which political actors must use to elaborate particular rules to apply to particular fact-finding procedures.[15] The legal contextualisation of the principle underlines its relational status. Precaution and the evidential basis for precaution alter in the light of the particular circumstances of production, the socio-economic features of particular production processes, as well as with regard to the legal culture within which evidence for precaution must be established.

The recognition that the evidential basis for precaution and the evaluation of risk will necessarily fluctuate in light of institutional, social and economic contexts raises, in its turn, new questions about the renewed emphasis laid upon the importance of 'participation' within governance. At one level, the move towards the securing of a greater degree of public participation within risk governance structures might be considered to be part of the overall effort to improve regulatory institutional credibility through greater participation and transparency and the consequent enhancement of public trust in the risk management regime. However, once we have admitted that risk management is itself a necessarily political process, entailing the weighing up of the relative substantive costs and benefits of fluctuating interests, the inevitable political contestation that such processes entail may also be argued to necessitate public participation within the executive for other efficiency-led and normative reasons.

Thus, participation, and more particularly public participation within institutional structures of risk governance, can serve a variety of rationales. As has been

13 H. Rothstein, in this volume.

14 H. Rothstein, in this volume.

15 See V. Walker, in this volume.

suggested, in stark contrast with traditional bureaucratic structures, whereby delegation was itself considered to be a manifestation of public trust in the efficacy of the executive process, and further, was designed to overcome complexity in regulatory matters, trust in modern risk management can only be assured where the public is afforded participatory tools, which allow it to oversee each stage in the management of complex issues. Public participation within executive structures can thus also be viewed to be a part of a general normative scheme of government that demands that executive action must always be integrated within democratic decision making. Participation, in this constellation, is accordingly seen as a vital element of democratic legitimacy. Finally, participation may also be conceived of in an 'instrumentalist-normative light', focusing on the quality of the outcome of the decision-making process, and thus being aimed at the enhancement of the quality of decisions.[16]

In this latter perspective, the recognition that scientific evidential bases are not monoliths, nor are they indisputable truths in their own right, but are, instead, required to structure and constrain debate in whichever material and institutional context it arises, has as its necessary corollary an alteration in the significance that is attached to the material views and opinions which participation brings to the risk management and risk assessment process. In this context, participation does not simply serve abstract normative goals of government such as enhancing trust or meeting democratic requirements, but also acts *as a part of knowledge creation itself*, as a material contribution to the evidential bases for the assessment and management of risk. In this way, participation thus aims to enhance the *quality both of scientific opinion and of the management decision*. By allowing citizens and/or stakeholders to provide knowledge about the scientific issues at stake on both a scientific/technical level, as well as on the level of ethical and social values, scientists are confronted with knowledge within a wider context, which also allows for lay knowledge to be introduced into the process of the production of 'hard science' knowledge (see Wynne 2001). In addition, allowing stakeholders and/or citizens to participate in management decision making may also enhance the quality of final decisions, as they are then able to express themselves on the management options/preference at issue, thus augmenting the knowledge-base for decision making.

Participation as a contribution to knowledge creation thus seems to form a sensitive response to the threats thrown up by a global risk governance regime. Ameliorating the potential 'inhumanity',[17] insensitivity and opaqueness of bureaucratic and scientific rationales, participation as knowledge creation can be argued to represent a sea-change within conceptions of governance and to be a positive response to the complexity of uncertain risks. However, participation as knowledge contribution must also be recognised to give rise to its own particular problems in the institutional structuring of risk governance. In contrast to traditional

16 See Harremoës *et al.* 2002. Stirling makes a threefold distinction for participatory engagement rationales: *normative democratic* ('because it is the right thing to do'); *substantive* ('because it leads to better decisions') and *instrumental* ('because it facilitates particular favoured decisions'), Stirling 2003: 381–401.

17 See M. Everson, in this volume.

bureaucracies, which ensured unitary and universal decision making through the exclusion of public participation from implementation processes, the re-evaluation of participation as a positive contribution to knowledge creation also demands that we identify institutional mechanisms and procedures that reconcile potentially irreconcilable rationalities of science and ethics, and which further guard against executive capture by inappropriate interests, or even an utter collapse in the executive function as plural processes of knowledge creation descend into meaningless and fruitless conflict between varied views and interests. Historically, trust was a communitarian good established within normal political processes. It predated and justified delegation in the effort to reduce regulatory complexity.

4 THREE MODELS OF PLURAL RISK GOVERNANCE

In the preceding sections we argued that, within the traditional models of bureaucracy maintained within the nation states of modernity, the major concern was one of ensuring the authority of bureaucratic rationales and decision making through a strict delimitation between political processes of policy and decision making and bureaucratic processes of implementation. The plurality of interests which circle each regulatory task were first neutralised within the conventional democratic processes of the national polity; subsequently a unitary will for action was transmitted to an implementing executive. Within plural global risk governance structures contestation continues between scientific and ethical/social rationales, as well as between diverse interests, from the moment of problem definition through to the point of regulatory intervention and the establishment of a precautionary approach. Here, the problem is a heightened one, of the identification of a principle that might both reconcile conflicting rationalities and legitimate a final (universal) decision, which transcends all particularistic interests that arise within particular constellations of risk.

Contributions to this volume, drawn from a variety of disciplines, provide us with three models within which we might begin to conceive of an institutional structure of plural risk governance within which the dangers of particularistic plural contestation and a lack of final regulatory authority might be effectively combated. For the political scientist Andreas Klinke, the primary problem is one of the identification of a universal rationality of 'justice' within which scientific and ethical-social rationalities may be reconciled and the varying cost-benefit calculations of individual actors be conflated. The process of global risk management must be dedicated to the identification of a 'common good' that will then legitimate final decision making. However, *'the common good-orientation' of risk management strategies* also raises the question of inclusion or exclusion, of whose good ought to be taken into account and the troublesome issue of, what, substantively-speaking is the common good'.[18] To Klinke, a deliberative conception of the common good is the only possible outcome. Certainly, 'resort may be made to the category of justice'; however, justice will necessarily be a 'relational' concept, to be established in each concrete case of

18 A. Klinke, in this volume.

risk management by virtue of cognitive reflection by and between all interested parties.

At the practical level of institutional design, global schemes of risk governance and processes of risk management must thus be informed by, and are only legitimated in the light of, an 'inclusive [form of] risk governance [made up of] discourse, deliberation and public participation'. Publicly acceptable common good rationality is a political product, whereby policy making and advisory bodies must consider and condense unadulterated and reliably collated public opinion and input throughout the whole of the risk governance process. The model is one that locates authority for final decision making within constitutive deliberation, whereby no one rationality can ever claim to represent and embody objective criteria for decision making: the common good is an epistemological product of concrete deliberation.[19]

The notion that decisional authority can never be derived from one single rationality, but must, instead, be teased out of deliberation between competing and contested rationalities is one that science also recognises. In particular, Harry Kuiper's description of the role of scientific experts in risk regulation amounts to a second model, *a model of 'sound science'*. The notion of sound science extends deliberation into the process of risk assessment and combats public sensitivity about science by contrasting scientific rationales with varying public ethical and social concerns at the very point of the creation of the scientific knowledge base. In this model, active stakeholder participation may occur at a number of levels: for example, (i) during the process of problem identification; (ii) during the organisation of the risk analysis process, and above all in decisions about who should participate within that process; (iii) in relation to the identification of the relevant technical, social and economical parameters that should be applied during risk analysis; (iv) with regard to the establishment of judgement values on the acceptance and mitigation of identified and characterised risks; and (v) with regard to the measures to be taken to monitor and control risk factors that have already been released into the environment.[20]

However, a pivotal point to note here is that although the common good cannot be found within any purportedly 'objective' rationality (scientific, bureaucratic, social or ethical) and must, instead, be established by the constant deliberative process of cross-referencing between competing rationalities, the institutional structures and procedures of global risk governance must also take care never to dilute the individual rationalities that are brought to bear upon the search for a common good and decisional authority. Science must not be contaminated by ethical considerations. Likewise, the ethics and social mores current amongst and supported by a wider process of public participation may not simply be set aside with reference to scientific criteria. This process of constitutive deliberation founded within mutual respect and cross-referencing between rationalities likewise finds a supportive partner within the disciplines of law and administrative design.

A third model, 'administrative constitutionalism' (Fisher 2007) or 'reflexive proceduralism' (Everson 2005; Everson and Eisner 2007), thus focuses upon a reorientation of the logics that drive institutional administrative design and legal oversight

19 Klinke in this volume.

20 H. Kuiper, in this volume.

of risk regulation. Neither the institutions of risk management nor the law that oversees them can claim to embody or apply substantive criteria to legitimate constitutive deliberation. Constitutive deliberation cannot be tested or assured simply within the logic of scientific discourse. Nor can it be measured against ever changing ethical and social mores. Accordingly, both the notion of administrative constitutionalism and the notion of reflexive proceduralism aim to secure a change within administrative and legal cultures. The administration may no longer simply rely on instrumental rationalism. Law cannot simply promote science. Instead, both administrative design and law must be dedicated to ensuring that constitutive deliberation between competing rationalities and interests is promoted and structured to ensure respect for contestation within the risk governance regime and, further, to the establishment of a clear set of procedures and rules which address conflict. Most importantly, legal and institutional structures guiding constitutive deliberation are not simply concerned with the provision of a neutral forum for debate between conflicting rationalities. Instead, both aim to ensure the quality of this debate by ensuring that each scientific, rational or ethical rationality promoted within the global risk governance regime is not simply subsumed within an obfuscating melting pot of values, but instead retains its own integrity and, thus, ability to convince in concrete cases. Thus, concrete administrative and legal structures are likewise used to enhance the philosophy of constitutive deliberation, further strengthening discursively established legitimacy through procedural values of transparency, participation, independence and excellence.

5 PROBLEMS OF GLOBAL RISK GOVERNANCE IN PRACTICE

Through the case studies we present in this volume, we aim to understand the dynamics of interaction between national, European and international risk regulation and the institutions of risk management. With its constitutionalised precautionary principle and its ever more differentiated institutional efforts to rationalise the process of risk regulation and scientific uncertainty, the European Union might initially appear to have developed the most streamlined of responses to risk and scientific uncertainty. However, when we investigate the examples of food and GMO regulation, the further hidden subtleties and complexities of risk and regulatory intervention become apparent. As the case studies demonstrate, long-standing contestation between industrial and consumer interests, which are difficult to maintain in equilibrium within institutional structures, bedevil processes of risk assessment and risk management. Which forms of food might be deemed safe? Should we pay greater attention to the efficiency-driven demands of the global food market for consolidated foods standards than to local perceptions of food as a product anchored within ethical and social values? How might a European executive best mediate between global trade interests and national/local preconceptions about the cultural embedding of food? By the same token, case studies on GMOs unveil and reveal the difficult demands made upon a European executive in relation to the structuring of public participation within the regulatory regime and concomitant effort to reconcile the ethical and social demands that public participation entails with the more rational interests and outlook of a global market, as well as with

European and global institutions of legal regulatory oversight. Both case studies prove to be exemplary of the manner in which 'contested governance' and (dis)-trust both challenge the legitimacy of existing institutional arrangements (Ansell and Vogel 2006: 10).

Above all, the current global framework for risk governance, encompassing national regulation, supranational regimes and international regulatory bodies and treaties, is still strongly characterised by inherent tension between instrumentalist rationality and demands that political participation and, above all, the ethical and social values which participation entails, be better structured and given a clearer profile within risk governance structures. In practice, the global risk regime presents us with a paradox, a dual and intertwined process of re-scientification and re-politicisation, whereby neither scientific/technical rationales nor political deliberation are properly structured in order adequately to ensure the integrity of the risk governance regime.

As noted, maintenance of the integrity of scientific discourse is a vital component within risk governance regimes. Scientific discourse is a universal discourse that creates objective values, which may be tested and which in turn may be used to test the validity claims of other political, social or ethical discourses; above all, science may be used to unveil hidden motivations, such as protectionism or the hidden evolution of, say, health protection policies within competing rationalities. At the same time, however, scientific rationalities, if never challenged within competing discourses, can prove to be insensitive to established ethical values and simple social realities. If further embedded within expansionist executive and bureaucratic logics and rationales, science and technical rationality might be argued to bear the potential to disenfranchise necessary political debate and to contribute to the expansion of a hegemonic executive function.

Pressures for the re-scientification of the European and global risk governance regimes are manifold. However, perhaps the most powerful of pressures for re-scientification remains the 'global' nature of trade, which, when taken together with the political aspirations of individual sections of the global risk governance executive, sees actors motivated to use the universal rationality of science to gain the upper hand within interconnected national, supranational and international regimes.[21] Thus, for instance, we witness the curious efforts of the European Commission to colonise the standards-making procedures of the Codex Alimentarius Commission through the effort to assert the overwhelming scientific excellence of the activities of the European Food Safety Authority (see Vos and Wendler 2006: 128). So, the argument is made, this excellence should – for wholly rational reasons – be deployed in the global effort to identify a 'state of the art' for the food standards that will apply to the whole of global trade. A fine and worthy endeavour? Or, perhaps not: the Commission's efforts to colonise the Codex are surely also informed by political motivations and, more particularly, by the WTO recognition of the Codex as a state-of-the-art set of standards which might then form the evidential basis for evaluation of potentially restrictive precautionary regulation at national and supranational level.[22]

21 See J. Scott, in this volume.
22 See M. Matthee, in this volume.

Science has become a tool in the endless controversy between US and European regulatory regimes, which centres on WTO dispute settlements (see Scott 2007; Prévost 2007).[23] The exact significance of scientific rationality within this dispute is highly opaque. The GMO dispute, recently heard by a WTO panel, presents us with a scenario whereby the EU has chosen to allow its Member States to continue to apply precautionary regulatory provisions, which appear, in the eyes of the US regulatory regime, to have very little to do with scientific and market rationalities and, instead, to represent the continuing preoccupation of European market cultures with the maintenance of cultural traditions within modes of production (Everson and Joerges 2007). Above all, the continuing restrictions placed upon GMOs reflect a 'European' notion that a (food) product is more than an end product but also encompasses the mode of its production: cheese is only cheese and beer is only beer where the same production methods have been used for generations (see Everson and Joerges 2007). The old-world 'feudalism' of such constructions is a necessary affront to US market liberalism; an affront which the US seeks to overturn with reference to scientific rationality. In this view, the European notion of precaution is context-based, founded not in rational, objective and universal criteria but in the social constructions of European markets, taking into account, alongside scientific rationales, the further legitimate and lifestyle concerns of European citizens. As this volume demonstrates, however, the WTO panel system appears to be singularly ill-equipped to tackle this issue directly.[24]

What, then, of the strategic use of European science to capture and colonise the Codex? Are we witnessing the de-politicisation of the Codex Commission and the establishment of a hegemonic rational discourse of science? Alternatively, is this trend just one further strategic European effort to assert its context-based evidential bases above US market liberalism and scientific rationality? The intertwined, yet not fully integrated structures of governance within the global trade market, make it very difficult to determine what form of science and what form of executive political action is taking place.[25]

The strategic use of science perhaps has its most important manifestation within the global context of risk governance. However, this is not to say that re-scientification and the use of science to dominate political debate is not also present at more local levels. Above all, national authorities within the European Union have often been forced to deploy scientific rationality, not simply since they embody empirical truths, but rather since they are a convenient tool to set aside inconvenient interests that may block trade in particular products; a trend most apparent within the early efforts to establish new scientific structures for food regulation in France.[26] By the same token, however, they may also be used to create or maintain barriers to trade. Thus, French authorities were also quick to seize upon science and the notion of scientific uncertainty to justify their continuing refusal to lift their ban on British beef following the BSE crisis.[27]

23 See J. Scott, in this volume.
24 See M. Everson, in this volume; Ch. Joerges, in this volume; see also Everson and Joerges 2007.
25 See Ch. Joerges, in this volume.
26 Noiville, in this volume.
27 J. Besançon and O. Borraz, in this volume.

So, what is the real danger posed by re-scientification and of the spread of instrumental rationalism through global structures of risk governance? Is it one that a scientific rationality with no sensitivity towards human social and ethical concerns will simply sweep away all of our more refined notions that goods are also the sum effect of their socially embedded modes of production; a tendency perhaps seen most clearly in the tortuous re-alignment of once hierarchical structures of political control of foodstuffs in Poland to suit the demand of the integrated European market for a clear distinction between risk assessment and management?[28] Alternatively, is it one that an ever expanding global executive function poses a danger to the integrity of the evidential scientific knowledge base for decision making, proving itself all too willing to use and misuse science in a strategic manner, which obscures an underlying confusion of scientific, ethical and social rationalities?

Clearly, the solution to both such dangers is a re-politicisation of the risk governance regime, which makes use of the legitimating quality of ethical and social values within the deliberatively constitutive debate on the nature of risk and the status of scientific uncertainty. The integrity of science itself can surely only be assured where transparent frameworks of discourse recognise the contested nature of risk governance, allowing political and ethical concerns to be given explicit expression rather than be hidden within or behind instrumentalist scientific rationalities. At the same time, however, participation, allowing for the expression of social and ethical values, can help to place truly universal scientific rationality in its necessarily embedded social context, enabling the establishment of equilibrium between competing and contested discourses.

However, at a practical level of risk regulation we can again see that equilibrium is far more easily established in theory than in practice. The problem is not simply one that participation tends only to occur at national level and cannot easily be accommodated within the bureaucratic and legal rationalities that characterise the interlinking institutions of risk governance within the global trade regime. The structures of the Codex Alimentarius Commission are thus not easily opened up to diffuse public debate and instead can only be made accessible to stakeholders, with all the fears of regulatory capture that such a constellation gives rise to. By the same token, however, the legal rationality of, say, WTO panels is of necessity closed to direct public interest participation: law decides issues in isolation. Rather, the problem is a far deeper one of a failure to identify the criteria that allow for the reconciliation of 'incommensurate rationalities'. Max Weber's fears about 'inhuman' bureaucracy still hang heavy over all of our modern efforts to establish a universal form of decision making that obtains its authority from the preparedness of all parties to decision making to recognise the quality of the final decision.

In the absence of one overarching rationality, which allows the process of contestation to be brought to its natural conclusion through the exclusion of all competing rationalities from the final decision, the habitual tendency to tolerate badly structured public participation is still visible. Worse still, participation may be misused: thus, GMO debates in both the Netherlands and the UK reveal that participation is not viewed as a means to enhance the *quality* of debate and the decision by means of mutual re-adjustment of the evidential bases for scientific uncertainty,

28 A. Surdej and K. Zurek, in this volume.

but is instead reduced down to its lowest common denominator, with the UK Government viewing participation as a means to educate the public in scientific rationalities[29] and the Dutch Government treating participation as a simple exercise in democratic legitimation and trust enhancement. Final decisions were still apparently taken with reference to the rationality criteria of science and the market, leaving the indelible impression that all social and ethical criteria raised in debate were simply extraneous to the final decision-making process.[30]

6 THE FUTURE OF RISK GOVERNANCE: THE QUALITY OF PARTICIPATION AND TRANSPARENCY

In the effort to re-establish the credibility of risk governance following the BSE crisis many institutional and procedural reforms, encompassing greater independence for the scientific knowledge-base and greater public participation within decision making, have, at the very least, helped policy makers, the public and academics in their efforts to enhance the quality and legitimacy of decision making on risk and uncertain risk. However, each reform also reveals the complexity of the regulatory problem to be addressed as the gap between scientific rationality and trust has proved to be difficult to address in practice.

However, in the continuing effort to bridge demands for safety and for trust we can now begin to sketch out the vital elements within an effective global risk governance regime. The conceptualisation of participation also helps us to identify in which cases and under which conditions participation should be allowed. Above all, participation must serve to improve the quality of decision making and be recognised as a vital substantive element within the knowledge base for decisions on scientific uncertainty. The substantive rationale for participation pleads for some form of participation by stakeholders within science making itself, such that knowledge can be transferred to the risk assessors, which will lead to better scientific opinions. Using a metaphor from the theatre, Stephan Hilgartner suggests that, when considering principles of transparency and participation, we should not become overly obsessed about the distinction made between the on-stage and backstage performance of science making (and decision making). Instead, each criterion should be viewed in the illuminating light of the creation of public spheres in which differences in opinion can be ventilated and viewpoints be exchanged in discussions between all relevant parties (Hilgartner 2000). Other authors suggest that expert bodies should be prepared to talk openly about scientific uncertainty, and reveal the uncertainties at stake, thus lessening the danger that risk managers will merely hide behind science and experts.[31] This would imply that scientific bodies should not only include experts on the relevant issues of uncertain risks, but also experts who are tolerant towards uncertainty who might, using language that is accessible to the public, then 'neutralise' the production of plausibility proofs. Further reform suggestions relate to the proceduralisation of the precautionary

29 M. Lee, in this volume.

30 H. Somsen, in this volume.

31 M. van Asselt, E. Vos and B. Rooijackers, in this volume.

principle and the stimulation of more independent research carried out by public scientific bodies themselves.[32]

Linking these empirical reform suggestions back to the structural theories of administrative constitutionalism and reflexive proceduralism, future global risk governance should seek to establish its own 'Constitution', which not only secures the vital independence and transparency of scientific advice, but also guarantees public participation, whether by stakeholders or a wider public, in order to ensure that scientific rationality, even as it is used to discipline the potential irrationalities of political debate, is nonetheless not the sole criterion for risk decision making. Instead, individual rules must be developed within the ambit of a procedural understanding of the precautionary principle, which recognises the case-specific context of a definition of scientific uncertainty and which ensures rationalisation of public participation and a widening of the knowledge base upon which precaution is established. Rationality in this latter sense in inextricably linked with notions of transparency. Decision making in situations of uncertain risks can and often must also be political in nature. The theatre metaphor teaches us that we should not expend unnecessary energy opening up and shedding light on the 'backstage' activities of scientific and political bodies. Instead, we should seek to create common public areas of discussion. If we demand that scientific and political bodies should cease to be secretive about their 'backstage' activities, we do so in the hope that transparency about the politics, science and values that revolve around the institutions of risk governance will ensure that no capricious or arbitrary decision making has taken place and that scientific, market and non-market values have been properly balanced against one another.

32 M. van Asselt, E. Vos and B. Rooijackers, in this volume.

BIBLIOGRAPHY

Ansell, C.K. and Vogel, D. (2006) *What's* the *beef?: The contested governance* of *European food safety*, Cambridge, MA: MIT Press.

Van Asselt, M.B.A. and Vos, E. (2006) 'Precautionary principle and the uncertainty paradox', *Journal of Risk Research* 9(4): 313–36.

Beck, U. (1986) *Risikogesellschaft. Auf dem Weg in eine andere Moderne*, Frankfurt am Main: Suhrkamp Verlag.

Beck, U. (2005) *Power in the Global Age: A new global political economy*, Cambridge: Polity Press.

Everson, M. (2005) 'Control of Executive Acts: The Procedural Solution. Proportionality, State of the Art Decision-Making and Relevant Interests', in D. Curtin *et al.* (eds), *EU Constitution: the Best Way Forwards* (Proceedings of the Asser Colloquium 2004), Nijmegen: Asser Institute.

Everson, M. and J. Eisner (2007) *The Making of a European Constitution: Judges and Lawyers beyond Constitutive Power*, Abingdon and New York: Routledge-Glasshouse.

Everson, M. and Joerges, Ch. (2007) 'Consumer Citizenship in Postnational Constellations?' in K. Soper and F. Trentmann (eds), *Citizenship and Consumption*, New York: Palgrave Macmillan (proof stage).

Fisher, E. (2007) *Risk Regulation and Administrative Constitutionalism*, Oxford: Hart Publishing.

Harremoës, P., Gee, D., MacGarvin, M., Stirling, A., Keys, J., Wynne, B. and Guedes Vaz, S. (2002) *The Precautionary Principle in the 20th Century: Late Lessons from Early Warnings*, London: Earthscan.

Hilgartner, S. (2000) *Science on Stage: Expert Advice as Public Drama*, Stanford, USA: Stanford University Press.

Masson-Matthee, M. (2007) *The Codex Alimentarius Commission and its Standards*, The Hague: T.M.C. Asser Press.

Prévost, D. (2007) 'Opening Pandora's Box: The Panel's Findings in the EC-Biotech Products Dispute', *Legal Issues of Economic Integration* 34(1): 67–101.

Scott, J. (2007) *The WTO Agreement on Sanitary and Phytosanitary Measures. A Commentary*, Oxford: OUP.

Stirling, A. (2003) 'Beyond Public Perceptions of Gene Technology: Community Participation in Dietrich and Schibeci', *Public Understanding of Science* 12: 381–401.

Vos, E. and Wendler, F. (eds) (2006), *Food Safety Regulation in Europe. A Comparative Institutional Analysis*, Antwerp: Intersentia.

Weber, M. (1969) *Economy and Sociology*, G. Roth and C. Wittig (translators and editors), vol. 2, Berkeley: University of Berkeley Press, Chapter 7.

Weingart, P. (1999) 'Scientific expertise and political accountability: Paradoxes of science in politics', *Science and Public Policy* 26(3): 151–61.

Wynne, B. (2001) 'Creating public alienation: expert cultures of risk and ethics on GMOs', *Science as Culture* 10(4): 445–81.

Part I

Regulating uncertain risks

Chapter 2

Opening Pandora's box: contextualising the precautionary principle in the European Union

*Elizabeth Fisher**

Over the last decade, the precautionary principle has become one of the most high-profile and contentious principles within European Union (EU) risk regulation and the principle has given rise to a burgeoning body of complex primary and secondary material as well as an overwhelming variety of arguments about its nature and validity (O'Riordan *et al.* 2001).[1] In particular the principle has seemingly become a 'touchstone' for thinking about the challenges involved in regulating risk in a globalising world. Concerning both, the internal and external exercise of state power (de Sadeleer 2002; Wiener and Rogers 2002), the European principle of precaution, and the academic debate which surrounds it within an EU context, proves to be an exemplary starting point for further consideration of, and comparison between, national, EU and international regulatory models for risk standard setting.

My aim in this chapter is to examine a number of important issues for thinking about the precautionary principle in the EU and thus open up a Pandora's box of issues for inquiry and debate throughout the volume. In the first section, I give a brief overview of some of the key features of the precautionary principle including how the principle is a legal principle concerned with regulating the process of decision making and how the principle's interpretation and operation depends upon the particular legal culture within which it operates; a phenomenon which is confirmed in subsequent case studies within the volume (Fisher 2002). The second section analyses, from a conceptual perspective, the typical contexts the principle applies in and shows how the principle applies to both the internal and external exercise of state administrative power. In both cases the operation of the principle raises issues of 'administrative constitutionalism'; that is issues concerning how public administration should be constituted and limited to ensure it is legitimate (Fisher 2007). While how such issues manifest themselves is unique to a legal culture, there are also common understandings of administrative constitutionalism that can be seen in different jurisdictions; in particular, notions of administrative constitutionalism that draw upon 'rationalist-instrumentalist' traditions, and notions that derive from a 'deliberative-constitutive' vision of legitimate administration.

* I would like to thank the editors for constructive feedback on earlier versions of this paper. Any errors or omissions remain my own.

1 I should stress that the principle also has an important role to play in other jurisdictions, in particular Australia.

The third section considers the operation of the precautionary principle in the EU. I show how there are at least six overlapping spheres of operation of the principle in the EU context. Considering these contexts side by side highlights: the pluralistic nature of administrative power and administrative constitutionalism in the EU; the fact that the same decision makers are subject to different regimes of administrative constitutionalism; and that the operation of power in these different contexts is interdependent. In the fourth section, I discuss the way in which widespread application of the European Commission's Communication on the Precautionary Principle[2] has resulted in the promotion of a particular (rational-instrumentalist) model of administrative constitutionalism and an assumption that one set of guidelines about the principle can apply in all the contexts the principle operates in. In the final section, I discuss the tension that I see as inherent in the above discussion. On the one hand, there is a need to recognise that how the principle is interpreted and applied is determined by legal culture and context. As such, there are limits to thinking in general terms about the principle and its implications for decision making. On the other hand, there is an increasing tendency to characterise the precautionary principle in generic and almost functional terms as a principle that can be easily transplanted from one context to another.

Before starting I should stress that this chapter does not attempt to be a comprehensive account of the precautionary principle in the EU. For that, readers will need to look elsewhere (Christoforou 2002; da Cruz Vilaca 2004; Scott 2004; Scott and Vos 2002).

I THE PRECAUTIONARY PRINCIPLE AND THE IMPORTANCE OF CONTEXT

Before considering the principle in the EU context, it is important to understand some basic features of the principle. The precautionary principle is a principle that is concerned with regulating the exercise of state regulatory power in relation to environmental and public health problems where collective knowledge of those problems is scientifically uncertain. The principle nearly always applies to standard setting and risk appraisal – that is the process of deciding whether to authorise a product or activity – and it primarily applies to public decision makers.

Official histories of the precautionary principle identify its roots in West German environmental policy in the late 1970s. It then rose to international prominence in the late 1980s (Trouwborst 2002).[3] Such histories often assume linearity in the development of the principle, while in reality the principle has been simultaneously developed in numerous different legal cultures (Fisher 2002). The precautionary principle was first included in Article 174(2) (then Article 130r(2)) of the EC Treaty in 1992 as a principle that Community environmental policy 'shall be based on'.

2 European Commission, *Communication on the Precautionary Principle*, COM(2000) 1, 2 February 2000, Brussels.

3 I say 'official' because, while this was no doubt the development of the version of the precautionary principle as we presently understand it, concepts of precaution can be seen in nearly all administrative regimes. See Fisher 2007.

However, before and after that date the principle, and associated ideas of precautionary action, were being developed by Community institutions in areas other than environmental policy[4] as well as by Member States (de Sadeleer 2000; Fisher 2001; Godard 2006; von Moltke 1988). This concurrent maturing of the principle has led to it having many different formulations. With that said the most common version of it is that which has been developed in the international environmental law context. To paraphrase – where there is a threat to human health or environmental protection a lack of full scientific certainty should not be used as a reason to postpone measures that would prevent or minimise such a threat.[5]

Three basic features of the principle can be evidenced from this formulation. The first is that the principle is directly concerned with scientific uncertainty in environmental decision making in that it states that 'lack of full scientific certainty should not be used as a reason' not to take measures. The complexity of scientific uncertainty and the problems it creates for 'factual' decision making should not be underestimated (Wynne 1992). Scientific uncertainties arise in relation to risk regulation because of the *ex ante* nature of standard setting and risk appraisal, the need to operate on the basis of regulatory science, not research science; and the fact that scientific knowledge in this area is plagued with methodological and epistemological problems (Dovers and Handmer 1999; Jasanoff 1990). Indeed, the precautionary principle highlights the lack of ontological security in this area of public action and in particular the provisional nature of scientific knowledge (Jasanoff and Wynne 1998). Moreover, such scientific uncertainty tends to complicate other features of intractable environmental problems such as their polycentricity and socio-political ambiguity (Fuller 1978; Klinke and Renn 2002).

Second, the precautionary principle does not direct a particular outcome to occur. This is consistent with the status of the principle as a legal 'principle', rather than a rule or a legal norm (Dworkin 1977; Fisher 2002) as well as with the fact that in circumstances of scientific uncertainty it would be illogical to talk in terms of outcomes (Mckinney and Hammer Hill 2000). Rather than being concerned with outcomes the principle regulates the way in which a decision is made, or in other words the decision-making *process* (Jowell 2000).[6] As the principle is concerned with process, it requires decision makers to reflect on how they justify their decisions, what factors are relevant to a decision, how that decision should be made, and who should be involved in the decision-making process. In particular, the principle is concerned with the reasons for a decision in that it states that in circumstances of scientific uncertainty a lack of certainty cannot be used as a reason for a decision.

Third, and following on from this, the principle's operation will largely depend on the institutional and cultural context in which it operates. In particular, what is deemed to be an acceptable process pursuant to the principle will depend on normative understandings of good decision-making processes embedded in a

4 Eg Case T-74/00 *Artegodan GmbH v Commission* [2002] ECR II-4965. Art. 6 is often used as a justification for the principle applying in other sectors.

5 A version of this definition can be found in Principle 15 of the Rio Declaration on Environment and Development; the Preamble of the Convention on Biological Diversity; and Article 10(2) of the Cartagena Protocol on Biosafety. For other formulations of the principle, see Harding and Fisher 1999 at Annex A.

6 A distinction should be made between process and procedure.

specific institutional context. This means that the principle's operation is highly flexible, a fact again consistent with its status as a legal principle, and which can best be seen by the fact that the different 'operational' parts of the principle – the 'triggering threat', the basis of action, and the measures to be taken – are capable of differing definitions. Thus, for example, a 'threat' can be defined: in quantitative terms as a certain level of risk; as a hazard; as a qualitative level of protection; and/or as a certain state of affairs that is deemed undesirable (Jaeger *et al.* 2001; Stirling *et al.* 2006). Moreover, as the principle gives negative guidance what is deemed as an acceptable course of action pursuant to the principle cannot only be determined by the principle alone but also requires reference to other factors.

How the principle is interpreted and applied will depend on socio-political and legal culture (Fisher 2002). Roughly speaking, 'the idea of legal culture points to differences in the way that features of law are themselves embedded in larger frameworks of social structure and culture which constitute and reveal the place of law in society' (Nelken 2001: 25). Legal culture is particularly important as the principle would never be found to require a process of decision making that was irreconcilable with more general legal understandings of reasonable action within a jurisdiction (Fisher 2001). The important thing to appreciate here is that there is no universal formula for applying the precautionary principle just as there can be no formula for applying any other legal principle such as fundamental rights or proportionality (Deville and Harding 1997). While the principle requires decision makers to focus on the problems of scientific uncertainty in decision making, the actual nature of it will depend on the surrounding legal, institutional and socio-political context. As this is the case it comes as no surprise that the principle has given rise to diverse bodies of jurisprudence in different jurisdictions (de Sadeleer 2002; O'Riordan, Cameron and Jordan 2001).

From the scholar's perspective this may seem a little disheartening. Grand theories about precaution seem to dissipate into a series of culturally specific examples, and attempts to draw comparisons and identify commonalities are, as the following case studies also demonstrate, hampered by the uniqueness of legal culture. Yet, while legal culture is important it should not be emphasised at the cost of ignoring the fact that the precautionary principle, while taking on very different meanings, tends to operate in similar contexts in different jurisdictions. The next section considers those contexts.

2 CONTEXTS OF OPERATION

As already noted, the principle is primarily a public law principle. In so being, it can apply to both the internal and external exercise of state authority (Fisher 2002; Godard 2006; MacCormick 1999). The principle's relevance in such contexts may be to: the design of the decision-making process, a particular decision, and/or to the process of holding the decision maker to account through legal or some other type of proceedings. In this last regard, the application (or non-application) of the principle may be subject to review and/or the principle may be a standard by which decisions are judged.

2.1 Application to the internal exercise of state sovereignty

From the internal perspective, the precautionary principle is a principle that governs what is understood as legitimate regulatory action in circumstances of scientific uncertainty. An overlooked feature of such action is that it is invariably administrative in form due to the resource-intensive nature of standard setting and risk appraisal (Fisher 2007; Fisher and Harding 2006).[7] These activities require the collection and evaluation of large amounts of information, the identification and consideration of expert opinion, the communication between numerous different actors, and the application of legislative prescriptions to specific complex circumstances. In a conventional separation of powers context, neither an elected body nor a court can provide an adequate forum for these activities to take place (Fisher 2007).

Stressing the administrative nature of standard setting and risk appraisal and thus of the principle's application is not mere pedantry on my part. It is essential in understanding the nature of the principle and the challenges involved in its application. As already noted, what is understood to be a legitimate interpretation and application of the principle will depend on context. As that context is public administration, then, the principle must be understood against the background of understandings about the role and nature of public administration. Indeed, one of the reasons why the principle is so contentious is because in having removed 'the facts' as a reason for a decision, the principle is seen by some as being little more than an excuse for arbitrary administrative decision making since a decisional factual basis has always been a more conventional way of ensuring the accountability of public administration (Marchant and Mossman 2004; Sunstein 2005). For others, however, the principle promotes good public administration because the principle allows for a more reflexive and pluralistic administrative process that takes into account the complexity of decision making in this area (Klinke and Renn 2002; Stirling 2001).

Indeed, what different perspectives on the principle highlight is that there is very little agreement about public administration. Administrative bodies occupy a necessary but awkward space in liberal democracies and there is a considerable polarisation of views over what the nature and form of legitimate public administration is and should be (Cook 1996; Mashaw 2002). This is particularly the case in relation to risk regulation because standard setting in this area requires delegation of large amounts of discretionary authority to public administration in circumstances of scientific uncertainty and socio-political conflict over the role of the state (Douglas and Wildasky 1982). As a legal principle, and like all law in this area, the precautionary principle is integral to the process of constituting decision makers, limiting their powers, and holding them to account. As such, legal debate will often be about whether a particular interpretation of the principle accords with received understandings of the role and nature of public administration (Fisher and Harding 2006).

7 In saying this I am not saying that the principle cannot be applied by either the legislature or the judiciary independently of any form of administrative action. They can be, but these cases are rare exceptions.

These debates are debates over administrative constitutionalism in that they are normative debates over what the role of law should be in ensuring legitimate administrative governance. Moreover, because of the contested nature of public administration, debates over administrative constitutionalism are ongoing as legal actors are constantly questioning and challenging the role and nature of administration. Understandings of administrative constitutionalism are unique to a particular legal culture, but at the same time there are basic normative understandings about the role and nature of public administration that are common across most jurisdictions. In particular, two paradigms of administrative constitutionalism have tended to dominate risk regulation – the deliberative-constitutive and the rational-instrumental (Fisher 2007). The former characterises the role of public administration in flexible and discretionary terms, while the latter understands the role of public administration more as a 'Weberian-type' agent of the legislature which executes a specific set of tasks. Each of these paradigms have their benefits and drawbacks and the simultaneous operation of them in most jurisdictions is arguably a desirable state of affairs as it reflects the difficult role of public administration in the risk regulation context.

This close interrelationship between the precautionary principle and administrative constitutionalism means that how the principle is defined, applied, and decision making pursuant to it subjected to review, will depend on ideas of administrative constitutionalism. This operates in two ways. First, different paradigms of administrative constitutionalism – rational-instrumental or deliberative-constitutive – will influence the manner in which the precautionary principle is interpreted and operationalised. Second, at the same time, academic debate has tended to more commonly characterise the precautionary principle as promoting a deliberative-constitutive understanding of public administration, since it requires a more flexible and less rule-bound approach to public decision making. Indeed, rational-instrumental understandings of the precautionary principle can appear to be less logical than deliberative constitutive understandings because inherent in them is a paradox – rational instrumental public administration ideally acts on a factual basis, but the precautionary principle highlights the problems posed by a reliance on a factual basis in circumstances of scientific uncertainty.[8] All in all, debates over the principle are in essence a continuation of debates over the role and nature of public administration. Whether the principle is accepted as valid, or how the principle is interpreted, will result in one paradigm being promoted over another.

It is also worth noting a number of other consequences of understanding the principle in terms of administrative constitutionalism. One is that the principle's operation does not involve a crude choice between democracy or science as some commentators have suggested (Morris 2000; Sunstein 2005) – all standard setting administrative regimes will draw on both science and democracy but the differences will be in how these terms are defined and how science and democracy are understood to interrelate (Fisher 2007). Likewise, the populist shorthand for

8 The best example of a rational-instrumental interpretation of the precautionary principle is the European Commission's Communication on the Precautionary Principle, above, note 2. For a discussion see Fisher and Harding 2006. Rational-instrumental interpretations also arise when decision makers are understood in adjudicatory terms. See *Conservation Council of South Australia v Development Assessment Commission & Tuna Boat Owners Association (No 2)* [1999] SAERDC 86 and Fisher 2007.

describing the precautionary principle as a 'shifting of the burden of proof' is a misconceived one. Burdens of proof are relevant to the evidentiary responsibility of parties in a courtroom and not to the legitimate exercise of administrative power (Fisher 2001).[9]

2.2 External exercise of state sovereignty

The precautionary principle does not only relate to exercises of internal state authority, however, but also to the exercise of external state authority. This may be relevant to how a state operates in an international, trans-national or supranational context. In these circumstances, the principle acts as a reason to require sovereign states to take action (Cameron and Abouchar 1991; Trouwborst 2002) or acts as a reason for a state to derogate from their international obligations (Bohanes 2002).[10] Obligations that fall into the former category have invariably taken a soft law form outside the supranational context and have tended to be considered in the context of international environmental regime building (Scott 2001). Examples that fall into the latter category have had the higher profile and been the subject of more commentary (Bohanes 2002; Button 2004; Perez 2004).

In each case the precautionary principle needs to be interpreted in light of the framework of legal obligations, the purpose of such regimes, and the legal culture. As with the exercise of internal state authority there is likely to be profound disagreement over what is the purpose and nature of legal provisions and this will be reflected in legal frameworks and dispute resolution processes. Thus, for example, in the EU setting, there has been an evolution in the jurisprudence over the fundamental freedoms which has resulted in not only a metamorphosis in understanding what is the nature of such freedoms but also when is it legitimate for a state to derogate from their trade obligations (Barnard 2004). Likewise, it is not clear whether the World Trade Organisation (WTO) Sanitary and Phytosanitary (SPS) Agreement is either an elaboration of what is understood to be unjustifiable discrimination or a more ambitious regime designed to minimise regulatory heterogeneity (Fisher 2007). In all cases a variation in what is understood to be the purpose of trade obligations will result in a variation in how the precautionary principle is defined and assessed.

While the ways in which the precautionary principle operates in the internal and external spheres are theoretically distinct, there is a very close conceptual relationship between the two. It is close in two senses. First, exactly the same institutions are nearly always used for the internal and external exercise of state authority. This is particularly the case in an era in which non-discriminatory risk regulation measures are subject to trade obligations due to the fact that national risk regulation standards *prima facie* will be the subject of trade obligations.[11] Second, and adding more complexity to the matter, what is a 'reasonable' exercise of external state authority

9 This is not to say that burdens of proof, or perhaps more appropriately 'burdens of persuasion', will not have a role to play in regulatory design. See also Jones and Bronitt 2006.

10 The most obvious example here is the role that the principle has played in WTO Sanitary and PhytoSanitary Disputes. See Appellate Body Report, *European Communities – Measures Concerning Meat and Meat Products (Hormones)*, 16 January 1998, WT/DS26/AB.

11 For an example of a discussion of this overlap see McNelis 2001.

will involve a determination of what is an appropriate model of administrative constitutionalism to be operating in that context. This is because in deciding what is a 'reasonable derogation' reference must not only be had to the purposes of trade regimes, but also to common understandings about how risk regulation standards are set. As risk regulation standard setting is administrative, implicit in those common understandings are understandings of administrative constitutionalism. This is obvious when one turns to commentary that discusses whether a state can utilise the principle in derogating from their trade obligations. Whether a commentator thinks a state can or not depends on what that commentator thinks is rational and non-arbitrary decision making which in turn depends on principles of administrative constitutionalism (Bohanes 2002; Majone 2002b; McNelis 2000).

This relationship between trade law and administrative constitutionalism has not been commonly recognised (Fisher 2007) and it is useful here to briefly elaborate on this point in the EU context to show the importance of it. Over the last 30 years the European Court of Justice (ECJ) has produced a complex body of case law concerning what is the nature of the free movement of goods obligation under Article 28 EC Treaty and when a Member State can derogate from that obligation. Maduro has argued that this case law is an example of the ECJ engaging in economic constitution building and the Court has encouraged Member States to harmonise their regulatory approaches (Maduro 1998). This thesis is undoubtedly correct but the problem is, as he explicitly notes, that the case law concerning Member State risk regulation measures does not fit his thesis. This is because his thesis concerns the harmonisation of regulatory outcomes and in the risk regulation cases the Court has allowed a proliferation of different regulatory outcomes, much more so than in other areas.[12] Yet, if one looks at the cases that do not conform to Maduro's thesis through the lens of administrative constitutionalism one can see that while Maduro's thesis is correct, his focus is wrong. In the risk regulation cases it is not outcomes that the Court is harmonising but ideas of administrative constitutionalism. In these cases the Court is scrutinising carefully the process by which risk regulations are set and assessing those processes against commonly understood ideas of administrative constitutionalism in the EU context. The focus of the Court in these decisions is upon the process of decision making – the reasons for the decision, who the state consulted, the information they relied on, and so on – to establish whether the state was exercising their power reasonably (Fisher 2007).[13] Moreover, in making that determination the Court is clearly influenced by how similar decisions are being made in other Member States and at the Community level.[14] In other words, the Court's ('majoritarian') harmonisation approach is, by and large, informed by common understanding of 'reasonable' administrative process on the part of Member States, taking into account ideas of administrative constitutionalism that exist in the traditions of the Member States and the Community.

12 This statement only stands true where there has been no harmonisation. See Case 174/82 *Sandoz BV* [1983] ECR 2445 at para 11 and Case 54/85 *Mirepoix* [1986] ECR 1067 at para 13.

13 Case 54/85 *Mirepoix* [1986] ECR 1067; Case 53/80 *Koninklijke Kaasfabriek Eyessen BV* [1981] ECR 409; and Case C-473/98 *Kemikalienspektionen v Toolex Alpha AB* [2000] ECR I-5681.

14 Case 304/84 *Müller* [1985] ECR 1511; Case 247/84 *Motte* [1985] ECR 3887; Case 178/84 *Commission v Germany* [1987] ECR 1227; and Case 176/84 *Commission v Greece* [1987] ECR 1193.

3 THE PRECAUTIONARY PRINCIPLE IN THE EU

The discussion so far has highlighted the fact that while each example of the precautionary principle is dependent on context and legal culture, there are common themes that arise in the principle's application, in particular that of administrative constitutionalism. When one turns to the EU context, one can begin to see the importance of culture, context and administrative constitutionalism. This is best evidenced by applying the internal/external authority schemata above to the precautionary principle's application in the EU. When one does this, at least six overlapping spheres of operation of the precautionary principle can be identified (Fisher 2002). These are:

a *The application by Community institutions in carrying out their international obligations.* This may include where the principle is being used to reinforce those obligations[15] or, more controversially, where the principle is being used to derogate from those obligations.[16] In most cases, such decisions will actually be exercises of internal Community power and thus the decisions will be of committees, agencies, the Commission, Parliament and the Council. In determining what is 'reasonable state action', however, the context is an external one and regulated by international agreements.[17]

b *The application by Community institutions in exercising their power pursuant to a Community regulatory regime.* Community institutions may rely on the principle in the creating of a new legislative/regulatory scheme[18] and/or in the exercise of power in relation to a specific product or activity.[19] The principle may be utilised by a range of different institutions including the Commission, committees and agencies but because of the rules concerning delegation in the EU these decisions will nearly always be attributed to the Council.[20]

c *The application of the principle by Member States when operating pursuant to Community regulatory regimes or competence.* The principle may be relevant to the mode in which Member State authorities choose to interpret a directive[21] and

15 Eg Cartagena Protocol on Biosafety.

16 Panel Report, *EC Measures Concerning Meat and Meat Products (Hormones) – Complaint by the United States,* 13 February 1998, WT/DS26/R/USA and Appellate Body Report, *European Communities – Measures Concerning Meat and Meat Products (Hormones),* 16 January 1998, WT/DS26/AB.

17 Fisher 2006b and Appellate Body Report, *Australia – Measures Affecting Importation of Salmon,* 20 October 1998, WT/DS18/AB/R.

18 Council Regulation (EC) No 2371/2002 of 20 December 2002 on the conservation and sustainable exploitation of fisheries resources under the Common Fisheries Policy, [2002] *OJ* L358/59.

19 Eg Article 7 of Regulation (EC) No 178/2002 of the European Parliament and of the Council of 28 January 2002 laying down the general principles and requirements of food law, establishing the European Food Safety Authority and laying down procedures in matters of food safety, *OJ* L31/1, as amended by Regulation (EC) No 1642/2003 of the European Parliament and of the Council of 22 July 2003, [2003] *OJ* L245/4.

20 Case 9/56 *Meroni v ECSC High Authority* [1957–58] ECR 133.

21 Eg Case C-318/98 *Fornasar* [2000] ECR I-4785 at para 37 and Case C-9/00 *Palin Granit OY and Vehmassalon Kansanterveystyön Kuntayhtymän Hallitus v Lounais-Suomen Ympäristökeskus* [2002] ECR I-3533 at para 23.

to the type of discretion that they have pursuant to that directive.[22] At the Member State level, application will be by national administrators or by courts drawing on national and EU legal principles.[23]

d *The application of the principle by Member States where there is a Community regulatory regime but a Member State wishes to rely on the principle in derogating from the obligations of that regime.* This may involve cases where the Member State is relying on specific provisions of a directive or regulation[24] or provisions of the Treaty such as Articles 95(4) and 176.[25]

e *The application of the principle by Member States where there is no Community regulatory regime but application* prima facie *infringes other Community obligations.* The most obvious example here is where such application *prima facie* infringes Article 28 EC Treaty.[26] The legal question which arises is whether a Member State is justified in taking such action under either Article 30 EC Treaty or the Cassis mandatory requirements doctrine.[27] In such cases a Member State must establish that their prohibitions of restrictions shall not 'constitute a means of arbitrary discrimination or a disguised restriction on trade between Member States'.[28] Broadly speaking, this requires a Member State to establish that the measure is necessary, appropriate and proportional.

f *The application of the principle by Member States in matters with no relationship to EU law.* This will include areas such as town planning and will often be in the context of well entrenched statutory regimes.[29]

Four important features of the application of the precautionary principle in the EU are apparent from this list.

First, it is clear that a diverse range of administrative institutions operating at the national and Community level are involved in the application of the precautionary principle. These institutions include: a network of national administrations; a panoply of different types of committees; the European Commission; and a range of Community agencies.[30] This is even the case where the Council is vested with the formal role of passing risk regulation standards. These institutions take many different forms and will be operating in different legal cultures. From the perspective of thinking about the precautionary principle the range of different institutions means that there will be a range of different legal contexts that the principle is

22 Case C-236/01 *Monsanto Agricoltura Italia SpA v Presidenza del Consiglio dei Ministri* [2003] ECR I-8105 at paras 110–12 and Case C-127/02 *Landelijke Vereniging tot Behoud van de Waddenzee v Staatssecretaris van Landbouw, Natuurbeheer en Visserij* [2004] ECR I-9405.

23 Case C-293/97 *Standley* [1999] ECR I-2603 and Case C-318/98 *Fornasar* [2000] ECR I-4785.

24 Case C-6/99 *Association Greenpeace France v Ministère de l'Agriculture et de la Pêche* [2000] ECR I-1651.

25 Case C-3/00 *Denmark v Commission* [2003] ECR I-2643.

26 Case C-95/01 *Criminal Proceedings Against Greenham and Abel* [2004] ECR I-1333 and Case C-41/02 *Commission v Netherlands* European Court Reports, 2 December 2004.

27 Case 120/79 *Rewe-Zentral AG v Bundesmonopolverwaltung für Branntwein* [1979] ECR 649.

28 Article 30 and *ibid.*

29 *R (On the Application of Thomas Bates & Son Ltd) v Secretary of State for Transport, Local Government and the Regions* [2005] 2 P & CR 11 and *R (On the Application of Davies) v Carmarthenshire County Council* [2004] EWHC 2847.

30 One could include international organisations as well. See for example Case C-198/03P *Commission v CEVA Santé Animale SA* ECR 12 July 2005.

applying in. At the national level, these contexts are relatively conventional, albeit controversial. The same is not true in relation to the Community level and care needs to be taken with the concept of 'administration', particularly as the EU is a polity that does not conform to the separation of powers doctrine. Rather institutional development has adhered (although not always strictly) to the very different ideal of institutional balance (both in its horizontal and vertical sense) (Prechal 1998), which has little room for the growth of an administrative arm of EU governance.[31] I use the term 'administrative' here simply to refer to institutions that have had their tasks delegated to them from a primary decision maker.

Second, and following on from this, how the principle is applied and interpreted will be influenced by debates over administrative constitutionalism operating in each specific context and legal culture (Fisher 2005; Fisher and Harding 2006). Some of those debates will be occurring at the national level, some at the Community level, and some involving both. Those with a Community aspect are particularly complex because of the *sui generis* nature of the EU and the fact that there is no agreement over what is EU administrative space. Recent discourses over comitology and the role of other committees are a good example of this (European Institute of Public Administration 2000; Joerges and Vos 2000) but the same is true in relation to the role of national administration in both implementing and participating in EU regulatory schemes (Demmke and Unfried 2001).[32] Moreover, in many cases that debate has been hampered by a lack of basic information about such institutions which has only begun to be remedied in the last several years (Vos 1999). Debates over administrative constitutionalism have also overlapped with more general debates over constitutionalism, a fact due to the non-elected nature of most Community institutions (Bignami 1999; Joerges *et al.* 2002; Lindseth 1999).

From the perspective of the precautionary principle, what all this means is that it is absurd to expect consistent interpretation and application of the principle. This is in two senses. In the first sense, it means that in any particular context there will be debates over what are the appropriate understandings of administrative constitutionalism to apply to that context. In other words, whether decision making should be on the basis of the deliberative-constitutive or rational instrumental paradigm. Thus, for example, as will be seen below, whether the European Commission's Communication on the Precautionary Principle (Commission of the European Communities 2000) is seen to be valid or not has depended on whether the rational-instrumental paradigm of administrative constitutionalism it promotes in the Community context is viewed as valid. Likewise, differing interpretations of what is understood by 'risk assessment' under the WTO SPS Agreement are dependent on what model of administrative constitutionalism is relied on in interpreting that Agreement.[33] Thus, for example, in *EC-Hormones* the Panel interpreted the Agreement in rational-instrumental terms while the Appellate Body interpreted

31 Case 9/56 *Meroni v ECSC High Authority* [1957–58] ECR 133. The basic point to note here is that the ECJ's refusal to allow delegations of powers to institutions not named within the treaties precludes the establishment of a new and distinct EU administrative arm.

32 See the discussion in Case C-6/99 *Association Greenpeace France v Ministère de l'Agriculture et de la Pêche* [2000] ECR I-1651.

33 Article 5.1 and Annex A.4.

it in deliberative-constitutive terms (Fisher 2006b).[34] The second sense in which it is improper to expect a consistent interpretation of the precautionary principle is that the nature of debates over administrative constitutionalism will vary from context to context. Thus, for example, the type of unilateral action held to be reasonable for a Member State to take when there is no harmonised scheme, and when there is one, are clearly different categories – the latter one being shaped by the recognition of the importance of co-operation between all Member State administrations and Community administration.[35] Moreover, and looking more widely, the ECJ has developed a very different jurisprudence over the validity of Community precautionary action as compared to that concerning when it is valid for a Member State to derogate from their Article 28 obligations. In the former category, the Court's approach has been shaped by emerging understandings about the role and nature of Community institutions and the role of judicial review in holding them to account.[36] In the latter category the Court's jurisprudence is a product of understandings about the nature of Article 28 EC Treaty, harmonised regimes, and understandings of administrative constitutionalism common among Member States.[37]

Third, there is clearly an institutional overlap between these different categories with only category f) artificially not doing so.[38] In other words, the same institution can find itself subject to two different discourses over administrative constitutionalism operating in different legal cultures. Thus, for example, categories a) and b) will nearly always overlap as they did when the EU banned the use certain growth hormones in beef cattle.[39] In that case, the SPS regime required the decision makers to base their measure on a risk assessment, albeit not defining what that meant, while the EU framework did not. A similar problem of overlapping discourses of administrative constitutionalism can also be seen in regard to cases falling into category e).[40] Thus, for example, in *Toolex Alpha* a decision by Sweden to ban a certain chemical was entirely consistent with the principles of administrative constitutionalism operating within Swedish legal culture. The question for the ECJ, however, was whether Sweden's regulatory action was consistent with what were understood to be as valid administrative constitutionalism norms for Member States to rely on in derogating from Article 28 EC Treaty.[41] Moreover, those that fall into

34 Panel Report, *EC Measures Concerning Meat and Meat Products (Hormones) – Complaint by the United States*, 13 February 1998, WT/DS26/R/USA and Appellate Body Report, *European Communities – Measures Concerning Meat and Meat Products (Hormones)*, 16 January 1998, WT/DS26/AB.

35 Consider the reasoning in Case C-6/99 *Association Greenpeace France v Ministère de l'Agriculture et de la Pêche* [2000] ECR I-1651.

36 Eg Case C-331/88 *FEDESA* [1990] ECR I-4023; Case C-180/96 *United Kingdom v Commission* [1998] ECR I-2265; and Case C-352/98 *Bergaderm & Goupil v Commission* [2000] I-5291.

37 Case 53/80 *Koninklijke Kaasfabriek Eyessen BV* [1981] ECR 409; Case 54/85 *Mirepoix* [1986] ECR 1067; Case 304/84 *Müller* [1985] ECR 1511; and Case C-473/98 *Kemikalienspektionen v Toolex Alpha AB* [2000] ECR I-5681.

38 I say artificially because the reality is that even in this category decision making will be influenced by EU law. See *R v Secretary of State for Trade and Industry ex parte Duddridge* [1995] Env LR 151 and *R (On the Application of Amvac Chemical UK Ltd) v Secretary of State for Environment Food and Rural Affairs* [2001] EWHC Admin 1011.

39 Case C-331/88 *FEDESA* [1990] ECR I-4023 and Appellate Body Report, *European Communities – Measures Concerning Meat and Meat Products (Hormones)*, 16 January 1998, WT/DS26/AB.

40 Case C-95/01 *Criminal Proceedings Against Greenham and Abel* [2004] ECR I-1333.

41 Case C-473/98 *Kemikalienspektionen v Toolex Alpha AB* [2000] ECR I-5681.

categories c) and d) are particularly problematic because it is not obvious what the analytical starting point should be (Bignami 2004). Should these be considered as examples of the exercise of Member State external sovereign authority or as examples of the internal exercise of authority pursuant to a statutory regime? In all these cases, ideas of administrative constitutionalism will be drawn from a range of national, supranational and transnational sources.[42]

Fourth, and following on from this, there is also a close interrelation between these different exercises of administrative power. Thus, for example, because the exercise of Community power in this area is so heavily dependent on the operation of comitology committees it means that Community administrative action often has as its impetus Member State action.[43] Likewise, because many regulatory regimes are in the form of shared administration, they require the concurrent exercise of administrative power by different Member States and Community institutions.[44] Take, for example, the decision-making processes which were subject to review in *Pfizer*,[45] one of the first CFI decisions which examined the principle. The case concerned a regulation that banned the use of certain antibiotics in animal feedingstuffs because of the potential but unproven risk that such use may lead to antibiotic resistance in humans. The regulation was the result of a decision-making process under Directive 70/524/EEC concerning additives in feedingstuffs.[46] The process was begun by Denmark (followed later by other Member States), exercising its right to apply a safeguard clause under Article 11 of that Directive by putting forward a dossier to the Standing Committee on Animal Feedingstuffs, a comitology committee.[47] Further information was collected, the Scientific Committee on Animal Nutrition was consulted, and ultimately the Standing Committee voted on the measure. What can thus be seen is that the ultimate regulation was the product of decision making by a series of interrelated administrative institutions. This is even more the case when one considers the different institutions which were also involved in identifying antibiotic resistance as a problem.[48]

What all the above highlights is that it is very difficult to make generalisations about how the precautionary principle operates in the EU. There are too many administrative contexts and too many different debates over administrative constitutionalism for that to be the case. At the same time, however, there are a series of overlaps and interdependencies between different administrative institutions. The problem is that while once there was some appreciation of these complexities this would no longer seem to be the case. This is the focus of the next section.

42 See the use of OIE risk assessment methodology in Appellate Body Report, *Australia – Measures Affecting Importation of Salmon*, 20 October 1998, WT/DS18/AB/R. For an analysis see Perez 2004.

43 As was the case in the regulatory action reviewed in Case T-70/99 *Alpharma v Council* [2002] ECR II-3495 and Case T-13/99 *Pfizer Animal Health SA v Council* [2002] ECR II-3305.

44 See the regulatory action reviewed in Case C-6/99 *Association Greenpeace France v Ministère de l'Agriculture et de la Pêche* [2000] ECR I-1651.

45 Case T-13/99 *Pfizer Animal Health SA v Council* [2002] ECR II-3305.

46 Council Directive 70/524/EEC of 23 November 1970 concerning additives in foodstuffs, [1970] *OJ* L240/1, as amended by Council Regulation EC No 2821/98 of 17 December 1998 as regards withdrawal of certain antibiotics, [1998] *OJ* L351/4.

47 Article 24 of the Directive and Case T-13/99 *Pfizer Animal Health SA v Council* [2002] ECR II-3305 at paras 29–59.

48 *Ibid.*

4 THE EUROPEAN COMMISSION'S COMMUNICATION ON THE PRECAUTIONARY PRINCIPLE

Throughout the 1990s, the principle and associated ideas of precaution were relied on by both the Community and Member States but rarely was there any detailed discussion of the principle and its consequences. With that said, a complex body of jurisprudence was developed by the CFI and ECJ in relation to when and on what basis various categories of precautionary action were valid (Scott and Vos 2002). What is clear from that body of case law is that understandings of reasonable administrative action were being shaped by a range of different factors including norms of administrative constitutionalism.[49] Indeed, a clear difference in approach can be seen in how the ECJ considered and analysed precautionary action in the different contexts.[50] With that said it is interesting to note that while the validity of action would depend on context, the courts – particularly when reviewing the validity of Member State action – were clearly being affected by the policy and administrative constitutionalism norms promoted by Community regulatory regimes.[51] There were, however, no universal requirements for a risk assessment although a careful scrutiny of information by the decision maker was required.[52] In this regard, it is useful to remember that risk assessment is itself largely a product of regulatory politics (Fisher 2006a; Jasanoff 1986).

By the end of the 1990s, there was an increased perception of a need for there to be more authoritative guidance about the nature of the precautionary principle, what it entailed, and when it could be applied. In February 2000 the European Commission published a Communication in which it outlined how *it* would apply the principle. The Communication was silent on which contexts it was planning to use it in, but clearly the Commission's concern was to explain how administrative power would be exercised in categories a) and b). First, the Communication was explicitly designed to show that EU decision making pursuant to the precautionary principle was consistent with how the WTO SPS Agreement had been interpreted in WTO dispute settlement proceedings (Majone 2005).[53] The second purpose of the Communication was to promote the 'accountability' of Commission decision making, something that was seen as of mounting importance in light of Commission corruption scandals (Craig 2000), the controversy over the Community's action in relation to BSE (Chambers 1999), new empirical insights into Community decision making (Vos 1999) as well as the growing obviousness of a democratic deficit (Weiler 1999). Moreover, there was an increasing interest in delineating the 'administrative' institutions of Community governance and constituting and

49 Compare Case 174/82 *Sandoz BV* [1983] ECR 2445; Case C-331/88 *FEDESA* [1990] ECR I-4023; and Case C-6/99 *Association Greenpeace France v Ministère de l'Agriculture et de la Pêche* [2000] ECR I-1651.

50 Refer to the cases discussed above.

51 Case C-67/97 *Anklagemyndigheden v Ditlev Bluhme* [1998] ECR I-8033.

52 Case 176/84 *Commission v Greece* [1987] ECR 1193 and Case 178/84 *Commission v Germany* [1987] ECR 1227.

53 Appellate Body Report, *European Communities – Measures Concerning Meat and Meat Products (Hormones)*, 16 January 1998, WT/DS26/AB. There appears to be no appreciation that the WTO Dispute Panel and Appellate Body ruled differently in the *Hormones* dispute settlement process (Fisher 2006b; Perez 2004).

controlling their power accordingly (Bignami 1999; Craig 1997; Majone 2002a; Vos 2000). In this regard, the Commission's Communication should be seen in the context of a number of other Commission documents at that time which had as their concern the regulating of 'administrative' decision making within the Community (Commission of the European Communities 2000; 2001; 2002).

It is useful to briefly outline the main features of the Communication guidelines. In the Communication standard setting and risk appraisal are understood to involve a scientific process of risk assessment; a political process of risk management; and risk communication.[54] Theoretically, the Communication relates to risk management but the principle only applies when a risk assessment has identified a 'potential risk' and the uncertainties surrounding it. When a risk assessment does identify a potential 'negative effect' after a scientific evaluation has been done, then, as part of risk management, there must be a decision to act or not to act and the precautionary principle will directly apply to this. In deciding this question, the Communication stresses the need for there to be an assessment of the uncertainties involved in the evaluation, and an assessment of the possible consequences of inaction, or waiting for more scientific information. The process of applying the principle must be transparent and inclusive, particularly in assessing the consequences of different forms of action and inaction. The Communication, however, describes this as a 'political decision' and provides few guidelines for this process of evaluation. What the Communication does do, however, is set out a series of standards by which the measures to be taken must be judged. Any measures taken pursuant to the principle must be proportional, non-discriminatory, consistent, based on an examination of potential costs and benefits, subject to revision in light of new data, and capable of assigning responsibility for the production of more scientific evidence.

I wish to note two features of the Communication here, both of which I consider together below. First, the Communication is promoting a rational-instrumental understanding of the precautionary principle. Second, the Communication has been understood as a set of universal guidelines that can apply to all contexts.

The Communication is a perfect example of how the precautionary principle is concerned with regulating the process of decision making on the basis of a particular model of administrative constitutionalism. The Communication is based on a 'rational–instrumental' model and, as such, its guidelines are a good example of the problems of trying to apply precaution in a regime that defines a valid decision as a factual one (Fisher and Harding 2006). Likewise, the responses to the Communication were very much in terms of whether it promoted the model of public administration that the responder deemed valid (Majone 2002b; Sunstein 2005). Graham and Hsia praised the Communication for the orderly process it created which 'requires the kind of formal policy analysis' taught in 'schools of public policy and public administration' while also criticising it for allowing the unchecked exercise of discretion (Graham and Hsia 2002). The European Council published a resolution in reply to the Communication in which it broadly agreed with it, although it placed

54 This characterisation is a direct product of earlier accountability crises in public administration where the division between science and politics was perceived as a way of ensuring that decision makers did not usurp power (Fisher 2006b).

greater stress on the importance of deliberation and the role of values, thus arguably a more deliberative-constitutive approach to standard setting (European Council 2000). A similar type of response could also be seen from the Committee on the Environment, Public Health and Consumer Policy of the European Parliament (Committee on the Environment, Public Health and Consumer Policy of the European Parliament 2000). In all cases the focus was on whether the Communication would aid 'rational' decision making, where what was understood as 'rational' was defined in accordance with understandings of administrative constitutionalism.

In 2001, the Communication clearly influenced a European Free Trade Association Court case concerning whether Norway was justified in banning vitamin- and iron-enriched cornflakes.[55] The Communication was not cited in the case but the Commission was a party and the Court's description of legitimate action pursuant to the precautionary principle paraphrased the Communication. The first substantive EU case law in which the precautionary principle was considered was in 2002 by the CFI in *Pfizer* and *Alpharma*, the former being discussed above.[56] The Court, in two lengthy judgments, upheld the regulation. There is no room here to go into the details of those decisions but there are two important things to note. First, the cases were primarily concerned with the CFI's review of the process of decision making and the consideration of the legal arguments in relation to the precautionary principle overlapped with legal arguments in relation to procedural impropriety, proportionality and manifest error of assessment. The decision is thus a good example of how the principle raises issues of process and administrative constitutionalism. Second, in considering whether there had been a proper application of the precautionary principle the CFI adhered to the Communication guidelines in its interpretation of the precautionary principle even though the Communication had not been published at the time the Regulation had been passed. After a lengthy and not always straightforward analysis of the principle the CFI stated:

> So, where experts carry out a scientific risk assessment, the competent public authority must be given sufficiently reliable and cogent information to allow it to understand the ramifications of the scientific question raised and decide upon a policy in full knowledge of the facts. Consequently, if it is not to adopt arbitrary measures, which cannot in any circumstances be rendered legitimate by the precautionary principle, the competent public authority must ensure that any measures that it takes, even preventive measures, are based on as thorough a scientific risk assessment as possible, account being taken of the particular circumstances of the case at issue. Notwithstanding the existing scientific uncertainty, the scientific risk assessment must enable the competent public authority to ascertain, on the basis of the best available scientific data and the most recent results of international research, whether matters have gone beyond the level of risk that it deems acceptable for . . . That is the basis on which the authority must decide whether preventive measures are called for.
>
> Furthermore, a scientific risk assessment must also enable the competent

55 Case E-3/00 EFTA *Surveillance Authority v Norway* [2001] 2 CMLR 47.

56 Case T-13/99 *Pfizer Animal Health SA v Council* [2002] ECR II-3305 and Case T-70/99 *Alpharma v Council* [2002] ECR II-3495.

> authority to decide, in relation to risk management, which measures appear to it to be appropriate and necessary to prevent the risk from materialising.[57]

This statement paraphrases much of the logic of the Communication. One can also see that there is a real tension in this statement between requiring a decision maker to base its decision on the facts and for it to act on other grounds in circumstances of scientific uncertainty (Fisher and Harding 2006; Lee 2005).[58] That tension makes the guidelines problematic to the point of being unworkable (Fisher 2006a).

Despite these problems in the guidelines they, and the interpretation they have been given by the Court, have been the basis for the ECJ and CFI assessing the validity of precautionary action and the application of the precautionary principle ever since.[59] In particular the CFI and ECJ have required those bodies under review to carry out as thorough a risk assessment as possible before applying the precautionary principle. The Communication has been used as the basis for assessing the validity of decision making in categories c),[60] d),[61] e)[62] and even f)[63] as well as being argued in relation to Article 230 (category b) cases).[64] Likewise, the ECJ's past case law has been re-interpreted as being consistent with the Commission's guidelines, even though those cases arguably promote a deliberative–constitutive not rational–instrumental understanding of administrative constitutionalism.[65] There has been little discussion about the relevance or appropriateness of the Communication guidelines being applied to these different contexts. Moreover, a certain pedantry can be seen in the application of the guidelines and there have been a number of cases in which the principle has not been found to apply because the principle should only apply: to provisional risk management measures;[66] where there is something more than a 'hypothetical' risk;[67] where there is scientific, as opposed to other types of, uncertainty;[68] and not to cases where the risk is well

57 Case T-13/99 *Pfizer Animal Health SA v Council* [2002] ECR II-3305 at paras 162–3.

58 Highlighted in Case C-192/01 *Commission v Denmark* [2003] ECR I-9693 at para 101 of the Advocate General's Opinion.

59 At the same time the principle is used to justify in quite general terms the promotion of health protection over economic issues. See Case T-177/02 *Malagutti-Vezinhet SA v Commission* European Court reports, 10 March 2004.

60 Case C-127/02 *Landelijke Vereniging tot Behoud van de Waddenzee v Staatssecretaris van Landbouw, Natuurbeheer en Visserij* [2004] ECR I-9405.

61 Case C-236/01 *Monsanto Agricoltura Italia SpA v Presidenza del Consiglio dei Ministri* [2003] ECR I-8105.

62 Case C-192/01 *Commission v Denmark* [2003] ECR I-9693. Case C-41/02 *Commission v Netherlands* 2 December 2004; Case C-95/01 *Criminal Proceedings Against Greenham and Abel* [2004] ECR I-1333; and Case C-24/00 *Commission v France* [2004] CMLR 25.

63 *R (on the application of Amvac Chemical UK Ltd) v Secretary of State for Environment, Food and Rural Affairs* [2001] EWHC Admin 1011 and (*Interdepartmental Liaison Group on Risk Assessment* 2002).

64 Case T-74/00 *Artegodan GmbH v Commission* [2002] ECR II-4965; Case C-286/02 *Bellio F.lli Srl v Prefettura di Treviso* [2004] EC I-3465; Case C-434/02 & C210/03 *Arnold Andre GmbH & Co. KG & Swedish Match* AG Geelhoed's Opinion, 7 September 2004; and Case C-244/33 *France v Parliament* [2005] 3 CMLR 6.

65 See the interpretation of Case 174/82 *Sandoz BV* [1983] ECR 2445 in the Advocate General's Opinion in Case C-192/01 *Commission v Denmark* [2003] ECR I-9693.

66 Case C-453/03 *ABNA Ltd v Secretary of State for Health* ECR 2005, Opinion of Advocate General, 7 April 2005.

67 Case C-244/33 *France v Parliament* [2005] 3 CMLR 6 per Advocate General.

68 Case C-434/02 & C210/03 *Arnold Andre GmbH & Co. KG & Swedish Match* ECR 2004, Advocate General Geelhoed's Opinion, 7 September 2004.

known.[69] Indeed, it would seem that the principle is being treated more as a 'bright line' rule which dictates certain action in particular situations rather than a flexible principle that might result in a variety of outcomes.

Moreover, in discussing EU risk regulation, there have been three tendencies which are a product of the current approach to thinking about the precautionary principle. First, the precautionary principle has become synonymous with risk management even though the relationship between the two is a product of the SPS Agreement and the promotion of a rational-instrumental paradigm (Fisher 2006b; Fisher and Harding 2006). There has been little recognition of the fact that risk assessment is a flexible regulatory construct or that the principle may operate separate from risk management. Second, the precautionary principle has been treated as shorthand for describing the whole of European risk regulation (Kogan 2005; Wiener and Rogers 2002). The principle is described as a 'central guideline' of EU consumer policy (Strünck 2005) and there seems little appreciation that the principle may have different meanings. Third, and following on from this, there appears to be little appreciation in some quarters that the principle is operating in different contexts and that this will result in different interpretations of the principle and different outcomes (Marchant and Mossman 2004; Sunstein 2005). Indeed the variation of definition is largely seen as a weakness of the principle rather than reflecting its context-bound nature.

All of the above is somewhat ironic. While the Commission described its Communication as a contribution to the 'ongoing' debate, the result of its publication has been to silence that debate (European Commission 2000). The principle has become a set of fixed rules and as such has required decision makers to apply a rigid framework for decision making rather than adapting their decision-making process to the problem at hand. There has been a shift away from thinking about the reasonableness of administrative process and rationality to thinking in terms of a formula. This is particularly odd when the Communication is not particularly logical and the ECJ and the CFI are increasingly discussing principles of administrative constitutionalism while reviewing complex administrative decision making in areas where the principle is not being applied.[70]

5 OPENING PANDORA'S BOX

What all of the above highlights is that there is, at present, an inherent tension in thinking about the role of the precautionary principle in EU risk regulation. This tension is between recognising the context- and culture-bound nature of the precautionary principle and of the promotion of a single approach to thinking about the principle. I deal with each briefly below. I should stress that in identifying this tension I have no answers to it.

A study of the precautionary principle and EU risk regulation requires an

69 Case E-4/04 *Pedicel AS v Sosial- OG Helsedirektoratet* (Directorate for Health and Social Affairs) [2005] 2 CMLR 7.

70 Case C-378/00 *Commission v Council* [2003] ECR I-937 and Case C-198/03P *Commission v CEVA Santé Animale SA* ECR 12 July 2005.

engagement with diversity – diversity of contexts, legal cultures, institutions, and ideas of administrative constitutionalism. As such, the principle has an important role in helping scholars and decision makers to think about an overlooked aspect of European integration – administrative power. To modify fashionable terminology, the principle is concerned with the 'thru-put' legitimacy of European administrative institutions, rather than with input and output legitimacy which have tended to be the focus of European integration scholarship (Scharpf 1999). In particular, there is a need to abandon quite vague concepts such as EU 'regulatory space' (Scott 2001) and the 'regulatory state' (Majone 1996) and replace them with a frame of inquiry which pays far more attention to legal and institutional detail and the way in which different paradigms of administrative constitutionalism operate (Fisher 2004). The precautionary principle's operation is likely to be controversial and its operation requires scholars, lawyers and policy actors to take a 'hard look' at the institutional arrangements for regulating risk (Stirling, Renn and van Zwanenberg 2006).[71] This 'hard look' is particularly challenging in the EU context because there is no settled concept of the administrative sphere. While the challenges involved in needing to think about the diverse and pluralistic nature of European administrative power should not be underestimated, nor are they particularly new to scholars and decision makers. Issues concerning the supremacy of one legal culture over another (Weiler 1999), regulatory integration (Joerges and Dehousse 2002) and legal pluralism (La Torre 1999; Snyder 1999) are constant features of European integration and the *raison d'être* of EU lawyers. The principle, by highlighting administrative constitutionalism in the EU, is simply adding another dimension to practical and theoretical inquiries about EU integration (Everson 1999). This fact has not gone ignored by commentators. Ladeur in reviewing the *Pfizer* case noted, after considering the intergovernmental decision-making processes at its heart, that:

> the multi-polar character of the European administrative system might even turn out to be well adapted to the setting up of such a network-like structure of decision-making, thus enabling learning processes, mutual comparison, and experimentation with different types of relationships and co-ordination.[72]

Ladeur's comments suggest that the operation of the precautionary principle is an opportunity to explore more closely the nature of administrative power in the EU. I would wholeheartedly agree, but be more circumspect about the opportunities for 'learning processes, mutual comparison, and experimentation'.

This is due to the developments seen above which have resulted in an approach to the precautionary principle, which point in an opposite direction from those that emphasise the diversity of legal culture and administration in the EU. Over the last five years at least, there has been an increasing tendency to think about the precautionary principle in universal and formulaic terms. Not only has there been very little questioning of the logic of the European Commission's Communication, but it

71 I use the term 'hard look' on purpose to invoke the 'hard look' debates of US law in the 1970s. See *Ethyl Corp v EPA* 541 F 2d 1 (DC Cir 1976).

72 Ladeur 2003: 1479.

has also been applied to all the contexts in which the principle is operating. Tentatively, I advance two possible reasons why this has occurred, both of which are closely tied to the process of European integration, albeit in different ways.

First, as Maduro argued as part of his economic constitution thesis, norms at the Community level are the most desirable basis for constitution building (Maduro 1998). As such, the Commission's Communication, despite its explicit statement about its limited applicability, has become a standard for judging the exercise of all administrative power in the EU because it is an authoritative 'harmonised' understanding of the principle. This is even though those guidelines are the product of specific debates over administrative constitutionalism in areas that do not relate to how a Member State exercises power. If this is the case, then inherent in integration is a tendency towards harmonising administrative constitutionalism. It is only a tendency, however, and this does raise the question of whether such harmonisation is inevitable.

Second, the reality is that due to the interconnection between different forms of state action the same rules apply even if there is no attempt to build an economic constitution. Thus, for example, a Member State applying to derogate under Article 95(4) EC Treaty must apply to the Commission to do so, which will assess that decision on its own internal guidelines (Scott and Vos 2002). The close interdependence and overlap between the different contexts require, as a matter of practical reality, different decision makers to take the same approach. In other words, inherent in the process of European integration may be a necessity to harmonise approaches to administrative constitutionalism. If this is the case, and I suspect it is not, then this raises some very difficult questions about the legitimacy of integration, which has tended to at least give lip service to the importance of national legal cultures.

What this tension, as well as my analysis above, highlights is that there are numerous unanswered questions concerning the operation of the precautionary principle in the EU as well as the development of risk regulation regimes more generally. Indeed, by analysing the relationship between the precautionary principle, legal culture, and administrative constitutionalism in the EU, I am literally opening up a Pandora's box of issues for scholars and decision makers. The image of Pandora's box is a hackneyed one, but I think particularly apt for this context because the analysis above is not simply identifying future lines of inquiry but also highlighting how European integration raises some very difficult issues that, once identified, are not easily solved. For those that have tended to view the principle in universal terms, it is clear that this is the wrong approach, as far more attention needs to be paid to particular contexts and legal culture. At the same time, however, the experimentalism and diversity that some have argued for may not be practically possible – uniformity may be the only realistic approach in the EU to thinking about the precautionary principle and risk regulation. Moreover, to add to the complexity, what is overwhelmingly clear is that there is a close interrelationship between risk regulation and European integration – the operation of the principle highlighting the ways in which the harmonisation of regulatory regimes is not a straightforward task.[73] In particular, I would argue that the tension between diversity and uniformity

73 Jasanoff has pointed to the same relationship in the context of EU biotechnology regulation. See Jasanoff 2005.

in thinking about the principle and administrative constitutionalism reflects a wider tension in the process of integration.

6 CONCLUSION

For those wishing for the precautionary principle to be a neat and simple formula, this chapter will have been a grave disappointment. Rather in this chapter I have opened up a Pandora's box of issues concerned with the nature of administrative power in the EU by doing the following. I have shown how the precautionary principle is a flexible legal principle, the operation of which will depend on context and legal culture. I have identified the fact that the principle applies to both the internal and external exercise of state power and, in so doing, raises issues of administrative constitutionalism. I have examined the EU context and shown how the principle has six overlapping spheres of operation which highlight: the diversity of public administration and administrative constitutionalism in the EU; the fact that decision makers are subject to competing discourses over administrative constitutionalism; and that the different spheres of operation are interdependent. I have shown how there is an increasing trend to thinking of the precautionary principle in monolithic terms. Finally, I have highlighted that there is an inherent tension between diversity and uniformity involved in the operation of the precautionary principle in the EU. As noted, I also have no answers to the tensions that are inherent in the operation of the principle of precaution. Nonetheless, the particular tensions which are revealed by a peculiarly European debate on precaution prove to be highly instructive, being reproduced as the following chapters demonstrate, on all national, supranational and international level of the application of the principle of precaution.

BIBLIOGRAPHY

Barnard, C. (2004) *The Substantive Law of the EU: The Four Freedoms*, Oxford: Oxford University Press.

Bignami, F. (2004) 'Foreword', *LCP* 68: 1–20.

Bignami, F. (1999) 'The democratic deficit in European rulemaking: a call for notice and comment in comitology', *Harv Int'l LJ* 40: 451–515.

Bohanes, J. (2002) 'Risk regulation in WTO law: a procedure-based approach to the precautionary principle', *Colum J Transnat'l L* 40: 323–89.

Button, C. (2004) *The Power to Protect: Trade, Health and Uncertainty in the WTO*, Oxford: Hart Publishing.

Cameon, J. and Abouchar, J. (1991) 'The precautionary principle: a fundamental principle for the protection of the global environment', *BC Int'l & Comp L Rev* 14: 1–17.

Chambers, G. (1999) 'The BSE crisis and the European Parliament', in C. Joerges and E. Vos (eds), *EU Committees: Social Regulation, Law and Politics*, Oxford: Hart Publishing, 95–106.

Christoforou, T. (2002) 'The origins and content of the precautionary principle in European community law', in C. Leben and J. Verhoven (eds), *Le Principe de Précaution – Aspects de Droit International et Communautaire*, Paris: Pantheon Assas, L.G.D.J. Diffuseur, 205–30.

Cook, B. (1996) *Bureaucracy and Self Government: Reconsidering the Role of Public Administration in American Government*, Baltimore: Johns Hopkins University Press.

Craig, P. (2000) 'The fall and renewal of the Commission: accountability, contract and administrative organisation', *ELJ* 6: 98–116.

Craig, P. (1997) 'Democracy and rule-making within the EC: an empirical and normative assessment', *ELJ* 3: 105–30.

da Cruz Vilaca, J. (2004) 'The precautionary principle in EC law', *EPL* 10: 369–406.

Demmke, C. and Unfried, M. (2001) *European Environmental Policy: The Administrative Challenge for the Member States*, Maastricht: European Institute of Public Administration.

Deville, A. and Harding, R. (1997) *Applying the Precautionary Principle*, Sydney: Federation Press.

Douglas, M. and Wildasky, A. (1982) *Risk and Culture*, Berkeley: University of California Press.

Dovers, S. and Handmer, J. (1999) 'Ignorance, sustainability and the precautionary principle', in R. Harding and E. Fisher (eds), *Perspectives on the Precautionary Principle*, Sydney: Federation Press, 167–89.

Dworkin, R. (1977) *Taking Rights Seriously*, London: Duckworth.

European Council (2000) *Council Resolution on the Precautionary Principle*, Nice European Council Meeting: Presidency Conclusions.

European Institute of Public Administration (2000) *Governance by Committee: The Role of Committees in European Policy Making and Policy*, Maastricht: European Institute of Public Administration, Research Paper 00/GHA.

Everson, M. (1999) 'The constitutionalisation of European administrative law: legal oversight of a stateless internal market', in C. Joerges and E. Vos (eds), *EU Committees: Social Regulation, Law and Politics*, Oxford: Hart Publishing, 281–310.

Fisher, E. (2007) *Risk Regulation and Administrative Constitutionalism*, Oxford: Hart Publishing.

Fisher, E. (2006a) 'Risk and environmental law: a beginner's guide', in B. Richardson and S. Wood (eds), *Environmental Law for Sustainability: A Critical Reader*, Oxford, Hart Publishing, 97–127.

Fisher, E. (2006b) 'Beyond the science/democracy dichotomy: the World Trade Organisation sanitary and phytosanitary agreement and administrative constitutionalism', in C. Joerges and E.-U. Petersmann (eds), *Transnational Trade Governance and Social Regulation: Tensions and Interdependencies*, Oxford: Hart Publishing, 327–51.

Fisher, E. (2005) 'Precaution, law and principles of good administration', *Water Science and Technology* 52: 19–24.

Fisher, E. (2004) 'Unpacking the toolbox: or why the public/private divide is important in EC environmental law', in J.-B. Auby and M. Freedland (eds), *The Public Law/Private Law Divide: une entente assez cordiale?*, Paris: L.G.D.J. Diffuseur, 215–42.

Fisher, E. (2002) 'Precaution, precaution everywhere: developing a "common understanding" of the precautionary principle in the European Community', *MJ* 9: 7–28.

Fisher, E. (2001) 'Is the precautionary principle justifiable?', *JEL* 13: 317–34.

Fisher, E. and Harding, R. (2006) 'The precautionary principle and administrative constitutionalism: the development of frameworks for applying the precautionary principle', in E. Fisher, J. Jones and R. von Schomberg (eds), *Implementing the Precautionary Principle: Perspectives and Prospects*, Cheltenham: Edward Elgar, 113–36.

Fuller, L. (1978) 'The forms and limits of adjudication', *Harv L Rev* 92: 353–409.

Godard, O. (2006) 'The precautionary principle and catastrophism on tenterhooks: lessons from constitutional reform in France', in E. Fisher, J. Jones and R. von Schomberg (eds), *Implementing the Precautionary Principle: Perspectives and Prospects*, Cheltenham: Edward Elgar, 63–87.

Graham, J. and Hsia, S. (2002) 'Europe's precautionary principle: promise and pitfalls', *Journal of Risk Research* 5: 371–90.

Harding, R. and Fisher, E. (eds) (1999) *Perspectives on the Precautionary Principle*, Sydney: Federation Press.

Interdepartmental Liaison Group on Risk Assessment (2002) *The Precautionary Principle: Policy and Application*, available at: <http://www.hse.gov.uk/aboutus/meetings/ilgra/pppa,pdf>.

Jaeger, C., Renn, O., Rosa, E. and Webler, T. (2001) *Risk, Uncertainty, and Rational Action*, London: Earthscan.

Jasanoff, S. (2005) *Designs on Nature: Science and Democracy in Europe and the United States*, Princeton: Princeton University Press.

Jasanoff, S. (1990) *The Fifth Branch: Science Advisers as Policy Makers*, Cambridge: Harvard University Press.

Jasanoff, S. (1986) *Risk Management and Political Culture: A Comparative Study of Science in the Policy Context*, New York: Sage Publications.

Jasanoff, S. and Wynne, B. (1998) 'Science and decision making', in Rayner, S. and Malone, E. (eds), *Human Choice and Climate Change – Volume One*, Pacific Northwest National Laboratory: Battelle Press, 1–87.

Joerges, C. and Dehousse, R. (eds) (2002) *Good Governance in Europe's Integrated Market*, Oxford: Oxford University Press.

Joerges, C., Mény, Y. and Weiler, J. (eds) (2002) *Mountain or Molehill: A Critical Appraisal of the Commission White Paper on Governance*, Florence: European University Institute.

Joerges, C. and Vos, E. (eds) (2000) *EU Committees: Social Regulation, Law and Politics*, Oxford: Hart Publishing.

Jones, J. and Bronitt, S. (2006) 'The burden and standard of proof in environmental regulation: the precautionary principle in an Australian administrative context', in E. Fisher, J. Jones and R. von Schomberg (eds), *Implementing the Precautionary Principle: Perspectives and Prospects*, Cheltenham: Edward Elgar, 137–59.

Jowell, J. (2000) 'Of vires or vacuums: the constitutional context of judicial review', in C. Forsyth (ed.), *Judicial Review and the Constitution*, Oxford: Hart Publishing, 327–39.

Klinke, A. and Renn, O. (2002) 'A new approach to risk evaluation and management: risk-based, precaution based, and discourse based strategies', *Risk Analysis* 22, 1071–94.

Kogan, L. (2005) *Exporting Precaution: How Europe's Risk Free Regulatory Agenda Threatens American Free Enterprise*, Washington: Washington Legal Foundation.

Ladeur, K.-H. (2003) 'The introduction of the precautionary principle into EU law: a pyrrhic victory for environmental and public health law? Decision-making under conditions of complexity in multi-level political systems', *CML Rev* 40: 1455–79.

Lee, M. (2005) *EU Environmental Law: Challenges, Change and Decision-Making*, Oxford: Hart Publishing.

Lindseth, P. (1999) 'Democratic legitimacy and the administrative character of supranationalism: the example of the European Community', *Colum L Rev*, 628–738.

MacCormick, N. (1999) *Questioning Sovereignty*, Oxford: Oxford University Press.

Maduro, M. (1998) *We, the Court: The European Court of Justice and the European Economic Constitution*, Oxford: Hart Publishing.

Majone, G. (2005) *Dilemmas of European Integration: The Ambiguities and Pitfalls of Integration by Stealth*, Oxford: Oxford University Press.

Majone, G. (2002a) 'Delegation of regulatory powers in a mixed polity', *ELJ* 8: 319–39.

Majone, G. (2002b) 'What price safety? The precautionary principle and its policy implications', *Journal of Common Market Studies* 40: 89–109.

Majone, G. (1996) *Regulating Europe*, London: Routledge.

Marchant, G. and Mossman, K. (2004) *Arbitrary and Capricious: The Precautionary Principle in the European Union Courts*, Washington DC: The AEI Press.

Mashaw, J. (2002) 'Deconstructing debate, reconstructing law', *Cornell L Rev* 87: 682–89.

Mckinney, W. and Hammer Hill, H. (2000) 'Of sustainability and precaution: the logical, epistemological, and moral problems of the precautionary principle and their implications for sustainable development', *Ethics and the Environment* 5: 77–87.

McNelis, N. (2001) 'The role of the judge in the EU and WTO: lessons from the BSE and hormones cases', *Journal of International Economic Law* 4: 189–208.

McNelis, N. (2000) 'EU communication on the precautionary principle', *Journal of International Economic Law* 3: 545–51.

von Moltke, K. (1988) 'The Vorsorgeprinzip in West German environmental policy', in Royal Commission on Environmental Pollution (ed.), *Best Practicable Environmental Option – 12th Report*, London: HMSO, 57–70.

Morris, J. (2000) 'Defining the precautionary principle', in J. Morris (ed.), *Rethinking Risk and the Precautionary Principle*, Oxford: Butterworth-Heinemann, 1–21.

Nelken, D. (2001) 'Towards a sociology of legal adaptation', in D. Nelken and J. Feest (eds), *Adapting Legal Cultures*, Oxford: Hart Publishing, 7–55.

O'Riordan, T., Cameron, J. and Jordan, A. (eds) (2001) *Reinterpreting the Precautionary Principle*, London: Cameron May.

Perez, O. (2004) *Ecological Sensitivity and Global Legal Pluralism*, Oxford: Hart Publishing.

Prechal, S. (1998) 'Institutional balance: a fragile principle with uncertain contents', in T. Heukels, N. Blokker and M. Brus (eds), *The European Union after Amsterdam*, The Hague: Kluwer Law International, 273–95.

de Sadeleer, N. (2002) *Environmental Principles: From Political Slogans to Legal Rules*, Oxford: Oxford University Press.

de Sadeleer, N. (2000) 'The enforcement of the precautionary principle by German, French and Belgian courts', *RECIEL* 9: 144–51.

Scharpf, F. (1999) *Governing in Europe: Effective and Democratic?*, Oxford: Oxford University Press.

Scott, C. (2001) 'Analysing regulatory space: fragmented resources and institutional design', *PL*, 329–53.

Scott, J. (2004) 'The precautionary principle before the European courts', in R. Macrory (ed.), *Principles of European Environmental Law*, Groningen: Europa Law Publishing, 51–67.

Scott, J. and Vos, E. (2002) 'The juridification of uncertainty: observations on the ambivalence of the precautionary principle within the EU and WTO', in C. Joerges and R. Dehousse (eds), *Good Governance in Europe's Integrated Market*, Oxford: Oxford University Press, 253–86.

Scott, S. (2001) 'How cautious is precautious? Antarctic tourism and the precautionary principle', *ICLQ* 50, 964–71.

Snyder, F. (1999) 'Governing economic globalisation: global legal pluralism and European law', *ELJ* 5: 334–74.

Stirling, A. (2001) 'The precautionary principle in science and technology', in T. O'Riordan *et al.* (eds), *Reinterpreting the Precautionary Principle*, London: Cameron May, 61–94.

Stirling, A., Renn, O. and van Zwanenberg, P. (2006) 'A framework for the precautionary governance of food safety: integrating science and participation in the social appraisal of risk', in E. Fisher, J. Jones and R. von Schomberg (eds), *Implementing the Precautionary Principle: Perspectives and Prospects*, Cheltenham: Edward Elgar, 284–315.

Strünck, C. (2005) 'Mix up: models of governance and framing opportunities in US and EU consumer policy', *Journal of Consumer Policy* 28: 203–30.

Sunstein, C. (2005) *Laws of Fear: Beyond the Precautionary Principle*, Cambridge: Cambridge University Press.

La Torre, M. (1999) 'Legal pluralism as evolutionary achievement of community law', *Ratio Juris* 12: 182–95.

Trouwborst, A. (2002) *Evolution and Status of the Precautionary Principle in International Law*, The Hague: Kluwer International.

Vos, E. (2000) 'Reforming the European Commission: What role for EU agencies?', *CML Rev.* 37: 1113–34.

Vos, E. (1999) *Institutional Frameworks of Community Health and Safety Legislation: Committees, Agencies and Private Bodies*, Oxford: Hart Publishing.

Weiler, J. (1999) *The Constitution of Europe: Do the New Clothes Have an Emperor?*, Cambridge: Cambridge University Press.

Wiener, J. and Rogers, M. (2002) 'Comparing precaution in the United States and Europe', *Journal of Risk Research* 5: 317–49.

Wynne, B. (1992) 'Uncertainty and environmental learning', *Global Environmental Change* 2: 111–27.

Part II

National systems on food and biotechnology

Section 1: Case studies on food regulation

Chapter 3

Uncertainties in regulating food safety in France

Olivier Borraz and Julien Besançon

This chapter commences by making a distinction between 'scientific uncertainty' and 'regulatory uncertainty'. The distinction is not mere sophistry. Instead, as the case study on the regulation of foodstuffs in France readily demonstrates, it is important to always bear both of these concepts in mind, since regulatory uncertainty (within the institutions of foodstuffs regulation) appears also to have a corresponding effect upon the severity of impact of cases of scientific uncertainty.

In the growing literature on risk regulation, uncertainty has become a useful notion to delineate and identify the difficulties that regulators must confront when managing highly controversial issues. The notion generally refers to the state of scientific knowledge ('known unknowns', but now also 'unknown unknowns'). Social scientists have largely focused on the construction of uncertainty (Wynne 1992); how it is handled by risk managers (Jasanoff 1990); or under what circumstances the precautionary principle applies (Noiville 2003). By contrast, they have less rarely acknowledged the existence of other types of uncertainties, such as those relating to the behaviour of agents and organisations in relation to hazardous activities or substances. Less often still have they analysed uncertainties in the way regulation is designed and implemented.

Yet, as Hood *et al.* (2001) have shown, many risk regulation regimes are characterised by a substantial disconnection between the different institutions in charge of producing rules, as well as between the different components of the regulatory process: fragmented institutional settings make it hard to determine who is in charge of a particular task; there is often haziness between regimes as regards who is responsible for what; the division of standard setting, enforcement and monitoring produces functional 'underlaps' rather than redundancy – and it is often in the interest of established institutional players to keep functional components separate rather than to bring them together.

Furthermore, ever since the pioneering works of Pressman and Wildavsky, policy studies have widely acknowledged the fact that the process of implementation rarely satisfies the 'great expectations' placed in rules by regulators, but rather often results in distortion or clear cases of non-compliance (Pressman and Wildavsky 1973). Likewise, commentators have also noted that the implementation phase is less a matter of strict application of the law and more a time of intense policy making (Lascoumes 1994). Seen in this light, scholars should make a greater effort to analyse what is actually taking place on the level of implementation, asking themselves whether such actions have aided or retarded a reduction in risk.

The French food safety regulation regime possesses a highly complex and fragmented institutional character and is further distinguishable in relation to the significant range of actors who are in charge of implementing national regulation. This includes not only national administrations (with their central and field services), political actors, local government, and scientific and technical bodies, but also agro-business agents (farmers, producers and retailers), who play a key role, alongside public entities, in implementing public rules and producing their own private standards and labels.

What we wish to argue is that such a situation fosters uncertainty, since it makes it harder to anticipate and coordinate the behaviour of different agents. In turn, this uncertainty can play a determinant role in the emergence of risk issues, by triggering crises, amplifying controversies or putting a problem on the public agenda. In fact, as this case study demonstrates, scientific uncertainty is often a by-product of tensions within the foodstuffs regulatory regime. In other words, risk often arises within food production due to the mismanagement of food issues by the bodies in charge of their regulation. This mismanagement is a direct result of the complex and fragmented nature of the regulatory system, of a lack of coordination, of the opposition between multiple interests and professional cultures, and of incomplete circulation of information. We term this 'regulatory uncertainty'; that is, attitudes and behaviours of the various agents within the regulatory regime responsible for the production, implementation and monitoring of rules, where such attitudes and behaviours cause uncertainty in the minds of other agents who are not able to predict or anticipate them and adjust their own behaviour accordingly.

Within the foodstuffs regulatory regime, regulatory uncertainty is not a direct result of its complex and fragmented nature – after all, most regimes are complex and fragmented – but rather derives from a series of shifts that have destabilised the previous regime and its coordinating procedures (ie procedures that had as their major aim predictability for all the different agents); these shifts have introduced new opportunities along with new constraints upon those agents who wish to play a role in the coordination of the new regime.

We start by describing the foodstuffs regulation system before the BSE crisis and the deep-seated modifications in the foodstuffs regulatory regime that the crisis prompted. We then move on to analyse tensions and conflicts within the new regime and their subsequent impact upon the emergence of risk issues, and even crises.

I FOOD SAFETY REGULATION BEFORE THE BSE CRISIS: CONFLICTING GOALS AND ACTORS

As we shall demonstrate, the history of foodstuffs regulation and agriculture in France is one of increasing instability. While some authors argue that instability was caused by the BSE crisis, we contend that it is instability due to changes in the regulation regime which in fact contributed to that crisis (Borraz, Besançon and Clergeau 2006).

Public authorities in France have traditionally been preoccupied with ensuring food safety. Before the Revolution, regulations were passed by cities or counties to protect populations from rotten meat or poisoned water (Ferrières 2002). In the 19th century, when chemical substances were frequently added to foodstuffs, laws were passed on products like meat, butter and wine. These regulations were mostly aimed at preventing frauds and falsifications and at securing fair competition; considerations of public health and consumer protection, although present, were only secondary (Stanziani 2005).

It is only at the beginning of the 20th century that general laws were passed: in 1902, a 'hygienist' law set in motion the creation of a system of public health (with, for example, compulsory declaration of transmissible diseases); and in 1905, at the request of agro-food producers, a law was passed to fight against frauds in foodstuffs, which also provided for the creation of a Fraud Inspectorate within the Ministry of Agriculture to centralise the preparation of regulation and the implementation of controls. Nonetheless, economic and trade objectives still prevailed over issues of public health.

During the 20th century, regulation was passed to regulate new products or substances, such as additives or artificial colourings, in line with the demands of increasingly internationalised markets. However, a distinct and coherent set of institutions and policies to manage food safety was never established. Food safety fell instead to the Ministry of Agriculture, which placed responsibility on two different departments: the Fraud and the Veterinary Inspectorates. The former dealt with frauds and falsifications with regard to packaged foods, also controlling the implementation of standards and norms by industry and retailers; the latter was concerned with the quality and safety of meat and meat-based products and with the sanitary control of farms and slaughterhouses. Although complementary, these two departments competed with each other over prerogatives and approaches.

From the 1950s onwards, foodstuffs regulation formed a part of a strongly integrated agricultural model of co-management between State authorities and farmers' unions (Müller 1984). Within this regime, food safety was not a priority: even if consumer protection was taken into account, the main purposes of regulation were the development of agro-food business and the defence of the farmers' interests. Regulation promoted a model of intensive agriculture, whose main concern was to strengthen productivity and develop trade according to the goals of the European Common Agricultural Policy (CAP). The major priority was food security, rather than food safety, ie the production and provision of food in sufficient quantities for internal consumption and exports rather than combating adverse health effects.

In 1985, the Fraud Inspectorate was transferred from the Ministry of Agriculture to the Consumer Affairs department of the Ministry of Economy and Finance. From this time, two ministries were in charge of food safety regulation and control. Both worked closely with farmers, agro-food producers and retailers. The Ministry of Health, meanwhile, continued to play only a minor role. Even though it managed the *Conseil Supérieur d'Hygiène Public de France*, a scientific advisory body with responsibilities in the field of public health, other expert committees were created within the Ministries of Agriculture or Consumer Affairs to support their own regulatory activities.

By the mid-1980s, this model was coming under pressure. First, external pressures began to have an impact. With the construction of the European Common Market, food safety regulation became motivated by the desire to lift all obstacles capable of impeding the free movement of goods. From the 1980s onwards, derogations from European free movement provisions were only possible where it could be demonstrated that health, safety or consumer interests were under threat. Although

European regulators aimed to overcome these potential obstacles through legal harmonisation, the perception within France was that the definition of common health and safety norms was not based on a high degree of protection in terms of public health, but rather – given the large-scale reliance on primary rather than secondary EU law – was derived from the identification of the smallest common denominator acceptable, based on all the available scientific data. Trade negotiations at worldwide level, first in GATT (General Agreement on Tariffs and Trade) and later WTO (World Trade Organization), also aimed to reduce trade barriers. The signature of the 1994 Sanitary and Phytosanitary agreement, by which states recognised the norms of Codex Alimentarius as the basis for food trade regulation, compelled France to strengthen its scientific expertise if it wanted to use stricter norms than those provided by Codex. Thus, in order to achieve free market rules and procedures, scientific expertise was given a specific role in the regulatory process.[1]

Second, however, the traditional foodstuffs regulatory regime also faced internal pressures. The intensive agricultural model was put into question by the CAP crisis and its reform in the early 1990s (reduction in subsidies, production levels and growing environmental awareness). Farmers were accused of environment pollution. Consumers, growing concerned about health and environmental issues were calling for increased foodstuffs variety and quality and, by the end of the 1970s, were organising campaigns against junk food, unsafe additives and beef hormones.

Alongside these changes, deeper transformations were taking place in foodstuffs regulation, with the development of private rule making. The role of private actors in the management of foodstuffs safety has been continuously growing since the 1980s. In 1983, a law on consumer safety[2] asserted the principles of product safety for public health: it reinforced the control powers of State authorities and required that firms implement systems of auto-control.

Given the lack of state supervision resources, this system displays a clear preference for private auto-control, with public intervention measures defining objectives or thresholds, and with the private sector being expected to adopt the necessary implementation measures to achieve these objectives. This facilitates State control of procedures; meanwhile, responsibility is delegated to private actors to exercise controls. This public-private partnership aims to guarantee the safety of food products through a flexible system adapted to the development of innovations and the free movement of goods.[3]

A further policy instrument developed was that of labelling. Prior to the 1980s, the labelling of food products was controlled by the State. Labels indicated origins

1 European Member States were prompted to organise their own processes of expertise under the pressure of a 1993 directive on scientific cooperation. In France, the *Centre national d'études et de recommendations sur la nutrition et l'alimentation* was charged with the coordination of scientific research institutions (Clergeau 2000).

2 Law 83–660 of 21 July 1983 on consumer safety, *Loi 83–660 du 21/07/1983 relative à la sécurité des consommateurs et modifiant diverses dispositions de la loi du 01–08–1905.*

3 The same strategy was adopted within the EU with the achievement of the common market and the use of the 'new approach' for harmonisation. France played an important role in the adoption of the European Council Directive 93/43/EEC ([1993] *OJ* L175), which fixes general rules of hygiene for food products and requires that firms adopt procedures of auto-control based upon the HACCP (Hazard Analysis Critical Control Point) method.

of the product (place and methods of production). The best known of these labels are the *appellations d'origine*, created in 1919, which became the AOC (*Appellations d'Origine Contrôlée*) overseen by the INAO (*Institut National des Appellations d'Origine*) in 1935; but many others abound.[4] In 1988, the *Commission nationale des labels et certifications de produits* took responsibility for delivering certifications of conformity with national specifications. Public authorities and farmers' lobbies alike had come to the conclusion that labels could offer a solution to the financial and distributional crisis that agriculture was now confronting and, in particular, would answer public quality concerns (Sylvander 1995). By 1995, 'specific quality products' made up 10 per cent of the agro-food market. They were now seen as an important source of growth rather than a supporting mechanism for smaller producers.

In turn, however, labels were to be challenged by other quality 'marks', including major retail 'brands' used by retailers to exert price pressure upon producers and also to subject producers to their own quality standards and control procedures (audits and quality insurance). In some cases, these brands were produced by retailers acting on their own and then imposed on their suppliers; in others, they were negotiated between retailers and professional groups in a specific field. Thus, food production witnessed a proliferation of labels and quality marks through which producers, industry and retailers guaranteed the quality of their products (origin, ingredients and production methods) and their compliance with public regulation.

Quality, accordingly, became an important component of food policy. It also reflected structural changes in the foodstuffs regulation system, more particularly, the growing strength of major retailers and their battle with producers, which focused upon their desire to lower prices and provide consumers with a larger variety of quality products.

All the above changes prompted public authorities and professionals to adapt. It is during this period that the first major crisis (BSE) hit, followed shortly thereafter by the controversy over GMOs. While it is commonplace to consider that these events destabilised French agriculture and the foodstuffs regulatory regime, we suggest that it is the shifts within the destabilised regime that made it possible for these events to occur, or at least that amplified their impact. Furthermore, as we will see later, these crises did not impact upon such structural change, but actually served to reinforce it.

2 THE BSE CRISIS AND THE REFORM OF THE FRENCH FOOD SAFETY REGULATION REGIME

With the BSE crisis of 1996, food safety became a salient issue on the public agenda. It revealed important dysfunctions both in beef industry practices and in their supervision by the State. But the crisis also echoed the blood transfusion scandal of

4 A definition of the specifications to be respected in order for a product to benefit from an AOC is first worked out by the producers and approved by the INAO, followed by the ministries of Agriculture and Finance. Other quality labels are the *Label Rouge* founded in 1960, dietetic products in 1966, biological food or mountain label in 1985.

the mid-1980s, making health safety a political priority. To most observers, the BSE crisis raised many of the same issues, albeit in a different sector. Subsequently, food safety became a sub-category of a more general theme: health safety (which encompasses drugs, medical, food, occupational and environmental safety).

The consequence was a reform of the foodstuffs regulatory regime. It was to adopt the more general features of a modern and efficient system of health safety regulation. The keywords were, alongside accountability: scientific excellence, transparency and independence.[5] The use of these principles suggested that the scandals were the result of a regulatory regime marked by policy-capture by private interests, a lack of transparency in the decision-making process, the absence of any diversity or discussion among experts, and insufficient resources or lacking will to control the implementation of rules. Thus, future avoidance of crisis and efficient regulation of future foodstuffs safety was assumed to be dependent upon: the provision of independent expertise; the establishment of a clear separation between risk assessment and management; the facilitation of discussion and debate; and a clear definition of responsibilities and control mechanisms.

2.1 AFSSA: new actor in the risk regulation regime

The 1998 law on health safety[6] upheld these principles, creating a set of agencies in charge of risk assessment. As regards food safety, AFSSA (*Agence Française de Sécurité Sanitaire des Aliments*) was to act as an independent agency assessing risks on the basis of expert knowledge, while the InVS (*Institut de Veille Sanitaire*) was to trigger alerts in case of epidemics due to food contamination and identify the culprits. The creation of these agencies potentially challenged the previous regulatory regime applying both to food safety and to food production.

Their origins are grounded in the development of public health policies going back to the beginning of the 1990s in France: after the blood transfusion scandal, it appeared necessary to reinforce the expertise and management capacities of the Ministry of Health by creating independent agencies in charge of regulating health safety with regard to drugs, blood or transplants. These agencies were to provide scientific risk assessment to help in the development of health regulation, to improve the transparency of the decision-making process and to apply the precautionary principle when confronted with scientific uncertainty. By the same token, the administration bodies in charge of economic functions were to be distanced from those with control and police missions (Tabuteau 2002). With the BSE crisis, several parliamentary reports suggested the creation of a new agency dedicated to food safety (Mattei and Guilhem 1997; Huriet and Descours 1997). The process of the creation of AFSSA was destined to unfold with an eye to the same guiding principles mentioned above, and thus was primarily concerned with the

5 These principles had already formed the basis for reform within the European expertise system in 1997. European Commission, *Green Paper: the general principles of food law in the European Union*, COM(1997) 176 final, 30 April 1997, Brussels.

6 Law 98–535 of 1 July 1998 concerning public health surveillance and the monitoring of products intended for human consumption, *Loi n° 98–535 du 1er juillet 1998 relative au renforcement de la veille sanitaire et du contrôle de la sécurité sanitaire des produits destinés à l'homme.*

untangling of the close relationships maintained between powerful agro-business lobbies and State officials. Economic interests were no longer to prevail over health safety issues. After a heated debate between the relevant administrations, ministries and members of Parliament over the institutional structure and the powers of the agency, the law was passed and AFSSA was created on 1 April 1999 as a governmental agency reporting to three ministries: Health, Agriculture and Consumer Affairs.[7]

The agency's objective is 'to ensure food safety, from the production of raw materials right through to distribution to the consumer'. It has three main missions: 1) the assessment of nutritional and health risk for all categories of foodstuffs; 2) a research and scientific support function, notably for animal health and diseases of animal origin; 3) to issue, suspend or remove licences for the sale of veterinary drugs. As regards risk assessment, AFSSA may receive referrals from its three supervising ministries, along with consumer associations; equally, the agency may choose to make its own 'self-referral'. Three types of questions can be addressed to the agency. First, AFSSA must be consulted on all food safety draft legislation: laws, decrees, orders and transpositions of European regulation. Second, it must be asked for recommendations on individual decisions relating to a market licence (eg new additives or mineral water licences). Third, it can be asked for advice in emergency situations or on general issues.

Despite the Senatorial commission's wish, but due to pressures from the ministries of Agriculture and Consumer Affairs, the law separated risk assessment from risk management, the latter remaining in the hands of the central administrations. But the law also provided for a close connection between the two tasks: despite the fact that the agency does not have any policing or control powers, it does and can issue opinions and formulate risk management proposals, as well as review the efficiency and quality of market control systems, as well as their suitability in terms of the objectives being pursued and their independence. The Agency has access to the information gathered by control authorities and can request that measures be implemented. However, central government authorities take the final decision and are free to decide whether or not to follow the Agency's recommendations.

2.2 Enhancing the role of science in the decision-making process

The 1998 law gave the Agency the task of rationalising the system of expertise. The Agency began by taking on the role of the many committees that had previously worked under the supervision of ministries. It also facilitated the dedication of greater means to the provision of expertise: a special department with a staff of 60 was created and made responsible for the assessment of nutritional and food safety risks. This department coordinates the work of 250 scientific experts

7 The agency has an administrative board composed of representatives of the State, consumer organisations, trade organisations from agriculture and industry, the retail and distribution sectors, the veterinary pharmaceutical industry and representatives of the agency's staff. The board is responsible for the annual report, the investment programmes, the budget and the accounts. A scientific board monitors the consistency of scientific policy. But power is essentially in the hands of the CEO, named by the government and responsible for the decisions, opinions and recommendations issued by the agency.

belonging to 10 external specialised committees on different types of food-related risks. These experts, drawn from a variety of disciplines and institutions, are appointed following a public call for applications. To accomplish its missions, AFSSA can also rely on the work of 13 research laboratories employing 600 people. The quality of risk assessment has undoubtedly improved, having greater collective elements and being based on peer-review.

Efforts have been made to ensure the independence of risk assessment from political and economic interests. The agency has facilitated the clearer separation between risk assessment and political decisions, so that, formally speaking, there is less possibility for scientific opinions to be influenced by economic or political considerations. Private sector representatives have been excluded from expert committees and research programmes are exclusively funded from the public purse. Experts working for the agency must declare potential conflicts of interests and these are made public.

Finally, the expertise system has become more transparent: due to the implementation of quality management procedures, important progress has been made in tracing assessment procedures, from the political request for expertise to the expert scientific opinion. Whereas, in the past, opinions of scientific committees were not always made public, all of the AFSSA's recommendations figure on the agency's website.

Through the provision of scientifically based and independent advice, AFSSA has become a strong instrument for legitimating policies. The separation between risk assessment and risk management and the compulsory publication of scientific advice has allowed for a more transparent regulatory regime: in turn, regulators now take scientific opinions into account when deciding policy measures. Administrations have systematically followed advice given on market-entry licences and the agency provides strong scientific and technical aid on legislative drafting and implementation control. As a noteworthy example, since 1999, AFSSA has published a number of recommendations on BSE risk control measures: deploying the precautionary principle, it has recommended new protective measures, including further restriction on the use of materials from cattle that are at risk, the application of BSE detection tests, and a ban on animal proteins used in animal feed. During the second BSE crisis in October 2000, the Ministry of Agriculture drew heavily on such recommendations in the effort to restore public trust in the beef industry (see below for full details of the crisis).

AFSSA has likewise proved efficient during several food crises. In its first year of existence, it dealt with dioxins in chicken and eggs, contamination in Coca-Cola and two Listeria epidemics (Besançon, Borraz and Grandclément-Chaffy 2004). In each case, the agency gave a scientific opinion on the level of risk for public health that was immediately followed by risk managers. More contentiously, AFSSA also attracted increased public support and international attention in 1999, when its advice (based upon the precautionary principle) was deployed by the French government as justification for maintaining an embargo on British beef, in opposition to advice provided by the Scientific Steering Committee of the European Commission (see below).

AFSSA has also launched long-term assessment procedures, such as the classification of foods in terms of Listeria risks, the extrapolation of the risks posed by avian influenza, as well as the detailing of the benefits and risks of GMOs. In 2001, it helped the Ministry of Health promote a policy on nutrition by creating consumer and industry guidelines. Various of these tasks (reduction of salt in pre-packaged food) are undertaken in collaboration with professional representatives and consumer movements, who can provide data useful for risk assessment. Additionally, AFSSA seeks to influence public debate: when the 2004 law on public health was being discussed, the agency publicly supported measures to reduce sugar consumption (bans on foodstuffs vending machines in schools and stricter control of advertising). The agency has adopted an offensive communication style, with its former director often expressing his opinions in public debates on issues like GMO.

A generally positive appraisal of AFSSA's impact on public regulation highlights the manner in which it has increased the efficiency, transparency and influence of the decision-making process (Besançon 2003). The scientific independence, together with the strong leadership demonstrated by its first director, have proven decisive in re-establishing a firm link between scientific expertise and consumer trust. The role of science and the representation of public health interests have thus been enhanced within the foodstuffs regulatory regime. AFSSA, accordingly, has a highly positive image within the media and is strongly supported by consumer movements.[8]

2.3 Mixing public and private regulation

Alongside risk assessment reform, however, the risk regulation regime has also pursued a mixture of private and public intervention. While important reforms were undertaken within different government departments responsible for food safety, a more decisive reform focused on the role of private actors.

Within the public sector, risk regulation remained divided between three ministries that launched reforms to improve the management of food-related risks and crises.[9] The government called for science-based regulation, a clear distinction between economic and public health issues, and – in cases of scientific uncertainty – the application of the precautionary principle (Kourilsky and Viney 2000). The *Direction Générale de l'Alimentation* (DGAL), the department in charge of food production and safety within the Ministry of Agriculture, was reformed in 1997: it no longer plays a role in the formation of economic policies, but is solely in charge of the safety of food products. Equally, in 2001, the veterinarian field services gained independence from the other field services of the Ministry of Agriculture, providing the DGAL with its own local agents.[10] The Fraud Inspectorates within the Ministry of

8 In 2004, several public reports acknowledged the improvement in risk assessment and the important role that AFSSA plays in re-establishing a normal level of consumer confidence in risk management.

9 The Ministry of Agriculture is in charge of animal and plant health, safety of meat and meat-based products used for animal and human consumption, and the inspection of farms, factories and slaughterhouses. The Ministry of Consumer Affairs is in charge of the safety of products; it prepares regulations and controls quality and labelling of all transformed foodstuffs. The capacity of the Ministry of Health to regulate food safety remains weak: it is mainly in charge of nutrition policies and water quality.

10 Possessing 200 agents in central administration, the DGAL can also count on 4,400 agents in decentralised services, distributed between the 100 departmental veterinary services and the 22 regional services for the protection of plants.

Consumer Affairs and the *Direction générale de la Santé*, the department in charge of public health within the Ministry of Health, were also reformed in order to enhance their capacities to manage food and health crises.

In 1999, the law on agriculture[11] defined a policy for implementing food safety and augmented the prerogatives given to the field services (thus enhancing oversight over the animal food industry). This was followed, in 2002, by a directive of the Ministry of Agriculture strengthening food safety 'from the farm to the fork' and promoting a general principle of traceability for all food products: private actors, defined as accountable for the safety of their products, were asked to improve their surveillance and control systems. Public regulation fostered the use of standards (established by professionals and certified by private standardisation bodies), the use of good practice codes (formulated by food business agents, examined by AFSSA and validated by public authorities), and the implementation of HACCP quality methods. Even if standardisation was already familiar within the food industry, the various foodstuffs crises had also supplied the public authorities with further justifications for delegating more controls to the business, and for increasing the degree of accountability in case of non-compliance. Furthermore, traceability was extended to farm products, previously only subject to very limited and often ineffective regulatory measures. In both cases, issues of safety, historically not a part of the privatisation trend, reinforced the process of standardisation; the move from public to private actors in the management of food safety was intensified. Formally speaking, the State remains in charge of approval and monitoring, but relies on private actors to enforce and apply public rules through the adoption of self-regulation and standardisation.

Alongside this deepening trend, the private sector initiated its own reform. In particular, the food crises strengthened quality-labelling trends, initially not a measure concerned with food safety. However, food safety crises that enhanced public perception of risk were met with an industry-led emphasis upon 'quality'; a measure which it considered adequate to restore consumer trust in the safety of food products – 'quality' now referred both to the origins and to the safety of the product. In the wake of the BSE crisis, a new label, *Viande Bovine Française*, was created to support the French beef market by certifying the quality and the safety of the food the animals had been given. Retailers, quickly followed by the agro-food industry, issued labels for GMO-free products and food that respected strict methods of production in order to eliminate all risks. Often, these measures were not based on any legal specifications or scientific data; firms simply considered that suspicion about a given product or its methods of production, which gave rise to consumer fear, should be countered with strong measures. In truth, the real risk here was not one posed to consumer health and safety; but rather one posed to industry profit in the wake of the BSE crisis.

The BSE crisis also gave major retailers the opportunity to enter into negotiations with producers of fresh farm products, in order to promote new *marques de filières* (brands tied to a specific product). Whereas the previous brands concerned solely transformed food products, the new brands were worked out with the producers of fresh products, then approved by the Ministry of Agriculture as certified products.

11 Law 99–574 on Agriculture of 9 July 1999, *Loi n° 99–574 du 9 juillet 1999 d'orientation agricole.*

Compliance with the specifications was overseen by third party certification companies. Subsequently, however, quality labels given out by the Ministry of Agriculture came under strong pressure from private labels – public labels, thus, either included health safety measures, based on minimal scientific data, to compete with private labels, or they excluded such safety measures, and were then accused of being too lax (Borraz and d'Arcimoles 2003).

In summary, both the development of standardisation and the success of 'new' quality labels (combining issues of origin and safety) heralded an important transformation in the process of the implementation of regulation. Public authorities defined objectives on the basis of stronger scientific advice, but private actors enjoyed greater autonomy in adopting the necessary means to achieve compliance in the implementation of standards and of other self-defined procedures and restrictions, and in enforcing regulatory respects. This situation, however, raises the thorny question of regulatory effectiveness, or the system's capacity to ensure that rules are correctly applied and produce the expected results. By delegating more controls to third-party actors and private firms themselves, public authorities acknowledged that they lacked the necessary means to enforce their own rules. But just how effective is public and private oversight? As the following section argues, this question remains a major source of uncertainty within the French foodstuffs regulatory regime.

3 REGULATORY UNCERTAINTY

The reform detailed above accordingly left some key questions unanswered: who is in overall charge of food safety; who has the capacity to coordinate the complex system of private and public agents managing food safety; which norms, principles and knowledge should inform foodstuffs regulation? Above all, during the period of destabilisation which the reform had occasioned, the absence of any central coordinating procedure, the introduction of new agents within the system, the efforts of existing agents to 'find their place' within the system and to demonstrate their capacities and resources, introduced further instability and subsequent uncertainty. Albeit not readily visible, this uncertainty undoubtedly contributes to the system's present vulnerability.

Several particular issues cause a high level of uncertainty within the reformed regime. Most notably, as we have seen above, a lack of state resources reduces public capacity to oversee or coordinate the fragmented regime; as a consequence, the task has largely been transferred to a private sector, which has combined public goals with its own market aims (confusion of aims within labelling). The following section focuses on three further problems which create vulnerability within the system and are thus a source of uncertainty and, potentially also, heightened risk: 1) the controversial separation made between risk assessment and risk management has resulted in endemic strains and sporadic conflicts between government and AFSSA; 2) the risk regulation regime lacks socio-economic expertise and any means of organising deliberation between stakeholders; 3) finally, within the setting of the European Union, multi-level governance has led to an increased danger of conflict between national and European expertise and principles of regulation.

3.1 Restrictions upon the influence of AFSSA

Although AFSSA provides independent recommendations, its exact degree of scientific independence is constrained by the fact that the agency works under the supervision of three ministries. AFSSA is accordingly constrained in the planning of its work by the annual budgets allocated by each of the ministries; all three currently refuse to contemplate multi-year determination of objectives and budgets, which would provide the agency with financial stability. Furthermore, during the years 1999 to 2003, central administration also interfered in the capacity of AFSSA to produce its own expertise, both by generating a large number of referrals that restricted the agency's ability to engage in independent research, and through participation in expert committees, initially only with the aim of offering data and clarifying questions, but becoming, with time, quasi-full-time members of these committees.

More generally, with regard to expertise generation, although AFSSA has its own laboratories, it is also dependent upon data produced by many other institutions: the multiple field services and inspectorates of the different ministries, the complex system of public-funded research institutions, the vast number of public- and private-funded laboratories and professional technical centres, the three layers of local government with some form of engagement in health safety, the other health agencies, the historically powerful farmers' organisations. The agency has little capacity to influence their agendas and objectives. Such a situation carries many uncertainties, in particular as regards the flow of information between the different agents: AFSSA has no capacity to oversee the production of data and/or detect a new and unknown virus or disease in its early stage. More alarming, perhaps, there is also a lack of data on highly sensitive issues such as water quality or the use of pesticides; data which has either not been collected, not been transferred to the central State services, or not been analysed.

In sum, AFSSA is far more dependent upon central government than would ideally be the case. The previous director often underlined the opinion that the agency is 'a dependent organisation giving independent advice' (Hirsch 2001). This situation has encouraged its staff to promote procedures that guarantee independence in the expertise process, going as far as engaging in quality insurance procedures and the standardisation of expertise production.[12] AFSSA is thus engaged in a process of bureaucratisation, seeking insulation from outside pressures along with higher predictability through stronger rules and procedures. Yet, such a bureaucratic evolution potentially makes it difficult to simultaneously promote more open and deliberative methods with outside interest groups (Benamouzig and Besançon 2005).

Moreover, the exact role of AFSSA within the decision-making process remains opaque. The different ministries, and most notably the Ministry of Agriculture, wish to restrict AFSSA's activities to scientific risk assessment, even though the law provides for a connection between risk assessment and risk management. When

12 As of 2003, representatives from the three supervisory ministries are no longer allowed to participate in the committees, except at the agency's demand. Guidelines have been implemented to standardise the expertise process and AFSSA has taken the lead in the production of an official AFNOR standard for quality of expertise.

the agency formulates policy recommendations, including risk management procedures, it opens itself up to accusations that it may be trespassing on the competences of ministries – the same bodies who often turn to the agency for advice on risk management measures. This confusion is all the more acute given the status of the opinions published by AFSSA. These consist of a risk assessment report produced by an expert committee, to which is added the general advice of the agency, sometimes with policy recommendations. In a limited number of cases, the agency has been criticised by experts who have claimed that its reports do not exactly reproduce, or have misrepresented, the scientific advice given. Although such instances are rare, their underlying cause – the uncertainty over the degree to which the agency might include risk management considerations within its advice – highlights continuing ambiguity in the status of the agency, and continuing doubt about its role within policy making. Despite the fact that many arguments can be brought to demonstrate the difficulties of separation of risk assessment from risk management, a 2005 parliamentary report – though complimentary with regard to the role and impact of the agency within the French foodstuffs regulatory regime – regretted the fact that the agency often pressurised government with its public recommendations and proactive media presence and seemed unwilling to allow ministries to decide for themselves (Saunier 2005).

More importantly, AFSSA also lacks the capacity to control, monitor and evaluate the decisions taken by the ministries on the basis of its recommendations, as it should legally do. It has no capacity whatsoever to oversee the implementation of decisions by administrative services or private firms. The data collected either by the inspectorate services of the Ministries of Agriculture and Consumer Affairs, or through procedures of auto-control within agro-food firms, is rarely made public. In other words, if some progress has been made in the production of information by agro-food business, this is essentially to the benefit of the inspectorate bodies, which often choose to work hand-in-hand with the firms rather than adopt a more rigorous stance towards them.

These shortcomings in the positions of AFSSA offer, it may be argued, an explanation for the fact that risk regulation within France still remains a source of conflict (Besançon 2005). AFSSA has provided a greater degree of knowledge and expertise; by the same token, the Ministry of Health and other public health officials have made use of this expertise in the efforts to redirect the regulatory system away from economic objectives in favour of health objectives, sometimes arguing for the creation of precautionary policies. A new actor within the regulatory regime, AFSSA has thus changed the rules of the inter-ministerial game, at the same time, however, also creating new tensions between the agency and its supervisors and between regulators themselves. For example, the Listeria crises of 1999–2000 were intensified by dysfunctions in risk management and communication between the three ministries in charge of food safety. What started out as a routine alert became a full-blown crisis by virtue of the industry-protecting and blame-shifting strategies pursued by the Ministries of Agriculture and Consumer Affairs, the information that was leaked to the press by the Ministry of Health, and by conflict on the use by health officials of epidemiological results to identify the contaminated food (and consequently the chain of producers and retailers). AFSSA argued that the presence of Listeria and risks to human health were the result of a complex system of interdependent relations, from the producers to the consumers, rather than the responsibility of an isolated actor. This approach appeared to imply that a systemic stance toward food-borne risks should be adopted; a stance that was supported by health officials, but that drew fire from the Ministries of Agriculture and Consumer Affairs, who were dedicated to protecting their particular sectors. The latter succeeded in restricting AFSSA to the task of scientific risk assessment and thus preserved their capacity to act within their sector (Besançon, Borraz and Grandclément-Chaffy 2004). Nonetheless, they also came together with the Ministry of Health to adopt a strategy for the better future management of Listeria alerts.

3.2 The lack of organised deliberation

An additional uncertainty arises in relation to the status of deliberation within the regulatory foodstuffs regime; an uncertainty that is heightened by continuing conflict on institutional responsibilities. Thus, the final decisions on French food safety remain firmly in the hands of the Ministries of Agriculture and Consumer Affairs, who work closely with the representatives of the farmers, agro-food firms and retailers they choose to consult. By creating AFSSA, government and legislators had intended to strengthen scientific risk assessment in the food safety regulation regime, but had not aimed to alter the general equilibrium within this regime. AFSSA's success results mainly from its capacity to legitimate risk management and enhance public confidence in the policy process. But the institutional configuration still holds many ambiguities, leading AFSSA and its supervisors to play on the boundaries of risk assessment and risk management (Jasanoff 1990). This often turns out to be a source of controversy, as it highlights the uncertain behaviour of various different agents, each of which pursues their own interests.

The separation between risk assessment and risk management is always controversial, mainly because it is incomplete. To evaluate an estimated risk, it is necessary to compare the risks and the benefits, the costs and the benefits of a measure of risk reduction, the potential risk tradeoffs or the relative risks. Within this process values are mobilised that refer to political, economic, social, professional and even ethical criteria. Yet, in France, this phase of value accumulation is often forgotten since channels that would allow for official consultation of the different stakeholder groups (producers, industry, retailers, consumers) are poorly organised.

AFSSA's legal mandate gives it no competence to include economic, political or social considerations within its risk assessment. Scientific experts from private firms and lobby representatives were excluded from expert committees. The agency can use *ad hoc* hearings to consult private interests on the cost or technical feasibility of a measure before issuing a recommendation; but this is neither a systematic procedure, nor one that is officially promoted, the agency being careful to maintain its reputation of independence. This is one of the major weaknesses within AFSSA, on which basis its recommendations are often criticised by political, administrative and private actors, since they are founded solely on scientific assessments and sometimes represent high-cost/low-feasibility solutions that pay scant attention to important social and economic impacts. This failure weakens the agency in that it can be criticised for making unrealistic recommendations. For example, in October 2001, AFSSA recommended a ban on the consumption of sheep bowels on the basis that BSE might in the future be found in these materials. The President of the Republic, opening the annual agriculture exhibition, criticised the agency's opinion, which was not based, according to him, on any new scientific proof, and further accused the agency of aggravating the public's fears. An underlying issue was, of course, the fact that implementation of this recommendation would have an adverse economic impact on sausage producers; as a consequence, and despite further recommendations, government never followed them. However, by the same token, were AFSSA to attempt to integrate technical or economic data within its recommendations, it would also draw fire for making recommendations on the basis of data that is foreign to strict scientific data, and thus for acting as a political entrepreneur rather than a scientific expert.

This particular weakness highlights the fact that the French foodstuffs safety regime has given insufficient thought to the coherent integration of the views of organised interests. The *Conseil National de l'Alimentation* (CNA), an advisory committee created in 1985 to represent these different interests, would like to play a role following upon the scientific assessment phase. However, its legitimacy remains weak: it comes under the direct authority of the Ministry of Agriculture; its consultation is not compulsory; it has no clear procedural rules; there is little actual deliberation among its members; advice is often asked on very general issues; and its recommendations are published after a long delay. Thus, in most cases, the consultation of organised interests falls to the ministries, who rely on pre-existing networks, lobbies and policy communities rather than consult with a large panel of representatives or engage in open discussion. As a consequence, a certain number of actors remain excluded from the decision-making process while the criteria upon which decisions are based are rarely made explicit and debatable. Two counterexamples actually confirm this point: the citizens' conference on GMOs in the spring of 1998 and the *Etats généraux de l'alimentation* held in 2000 gave a number of stakeholders the opportunity to take part in a general debate; yet, in both cases, these consultations had little or no impact on the decisions taken (Joly and Marris 2003).

Furthermore, there exists for the moment no organised socio-economic expertise, i.e. expertise produced by social scientists assessing the economic and social costs, consequences, risks and benefits of a given product, activity or decision. Once again, the consequence is that such expertise is produced by the ministries' central services for their own use, without any peer-review, let alone any discussion. The CNA has suggested, in a report published in early 2005, that socio-economic expertise should be formally organised, along with a separate process of consultation with stakeholders.[13] To date this proposal has not been adopted.

3.3 The multi-level governance of food safety issues

Finally, a third source of regulatory uncertainty arises within the French regime due to the increasing activities of the EU following the BSE crisis, and the subsequent national-European scientific clashes that have followed upon increasing EU prerogatives in food safety regulation. In 1997, the European Commission reformed its

13 CNA (2005) Position n° 50 *Propositions pour la mise en place d'une expertise socio-économique dans le cadre de l'analyse des risques alimentaires.*

risk assessment and risk management procedures and in 2000, a White Paper led to the adoption of a General Food Law and the creation of the European Food Safety Authority (EFSA).[14] Food safety regulation has become multi-level, shared between national and European authorities, and, despite the fact the French and European food safety regimes rest upon the same foundations (science-based regulation, the separation between risk assessment and risk management, a reliance on private standards), tensions have developed between the different levels of government.

The conflict over the embargo on British beef offers a case where scientific expertise lies at the root of controversy. In 1998, the European Scientific Steering Committee (SSC) published its recommendation to lift the embargo imposed in March 1996, on the basis of the technical scheme for exportation (DBES) that had been elaborated by British authorities. The European Commission decided to go ahead and lift the ban;[15] and the French Ministry of Agriculture undertook to transpose this decision into national regulation. AFSSA, which the public authorities had not seen fit to consult, was successful in forcing the Ministry to request its advice; more importantly still, the minister proclaimed that whatever the result, he would follow the agency's recommendation. In September 1999, the committee within AFSSA in charge of BSE produced a recommendation in conflict with the views of the SSC. In particular, it concluded that, even were the British scheme satisfactory on paper, the real issue was how the DBES would be implemented – and on this point, AFSSA felt there was not enough data to prove its effectiveness. The SSC had indeed given its advice under the postulate that the measures were effective but did not feel it was its role to assess this effectiveness. AFSSA considered that, until proof was available on effective implementation, it was necessary to adopt the precautionary principle since the risk could not be clearly assessed (Setbon 2004). The French government followed the advice and maintained the embargo, thus beginning a conflict with the European Commission. In the autumn of 1999, the SSC and AFSSA tried to come to an agreement while French and British authorities negotiated further measures. In December, however, AFSSA still felt that a risk of infected beef meat being introduced to the continent existed and that, on this basis, the ban should be maintained. Early in 2000, the Commission decided to challenge the decision before the European Court of Justice.[16] The embargo was finally lifted by France in October 2002, on the basis of the data collected by British authorities, which showed that the risk was now the same in Great Britain and in France. In this case, not only did French and European scientific experts diverge within their analysis of the existing data, but the French authorities followed AFSSA in promoting the precautionary principle, thus setting an immutable standard for decision making in the field of food safety. This posture was all the more acceptable to government and the public given that the French beef industry was still weak. By

14 European Commission, *White Paper on Food Safety*, COM(1999) 719 final, 12 January 2000, Brussels. Regulation (EC) 178/2002 of the European Parliament and of the Council of 28 January 2002 laying down the general principles and requirements of food law, establishing the European Food Safety Authority and laying down procedures in matters of food safety, [2002] *OJ* L31/1.

15 Commission Decision 96/239/EC of 27 March 1996 on emergency measures to protect against bovine spongiform encephalopathy, [1996] *OJ* L78/47.

16 See Case C-1/00, *Commission v France* [2001] ECR I-09989.

maintaining the ban, the French government was able to protect the sector from reductions in consumer confidence, public opinion being in favour of the embargo.

As of 1 January 2005, the General Food Law has become effective in all Member States. It provides a common framework and defines the guiding principles in the management of food safety: regulation must be based on a risk analysis, the precautionary principle may be applied in situations of scientific uncertainty, standardisation is a useful instrument in the implementation of regulation. Furthermore, new hygiene rules were adopted in 2004 by the European Parliament and the Council and have been applicable since 1 January 2006.[17] These new rules apply a 'farm to table' approach, harmonise and strengthen public controls, encourage the use of HACCP for all food business operators and the development of good practice codes. These rules might have a powerful impact in the future on national regulatory frameworks. For the moment, however, French food safety regulation remains divided between three ministries, each referring to its own set of rules: will the construction of a common European foodstuffs regulation, which is compulsory for all Member States, encourage them to merge and adopt a unique national food law?[18] Or will it produce further tensions and foster conflicts?

As for EFSA, its position *vis-à-vis* the network of national food safety agencies is not clear; more precisely, it is still a matter of debate as to the role the agency would like the network to play. Will EFSA depend on this network to promote a common approach to risk analysis? And will this in turn reduce potential conflict between national and European levels of government? Or, on the contrary, will EFSA attempt to produce its own expertise without relying on the national agencies, thus potentially fostering new controversies? For the moment, French officials believe the second option to be more probable.

4 CONCLUSION

The reforms of the food safety regulation regime undertaken at the end of the 1990s in France have amplified the level of regulatory uncertainty – while failing to create a coherent set of institutions and policies on food safety. The regulatory system is more fragmented and coordination more difficult than ever. By creating AFSSA, government and legislators intended to strengthen scientific risk assessment in the food safety regulation regime. And indeed, decisions taken by the public

17 Regulation (EC) 852/2004 of the European Parliament and of the Council of 29 April 2004 on the hygiene of foodstuffs, [2004] *OJ* L139/1; Regulation (EC) 853/2004 of the European Parliament and of the Council of 29 April 2004 laying down specific hygiene rules for food of animal origin, [2004] *OJ* L139/55; Regulation (EC) 854/2004 of the European Parliament and of the Council of 29 April 2004 laying down specific rules for the organisation of official controls on products of animal origin intended for human consumption, [2004] *OJ* L139/206; Regulation (EC) 882/2004 of the European Parliament and of the Council of 29 April 2004 on official controls performed to ensure the verification of compliance with feed and food law, animal health and animal welfare rules, [2004] *OJ* L165/1.

18 In a recent opinion on the implementation of the new European regulations, the CNA has encouraged such a shift (2004, *Avis n° 48 sur la préparation de l'entrée en vigueur, au 1er janvier 2005, de certaines dispositions du règlement CE n° 178/2002 du Parlement européen et du Conseil qui concernent les entreprises*).

authorities seem more firmly based on scientific opinion. The role of science and public health objectives has been enhanced, giving greater legitimacy to political decisions. As the management of food safety addresses issues of perceived as well as objective risk, AFSSA has strengthened public confidence in the policy process. But the institutional configuration still holds a number of ambiguities, allowing AFSSA and its supervisors to play around on the boundaries of risk assessment and risk management.

Coordination between the multiple agents managing food safety also remains opaque as it tends to be ensured by private firms and retailers. The regime relies to an ever increasing degree on private auto-regulation and standards to implement public rules. Simultaneously, private actors adopt labels that add supplementary restrictions to ensure compliance with consumer needs. Yet, the regime's vulnerability lies not so much in this situation than in the fact that the role of private enforcement, along with the lack of State resources to enforce regulation, is not officially acknowledged. The system continues to rest on the myth that regulation is being effectively implemented under the strict supervision of State field services. But this no longer corresponds with the real situation.

Thus, on the one hand, the reality of food safety regulation is one of a growing role for private sector auto-regulation and third-party enforcement, along with the fact that the State has limited capacities to oversee and ensure effective implementation. On the other hand, the ministries in charge of food safety have gone a long way to prevent the occurrence of a new crisis or scandal (with its economic and political consequences) by carefully organising their risk communication procedures and adopting blame-prevention strategies. Their success rests largely on the existence of AFSSA. But by refusing to organise the creation of a body of a socio-economic expertise or clear deliberation channels with private interests and NGOs, by restricting the capacity of AFSSA to control and monitor implementation, by doing little to combat fragmentation in the regime, and by refusing clearly to acknowledge the role of the private sector in the enforcement of regulation, public authorities have created further uncertainties which could, in due time, foster new risks and crises.

Meanwhile, recent changes within the European food safety regulation regime have impacted heavily on the French regime. Although they might favour a move toward a more integrated and coordinated approach to food safety, these changes could also foster conflict between the different ministries and agencies, as well as between French and EU administrations and scientific authorities; further, they may highlight the insufficient means the administration has to ensure the implementation of regulation, the unclear separation of roles between public and private oversight bodies, and the many uncertainties in the control and monitoring of food safety regulations. All in all, they could very well be a further source of regulatory uncertainty.

BIBLIOGRAPHY

Benamouzig, D. and Besançon, J. (2005) 'Administrer un monde incertain: les nouvelles bureaucraties techniques. Le cas des agences sanitaires', *Sociologie du Travail* 47(3): 301–22.

Besançon, J. (2005) 'L'Agence française de sécurité sanitaire des aliments: rationalisation de l'expertise et régulation des risques', in C. Lahellec (ed.), *Risques et crises alimentaires*, Paris: Editions Lavoisier, 81–108.

Besançon, J. (2003) *Évaluation de l'Agence française de sécurité sanitaire des aliments. Étude auprès des publics et personnels de l'agence*, Paris: CSO.

Besançon, J., Borraz, O. and Grandclément-Chaffy, C. (2004) *La sécurité alimentaire en crises. Les crises Coca-Cola et Listeria de 1999–2000*, Paris: L'Harmattan.

Borraz, O. and d'Arcimoles, M. (2003) 'Réguler ou qualifier. Le cas des boues d'épuration urbaines', *Sociologie du Travail* 45(1): 45–62.

Borraz, O., Besançon, J. and Clergeau, C. (2006) 'Is it just about trust? The practical reform of French food safety regulation' in C. Ansell and D. Vogel (eds.), *What's the Beef? The Contested Governance of European Food Safety*, Cambridge: MIT Press, 125–52.

Clergeau, C. (2000) *Le processus de création de l'Agence française de sécurité sanitaire des aliments. Généalogie, genèse et adoption d'une proposition de loi*, Paris: ENSA Rennes, IEP de Paris.

Ferrières, M. (2002) *Histoire des peurs alimentaires*, Paris: Seuil.

Hirsch, M. (2001) 'L'expertise scientifique indépendante dans un établissement public: l'exemple de l'Agence française de sécurité sanitaire des aliments' in Conseil d'Etat, *Rapport public 2001*, Paris: La Documentation française, 227–38.

Hood, C., Rothstein, H. and Baldwin, R. (2001) *The Government of Risk. Understanding Risk Regulation Regimes*, Oxford: Oxford University Press.

Huriet, C. and Descours, C. (1997) *Renforcer la sécurité sanitaire en France. Rapport d'information n° 196*, Paris: Sénat.

Jasanoff, S. (1990) *The Fifth Branch. Science Advisers as Policy Makers*, Cambridge: Harvard University Press.

Joly, P.B. and Marris, C. (2003) 'A la recherche d'une démocratie technique. Enseignements de la conférence citoyenne sur les OGM en France', *Natures, Sciences et Sociétés* 1: 3–15.

Kourilsky, P. and Viney, G. (2000) *Le principe de précaution. Rapport au Premier Ministre*, Paris: Odile Jacob.

Lascoumes, P. (1994) *L'éco-pouvoir: environnements et politique*, Paris: La Découverte.

Mattei, J.F. and Guilhem, E. (1997) *De la 'vache folle' à la 'vache émissaire', rapport d'information n° 3291*, Paris: Assemblée Nationale.

Müller, P. (1984) *Le technocrate et le paysan. Essai sur la politique française de modernisation de l'agriculture de 1945 à nos jours*, Paris: Editions Ouvrières.

Noiville, C. (2003) *Du bon gouvernement des risques*, Paris: PUF.

Pressman, J. and Wildavsky, A. (1973) *Implementation*, Berkeley: University of California Press.

Saunier, C. (2005) *Le renforcement de la veille sanitaire et du contrôle de la sécurité sanitaire des produits destinés à l'homme: application de la loi du 1er juillet 1998*, Rapport n° 2108 de l'Office Parlementaire d'Évaluation des Choix Scientifiques et Techniques, Paris: Assemblée Nationale et Sénat.

Setbon, M. (ed.) (2004) *Risques, sécurité sanitaire et processus de décision*, Paris: Elsevier.

Stanziani, A. (2005) *Histoire de la qualité alimentaire (XIXe–XXe siècle)*, Paris: Seuil.

Sylvander, B. (1995) 'Conventions de qualité et institutions: le cas des produits de qualité spécifique' in F. Nicolas and E. Valceschini (eds), *Agro-alimentaire: une économie de la qualité*, Paris: INRA Editions, Economica, 167–84.

Tabuteau, D. (2002) *La sécurité sanitaire*, Paris: Berger Levrault.

Wynne, B. (1992) 'Carving out science (and politics) in the regulatory jungle', *Social Studies of Science* 22: 745–58.

Chapter 4

The origins of regulatory uncertainty in the UK food safety regime

Henry Rothstein

1 INTRODUCTION

Acting under uncertainty is a problem that pervades risk regulation across policy domains, from radioactive waste and climate change to vaccination and mobile phones, to take just a few examples. In the UK, nowhere has the problem of uncertainty been more evident than in the food domain, where there seem to be never ending conflicts over the safety or dangers of food additives, pesticides, plastics packaging, growth hormones and genetically modified organisms. The BSE crisis even contributed to the downfall of the Conservative government in the UK in 1997 and led to the reorganisation of food safety policy making with the establishment of a new Food Standards Agency (FSA) in 2000. The FSA set out to chart a new course for risk regulation that attempted to manage food safety risks by being more open, consumer-orientated and precautionary. The reform of the regime has had some success, but the FSA has been confronted with managing a range of uncertainties that have their origin not just in science but also in the practice of regulation itself. This chapter will examine these uncertainties and the difficulties that the FSA has experienced in addressing them.

Much debate on risk regulation understandably tends to focus on scientific uncertainty. Regulators often find themselves dealing with risks that sit at the horizons of knowledge and regularly confront the dilemma of acting on false positives or false negatives (see Shrader-Frechette 1991). Past failures, such as thalidomide and BSE, have strengthened support for precautionary policy stances, but imposing regulatory restrictions that turn out to be unnecessary can present obvious downsides for society if it means missing out on potential benefits, or if old risks are replaced by new and potentially worse risks. A central question for risk regulation, therefore, is how to balance precautionary and resilient policy stances when trading off these two types of regulatory error.

Risk regulation, however, faces other uncertainties beyond those that are scientific. Regulators, for example, face normative uncertainties in determining the distribution of the costs and benefits of regulation. The problem is how the interests of different groups in society should be traded off against each other, and, indeed, more generally, how we interpret the concept of the public interest (see, for example, Feintuck 2004). Is the public interest, for example, best served by facilitating the exercise of private choices, by establishing a superior standard of rational and 'right' wisdom, by simple majority opinion, or through deliberative processes of government? Different conceptions of the public interest often lead to highly inconsistent policy outcomes. A classic example is found in regimes regulating radiation safety, where conflicting interpretations of the public interest mean that health care workers can be legally exposed in the workplace to greater radiation risks from the naturally occurring radioactive gas, radon, than from x-ray equipment.

Risk regulation also highlights the uncertainties of the capacity and effectiveness of regulatory institutions within a regulatory regime to take decisions and implement controls (Hood *et al.* 2001). Effective risk regulation is fraught with difficulty when regulatory regimes are fragmented, for example, between international standard setting and local enforcement, or when risks cross national jurisdictions or fit uncomfortably with legal frameworks. Too often crises have been the result of regulatory incoherence, where regime complexity has led to gaps in implementation or detection, or components of regulatory regimes have failed. Enforcement failures, for example, were an important contribution to the 1996 *E. coli* 157 food poisoning outbreak, which killed 30 people in Scotland, and more infamously the BSE debacle in which inspectors failed to prevent BSE-infected meat contaminating the animal and human food chain during the early 1990s (Rothstein 2003a).

Recent years have seen a range of innovative regulatory reforms in response to such problems in a number of policy domains. Scientific uncertainty has been addressed by attempts to improve the quality and transparency of scientific advice and clarify its role and limits within decision making. That trend has been an important feature of the reorganisation of scientific advisory committees and the creation of agencies within the European Commission and Member States in the domains of food, environment and occupational health and safety. Risk assessment has been given greater emphasis as the evidentiary basis of decision making from national governments to the World Trade Organization. At the same time, the so-called 'precautionary principle' has also become embedded within many regulatory frameworks.

Normative uncertainties of how to distribute the costs and benefits of decision making have been addressed by greater emphasis on open and more participative forms of decision making to help inform a wide range of social and ethical judgements within decision making, and to strengthen the legitimacy of regulatory processes. For example, at the international level, the Århus Convention of 2001 was designed to improve access to information and public participation in environmental decision making. And in the UK, new government commissions and agencies in the domains of GMOs, food and human fertilisation, and the government sponsored GM debate – GM Nation – in 2003 have also attempted to make decision making more inclusive.

Institutional uncertainties have also been addressed in a number of policy domains by attempts to improve the coherence and effectiveness of organisationally complex regulatory regimes both within and between nation-states, such as consolidating fragmented policy functions within agencies and attempting to join up policy with enforcement. There has also been greater interest in innovative methods of control, such as co-opting non-state actors in regulation through processes of co-regulation or third party accreditation. The increased bureaucratic scrutiny and control of regulatory performance that has accompanied the creation of regulatory agencies has also focused attention on the extent to which regulatory regimes are delivering their intended goals. Within the UK, for example, regulatory regimes far removed from those concerned with health and safety have adopted risk as a decision-making instrument to improve the targeting of regulatory resources (Rothstein 2006).

But such attempts to reform and improve risk regulation have created further challenges. More knowledge can help regulation by reducing uncertainty, but it can also introduce further dilemmas by making us aware of what we don't know, or by introducing further conflicting evidence. More sensitive chemical detection methods, for example, put pressure on regulatory systems to manage ever more chemical risks.

Moreover, as regulators attempt to legitimate their management of regulatory objects in bureaucratic terms through complex risk assessments, regulators also need to work harder to legitimate their practice in the eyes of the public. Yet, as public participation emerges as a regulatory norm, so the need emerges to elaborate legitimate criteria for consultation and how views should be traded off against other interests and the institutional constraints of decision making.

Finally, attempts to improve the coherence of regulatory regimes and to make them accountable for their inevitably limited capacity to assess and manage regulatory problems, have amplified the institutional risks confronting regulators. Indeed, pressures towards 'good governance' could be argued to be behind 'risk' concepts colonising regulatory regimes far removed from traditional health, safety and environmental domains. As Luhmann has observed, the concept of 'risk' anticipates and legitimates the possibility of failure by transforming decision making into probabilistic assessments of success and failure (Luhmann 1993). From that perspective, the concept of 'risk' both frames the objects of regulation as well as reflexively anticipates the inevitable limits of regulatory success (Rothstein, Huber and Gaskell 2006). But heightened institutional risks, for example, created by greater openness, can lead to blame-shifting responses whereby regulators seek to manage their own institutional risks sometimes at the expense of managing risks to society.

In general, therefore, the uncertainties that regularly beset regulation are not just scientific in nature, but also have their origin in fundamental normative and institutional uncertainties of regulation itself. Those uncertainties pose important challenges to the reform of risk regulation regimes and it is, therefore, of considerable interest to study how those challenges have been met. In order to do so, this chapter will examine reforms to the regulation of food safety in the UK. Food safety regulation faces many of the challenges discussed above; often dealing with uncertain science, involving a wide range of public, private and state actors who often have conflicting stakes in regulatory processes and outcomes, and entailing complex and multi-tiered regulatory regimes. It is, therefore, of interest how the new Food Standards Agency has managed to address these challenges.

2 REFORM OF THE UK FOOD SAFETY REGIME

In the 1990s, food safety came to symbolise the problems afflicting risk regulation in the UK. Scientific advisory systems were weak and the practices of risk assessment were often confused with risk management (see, for example, Lord Phillips *et al.* 2000). Decision making was famously secretive, which compounded the inherent conflicts of interest posed by the Ministry of Agriculture, Fisheries and Food's (MAFF) dual responsibilities for food safety and the promotion of food and agriculture business. The regime was also fragmented; there was poor communication between MAFF and its weak policy partner, the Department of Health, and there was little evidence of connection between central government policy making and local government enforcement.

After a spate of crises, culminating in BSE, MAFF was finally replaced in 2000 by a dedicated non-departmental agency, the Food Standards Agency, which comprised a stakeholder style Board of up to 12 members with a balance of skills and interests and a large supporting bureaucracy. That institutional reform addressed many of the problems that had afflicted the old regime. To improve the evidential basis of decision making, the FSA attempted to separate out risk assessment and risk management processes, its scientific advisory committees held at least some meetings in public and made evidence available on request, and the precautionary principle was adopted in cases of residual scientific uncertainty (FSA 2001: 23). To improve the representation of the public interest in decision making, conflicts of interest were reduced by removing responsibilities for food and agriculture business promotion, and possibilities for direct political interference were restricted by giving the agency the right to publish its advice to ministers. The FSA Board also held its meetings in public and carried out extensive consultation with consumer groups to combat concealment of bias, improve decision making and enhance public confidence. And, finally, to improve the institutional coherence of the regime, food safety responsibility was consolidated within the FSA and it was given extended monitoring powers over local government enforcement.

The reforms to the regime were encapsulated by the FSA's adoption of three core guiding principles 'putting the consumer first', 'being open and accessible' and 'being an independent voice' which the FSA promulgated widely during its first five years (FSA 2000). Many of these reforms have found a favourable response among the FSA's key constituents. Consumer groups have given the agency qualified support, food retailers have been encouraged to see the FSA's focus on the food chain rather than just farmers, and survey work suggests that overall consumer confidence in the agency has risen from 50 to 60 per cent (FSA 2003a).

The FSA has, however, been confronted by a number of problems that have involved conflicts with business groups, consumer groups and the European Commission that have been difficult to resolve. Close examination of some of these cases illustrates the diverse origins of regulatory uncertainty facing the FSA and the challenges it has faced in resolving those uncertainties. This chapter will now examine three particular problems that the FSA has tackled in its first five years of existence. These cases will variously focus on the dilemmas of taking precautionary action, the institutional constraints on improving consumer protection and the problems of institutionalising consumer consultation. The chapter draws upon a range of documentary sources, attendance at FSA public meetings, and in-depth face-to-face and telephone interviews with state officials and scientific advisors at both the UK and EU level, and business and consumer representatives who have had to remain anonymous for confidentiality reasons.

3 DILEMMAS CONFRONTING THE REFORM OF THE FOOD SAFETY REGIME

3.1 Slipping on sausage skins: the uncertainties of taking precautionary action

The first case highlights the uncertainties of precautionary decision making and concerns the European Commission's rejection of the FSA's proposed precautionary ban in 2002 on natural sausage casings made from sheep intestine (for further detail, see Rothstein 2004). The case arose early in the life of the FSA and stemmed from concerns that BSE might also exist within sheep and goat flocks. Although no cases of BSE in sheep and goats had been found, it was known that they had consumed the same feed that had infected cattle; they were experimentally susceptible to the disease; and any infectivity, if present, was likely to be distributed throughout the carcass. BSE, however, was difficult to distinguish from the disease scrapie, which was endemic in sheep and goat flocks, and it was unclear whether flocks were free of BSE or if scrapie was masking BSE infection. Indeed, one important UK-government-funded study infamously had to be abandoned in 2001 after it was discovered that samples had been contaminated by cattle brains.

In 2001/02 the FSA held an open meeting and convened a small stakeholder group to consider whether further controls should be introduced in addition to those already in place in relation to certain sheep and goat organs. The stakeholder group was presented with two conflicting studies. The first study suggested that natural sausage casings made from sheep intestines could contribute up to one-third of the total exposure to potential BSE risks from sheep should they be infected (FSA 2002a). The second study conversely suggested that processing practices significantly reduced the potential risks from casings, leaving carcass meat to contribute four-fifths of potential exposure (DNV 2001). Faced with that conflict, the stakeholder group took a precautionary view of the risks arising from natural sausage casings and recommended that they should be banned. The FSA Board decided to recommend that advice to the European Commission and issued general advice in the meantime that consumers could reduce their theoretical risk by avoiding sausages with natural casings, and meat from older sheep and goats. The Board also explicitly stated, however, that it did not advise against the consumption of sheep and goat meat.

The Board's recommendations caused predictable furore among UK and European natural sausage casings manufacturers, who lobbied the European Commission. The EC's Scientific Steering Committee (SSC) reviewed the evidence including additional work submitted by the casings manufacturers and concluded that potential risks from casings were minimal compared to other cuts of meat, and further made the risk management recommendation that no more action should be taken until what is a theoretically possible risk becomes a probable risk (SSC 2002a; 2002b). The EC consequently rejected the FSA's proposed ban but instead struck a compromise deal that put an already widely observed voluntary ban on a part of the intestine called the ileum on a statutory footing.

At first sight, this case suggests that the FSA's attempt to be consultative and precautionary was defeated by a combination of business lobbying and European scientific advisors extending their remit from providing advice on risk assessment to risk management. But analysis of the controversy reveals that the conflict was underlain by fundamental uncertainties facing regulators in taking precautionary decisions.

The first problem the case highlights is the methodological difficulty of determining a precautionary course of action when confronted with scientific uncertainty. While the stakeholder group and the FSA based their recommendation on evidence that suggested casings presented significant risks, the SSC put greater emphasis on other evidence that suggested normal carcass meat potentially presented considerably greater risks than casings. From that latter point of view, as one ex-member of the Spongiform Encephalopathy Advisory Committee (SEAC), the UK expert committee on BSE, put it, 'if you want to reduce the risk by 50 per cent, it would be more consistent to cut every sheep in half and throw half away'. Scientific uncertainty, in this case, created significant scope for conflicting policy options to be equally defined as precautionary.

The second related problem the case highlights is the normative difficulty of how the costs and benefits of precautionary decision making should be distributed. While the precautionary principle has become central to EU risk regulation, it is balanced by the principle of proportionality, which is also enshrined in EU law, and which requires the maintenance of 'a proper balance' between the purposes of administrative action and the adverse effects of that action (eg see De Smith, Woolf and Jowell 1995: 593–8). Yet the identification of proportionate action, like precaution, is highly dependent on choice of evidence and the framing of risk management questions. The FSA argued on the basis of the first study that its recommended ban reconciled the need for both precautionary action and proportionality; natural casings sales in the UK came to £6.5 million and only accounted for a sixth of the UK sausage market, whereas a ban on mature sheep meat could cost £115 million in lost sales and decimate the UK sheep industry. Given that there was no evidence that BSE was present in flocks, no one was arguing that sheep meat should be banned. But on the basis of the second study, it was not clear that it was proportionate or consistent to ban natural casings if carcass meat, which was more widely consumed, presented greater risks. Certainly in the EU market, the proportionality argument was harder to sustain given that casings sales came to £200 million and related sausage sales to much more – Germans, for example, eat 11 million sausages with natural casings each day.

This policy conflict also highlights a third institutional uncertainty of what constitutes 'due process' for risk decision making. Much has been made of the FSA's new open and inclusive approach to decision making, but analysis of the decision-making process shows how outcomes were highly sensitive to the differential representation of interests within decision making, creating considerable scope for policy conflict.

The FSA's stakeholder group was established to help represent the balance of views on different options. While the stakeholder group included consumer representation, however, it was dominated by the FSA and other state-related personnel or advisors, and crucially did not include representatives from the natural sausage casings industry.[1] Instead the casings industry had just two weeks following the

1 Out of 12 members, there were five FSA representatives including the Chief Executive, Board Chairman and Deputy Chair, two scientists that sit on government advisory committees, a representative of the Meat and Livestock Commission (MLC) – a non-departmental public body – a representative from the Welsh Assembly Government, a farmers' representative and two consumer representatives.

publication of the stakeholder report to make its case before the FSA Board met to consider the issue: 10 weeks short of the minimum recommended as best practice. The FSA's Chief Executive robustly defended this process on the grounds that the agency was designed to 'insulate decisions on food issues from "special pleading" ' (FSA 2002e). The flip side of that argument, however, was that the decision-making process marginalised inputs from a key group that had an important stake in policy outcome.

Moreover, independent scientific advice was also surprisingly marginalised. SEAC was not asked to give a formal opinion on the scientific evidence, but instead scientific advice was provided by the chair of SEAC, who sat on the stakeholder group. Subsequent interviews with members of SEAC revealed that the FSA's interpretation of the evidence was far from unanimously supported. That significantly contrasted with the European process, which provided a greater opportunity for the casings industry to argue its case and the SSC to evaluate the evidence.

This case, therefore, highlights how scientific, normative and institutional uncertainties provided significant scope for conflict on what constitutes precautionary action. While the conflict could be explained by the FSA being more precautionary, proportionate and inclusive, alternative framings made the FSA recommendation look inconsistent, disproportionate and subject to inadequate consultation. From that latter point of view, the conflict was better explained by the FSA's opportunistic need for an 'early win' to demonstrate its credentials as the consumer's champion by picking on the small natural casings market in the UK which minimised the potential for a public backlash while limiting the business risks to the UK sheep industry. By contrast, the EC was under less pressure to demonstrate its consumer credentials and the configuration and mobilisation of European business and consumer interests suggested that such a ban was politically unsaleable in the absence of evidence that BSE was actually in the sheep flock.

3.2 Warning! This regime may contain gaps: institutional constraints on improving consumer protection

The second case illustrates the institutional constraints on reforming risk regulation regimes to improve consumer protection, and concerns the limited improvements the FSA has been able to make to the management of food allergen risks (for further detail, see Rothstein 2005). Almost 2 per cent of adults and up to 8 per cent of children are thought to have a food allergy. While most reactions are not fatal, there are approximately 10 confirmed deaths from food-induced anaphylaxis each year, and possibly more deaths from food-related asthma that are unrecorded. Over two-thirds of those deaths arise from commercial catering, where often ingredient control is relaxed and cross-contamination happens easily (Pumphrey 2000). During the 1990s, when food allergy emerged as an increasingly recognised and widespread problem, MAFF had done little to improve consumer protection other than establishing a programme of basic scientific research into allergens. In 2003, however, the FSA announced a major policy initiative on food allergens in line with its commitment to 'put consumers first' (FSA 2003b).

The basic regulatory challenge posed by food allergens is to ensure the provision of reliable information to help consumers make rational consumption decisions. Ideally, that challenge might be met with rules to ensure businesses throughout the supply chain provide robust information on ingredients and contaminants; enforcement mechanisms to ensure business compliance; and awareness raising to ensure that allergic consumers are alert to their responsibilities, such as reading food labels or inquiring whether foodstuffs contain allergens.

The FSA managed to improve some aspects of consumer protection. The agency continued to support MAFF's basic research programme but it also improved advice to caterers, enforcers and consumers. The FSA also helped improve the European labelling regime for pre-packed food to require listing of the main allergenic ingredients and close a loophole that exempted labelling constituents of compound ingredients that comprised less than 25 per cent of foodstuffs.

The FSA, however, failed to improve the regime in a number of key respects. Most importantly, serious gaps in the law remained. Unlike pre-packed food, there were no specific rules on declaring allergenic ingredients of catered or foods sold loose, despite these being the greatest source of allergen risks. These gaps in the law contrasted starkly with legal requirements for all food businesses to declare genetically modified food ingredients since 2000. Nor were there rules on declaring contaminants of any food; 'may contain' warnings remained voluntary and continued to be inconsistently applied. In the absence of clear criteria for legal compliance, there was wide variation in business and consumer behaviour. One study, for example, found that one-fifth of take-away meals requested to be peanut-free contained peanut protein (Leitch *et al.* 2005). Moreover, while the FSA encouraged local government food safety inspectors to take a more vigorous approach, in practice, they rarely inspected or enforced the law, even following fatal incidents. Allergic consumers, therefore, continued to play Russian roulette with their food purchases and had to put their trust in businesses to provide them with robust information.

Despite the FSA's high intentions to improve consumer protection, the FSA failed to deliver a robust regime because it was unable to resolve a range of uncertainties. The first set of uncertainties concerned the risks posed to consumers. Scientific uncertainty about safety thresholds meant that it was difficult to set legal standards for trace contaminants. Moreover, consumers faced further uncertainties in assessing the accuracy of information provided by food retailers and caterers about the presence of allergenic ingredients in loose and catered foods. The FSA could have taken a precautionary approach to these problems by setting non-zero risk thresholds for contaminants, requiring caterers to declare or at least keep records of the use of allergenic ingredients, and encouraging greater use of 'may contain' warnings. The FSA, however, did not do so.

The FSA's resistance to taking a precautionary approach can best be understood by examining the normative uncertainties of how best to serve the public interest. On the one hand, the FSA was committed to putting consumers first, which the FSA has publicly interpreted as taking a precautionary approach in cases of uncertainty. On the other hand, food allergens affect only a minority of consumers, and although polls suggested that just under one-third of the population wanted tougher controls, regulation would have imposed an unequal distribution of costs and benefits on allergic and non-allergic consumers. Moreover, caterers were resistant to the introduction of onerous, difficult and potentially expensive controls on allergens in catered foods. Caterers were particularly concerned about legal liabilities because failures would be readily identifiable if customers suffered allergic reactions. Further controls could spawn ubiquitous 'may contain' warnings that restricted the market for allergic consumers and even possibly undermined the risk management value of such warnings. Moreover, if foods disappeared from menus, the potential general public opinion backlash could create a public relations headache for the FSA. Assessment of the public interest, therefore, entailed a complex series of risk-risk trade-offs that included the institutional risks posed to the FSA itself.

Moreover, at the heart of the issue was a fundamental normative uncertainty about the allocation of rights and responsibilities for risk management. Some, mainly caterers, viewed food allergen risks as a consumer health problem and, therefore, out of the ambit of conventional food safety law with responsibility borne by the consumer rather than the supplier. From that perspective, the state's main role was in health care provision and advice. Allergic consumers, in contrast, argued that allergens needed to be treated as food safety risks if they were to have robust information on ingredients and contaminants. From that point of view, the state's main role was to use the instrument of food safety regulation to assist consumers to manage their exposures. The FSA failed to resolve this normative uncertainty, preferring the view that it was for the courts to decide (Hattersley 2004).

Even if the FSA had decided that the public interest was best served by introducing regulatory controls on information provision for catered and loose foods and contaminants, it was confronted by institutional constraints on how best to achieve its aim. In particular, the multi-level governance dimension of the food safety regime limited the FSA's power to change EU rules. The FSA could have unilaterally introduced tougher controls on catered and loose foods in the absence of EU rules, given the putative risks to health and, in principle, the issue did not present an intra-community trade issue. But such an option posed considerable institutional risks for the FSA if it was challenged in the European Court and demanded resources and policy skills probably beyond the agency's capacity. Instead, the FSA trod politically safer ground by building on pre-existing regulatory frameworks to develop allergen labelling for pre-packed foods, but encouraging only voluntary action for loose foods and catering even though they posed the greatest risk.

The multi-level governance regime also restricted the ability of the FSA to improve the enforcement of controls that did exist. The problem was that food safety enforcement was the responsibility of local authorities and, because it was financed out of general funds provided by central government, it often lost out to other locally politically pressing issues. For example, one audit of controls at the port of Dover found that only 10 out of 100,000 food imports had been checked over the previous two years, and mandatory controls on high-risk foods had simply not been carried out (FSA 2003c: 8). Another study found that inspection targets were met in London and other areas by focusing on lower- rather than higher-risk-rated activities because of under-funding and staff recruitment and retention problems (FSA 2002b: 16).

The FSA has had some scope to improve enforcement controls by using its power to audit and name and shame local authorities, and to provide its own funding to improve enforcement activities (FSA 2005). But allergens were always going to take a back seat to other, often less serious or non-risk issues. Local authorities only had a total staff of about 1,500 inspectors, yet there were several hundred thousand catering establishments, and it was difficult enough to get basic food hygiene messages through such as hand washing, let alone messages on food allergens. Moreover, inspectors had low levels of understanding of the issue and recourse to law was difficult because it was expensive, there was a lack of clear legal compliance criteria, and cases often hinged on unwitnessed dialogue between businesses and, sometimes deceased, customers prior to consumption.

This case, therefore, shows that the constraints on improving consumer protection can go beyond uncertainty in scientific knowledge. Problems such as food allergens show that regulators are additionally confronted by fundamental normative uncertainties about the distribution of costs and benefits of regulation, the allocation of rights and responsibilities for risk management, and institutional uncertainties that can mitigate against the establishment of a robust regime for policy making and enforcement.

3.3 It's all just talk: the uncertainties of institutionalising consumer consultation

The third and final case illustrates the uncertainties of participative regulation and concerns the failed attempt to institutionalise consumer consultation within the FSA through the establishment of a Consumer Committee (for further detail, see Rothstein 2007). Participative approaches to regulation have become the *sine qua non* of the reform of risk regulation regimes. Broadening the range of public actors involved in decision making, so it is argued: can help reduce information asymmetries within risk bureaucracies by generating information about policy problems, particularly in relation to relevant social practices and attitudes; inform a wide range of social and ethical judgements; and strengthen the legitimacy and efficiency of regulatory processes.

In 2002, the FSA established a Consumer Committee, which comprised up to six representatives from consumer organisations and six publicly appointed lay members to provide advice to the Agency on issues of consumer concern; consultation methodologies and practices; and the Agency's strategic objectives. At first, the Committee was welcomed by all, but by 2005, relations between the FSA and the Committee had soured. Committee members felt ignored and the FSA felt that the Committee was trying to exceed its remit. At the end of the year, the FSA abolished the Committee altogether and instead focused on other *ad hoc* consumer engagement activities.

A number of cases came to symbolise the problems. In one case, the FSA recommended that the EU ban the addition of non-poultry proteins to chicken and limit added-water to 15 per cent. The Consumer Committee subsequently supported the general direction of policy but criticised the FSA for not banning the addition of water to chicken completely. The FSA, however, challenged the Committee's expertise and representativeness and was concerned that the Committee had elected to discuss the issue after the Board had already made its recommendation. In a second case, the Committee welcomed the FSA's initiative in 2002 to prioritise low income consumers, but over time began to believe that the FSA was procrastinating by focusing on undertaking primary research rather than acting on the basis of existing data. The FSA argued conversely that it needed a stronger evidence base for action. And in a third case, the Committee again supported the general direction of the FSA's policy initiative to control food promotion to children, but was concerned that the FSA's decision to pursue voluntary rather than mandatory controls would be inadequate.

The conflicts that arose between the FSA and its Consumer Committee highlighted three core uncertainties facing risk bureaucracies in consulting consumers. The first uncertainty concerned the contested status and kinds of knowledge contributed by the Committee. The Committee was established as a deliberative forum for its generalist members but as a consequence of its generalist character, it sometimes had little novel evidence to contribute about regulatory problems that was not already well known. Members themselves recognised that sometimes they were unclear about technical issues and sometimes missed what the Agency perceived to be the important questions. Certainly, in cases such as water in chicken that involved highly technical questions, Agency officials did not perceive the Committee to have sufficient expertise to be consulted. At times, however, Committee members felt that Agency officials too readily dismissed their contributions or ignored them in favour of the contributions of organised business interests. Committee members, for example, criticised the FSA's use of an industry study that purported to show consumer preferences for chicken with added water, but which remained commercially confidential.

The value of the Committee's contributions were most obviously contested in relation to its representation of consumer views. The Committee did not have resources to undertake opinion polls or other public attitude research but members of the Committee argued that what they lacked in terms of public representativeness, they gained in terms of ongoing institutionalised deliberation of issues at greater depth than could be achieved by polling exercises. But the virtue of such consumer representation was also its vice. By using *ad hoc* lay representatives and consumer NGOs to stand for consumers, the FSA perceived the Committee's contributions to represent neither majority opinion nor the views of the 'hard to hear' consumers. That created scope for conflict between the Committee and the FSA on a number of occasions.

In part, however, these conflicts also originated from the way in which the Committee and the FSA framed evidence, problems and solutions. The FSA was constrained to act on issues from within regulatory frameworks and according to bureaucratic norms that framed the questions it could ask, the kinds and standards of evidence it could consider, and the policy solutions it could pursue. The Consumer Committee, however, was not so constrained and conceived of issues within different framings so that information that it saw as relevant to the problem often did not easily fit with regulatory expectations. One example was the clash over the evidential standards needed for action on low income consumers. Another example was water in chicken, which the FSA viewed as a problem of trying to establish a robust regulatory framework, but the Committee viewed as a more general problem of domestic cooking skills, catering techniques and the type and quality of produce on offer to consumers. Conflicts between the FSA and the Consumer Committee were, therefore, often underlain by incommensurabilities of understanding and resolving such conflicts was always going to prove difficult.

The second uncertainty concerned the normative distribution of the costs and benefits of regulation. In particular, the absence of commonly agreed benchmarks for assessing consumer interests led to contested assessments of whether policy put consumers first or not. The Consumer Committee argued that cases such as the failure to ban water in chicken and the promulgation of voluntary rather than mandatory controls on food promotion to children suggested that the FSA was overly favouring business interests at the expense of the consumer. The FSA argued conversely in those cases that their actions to ban animal proteins, control water in chicken and address food promotion to children were good examples of 'putting consumers first'. From the FSA's perspective, widespread consumption of chicken with added water, particularly among lower income consumers, suggested that there might be a consumer interest in retaining such products. And the FSA's scope for action on food promotion to children was constrained by more than just powerful business lobbies, but also by other factors such as the potential impacts of mandatory controls on school incomes and the overlapping responsibilities of the communications regulator Ofcom, which had been unsympathetic to the idea of mandatory controls.

Different conceptions and assessments of the public interest can lead to very different policy responses, as has been discussed already in this chapter in relation to natural sausage casings and food allergens. Neither the FSA nor the Consumer Committee had well-worked-out ideas about how to navigate these difficult waters, other than establishing the procedural need to 'understand and take full account of the broad range of consumer views and perspectives' in decision making (FSA 2002c: 2). For the FSA, that did not mean, however, 'just doing what consumers, or consumer organisations, say they want us to do' (FSA 2002d: 1). That, however, begged the question of how consumer views should inform decision making, and how they should be balanced against other factors, such as commercial interests, to give substance to the concept of 'putting consumers first'.

Uncertainty in the concept of 'putting consumers first' meant that whoever laid claim to representing consumer interests could lay claim to having a say in policy. If the Consumer Committee claimed to represent consumers then when FSA outcomes did not align with its view, the implication was that consumers were not being put first. But for the FSA, the Committee's views were conceived as only a partial and sometimes biased indicator of consumer views. Indeed, for one FSA official interviewed by the author, the Committee offered an opportunity for some consumer groups to get 'a second bite of the cherry'.

The procedural conception of 'putting consumers first', however, highlighted a third set of uncertainties concerning the procedural legitimacy of consultation. For example, the organisation of the Committee's work proved to be a point of tension between the Committee and the FSA and lessened the Committee's support for the consultation process. The Committee had little time to consider issues in half-day quarterly meetings; the issues it discussed, such as water in chicken, were often poorly synchronised with the course of policy development; and sometimes it was unclear what questions the Committee was being asked to consider. Sometimes, it seemed that the Committee was merely being asked to 'rubber stamp' decisions. Moreover, the Committee was poorly integrated into the Agency; members complained that the secretariat failed to effectively communicate the Committee's views throughout the Agency and provided insufficient feedback on how the Committee's views had been used. From the FSA's point of view, however, there would always be practical constraints on how much time was available for consultation, and the Committee was seen to sometimes exceed its remit by inappropriately investigating issues on its own initiative or demanding responses that the Agency felt no obligation to respond to.

But these problems reflected deeper conflicts about the constitutional role of the Committee within the FSA. Committee members saw themselves as having a check and audit function; it should be like 'an outside body looking in . . . it should be able to hold the Agency to account', as the Chair of the Committee put it. It was not expected that the Committee's views would always be followed, but members felt that the FSA should provide an explanation if it did not act upon its recommendations.

By contrast, the FSA broadly conceived the Committee as a useful resource to be called upon when necessary, although there was some difference of opinion as to the role of such a resource. Some FSA Board members felt there was a need, as one put it at a board meeting in July 2005, for a 'separate stream of consumer advice beholden to no-one'. But other Board members were concerned to avoid deadlocked constitutional conflicts that could arise if the Committee was conceived as holding the Agency to account; 'that is what the Board does', as another Board member put it. The absence of clarity of the Committee's role and purpose certainly created wide scope for conflicts.

The conflicts between the Consumer Committee and the FSA, therefore, were underlain by uncertainties over the nature of evidence, normative conflicts of what constitutes the public interest, and the institutional role of consumer consultation in decision making. The FSA saw the Consumer Committee as an opportunity to provide procedural legitimacy for decision-making processes, but that goal raised the expectations of Committee members to have a substantive input into the evidential basis of decision making and policy outcomes. In the end, both the FSA and the Consumer Committee were disappointed, and the Committee was disbanded.

4 CONCLUSIONS

The FSA is one of a new breed of risk regulation agencies in Europe that has pioneered the role of precaution, openness and participation, and the importance of improving regulatory implementation to better serve and protect the public. Created at a time when public trust in the UK government to adequately manage food safety was at an all-time low, the FSA has undoubtedly achieved some success in enhancing public confidence over its first five years of operation. This chapter, however, has used a number of cases to examine how successful the FSA has been in improving regulatory outcomes. The cases, of course, represent just a small fraction of issues that the FSA has dealt with in its first five years. It would, therefore, be inappropriate to simply read over from one issue to another and also not to recognise the steep learning curve that the FSA has been on. Nevertheless, the cases highlight at least five of the cross-cutting fundamental constraints and uncertainties facing reform of food safety regulation and risk regulation regimes in general.

First, the cases illustrate the difficulties and uncertainties of operationalising the precautionary principle. The BSE in sheep case, for example, reveals methodological uncertainties posed by the adoption of the precautionary principle in cases of scientific uncertainty. The problem is that inherent flexibility in the concepts of precaution and its companion principle, proportionality, mean that when confronted with conflicting evidence, conflicting policy options can be equally construed as precautionary and proportionate depending on the choice of evidence and problem framings. In the BSE in sheep case, what was understood as precautionary and proportionate depended on how conflicting scientific studies on risks from casings were interpreted; whether action was determined solely on the basis of risks from casings or the relative risks of casings and carcass meat; and whether economic calculations took into account the UK or the wider EU market. That case suggests that conflicts over the precautionary principle may be more deeply seated than the more obvious normative conflicts about the distribution of regulatory costs and benefits when acting under uncertainty.

Second, and relatedly, inconsistencies in the way that the FSA has taken decisions highlights the uncertainties of expertise and evidence within the decision-making process. In the BSE in sheep case, for example, the FSA's stakeholder consultation process brought consumer representatives into the decision-making process, but the key business stakeholder was excluded and scientific advice took a surprisingly minor role. That contrasted with the EC's reliance on its scientific expert committee as the legitimate source of advice. Similarly, questions about expertise and representativeness were the source of conflict between the Consumer Committee and the FSA on the legitimacy of members' contributions to policy knowledge and policy prescriptions. In that case, conflicts were underlain by misalignments between the ways in which the Committee framed evidence, problems and solutions and the bureaucratic norms, constraints and expectations of the FSA. These examples suggest that scientific knowledge does not provide an uncontested universal evidential basis for decision making, but instead what stands for acceptable expertise and evidence is subject to negotiation dependent on local and case-specific institutional practices and understandings.

Third, the cases highlight the normative uncertainties of how to improve risk regulation in what might be termed the 'public interest'. The FSA, for example, was inconsistent in operationalising its principle of 'putting consumers first', in so far as it recommended a precautionary ban on natural sausage casings, yet left consumers to play Russian roulette with food allergens. It is, of course, not surprising that 'putting consumers first' is a problematic concept. The phrase is suggestive of directing regulators to limit the exercise of private power in pursuit of objectives valued by consumers. But regulatory decisions are rarely straightforward choices between 'consumer' and 'other' interests, but entail complex trade-offs between different interests such as consumer choice and consumer health, the rights of minorities, conflicting business interests, competing demands on resources and even the institutional risks attaching to the agency for unpopular decisions. Indeed, the allergens case highlights how fundamental uncertainties about the allocation of rights and responsibilities in managing risk can have a significant impact on the coherence and efficacy of consumer protection regimes. Certainly conflicting understandings of what it means to 'put consumers first' created tensions between the Consumer Committee and FSA. In the absence of any substantive conceptual elaboration of what should be protected in the name of consumers and how, it is unsurprising that there is little consistency in the way that the interests of private and public groups are translated into, and legitimated as, 'putting consumers first'.

Fourth, and following on from that point, the case of the Consumer Committee suggests that participative processes may have relatively little impact in shaping resolution of such uncertainties, and can even exacerbate problems. The minimal or equivocal impact of the Committee on shaping the evidential basis of decision making, policy outcomes and procedural legitimacy highlights institutional uncertainties about the role and purpose of participation. In that case, the FSA saw the Committee primarily in instrumental terms of providing procedural legitimation by co-opting public opinion-formers, but largely rejected the potential methodological value or normative role of participation in improving the robustness or justice of decision making. In contrast, Committee members resisted being positioned as an endorsement body without substantive input into the evidential basis of decision making and influence over policy outcomes.

The Consumer Committee case, however, also suggests that resolution of such conflicts may depend on trade-offs between competing conceptions of the purposes of participation. If participation, for example, is designed to contribute specialist information about policy questions such as social contexts or public attitudes, then that may be at the expense of its instrumental value in bringing in more generalist public representatives and opinion-formers who may approach problems differently. Or if participation is designed to co-opt public opinion-formers, then that may undermine its usefulness in improving the evidential basis of policy.

Fifth, and finally, the cases illustrate the institutional dilemmas facing regulatory agencies in achieving their goals when working within complex regulatory regimes. While the FSA was established to make a difference to food safety regulation, its impact has been constrained because it is only one actor within a complex multi-level regime that stretches from international policy making down to local authority enforcement and even involves non-state regulation by commercial intermediaries. The FSA's limited ability to act within the EU context, for example, was shown by the EC's rejection of the FSA's recommended ban on natural sausage casings, and the FSA's preference for improving existing regulatory frameworks for food allergens in pre-packed food rather than unilaterally introduce new rules for food allergens in catered and loose foods.

At the UK national level, the FSA has been further constrained by the overlapping responsibilities of other government departments and regulators, which have different ways of working and policy priorities. One example was the case of food promotion to children, where the FSA's scope for action was constrained by the communications regulator Ofcom. And the FSA's role in shaping the enforcement of food safety regulation on the ground has been further constrained by the separation of responsibilities between the FSA and local authorities. Incoherence between standard-setting and enforcement has long been an important factor in past food safety crises, and uncertainties in the scope for improvement was an important constraint on tightening up the control of food allergen risks.

The cases show that the origins of regulatory uncertainty go beyond simple scientific uncertainty, but also encompass uncertainties in the conception of consumer interests and preferences; how regulatory costs and benefits should be distributed; the purposes and role of participative processes; and how to overcome constraints of regulatory architectures that cross multiple levels of governance and policy domains. For regulatory bodies charged with improving risk regulation, a commitment to putting consumers first will only add value if accompanied by careful identification of these methodological, normative and institutional uncertainties and analysis of how they can best be addressed.

BIBLIOGRAPHY

DNV Consulting (2001) *Risk of Exposure to BSE Infectivity in UK Sheep (for Food Standards Agency)*, London: DNV Consulting.

Feintuck, M. (2004) *'The Public Interest' in Regulation*, Oxford: OUP.

Food Standards Agency (FSA) (2005) 'Food Standards Agency provides £10 million for local authorities to promote new food safety initiative', *Press Release 2005/0582*, London: FSA, 23 May 2005.

Food Standards Agency (FSA) (2003a) *Consumer Attitudes to Food Standards*, London: FSA.

Food Standards Agency (FSA) (2003b) 'Progress on agency plan to help food allergic consumers', *FSA Paper 03/09/04*, 11 September 2003.

Food Standards Agency (FSA) (2003c) *Report on the Food Law Enforcement Service: Dover District Council and Port Health Authority 2–4 December 2003*, London: FSA.

Food Standards Agency (FSA) (2002a) *BSE and Sheep: Report of the Core Stakeholder Group*, London: FSA.

Food Standards Agency (FSA) (2002b) *Report on Local Authority Food Law Enforcement in the UK*, London: FSA.

Food Standards Agency (FSA) (2002c) *Consumer Involvement in Agency Policy Making*, FSA 2 November 2004, London: FSA.

Food Standards Agency (FSA) (2002d) *Putting Consumers First*, ConsComm D0006/02, London: FSA.

Food Standards Agency (FSA) (2002e) 'Minutes of the Food Standards Agency Board Meeting', 11 July 2002, London: FSA.

Food Standards Agency (FSA) (2001) *Strategic Plan 2001–2006 Putting Consumers First*, London: FSA.

Food Standards Agency (FSA) (2000) *Statement of General Objectives and Practices*, London: FSA.

Hattersley, S. (2004) 'Personal communication with S. Hattersley, Head of Branch 2, Chemical Safety and Toxicology Division', Food Standards Agency, 9 February 2004.

Hood, C., Rothstein, H. and Baldwin, R. (2001) *The Government of Risk: Understanding Risk Regulation Regimes*, Oxford: Oxford University Press, 2nd edition (2004), Spanish translation (2006) *El Gobierno del Riesgo*, Barcelona: Editorial Ariel.

Leitch, I., Walker, M. and Davey, R. (2005) 'Food allergy: gambling your life on a take-away meal,' *International Journal of Environmental Health Research* 15(2): 79–87.

Lord Phillips of Worth Matravers, Bridgeman, J. and Ferguson-Smith, M. (2000) *The BSE Inquiry: Volume 1*, London: The Stationery Office.

Luhmann, N. (1993) *Risk: A Sociological Theory*, Berlin: de Gruyter.

Pumphrey, R. (2000) 'Lessons for management of anaphylaxis from a study of fatal reactions', *Clinical and Experimental Allergy* 30: 1144–50.

Rothstein, H. (2007) 'Talking shops or talking turkey? Institutional constraints to proceduralising consumer representation in risk regulation', *Science, Technology and Human Values* 32(5): 582–607.

Rothstein, H. (2006) 'The institutional origins of risk: a new agenda for risk research', *Health, Risk and Society* 8(3): 215–21.

Rothstein, H. (2005) 'Escaping the regulatory net: why regulatory reform can fail consumers', *Law & Policy* 27(4): 520–48.

Rothstein, H. (2004) 'Precautionary bans or sacrificial lambs? Participative regulation and the reform of the UK food safety regime', *Public Administration* 82(4): 857–81.

Rothstein, H. (2003a) 'Neglected risk regulation: the institutional attenuation phenomenon', *Health, Risk and Society* 5(1): 85–103.

Rothstein, H. (2003b) 'Risk management under wraps: self-regulation and the case of food contact plastics', *Journal of Risk Research* 6(1): 61–74.

Rothstein, H., Huber, M. and Gaskell, G. (2006) 'A theory of risk colonisation: the spiralling regulatory logics of societal and institutional risk', *Economy and Society* 35(1): 91–112.

Scientific Steering Committee (SSC) (2002a) 'Complement to the SSC opinion of 4–5 April 2002 on safe sourcing of small ruminant materials, with special reference to the safety with regard to BSE risks of sheep intestines and casings', Brussels: European Commission, 12–13 September 2002.

Scientific Steering Committee (SSC) (2002b) 'BSE: result of the Scientific Steering Committees', Press Release, IP/02/1314, Brussels: European Commission, 17 September 2002.

Shrader-Frechette, K. (1991) *Risk and Rationality*, Berkeley: University of California Press.

De Smith, S.A., Lord Woolf and Jowell, J. (1995) *Judicial Review of Administrative Action*, 5th edn, London: Sweet and Maxwell.

Chapter 5

The Dutch regulatory framework for food – risk analysis based food law in the Netherlands

*Bernd M.J. van der Meulen**

1 INTRODUCTION

This chapter explores the evolution in the Netherlands of a regulatory system – policy, legislation and institutions – for risk analysis in food.

Section 2 describes the policy arena at government level. Section 3 focuses on the enforcement of food law in general and on the role of the food safety authority in particular. Section 4 introduces the EU law concept of risk analysis and the way in which it has been implemented in the Netherlands. Section 5 places this concept in the context of the general framework of Dutch administrative law. Section 6 analyses what little case law is available so far on this subject. Section 7 discusses how the concept of risk analysis is applied in practice by the food safety authority. Finally, section 8 draws some conclusions from the discussion in this chapter.

2 FOOD LAW AND POLICY IN THE NETHERLANDS

2.1 Competition between ministries

Food safety is a contested area in Dutch politics. For decades influence has been moving back and forth between two ministries. Today, both the Ministry of Public Health, Welfare and Sport (*Ministerie van Volksgezondheid, Welzijn en Sport, VWS*) and the Ministry of Agriculture, Nature and Food Quality[1] (*Ministerie van Landbouw, Natuur en Voedselkwaliteit, LNV*) have competences in the field of food policy, food law and its enforcement. The demarcation of competences has been a point of dispute for many years. Traditionally the Ministry of LNV was the voice of the Dutch agriculture sector. This sector represented a substantial part of the Dutch population and was so thoroughly organised and influential that it was often referred to as 'the green front'. However, the influence of agriculture on society and politics in the Netherlands has been declining steadily. This has had its impact on food safety policy as well.

In 1995, a division of tasks between the Ministries of Health, Welfare and Sport

* Many thanks for their very useful remarks and suggestions to Aaron Underwood Chase, Michelle Everson, Michael Fogden, Annelies Freriks, Margaret Rosso Grossman and Anna Szajkowska.

1 Previously called the Ministry of Agriculture, Nature Conservation and Fisheries.

(hereinafter VWS) and Agriculture, Nature and Food Quality (hereinafter LNV) was laid down in a protocol.[2] VWS was to have primary responsibility for matters pertaining to public health and consumer protection. LNV was to have primary responsibility for animal health and welfare and the marketing of agricultural products. LNV aimed, among other things, to increase trade in agricultural products by laying down or promoting quality standards for food products. Despite this protocol both Ministries try from time to time to extend their responsibilities, recently during the debates about the setting up of a national food authority (see below).

In October 2001, a discussion in Parliament on food safety led up to the decision that VWS should have primary responsibility for food safety. A few years later, however, the restructuring of European food safety law, and in particular the entry into force of the hygiene package,[3] raised the question whether it was necessary to reconsider yet again the division of competences between the two Ministries. Two consultants were engaged and presented three options in their report: two sharing responsibilities between VWS and LNV, the third concentrating all responsibilities within LNV (Van Hoogstraten and Folkerts 2005). The report failed to give reasons why the option that has been followed by the EU – in which major responsibilities are concentrated within the department of Health (the so-called 'total-option') – was rejected, possibly reflecting the power base re-established by LNV.[4]

The Ministers chose a shared responsibility option, the so-called 'health-option'.[5] VWS is given sole responsibility for all public health issues and, in particular, for the hygiene package with the exception of slaughter and meat inspection and official controls in this context. All matters pertaining to food quality and the food production chain, feed, animal welfare and animal health remain with the Minister of Agriculture. In practice, this results in VWS actions in the case of food safety problems in food processing and distribution and in LNV actions during the stage of delivery and production. As a result, two Ministries remain responsible for the implementation of food law. It is unclear who has the final responsibility in the case of differing views.[6]

2 *Kamerstukken II (Proceedings of the Second Chamber of Parliament)*, 1994/95, 23900 XIV, No. 48. Official Dutch documents can be found at: <www.overheid.nl>.

3 Regulations (EC) No. 852/2004 of the European Parliament and of the Council of 29 April 2004 on the hygiene of foodstuffs, [2004] *OJ* L139/1; Regulation (EC) No. 853/2004 of the European Parliament and of the Council of 29 April 2004 laying down specific hygiene rules for food of animal origin, [2004] *OJ* L226/22; Regulation (EC) No. 854/2004 of the European Parliament and of the Council of 29 April 2004 laying down specific rules for the organisation of official controls on products of animal origin intended for human consumption, [2004] *OJ* L139/1; and Directive 2004/41 of the European Parliament and of the Council of 21 April 2004 repealing certain directives concerning food hygiene and health conditions for the production and placing on the market of certain products of animal origin intended for human consumption and amending Council Directives 89/662/EEC and 92/118/EEC and Council Decision 95/408/EC, [2004] *OJ* L195/12.

4 *Kamerstukken II*, 2005–2006, 30 400, Nos 1–2.

5 Constitutionally, competences rest with government as a whole. For this reason it is possible that the competences of Ministers are delineated by mutual consent and laid down in a protocol or a letter.

6 See *Kamerstukken II*, 2005–2006, 30 400, Nos 1–2.

2.2 Legislation

Dutch food law can be characterised as economic regulatory law. The current legislation dates back to 1919 when the first national Consumer Products Safety Act[7] (*Warenwet*) was published. It is a framework Act that provides the legal basis for statutory legislation in the form of Orders in Council[8] and Ministerial Orders[9] on food and non-food matters.[10] Prior to 1919 food law provisions were issued at municipal level. At present, the 1919 Act is still used, but has been considerably amended and expanded. The major objectives of the Act are the protection of public health, safety, fair trade and proper information about products.[11] Several other Acts also contain food law provisions. All in all, food law in the Netherlands has a rather complicated structure of diverse (framework) Acts and pieces of delegated legislation.

The European call for simplification and deregulation did not bypass the Netherlands. At roughly the same time that the Molitor report[12] suggested a drastic restructuring of European law including food law, a report on food legislation was published in the Netherlands[13] in the context of an extensive project aimed at raising the overall quality of legislation through deregulation, market mechanisms and other quality measures (*Marktwerking, Deregulering en Wetgevingskwalieit: MDW*). The report advocated drastic restructuring and simplification.[14] Government asked for follow-up advice on whether Dutch food law should be re-codified into one single act. The expert chosen was the godfather of the General Administrative Law Act, Professor Martin Scheltema. His suggestion to undertake such restructuring (Scheltema 1997) met with little enthusiasm from the various stakeholders. Therefore government was all too happy to postpone action until the EC Green Paper on Food Safety had resulted in concrete measures, more particularly the famous White Paper on Food Safety with its Action Plan on Food Safety aimed at a restructuring of both EU and national food law.

After the entry into force in 2002 of Regulation 178/2002,[15] the General Food Law, with its common definitions and principles for European and national food law in the EU,[16] one would have expected a fresh restructuring of food legislation. Little could be further from the truth, however. No indication can be found that Dutch legislators are considering any major restructuring.

7 Or Commodities Act, Act of 28 December 1919, Statute Book (*Staatsblad*) 1935, 793.

8 Usually referred to as '*Warenwetbesluiten*'.

9 Usually referred to as '*Warenwetregelingen*'.

10 Such as toys and cosmetics.

11 Article 3, Consumer Products Safety Act.

12 European Commission, *Report of the Group of Independent Experts on Simplification of Legislation and Administration*, COM(1995) 288 final/2, 21 June 1995, Brussels.

13 6 June 1996; *Kamerstukken II*, 1995/96, 24 036, No. 24.

14 See for a press release (in Dutch) dated 5 September 1997: <http://www.minvws.nl/persberichten/zzoude_directies/gzb/levensmiddelenwetgeving_verder_vereenvoudigd.asp>.

15 Regulation (EC) No. 178/2002 of the European Parliament and of the Council of 28 January 2002 laying down the general principles and requirements of food law, establishing the European Food Safety Authority and laying down procedures in matters of food safety, [2002] *OJ* L31 (hereafter: 'the General Food Law' or GFL).

16 See E. Vos, in this volume.

2.3 Public consultation

Before amending the Consumer Products Safety Act or statutory legislation based on this Act, consultation takes place via the Regular Consultation Meeting on the Consumer Products Safety Act (*Regulier Overleg Warenwet*).[17] This Meeting consists of representatives from the food industry and trade, consumers, the Ministries of VWS and LNV, the Food and Consumer Product Safety Authority and relevant public industrial organisation(s). The Meeting discusses draft European food legislation,[18] domestic food legislation and policy intentions as regards the Consumer Products Safety Act. In principle, the Meeting tries to reach consensus about the subjects discussed. In practice, it plays an important intermediary role between the government and social actors involved in food law. The Meeting plays a role in light of Article 9 of the General Food Law, which states that there should be open and transparent public consultation, directly or through representative bodies, when drafting, evaluating and revising food law.

2.4 Research

The responsibility for (government) research on food safety in the Netherlands has not been concentrated in one single body. The major bodies carrying out such research are the RIVM Institute for Public Health, Environment and Nature and the RIKILT Institute of Food Safety.[19] RIVM is under the responsibility of the Ministry of Housing, Spatial Planning and the Environment (*Ministerie van Volkshuisvesting, Ruimtelijk Ordening en Milieu: VROM*). RIKILT has been privatised and is part of Wageningen University and Research Centre (WUR). WUR is financed by the Ministry of LNV, but is independent in its policy.

From 1999 up until 2005, pre-market safety assessment of novel foods was undertaken by the Dutch Health Council (*Gezondheidsraad*). The Health Council, established in 1902, is an independent scientific advisory body. Its mission is 'to advise the government and parliament on the current level of knowledge with respect to public health issues'.[20] The Health Council receives most requests for advice from four Ministries: VWS, VROM, LNV and Social Affairs & Employment. The Council can publish advisory reports on its own initiative. It usually does this in order to draw attention to developments or trends that are thought to be relevant to government policy. Most Health Council reports are prepared by multidisciplinary committees of Dutch or, sometimes, foreign experts who are appointed in a personal capacity. The reports are available to the public.[21]

17 Protocol for the Regular Consultation Meeting on the Commodities Act of 18 December 1996, Government Gazette (*Staatscourant*) 1996, No. 246.

18 For instance, the agenda of the meetings of the Standing Committee on Food Safety and Animal Health is discussed in the Netherlands via this forum.

19 See: <http://www.rivm.nl/> and <http://www.rikilt.wur.nl/UK/>. In 2004 RIVM published an extensive study on the food situation in the Netherlands: 'Ons eten gemeten'. It provides information on consumption patterns, health, food safety, government policy, risk perception, etc. See: <http://www.rivm.nl/bibliotheek/rapporten/270555007.pdf>; the report has been translated under the title: 'Our food, Our health', available at: <http://www.rivm.nl/bibliotheek/rapporten/270555009.html>.

20 Article 21, Health Act.

21 See: <www.gr.nl> or <www.healthcouncil.nl>. For instance: Health Council of the Netherlands (2002) *Safety Assessment of Novel Foods*, The Hague, publication No. 2002/05VNV.

Since 1 January 2005 the responsibility for the assessment of novel foods has been moved from the Health Council to the Medicines Evaluation Board (MEB) (*College ter Beoordeling van Geneesmiddelen*). The duties of the MEB are laid down in article 29, paragraph 1 of the Medicines Act. The MEB is an executive body with the authority to approve or reject medicinal products or to delete them from the Register on the basis of statutory criteria. Authorised medicinal products may be marketed in the Netherlands.[22] The shift of evaluation of novel foods to the MEB is not as odd as it may seem at first sight. The pre-market safety clearance procedure of novel foods resembles the approval of medicinal products in several ways. Finally, in the private sector, the most important body dealing with food safety research is TNO (*Nederlands Instituut voor Toegepast Natuurwetenschappelijk Onderzoek: the Dutch Institute for Applied Natural Science*).[23]

3 ENFORCEMENT OF FOOD LAW

Enforcement of food law in the Netherlands can be subdivided into four phases of a mixed administrative law and criminal law nature:

- supervision (administrative law);
- investigation (criminal law);
- prosecution (criminal law); and
- sanctioning (administrative law or criminal law).

The Food and Consumer Product Safety Authority (*Voedsel- en Warenautoriteit, VWA*) plays an important role with regard to supervision and investigation.

3.1 Supervision and investigation

3.1.1 Developments

Towards the end of the last century awareness grew that the distribution of powers and responsibilities in the field of food safety was incidental and haphazard. Restructuring and centralisation within a national food safety authority was advocated by varied interests. In mid 2001, under the responsibility of the Minister of LNV, a temporary Dutch Food Authority was set up with the objective of (re)gaining and retaining consumer confidence following several well-known food scares. Thereafter, following social and political debate, the Food and Consumer Product Safety Authority (VWA) was set up in July 2002 as a successor to the temporary Dutch Food Authority.[24] Unlike the temporary Food Authority, the VWA not only covers the food chain, but also has authority over non-food matters. In this its competence mirrors the scope of the Consumer Products Safety Act.

22 See: <www.cbg-meb.nl>.

23 And for other scientific research as well. See: <www.tno.nl>.

24 Decree on the Organisation of the Food and Consumer Products Safety Authority, *Staatscourant* 2002, No. 127. See: <www.vwa.nl>.

At the insistence of Parliament, the VWA was brought under the responsibility of VWS.[25] This situation did not last long, however. When a new government took office in 2003 it decided to transfer authority for VWA from the VWS to LNV. The VWA is mainly responsible for controls, but also for risk assessment and risk communication. The VWA has the same objective as its predecessor, namely to (re)gain and retain consumer confidence in food safety. It issued a mission statement stating that it would 'visibly reduce risk'.[26]

3.1.2 The position of enforcement agencies

In 2001, the Ministry of the Interior published a policy paper on the position of enforcement agencies.[27] It was deemed essential that such agencies work independently, transparently and professionally. To this end the function of law enforcement should be recognisable as a separate function within the bureaucracy. Three relationships should be taken into account:

a the relationship between the enforcement agency and the public subject to enforcement;
b the relationship between enforcement and policy; and
c the relationship between the agency and the responsible Minister.

First of all, the enforcement agency should not be otherwise involved in the field falling under its responsibility. This may seem self-evident, but the Netherlands has a strong corporatist tradition, which means that quite often the sector is involved in its own regulation. Second, policy interests should not dilute enforcement. Finally, enforcement should not be influenced by political considerations.

For these reasons, enforcement responsibilities should lie high up within the bureaucratic hierarchy – directly under the Minister or, in cases where the State itself is present in the field, not only as an arbiter but also as a player, enforcement should be positioned outside the Ministry. In the latter situation, implementation takes place through so-called autonomous administrative bodies (*Zelfstandige bestuursorganen: ZBOs*). ZBOs are not subordinate to the Minister. Only ministers and no other civil servants are answerable to Parliament. Ministers answer for their own actions and for those of their subordinates. The upshot of this is that democratic oversight does not go any further than the Minister's authority. Because of the democratic deficit that is inherent to ZBOs, this structure is only used if one of three criteria is met:

25 *Kamerstukken II*, 2001–2002, 26 991, No. 54–55.

26 Dutch Food and Consumer Product Safety Authority (VWA) *Vision for the Future 2004–2007*, 9 (<www.vwa.nl>): 'The Food and Consumer Product Safety Authority has formulated the following mission statement "To work towards visible risk reduction for food and consumer products with regard to public health, animal health and animal welfare".'

27 Ministerie van Binnenlandse Zaken en Koninkrijksaangelegenheden (2001) *De kaderstellende visie op toezicht*, The Hague, available at: <http://www.videnet.nl/download/?noGzip=1&id=3863625>. A new version has been published in 2005, available at: <http://www.minbzk.nl/63510/aanbiedingsbrief>.

a there are no discretionary powers. Decisions to be taken are determined by law;
b decisions taken by the body are determined by expertise not by a weighing up of interests and policy alternatives;
c the state is commercially involved in the social field under control of the body.

ZBOs are popular for not being political. At the same time they are suspect for not being democratic. In the Netherlands, independence is often established with reference to this form of body.

3.1.3 Constitutional position of the VWA

Despite the considerations in the policy paper the VWA is not a ZBO; therefore it is within the scope of parliamentary oversight. The legal position of VWA is rather more complicated. Its civil servants are subject to the management of the Minister of the LNV, but they may exercise duties under the authority of the Minister of the VWS as well, or – if they use investigative competences – under the authority of the Minister of Justice.

Within the bureaucratic hierarchy, the VWA is positioned directly under the LNV Minister. More precisely, the VWA is an entity within the LNV Ministry, but is not physically located within the department. As a law enforcement agency, VWA does not deal with policy issues, the issuing of legislation or relationships with other ministries. These remain the responsibility of the LNV Minister. Food safety policy and legislation, however, is mainly the domain of the VWS Minister.

The VWA's independence is qualified. The VWS Minister (not LNV) retains the legal power to take the most important enforcement decisions. In addition, both the LNV and the VWS Ministers have the power to issue instructions to the VWA to preserve their own responsibility and accountability to Parliament. In order to maintain some distance and encourage factual independence, the relationship between the Minister and the VWA must be transparent. Transparency may prove an effective check. At the least, it will expose ministerial intervention to political and public oversight. Briefly stated, the VWA cannot be classified as a general type of Food Safety Authority, with enforcement powers, like its counterparts abroad, but neither is it a ZBO. The VWA will have to find its own way without much of an example to adhere to.

3.1.4 Organisation of the VWA

The VWA now incorporates the former Inspectorate for Health Protection and Veterinary Public Health (*Keuringsdienst van Waren, KvW*) and the former National Inspection Service for Livestock and Meat (*Rijksdienst voor de keuring van Vee en Vlees, RVV*). The major justification for the merger of these two enforcement bodies is the better coordination of their activities. The VWA consists of a General Inspectorate in The Hague and Regional Inspectorates. The central unit consists of three directorates: 1) Directorate Implementation, Enforcement & Surveillance, 2) Directorate Inspection Strategy & Communication, and 3) Directorate of Operations. In addition, VWA maintains an Office for Risk Assessment (see below). VWS and LNV retain their responsibility for policy and legislation; but, the VWA may also advise the Ministries in these fields. Initially it was intended that the RIVM and RIKILT would be integrated into the VWA as well, but this plan was later abandoned. As a consequence, the VWA is more concerned with enforcement rather than risk assessment. In its annual reports, VWA presents risk assessment, supervision and risk communication as a 'strategic triangle', thus underscoring the interrelationship VWA perceives between these three responsibilities (VWA 2004).

In conclusion, the responsibilities of the Dutch VWA seem to differ from those of food safety authorities in other European countries. For instance, in the United Kingdom, the Food Standards Agency carries out research on food safety, but is not immediately responsible for undertaking practical food safety enforcement; this is generally undertaken by local authorities. In France, the *Agence Française de Sécurité Sanitaire des Aliments* focuses on risk assessment.

3.1.5 Competences

The major responsibilities of the VWA are:

a supervising and inspecting foodstuffs; these inspections encompass:
- basic supervision of compliance with all provisions which have been laid down in legislation;
- supervision of legally prescribed food safety systems (eg HACCP);
- additional supervision in areas where there is already another public or private enforcement body active;[28]

b setting up programmes for research on food safety and coordination of food safety research, which will be carried out by several public and/or private organisations; and

c communicating information about its activities.[29]

The VWA is the principal authority within the Netherlands with both *supervisory* and *investigative* powers, established in line with the Consumer Products Safety Act, the General Administrative Law Act[30] (*Algemene wet bestuursrecht, Awb or GALA*) and the Economic Offences Act (*Wet op de Economische Delicten*).[31] The fact that inspectors have both supervisory and investigative competences is referred to as a 'two hats issue'. When an inspector discovers an infringement of food law during a supervision visit that needs further action, s/he must put on her/his other hat, clearly indicating to the company that s/he is changing her/his role from supervisory to investigative officer. As soon as the company becomes subject to investigation, the inspector must respect all the rights of defence under criminal law and read the company its rights, especially the right to remain silent.

28 For instance, in the dairy sector, the Netherlands Controlling Authority for Milk and Milk Products (*COKZ, Centraal Orgaan voor Kwaliteitsaangelegenheden in de Zuivel*, <www.cokz.nl>) carries out controls that are supervised by this Inspectorate.

29 The Netherlands Nutrition Centre (*Voedingscentrum*) will remain responsible for general nutrition communication and information to consumers (<www.voedingscentrum.nl>).

30 Act of 4 June 1992, *Staatsblad* 315. English translation, available at: <http://www.justitie.nl/images/Engelse%20tekst%20Awb_tcm34-2020.pdf> or <http://www.justitie.nl/images/Wettekst%20Awb%20Engelse%20Versie_tcm34-2121.pdf>.

31 Act of 22 June 1950, *Staatsblad* 258.

An interesting example of this issue can be found in criminal case law.[32] Law establishes an obligation to cooperate with supervisory officers and to provide information they demand, and likewise criminalises non-compliance. By contrast, Article 6 of the European Convention on the Protection of Human Rights and Fundamental Freedoms and Dutch criminal law ensure rights of defence with regard to investigative officers, including a right not to assist in self-prosecution. The Court of Appeal in Leeuwarden was required to decide on this issue when a VWA supervisory officer was denied access he requested to documentation on the handling of high-risk materials during an inspection visit to a slaughterhouse. The refusal was subsequently reported and gave rise to a criminal prosecution, as well as the question of whether the officer concerned could use his powers as investigative officer to report on a crime committed against him in his role of supervisory officer. The relevance of the question probably lies in the weight the report carries as proof in criminal proceedings. In the case at issue a report by an investigative officer would be sufficient proof to condemn the accused while the report of a supervisory officer would probably require additional proof. The Court of Appeal ruled that, in this case, the officer was indeed entitled to apply investigative powers. As a result the accused was condemned for resisting a supervisory officer in the exercise of his duties.

Inspectors have several measures at their disposal to halt a violation of food law, such as a warning, a report as a first stage to imposition of an administrative fine, a police report, which can be sent to the Public Prosecutions Department, and seizure of foodstuffs. In case of an infringement that needs direct action, the Public Prosecutions Department can impose provisional measures on the accused, and a court can even temporarily close down the company in part or in whole.

3.2 Prosecution

Prosecution of food law infringements falls under the responsibility of the Public Prosecutions Department. The Public Prosecutions Department will only bring the most severe infringements to court. Most infringements are dealt with under administrative law.

3.3 Sanctions

Sanctions can be imposed either by criminal courts or by the Minister of Health. An administrative fine was added to the spectrum of sanctions that the Minister of Health can impose for breach of the Consumer Products Safety Act in 2000. This administrative law measure is now used for the majority of infringements of the Consumer Products Safety Act. The fines are rather modest for larger companies.[33] Generally speaking, the amounts range from €450 for infringements by smaller companies (fewer than 50 employees) to €900 for larger companies (more than 50 employees). Fines for more severe infringements range from €680 for smaller companies to €1,360 for larger companies.

32 Gerechtshof Leeuwarden, 24 February 2005, *LJN*: AU1224.

33 Continued infringements can be sanctioned repeatedly, which increases the amount of the penalty payment.

3.4 Supervision of controls

The Ministry of Agriculture has published a policy paper called Supervision of Controls (*Toezicht op controle*[34]) indicating that it intends to shift its own emphasis from the basic supervision of products to system supervision and additional supervision, which audits quality assurance systems within companies and which allows for third-party inspections on a private law basis. In particular, the new approach emphasises public-private cooperation, with business operators taking responsibility for compliance, and inspection agencies checking their control systems (Freriks 2005; Van der Meulen and Freriks 2006).

4 THE CONCEPT OF RISK ANALYSIS

4.1 The General Food Law

On 21 February 2002, (EC) Regulation 178/2002, generally known as the General Food Law (GFL), entered into force. This regulation provides the common principles and definitions for a safety-oriented redrafting of food law in the European Union, both at Community level and at national levels.

In Article 5, the GFL gives the general objectives to be served by food law:

1 Food law shall pursue one or more of the general objectives of a high level of protection of human life and health and the protection of consumers' interests, including fair practices in food trade, taking account of, where appropriate, the protection of animal health and welfare, plant health and the environment.
2 Food law shall aim to achieve the free movement in the Community of food and feed manufactured or marketed according to the general principles and requirements in this chapter.

In other words, food legislation should be about one of two things: protection of health or protection of (other) consumer interests. The principles set out in the following articles correspond with this distinction. Article 8 concerns the protection of consumer interests with regard to fraud, adulteration and other misleading practices. More importantly, for this chapter, Articles 6 and 7 deal with health protection.

Article 6(1) GFL provides:

> In order to achieve the general objective of a high level of protection of human health and life, food law shall be based on risk analysis except where this is not appropriate to the circumstances or the nature of the measure.

The determination of what degree of protection health requires is defined as a scientific question,[35] and Articles 6 and 7 provide principles for the procedural

34 See: <http://www.minlnv.nl/cdlpub/servlet/CDLServlet?p_file_id=13984>.

35 This conforms with the principles that apply to standard setting in the context of the Codex Alimentarius as well as with the EU's obligations under the SPS-Agreement.

framework for answering this question in any given case. Risk analysis is defined by the law as a three-step procedure of risk assessment, risk communication and risk management.[36] Article 6 only elaborates risk assessment and risk management:

> 2 Risk assessment shall be based on the available scientific evidence and undertaken in an independent, objective and transparent manner.
>
> 3 Risk management shall take into account the results of risk assessment, and in particular, the opinions of the Authority referred to in Article 22,[37] other factors legitimate to the matter under consideration and the precautionary principle where the conditions laid down in Article 7(1) are relevant, in order to achieve the general objectives of food law established in Article 5.

From this provision it is clear that risk assessment is seen to be a scientific matter. Generally, advice would be given on it by an independent entity, such as the European Food Safety Authority (EFSA). The concept is defined narrowly in Article 3(11) GFL in the sense that it focuses on hazards that are directly related to food.[38]

Risk management in turn is defined as a decision-making process: selecting prevention and control options. In practice the expression 'risk management' may also be applied to the options chosen – the actual action taken to deal with the risk – but the powers for these have to be found elsewhere. Article 6(1) GFL sees risk management as a major part of food law. 'Food law' in turn can be anything: 'laws, regulations and administrative provisions governing food in general, and food safety in particular'.[39] This definition, however broad it is, seems to cover mainly legal acts. It is less clear if and to what extent it covers factual enforcement acts. As we will see in the context of the precautionary principle, this lack of clarity may have significant consequences.

Article 6(3) GFL states that risk management shall take into account 'other factors legitimate to the matter under consideration'. These other factors may include knowledge about food safety that is distinct from scientific risk assessment, for example, 'experience'.[40] Article 6 GFL likewise places the burden to prove that a measure of food law is necessary from a scientific point of view upon the legislature. Article 7 nonetheless reduces this burden somewhat. On the basis of the precautionary principle, risk management measures may be taken in situations where risk assessment is as yet inconclusive:

36 GFL, above, note 15, Article 3(10).

37 Eg EFSA.

38 As defined in Article 3(14) GFL, above, note 15. We can think here of the regulatory texts on pre-market approval of food additives, genetically modified foods and (other) novel foods and the setting of maximum levels for pesticide and veterinary residues and (other) contaminants.

39 GFL, above, note 15, Article 3(1).

40 The Novel Foods Regulation (Regulation (EC) No. 258/97 of the European Parliament and of the Council of 27 January 1997, [1997] *OJ* L043), for example, accepts foods that have a history of safe use in the EU regardless of whether any specific scientific knowledge exists with regard to these foods.

1 In specific circumstances where, following an assessment of available information, the possibility of harmful effects on health is identified but scientific uncertainty persists, provisional risk management measures necessary to ensure the high level of health protection chosen in the Community may be adopted, pending further scientific information for a more comprehensive risk assessment.

2 Measures adopted on the basis of paragraph 1 shall be proportionate and no more restrictive of trade than is required to achieve the high level of health protection chosen in the Community, regard being had to technical and economic feasibility and other factors regarded as legitimate in the matter under consideration. The measures shall be reviewed within a reasonable period of time, depending on the nature of the risk to life or health identified and the type of scientific information needed to clarify the scientific uncertainty and to conduct a more comprehensive risk assessment.

4.2 Implementation of the General Food Law in the Netherlands

What, then, of the place of these principles within Dutch food law? Initially, the GFL was only partially implemented within Dutch law by means of an Act of Parliament and a piece of delegated legislation.[41] These two pieces of legislation do little more than turn breaches of Articles 12, 14, 18 and 19 GFL into offences. This approach to implementing the GFL is explained in the Explanatory Memorandum to the Order in Council (the delegated legislation), stating that the GFL, like all other regulations, is binding in its entirety and directly applicable in all Member States of the European Union. For this reason it is deemed not to be necessary to transpose the regulation into national legislation. Criminal sanctions, however, must be stipulated.

This interpretation seems to do little justice to the ambitions of the GFL. Its general concepts, principles and procedures are not only designed for Community level, but also for the Member States. As expressed in Recital 5, it aims: 'to approximate these concepts, principles and procedures so as to form a common basis for measures governing food and feed taken in the Member States and at Community level'. Approximation of concepts and principles in the food laws of Member States is an aim one would expect in a directive rather than in a regulation. In fact, the Action Plan on Food Safety – the Annex to the White Paper on Food Safety[42] – included a plan to create a General Food Law *Directive*. Though a regulation was ultimately adopted, the General Food Law retains much of the character of a directive in that it intends to harmonise both European and national food law.

41 *Wet van 13 april 2004, houdende wijziging van de Warenwet, de Bestrijdingsmiddelenwet 1962, de Diergeneesmiddelenwet en de Wet op de economische delicten, teneinde deze af te stemmen op verordening (EG) nr. 178/2002, Staatsblad 2004, 164; Besluit van 1 juli 2004, houdende wijziging van diverse Warenwetbesluiten in verband met verordening (EG)* No. 178/2002, Staatsblad 2004, 408: Act and Order respectively changing existing legislation to conform with the GFL, above, note 15.

42 European Commission, *White Paper on Food Safety*, COM(1999) 719 final, 12 January 2000, Brussels.

Article 4(3) sets a deadline for the implementation of this regulation/quasi-directive, and in particular Articles 5–10. In Germany the legislature completely reworked national food legislation in order to comply with this requirement.

In the Netherlands, by contrast, only a few minor adjustments have been made. The definition of 'food' was adopted[43] and various measures taken in order to ensure independent risk assessment (see below). Beyond that, however, the risk analysis principle applies in the Netherlands simply as part of directly applicable EU law.

5 DUTCH ADMINISTRATIVE LAW

5.1 Decision making

Because the principles set out in the GFL have been implemented in the Netherlands only to a limited extent, it is all the more important to apply existing Dutch law in conformity with EU law. Happily, the interpretation of the risk-analysis principle as a decision-making principle that requires both risk assessment and a weighing of alternatives to take place prior to implementation of sanitary measures fits seamlessly with the requirements that Dutch administrative law generally places on public decision making. These requirements, known as the general principles of proper administration, were developed within the case law of the Dutch administrative courts and were codified in 1992 in the General Administrative Law Act (GALA).

5.1.1 Establishment of the facts

Before an administrative body can take a decision, it must establish the relevant facts of the case:

> When preparing an order[44] an administrative authority shall gather the necessary information concerning the relevant facts and the interests to be weighed (Article 3:2 GALA).

5.1.2 Weighing of interests

Before taking its decision the administrative body must weigh up the interests of all parties concerned:

> 1 When making an order the administrative authority shall weigh the interests directly involved in so far as no limitation on this duty derives from a statutory regulation or the nature of the power being exercised.
> 2 The adverse consequences of an order for one or more interested parties may not be disproportionate to the purposes to be served by the order (Article 3:4 GALA).

43 *Staatsblad* 2005, 623.

44 According to Article 3:1 (1) GALA, 'Order' means a written decision of an administrative authority constituting a public law act.

Risk assessment, as prescribed in the GFL, can be seen as an important part of the process of the establishment of the facts. Usually the administrative body will need the help of experts. If this is demanded by law,[45] further GALA provisions apply. Thus, for example, the decision must detail expert advice[46] and, where it departs from that advice, must give its reasons for doing so.[47]

5.2 Judicial review

5.2.1 Procedures

Interested parties can challenge all administrative decisions (orders) on the basis of the GALA. Such decisions can be contested first by lodging an objection with the body that took the decision and thereafter by lodging an appeal with the competent administrative court. The competent administrative court with regard to the VWA or the Minister of Health is the District Court in Rotterdam. In economic cases, such decisions are subject to appeal before the Industrial Appeals Board (*College van Beroep voor het bedrijfsleven*).

5.2.2 Weighing of interests

Under Dutch administrative law, the weighing of alternatives is the prerogative of administrative bodies, which usually enjoy a wide margin of discretion. Within the limits of this discretion, the courts only check whether a decision is arbitrary in nature. A decision is considered arbitrary if the administrative body could not, in all reasonableness, arrive at it. This is the case if the decision taken does not reflect a process of the weighing of interests. The courts then assume that such a weighing has not taken place.

5.2.3 Establishment of facts

In theory, administrative bodies do not enjoy discretion in the establishment of facts, meaning that Administrative courts theoretically have wide powers of review over the process. Experience nonetheless demonstrates that courts limit themselves to ascertaining whether the administrative body concerned has acquired sound scientific advice. Van den Berg (1999) has shown that, although the courts can themselves refer to independent experts, plaintiffs generally only have a chance of successfully contesting an administrative decision based on scientific advice where they can produce countervailing scientific opinions.

As noted, the District Court in Rotterdam is competent in economic matters, including food law. In its case law, the Court has taken the stance that the degree of restraint in judicial review must increase in line with the complexity of the

45 At present it remains somewhat unclear if an expert opinion given in the context of risk assessment is to be considered as prescribed by law in the sense of the GALA.

46 Article 3:8, GALA.

47 Article 3:50, GALA.

economic assessment.[48] This might mean that the establishment of scientific facts is also becoming a matter for administrative discretion, sheltered from judicial review.

6 CASE LAW

So far no case law has appeared on risk analysis in administrative law. There are a few interesting cases, however, in civil and criminal law.

6.1 Civil law

In civil law two cases involving the VWA are worth mentioning. Both cases are preliminary proceedings. The first was heard by the District Court of The Hague in 2005:[49] *Sara Lee Household and Bodycare International BV v Consumentenbond and Bureau Européen des Unions des Consommateurs* (BEUC) (Dutch and European Consumers' organisations). The second was heard by the District Court in Amsterdam in 2005:[50] *Laurus BV/Super De Boer* (a chain of supermarkets) *v Vereniging Milieudefensie* (Friends of the Earth Netherlands). In both cases companies took action against public warnings about their products issued by private organisations. The question at issue was one of whether these public warnings constituted a tort.

The first case concerned air fresheners. The reasoning, however, is also relevant for food safety matters. The consumers' organisations had issued press releases titled: 'Foul-smelling whiff from air fresheners!' and 'Indoor air pollution and air fresheners, a smoke screen'. They warned that several air fresheners spread irritating, allergenic and carcinogenic substances, such as benzene and formaldehyde. Vulnerable people – pregnant women, children, people prone to allergies – were told to avoid them. In January 2005 BEUC published a report: 'Emission of chemicals by air fresheners, Tests on 74 consumer products sold in Europe', stating:

> This test conducted on 74 air fresheners, incense types, natural products, scented candles, electric diffusers, liquids, gels and aerosols and the associated bibliographical research have allowed us to reach the following important conclusions:
>
> - Total VOC emissions from virtually all the products tested occur at a concentration higher than 200 (g/m^3) after 2 hours of use. This represents a substantial increase in indoor air pollution.
> - Among the substances emitted, the presence of several carcinogens, benzene and formaldehyde, is a matter of concern. Benzene is emitted, after 1 hour 30 minutes' burning, at a concentration of over 220 (g/m^3) by the Ushuaia fleur de Vanille stick. It is also emitted by scented candles and liquid air fresheners in a high concentration. Given the particularly high levels, it seems necessary to conduct further research on a wider number

48 Rb. Rotterdam 21 June 2001, *AB* 2001, 331, m.nt. Boogers.
49 *LJN*: AS8908.
50 *LJN*: AR8854.

> of incense products. Formaldehyde poses the same problem as benzene. High concentrations are emitted by incense (> 65 (g/m^3)), while the toxicological reference value for chronic exposure by inhalation is set at 10 (g/m^3) by the ATSDR. Three candles and one electric diffuser registered a high concentration of formaldehyde.

This report was supplemented by a report from the University in Leuven (Belgium) stating:

> In most situations, sporadic or occasional use of these chemicals is unlikely to cause adverse health effects. However, given the detailed uncertainties, it is advisable to refrain from regularly using several of these products, especially when there is a risk of exposure to the following groups:
>
> - Subjects with asthma and other allergic diseases (. . .).
> - Children (. . .).
> - Pregnant women and women who are breast feeding (. . .).

On 3 February 2005 TNO tried to duplicate the BEUC study:

> The present study was undertaken to reproduce, as far as is possible, the emission of selected volatile compounds as a consequence of the operation of air fresheners under conditions that seemed to have been applied in the earlier BEUC study. (. . .) The concentrations measured after operation of the air fresheners are, in general, of the same order of magnitude as the background concentrations.
>
> As a consequence, where individual deviations were established, it was impossible to judge whether and to what extent release from the air fresheners may have contributed to these deviations as a fluctuation in background release may also have been involved. Repetitive measurements on the same types of air fresheners would be required in order to assess the contribution of releases from air fresheners in detail and to allow for reliable statistical evaluation.
>
> Comparison of the results of the present study with the BEUC study is difficult on the basis of the limited information given within the BEUC study at the date of issue of this report. (. . .) For benzene, levels exceeding 5 (g per m^3) were reported for several products tested in the BEUC study, while in the present study all levels remained below 5 (g per m^3).

RIVM and VWA also took the position that no risk to public health existed.

The court argued that the public reputation of the consumer organisations was such that their opinions would have a considerable degree of influence. As a consequence, they would be required always to exercise great caution. The court based its judgment on the limits set by WHO: 8 (g/m^3) for benzene and 13 (g/m^3) for formaldehyde. According to TNO, RIVM and VWA these levels were not surpassed. As BUEC did not want to disclose the identity of the laboratory that had undertaken their research, the Court ruled that these findings (established by independent authorities) had not been refuted. An injunction was issued since the consumers organisations had not sufficiently substantiated their allegations.

In the second case, Laurus BV/Super De Boer acted against allegations about pesticide residues on their grapes made by Milieudefensie. The residue levels were found to be higher than those registered in other supermarkets and surpassed statutory limits. Laurus BV/Super De Boer nonetheless argued that it was misleading to label the residues as 'poison'. The authority responsible for setting the maximum level of permitted residue limits (MRLs) had recently issued 'import tolerances' in preparation for the introduction of more lenient MRLs. Likewise, the Netherlands Nutrition Centre and the Minister of Public Health had expressed the opinion that excess residues did not pose a health risk and that new MRLs should be introduced.

The Court reasoned that Milieudefensie freedom of speech could only be curbed if this was provided for by law and necessary within a democratic society. This might be the case if information provided were false or misleading. The levels were established by TNO. This in itself was reason enough for the court to accept them as correct since Laurus BV/Super De Boer had not contested them. The fact that statutory MRLs were exceeded was sufficient to justify Milieudefensie's actions. They did not need to take into consideration the changing views of VWA and other authorities.

6.2 Criminal law

A criminal case heard by the District Court of Leeuwarden[51] and the Court of Appeal of Leeuwarden[52] concerned the Dutch equivalent to Article 14 GFL: a ban on unsafe food. The provision concerned Article 18 of the Consumer Products Safety Act. The defendant was accused of selling food supplements in 2002, registering levels of benz(a)pyrene of about 7.5, 9.5, 11.7, 22.5 and 28.4 micrograms per kilogram product. The defendant argued that he should not be held accountable because the producer had certified the reliability of the product. Further the legal norm 'unsafe food' was too vague a basis for a criminal conviction.

The courts ruled that a trader in food should keep himself informed about developments concerning safety and health with regard to products in his line of business. Certification by the producer does not free the trader from the obligation to form his own opinion on the safety of the products he is selling. With regard to benzo(a)pyrene the evidence was as follows:

- a in 1987 the International Agency for Research on Cancer had categorised it as 'probably carcinogenic';
- b on 15 December 1999 the Minister of VWS stated in a letter to Parliament that the safety level is between 20 and 40 nanograms per kilogram bodyweight;
- c by letter of 8 May 2000, this level was adjusted to 5 nanograms;
- d in November 2001 RIVM issued a report giving a Virtually Safe Dose of 5 nanograms, or 0.5 nanogram in combination with other polycyclic aromatic hydrocarbons (PAHs).

An expert testified that it had to be assumed that in the food supplements concerned, benzo(a)pyrene appeared in combination with other PAHs, and that

51 Rechtbank Leeuwarden 28 May 2004, *LJN*: AP1271.

52 Gerechtshof Leeuwarden 30 November 2006, *LJN*: AZ3591.

therefore the level of 0.5 nanogram per kilogram bodyweight should be taken as standard. If the supplements were used according to the instructions of use, this level would be surpassed by a considerable degree. VWA had measured the levels present within the product. The Court of Appeal subsequently rejected the argument that the defendant was familiar with the Minister's 1999 letter, but not that of May 2000. A trader must heed the warnings issued by the competent authorities. It also rejected the defendant's arguments against the validity of the methods applied by VWA, adopting the observation given by the expert that VWA knows how to generate reliable results. At first instance the Court had ruled on this point, stating that on the basis of experience it accepts the validity of VWA measurements. The defendant had not produced any counter evidence from TNO. A report from an Italian laboratory that the defendant did bring forward did not convince the Court.

6.3 Risk assessment in case law

The cases discussed in this section are too few for solid conclusions, but they indicate that, within Dutch case law, risk assessment is not only a basis for public standard setting. The results also apply immediately to food business operators – even in criminal law – through the general ban on unsafe food that is now laid down in Article 14 GFL.

Although, in theory, the results of risk assessment may be judicially scrutinised, the courts appear to be willing simply to accept the verdicts of VWA, RIVM and TNO on the basis of their reputation. Food business operators who want to defend themselves from such risk assessment must make recourse to scientific advice, which has at least the same stature.

7 RISK ANALYSIS IN VWA PRACTICE

7.1 Independent risk assessment by VWA?

Article 6(2) GFL requires risk assessment to be undertaken in an independent, objective and transparent manner. Against this background the EFSA has been given a degree of independence from the European Commission, much like a ZBO in the Netherlands. EFSA's independence is intended to ensure a functional separation of the scientific assessment of risk from risk management decisions, because scientific risk assessment should not be swayed by policy or other external considerations. This is designed to guarantee impartiality and objectivity.

Recently a bill has been enacted aiming to guarantee VWA's independence in matters of science-based risk assessment and the issuing of advice.[53] On the one hand, 'Chinese walls' have been erected within the VWA. Civil servants engaged in risk assessment may not exercise duties relating to supervision, investigation and sanctioning. The director of the Office of Risk Assessment decides on the content of these assessments and of the advice based thereon. The VWA's Inspector-General

53 *Wet van 26 april 2006 tot regeling van een onafhankelijke uitoefening van risicobeoordeling door de Voedsel en Waren Autoriteit (Wet onafhankelijke risicobeoordeling Voedsel en Waren Autoriteit), Staatsblad* 2006, 247.

must forward these documents to the Minister and make them known to the general public. On the other hand, the power of the Minister of Agriculture to issue orders to VWA is limited. In matters of risk assessment, orders may be given only in writing. Any order given will be mentioned in the official gazette. This approach upholds the Minister's political responsibility and protects scientific risk assessment from undue interference. Nevertheless, this structure looks rather fragile, providing only for a minimum degree of independence.

7.2 Risk assessment by VWA

In its Annual Reports, the VWA describes its risk assessment activities as follows (VWA 2004):

> The VWA's Department of Research and Risk Assessment bases its work on scientific knowledge and insight. It plays an important role in detecting potential problems. The aim is to detect potential risks at the earliest possible stage, take appropriate supervisory measures, propose standards and initiate an information programme. For this purpose there are regular consultations with international colleagues. After all, events can sometimes take place abroad, which may pose a potential future risk to the Netherlands, and vice versa.

The examples elaborated show a certain tendency to take shortcuts from risk assessment to enforcement. Apparently VWA's different activities mutually affect each other:

> In the recent past there were various problems in the animal feed sector, such as animal feed chains contaminated with MPA and the dioxin affair. The Minister of LNV asked the VWA to conduct an analysis of the animal feed chain to elucidate the flows of raw materials. For this reason, in 2003 particular efforts were made to analyse the flow of raw materials and to chart the activities of the various parties involved. In this way the VWA managed to locate sections of the animal feed chain which had previously slipped through the net of inspection and still posed safety concerns or about which not enough was known. This enables the VWA to exercise additional control measures where they are needed most.

This example shows that establishment of the existence of risk may well go beyond the definition of risk assessment in the GFL because it does not limit itself to dealing with exposure to hazards (as defined), but takes management structures in the food chain into consideration as well.

7.3 Risk management by VWA

What is risk management? More precisely, which measures can be taken on the basis of the decision procedure described above? Elsewhere I have written that risk management encompasses 'legislation, enforcement and everything in between' (Van der Meulen and Van der Velde 2008: 268). As far as the VWA is concerned, risk management measures are limited to enforcement as VWA hardly has any other powers.

In its Annual Reports, VWA draws attention to various enforcement activities, like the enforcement of the prohibition on selling alcohol to minors under 16 and its role in fighting avian influenza. Priorities are set on the basis of risk assessment (VWA 2004):

> Many consumers take food supplements for their health, although the ingredients of these products sometimes give cause for concern. In 2002 the VWA detected PACs (polycyclic aromatic carbonates) in some of these products. It is possible that these substances are carcinogenic. After consultations with the National Institute for Public Health and the Environment (RIVM), the VWA laid down enforcement standards on the basis of the available data and began a system of prioritised enforcement in 2003.

7.3.1 Precaution

Decisions dealing with food safety risks will not always be triggered by infringements by food business operators of food (safety) law. They may also arise due to new scientific insights and even scientific uncertainty. Article 7 GFL allows for provisional measures in cases where the possibility of harmful effects is identified, but scientific uncertainty persists.

However, where no individual food business operator can be accused of infringing of food (safety) law, questions arise about the ability of public authorities to tackle the specific problem and properly to balance conflicting interests. As a rule, enforcement powers are based on the existence of an (at least potential) infringement of a legal prescription. The GFL includes a general ban on unsafe food (Article 14(1) GFL). However, in the cases of scientific uncertainty to which the precautionary principle applies, per definition, no proof of infringement exists. This makes it tricky to apply enforcement measures. An applicable norm should be formulated first by an administrative body with the power to set such a norm. No such power has been granted the VWA.

The VWA seems unperturbed by this lack of appropriate legal powers to apply the precautionary principle. In 2005 it published a policy paper on its role as an inspection and enforcement agency (VWA 2005a). In this paper it advocates a 'problem oriented approach'. This is explained as meaning that if a problem presents itself, this problem must be taken care of regardless of whether any legislation applies. If no legislation applies to the problem at hand, according to the VWA, one has to look beyond the legal framework.[54] Although this position is indefensible, from a rule of law point of view, it has not yet been challenged.

What would be needed to ensure effective risk management in all situations is the introduction of instruments that do not depend on the existence of infringements, but are based instead on the existence of probable food safety risks. As a rule, such risk management measures will affect the economic position of food business operators. In Dutch case law, a principle of French origin, called the principle of '*égalité*

54 On this basis, for example, the use of carcinogenic colourings for tattooing has been taken on by VWA. Legislation taking care of this issue appeared only on 20 November 2006 (*Staatsblad* 2006, 627).

devant les charges publiques' (equality in the face of public burdens) has been adopted. This principle says that individuals (natural or legal persons) should not be made to suffer unduly for measures taken for the common good. If it is necessary to sacrifice the interests of the individual for the common good, the individual concerned should be financially compensated. I am not aware of any precedents, but it seems likely that, under Dutch administrative law, the financial losses of food business operators caused by precautionary measures will have to be carried by the public authorities.

7.3.2 Risk communication by VWA

Both the Codex Alimentarius and General Food Law regard risk communication as an integral part of risk analysis. Furthermore, the GFL identifies transparency as a principle of food law (Articles 9 and 10). The 2003 VWA Annual Report accordingly formulated a general vision for risk communication:

> The VWA uses risk communication to provide clear information about which risks certain products pose. In some cases this means above all placing risks in their context, thereby making it clear that the risks involved are not insurmountable for the consumer. The consumer can use the information to adapt his or her behaviour accordingly. The VWA bases its messages on scientifically underpinned risk assessment. In practice, the website is the most important means of communication. On the site, the consumer can find information about risks which the VWA has investigated, featuring practical examples written in a clearly accessible style (VWA 2004).

Dutch legislation does not grant any specific powers in this respect; therefore the general legal framework applies. In the Netherlands, the 1980 Freedom of Information Act[55] (*Wet openbaarheid van bestuur: Wob*) empowers all citizens to ask public authorities for information on all their activities and provides the authorities with a legal basis for informing the public. These authorities must decide whether to supply information by weighing issues of transparency against specific interests, such as privacy and trade/commercial secrets. As a result, documents are usually released in whole or in part and questions are answered.

This framework does not seem to be entirely satisfactory for the VWA. The 2004 Annual Report mentions some complications:

> In May 2004 VWA found 125 kilos of rotten meat at a meat products manufacturer in Coevorden. As the company's hygiene also left a lot to be desired, VWA started the procedure for withdrawing the company's recognized status. As a result, the company was no longer permitted to manufacture meat products. In accordance with the rules, VWA did not disclose the name of the business involved. However, another meat-processing company based in Coevorden requested disclosure of the name on the grounds that the negative

55 For an English translation (labelled Government Information (Public Access) Act) see: <www.minbzk.nl/actueel/publicaties/9070/act-on-public-access>.

publicity was affecting its reputation and turnover, even though it was entirely blameless. VWA was not able to comply with this request on account of legal objections (VWA 2005).

In a policy document, VWA considers going beyond the current legal limits by using publicity as an enforcement tool: naming and shaming perpetrators by disclosing their names through black lists (VWA 2005a), probably on the internet. The LNV and VWS Ministers have elaborated upon this line of thought.[56]

Both at the national level and with colleague authorities in the Forum of European Food Law Enforcement Practitioners,[57] VWA discusses the possibility of disclosing inspection results. On the one hand this is seen as a method to empower consumers to make informed choices, on the other hand it is expected that it will stimulate compliance. This way of thinking is new in the Netherlands. As far as disclosure is used to coerce businesses to compliance, it must be seen as a sanction. The legislature will have to decide whether or not to condone it in law.

8 CONCLUSIONS

The principle that food law is based on risk analysis was introduced into Dutch food law by the GFL. Risk analysis is a decision-making method consisting of science-based risk assessment and a weighing of alternative regulatory solutions. This method seems to fit well within the general requirements on decision making under Dutch administrative law. The application of the principle in practice is more colourful than was envisaged by the General Food Law.

At present the Ministry of Public Health is responsible for food safety policy and legislation, but the Ministry of Agriculture manages the Dutch Food and Consumer Product Safety Authority (VWA). The VWA is first and foremost an enforcement agency, but it is also responsible for coordinating risk assessment. As far as this responsibility is concerned, the powers of the Minister over the VWA have been restrained by law in order to ensure that risk assessment is undertaken in an independent manner. Nevertheless the VWA itself combines responsibilities in risk assessment with risk management responsibilities (eg enforcement).

In practice, risk assessment looks beyond exposure to food-borne hazards and includes HACCP-type analyses of the food chain. Equally, other legitimate 'factors' contributing to risk management may also rely heavily on science, in particular, economic science.

Risk management takes the form of legislation, industry self-regulation, and also case law, in particular, where vague requirements in food law are fleshed out by scientific insights. Criminal sanctions may be applied to food businesses that do not comply with the most recent scientific findings.

Traditionally administrative bodies enjoy a large margin of discretion in the weighing of interests, but not in the establishment of the facts. The trend seems now

56 In a letter to the Chairman of the second Chamber of Parliament, dated 30 August 2006, *Kamerstukken II*, 2006–2007 26 991, nr. 143.

57 See <www.FLEP.org> and in particular on transparency <http://www.flep.org/workshops.html>.

to be one of also giving administrative bodies a broad margin of discretion in relation to scientific assessment. In particular the VWA opinions and those of the established research centres RIVM and TNO carry particular weight before the courts.

Risk assessment is used as a basis for setting priorities in enforcement and even for applying enforcement powers to situations that are not as such illegal, but are undesirable from a scientific point of view.

Communication on risk seems to be developing into an independent instrument to empower consumers to make informed choices and to coerce compliance with food safety requirements.

BIBLIOGRAPHY

Van den Berg, B. (1999) *Deskundigheid in het geding: een vergelijkend onderzoek naar de inbreng van deskundigheid bij de administratieve en civiele rechter*, The Hague: BJu.

Freriks, A.A. (2005) 'Toezicht op toezicht', in Ch.W. Backes, P.J.J. van Buuren, G.T.J.M. Jurgens and R.J.G.M. Widdershoven (eds), *Lex Dura, Sed Lex, Opstellen over de handhaving van het omgevingsrecht*, Deventer: Kluwer, 57–71.

Gorny, D. (2003) *Grundlagen des europäischen Lebensmittelrecht. Kommentar zur Verordnung (EG) Nr. 178/2002*, Hamburg: Behr's Verlag.

Van Hoogstraten, St. and Folkerts, H. (2005) *Wie houdt ons voedsel gezond? Een advies over De taakverdeling tussen de departementen van LNV en VWS op het vlak van voedselveiligheid*, PLW 05–188a NL/vv.

Lugt, M.J. and Van der Meulen, B.M.J. (2002) *Policing Food Safety. Regulatory reform in the Netherlands*, paper presented at the 2002 UMAU (Union Mondiale des Agraristes Universitaires) conference in Sienna, Italy. Published in A. Massart *et al.* (eds) *Prodotti Agricoli e Sicurezza Alimentare. In memoria del Prof. Louis Lorvellec*, Milano: Giuffrè editore, 369–83.

Van der Meulen, B.M.J. (2006) 'Haalt de Warenwet 2007? Deel I Implementatie van EG-Verordeningen; Deel II Implementatie van Verordening 178/2002', *Journaal Warenwet* 7(3), 6–14 and 7(4), 6–15.

Van der Meulen, B.M.J. and Freriks, A.A. (2006) 'Millefeuille. The emergence of a multi-layered controls system in the European food sector', *Utrecht Law Review* 2(1), 156–76, available at: <http://www.utrechtlawreview.org/publish/articles/000022/article.pdf>.

Van der Meulen, B.M.J. and Van der Velde, M. (2008) *European Food Law Handbook*, Wageningen: Wageningen Academic Publishers. <http://www.wageningenacademic.com/foodlaw>.

Scheltema, M. (1997) *Naar één levensmiddelenwet*, 28 November 1997, available at: <http://ikregeer.nl/zoek/dossier/24036::40>.

VWA (2005a) *Zicht op toezicht. Effectief toezicht houden, hoe doe je dat?*, available at: <http://www.vwa.nl/portal/page?_pageid=119,1639827&_dad=portal&_schema=PORTAL&p_file_id=10725>.

VWA (2005b) *Annual Report 2004*, VWA: The Hague.

VWA (2004) *Annual Report 2003*, VWA: The Hague.

Chapter 6

Food safety in Poland: standards, procedures and institutions

Aleksander Surdej and Karolina Żurek

1 INTRODUCTION

The perspective of accession to the EU has been the most important factor influencing transformation within the Polish food safety regime since the mid-1990s. The core of transformation has been the adjustment of the Polish food safety regime to satisfy the criteria found within EU food safety regulations. The EU negotiation position was clear: *the full adoption of the acquis communautaire is the precondition for Poland's accession to the EU.* This demand was accepted by Poland, which likewise did not request a transition period for the transposition of EU food safety law.[1] Nonetheless, the greatest accession challenge has not proven to be legal harmonisation, but rather practical implementation and adjustment of practices. The principal transition challenge has been posed by the shift from a system of administrative regulation and control to a regulatory system where responsibility for food safety is primarily placed upon producers.

In this chapter, we will describe the current state of the development of the food safety system in Poland by looking at the institutions which it comprises, and by analysing the reform of food safety legislation, as well as changes made with regard to inspection procedures. We will, however, begin with a brief look at the socio-economic context that frames the Polish agro-alimentary industry, which has, to a large extent, been determinative for the efficacy of the food safety system in Poland.

2 PREPARATION FOR EU ACCESSION

2.1 Historical background and socio-economic determinants of the agro-alimentary sector in Poland

Within the period of the Polish communist regime, agriculture was the most important economic sector, which still exhibited and was dominated by private ownership. Forced collectivisation attempts in the 1950s were not successful, which considerably reduced the scale of privatisation problems that had to be dealt with

1 Experts consider that Poland and other post-communist countries must engage in large-scale adjustments (Banati 2003: 89–93).

post-1989. Social problems flowing from the bankruptcy of state-owned farms in the 1990s hints at the difficulties that might have had to be faced had the whole of agricultural production been collectivised.

The common notion of Polish agriculture that stresses small-scale, traditional farms with low productivity and low income is largely a simplifying stereotype. Certainly, such farms do exist; however, Polish agriculture was, at the time of the EU accession, disadvantaged in relation to its counterparts in the old EU Member States, not only due to the size of farms and the legacy of the previous economic system, but also because of the lack of a comprehensive agriculture policy, modest subsidy support and limited exposure to competitiveness and quality-enhancing international trade.

In contrast to predominantly private farming, up until transition, the food industry was 80 per cent state-owned. Only at the beginning of the 1990s, thanks to privatisation and a rapid increase in private investment (also foreign), did the structure of ownership begin to change, and towards the end of that decade the share of state ownership in the sector dropped to 15 per cent.[2]

Analysis of compatibility between Polish and EU agriculture policies caused discomfort during accession negotiations. In addition to large-scale structural agriculture discrepancies, the major differences between Polish agricultural policy and the EU's common agricultural policy (CAP) appeared at the beginning of the accession process to be beyond any mode of reconciliation. Four major differences should be emphasised. First, the level of economic development, measured as domestic income *per capita*, was much lower in Poland than in any other existing Member State. Second, the percentage of the population employed in agriculture was much higher. Third, the agriculture and food production sector had far greater economic importance within Poland than in existing Member States; an importance which did not, however, derive from its higher level of development and efficiency, but rather by virtue of a comparatively lower level of development in other economic sectors. Fourth, the Polish economy was considered, from an institutional point of view, to be 'an economy in transition', while the economies of the European Union Member States could be called mature market economies. These differences impact in numerous ways. The lower level of economic development limits the economic surplus that can be transferred to agriculture via budgetary support in the form of agricultural subsidies or regulated (higher) prices. In addition, the high percentage of workers employed in the agricultural sector, together with the large number of producers, determines that a small measure of public support must be distributed among a large number of recipients, leading in effect to below-average support for investment and modernisation. Additionally, general low income levels outside the agri-food sector limits the development of income redistribution policies via the control of market prices, as all such interventionist activities are constrained by lower net purchasing power. This particular problem was the cause of great fears during the pre-accession period: concerns were raised that an increase in food prices under the influence of CAP would lead to significant wealth shifts from the general population to the agricultural sector;

2 See, for a detailed description of the structure, production patterns and development of Polish agriculture, Mertens 2001: 223–68.

furthermore, higher costs of food would generate general pressure to increase wages, which might also lead to a drop in overall economic competitiveness (Rowinski 1992).

As a result pre-accession Poland was not in a position to create a comprehensive public support system for agriculture mirroring that of the EU. By the same token, the transition from a centrally planned economy determined that Polish agricultural and food processing policy would also be called upon to tackle issues unknown to its EU counterparts (eg the privatisation of state farms and firms, as well as the creation of food wholesale and retail trade markets); a policy which was often accompanied by serious social tensions due to rapid growth of unemployment in rural areas and the relative impoverishment of farmers. All in all, these factors contributed to making it hard to develop a comprehensive domestic agricultural policy. During the 1990s, when under the pressure of the GATT, the EU was stabilising production of all major agricultural products, Poland was only beginning to build a system for the oversight of its agricultural production (Rowiński 1992: 40; Jurcewicz 1997: 31–5; Czyżewski 1997: 265–74).

In addition to the necessary structural changes undertaken in the early 1990s, Poland also initiated transformation and approximation processes within the institutional realm of the market economy. With a particular eye to EU accession, but also with the aim of supporting the creation and functioning of the market for agricultural products, two governmental agencies were established: the Agricultural Market Agency (*Agencja Rynku Rolnego – ARR*) and the Agency for the Restructuring and Modernisation of Agriculture (*Agencja Restrukuryzacji i Modernizacji Rolnictwa – ARiMR*). Even though their initial aims and scopes of activities – which suited the then prevailing domestic needs – differed significantly from their respective European counterparts, they were also established with an eye to their easy later transformation in order to perform the functions required by the CAP. The ARR was expected to take over interventionist agricultural functions; meanwhile, it was projected that the ARiMR would coordinate the EU structural policy at national level and administer EU funds and direct payments (Rowinski 1992: 42–3).

2.2 Polish food safety policy and preparation for the EU accession

Polish food safety legislation dates back to the interwar period (the first comprehensive food safety law was passed in 1929). The next major revision of legislation on food safety, health and nutrition was passed in Poland in November 1970. Poland has been a member of the Codex Alimentarius Commission since its inception, and the Polish Agricultural and Food Quality Inspectorate (once the Central Inspectorate for Standardisation) has long participated in the work of other international safety standard setting bodies. Basic food regulation passed during the communist period did not deviate from international standards. What was different, however, was the mode in which food safety law was implemented and, in particular, the communist state's overwhelming reliance on administrative and penal sanctions.

The economic transformation underway since the late 1980s has necessitated wide-ranging reform to foodstuffs regulations, largely as a result of the very different socio-economic context to which they originally applied. Nevertheless, it was not until the late 1990s and commencement of accession negotiations that reform was begun. Under pressure from the European Commission and the threat of the closure of a significant portion of Polish milk and meat production facilities, the question of food safety began to be viewed as a high priority issue by the Polish Government.[3]

Particular problems with the adoption and implementation of European food safety law before accession were to a large extent shaped by the previous mode of regulation and the institutional division of powers in this policy area. In pre-accession Poland, food safety was not subordinated to any one ministry, but two had a particular interest: the Ministry of Agriculture and Rural Development was responsible for food products of animal origin and the Ministry of Health for other types of foodstuffs. Both wished to maintain their dominance in their own fields. Thus, the first task was one of establishing smooth and effective cooperation between them and their respective subordinate bodies, control offices and laboratories.

The first general policy initiative taken by the Polish Government in cooperation with various interested parties was the formulation of the Polish Food Safety Strategy. In order to prepare a coherent strategy which would be acceptable to all partners and efficiently enforced, the Government sought participation of and consensus among all relevant actors. A special working group was accordingly established, composed of representatives of the Ministries involved, the Office of the Committee for European Integration (*Urząd Komitetu Integracji Europejskiej – UKIE*), the scientific institutes, the sanitary and veterinary inspectorates, as well as representatives from the food and feed sector and consumers' organisations. The task of the group was to prepare a document identifying the necessary improvements to be made, to plan the division of powers and responsibilities at all levels of the food safety system, and to lay down a timetable for the adoption of necessary legal and administrative adjustments. The Polish Food Safety Strategy, defining priorities with regard to the creation and maintenance of a food safety system which would ensure the minimum level of risk to health, was meant to serve as a solid basis for the implementation of a comprehensive, multi-sectoral system of public health in the area of foodstuffs, and its development constituted one of the conditions for successful preparation for EU membership.

The Polish Food Safety Strategy[4] was meant to incorporate all guidelines and policy recommendations laid down by the European Commission in its recommendation of 16 February 2001, 'Guidelines to prepare the Food Safety Strategy', which set out the main elements to be included in national programmes.[5] The Strategy was adopted by the Polish Government in February 2002 and submitted to the European Commission for approval. It consists of two sections. The first concerns the legal and organisational structure of the official food control system; the second lays down criteria for the evaluation of progress in the EU accession preparations. In substance, the Polish Food Safety Strategy follows the recommendations

3 *Oszczędźcie te rzeźnie*, in *Gazeta Wyborcza*, 4 March 2004.

4 Food Safety Strategy in Poland, Warsaw, 11 February 2002.

5 European Commission, *Guidelines to prepare the Food Safety Strategy*, 16 February 2001.

of the Commission White Paper on Food Safety,[6] the OECD's 'Compendium of National Food Safety Systems and Activities',[7] as well as the guidelines of the Codex Alimentarius Commission and the WHO. Among the main objectives of the Strategy, the document lists: (1) ensuring food safety throughout the food chain, starting with primary production and ending with food distribution and private consumption; (2) ensuring, *inter alia* through border control, that imported food meets the same or equivalent health quality norms and requirements as those applicable to domestically produced food; (3) ensuring harmonisation of Polish food law with European Union law, as well as its effective implementation; (4) ensuring effective and efficient control of the food chain; (5) ensuring continuous provision of reliable food safety information to the Government and the general public; and (6) building and strengthening the trust of domestic and foreign consumers in food safety and thereby establishing favourable economic conditions for Polish business.[8] The last objective clearly illustrates the awareness of the Polish Government that food safety would need to be ensured in order to enhance the competitiveness of Polish food products within the European market.

The Strategy begins with a description of the then existing national regulatory and institutional framework. It contains: (1) an overview of applicable Polish foodstuffs legislation; (2) a description of competent national authorities and the most significant supervision procedures; (3) a brief presentation of the national advisory bodies and entities providing scientific expertise in the field of food; (4) a description of the national system of hazardous products information.[9] Thereafter, the Strategy is devoted to the activities planned in preparation for the EU accession.

The point of departure for institutional reform was a desire that heightened effectiveness and efficiency within the foodstuffs regulatory regime would not require a revolution in the existing system, but could instead be secured by means of the building of links and strengthening of ties between existing regulators. The Strategy is, thus, built upon a detailed evaluation of current bodies and their procedures in order to identify deficiencies and to develop mechanisms for the creation of an integrated system of official food oversight. The need to strengthen control mechanisms was explicitly accepted. All levels of oversight required reform. At the basic, production level, emphasis was laid on more precise specification of the responsibilities of food and feed producers and on the defining of comprehensive safety assurance conditions and the introduction of internal control mechanisms, such as the HACCP system (see below). At the level of local official control, many necessary challenges were identified, the most important of which included the strengthening of the national inspection network and its readiness to cooperate with EU institutions, as well as the development of a uniform set of procedures and standards which local institutions would apply in undertaking their tasks. At the level of scientific expertise, the strategy envisaged the creation, identification and accreditation of series of laboratories, able to undertake all of the range of

6 European Commission, *White Paper on Food Safety*, COM(1999) 719 final, 12 January 2000, Brussels.

7 OECD, 'Compendium of National Food Safety Systems and Activities' of 15 May 2000, SG/ADHOC/FS(2000)5/ANN/FINAL.

8 Above, note 4, p. 5.

9 Above, note 4, Parts 1.3–1.5, pp. 1/25–1/30.

examinations required by the EU law. Finally, at central national level, the Strategy prioritised the definition of the rules of comprehensive and substantive cooperation between general Government administration and specialised official food control bodies.[10] In addition, the Strategy also highlighted a large number of cross-cutting problems, such as lacking technical capacity, shortage of trained personnel or inadequate financing. The Strategy further detailed measures for the improvement of food safety within Poland; beginning with specific legislative proposals, highlighting necessary institutional reforms and ending with budgetary proposals, which included expected financial assistance from the EU.[11] Annexed to the plan was a detailed timetable and implementation schedule.[12]

In summary, the Strategy proved to be a significant element within the accession process in the foodstuffs area, both providing a comprehensive reform action plan and committing the Polish Government and European institutions to mutually agreed goals and actions.

3 LEGAL AND INSTITUTIONAL FRAMEWORK OF FOOD SAFETY POLICIES IN POLAND

3.1 Food safety legislation

On 11 May 2001 Poland made a major effort to bring the general food legislation in line with the *acquis* by passing the Law on Health Conditions of Food and Nutrition,[13] hereinafter referred to as 'the Food Law'.[14]

The Food Law significantly altered the entire system of food safety regulation in Poland.[15] It started by defining the notion of 'food safety' as 'a set of complex conditions, which must be met and activities which must be undertaken at all stages of food production and food distribution in order to ensure safety for people's health and life' (Article 3(15)). These conditions and activities are translated into product and process standards. However, specific product and process standards do not form a part of this basic law: their formulation has been delegated to the Ministry of Health. The Ministry of Health also supervises the work of the State Sanitary Inspectorate, which carries out field controls with regard to all foods

10 Above, note 4, Part 2.1, pp. 2/1–2/4.

11 Above, note 4, Parts 2.2–2.4, pp. 2/5–2/49.

12 Above, note 4, Part 3, pp. 3/1–3/3.

13 Law of 11 May 2001 on Health Conditions of Food and Nutrition, unified text in *Journal of Laws*, No 31, Item 265, 2005, as amended.

14 Earlier the Law of 24 April 1997 on control of infectious diseases of animals, examinations of slaughtered animals and meat, and on the Veterinary Inspection (*Journal of Laws*, No 66, Item 752, 1999 as amended) was passed, which contains provisions concerning food of animal origin. With regard to non-health-related food quality, the most important piece of legislation is the Law of 21 December 2000 on Commercial Quality of Agricultural and Food Products (*Journal of Laws*, No 5, Item 44, 2001, as amended). Important modifications of the Polish Food Law were passed on 14 February 2003 and later on 30 October 2003.

15 This law transposes more than 80 EU Directives. In general, EU food safety standards were more stringent than Polish ones, but in some cases (various additives and preservatives) Polish food safety requirements were more restrictive than EU standards; see 'Links to the West', *Warsaw Business Journal*, 23 January 2003.

except food of animal origin, the oversight of which is delegated to the State Veterinary Inspectorate under the supervision of the Ministry of Agriculture.

The law recommended that the maximum allowed levels of food contamination be based on 'the outcomes of scientific research and in order to protect human health and life'.[16] This statement suggests that scientific expertise should play an absolute role in the setting of food safety standards; but, the law likewise relaxed this condition by stating that 'official inspection authorities can undertake preventive actions in order to protect human life and health, if those measures are proportional to the threat posed (*the precautionary principle*)' and where 'there is no scientific proof confirming the non-harmful characteristics of food items'.[17] The precautionary principle in its modern European form was a novelty within Poland and was introduced under EU influence. The accession negotiation commitment to faithful legal harmonisation left no room for discussion concerning its particular shape and scope within Polish law. It was, in effect, based thoroughly on the European prototype. Furthermore, the Food Law defined procedures applying to the creation of scientific expertise (Article 44(2.7)) and urged national laboratories and standard setters to draw on the best practice and experiences of EU laboratories.

In anticipation of regulatory problems related to biotechnological products the law defined 'novel food' (Article 3(26)) as 'substances or their compounds, which have not already been subject to human consumption'. Genetically modified food was considered a subcategory of novel food and its production or sale in Poland depended upon the decision of the General Sanitary Inspector. The Inspector checked if it is properly labelled and after reviewing scientific expertise, issued a decision allowing or forbidding its production or sale. The law also dealt with problems of the production of food from animals treated with hormones by setting a direct ban on such practices (Article 6). It conditionally approved (Article 8) the production or sale of irradiated food, if 'it does not pose a threat to human health or life and if it is technologically justified'; but it added that irradiation should not substitute normal hygiene practices or be applied to food which contains chemical substances serving to conserve or stabilise food (Article 8(2)). In addition, the law delegated the task of setting specific rules regarding irradiation to the Ministry of Health.

The law met the European transparency requirement by imposing on the State Sanitary Inspector the task of making public the register of decisions taken (Article 14(3)) together with all documentation on the admissibility procedure, thus allowing for public control of the impartiality of decisions taken. The law also responded to more recent evolutions within regulatory sciences, demanding that regulators facilitate consumer choice through enhanced information disclosure: for example, Article 24 required that all food and nutritional products should be labelled with all information essential for the protection of human health and life and in particular should detail: the composition of food products; the nutritional value; the presence of permitted additives; the expiry date; the instructions for use;

16 Article 7(2).

17 Article 45(2): 'In the case of the lack of credible scientific evidence confirming harmlessness of alimentary products, if the official body responsible for surveillance has justified suspicion about the harmfulness of these alimentary products, it can undertake early, and proportional to the threat, preventive activities aiming at the protection of health or human life (the principle of precaution)'.

and the name of the producer or the company which has placed the product on the market. Furthermore, the law determined that packaging 'should not mislead a consumer with texts or graphic signs' or 'should not attribute to the product nutritional values which it does not possess' (Article 24(2)).

As noted, a very significant shift within Polish regulation was that from reliance upon administrative or penal sanctions for purposes of enforcement to the direct imposition of responsibility for health and safety upon producers. Thus, pre-market approval procedures were abolished; meanwhile, Article 28 imposed a duty on companies producing to safeguard the effectiveness of food safety standards by carrying out internal inspections. It made the Hazard Analysis and Critical Control Points (HACCP) a basis for the internal inspection system, and stated that all large companies should implement and document the proper functioning of the HACCP control system as of the date of accession to the EU.[18] If a food company identified food safety problems, it had to spontaneously withdraw foodstuff from the market (Article 31). The state of food produced or treated in a given company could, however, also be verified *ex post* since all food companies are required to store samples of food products for a certain period of time and allow food inspections on request. Operators who produce foodstuffs or sell them in violation of food safety rules risk financial penalties or imprisonment up to two years (Article 49).

Article 40(c) of the Food Law made the Minister of Health responsible for cooperation with the European Food Safety Agency. In particular, the Ministry of Health sends a representative to the EFSA Advisory Forum, sends requests for EFSA scientific opinions and lodges the requisite scientific data on Polish food safety with EFSA. In this manner full cooperation of the Polish food safety authorities with EFSA was assured.

Following the accession, legislative efforts were undertaken in order to replace the 2001 Food Law with a new framework regulation. The Law on safety of food and feed of 25 August 2006[19] seems to mark an end to the adjustment and transition period and conforms with the 'New Approach' to food safety regulation developed by the European Union. In line with the EU Treaty provisions and policy,[20] the new law limits itself to providing a national framework for the direct application of European regulations. As a consequence, it makes very few substantive adjustments, dealing mostly with procedural matters and preparing a framework for enforcement of the directly applicable *acquis*. Nevertheless, despite some expectations and previous stipulations, the law makes no mention of the creation of a national food safety agency.

In summary, however, even though the establishment of a food agency was not

18 'First bakery with HACCP certificate does not haunt' (*Pierwsza piekarnia z certyfikatem HACCP nie straszy*) in *Gazeta Wyborcza*, 12 August 2003.

19 *Journal of Laws* No 171, Item 1225, 2006.

20 The adoption of the 'general food law' in form of Regulation (EC) No 178/2002 of the European Parliament and of the Council ([2002] *OJ* L31) heralded the change in the EU regulatory regime from a directive-based regime to a far more intrusive regulation-based regime. See, for the latest examples of such intense direct regulation, the two milestone hygiene regulations (Regulation (EC) No 852/2004 of the European Parliament and of the Council of 29 April 2004 on the hygiene of foodstuffs, [2004] *OJ* L226/3; Regulation (EC) No 853/2004 of the European Parliament and of the Council of 29 April 2004 laying down specific hygiene rules for food of animal origin, [2004] *OJ* L139/55).

undertaken, Polish food law appears to have been adjusted to meet EU food safety requirements on schedule. Equally, all important contemporary food safety issues would seem to have been addressed. Thus, at least a '*nominal*' harmonisation of Polish food law to meet EU standards has been achieved mainly in response to EU accession requirements, but also due to the country's commercial interest in the maintenance of its food exports (Post 2004).

The ambit of Polish food safety law also extends to encompass so-called 'veterinary legislation'. The European veterinary legislation has been transposed to the Polish legal system by means of five major framework laws and dozens of executive regulations, which, taken together, reproduce the very extensive veterinary *acquis*. At its core, veterinary law comprises: a law on veterinary control of trade (2003);[21] a law on veterinary border controls (2003);[22] a law on veterinary requirements for products of animal origin (2004);[23] a law on the protection of animal health and eradication of contagious animal diseases (2004);[24] and a law on veterinary inspections (2004).[25] In addition, three further pieces of legislation contain important veterinary provisions (the law on animal welfare (1997), the law on animal feedstuffs (2006) and the law on the system of identification and registration of animals (2004)). This enormous body of law has provided a basis for factual implementation of European veterinary standards with an aim of achieving the full 'from the farm to the fork' safety and control of foodstuffs.[26]

3.2 Institutional structure of the food safety system

Despite criticism expressed both by producers (Gronowska-Senger *et al.* 2002: 30–8) and by some scientific experts (Szponar and Molski 2000: 5, 8; Szponar *et al.* 2002: 116; 2003: 18, 25), the guiding notion that national administrative capacity could be strengthened within existing institutions was one that was maintained and implemented during the accession reform period. Reforms efforts accordingly focused on increasing coordination between existing administrative entities and on reinforcing their organisational capacities. Currently, the Polish food safety system comprises the following institutions:

1 The State Sanitary Inspectorate (*Państwowa Inspekcja Sanitarna*) created by the Law of 14 March 1985[27] and directly subordinated to the Minister of Health. Its major task is to protect public health, in particular by supervising the nutritional quality and health safety of food and other daily use products,

21 *Journal of Laws* No 16, Item 145, 2004.

22 *Journal of Laws* No 165, Item 1500, 2003.

23 *Journal of Laws* No 33, Item 288, 2004, replaced in 2006 by the law on products of animal origin of 16 December 2005, *Journal of Laws* No 17, Item 127, 2006.

24 *Journal of Laws* No 69, Item 625, 2004.

25 *Journal of Laws* No 33, Item 287, 2004.

26 Note, however, that in view of European hygiene law reform (see above, note 20) some of these measures will be amended or replaced in the near future. Legislative is already underway on the draft law on feedstuffs and the draft law on products of animal origin.

27 Law of 14 March 1985 on State Sanitary Inspectorate, *Journal of Laws* No 90, Item 575, 1998 with later amendments and the Ruling of the Minister of Health modifying competences of the General Sanitary Inspectorate of 30 December 1999, *Journal of Laws* No 111, Item 1315, 1999.

and to exercise an ongoing and preventive sanitary supervision function. The State Sanitary Inspectorate (SSI) controls compliance with the regulatory standards defining hygienic and health requirements on a daily basis; for example, conditions of production, transportation, storage and the sale of food as well as the conditions of mass catering. The SSI is led by the Chief Sanitary Inspector who is a member of the central Government administration. The Chief Sanitary Inspector is appointed and recalled by the Prime Minister, on the recommendation of the Minister of Health, and is supported in his tasks by the Chief Sanitary Inspectorate. The Inspector is supervised by and responsible to the Minister of Health.

2 The Veterinary Inspectorate (*Inspekcja Weterynaryjna*) established by the Law of 29 January 2004.[28] Its main objective is to supervise animal health and the safety of foodstuffs of animal origin with a view to protecting public health. The Veterinary Inspectorate oversees all stages of food production: control of animal welfare, control of feed production, oversight of slaughtering, control of the storage and processing of meat. In tandem with the Pharmaceuticals Inspectorate and the Inspectorate for the Commercial Quality of Agri-Food Products, the Veterinary Inspectorate also oversees production of pharmaceuticals for animals. The Inspectorate's founding statute organises the body along vertical lines; lower levels are subordinated to the higher, and all levels are made independent from the organs of general public administration.[29] The Inspectorate is led by the Chief Veterinary Doctor (CVD) who is directly responsible to the Minister of Agriculture and Rural Development. At slightly lower levels, 'Voyvod' Veterinary Inspectors direct and are responsible for inspections within the territory of their own administrative unit (Voyvodship), and are directly subordinate to the CVD. Finally, at the level of the most basic administrative unit, the Poviat (Province) Veterinary Inspector (directly subordinate to each Voyvod Veterinary Inspector) is responsible for routine inspections of abattoirs, meat producing plants, etc. within the region. Veterinary inspection at all levels is supported by a series of laboratories, including National Reference Laboratories accredited by the CVD. Veterinary (or sanitary) inspectors can take decisions about the withdrawal of foodstuffs from the market, the suspension of food production or even the closure of a plant – all these decisions might influence the market position of an enterprise.

3 Main Inspectorate of Plant Health and Seed Inspection (*Państwowa Inspekcja Ochrony Roślin i Nasiennictwa*) created by the Law of 18 December 2003,[30] whose main tasks include monitoring plant health conditions; the use of plant protection remedies and their production; verification and trade of seed material; protecting Poland's territory against pest organisms; protecting crops against pest organisms; preventing the spread of pests across the country; supervising correctness of trade and use of plant protection remedies.

28 Law of 29 January 2004 on the Veterinary Inspection, *Journal of Laws* No 33, Item 287, 2004.

29 The previously existing system, whereby different levels of veterinary inspection were carried out by bodies subordinated to organs of general public administration, was heavily criticised by the EU during the pre-accession period, as ineffective and vulnerable to political pressure and fraudulent misconduct. Organisational reform was, therefore, one of the important conditions for accession.

30 Law of 18 December 2003 on Plan Protection, *Journal of Laws* No 11, Item 94.

4 Agricultural and Food Quality Inspection (*Inspekcja Jakości Handlowej Artykułów Rolno-Spożywczych*) created by the Law of 21 December 2000.[31] The main task of the Inspectorate is to control the trade quality of agri-food products during all stages of production – from the farm, through to food processing and to wholesale trade – and reduction of health risks for consumers.
5 The State Trade Inspectorate (*Państwowa Inspekcja Handlowa*) operates in accordance with the Law of 15 December 2000 on Trade Inspection[32] and has broad competences to protecting consumers' interests and the economic interests of the state. The State Trade Inspectorate is responsible to the Office for Competition and Consumer Protection (*Urząd Ochrony Konkurencji i Konsumentów*).
6 The Customs Inspectorate (*Inspekcja Celna*)[33] which co-manages border veterinary, plant and seed protection and control, as well as the commercial quality of agri-products.

The institutions that operate within the Polish food safety system are diversified according to function; this situation, however, creates coordination problems. From the purely administrative point of view, the task of coordination rests with the office of the Prime Minister. Following a ruling of the Prime Minister of 28 June 2002, the responsibility for the substantive coordination of food safety system has passed into the hands of the Minister of Health. The Minister of Health is the formal head of the 'food safety team'; the heads of the Sanitary and Veterinary Inspections act as his substitutes. Membership of the food safety teams comprises representatives from other food oversight institutions (including the Minister of Finance in his capacity as head of customs), as well as representatives from the Ministry of Scientific Research; a measure designed to coordinate foodstuffs oversight with scientific research in this area.[34]

Alongside the formal coordination responsibilities assigned to the Minister of Health, the Government has sought to combat coordination problems by means of the establishment of an inter-sectoral team for food safety (*Międzyresortowy Zespół do spraw Bezpieczeństwa Żywności*), which is formally located within the Office of Prime Minister and is chaired by the Chief Sanitary Inspector and composed of representatives of all relevant institutions. The Minister of Agriculture has also created its own sectoral team for food safety (*Resortowy Zespół do spraw Bezpieczeństwa Żywności*).[35]

All intensive coordination efforts notwithstanding, the Minister of Health and the other rather *ad hoc* bodies described above only have access to soft coordination

31 Law of 21 December 2000 on Commercial Quality of Agricultural and Food Products, *Journal of Laws* No 5, Item 44, 2001.

32 Law of 15 December 2000 on the Protection of Competition and Consumer, *Journal of Laws* No 86, Item 804, 2003.

33 Law of 6 June 1997 on Customs Inspection, *Journal of Laws* No 71, Item 449, 1997.

34 No one scientific institution leads research on food safety issues in Poland. The most important scientific bodies include: the Institute of Food and Nutrition (*Instytut Żywności i Żywienia*), the State Sanitary Institute (*Państwowy Instytut Higieny*) and other scientific institutes subordinated to the Ministry of Health and the Ministry of Agriculture.

35 Although no formal role has been assigned to business associations representing food producers, they are very active within law-making processes and also strongly influence the implementation of standards.

tools, such as information exchange, the discussion and identifications of food safety priorities, which might or might not lead to proposals for legislative adjustment, or the creation of *ad hoc* working committees composed of experts drawn from the various oversight institutions. In summary, the Polish institutional food safety system does not yet appear to be adequately streamlined and is only cemented together by means of reference to the sense of common mission rather than clear organisational principles.

As mentioned above, Poland has taken the rather controversial step not to establish any integrated institution for scientific advice in risk assessment. Instead, Ministers in charge of food safety remain embedded in a network of various scientific institutes and laboratories, which fall under their respective supervision. They are reduced to using those scattered resources for their gathering of scientific advice in risk assessment. This rather extraordinary solution has received heavy criticism, but although a number of regulatory and political efforts have been made towards establishing a singular and well-integrated institution for scientific risk assessment, these have all failed at different levels of the decision-making process. In the course of application, this situation appears all the more problematic as it has left Poland without a strong and unified representation of 'national' scientific opinion which other states often have. This has naturally put Poland in a rather disadvantaged position in cases of conflict. A recent example may well illustrate the situation: It would probably be easier to argue in favour of safety of Polish products in the face of the Russian embargo on certain Polish foodstuffs if these arguments could be supported by solid and analytical background information provided by an internationally recognised scientific institution, representing the national scientific standpoint. It will thus be interesting to observe in which ways this case could affect the Polish approach towards the institutionalisation of scientific risk assessment in food safety. Will Poland be forced by circumstance and need to *adapt* to the common solution or will it rather attempt to answer to the need for scientific argument through a more independent *adoption* of institutionalisation? Admittedly, the eventual response to this dilemma will probably depend more upon situational constellations of political needs and scientific resources as well as infighting between these factors – nationally and internationally – than upon legal considerations. Yet, it is exactly through cases such as this one that we may observe why the political-scientific nexus should be considered central to the legal analysis of food safety and its risk assessment, in Europe and elsewhere.

3.3 Problems of regulatory implementation

Food safety policies are vulnerable to the threat of poor implementation. On the eve of formal EU enlargement in 2004, various voices were raised drawing attention to continuing concern about the ineffective implementation of EU food safety rules in new Member States, and, in particular, in Poland. The following seeks to review various developments within the Polish regulatory regime that may impact upon the effectiveness of the implementation of food safety rules.

Direct oversight of food processing plants is costly. As a comparative example, it should be noted that in 1998 the US Government employed 7,400 compliance inspectors and spent US$600 million on the inspection of meat and poultry in 6,200 plants; a ratio of 1.2 inspectors to each plant (May 2002: 156). By contrast, in 2001, 7,000 Polish meat plants were subject to oversight by the Veterinary Inspectorate, which then had a total of 4,450 employees; a ratio of 0.6 inspectors to each plant.[36] EU accession has slightly alleviated this situation, since external funding has been made available to support food safety policies and since those meat processing plants which did not meet EU food safety standards have subsequently closed. Such cost considerations clearly play a large role in the choice of policy that makes producers responsible for food safety. In line with general EU adjustments, the Polish regulatory regime has increasingly moved away from a system of *ex ante* administrative control to one in which the basic responsibility for food safety rests upon producers, while the state (via its specialised services) stipulates regulations and controls their implementation. HACCP is an important element within this strategy.[37]

Various Polish food businesses began to introduce HACCP as early as 1995 with an eye to improving their export position within the EU.[38] During preparation of the 2001 Food Law, however, the Government faced increased pressure from producers' organisations, who sought derogation from HACCP implementation for all companies employing fewer than 50 people. Although the Polish food law was eventually to impose HACCP upon all food producers, it has set temporal limits on implementation, demanding only that business initiate HACCP implementation prior to 1 May 2004 and giving no final date for full implementation, thus effectively delaying the full impact of the policy.[39] It is also important to note that introduction of the HACCP system in Poland has not merely necessitated wide-ranging alterations in production methods and renewal of technical equipment within processing plants, but also calls for fundamental behavioural adjustments (Konecka-Matyjek *et al.* 2005: 1–9); that is, changes in working practices and employee attitudes. This will prove to be a lengthy process; producers became fully aware of their heightened responsibilities during the reform period, but likewise evidenced much fear about liability and consequently sought to oppose proposed adjustments in the regime. Governmental action was needed not only to raise awareness and reduce the costs of reforms, but also to combat fear: both the fear of food business that it will not be able to manage reforms and the fear of the EU officials that Poland will not be in a position to guarantee safety of its food after accession. Accordingly, and making use of extensive EU technical and financial support, the Government developed a comprehensive information and training policy. The range of activities was very broad in order to reach all categories of recipients: mainly private producers responsible for implementation of the HACCP; and state inspectors responsible for oversight of implementation. The first group received support in the form of all sorts of manuals and guidebooks as well as training programmes. Both the Sanitary and Veterinary Inspectorates ran training programmes for their inspectors regarding the new regulations, the new

36 Calculations made by the authors based on the Report of the Supreme Chamber of Control from March 2003 (*Informacja o wynikach kontroli zadań nadzoru weterynaryjnego*).

37 Besides HACCP, large Polish food producers also belong to other certification systems, for example, ISO (the 9000 Series), GMP (Good Manufacturing Practices) and local certificates such as '*Dobre, bo polskie*' (It is good because it is Polish!), see Chodkowski 2004.

38 Do they implement HACCP or not? (*Wdrażają system HACCP czy nie?*), in *Gazeta Wyborcza*, 29 July 2003.

39 See *Gazeta Wyborcza* (Wrocław edition), 9 August 2004.

responsibilities placed upon the food business and methodologies for its control and evaluations.[40]

In January 2005, the Food and Veterinary Office undertook a survey to review implementation. Its overall results were in general positive; however, FVO inspectors also noted that the majority of control inspections are still focused on hygiene prerequisites, with subsequently little or no attention paid to the implementation of food safety procedures based on HACCP prerequisites. The Polish Government has responded, assuring FVO inspectors that further training programmes will be made available in the coming months for the training of local inspectors in the assessment of HACCP systems.[41]

Likewise, sound food safety policies are ideally founded within an efficient information collection system. One important element within information collection systems is the identification and registration of animals. The European Commission Regulation 494/98/EC of 27 February 1998 lays down the requirements for a system for the identification and registration of bovine animals.[42] Following those requirements, Poland has created a system for the Identification and Registration of Animals (*Identyfikacja i Rejestracja Zwierząt – IRZ*)[43] in order to monitor trade in animals. However, according to a review conducted in August 2004, approximately 30 per cent of registered entries contained insufficient or incoherent information.[44] With Regulation 178/2002[45] the European Union has created the RASFF (*Rapid Alert System for Food and Feed*), which seeks to collect information about immediate food safety threats and to evaluate them. Responding to the EU initiative, Poland has created its own Domestic System for Information about Harmful Food Products (*Krajowy System Informowania o Niebezpiecznych Produktach Żywnościowych*), located within the structure of the Chief Sanitary Inspectorate. Food producers are legally obliged to inform the relevant state administration about possible threats to human health and safety. Thus, on a more positive note, the Polish domestic system has been integrated into the RASFF since 2003.

In summary, the implementation of the new food safety regime within Poland can be evaluated in the light of the Veterinary Inspectorate's report of May 2003. According to this review, only 24 per cent of meat processing plants, supplying approximately 30 per cent of domestic production, met EU food safety standards.[46] Almost half (1,780) of the meat processing plants had committed themselves to

40 See, for example: Report of the activities of the State Sanitary Inspectorate in 2001–2005 (*Raport z działalności Państwowej Inspekcji Sanitarnej w latach 2001–2005*), Warsaw, September 2005, 49–51.

41 Final report of a mission carried out in Poland from 17 to 21 January 2005 in order to evaluate the official foodstuffs control system and in particular the implementation of controls on the hygiene of foodstuffs, 22 April 2005, DG(SANCO)/7521/2005-MR final.

42 Commission Regulation (EC) No 494/98 of 27 February 1998 laying down detailed rules for the implementation of Council Regulation (EC) No 820/97 as regards the application of minimum administrative sanctions in the framework of the system for the identification and registration of bovine animals, [1998] *OJ* L60/78.

43 Law of 2 April 2004 on the System of Identification and Registration of Animals, *Journal of Laws* No 91, Item 872, 2004.

44 Gaps in the IRZ system, in *Rzeczpospolita*, 9 September 2004.

45 Regulation (EC) No 178/2002 of the European Parliament and of the Council of 28 January 2002 laying down the general principles and requirements of food law, establishing the European Food Safety Authority and laying down procedures in matters of food safety, [2002] *OJ* L31/1.

46 Will Polish meat processing plants get transitional periods?, in *Gazeta Wyborcza*, 12 August 2003.

meeting EU standards by the date of accession and have succeeded in satisfying these obligations. However, a further 332 meat plants benefited from transitional measures up until 31 December 2007. This was not the only concession made on the part of the EU. The Polish Government was furnished with a further derogation in order to allow the majority of 'non-performing' meat processing plants to continue to sell their products to a local market (defined as the province of the plant's location and neighbouring provinces). As a consequence, earlier estimates of the number of small meat production businesses that will eventually close have been revised downwards from 1,500 to 300.[47]

4 CONCLUSION

According to the latest available data, the number of cases of food-related ill-health has decreased in Poland from 29,000 in 1996 to 26,700 in 2000.[48] Assessing the sanitary state of the country in 2004, the report of the State Sanitary Inspectorate details an improvement in the safety conditions prevailing within Polish food production and food trade facilities, with the proportion of businesses adjudged to have bad sanitary conditions decreasing from 14.5 per cent in 2001 to 8.6 per cent in 2004. The SSI has also clearly stated that it will strengthen control over the implementation of the HACCP system, as well as its adequate documentation.[49] Based on such data various food safety experts estimate that 88 per cent of food sold in Poland is fully safe.[50] As public opinion polls have shown, the Polish public tends to believe that domestic food is 'safe enough'.[51]

Whether correct or incorrect, public perception confirms the fact that EU membership requirements, rather than domestic pressure, has driven the process of reform of the Polish food safety system. Basic food safety principles have been drawn up, and institutional structures designed, in an effort to ensure conformity of the Polish food safety system with EU food safety law and to ensure its effective implementation. Although, in a final analysis, it is currently difficult to assess the degree of effectiveness of the Polish food safety system, it is important to note that the Polish Government has made a considerable effort to increase the effectiveness of food controls: restructuring the network of research laboratories which work to food inspectorates, reviewing the personnel and equipment available for food inspections, and beginning the process of building a new system of educational requirements and training for the staff of food control bodies.

Following completion of basic legislative and institutional adjustments, the quality of the Polish food system appears now to be dependent upon the quality of operational procedures and of day-to-day implementation practices and oversight.

47 *Oszczędźcie te rzeźnie*, in *Gazeta Wyborcza*, 4 March 2004.

48 'Food quality and food safety as a XXI century challenge', the materials from the conference organised by the Polish Senate on 25 February 2003.

49 Chief Sanitary Inspectorate, *Sanitary state of the country in 2004* (*Stan sanitarny kraju w roku 2004*), Warsaw, July 2005.

50 *Ibid*, presentation by Dr L. Szponar, Head of the State Institute of Nutrition Sciences.

51 When asked about the perception of food safety, Poles expressed far greater confidence in food produced exclusively from domestic components than imported food; see CBOS survey, November 2001.

BIBLIOGRAPHY

Banati, D. (2003) 'The EU and candidate countries: How to cope with food safety policies?', *Food Control* 2: 89–93.

Chief Sanitary Inspectorate (2005a) *Sanitary State of the Country in 2004 (Stan sanitarny kraju w roku 2004)*, Warsaw: Chief Sanitary Inspectorate.

Chief Sanitary Inspectorate (2005b) *Report of the activities of the State Sanitary Inspection in 2001–2005 (Raport z działalności Państwowej Inspekcji Sanitarnej w latach 2001–2005)*, Warsaw: Chief Sanitary Inspectorate.

Chodkowski, A. (2004) *Zapewnienie tożsamosci i dobrowolna certyfikacja artykułów rolno-spożywczych* (Assuring Identity and Voluntary Certification of agri-food products), paper presented at a conference *Czy chcemy żyć z GMO? Aspekty gospodarcze, ekologiczne I etyczne stososwania produktów GMO*, Warsaw, 4 March 2004, available at: <http://gmo-eko.net/referaty/chodkowski.doc>.

Czyżewski, A. (1997) 'Macroeconomic Interdependencies in the Process of Transformation of Agriculture', in P.-Ch. Müller-Graff and A. Stepniak (eds), *Poland and the European Union – Between Association and Membership*, 4 European Community Studies Association Series, Baden-Baden: Nomos.

Gronowska-Senger, A., Izdebski, H., Trochimczuk, G. and Czarnecki, J. (2002) *Prawo Żywnościowe i Strategia Bezpieczeństwa Żywności, Stanowisko Polskiej Federacji Producentów Żywności*, Warsaw: Polska Federacja Producentów Żywności.

Jurcewicz, A. (1997) 'Legal problems resulting from the assignment of new tasks to the agricultural sector in Poland', in P.-Ch. Müller-Graff and A. Stepniak (eds), *Poland and the European Union – Between Association and Membership*, 4 European Community Studies Association Series, Baden-Baden: Nomos.

Konecka-Matyjek, E., Turlejska, H., Pelzner, U. and Szponar, L. (2005) 'Actual situation in the area of implementing quality assurance systems GMP, GHP and HACCP in Polish food production and processing plants', *Food Control* 1: 1–9.

May, P.J. (2002) 'Social Regulation', in L.M. Salamon (ed.), *The Tools of Government*, Oxford: Oxford University Press, 156–216.

Mertens, H. (2001) 'Poland', in S. Goetz, T. Jaksh and R. Siebert (eds), *Agricultural Transformation and Land Use in Central and Eastern Europe*, Aldershot; Burlington, Vt.: Ashgate.

Post, D.L. (2004) *Diffusion of International Food Safety Standards: Developing Country Experiences*, Manchester: WP of Centre on Regulation and Competition, Manchester University.

Rowiński, J. (1992) 'Integracja Polski z Unia Europejska – niezbędne procesy dostosowawcze polskiej gospodarki żywnościowej', in M. Moroz (ed.), *Sprawy Rolnictwa i Gospodarki Żywnościowej w Umowach Polski ze Wspólnotami Europejskimi*, Warszawa: Fundacja im. Mikołaja Rataja.

Szponar, L. and Molski, M. (2000) 'Czy model brytyjski Food Standards Agency może być korzystnym rozwiązaniem dla poprawy istotnej części stanu zdrowia publicznego w Polsce?', *Żywność, Żywienie, Prawo a Zdrowie*, Rok XI, Supplement 2, Warszawa, 5 and 8.

Szponar, L., Stoś, K., Traczyk, I. and Turlejska, H. (2003) 'System bezpieczeństwa żywności w Polsce i krajach Unii Europejskiej – podstawy instytucjonalne', in L. Szponar, K. Stoś and I. Traczyk (eds), *System Bezpieczeństwa Żywności w Polsce – Wybrane Zagadnienia*, Prace IŻŻ, Warszawa: Instytut Żywności i Żywienia.

Szponar, L. *et al.* (2002) 'The concept of implementation of Food Safety Strategy in Poland', *Żywienie Człowieka i Metabolizm*, Rok XXIX, No 3, Warszawa.

Chapter 7

A default-logic model of factfinding for United States regulation of food safety

*Vern R. Walker**

1 INTRODUCTION

An important question about safety regulation is how different regulatory systems shape the relationship between law and science, and how they influence the public confidence in science-based decision making. Different process rules might impose different constraints on scientists, and different substantive rules will pose different questions to scientific researchers. What is needed for comparative work in this area of law is a conceptual model that is generic enough to analyse the relationship between risk assessment and risk management in multiple jurisdictions. This chapter introduces such a model, and uses it to analyse the regulation of food safety in the United States. The first part of the chapter describes the functional elements of a default-logic model for factfinding. The second part applies the model to food safety regulation in the United States, with particular attention to the distinction between risk assessment and risk management. The last part summarises a number of major conclusions from that analysis, with particular attention to issues that might arise across jurisdictions.

2 A DEFAULT-LOGIC MODEL OF FACTFINDING PROCESSES IN LAW

In order to achieve the generality of application needed for comparative work on a global scale, the model is based on the logic of legal reasoning. The first section describes the foundation of the model in current theories of default logic. The second section discusses three functional elements of default reasoning (rules, policies and evidence) in terms that are familiar to practitioners of legal reasoning. The third section discusses the synchronic and diachronic dimensions of the model.

* I wish to thank Nicole Irvin and Kevin Gick for their assistance in researching this chapter.

2.1 Default-logic foundations

During the last few decades, logicians have been developing formal models for practical reasoning that are useful in analysing legal factfinding.[1] Whereas traditional logic is axiomatic and deductive, default logic models what logicians call 'practical reasoning' or 'applied logic'. We use such reasoning patterns to warrant conclusions about objects and events in the real world, and we rely on those conclusions to guide our decisions and actions. Besides being practical, default logic is dynamic. The 'warrant' or 'support' relationship between premises and conclusion can change over time, as a result of adding new information to the corpus of knowledge or removing information from it. Also, different participants and institutions can play distinct roles in the proof process. Third, conclusions warranted by default reasoning are defeasible, meaning that new information can increase or undermine the previous warrant. Fourth, despite the defeasibility of the conclusions reached, default reasoning does warrant holding such conclusions in a provisional way, until new information in fact undermines the warrant for those conclusions. This means that default reasoning is presumptive, and must have some provisional claim to correctness.

The goal of default logic is to identify patterns or formal structures for modelling the practical and dynamic reasoning that we use every day. A line of reasoning is simply a pattern of propositions organised in such a way that some of the propositions (the 'premises' or 'reasons') warrant finding another proposition to be true (the 'conclusion'). Propositions, expressed in English by grammatical sentences, are by definition capable of having a truth-value – that is, of being either true or false.[2] While a default conclusion is considered true only tentatively, the reasoning pattern behind it should nevertheless warrant our making the presumptive inference from the available evidence.

2.2 Three functional elements of default reasoning: rules, policies and evidence

Default-logic models can be adapted to a particular domain of knowledge by emphasising functional elements frequently found in that domain and by adopting terminology familiar to that domain. For understanding the default structure of reasoning in a legal context, three types of propositions are particularly useful: rules, policies and evidence.

1 For discussions of the logic of default reasoning, see, eg, Kyburg and Choh Man Teng 2001; Pollock 1990; Prakken 1997; Toulmin, Rieke and Janik 1984; Walton 1996; 2002.

2 For comparative work across different legal systems, at least at the present stage of linguistic theory, any models of reasoning must be based on propositions (logical entities) rather than on sentences (linguistic entities). Different speakers can assert the same proposition to be true (for example, 'food poisoning caused the person's death') in different languages and with different linguistic expressions. Internationally agreed and binding factfinding processes that exhibit the rule of law (such as the dispute settlement process and trade agreements administered by the World Trade Organization) employ lines of reasoning that must be understood by every WTO Member, regardless of the different languages used by those Members.

2.2.1 Rules

Legal rules are conditional propositions established as true by legal authority. An example from tort law is: 'if the defendant's food product has an unsafe characteristic that departs from its intended design, then the food product contains a manufacturing defect'. From a logical perspective, this rule has the conditional form 'if p, then q' – where p and q stand for propositions, with p being called the 'antecedent' condition and q being the 'consequent' proposition. A rule states that proposition p's being true is a sufficient condition for the truth of q. Rules play an important role in warranting inferences. In a lawsuit seeking compensation for illness due to food poisoning, if the rule above is adopted in the jurisdiction, then we know that if the factfinder determines that 'the defendant's food product has an unsafe characteristic that departs from its intended design', then the rule directs the factfinder to conclude that 'the food product contains a manufacturing defect'.

A conditional proposition must satisfy certain criteria in order to be a legal rule. First, the conditional proposition must be properly adopted by a legal authority, so that it 'has the force of law'. Second, legal rules must be universal: they should apply in all situations in which the antecedent condition is satisfied. Any exceptions should be identified and governed by additional rules. Third, it is useful to categorise legal rules into three traditional types:

a substantive rules (eg, standards of food safety);
b procedural rules (eg, procedures for approving a food additive); and
c evidentiary rules (eg, rules for excluding or evaluating the probative value of evidence about food safety).

Legal factfinding processes are typically governed by procedural rules, in which a presiding authority (judge or regulatory official) and a factfinder (judge, regulatory official or jury) evaluate the evidence and find propositions to be true or false, while applying the substantive rules and any applicable evidentiary rules to the particular case (Walker 2003).

2.2.2 Policies

Policies are propositions that state reasons for or against adopting a rule. Policies are often classified as either teleological (prudential, or consequentialist) or deontological. A teleological policy argument posits the objective that we are trying to achieve by adopting or rejecting the rule, and asserts whether adopting the rule will help achieve that objective. For example, in torts, one policy objective is to increase economic efficiency through minimising the occurrence of accidents, and another is to minimise economic dislocation in society by spreading the cost of accidents among a class of beneficiaries. Particular rules may help or hinder achieving these goals. By contrast, a deontological policy of fairness to the food product supplier might favour placing the burden of producing evidence of the injury on the plaintiff. For any particular rule, there are often a large number of relevant policies, some of which weigh in favour of adopting the rule and others weigh against the rule. In a rational legal system, the rule-making authority would balance all competing policies in making decisions about rule adoption.

2.2.3 Evidence

Evidentiary propositions are statements about the world that provide the factual warrant for any findings of fact. Of particular interest in regulatory analyses are generalisations about groups of individuals or about members of groups. Examples of generalisations are: 'most commercial food products are safe'; 'product suppliers typically act in good faith'; and '6 per cent of the samples tested were contaminated'. Using these same examples, we can reformulate them (without change of meaning) into conditional propositions, as: '*in most cases, if* a product is a commercial food product, *then* it is safe'; '*in the typical case, if* someone is a product supplier, *then* he or she is acting in good faith'; '*in 6 per cent of the cases, if* it was a tested sample, *then* it was contaminated'.

Although generalisations resemble rules in being conditional assertions about groups, generalisations do not make a universal claim. Generalisations acknowledge that the consequent proposition is *not* true in *all* of the cases that satisfy the antecedent condition. Generalisations, unlike rules, are evaluated probabilistically and warrant inferences that are merely probabilistic. Moreover, unlike rules, generalisations depend for their inferential value on empirical evidence and common experience, not on legal authority. The problem of stating when the available evidence *should* warrant a generalisation, or *should* undermine the tentative truth of a generalisation, is a difficult problem of logic, probability and statistics.

2.3 The default-logic structure of factfinding reasoning

Because default logic is practical, dynamic, defeasible and presumptive, it is a particularly useful model in studying comparative law. The primary function of legal factfinding is to provide a legitimate basis for governmental action, and to guide governmental actions that are lawful. In law, we usually know in advance which propositions would make useful conclusions, and we proceed to construct arguments or lines of reasoning relevant to those conclusions, using legal rules, policies and evidence. The default-logic structure of such possible arguments has both synchronic and diachronic dimensions.

2.3.1 Synchronic models of acceptable arguments

A 'synchronic' logic model captures all acceptable lines of legal argument at a single point in time, without reference to changes in acceptability over time. At any one time, relative to any particular conclusion of importance in the legal proceeding (ie, a contested 'issue of fact'), particular legal rules are applicable and particular evidence is available. The synchronic default model addresses the question: what possible lines of reasoning are acceptable for or against that conclusion, given the applicable rules and the available evidence?

The set of all acceptable arguments leading to the conclusion can be represented graphically by an inverted 'tree', with the proposition at issue at the top (the root node of the inverted tree) and branches of propositions extending downward, as in Figure 7.1. Every node in the tree represents a proposition, and is capable of having a truth-value. The arrows pointing upward, which ultimately converge on the proposition at issue at the top, represent implication relationships. Implications are inferential relationships, expressed as conditionals ('*if*. . ., *then* . . .'). A conditional asserts that if the *antecedent* proposition is true (the proposition in the '*if*' clause), then the *consequent* proposition is also true (the proposition in the '*then*' clause). These trees are therefore called 'implication trees'. We build an implication tree downward from the proposition ultimately at issue, by asking at each new level which subsidiary propositions, if true, would warrant inferring the next higher proposition. The goal is to construct a tree that captures all of the lines of reasoning that are acceptable for proving the proposition at issue to be either true or false. Implication trees therefore 'evaluate upward': if lower propositions (which function as antecedents or premises) prove to be true, then they warrant finding higher propositions (consequents or conclusions) to be true.

At lower levels of the inverted tree, the branching necessarily multiplies because implications upward use multiple antecedents (premises) to infer a single consequent (conclusion). Many valid implications have conjunctive antecedent conditions, all of which have to be true in order to infer the conclusion: *if* B *and* C *and* D, *then* A. The top two levels of Figure 7.1 depict a conjunctive implication. Other implications involve disjunctive antecedent conditions, any one of which warrants

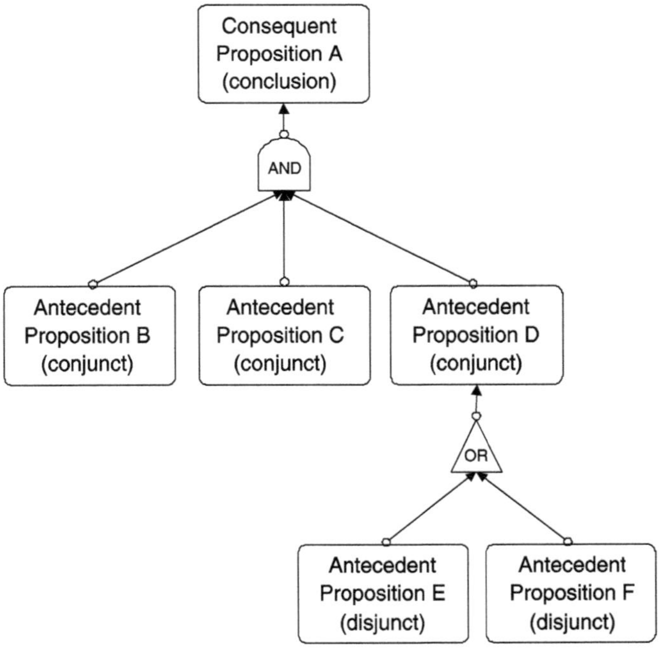

Figure 7.1

drawing the conclusion: *if* E *or* F, *then* D. (See the bottom two levels of Figure 7.1.) As we construct an implication tree downward from the proposition ultimately at issue, the logic of that proposition tends to proliferate branches by attaching conjunctions or disjunctions at the next lower level.

One other logical connective, besides conjunction ('AND') and disjunction ('OR'), is particularly useful in constructing implication trees for legal reasoning. In default-logic terminology, a 'defeater' is a proposition which, if true, defeats the line of reasoning to which it attaches. A defeater proposition that is *true* makes the proposition above it *false*, despite the truth value of any propositions lower in that branch of the tree. Defeaters attach to implication arrows, as shown by the connective 'UNLESS' in Figure 7.2. In law, both exceptions and affirmative defences exhibit defeater logic. For example, even if the plaintiff proves the normal elements of a *prima facie* case to be true, the defendant might fall under some legal exception, or have an affirmative defence (eg, based on the plaintiff's consent or conduct), or have immunity (eg, due to the defendant's status). If the defendant proves the defeating proposition to be true, then this defeats the plaintiff's *prima facie* case.

At some point down each branch of the tree, however, the legal rules must come to an end, and we reach a 'terminal node' of the implication tree. What makes such a terminal node have any particular truth-value is not a lower-level legal rule, but the probative value of the available evidence that is relevant to proving that terminal proposition. An important area of study in default logic is the structure of warrant patterns within the evidence. That is, the goal is to analyse how a reasonable factfinder should arrive at an evaluation of probative value for terminal propositions. While this paper cannot explore this problem in detail, we can say that inferences often are based on probabilistic generalisations, instead of on rules of law. Therefore, we can say that trees used to model legal reasoning have two major regions: the rule-based implications near the top of the tree and the generalisation-based inferences toward the bottom.

While the role of the presiding authority (the judge in a court) is to adopt and apply legal rules, the role of the factfinder is to evaluate the available evidence and

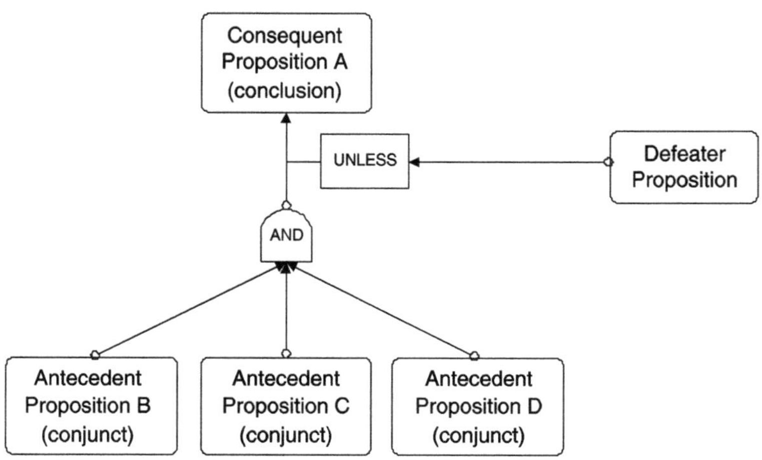

Figure 7.2

to assign truth-values to the terminal propositions of the implication tree. While the rule-based region of an implication tree has an identical structure for all cases in the jurisdiction at a given point of time, the generalisation-based portion of the reasoning is often unique to each case or proceeding. To guide the factfinder's reasoning in assessing the evidence, the legal authority might establish presumptions (generalisations that must function as default inference rules). Also, the legal authority might establish sets of relevant factors that the factfinder must take into account, or might establish sets of irrelevant factors that the factfinder is not allowed to take into account. Such instructions on relevance and such presumptions partially structure the evidence for the factfinder, but they might not legally determine (by themselves) any particular finding.

2.3.2 *Diachronic models of acceptable arguments*

If an implication tree models all possible lines of reasoning that are acceptable at any given time, based on all of the available legal rules, then it is also possible to model how implication trees change over time. This furnishes a 'diachronic' model of legal reasoning. In general, a default-logic model can change in either or both of two fundamental ways: the rule-based region of the implication tree can change by adding or pruning branches of legal rules, and the generalisation-based reasoning can change by attaching evidence to, or detaching evidence from, the terminal nodes of the tree. Such changes in the content of the evidence might also lead to a re-evaluation of the probative value or total weight of evidence.

The appropriate legal authorities can elaborate new legal rules, provided they follow the applicable legal rules for doing so. From the logical perspective, the function of policies (including legal principles) is to guide the dynamic process of constructing the rule-based regions of implication trees. Although the change in legal rules over time is usually gradual, the change in the evidence available in a particular proceeding is often rapid. A party in a lawsuit, or an investigating judge, or an administrative agency might introduce evidence for the record or remove evidence from that record. There might also be objections and arguments about the admissibility of evidence to the tree, either because the proffered evidence is not relevant to any terminal proposition or because there is some evidentiary rule excluding the particular item of evidence. Evidence might be admissible and relevant to some issues, but irrelevant as a matter of law to other issues. The diachronic model of default reasoning for any particular factfinding process can therefore become quite complex, as it captures all the changes in reasoning throughout the proceeding.

3 APPLYING THE DEFAULT-LOGIC MODEL TO FOOD SAFETY REGULATION IN THE UNITED STATES: FOOD ADDITIVES AND PESTICIDE RESIDUES

A model is useful if it simplifies a confusing mass of information, and organises it to help solve a particular problem or to answer a particular question. The food safety law of the United States certainly qualifies as such a confusing mass of information.

The primary statute for this law is the Federal Food, Drug and Cosmetic Act (FFDCA).[3] The default-logic model helps to clarify the complex law-science relationship within that regulatory system, with particular attention to the interplay between risk assessment and risk management. It may also suggest normative insights into the reasonableness of public confidence in science-based decision making within that system. In order to make this analysis manageable, this chapter compares only two regulatory sub-categories: food additives and pesticide chemical residues.

3.1 The statutory framework of rules and policies

Because all governmental factfinding is action-oriented, the place to begin the analysis is the action to be decided. For example, in the regulation of food, if the FDA considers particular articles of food to be unsafe, the agency may petition a federal district court to condemn the food.[4] In such a proceeding, the government asks the federal court to make the required findings that justify condemnation of the food. For example, the government might argue that the article of food is 'adulterated'.[5] Adulteration may result either from a food additive or from a pesticide residue, although it may also result from some other factor not considered in this chapter.

3.1.1 Adulteration due to a food additive

According to the statute, '[a] food shall be deemed to be adulterated . . . if it is or if it bears or contains . . . any food additive that is unsafe within the meaning of section 348' of Title 21 of the United States Code.[6] A food is therefore adulterated due to a food additive if two antecedent or subsidiary propositions are true: the article of food contains a 'food additive' and the food additive is 'unsafe'. Figure 7.3 shows this conjunctive implication.

Elaborating the left-hand branch of this logic, the statute defines a 'food additive' as 'any substance the intended use of which results or may reasonably be expected to result, directly or indirectly, in its becoming a component or otherwise affecting the characteristics of any food'.[7] Figure 7.3 contains a truncated version of an implication rule derived from this definition. An important qualification is that any substance qualifies as a 'food additive' only if it is not 'GRAS' – that is, not 'generally recognised as safe'.[8] Proving that the substance is GRAS defeats its classification as a

3 21 U.S.C. §§ 301 *et seq.*, as amended. All citations in this paper to sections of the United States Code reflect amendments through P.L. 109–73 (excluding P.L. 109–59), approved 23 September 2005.

4 See 21 U.S.C. § 334(a)(1).

5 *Ibid.*

6 21 U.S.C. § 342(a)(2)(C)(i).

7 21 U.S.C. § 321(s). This category includes 'any substance intended for use in producing, manufacturing, packing, processing, preparing, treating, packaging, transporting, or holding food', and specifically includes 'any source of radiation intended for any such use'. *Ibid.*

8 See 21 U.S.C. § 321(s). The acronym GRAS derives from the statutory provision that a substance is not a 'food additive' if it is 'generally recognized, among experts qualified by scientific training and experience to evaluate its safety, as having been adequately shown through scientific procedures (or, in

food additive. The 'Authority' note in Figure 7.3 highlights the point that every implication arrow that models an established legal rule must have an authoritative source associated with it. Here, the authority behind this exception (modelled as a logical defeater with the 'UNLESS' connective) is Section 321(s) of Title 21 of the United States Code. The 'Policies' note in Figure 7.3, attached to the 'Authority' note, indicates that behind the adoption of every legal rule there are policy considerations. These policy considerations suggest that we should model the property of being GRAS as a defeater – as an affirmative defence to be raised by a potentially affected party in the seizure proceeding. Consistent with such reasoning, courts have held that once a substance is determined to be a food additive, it is presumed to be unsafe, and the processor has the burden in a seizure proceeding of showing that the substance is GRAS.[9]

There is also a right-hand branch to proving adulteration due to a food additive: it requires a finding that the food additive is 'unsafe'. The statute establishes the presumption that a food additive is 'deemed to be unsafe' – a presumption that can be defeated if there is in effect a regulation 'prescribing the conditions under which such additive may be safely used', and the food additive and its use or intended use are in conformity with that regulation.[10] Figure 7.3 displays this presumption, and Figure 7.4 displays the statutory rules governing such a regulation. Because the affirmative defence is that the FDA has given prior approval in the form of issuing a regulation, the burden of proving safety is ultimately on a party seeking to prove this to the agency in a prior administrative proceeding.

A prior administrative determination of safety might be by regulation or by exemption.[11] Any person may petition the FDA to issue a regulation prescribing conditions of safe use for a food additive.[12] Such a petition 'shall, in addition to any explanatory or supporting data, contain . . . full reports of investigations made with respect to the safety for use of such additive, including full information as to the methods and controls used in conducting such investigations'.[13] This procedural rule places the burden of producing any available scientific evidence on the petitioner seeking the regulation. A statutory rule of evidence prescribes a list of relevant factors that the FDA must take into account in 'determining . . . whether a proposed use of a food additive is safe'.[14] Those factors specified in the statute include:

the case of a substance used in food prior to January 1, 1958, through either scientific procedures or experience based on common use in food) to be safe under the conditions of its intended use'. See *ibid.* The statute also excludes from the regulatory category of 'food additive' other important regulatory categories, such as pesticide chemical residues and colour additives. *Ibid.* This explicit exclusion avoids double regulation of the same substance, and also leaves 'food additive' as the default category for kinds of substances added to foods.

9 Eg *United States v 29 Cartons . . . An Article of Food, Etc.*, 987 F.2d 33, 35 (1st Cir. 1993); *United States* v. *Two Plastic Drums*, 984 F.2d 814, 816 (7th Cir. 1993).

10 See 21 U.S.C. § 348(a)(2).

11 A second branch of authorisation, besides regulation, is if there is an 'exemption' in effect and the food additive and its use or intended use conform to the terms of the exemption. 21 U.S.C. § 348(a)(1).

12 21 U.S.C. § 348(b)(1).

13 21 U.S.C. § 348(b)(2)(E).

14 21 U.S.C. § 348(c)(5). The word 'safe', as used in the subsection defining the term 'food additive' (and which includes the definition of GRAS), as well as in the section discussed here (Section 348), 'has reference to the health of man or animal'. 21 U.S.C. § 321(u).

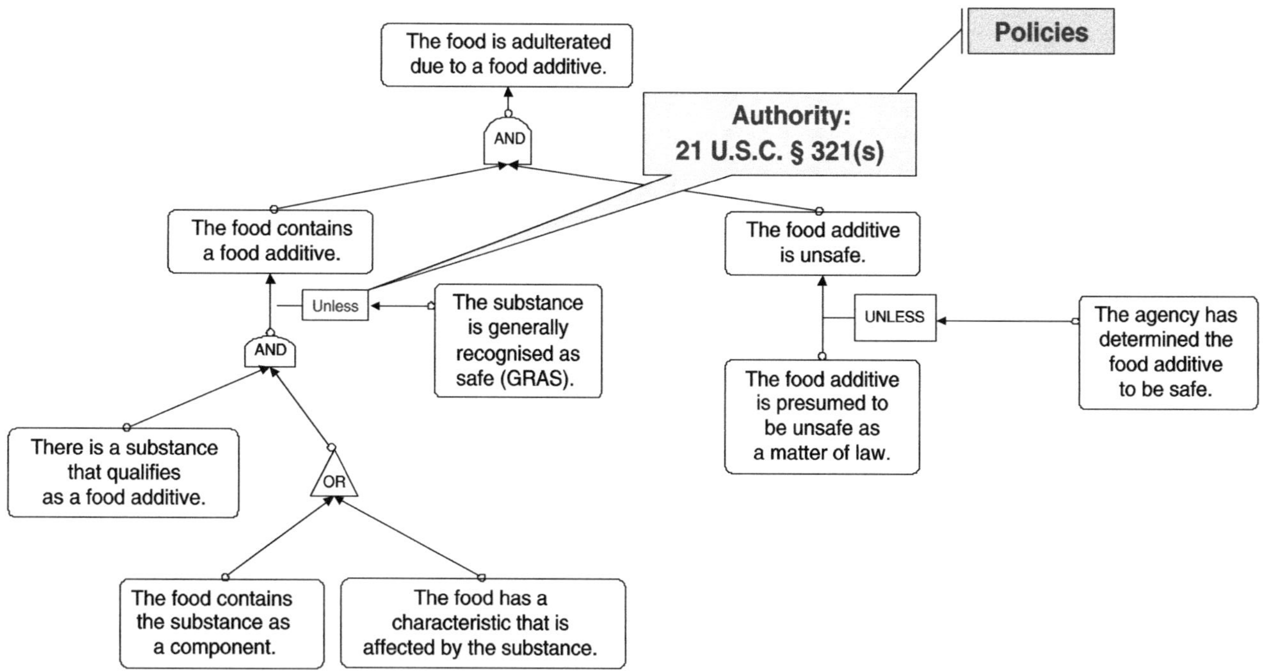
Policies
Authority:
21 U.S.C. § 321(s)
The food is adulterated due to a food additive.
AND
The food contains a food additive.
Unless
The substance is generally recognised as safe (GRAS).
AND
There is a substance that qualifies as a food additive.
OR
The food contains the substance as a component.
The food has a characteristic that is affected by the substance.
The food additive is unsafe.
UNLESS
The agency has determined the food additive to be safe.
The food additive is presumed to be unsafe as a matter of law.

Figure 7.3

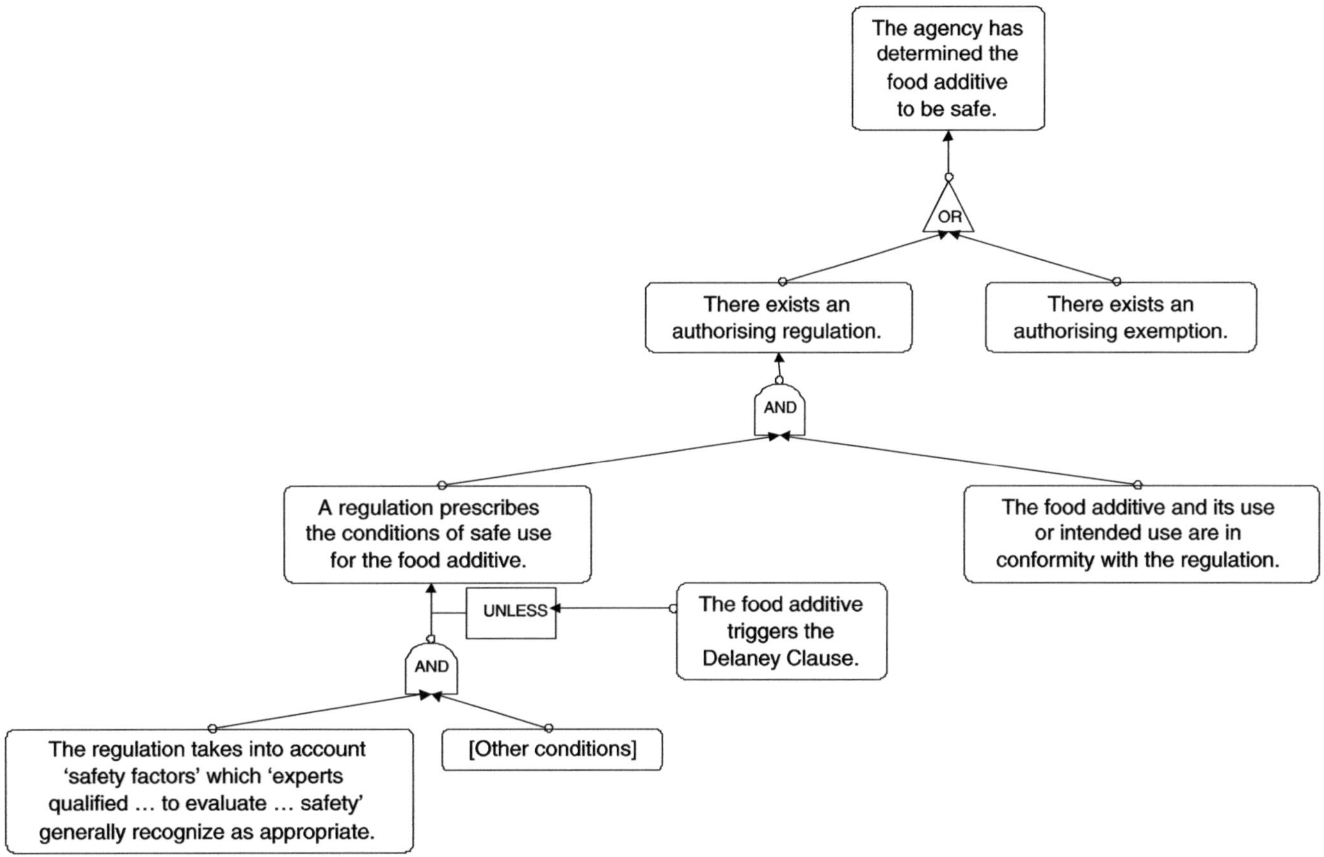
The agency has determined the food additive to be safe.
OR
There exists an authorising regulation.
There exists an authorising exemption.
AND
A regulation prescribes the conditions of safe use for the food additive.
The food additive and its use or intended use are in conformity with the regulation.
UNLESS
The food additive triggers the Delaney Clause.
AND
The regulation takes into account 'safety factors' which 'experts qualified … to evaluate … safety' generally recognize as appropriate.
[Other conditions]

Figure 7.4

- the probable consumption of the additive;[15]
- the cumulative effect of such additive in the diet;[16] and
- 'safety factors which in the opinion of experts qualified by scientific training and experience to evaluate the safety of food additives are generally recognized as appropriate for the use of animal experimentation data'.[17]

This last provision introduces the notion that there are in fact scientific experts 'qualified ... to evaluate the safety of food additives', and that such experts can identify 'safety factors which ... are generally recognized as appropriate' for extrapolating from animal experimentation data to conclusions about safety.

It is important to note that the factfinder making the administrative determinations is not a court, but the Secretary of Health and Human Services (HHS), whose Department includes the FDA.[18] It is likewise the Secretary of HHS who, in the regulation, prescribes 'the conditions under which such additive may be safely used',[19] and who therefore justifies issuing the regulation by finding that the use under such conditions is safe. Congress, however, prescribes the required finding of safety:

> No such regulation shall issue if a fair evaluation of the data before the Secretary . . . fails to establish that the proposed use of the food additive, under the conditions of use to be specified in the regulation, will be safe.[20]

Some implicit subsidiary rules are that the evidentiary basis for this finding must be in 'the data before the Secretary' and that there can be no warrant unless the finding is based on a 'fair evaluation' of that data.

The above provisions do not impose clear substantive constraints on the agency's use of discretion to decide what is in fact 'safe'. The agency's administrative elaboration of these statutory rules is discussed below. However, the statute itself adds an important rule through the so-called 'Delaney Clause' for food additives.[21] Figure 7.4 shows the logical connection of the Delaney Clause to factfinding about food additives. With some exceptions, the Delaney Clause provides that 'no additive shall be deemed to be safe if it is found to induce cancer when ingested by man or animal, or if it is found, after tests which are appropriate for the evaluation of the safety of food additives, to induce cancer in man or animal'.[22] The Delaney Clause imposes substantive constraints on the agency's discretion to determine that a food additive is 'safe', and here Congress is not deferring to

15 21 U.S.C. § 348(c)(5)(A). This includes the consumption 'of any substance formed in or on food because of the use of the additive'. *Ibid.*

16 21 U.S.C. § 348(c)(5)(B). This includes 'taking into account any chemically or pharmacologically related substance or substances in such diet'. *Ibid.*

17 21 U.S.C. § 348(c)(5)(C).

18 21 U.S.C. § 321(d).

19 21 U.S.C. § 348(c)(1).

20 21 U.S.C. § 348(c)(3).

21 There are three 'Delaney Clauses', which are found at 21 U.S.C. § 348(c)(3)(A) (food additives); 21 U.S.C. § 379e(b)(5)(B) (colour additives); and 21 U.S.C. § 360b(d)(1)(I) (new animal drugs).

22 21 U.S.C. § 348(c)(3)(A).

the opinions of experts 'qualified to evaluate the safety of food additives'. Congress is itself prescribing a risk management rule for food additives. Unfortunately, this chapter cannot explore further the logical structure within the Delaney Clause provisions.

3.1.2 *Adulteration due to a pesticide chemical residue*

Prior to enactment of the Food Quality Protection Act of 1996 (FQPA),[23] pesticide residues in food were regulated as food additives. With enactment of the FQPA, however, 'pesticide chemical residues' became a distinct regulatory category under the FFDCA. A diachronic default-logic model would show very different implication trees governing pesticide residues, before and after enactment of the FQPA. For example, a major change is that pesticide residues are no longer subject to the Delaney Clause for food additives, and determinations of safety given evidence of carcinogenicity may be warranted very differently for pesticide residues than they are for food additives.

The statute defines a 'pesticide chemical residue' as a residue, in or on a raw agricultural commodity or processed food, of a pesticide chemical or any other 'added substance' that is present 'primarily as a result of the metabolism or other degradation of a pesticide chemical'.[24] The statute uses a presumption similar to that adopted for food additives, and deems a food to be adulterated 'if it bears or contains a pesticide chemical residue that is unsafe'.[25] Figure 7.5 shows this statutory logic for pesticide residues. A pesticide residue is 'deemed unsafe' for regulatory purposes 'unless a tolerance for [its use] on such food is in effect . . . and the quantity of the residue is within the limits of the tolerance'.[26] A tolerance prescribes a ceiling quantity of residue, below which the food is not considered adulterated by reason of bearing or containing that residue.[27]

The United States Environmental Protection Agency (EPA) has general jurisdiction over the regulation of pesticides, and the EPA is the presiding authority and administrative factfinder in rulemaking proceedings about pesticide residues in food.[28] In order to establish a tolerance, the Administrator of EPA must determine that 'the tolerance is safe'.[29] The term 'safe' in this context means that

> the Administrator has determined that there is a reasonable certainty that no harm will result from aggregate exposure to the pesticide chemical residue,

23 Pub. L. No. 104–170, 110 Stat. 1489 (1996).

24 21 U.S.C. § 321(q)(2). The Administrator of EPA can also 'except' substances from the definition of 'pesticide chemical' or 'pesticide chemical residue' under certain conditions. 21 U.S.C. § 321(q)(3).

25 21 U.S.C. § 342(a)(2)(B).

26 21 U.S.C. § 346a(a)(1)(A). In parallel with food additives, an alternative regulatory means of categorising pesticide residues as safe is by issuing an exemption. 21 U.S.C. § 346a(a)(1)(B).

27 See 21 U.S.C. § 346a(a)(4).

28 See 21 U.S.C. § 321(hh), 346a(b).

29 21 U.S.C. § 346a(b)(2)(A)(i). The statutory prescription tying administrative action to factfinding about safety is particularly clear: '[t]he Administrator [of EPA] may establish or leave in effect a tolerance for a pesticide chemical residue in or on a food only if the Administrator determines that the tolerance is safe. The Administrator shall modify or revoke a tolerance if the Administrator determines it is not safe'. *Ibid.*

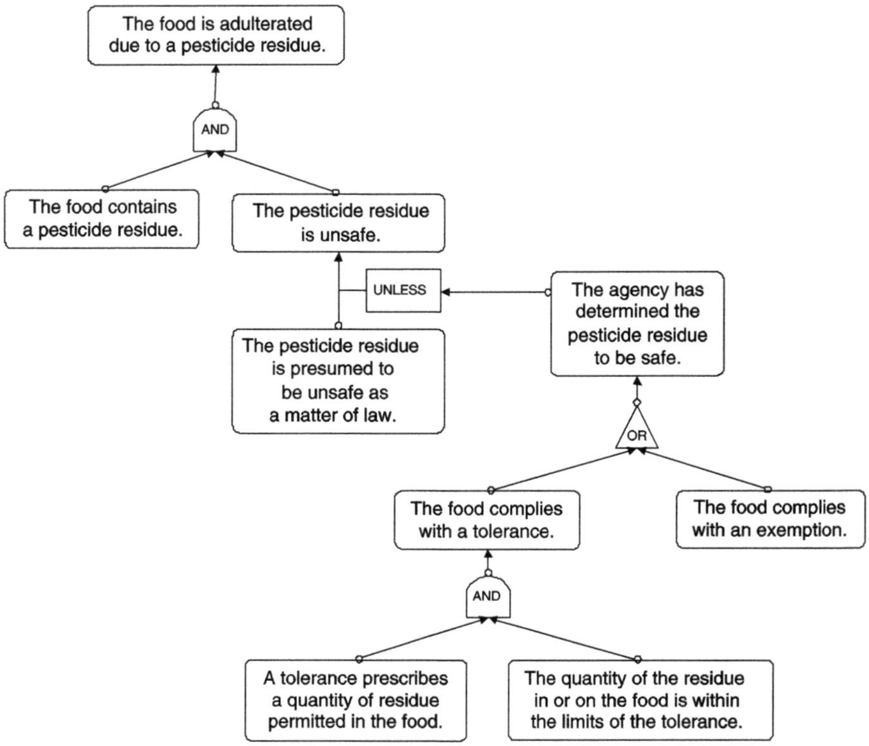

Figure 7.5

> including all anticipated dietary exposures and all other exposures for which there is reliable information.[30]

From the perspective of default logic, this statutory provision contains both an issue of fact to be determined ('that no harm will result . . .') and an evidentiary standard of proof ('that there is a reasonable certainty . . .'). The factfinder is the agency, and the burden of persuasion on this issue is effectively on the party petitioning the agency to set the tolerance. Unless the EPA makes a positive finding of safety, it cannot establish a tolerance and the pesticide residues will be deemed unsafe. Moreover, the statute creates important issues of fact for the EPA to determine, such as which dietary exposures are 'anticipated' and which exposure information is 'reliable'.

The statute prescribes a long list of relevant factors that the EPA must take into account in establishing a tolerance.[31] Some of these require consideration of what information is in fact available – information, for example, on dietary consumption

30 21 U.S.C. § 346a(b)(2)(A)(ii).
31 See 21 U.S.C. § 346a(b)(2)(D).

patterns and aggregate exposure levels, on the cumulative effects of substances that have common mechanisms of toxicity, and on the variability of sensitivity of major identifiable subgroups of consumers.[32] But the EPA must also consider the validity, reliability and completeness of the available data,[33] and may require petitioners to generate additional data. The EPA must also consider 'the nature of any toxic effect shown to be caused' by the pesticide residue.[34] Finally, in parallel with the provisions on food additives administered by the FDA, the EPA must consider 'safety factors which in the opinion of experts qualified by scientific training and experience to evaluate the safety of food additives are generally recognized as appropriate for the use of animal experimentation data'.[35]

In addition, Congress requires the EPA, when setting tolerances, to take special care with regard to infants and children. The EPA must assess the risk of pesticide residues based on available information about consumption patterns among infants and children, about the special susceptibility of infants and children (including *in utero* exposure), and about the cumulative effects on them of such residues and other substances that have a common mechanism of toxicity.[36] The agency 'shall ensure that there is a reasonable certainty that no harm will result to infants and children from aggregate exposure to the pesticide chemical residue'.[37] In the case of effects that exhibit a safe threshold of exposure, the agency must apply 'an additional tenfold margin of safety' in order to protect infants and children adequately, and 'may use a different margin of safety ... only if, on the basis of reliable data, such margin will be safe for infants and children'.[38] Figure 7.6 diagrams these statutory rules. These provisions establish important evidentiary rules about relevant and necessary evidence, procedural rules about additional findings that must be made, and substantive rules governing the setting of tolerances.

The statute also recognizes that there are pesticides and harms for which the EPA is not able to identify a safe tolerance due to a phenomenon called a 'nonthreshold effect'.[39] There are certain types of harm, such as carcinogenicity, for which current scientific theories and paradigms of experimental method do not allow us to identify an exposure threshold below which the pesticide residue is 'safe'. Such pesticides are often regulated differently than those that exhibit safety thresholds. As mentioned above, carcinogenic food additives are governed by a Delaney Clause. The FQPA took pesticide residues out of the category of food additives, however, and as a result residues of carcinogenic pesticides are now also governed by the rule

32 See 21 U.S.C. § 346a(b)(2)(D)(iii)–(vii).
33 See 21 U.S.C. § 346a(b)(2)(D)(i) and (viii).
34 See 21 U.S.C. § 346a(b)(2)(D)(ii).
35 See 21 U.S.C. § 346a(b)(2)(D)(ix).
36 See 21 U.S.C. § 346a(b)(2)(C)(i).
37 21 U.S.C. § 346a(b)(2)(C)(ii)(I).
38 21 U.S.C. § 346a(b)(2)(C)(ii)(II).
39 21 U.S.C. § 346a(b)(2)(B)(i)(I). This condition of having a 'nonthreshold effect' is that 'the Administrator is not able to identify a level of exposure to the residue at which the residue will not cause or contribute to a known or anticipated harm to human health'. *Ibid.*

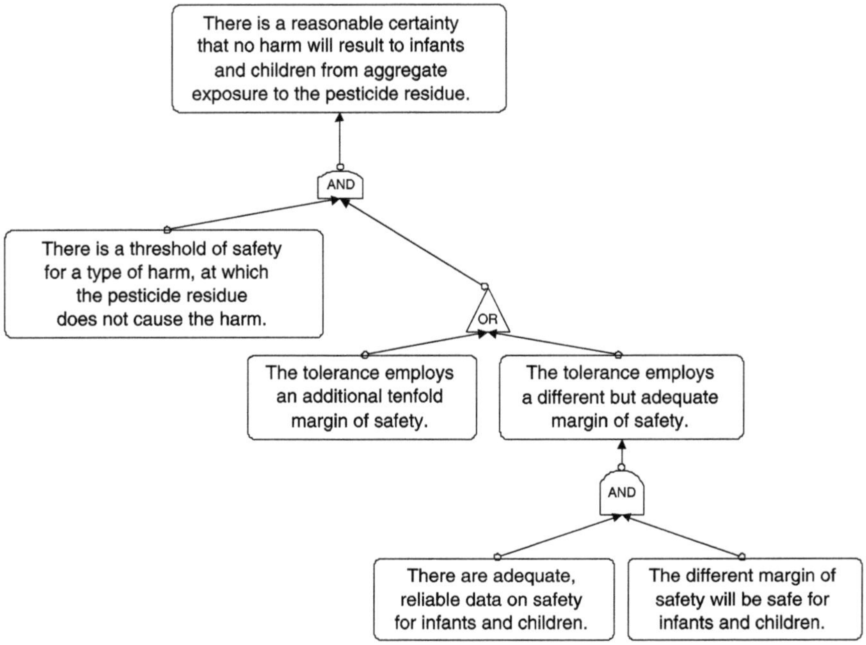

Figure 7.6

of 'a reasonable certainty that no harm will result'.[40] The House Report accompanying the FQPA shows that Congress expected the EPA to make such a finding when the lifetime risk of cancer is no greater than one in one million, calculated using conservative assumptions in risk assessment.[41]

Taken as a whole, the Food Quality Protection Act of 1996 established an extensive and complicated set of rules for establishing tolerances. Although some of the regulatory rule structure was already in place (such as the practice of quantitative risk assessment), and although the agency has made considerable effort to

40 21 U.S.C. §346a (b)(2)(A)(ii); see H.R. Rep. No. 104–669, pt. 2, at 36 (1996). Under the prior law, pesticide residues that concentrated in food processing triggered the regulatory provisions for food additives, including the food additive Delaney Clause. See *Les v Reilly*, 968 F.2d 985, 985 (9th Cir. 1992), *cert. denied sub nom.* National Agric. Chem. Ass'n v. Les, 507 U.S. 950 (1993).

41 H.R. Rep. No. 104–669, pt. 2, at 41 (1996), which states: 'In the case of a nonthreshold effect which can be assessed through quantitative risk assessment, such as a cancer effect, the Committee expects, based on its understanding of current EPA practice, that a tolerance will be considered to provide a "reasonable certainty of no harm" if any increase in lifetime risk, based on quantitative risk assessment using conservative assumptions, will be no greater than "negligible". It is the Committee's understanding that, under current EPA practice, . . . EPA interprets a negligible risk to be a one-in-a-million lifetime risk. The Committee expects the Administrator to continue to follow this interpretation.' See Cross 1997: 1164–5. This quantitative level of protection of one in one million is precisely the risk that the FDA had announced to be negligible or *de minimis*. Eg, *Public Citizen v Bowen*, 833 F.2d 364 (D.C. Cir. 1987). The FQPA also contains risk-management rules for 'eligible' nonthreshold pesticides that are conditioned on certain findings. See 21 U.S.C. § 346a (b)(2)(B); Smart 1998: 337–8.

elaborate administrative rules for the new provisions (such as those about protecting infants and children), the magnitude of the task ensures that progress will be slow.[42] The next section of this chapter extends the default-logic model beyond the statutory provisions, by incorporating a number of rules that the agencies have established.

3.2 The administrative elaboration of rules and 'science policies'

This chapter cannot summarise the complete rule structures that the FDA has elaborated for issuing regulations for food additives and that the EPA has elaborated for establishing tolerances for pesticide residues. The complexities of the statutory provisions ensure that the administrative extensions will be at least as complex as the statutory portion of the implication tree. The goal here is to discuss certain aspects of those extended trees that help us study the interaction between science and regulation, and in particular the interface between risk assessment and risk management. The discussion will therefore focus on the rules governing food additives and pesticides that exhibit thresholds of safety in animal studies, because those rules are older, more easily understood, and generally less controversial than safety testing for carcinogens.

3.2.1 Safety factors for food additives exhibiting safe thresholds

As mentioned above and as shown in Figure 7.4, the statutory scheme for food additives requires the FDA, when it issues a regulation prescribing the safe use of a food additive, to take 'safety factors' into account. As illustrated below, a safety factor is a quantitative factor used to create a margin of safety between the lowest level of concern in toxicological data and the level of human exposure to be allowed under a regulation. The statute requires the FDA to take into account those safety factors that 'experts qualified to evaluate safety' generally recognise as appropriate.

The shaded propositional shapes in the implication tree in Figure 7.7 capture the administrative rules that the FDA has elaborated in order to implement this statutory requirement. Such rules are binding federal law, but they were adopted under administrative authority granted to the agency by Congress, not enacted directly by Congress itself. Section 170.3(i) of Title 21 of the Code of Federal Regulations contains the FDA's definition of 'safe', as the word is used for food additives. Since the statute presumes that there are 'experts qualified to evaluate safety', the FDA defines 'safe' as meaning that there is 'a reasonable certainty in the minds' of those experts that the substance under consideration 'is not harmful under the intended conditions of use'.[43] Section 170.22 of the same title establishes the administrative

42 See, eg, the list of science policy issues and guidance documents available at: <http://www.epa.gov/pesticides/trac/science/#10-fold> (last visited 30 September 2005).

43 21 C.F.R. § 170.3(i). All citations in this paper to the Code of Federal Regulations are current through 27 September 2005.

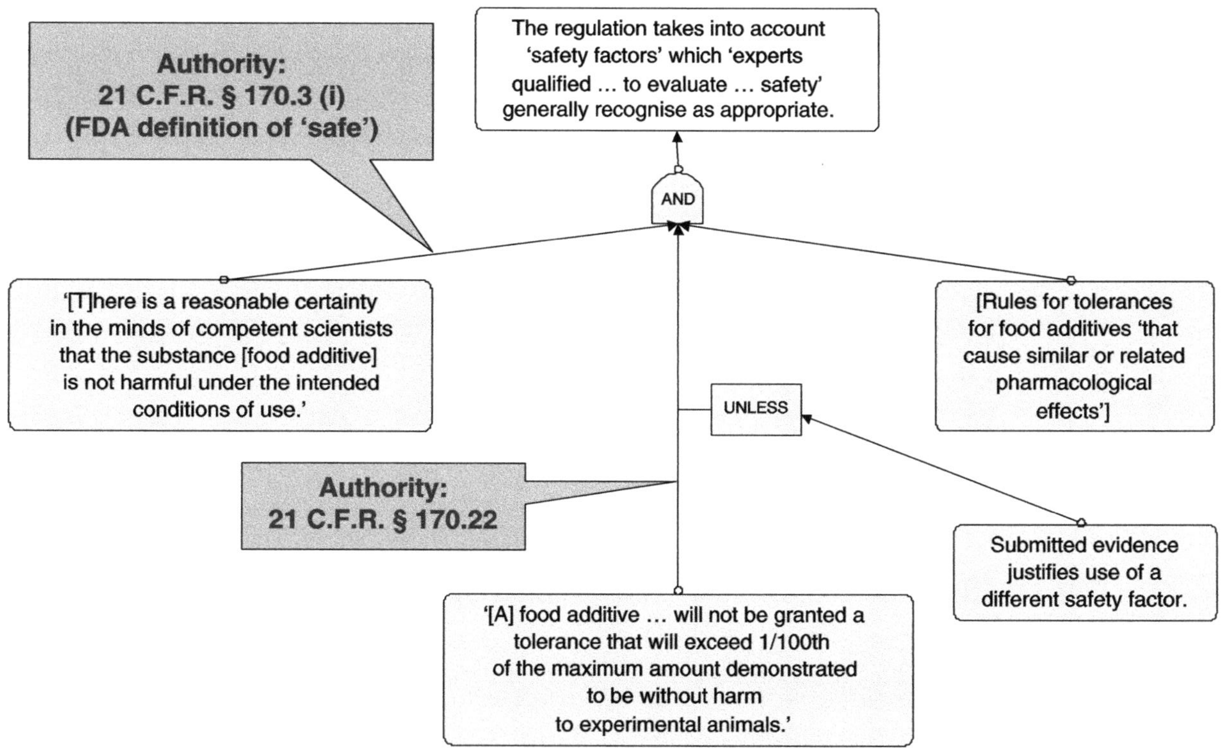
Authority:
21 C.F.R. § 170.3 (i)
(FDA definition of 'safe')
The regulation takes into account 'safety factors' which 'experts qualified … to evaluate … safety' generally recognise as appropriate.
AND
'[T]here is a reasonable certainty in the minds of competent scientists that the substance [food additive] is not harmful under the intended conditions of use.'
[Rules for tolerances for food additives 'that cause similar or related pharmacological effects']
UNLESS
Authority:
21 C.F.R. § 170.22
Submitted evidence justifies use of a different safety factor.
'[A] food additive … will not be granted a tolerance that will exceed 1/100th of the maximum amount demonstrated to be without harm to experimental animals.'

Figure 7.7

presumption that a safety factor of 100 is 'safe', unless the submitted evidence justifies use of a different safety factor.[44] Operationally, this means that when toxicity tests establish a 'maximum amount demonstrated to be without harm to experimental animals', then this dose is divided by 100, and that quotient is presumed to be a dose posing no harm to humans.

3.2.2 *Safety factors for residues of pesticides exhibiting safe thresholds*

By the time that Congress enacted the FQPA in 1996, the EPA had for nearly two decades employed a risk assessment methodology that Congress could reference.[45] Congress could also draw upon the FDA's administrative rules and practice elaborated for regulating food additives.[46] Congress used wording to define 'safe' for pesticide tolerances that is very similar to the wording that the FDA uses to define 'safe' in its food additive regulations: 'a reasonable certainty that no harm will result'.[47]

In approving tolerances generally, the EPA has developed an approach using a 'reference dose' (RfD).[48] The EPA calculates the RfD from the dose at which no adverse effects have been observed (the 'NOAEL') in animal toxicological studies, divided by all applicable safety or uncertainty factors. Typically, the safety factor used has been 100 – one factor of 10 'to account for uncertainties inherent in the extrapolation from laboratory animal data to humans' and another factor of 10 'for variations in sensitivity among members of the human population as well as other unknowns'.[49] This safety factor of 100 is the same factor traditionally used by the FDA for food additives (see above). Once safety factors have been applied to the NOAEL, therefore, the EPA presumes that the resulting RfD is a safe dose for humans – that is, dietary exposures lower than the RfD 'are generally not of concern' to the EPA.[50] Figure 7.8 shows the implication tree for this reasoning.

In adding an additional margin of safety for infants and children, the FQPA

44 21 C.F.R. § 170.22.

45 See, eg, the discussions of the EPA's risk assessment policies throughout National Research Council, Risk Assessment in the Federal Government: Managing the Process (1983) (the 'red book'); National Research Council, Science and Judgment in Risk Assessment (1994) (the 'blue book'). The EPA has more recently issued its revised 'Guidelines for Carcinogen Risk Assessment', EPA/630/P-03/001B, 25 March 2005.

46 The FQPA standard appears to track the FDA's administrative definition of 'safe' for food additives. See Cross 1997: 1162–3.

47 Compare 21 U.S.C. § 346a(b)(2)(A)(ii) with 21 C.F.R. § 170.3(i).

48 Environmental Protection Agency, 'Imidacloprid; Order Denying Objections to Issuance of Tolerance', 69 Federal Register 30,042, 30,044, 26 May 2004 (final order) (hereinafter 'Imidacloprid'). Cf. Environmental Protection Agency, Reference Dose/Reference Concentration (RfD/RfC) Technical Panel, 'A Review of the Reference Dose and Reference Concentration Processes', EPA/630/P-02/002F, December 2002 (final report).

49 'Imidacloprid', *supra* note 48, at 30,044.

50 *Ibid.*

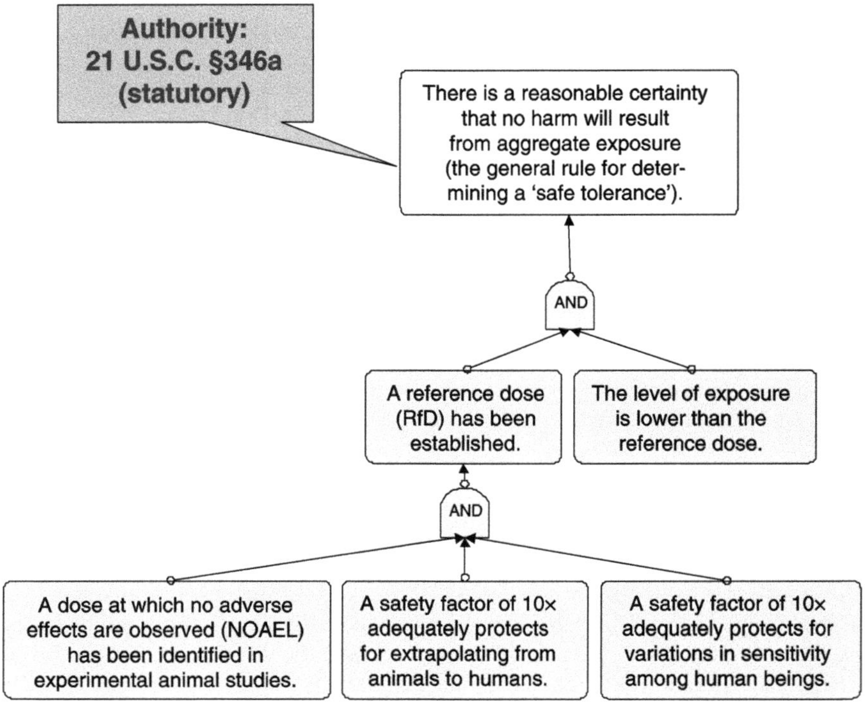

Figure 7.8

established a statutory presumption that an additional safety factor of 10 would be adequately protective, unless there are adequate, reliable data that establish that a different margin of safety is adequate.[51] An EPA order denying objections to issuing or re-establishing a tolerance for residues of the pesticide imidacloprid on blueberries illustrates both the kinds of rules that might elaborate this requirement further, and the fact that agencies can extend implication trees through case-specific factfinding as well as through generic rule making. The Natural Resources Defense Council (NRDC) had filed objections to tolerances for various pesticides – objections focusing on the potential risks posed to farm children and opposing the EPA's decision to use an additional margin of safety for infants and children that was different than the *ten*fold default value established by the FQPA. The EPA denied the validity of the NRDC's objections, and defended the use of a *three*fold 'children's safety factor', instead of an additional factor of 10.[52] The EPA had required the submission of a developmental neurotoxicity study, but decided after

51 See 21 U.S.C. § 346a(b)(2)(C)(ii)(II); 'Imidacloprid', above, note 48, at 30,044–5. For a discussion of the EPA practice regarding the FQPA safety factor, see Thayer and Houlihan 2004: 284–90.

52 'Imidacloprid', above, note 48, at 30,066.

reviewing the results that there were 'no residual uncertainties for pre-/post-natal toxicity' in the study.[53]

Moreover, the agency decided that a threefold safety factor is adequate to protect infants and children despite the lack of a NOAEL in an acute neurotoxicity study in rats.[54] Instead of requiring an acute study that identified a NOAEL (a dose with no observed adverse effect), the EPA decided to divide the *lowest* dose in the study at which adverse effects *were* observed (a 'LOAEL') by a factor of three as a method of estimating 'a projected NOAEL that is unlikely to be higher than the actual NOAEL'.[55] Against the NRDC's objections to this reliance on a threefold safety factor applied to the LOAEL, instead of to a NOAEL, the EPA asserted that '[w]hether a LOAEL provides a sufficient basis for a reasonable certainty of no harm finding is a question of scientific fact'.[56] The EPA gave three reasons for concluding that a safety factor of three applied to a LOAEL was adequate:[57]

1 The LOAEL used is comparable to LOAELs in other studies.
2 The LOAEL divided by 3 (the estimate of the missing NOAEL) is comparable to the NOAEL for the same effect (decreased motor activity) found in the developmental neurotoxicity study.
3 The study containing the LOAEL showed 'a good dose response which resulted in minimal effects on motor activity and locomotor activity at the LOAEL'.

Figure 7.9 displays possible rules implicit in this line of reasoning.

Although the EPA gave these three reasons for its 'high confidence' in finding a safe tolerance in the imidacloprid case,[58] the agency did not announce them as science policy rules for future cases, let alone conduct generic rule making to establish them as binding law. Instead, the agency stated that whether they are sufficient reasons for inferring safety is 'a question of scientific fact'. How such a characterization is likely to fare on judicial review is discussed in the next section. Before moving to that topic, however, it is important to notice several aspects of the logic in Figure 7.9. The default-logic analysis has arrived at a level of the implication tree where reasoning is generalisation-based rather than rule-based. Moreover, we have arrived at reasoning based on evidence specific to the imidacloprid tolerance proceeding. Finally, we can meaningfully ask about each of the three propositions at the lowest level of Figure 7.9:

53 *Ibid.* at 30,057. The NOAEL for the developmental neurotoxicity study (20 mg per kg body weight per day) was higher than the NOAELs previously identified (which ranged from 5.7 to 10 mg per kg per day). *Ibid.* This means that the EPA expected a tolerance based on the lower NOAELs also to be protective against developmental neurotoxicity. In assessing chronic risk, the EPA set the RfD using the NOAEL of 5.7 mg per kg per day. *Ibid.*, at 30,067.

54 *Ibid.*, at 30,057, 30,066–7.

55 *Ibid.*, at 30,066.

56 *Ibid.*

57 *Ibid.*, at 30,067. 'The acute toxicity endpoint was based upon a LOAEL of 42 mg/kg/day from an acute neurotoxicity study in rats'. *Ibid.* The estimate for the missing NOAEL was therefore 42 / 3 = 14 mg/kg/day. *Ibid.*

58 *Ibid.*, at 30,067.

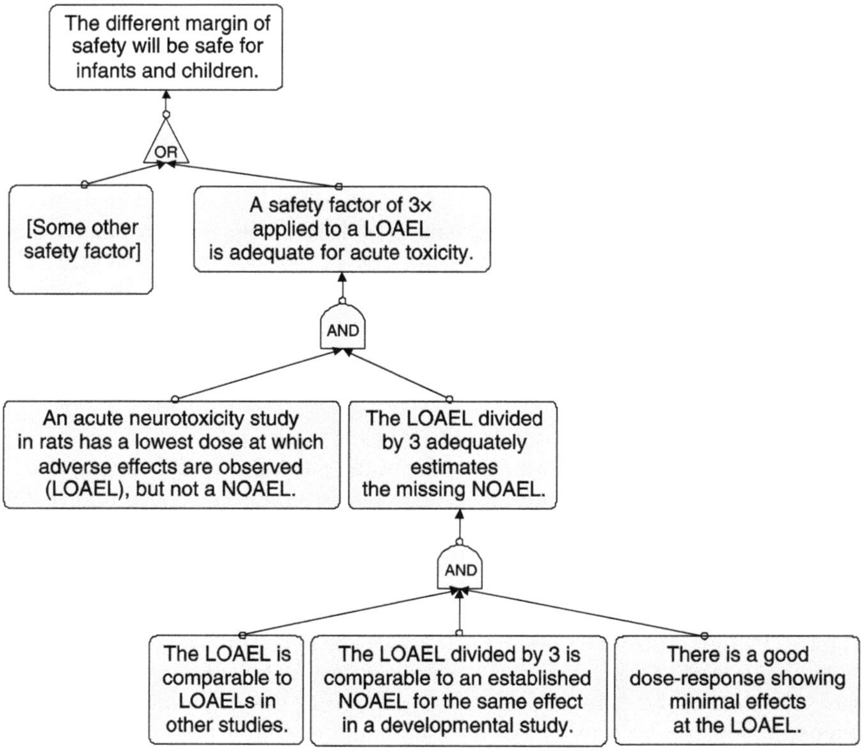

Figure 7.9

- Is it a scientific proposition or a policy statement?
- Is it properly considered part of risk assessment or part of risk management?
- Is it a prediction or a precautionary decision?

When the reasoning supporting the factfinding is analysed to the level of the evidence, it may no longer be clear why we would use such distinctions as 'science' v 'policy' and 'risk assessment' v 'risk management'. Indeed, perhaps we should wonder whether the distinctions themselves were ever clear. The concluding section of the chapter returns to this topic.

3.3 Judicial review of administrative proceedings

In the case of controversy as to the validity of an order issuing a regulation, generally any person who is adversely affected may petition a court for judicial review.[59] The reviewing court, however, is not empowered to make findings of fact *de novo*, based on its own evaluation of the evidence. It is typical, under United States law governing judicial review of agency determinations, that the court must defer to the

59 Eg, 21 U.S.C. § 348(g)(1).

agency's determinations of fact, provided there is some reasonable basis for the agency's finding.[60] In particular, with regard to judicial review of regulations concerning food additives, the statute prescribes that '[t]he findings of the Secretary with respect to questions of fact shall be sustained [by the court] if [they are] based upon a fair evaluation of the entire record' in the administrative proceedings.[61] The court is not empowered to receive new evidence (although under unusual circumstances it may order the agency to take such additional evidence[62]), and it has the power (only) 'to affirm or set aside the order complained of in whole or in part'.[63] As a general matter, therefore, risk assessment determinations are within the authority of the agency, not of the court. The court's authority is merely to set aside the agency's *action* if the court determines that the requirements for antecedent findings and justifying conditions are not satisfied.[64]

Besides receiving judicial deference on its findings of fact, the administrative agency generally has the authority to interpret the statute that it administers, by elaborating new substantive, procedural and evidentiary rules for implementing that statute. This is a complicated area of administrative law governed by the United States Supreme Court's case law under *Chevron*.[65] A point of critical importance in understanding the default logic of regulation is that an administrative agency often has discretion *either* to elaborate new *rules* governing its own authority *or* merely to regulate through *factfinding* when it applies the statutory rules to the evidence in the particular case. In the case of EPA regulation of pesticide residues in food, if the agency chooses to proceed by generic rule making, then the agency itself is both the factfinder and the rule maker, and the reviewing court must defer to it. If, however, the EPA chooses to forego generic rule making and regulates merely by issuing or denying tolerances for specific pesticides, then the agency can make its findings of safety in accord with informal administrative policies and still receive deference from a reviewing court. In the imidacloprid proceeding, the EPA emphasised that it considered its reasoning on the adequacy of the additional threefold 'children's safety factor' to be 'a question of scientific fact', and therefore entitled to great deference by the court. It is a fine line, however, between rule elaboration and scientific factfinding in the lower, generalisation-based inferences. Any court reviewing the adequacy of the evidentiary support for the lowest level of propositions in Figure 7.9 will certainly defer to the EPA's expert assessment,

60 See, eg, the Administrative Procedure Act, 5 U.S.C. § 706(2)(A) (providing that reviewing courts shall 'hold unlawful and set aside agency action, findings, and conclusions found to be . . . arbitrary, capricious, an abuse of discretion, or otherwise not in accordance with law'). Reviewing courts show great deference to administrative findings of fact about risk, especially when those findings are within the agency's expertise and are made on 'the frontiers of scientific knowledge'. Eg, *Environmental Defense Fund v EPA*, 548 F.2d 998 (D.C.Cir. 1977), *cert. denied sub nom.* Velsicol Chem. Corp. v. EPA, 431 U.S. 925 (1977).

61 See 21 U.S.C. § 348(f)(1)–(2), (g)(2).

62 21 U.S.C. § 348(g)(4) (authorising the court to so order 'if such evidence is material and there were reasonable grounds for failure to adduce such evidence in the proceedings below' before the agency).

63 21 U.S.C. § 348(g)(2).

64 From the logical perspective, the reviewing court has its own implication trees of required findings to justify its actions. The legal rules governing judicial action are separate and distinct from the legal rules governing administrative action.

65 *Chevron, U.S.A., Inc. v Natural Res. Def. Council*, 467 U.S. 837 (1984).

whether the court considers the agency to be engaged in factfinding or in a 'soft' form of rule making. In situations similar to this one, the agency has an incentive to evaluate the terminal propositions of the implication tree by means of policies guiding its own factfinding practice, instead of by more explicit rule making, because the agency retains maximum flexibility in future cases while achieving great deference from reviewing courts.[66]

4 CONCLUSIONS

The default-logic model enables us to understand, and to depict graphically and transparently, the functions of rules, policies and evidence in warranting a finding of fact in law. A synchronic model captures in a single implication tree every proposition that is relevant in warranting a finding. It therefore enables us to compare different regulatory programmes, involving different governmental institutions, regardless of the jurisdiction. The diachronic dimension of the default-logic model allows us to study, in a formal way, the evolution of regulatory warrant over time. This modelling of change allows us to investigate the causal dynamic among legislative institutions, executive agencies, and courts, as well as their interactions with scientific bodies, regulated constituencies, and consumer or environmental groups. A default-logic model for a finding synthesises the legal rules and the generalisation-based evaluation of the evidence into a single body of reasoning or warrant.

Within the United States regulatory system for food safety, the different implication trees for food additives and for pesticide chemical residues display similarities and dissimilarities. They show different levels of statutory rule making by Congress, or Congress's attempts to bind administrative discretion. In addition, those implication trees display different levels and methods of rule making by the two agencies involved – the FDA for food additives and the EPA for pesticide residues. The net result is different degrees of rule-based reasoning in the two trees, as distinct from case-by-case, generalisation-based reasoning about the evidence. Such differences in reasoning using the two trees may also influence the degree of effective judicial oversight of regulation. In general, the more rule-based reasoning there is within the warrant structure for factfinding, the more 'law there is to apply', and the more likely it is that a court can supervise an agency's reasonableness, consistency and transparency.

The models also allow us to analyse the synchronic and diachronic roles of scientists, scientific reasoning and scientific institutions within legal factfinding, with a particular focus on the interaction between risk assessment and risk management.

66 In other situations, the agency's options may be statutorily limited either to administrative rulemaking or to going to court for enforcement proceedings. For example, if the FDA petitions a court to seize particular articles of food, then the court will be the factfinder and the government must prove its case by a preponderance of the evidence. Eg, *United States v 29 Cartons . . . An Article of Food, Etc.*, 987 F.2d 33, 35 (1st Cir. 1993). Even if the district court judge in the latter situation is likely to be persuaded by the agency's position on the factual issues, nevertheless the factfinding process is no longer under the agency's own control. This creates an incentive for an agency to proceed by rulemaking, which makes the related factfinding process internal to the agency.

In governmental factfinding processes, scientific reasoning is always embedded within practical and prudential reasoning. If, for example, the governmental action to be justified is an instance of risk management (such as seizing a potentially harmful shipment of food), then one antecedent finding of fact is normally a finding of risk, which is in turn warranted by a risk assessment. The pressure exerted by the rule of law in the direction of transparent reasoning also operates on the role of scientific reasoning in warranting findings about risk. The implication tree extending into the risk assessment will make that reasoning more transparent.

A synchronic model of warrant for risk assessment may also show the way out of some conceptual quandaries about the interplay between science and regulatory policy. As the reasoning unfolds into ever-lower levels of the implication tree, we arrive at the kinds of concrete propositions at the bottom of Figure 7.9. At that level of elaboration, the content of each distinct proposition, as well as the evidence relevant to proving it true or false, allows principled solutions to such questions as:

- What procedures and burdens for producing evidence are appropriate?
- What kinds of evidence are relevant or irrelevant, or should be excluded from consideration for policy reasons?
- What amounts of which kinds of evidence are minimally necessary to warrant a finding?
- What amounts and kinds of evidence are sufficient to satisfy the appropriate standard of proof?
- Who is the appropriate factfinder?

Principled answers to such questions are often achievable for propositions with precise content, when they are not achievable for highly abstract propositions. Perhaps debating 'high-level' questions using such abstract concepts as 'risk assessment' and 'risk management', or even 'science' and 'policy', merely obfuscates principled solutions to the real underlying questions. It might be far more useful to model the reasoning down the tree as far as possible, and then to decide which propositions at the ends of the branches are best decided by scientists alone, by regulators alone, or by hybrid factfinding bodies designed specifically to decide particular types of propositions.

At a minimum, a default-reasoning model for factfinding about risk enables us to describe and compare the roles of scientists within different regulatory programmes. For example, different programmes might elaborate rules about science policies very differently, and the rule/evidence interface may occur at different levels of the reasoning. For example, a synchronic model will identify the mix of legal rules, generalisations and presumptions that are functioning in the risk assessment, depending on the content of the proposition at issue. A diachronic model may show the evolution of rule-based risk assessment and of generalisation-based risk assessment, as well as the interplay between risk assessment and risk management, and the interplay among legal institutions and scientific bodies (such as advisory committees). Such studies may be useful in evaluating the design of agencies such as the European Food Safety Authority – an independent agency that nominally has risk assessment authority only, without risk management authority.[67] There is also the important dynamic between domestic regulatory institutions and international scientific and regulatory bodies.

Finally, the default-logic model for food safety regulation in the United States suggests a very general comment about the Precautionary Principle. It is best to view the Precautionary Principle *not* as a positive *rule within* any legal implication tree, but rather as a high-level *policy* to use both in *elaborating rules* and in *applying those rules* in factfinding. Rather than being a propositional element within implication trees, the Precautionary Principle is a high-level policy that all decision makers should pursue in making decisions throughout the trees. This insight is consistent with the suggestion above that it is more productive to address concrete questions within the context of implication trees, than to debate abstract issues. Many debates over the Precautionary Principle may dissolve once we address questions that have more precise logical content. And a more informative Precautionary Principle may evolve from analyses of such concrete propositions.[68] In any case, success is more likely with the kind of transparent analysis provided by the default-reasoning model of factfinding.

67 See European Food Safety Authority, 'Legal Foundation', <http://www.efsa.eu.int/about_efsa/legislation/catindex_en.html> (last visited on 30 September 2005).

68 For discussion of an evolutionary approach to elaborating the Precautionary Principle, see Hickey and Walker 1995: 423.

BIBLIOGRAPHY

Cross, F.B. (1997) 'The consequences of consensus: dangerous compromises of the Food Quality Protection Act', *Washington University Law Quarterly* 75: 1155–206.

Hickey, J.E. Jr. and Walker, V.R. (1995) 'Refining the Precautionary Principle in international environmental law', *Virginia Environmental Law Journal* 14: 423–54.

Kyburg, H.E. Jr. and Choh Man Teng (2001) *Uncertain Inference*, Cambridge: Cambridge University Press.

Pollock, J.L. (1990) *Nomic Probability and the Foundations of Induction*, New York/Oxford: Oxford University Press.

Prakken, H. (1997) *Logical Tools for Modelling Legal Argument*, Dordrecht: Kluwer Academic Publishers.

Smart, J. (1998) 'All the stars in the heavens were in the right places: the passage of the Food Quality Protection Act of 1996', *Stanford Environmental Law Journal* 17: 273–351.

Thayer, K. and Houlihan, J. (2004) 'Pesticides, human health, and the Food Quality Protection Act', *William and Mary Environmental Law and Policy Review* 28: 257–312.

Toulmin, S., Rieke, R. and Janik, A. (1984) *An Introduction to Reasoning*, New York: Macmillan Publishing Co., Inc., Second Edition.

Walker, V.R. (2003) 'Epistemic and non-epistemic aspects of the factfinding process in law', *APA Newsletter* 3(1): 132–6; reprinted in (2005) *The Journal of Philosophy, Science and Law* 5, available at <http://www.psljournal.com/archives/all/walkerpaper.cfm>.

Walton, D. (2002) *Legal Argumentation and Evidence*, University Park: Pennsylvania State University Press.

Walton, D.N. (1996) *Argument Schemes for Presumptive Reasoning*, Mahwah: Lawrence Erlbaum Associates.

Part II

National systems on food and biotechnology

Section 2: Case studies on biotechnology regulation

Chapter 8

The French regulatory system on GMOs*

Christine Noiville

In late 2004, the President of the French Commission responsible for the risk assessment of genetically modified organisms (GMOs) posed a vital question:[1] why he asked, should GMOs still be the cause of such deep controversy within France, when they were early subject to a battery of the most stringent legal regulations, requiring in each and every case full assessment of risks posed to public health and the environment? Undoubtedly, the unprecedented political and legal conflicts which GMOs give rise to, as well as continuing doubts about the appropriate legal framework for their regulation, are not issues confined to France. Nonetheless, conflict within France is so intense that the peculiarities of the French case deserve particular attention as an exemplary indication of the problems that GMO regulation (as well as risk regulation in general) pose.

Rather than present French legal framework in all its technical detail,[2] this chapter seeks to highlight two questions: first, which particular shortcomings are evident within the French legal framework, when the matter is one of the regulation of GMOs; and second, how do the political and legal conflicts which the framework gives rise to play out in practice? In particular, the chapter demonstrates how, as a result of deficits within government regulations, courts have become a major arbitrator within the GMO debate; and while this may also be a part of a more general trend that has seen vast tracts of policy making 'judicialised', the extent of judicial activism in relation to GMOs is particularly noteworthy. Courts are thus not only strategically seized upon by the different stakeholders within the GMO political arena but, also, likewise, take their opportunity to fashion GMO regulation in a decisive manner.

I WHY DOES THE FRENCH LEGAL FRAMEWORK UNDERPERFORM?

Once again, given the overall complexities raised by scientific progress, there are clearly no simple legal answers to this broad question. Nonetheless, a part of the answer may be found within French legislation, specifically, in the law of 13 July 1992,

* This chapter was last updated in 2005.

1 M. Fellous, Oral Intervention, *Séminaire de restitution sur les impacts des OGM,* Ministère de la recherche, Paris, December 2004.

2 For a detailed review, see Noiville 2005.

together with its related decrees, which transposed Directives 90/219/EC and 90/220/EC into national law and set up a specific framework to oversee the contained use and deliberate release of GMOs.

On the one hand, these regulations are in line with major EU requirements. A competent authority has been set up to authorise releases or marketing. In most cases (for example, GM crops), responsibility for decision making lies with the Minister of Agriculture. In addition, however, various other Ministers also have complementary competences (the Health Minister for GM human body elements and the Consumer Minister for foodstuffs). Decisions are only taken following risk assessment undertaken by various *ad hoc* scientific commissions. Predominantly, assessment is carried out by the Biomolecular Engineering Commission (*Commission d'étude de la dissémination des produits issus du genie biomoléculaire – CGBM*); occasionally, however, the French Agency for Food Safety (*Agence française de sécurité sanitaire des aliments – AFSSA*) arranges for risk assessment in relation to foodstuffs or phytopharmaceutical products.

On the other hand, however, the French regulatory framework also appears to contain three distinct limitations.

The first limitation relates to the *understanding of risk assessment* found within the administrative culture. Without doubt, the competent French authorities do respect principles of risk assessment: when applications are made for licensing for deliberate release or marketing projects, the authorities do consult with the appropriate scientific commission and projects are reviewed in line with the major recognised risk regulation principles; in particular, the separation of risk assessment and risk management, independence and declaration of interests. However, the practice of assessment fails to meet current needs for two reasons.

First, and highlighting short-term problems, France has still not fully integrated Directive 2001/18/EC within national legislation,[3] even though the aim of this text is to strengthen and broaden the scope of assessment (Noiville and De Sadeleer 2002: 81). This situation is all the more noteworthy since France has recently

3 No more than it has transposed Council Directive 98/81/EC of 26 October 1998 amending Directive 90/219/EEC on the contained use of genetically modified micro-organisms, [1998] *OJ* L330/13. France has been condemned by the European Court of Justice for such a lack of transposition. See, particularly, as far as Directive 2001/18/EC of the European Parliament and of the Council of 12 March 2001 on the Deliberate Release into the Environment of Genetically Modified Organisms, [2001] *OJ* L106/1 is concerned, C-419/03, *Commission v France*, [2004] *OJ* C 228/15. A joint transposition of these two directives (98/81/EC and 2001/18/EC) was due to be debated after the preparation of a parliamentary report (Le Déaut, and Ménard 2005) but the projected bill (*Projet de loi relative aux OGM*, available at: <http://www.senat.fr>) has never been adopted.

As this paper was in press, though, the French government adopted several regulations transposing Directive 2001/18/EC and published in Official Journal n° 67, 20 March 2007:

- *Décret n° 2007–357 du 19 mars 2007 modifiant le décret n° 93–774 du 27 mars 1993 fixant la liste des techniques de modification génétique et les critères de classement des organismes génétiquement modifiés;*
- *Décret n° 2007–358 du 19 mars 2007 relatif à la dissémination volontaire à toute autre fin que la mise sur le marché de produits composés en tout ou partie d'organismes génétiquement modifiés;*
- *Décret n° 2007–359 du 19 mars 2007 relatif à la procédure d'autorisation de mise sur le marché de produits non destinés à l'alimentation composés en tout ou partie d'organismes génétiquement modifiés;*
- *Arrêté du 15 mars 2007 relatif à l'étiquetage des organismes génétiquement modifiés mis à disposition de tiers pour une utilisation confinée à des fins de recherche, de développement ou d'enseignement;*

incorporated the precautionary principle within its Constitution, giving higher normative recognition to the famous principle that obliges public authorities to take pre-emptive action in the case of serious and irreversible harm to the environment and to assess risks, even when scientific uncertainty exists about the degree of potential damage.[4] Second, however, at a substantive level, public funding for research is still not sufficient. Even though the public research purse may not be inexhaustible, too great a degree of reliance is placed on private-sector expertise for GMO assessments.[5] Likewise, although CGBM membership has been renewed, it is still, to a certain extent, made up of molecular biologists whose views on potential risk are preconditioned by the thesis that genetic engineering will allow for a much more precise and controlled construction of organisms and is therefore safer than traditional methods of reproduction.[6]

A second limitation within the regulatory framework is the *particular basis for public action within the GMO field*, with the simple process of risk assessment being falsely perceived to be sufficient for the acceptance of such products (Noiville 2003). Above all, in cases of scientific uncertainty, the notion that 'science' can inform a Minister's decision making is a simple tautology; a tautology all the more intense with regard to GMOs, which often pose questions far beyond the grasp of scientific assessment. In particular, two questions are absent from the underlying philosophy of the French regulatory framework, which should, logically, lie at the heart of all GMO regulation.

First, does the GMO in question offer any advantage and, if so, what is it and who benefits? This question is key, since risk (even minimal risk) is only worthwhile if there is potential gain. Both risk and advantage must be assessed in order to allow for a serious balancing of risk and advantage. AFSSA, for example, has given its

- *Arrêté du 15 mars 2007 modifiant l'annexe I de l'arrêté du 2 juin 1998 relatif aux prescriptions générales applicables aux installations classées pour la protection de l'environnement soumises à déclaration sous la rubrique 2680–1;*
- *Arrêté du 15 mars 2007 modifiant l'arrêté du 2 juin 1998 relatif aux règles techniques auxquelles doivent satisfaire les installations soumises à autorisation au titre de la rubrique 2680–2 de la nomenclature des installations classées pour la protection de l'environnement;*
- *Arrêté du 19 mars 2007 relatif à la dissémination volontaire dans l'environnement et à la mise sur le marché de certains produits composés en tout ou partie d'organismes génétiquement modifiés;*
- *Arrêté du 19 mars 2007 relatif à la collecte d'informations sur la mise en culture de végétaux génétiquement modifiés.*

4 *Charte de l'environnement*, Article 5, integrated into the Constitution by law n° 2005 204, 1 March 2005, *OJ* n° 51, 2 March 2005, p. 3696: '[w]hen the environment is at risk from serious and irreversible harm, even if this cannot be scientifically proven, public authorities must, through the application of the precautionary principle and according to their competences, implement procedures to assess the risks and adopt temporary and proportionate measures to prevent the damage occurring' ('*Lorsque la réalisation d'un dommage, bien qu'incertaine en l'état des connaissances scientifiques, pourrait affecter de manière grave et irréversible l'environnement, les autorités publiques veillent, par application du principe de précaution et dans leurs domaines d'attributions, à la mise en œuvre de procédures d'évaluation des risques et à l'adoption de mesures provisoires et proportionnées afin de parer à la réalisation du dommage*').

5 See, however, the CNRS programme *Impact des biotechnologies sur les agro-écosystèmes* and the new Agence nationale de la recherche *Programme national de recherche sur les OGM.*

6 *Code de l'environnement, Article L. 531–4; Décret n° 93–235, 23 févr. 1993, portant création de la Commission d'étude de la dissémination des produits issus du génie biomoléculaire,* OJ 24 February 1993, p. 2940. Available at: <http://www.legifrance.gouv.fr/>.

support to this formula in a recent report, which argues in favour of a more systematic assessment of advantage and risk, particularly in fields where 'scientific rationality' is very opaque (AFSSA 2004). A similar recommendation was strongly supported by the 'Economic and Social Committee'[7] in 1998 in a set of recommendations closing a public debate on GMO releases which also called for far stricter regulation. In particular, great emphasis was laid on an assessment of GMO 'utility' and a recommendation was made in favour of the 'immediate' establishment of a specific committee to this end. Whatever the means of implementation argued for, in summary, public debate often plays host to proposals that, as is the case for pharmaceuticals, a procedure should be established whereby benefits are clearly assessed along with risks, even though traditional risk-benefit analysis is undoubtedly complicated in relation to the scientific uncertainties created by GMOs.

However, the competent public authorities have yet to respond to such proposals and current legislation does not foresee comprehensive socio-economic assessment of benefits; it is the Minister who decides, on an inevitably empirical basis. The reasons for this neglect are twofold. Legally speaking, socio-economic assessment is somewhat hampered by Directive 2001/18 which, while not prohibiting this form of evaluation, does limit its evolution as a matter of fact, with Article 22 stating marketing prohibition or restrictions may only be justified with reference to health and environmental risk assessments.[8] More generally, France does not have a tradition of *a priori* assessment; traditionally, greater importance has been given to *ex post* control. Finally, as to the concept of 'benefit' itself, it is generally considered by French administration to escape any easy characterisation. The situation may nonetheless improve in the near future since discussion on the draft law transposing Directive 2001/18 into French law has raised the possibility of the creation of a Biotech Council (*Conseil des biotechnologies*), which would be composed of two chambers, with one assessing risks posed by GM technology, and another analysing its social and economic aspects. Should this project be successful (and implemented with a serious will), proper room might yet be created for the comprehensive appreciation of the acceptability of GMOs.

The second question arising in relation to GMOs concerns liability. Decisions to release GMOs will be followed by positive or negative effects. However, should any damage be inflicted upon goods, the environment or human health, the question remains as to who will be liable for payment of compensation. As legal history teaches us, scientific and technical development since the end of the 19th century has only been possible since it was founded within a distinct compact: risk was acceptable where it could be compensated for (Noiville 2003). However, not only has France not instituted any form of liability ahead of the European Community legislator, but Parliament has chosen to reduce and even exclude liability in certain cases based in line with the notion of 'development risk',[9] that is in cases where risk could not be foreseen when the product received market approval. Should the

7 *Conférence du Comité économique et social* (Babusiaux, Le Déaut, Sicard and Testart 2002).

8 Article 22: '. . . Member States may not prohibit, restrict or impede the placing on the market of GMOs, as or in products, which comply with the requirements of this Directive'. Above, note 3.

9 See Article 1386–11–4° of the French Civil Code.

notion of development risk extend to cover GMOs? This latter point is debatable and government, conscious that the GMO industry cannot evolve in the context of uncertainties about liability, have undertaken preparatory work for and may soon propose a liability and insurance framework.[10] In any case, the discussion on liability will be one of the most important issues raised during the transposition of Directive 2001/18 into French law.

The third and final limitation within the contemporary French framework for GMO regulation is the continuing *failure of the administrative system to provide the public with any real information on decision making*, and thus to temper the tone of public debate. The situation is incongruous: the 1992 Act contained a principle of 'public information' for all decisions on GMO releases or marketing. A political will certainly existed to take the process further than institute a simple 'communication' procedure; a notion that is clearly limited, at least when it is not conceived as an interactive process. However, the principle of 'public information' has been continuously misapplied, since it was considered from the outset to be prejudicial to the requirements of confidentiality and industrial secrecy.[11] Such intransigence within the administrative culture is confirmed by recent case law; as a matter of fact, the only reason that businesses seeking GMO authorisation must now justify their demands that various information remain confidential is that courts and judges have stepped in to apply this principle; the same holds true for the fact that public authorities must now inform the general public of test locations and also publish assessment proceedings.[12]

As far as public 'participation' is concerned, at the daily administrative level, it exists only in a minimalist form. Up until recently, the general public was only able to comment on decisions that had already been taken. Today, using the internet, the public can express its opinion prior to a decision being taken by the Ministry of Agriculture; however, there are no clear channels to demonstrate how, if at all, this public feedback impacts on Ministry decision making. In line with EU requirements, the law transposing Directive 2001/18 seems to impose the principle that the public should be 'effectively' consulted prior to each GMO release and should thus put an end to a situation widely open to criticism.

At a higher political level, however, efforts have been made to initiate public participation. In particular, two major public debates have been organised. In 1998, a 'citizens' jury'[13] was established by the *Office parlementaire d'évaluation des choix scientifiques et technologiques* – a parliamentary committee in charge of the early assessment of scientific and technical choices – in an effort to clarify the debate and to formulate recommendations to public authorities. Foreshadowing the public debate convened by the Economic and Social Committee in 2002,[14] the outcomes of this debate included demands for more democratic decision making, the establishment of a systematic risk-benefit analysis and the imposition of strict liability

10 See, in the project bill, the disposition obliging GMO producers to repair economic damages.

11 For examples, see case law cited in Noiville 2005.

12 *Ibid.*, n° 81 et s. See, for instance, Tribunal administratif de Paris, 1 March 2001, *Assoc. France Nature Environnement*, req. n° 0008412/7: Dr. adm. 2001, comm. n° 138 (location of GMO releases must be communicated to the public).

13 *Conférence de citoyens*, 20–21 June 1998, followed by the parliamentary report of Le Déaut 1998.

14 *Conférence du Comité économique et social* (Babusiaux, Le Déaut, Sicard and Testart 2002).

upon GMO producers. However, these demands were not taken into account by the authorities; although many were rational, they likewise created too many legal and political difficulties (see above). More importantly, the principle of citizen debate itself was generally seen as being prejudicial to the discretionary decision-making power of political authorities, and particularly to parliamentary supremacy.

In conclusion, not only do the French public authorities fail to conform with principles laid down in EU law (especially Directive 2001/18, not yet transposed in March 2007), but they have consistently been reluctant to apply recommendations made by public institutions; among these, those made by the Economic and Social Committee and those made by AFFSA and the *Office parlementaire d'évaluation des choix scientifiques et technologiques*, showing concern that regulation is applied *a minima*, or without due regard for public deliberation or socio-economic assessment. None of the reasons for this failing are peculiarly French in character: in other countries, regulatory frameworks are also characterised by a desire to foster national biotech development, as well as administrative jealousy about the retention of competences. Nonetheless, within France at least, a further turn of the mismanagement screw can be noted.

2 THE PRACTICE OF RISK REGULATION: ARBITRARY DECISION MAKING AND SHIFTS IN INSTITUTIONAL POWERS

One of the most striking features of the practice of risk regulation within France is the growing perception among a number of actors that public decision making is arbitrary in nature and, as a consequence of this, the evolution of practical strategies, designed to shift decision making to other institutions, in particular, to the courts. Once again, this tendency is not peculiar to France. The same preoccupation exists in other countries: governments cannot maintain exclusive control over decision making relating to GMOs, and other less 'traditional' regulatory authorities, such as 'agencies', which have joined the regulatory game. Nonetheless, within France the particular contours of this evolution deserve special attention, since they appear to have their own original and worrying dynamic, which has exacerbated a general tension within risk regulation to a particular degree: the tension between risk and judicial law making.

First of all, French dynamics are unique. First, opposition to the risk regime extends far beyond traditional actors (for example, NGOs). Instead, political actors have moved to create so-called *second opinion committees*, the most emblematic of which is the *CriiGen*,[15] founded in accordance with the model found within debate on nuclear matters (the *CriiRad*), and which has as its aim the fostering of transparency and the creation of a wide debate going beyond 'reasons of State'. Likewise there has been a rapid increase in direct action: one-third of all GMO trials have been destroyed by GMO opponents in the past few years. Most significantly, several thousand mayors have organised themselves into a 'front' and are attempting to

15 *Commission de recherche et d'information indépendante sur la génétique*, founded by former Minister of Environnement Corinne Lepage: available at: <www.criigen.org>.

deploy their local police powers to prohibit GM field tests and crops in their jurisdictions, even though such trials have been authorised by the Minister.[16] At this point, we are confronted with one of the key questions concerning risk management: what is the appropriate level of decision making, when potentially contradictory local, regional and international goals are at stake?

Furthermore, the will to redistribute decision-making powers is paralleled by the 'institutionalisation of conflict'. Thus, in France, protesters who destroy GMO field tests or crops expressly stake claim to the right to 'civil disobedience': they claim that when legislation is fundamentally unfair, civil citizens must fight it, even in ways that may be violent and illegal. In the name of the '*état de nécessité*' (Act of necessity), as defined by the French Criminal Code, they hold that they are in a position of 'absolute need' to commit such offences in order to fight the dangers posed. Struggle is based on the same idea as 'legal guerilla warfare' (*guérilla juridictionnelle*), a now well-known feature of the French model; in other words, the systematic legal challenging of product and release licensing.

As a result, final decision-making powers are sometimes shifting to judges. Since an increasing number of cases have now come to court, they are typically expanding upon their traditional role of applying the law. At one level, judges have been strict in applying the existing law. Severe sentences have been imposed upon GM protesters who have destroyed crops or field tests,[17] albeit that certain courts have recognised extenuating circumstances that 'general concern caused by developments that are possibly too rapid for society, can have serious consequences, especially for consumer health and the environment.[18] More generally, however, the courts argue that in a "democratic society" such as ours, a number of means of expression other than crop destruction are available to GM protesters [. . .] to make themselves heard and if they have chosen to commit offences, they must suffer the consequences' (Noiville 2005). By the same token, actions taken by mayors to impose local prohibitions have been tested against the classic French legal requirement of 'impending danger' (*péril imminent*). Thus, although courts do admit that mayors may have room for manoeuvre to disrupt uniform application of ministerial decisions, any GM prohibition on trials or releases enacted by a mayor must be justified with reference to the prevention of 'impending danger'. Needless to say, and given the inherent difficulties of 'proving' that GMOs pose real threats, this condition has rarely yet been considered to have adequately been fulfilled.[19]

At another level, however, judges have gone far beyond simple enforcement. Two very significant examples spring to mind: judicial monitoring of risk assessments and traceability (labelling).

2.1 Judicial monitoring of risk assessments

On the basis of the precautionary principle, judges have forced the administration to move far beyond brief assessments and to take all relevant scientific data into

16 Case law is quite hesitant about the legality of such prohibitions (see below).

17 See, eg, Cour de Cassation, Chambre criminelle, 7 February 2007, n° 06–80108.

18 See, eg, Tribunal de Grande Instance d'Orléans, 9 December 2005.

19 Even the contamination of non-GM crops is generally not considered as such. Some jurisdictions, however, state that the mayor can prohibit trials that take place around organic enterprises.

account, even data supported only by a minority of scientists. The *BT Maize* case ruled on by the Conseil d'État is emblematic of such a trend,[20] as is the more recent *Gaucho* case, where the same Conseil d'État stated that the Minister of Agriculture had failed to examine all of the elements necessary in order properly to adjudge whether the product in question was safe.[21]

Though incomplete at the level of judicial interpretation, this trend may be further reinforced by the recent constitutionalisation of the precautionary principle. Thus, for example, recent case law in fields as diverse as hunting and 'rave parties' have seen courts state that judicial decision making is now driven by new constitutional constraints: according to the courts, not only is the precautionary principle now 'constitutionally guaranteed', but 'environmental protection' has become a legal principle with the same status as other legal principle (that is, it is no longer subordinate to individual liberties).[22] A recent judgment and the particular appreciation made by Orléans 'tribunal' of risks posed by transgenic maize risks is characteristic.[23] The court stated that the constitutional consecration of the precautionary principle by the legislator imposes particular restraints upon GMO releases since these may give rise to the uncontrolled dissemination of modified genes into the environment.

Equally, although it might be exaggerated to pretend that the introduction of the precautionary principle into the constitution will fundamentally change the legal review process, courts are clearly taking care to examine the adequacy of public decision making more thoroughly. Thus, in the recent case that came before the Orléans tribunal, the judge combined the precautionary principle with the legal principle of contradiction to facilitate in-depth substantive analysis of risk assessments undertaken. He refused simply to take formal note of the scientific controversy on GMOs and instead directly examined all potential risks. Having referred to a wide variety of scientific and non-scientific publications, having taken note of uncontrolled dissemination of GM maize within the environment, as well as technical shortcomings within current anti-pollenisation barriers, he finally ruled that the GM Maize substance as stake was 'dangerous', or at least posed 'potential dangers'. The significance of this case cannot be understated: traditionally, courts have adopted a very narrow approach to the review of scientific evidence, rarely going into the 'substance of science', not simply since courts lack technical expertise, but also, since to do so would be to trespass upon a political decision-making process and the prerogatives of politicians to determine the course of scientific, technical and economic development. Another example of such an evolution may be found in a recent GMO case ruled by the Conseil d'Etat:[24] judging that the risks associated with a transgenic maize cannot be evaluated at a regional level and must instead be assessed at a local level, judges clearly cease to restrain their jurisprudence on scientific matters.

20 See, particularly, Conseil d'Etat, 25 September 1998, *Assoc. Greenpeace France*, req. n° 194348: *Juris-Data* n° 1998–050609.

21 Conseil d'Etat, 9 October 2002, *Union nationale de l'apiculture française*, n° 233876.

22 See, for example, Tribunal administratif, Châlons-en-Champagne, 29 April 2005, n° 0500828, 05008829 et 0500830.

23 Tribunal de Grande Instance, Orléans, 9 December 2005, n° 2345/S3//2005.

24 Conseil d'Etat, Fédération des syndicats agricoles MODEF, 28 April 2006, n° 274458–274459.

2.2 Judges and traceability (labelling)

In addition, courts have also taken a direct hand in the enforcement of one of the most crucial areas within the GMO regulatory framework, that of GMO labelling and traceability. Thus, even prior to the European Commission imposing a requirement that all seeds exceeding detection thresholds should be labelled, a number of French judges not only made this a clear requirement of French law, but also heavily fined seed companies selling unlabelled contaminated seed, even where the degree of contamination was proportionally very low. Interestingly, such decisions were justified and liability imposed in line with a subtle expansion of existing French law on misrepresentation and misleading advertising.[25] One series of cases focused upon the sale of partially contaminated soyabean from one firm to another that then took legal action. The final decision stressed that although contamination was fortuitous and extremely low, the extent of scientific controversy on GM products, as well as general political sensitivity, determined that 'a particular clear and prudent presentation' of the product was required. This judgment, whereby various legal tools and principles (precaution, information, contradiction, misleading advertising) are combined to facilitate judicial decision making, is exemplary for the manner in which judges have afforded themselves a growing influence over the regulatory framework for GMOs within France.

3 CONCLUSION

The case of the regulation of GMOs within France offers us a particular opportunity to analyse the problems created both by GMO regulation and by risk regulation in general. A particular feature of the French case is the lack of a 'social contract' between those who produce the risk (albeit an uncertain risk), those who manage it, and those who are mainly exposed to it. Therefore, the presence of a dual trend, whereby increasing strategic use is made of courts, which, in turn, have ceased to restrain their jurisprudence on scientific and technical matters, is unsurprising if a source of further uncertainty within the debate. Certainly, this author would hesitate to condemn judges who are no longer willing just to act as 'the mouthpieces of the law'. In this view, judicial decision making does not currently substitute for political judgement; and seeks instead to punish those who disregard the 'spirit' of existing legislation and law, taking advantage of the fact that the regulatory framework contains its own lacunae. However, it must also be recognised that the line between effective judicial enforcement and judicial activism is a thin one and the current danger that judges will be increasingly forced to bridge the gap left by legislators to become one of the few spaces for genuine democratic debate is a worrying one indeed.

25 TGI Carcassonne, *Reymond et Bonastre v Confédération Paysanne de l'Aude*, 12 May 2003; Cour d'appel Montpellier, *Reymond et Bonastre v Confédération Paysanne de l'Aude*, 29 July 2004; Tribunal correctionnel de Saumur, *Golden Harvest Zelder*, 2 December 2004. For a precise review, see Noiville 2005.

BIBLIOGRAPHY

AFSSA (2004) *Innocuité sanitaire des OGM?* Paris, available at: <www.afssa.fr>.

Babusiaux, C., Le Déaut, J.-Y., Sicard, D. and Testart, J. (2002) *Rapport à la suite du débat sur les OGM et les essais au champ*, Paris: Documentation française.

Le Déaut, J.-Y. (1998) *L'utilisation des organismes génétiquement modifiés dans l'agriculture et dans l'alimentation, Office Parlementaire d'Évaluation des Choix Scientifiques et Technologiques: Rapport Assemblée nationale n° 1054, et Sénat n° 545*, Paris: Assemblée Nationale Publishers.

Le Déaut, J.-Y. and Ménard, Ch. (2005) *Mission d'information sur les enjeux des essais et de l'utilisation des organismes génétiquement modifiés*, available at: <http://www.assemblee-nationale.fr/12/dossiers/ogm.asp>.

Noiville, C. (2003) *Du bon gouvernement des risques. Le droit et la question du risque acceptable*, Paris: Presses Universitaires de France, Collection Les Voies du Droit.

Noiville, C. (2005) *Jurisclasseur Environnement, OGM*, fascicule 2700, Paris: Lexis Nexis Publisher.

Noiville, C. and De Sadeleer, N. (2002) 'Les organismes génétiquement modifiés au regard du droit communautaire, examen critique de la directive 2001/18/CE', *Journal des Tribunaux de Droit Européen*, 81–5.

Chapter 9

The UK regulatory system on GMOs: expanding the debate?

Maria Lee

1 INTRODUCTION: RISK REGULATION IN THE UK

Agricultural biotechnology was for a long time defined in the UK as a purely scientific issue. Debate and concern that was not based on scientific evidence was dismissed as irrational, or at best irrelevant (Black 1998), and this narrow framework for decision making went along with a resistance to public involvement. This was very much in line with the UK's fairly opaque approach to decision making in technical or scientific policy areas more generally. It would, however, have been difficult for such an *overtly* narrow approach to genetically modified organisms (GMOs) to survive the media and public discussion of the issue in the late 1990s. In the UK as elsewhere, developments in agricultural biotechnology provoked unusual levels of public concern at this time, and major food retailers and processors began to avoid GM produce. Some sort of response was required of government. In 1999, an agreement was reached between government and the industry body, SCIMAC (the Supply Chain Initiative on Modified Agricultural Crops), that there would be no commercial cultivation of GM crops pending completion of certain scientific trials (relating specifically to the impact of the crop management regimes related to four different GM crops on farmland biodiversity). This 'moratorium' ran parallel with the EU-wide moratorium on authorisations of GMOs, which the UK government did not formally support. The UK moratorium had an explicitly scientific starting and end point: it was based on concern expressed by, among others, the government's advisor on biodiversity issues, English Nature, that GM herbicide-tolerant crops could have harmful effects on farmland biodiversity,[1] and was a temporary decision, pending the completion of further scientific investigation. However, this narrowly scientific 'precautionary' stance also created some time for more broadly based public discussion of the issues.

Agricultural biotechnology policy in the UK now recognises (at least in principle) the importance of public values and public participation. This shift of approach, or at least of rhetoric, reflects, and even exemplifies, more general changes in the UK approach to risk regulation. While it would be overly simplistic to explain evolution of thinking on risk by reference to one, or even a few, specific events, the discovery

1 Department of the Environment, Food and Rural Affairs, *The GM Dialogue: Government Response*, 9 March 2004, available at: <http://www.defra.gov.uk/environment/gm/debate/pdf/gmdialokgue-response. pdf>, para 5.4.

of a link between bovine spongiform encephalopathy (BSE or 'mad cow disease') in cattle and variant Creutzfeldt-Jakob Disease (vCJD) in human beings is a notorious episode in the regulation of risk in the UK. Government communication on the issue had emphasised reassurance, focusing on the safety of beef in a way that tended to suggest that transmissibility of BSE to humans was not possible.[2] The public reaction to the revelation of a link between consumption of beef and vCJD contributed to greater political awareness of the difficulties of regulating uncertainty, and considerable political attention was subsequently paid to uncertainty in the scientific process, to public perceptions of risks and to public values that fall outside traditional scientific assessments. Since the late 1990s, a number of influential reports on risk and decision making have brought the complexity of good decision making into the mainstream.[3] While the importance of science to the policy process is kept firmly in view, the trend is now to emphasise a more open and participative approach to environmental decision making than before, as well as the significance of moral, social and ethical concerns. The Department of Environment, Food and Rural Affairs' guidelines on risk, drawn up in this context of increased recognition of public input into risk decisions,[4] respond to many of the recent academic and political debates on risk regulation. While the main focus is on technical methods for the calculation and comparison of risk, considerable space is dedicated to the 'social aspects' of risk, including a discussion of questions of risk acceptability, risk perception, trust and distributive issues. Even if it is something of an afterthought, the recognition of the complexity and breadth of decisions on 'risk' is clear. This chapter will proceed from the observation that policy on agricultural biotechnology, and decisions on the authorisation of individual GMOs in the UK are not, in principle, expected to be based on a purely technical assessment of 'risk' to human health or the environment, but on a more broadly based decision-making process, incorporating a range of perspectives. In an attempt to reconcile the competing pressures from various sections of the public, from EU and international law, and from economic objectives, a complex and unusually extensive framework for expert advice and public consultation emerged in this field at the beginning of the decade.

This chapter will begin by examining the institutions involved in the regulation of agricultural biotechnology, before moving on to examine the government's extensive approach to consultation on GMOs: in 2003, a three-stranded 'dialogue' was completed, with a scientific review, an economic review and a 'public debate'. While government appears fully committed to inclusive decision making (both in respect of participants and in respect of factors taken into account), an examination of the government *response* to the public consultation, and of the legal and political context for decision making, suggests a lingering ambivalence. As we (arguably) emerge from the UK and EU 'moratoria', recent UK decisions on GMOs continue to rely heavily on scientific information and technical language. So, notwithstanding

2 See generally Phillips Report, *BSE Inquiry Report* (2000); for a review see Little 2001.

3 See especially Royal Commission on Environmental Pollution, 21st Report, *Setting Environmental Standards* (CM 4053, 1998). House of Lords Select Committee on Science and Technology, Session 2000–01, 3rd Report, *Science and Society*.

4 Department of the Environment, Food and Rural Affairs, *Guidelines for Environmental Risk Assessment and Management*, available at: <http://www.defra.gov.uk/environment/risk>.

a significant expansion of acceptable grounds of debate, and a much more inclusive process, considerable legal and political pressures continue to keep the acceptable rationales for decisions narrowly technical. I would not suggest that government decisions should follow 'public opinion' (even if that were possible when views diverge so widely). The level of direct and explicit engagement by government with the concerns of the public that go beyond the scientific (including concerns that our ignorance in this area is too great to proceed, or that the benefits of the technology are too uncertain or too narrowly distributed), however, provides at best an anti-climactic end to a brave process.

2 THE REGULATORS

In most cases, the British regulators of agricultural biotechnology will be feeding into an EU-wide decision, either through contributions to technical risk assessment or through 'comitology' and Council, and UK law fits into a complex regime of regulation at EU level.[5] Part VI of the Environmental Protection Act 1990 (the Act) provides the basic statutory framework for the regulation of release of GMOs, supplemented and amended by the Genetically Modified Organisms (Deliberate Release) Regulations 2002 (the Regulations).[6] These pieces of legislation together implement the Deliberate Release Directive 2001/18.[7] The Food and Feed Regulation 1829/2003[8] replaces the Deliberate Release Directive in respect of GMOs intended for food or (animal) feed use, although if that GMO is also to be deliberately released into the environment (for example as a crop), it is supplemented by the provisions of the Deliberate Release Directive relating to environmental risk assessment.

The Department of the Environment, Food and Rural Affairs (DEFRA) is the government department responsible for environmental protection, and also for the consideration of applications for the deliberate release of GMOs, feeding into both the technical and the political stages of the process under Directive 2001/18,[9] as well as granting or refusing authorisations when a 'Community' decision is not required. The retention of decision-making authority by the government department itself may reveal the perceived political sensitivity of this area; the independent agency more usually responsible for environmental decisions, the

5 I will refer to 'UK' institutions for the sake of simplicity. A relatively complex system of devolution exists in the UK: Scotland, Wales and (although its assembly is currently suspended) Northern Ireland have devolved parliamentary assemblies, with different powers and responsibilities in each case. There is in principle some room for distinctive policies on GMOs, for example, the long debate on the possibility of a 'GM-free Wales' (policy statement of the Welsh Department for Environment, Planning and Countryside on GMOs, available at: <http://www.countryside.wales.gov.uk/fe/master.asp?n1=4&n2=152>, accessed May 2005). The UK government retains responsibility for implementing EU law and for complying with international agreements.

6 SI 2002/2443.

7 Directive 2001/18/EC of the European Parliament and of the Council of 12 March 2001 on the Deliberate Release into the Environment of Genetically Modified Organisms, [2001] *OJ* L106/1.

8 Regulation (EC) No. 1829/2003 of the European Parliament and of the Council of 22 September 2003 on genetically modified food and feed, [2003] *OJ* L268/1.

9 Above, note 6, Regulation 23.

Environment Agency, has no direct role in the regulation of GMOs.[10] By contrast, the Food Standards Agency is responsible for GM food and feed, providing input to the EC-level risk assessments when required under the Food and Feed Regulation; the Food Standards Act 1999 created the Food Standards Agency and amended the Environmental Protection Act 1990 to reflect the role of the Agency in GMO regulation. The Food Standards Agency has no express environmental responsibilities, but in terms of food, its remit is potentially wide: its 'main objective' is to 'protect public health [. . .] and otherwise to protect the interests of consumers in relation to food'.[11]

Until relatively recently, government was advised on biotechnology issues by a number of disparate bodies, arrangements criticised as fragmented and lacking in transparency.[12] Two main advisory bodies now address the deliberate release of GMOs:[13] the AEBC (Agriculture and Environment Biotechnology Commission) and ACRE (Advisory Committee on Releases into the Environment). ACRE is perhaps the more conventional body. Every application involving a deliberate release of a GMO goes to ACRE, a statutory body[14] whose main function is to give advice to Ministers on the risks to human health and the environment from the release and marketing of GMOs. In its early days, ACRE was dominated by those with links to the industry.[15] Membership now is much less one-sided,[16] and ACRE also claims 'a continuing commitment to openness and transparency'. Agendas and minutes are published on its website, as is advice to Ministers, a summary of which in any event must be published on the statutory 'register of information' on GMOs.[17] ACRE focuses on scientific and technical risk assessment, and does not seem to see its role as involving consideration of broader political issues, leaving political questions to DEFRA, the primary recipient of ACRE advice.

These attempts to draw bright lines between *technical* and *political* decision making, the 'risk assessment'/'risk management' dichotomy so familiar to environmental lawyers,[18] do at least recognise the evaluative nature of risk decisions. Such a dichotomy, however, raises some important concerns, not least in that it implies that the science can be isolated from value judgements, which are made later in time by a different set of decision makers. Professional and personal values can, however, imperceptibly enter the scientific process through the necessary exercise of judgement. I will discuss below the assumption that the appropriate comparator against which the environmental performance of GM crops should be judged is

10 The Environment Agency operates in England and Wales.

11 Food Standards Act 1999, section 1(2).

12 See Environmental Audit Committee, 1998–1999 Fifth Report, *Genetically Modified Organisms and the Environment: Coordination of Government Policy*, HC 384-I.

13 The Advisory Committee on Novel Foods and Processes (ACNFP) and the Advisory Committee on Animal Feedingstuffs (ACAF) provide scientific advice to the Food Standards Agency and ACRE.

14 Section 124, Environmental Protection Act 1990. ACRE existed before the 1990 Act.

15 Although see the discussion of representation on ACRE, Levidow and Tait 1993: 193. A 1999 Friends of the Earth press release suggests the potential isolation of the NGO member, available at: <http://www.foe.co.uk/resource/press_releases/19990120000147.html>.

16 Register of interests, available at: <http://www.defra.gov.uk/environment/acre/about/index.htm>.

17 Above, note 6, Regulation 34.

18 See, for example, European Commission, *Communication on the Precautionary Principle*, COM(2000) 1, 2 February 2000, Brussels.

contemporary 'industrial' farming; this implies a judgement about the 'acceptable' level of environmental harm associated with farming. Similar exercises of judgement, and similarly value-laden assumptions, will very often form part of a risk assessment. To take a well-known example from the environmental field, the simplification of complex problems into a number of discrete issues is often a necessary and legitimate part of scientific progress. It can, however, lead to neglect, for example, of interactions between different substances or between and within ecosystems; and as well as providing space for error, it arguably points towards a fundamental and systematic failure to appreciate the complexity and sensitivity of environmental resources. A too-rigid dichotomy between risk assessment and risk management can undermine efforts to expose and examine the values inherent in risk decisions, as political decision makers are tempted to use the apparent neutrality and objectivity of the 'facts' as revealed by science to justify their decisions.

Turning back to the second main advisory body involved in agricultural biotechnology, the AEBC is also in some respects a conventional approach to defusing controversial issues by reference to an 'expert' committee. Its membership and remit, however, are very different from ACRE, and to a large degree the AEBC escapes the attempt to separate science and politics. The AEBC was set up in 2000 to provide strategic advice to government. It specifically addresses the ethical and social issues associated with agricultural biotechnology, as well as the science. The AEBC is designed to be an open institution, with meetings held in public, and published minutes and agendas. It is said to be 'a new form of institutional, multi-stakeholder, consultative body'.[19] While membership is individual rather than representative of particular constituencies, members have been drawn from all sections of the debate on GMOs, including the biotech industry and those sceptical of agricultural biotechnology. The tension between the views of members may have been intended as part of a broader effort to work towards consensus and overcome polarisation on agricultural biotechnology. In this respect, the importance of 'deliberation' within the group has been stressed by the Chair, and it seems that changes of approach by individual members during the course of internal debate are not unheard of, albeit predictably rare given the established positions of the members.[20] The nature of the membership seems primarily, however, to have been an attempt to improve the legitimacy of the body (and by association of the regulatory framework) by a level of representativeness, allowing different sides of the debate to feel that their voices have been heard.[21]

As a formal space for ethical and social issues to enter into the regulatory arena, the AEBC was an important innovation. While the precise role of the AEBC has been ambiguous,[22] the profile it creates for non-technical issues is perhaps most important for current purposes. And from this perspective, the AEBC has successfully provided 'a thorough exploration of the issues that divided the main stakeholder groups in an open transparent process',[23] which could have been difficult to

19 Horlick-Jones *et al.* 2004: 14.

20 Williams 2004: para 4.3.

21 Steele 2001: 415; Above, note 20, para 3.4.

22 In particular whether it is an 'investigative/analytic body', a 'stakeholder/consensus forming body' or a hybrid: above, note 20, para 3.8.

23 Above, note 20, para 6.30.

achieve in a more technical advisory body. The task of the AEBC has been described as 'mission impossible',[24] because of the deep controversy over the issues, limited public understanding of or confidence in advice, and the background of polarisation over the issue: even within the AEBC, '[t]here were deep disagreements over the intellectual framework for the debate'.[25] In a sense, however, this is one of the distinctive contributions of the AEBC. It has by now been very well observed that the dispute about GMOs extends to the very identification of the questions that need to be asked: technical, scientific, ethical, economic;[26] for these disputes to come out in this forum is entirely appropriate. Arguably, less flexible terms of reference could have cut short some of the most sensitive discussions. Moreover, in spite of the challenges, the AEBC has produced consensus reports (albeit highlighting areas of internal disagreement) and on some issues, for example its recommendation that there be a 'public debate' on GMOs (discussed below), it has been both influential and radical.

The AEBC was wound up in April 2005. There has inevitably been speculation about the inconvenience of some of the AEBC's recommendations to government, but we can simply note that a routine review of the performance of the AEBC recommended its winding up,[27] and that the AEBC did not dissent from the main thrust of this review.[28] Given the development of the policy background, it was argued that the AEBC 'is likely to face increasing difficulty in finding areas within its current terms of reference on which it can make a distinctive contribution'.[29] Some of those consulted during the review raised the possibility that the AEBC be replaced with an advisory body of broader scope, which could address issues of agriculture and environment more generally than biotechnology, and government has referred to this as a possibility,[30] although without proposing any new body. This may represent the beginnings of a shift of approach in the UK, an effort to move the focus from GMOs specifically, to the environmental impact of agriculture more generally.[31] This has certain attractions, particularly the possibility of subjecting the different harms done by conventional agriculture to the same sort of thorough debate as GMOs. However, biotechnology is regulated separately from the broader pursuit of agriculture, and there must be concerns about losing the AEBC's contribution to that regulatory process.

There is clearly a danger that the loss of the AEBC will marginalise the status of social and ethical factors in the regulation of agriculture biotechnology; to lose this broader perspective would be a major step backwards in risk regulation, and

24 Above, note 20, para 3.5.
25 Above, note 20, para 1.2.
26 Above, note 1.
27 Above, note 20.
28 *AEBC Members' Reaction to the Review and the Future of the AEBC*, 18 January 2005, available at: <http://www.aebc.gov.uk/aebc/reports/members_response_aebc_review.pdf>.
29 Above, note 20, para 8.8.
30 *Government Response to the Review of the Agriculture and Environment Biotechnology Commission*, April 2005, available at: <http://www.ost.gov.uk/policy/bodies/aebc_review_apr05.pdf>.
31 ACRE hints at a similar shift, ACRE, *Advice on the implications of the farm-scale evaluations of genetically modified herbicide tolerant crops*, 13 January 2004, available at: <http://www.defra.gov.uk/environment/acre/pubs.htm>; as does Secretary of State Margaret Beckett's Statement on GM Policy, 9 March 2004, para 16, available at: <http://www.defra.gov.uk/corporate/ministers/statements/mb040309.htm>.

somewhat out of line with the increasingly confident recognition by government of the importance of these broader aspects of 'risk'. Such a mismatch between presentation and practice is not, however, unusual in the very difficult policy area of agricultural biotechnology, as we will see.

3 COMMERCIALISATION OF GMOs IN THE UK: *GM NATION?*

The UK has held an elaborate consultation process over the commercialisation of GMOs. There are obligations of publicity in respect of applications for consent to release/market GMOs, but without any real detail as to consultation, and there is simple, even pro-forma, reference to public comments in DEFRA assessment reports on particular applications. Much more ambitiously, government initiated the 'GM Dialogue' in 2003. This comprised three strands: a study into the overall costs and benefits of GM crops by the government's Strategy Unit; a review of the science led by government scientific advisors in conjunction with an independent panel of academics; and a public debate.

The most common and long-standing method of involving the public in decision making in the UK is a process of written consultation. The science and economic reviews both relied heavily on this traditional consultation process, with outsiders (largely experts) providing information to decision makers, without necessarily interacting with each other or the organisers in a significant way. Written consultation was also an important feature of the 'public debate', but by no means the most visible or significant part. This section will look at each of the three 'strands' of the process in turn.

3.1 The economics review

The government's Strategy Unit carried out a study into the overall costs and benefits of GM crops, including their effect on conventional and organic farming interests, resulting in a lengthy report, *Field Work: Weighing up the Costs and Benefits of GM Crops*.[32] The team working on the study was self-defined as 'multi-disciplinary', with experience in 'economics, science, policy-making and issues affecting developing countries', from inside and outside the civil service. There is an effort to reassure through the status of those involved, by an attempt at 'neutrality' rather than an attempt to bring on board opposing positions: no member of the team had worked for organisations with a financial interest in GM crops or food or associated with campaigning activities on GM.[33] Consultation seems to have been wide, including workshops and bilateral discussions with 'stakeholders', as well as the invitation of submissions from the public through the website. Input was, because of the specialist nature of the discussion, and as acknowledged in the report, on the whole limited to those with an existing 'interest' in the issue.

The prominence given to economics in environmental policy creates concern

32 Cabinet Office, available at: <http://www.strategy.gov.uk/work_areas/gm_crops/index.asp>.
33 *Ibid.*, p. 122.

that important uncertainties and value judgements will be hidden from view behind a display of apparently inevitable numbers. Any attempt to simplify the complex issues surrounding GMOs and to shelter from criticism behind a façade of objectivity would have been resisted, and probably counter-productive. The report is decidedly circumspect. It emphasises the limited evidence and data on which it is based, and makes 'no attempt to provide a single "net present value" of total costs and benefits; neither has the study attempted to make policy recommendations'.[34] Instead, it paints a complex picture that emphasises the difficulty of the *political* judgements to be taken. It resorts predominantly to assessing the pros and cons of different regulatory approaches, setting out results based on five possible 'scenarios' for the future of GM agriculture in the UK,[35] incorporating varying public attitudes and varying regulatory regimes, as well as considering the possibility of 'shocks and surprises'. It also emphasises that the costs and benefits will be different for each GMO, and that a case-by-case approach is appropriate.

I will not attempt to summarise the findings of the study. The then Secretary of State for the Environment, Margaret Beckett, however, summed up the results to the House of Commons as follows:

> The costs and benefits study concluded that the GM crops currently available offer only some small and limited benefits to UK farmers, but that future developments in GM crops could potentially offer benefits of greater value and significance even in the United Kingdom.[36]

This is far from capturing the nuanced picture presented in the report, but is a perhaps understandable effort of the politicians to produce a brief public response; interesting, given the concern that it is *economic* assessments that misleadingly avoid the necessary complexity of political judgements.

3.2 The science review

The Science Review was set up to consider the current state of the science behind GM issues, including clarifying the state of knowledge and areas of uncertainty, basing its conclusions on peer reviewed work. The review was led by the government's Chief Scientific Advisor, working with the Chief Scientific Advisor to DEFRA, with independent advice from the Food Standards Agency. It was a very open process. The GM Science Review Panel produced two reports, in September 2003 and January 2004.[37] The second provided a period, in which comments could be received on the first report, new scientific information could be considered, and the results from the public debate and the farm scale evaluations (to be discussed

34 *Ibid.*, para 1.5.4.

35 *Ibid.*, Chapter 4.

36 Secretary of State, above, note 31.

37 GM Science Panel, *GM Science Review: First Report: An Open Review of the Science Relevant to GM Crops and Food Based on the Interests and Concerns of the Public* and *GM Science Review: Second Report: An Open Review of the Science Relevant to GM crops and Food based on Interests and Concerns of the Public*, available at: <http://www.gmsciencedebate.org.uk>.

below) could be taken into account. There was no substantial change in conclusions, albeit some clarifications were made.

One of the most important functions of the Science Review was to identify gaps in knowledge, reaching more widely than the case-by-case review under the regulatory scheme. The government, however, responded to this element of its work variously by referring to the safety assessments in the regulatory process, or by promising/referring to new research.[38] One of the key findings of the Review (according to the government) was the conclusion that 'GM is not a single homogeneous technology', and so blanket judgements cannot be made.[39] The Review examined a number of common concerns about GM crops and, in the words of the Secretary of State, 'reported no verifiable ill-effects from extensive human and animal consumption of products from GM crops over 7 years, and it concluded too that current GM crops were very unlikely either to invade the countryside or to be toxic to wildlife. The most important environmental issue identified was indeed the effect on farmland wildlife which was the subject of our extensive trials – the largest carried out in the world.'[40]

The 'extensive trials' referred to by the Secretary of State were the 'Farm Scale Evaluations' (FSEs), scientific studies addressing the biodiversity impact of particular GM crops at the farm level. While not formally part of the Science Review, the results of three of four FSEs became available at around the same time as the results from the three strands of the GM Dialogue.[41] The completion of the FSEs had been a central element of the agreement, mentioned in the introduction to this paper, between government and SCIMAC, to postpone commercialisation of GM crops in the UK. The results of the FSEs are public documents, published as a series of papers in a themed issue of the *Philosophical Transactions of the Royal Society*; a non-technical summary, aimed at a wider public, was also published.[42]

The FSE results were published in 2003 for genetically modified herbicide tolerant (GMHT) spring-sown oilseed rape, GMHT beet and GMHT forage maize. The results were described as 'remarkably consistent and clear' over the range of sites tested.[43] In essence, the FSE results showed that GMHT spring-sown oilseed rape and GMHT beet, with their associated herbicide regimes, resulted in lower levels of field biodiversity than was the case for their conventional counterparts managed conventionally. GMHT forage maize with its herbicide regime, by contrast, resulted in greater levels of field biodiversity than was the case for its conventional equivalent, conventionally managed.[44] The results are claimed only to apply to particular management regimes; uncertainties enter in if future management techniques (either for the GM crop, or for the conventional comparator) vary.[45]

38 DEFRA, above, note 1, Annex 2.

39 DEFRA, *ibid.*

40 Secretary of State, above, note 31.

41 The fourth is winter oilseed rape, and the results were published in March 2005, available at: <http://www.defra.gov.uk/environment/gm/fse/index.htm>.

42 Available at: <http://www.defra.gov.uk/environment/gm/fse/index.htm>.

43 GM Science Review, Second report, above, note 37, para 3.4. See also ACRE, above, note 31; see also ACRE, *Response to Open Letter from AEBC on the Wider Issues Raised by the Farm Scale Evaluations*, available at: <http://www.defra.gov.uk/environment/acre/advice/pdf/acre_advice57.pdf>.

44 ACRE, above, note 31.

45 GM Science Review, Second Report, above, note 37, para 3.8.2.

The FSEs have been controversial. To take one particular issue,[46] a parliamentary committee judged the benchmark of conventional farming against which the GM crops were measured to be 'unambitious'; and the comparison between GMHT forage maize and a conventional crop that relied on a herbicide (atrazine), the use of which was soon to be phased out, was described as 'invalid'.[47] Irrespective of the particular criticism of the atrazine issue, it is clear that GM agriculture is going to look better in terms of biodiversity when judged against highly industrialised intensive farming than against, for example, organic farming. The degree of professional judgement (rather than neutral technical know-how) involved in risk assessment is blatantly clear when looking at the FSEs. The 'norm' is assumed to be heavily industrialised farming, and although in this case the 'norm' was in principle controllable by government as well as scientists, this provides another reminder that attempting to maintain a rigid distinction between consecutive phases of 'technical' risk assessment and 'political' risk management is not always possible. The information on which government relies to make its decisions is framed by a deeply value-laden decision, which in many cases would be hidden by its apparently technical nature. The outcry that met the results of the FSEs, however, also illustrates the potential for transparency of scientific assessment to bring judgements and alternatives into the open.

The FSE results were passed to ACRE as well as government, and ACRE provided advice to government to the effect that if managed and grown as in the trial, the GMHT beet and spring-sown oilseed rape would produce adverse effects under Directive 2001/18 compared to conventionally managed crops.[48] It is for applicants to provide evidence on alternative, less damaging, management strategies. With respect to the GMHT maize, which would not have adverse effects, ACRE advised that any commercial cultivation be limited to the conditions of the FSEs 'or conditions that have been shown not to result in adverse effects'[49] and that 'studies are initiated immediately' to consider the validity of the results given the phasing out of atrazine.[50] DEFRA has stated that when seeking renewal of authorisations, new evidence providing a comparison against conventional practice current at that time will be required.[51]

3.3 The public debate

Described by its organisers as an 'unprecedented event – a special public debate before a potentially far-reaching change in public policy',[52] the public debate strand of the GM dialogue went under the mildly sinister title of '*GM Nation?*'. It

46 ACRE, above, note 31, outlines further concerns.

47 Environmental Audit Committee, 2003–2004 Second Report, *GM Foods – Evaluating the Farm Scale Trials* HC 90-I, Conclusion, paras 1 and 14.

48 ACRE, above, note 31.

49 *Ibid.*, para 38.

50 *Ibid.*, para 39.

51 DEFRA, *Government Response to the Environmental Audit Committee Report: GM Foods – Evaluating the Farm Scale Trials*, Second Report, Session 2003–04.

52 *GM Nation? The Findings of a Public Debate* (2003), available at: <http://www.gmnation.org>.

constituted a self-consciously deliberative and inclusive exercise.[53] While serious criticisms have been made of the process, this has generally been in the context of an acknowledgement of the experimental nature of the process, and financial and time limitations.[54]

The public debate followed a recommendation of the AEBC in its report *Crops on Trial*.[55] *GM Nation?* was run by a steering committee, at arm's length from government, chaired by the chair of the AEBC, and with several members from the AEBC. The core activity of *GM Nation?* was a series of public meetings around the country, including a small number of high-profile regional events, together with a larger number of smaller local meetings, from which written feedback was provided to the Steering Committee. The *GM Nation?* public meetings tended on the whole not to follow the traditional approach to public meetings in the UK. Rather than revolving around platform addresses from experts, followed by questions from the floor, and in line with the deliberative ethos of *GM Nation?*, attendees were encouraged to listen and engage with other opinions, as well as put forward their own views. *GM Nation?* was an interesting and innovative novel approach to public participation, moving beyond (although including) simpler forms of written consultation, allowing or encouraging engagement between the participants.

The public meetings were not supposed to be representative, either of the general population or of public views on GMOs. There was some concern, however, that the results from the public meetings would not adequately reflect the breadth of public opinion: going to a public meeting 'is an unusual activity'; and 'people who go to public meetings and events are self-selected'.[56] The public meetings were for this reason supplemented by a 'Narrow but Deep' strand to the debate, designed as a 'test' to the public meetings. The Narrow but Deep strand involved a number of further group discussion exercises, with constructed samples of public representation. This was supposed to be a 'control' for the concern that the conclusions from the *GM Nation?* meetings would be unrepresentative, allowing for the possibility of the 'silent majority'.

The *GM Nation?* process swept up the 'other' issues that provoke concern about GMOs, as well as allowing lay discussion of scientific and economic issues. The initial AEBC recommendation that there be a public debate speaks of the need to 'expose, respect and embrace the differences of view which exist, rather than bury them'.[57] There appeared to be no attempt to impose a framework of 'acceptable' ways of discussing the 'problem'; indeed, the principle followed was that the public frame the issues for the debate, by means of a number of discussion workshops, and that questions raised by the public would feed also into the scientific and economic reviews.[58]

53 Its record in both of those respects is mixed, Understanding Risk Team, above, note 19.

54 *Ibid.*; Environment, Food and Rural Affair Select Committee, Session 2002–2003, 18th Report, *Conduct of the GM Public Debate*, HC 1220.

55 AEBC, *Crops on Trial* (2001), available at: <http://www.aebc.gov.uk>.

56 *GM Nation?*, above, note 52, paras 78–9. The Understanding Risk Team, above, note 19, found 'substantial evidence at the public meetings of participation by large numbers who were politically engaged in the issue; in the sense that beliefs about GM appeared to form part of a wider *Weltanschauung*'.

57 AEBC, above, note 55, para 21.

58 *GM Nation? The Findings of a Public Debate*, above, note 52, paras 14–18.

Perhaps the simplest observation to be drawn from *GM Nation?* is that '[a]mong the participants in the debate there are many more people who are cautious, suspicious or outrightly hostile about GM crops than there are supportive towards them'.[59] Further, 'the public do not view GM as purely a scientific, or environmental, or economic, or political or ethical issue. All of these aspects are important to them. It follows that the public accept no single arbiter of decisions to be made about GM.'[60] This illustrates nicely the complexity of public opinion on agricultural biotechnology: one of the striking aspects of the factors raised by the participants is that 'there are so many of them'.[61]

By its examination of the Narrow but Deep strand, the Report of *GM Nation?* concluded that the general population does not express views identical to the active participants in the public meetings, but that 'they are *not* a "silent majority" in the original Nixonian sense of being a completely different audience with different values and attitudes from an activist minority'.[62] There were many shared concerns between the Narrow but Deep group and the other participants, although the former were 'more prepared to acknowledge potential benefits from GM crops'.[63] While the official report of the Debate attaches relatively little importance to this distinction, others are particularly concerned that this willingness to acknowledge benefits could be a very significant element of more general public views.[64] The DEFRA response to the public debate picked up on this, accepting that the findings of the debate 'broadly reflect the current state of public opinion on GM' and that 'people are generally uneasy about GM crops and food, and that there is little support for early commercialisation of GM crops in this country',[65] but also noting that 'the results suggested that the general public may have a lower degree of outright opposition to GM than the participants in the debate, while still being very cautious'.[66] The Narrow but Deep group, however, also suggested that people become more hostile the more they learn. This is disturbing for anyone who still hopes to 'educate' the public into accepting biotechnology, although there have been suggestions that this very important conclusion has been drawn on the basis of 'flimsy evidence'.[67]

Both the inclusion of the Narrow but Deep strand and the reactions after the debate suggest some concern about the level of pre-existing 'interest' among participants in the public debate. We might note that there was no similar concern about the 'representativity' or identity of consultees in the economic and scientific limbs of the process. There seems to be an implicit assumption that the economic or scientific information is capable of objective assessment, or perhaps that expertise precludes any bias that might be of concern. 'Expertise' is, however, seen as a mixed blessing when it comes to the non-scientific public debate, in respect of which the prior engagement of the participants can be interpreted as bias.

59 *Ibid.*, para 41 (emphasis omitted).
60 *Ibid.*, para 42 (emphasis omitted).
61 *Ibid.*, para 42.
62 *Ibid.*, para 195.
63 *GM Nation?*, above, note 52, para 205.
64 Understanding Risk Team, above, note 19.
65 DEFRA, above, note 1, para 3.2.
66 DEFRA, above, note 1, Executive Summary, para 7.
67 Understanding Risk Team, above, note 19, para 5.8.

3.4 Conclusions

The purposes of public consultation are rarely clear, and the GM dialogue was no exception. Indeed, there was considerable confusion retrospectively as to precisely what *GM Nation?* was intended to achieve.[68] There is clearly an effort to make all parties feel that they have sufficient say in decision making; also to bring into the fold a range of information that would be difficult to locate in a single bureaucracy – including external information on the economics and the science, but more strikingly, information on public views.

4 THE GOVERNMENT RESPONSE: A BROADLY BASED DECISION?

Government had undertaken to respond to the results of the GM Dialogue, notwithstanding 'widespread cynicism' about the impact of the debate on decision making.[69] The 'institutional body language' of government may have been problematic: a number of ministers had made clear their support of GM, and the Prime Minister had criticised anti-GM protestors before the debate got underway.[70] Nevertheless, the 'dialogue' was unique for the UK, and at the very least its political riskiness suggests a commitment to engage with public debate on this issue.

Government made a joint response to the three strands of the dialogue, together with the results of FSEs, and an AEBC report on *Co-existence and Liability*,[71] 'a uniquely diverse body of evidence on which to base our decisions'.[72] Government claims to 'take public concern very seriously' and to have 'weighed public opinion alongside the scientific evidence'.[73] It accepts that people are 'generally uneasy', and that there is 'little public support for early commercialisation'.[74] The government response acknowledges the 'complex range of issues and concerns' that shape people's views on biotechnology,[75] reinforcing its acknowledgement of the legitimacy of issues going beyond technical assessments of risk to health and the environment. The government claims to have 'taken into account a range of different policy objectives: environmental protection, food safety, consumer choice, sustainable food and farming, thriving rural communities, science and innovation, industrial competitiveness, international development, and trade'. There is no suggestion that they have a purely technical or scientific decision to make: to borrow from Andrew Dobson in another context, we might be forgiven for thinking that 'government and its advisers had fully grasped the normative dimension' of decision making on GMOs, 'and was determined to factor it into decision making'

68 Understanding Risk Team, above, note 19.
69 *Ibid.*
70 Understanding Risk Team, *ibid.*, p. 35.
71 (2001), available at: <http://www.aebc.gov.uk>.
72 DEFRA, above, note 1, executive summary para 10.
73 *Ibid.*, Executive Summary, para 1.
74 *Ibid.*, Executive Summary, para 7.
75 *Ibid.*, Chapter 3, para 3.1.

(Dobson 2003: 153). The government response, however, turns very quickly to its commitment to 'evidence-based policy-making'.[76]

As it goes through 'each of the concerns raised in the public debate', the focus is on responding to those concerns through rigorous safety and approval processes. The concerns are listed as follows: (1) caution and precaution; (2) protecting human health; (3) protecting the environment; (4) providing choice for consumers; (5) providing information; (6) openness and transparency; (7) gaps in scientific knowledge; (8) developing countries; (9) no need for GM crops?; (10) ethical issues.[77] The response of government to the first six issues is basically to explain how both current regulatory practice and available scientific information, including that gained during the dialogue, respond to these issues. Public concern is met simply with reassurance, by reference to scientific evidence and its use by regulators.

The last four criteria are potentially more challenging, not obviously susceptible to this type of reassurance, but the government response is not ambitious. On gaps in scientific knowledge, the government acknowledges uncertainty, and promises further research. This reductionist approach to scientific uncertainty, placing faith in more or better science, rather misses the point. We face much more profound dilemmas around ignorance (we don't know what we don't know) and indeterminacy (the unpredictability of real life ecological and human systems) in this area;[78] lack of knowledge was a key concern in *GM Nation?* On the question of developing countries, government asserts the value of developing countries making their own decisions on GM crops; clearly true, but EU policy will have a very significant influence on those decisions. And on the need for GM crops, government cites the Economic Review to the effect that while there is currently limited economic value to the UK in GM crops, they have the potential to offer greater benefits. The final question of ethical issues are met with the citation of the Nuffield Council on Bioethics, to the effect that 'there is an ethical obligation to explore [the] potential benefits [of agricultural biotechnology] responsibly, in order to contribute to the reduction of poverty, and to improve food security and profitable agriculture in developing countries'. The Nuffield Council, in the cited report,[79] roundly dismisses the notion that ethical concerns should limit development of biotechnology, beyond questions of safety (that is, the ethical implications of harming the environment or the health of farmers), and dismisses any attempt to distinguish between forms of agriculture on the basis of their 'naturalness'. The appeal of 'expertise' when faced with the prospect of having to engage with competing ethical perspectives on new technology is clear.

Policy on agricultural biotechnology was not subject to radical revision following the GM Dialogue, albeit that policy was explained in such a way as to respond to particular concerns: each strand was found to support the existing 'case-by-case' approach. At the time of the conclusion of the GM Dialogue, decisions also fell to

76 DEFRA, above, note 1, Executive Summary, para 11.

77 *Ibid.*, Chapter 5 (numbering added).

78 Following Brian Wynne, see for example Wynne 1992: 111.

79 Nuffield Council on Bioethics, *Genetically Modified Crops: the Ethical and Social Issues*, 1999, available at: <http://www.nuffieldbioethics.org/go/print/ourwork/gmcrops/introduction>.

be made on a number of particular applications relating to those crops that had been subject to the FSEs.[80] The government relied heavily on the FSEs (and advice from ACRE and the Science Review), rather than broader issues raised in the debate, to explain its decisions. Neither the beet nor the spring-sown oilseed rape were thought to satisfy the regulatory requirements for authorisation. The maize considered by the FSEs had received EU-level approvals before the moratorium, under the old legislation on GMOs. This GMO was allowed to go ahead in the UK, conditional upon the crop management regime being consistent with that tested in the FSE. A fresh application would be required under the new legislation by 2006 in any event, at which time the 'atrazine' issue would be revisited. Bayer CropScience, however, decided to discontinue further efforts to commercialise its GM forage maize variety in the UK, because of 'a number of constraints on this conditional approval before the commercial cultivation of GM forage maize can proceed in the UK'.[81]

The decision on GMHT maize purported to allow commercial cultivation, and purported to rest on very specific scientific information. Whether the response from Bayer was anticipated by government is another matter for the conspiracy theorists, but the way that this played out at least raises questions about the transparency of decision making. More generally, if it is the case that the decisions made at this time are based at least in part on the results of the public debate, genuine transparency would need to be reflected much more clearly in the explanation of the decisions.

There are really two concerns here, partially contradictory, but fundamentally connected, and going to the heart of the transparency and accountability of decision making. First, it is possible that political decisions made to respond to public opinion have been 'dressed up' as *scientific* decisions. Second, the depth and extent of public concern has not received a full response from government. Again, the point is not that 'public opinion' should be followed in all cases: there is rarely a monolithic public opinion *to* follow, and in any event, public opinion can be manipulated, difficult to identify, and discriminatory, ignorant or ill-informed. A major public debate such as that in *GM Nation?*, however, allows an examination of the basis for different strands of public opinion: is it based on legitimate ethical or social values, even if incoherently expressed, or is it based on ignorance and superstition? A government response that engages openly with the underlying basis for public concern (however difficult and controversial the identification of that underlying basis inevitably is) would have a number of benefits, aside from the virtue of democratic responsiveness. It would put into practice the basic acceptance that agricultural biotechnology policy is not a wholly scientific question, but one resting on fundamental values about how we wish to feed ourselves; government could ultimately prefer a particular scientific view, but on the basis of an explanation that, for example, in this case the dangers of ignorance are worth running just as they have been with earlier technological developments. Engagement with the

80 For a complete review of decisions taken, available at: <http://www.defra.gov.uk/environment/gm/regulation/registers.htm>.

81 Bayer CropScience Press Release, 31 March 2004, available at: <http://www.bcsbioscience.co.uk/documents.asp?sec=3&con=31&section=4>.

basis of public concern would also allow the 'public opinion' to be challenged by competing public opinion in a way that is not possible if a political decision is justified by a convenient scientific framework; this in turn provides a level of 'check' on the risk of succumbing to ignorance or prejudice in the rush to public participation.

5 THE LEGAL AND POLITICAL CONTEXT

Government policy ostensibly recognises and accepts the breadth of factors relevant to decisions on GMOs. This reflects more general government policy on risk, which acknowledges the legitimate consideration by decision makers of a wide range of factors, albeit with little guidance on the relative importance of those different factors in particular cases.[82] However, this rhetorical responsiveness to a full range of considerations has proven difficult to match by the actual practice of decision making, where government has tended to go back to expert advice, and scientific information; a number of pressures tend towards this narrowing of the decision.

In particular, the legal framework tends to focus on environmental and human health issues, pointing towards the importance of science. There has been relatively little direct judicial discussion of the relevance of public concern in environmental (or indeed other) regulation. An administrative court decision in *Amvac* is suggestive of its 'supporting' role.[83] This case was concerned with the withdrawal of authorisation for a chemical used in pesticides.[84] The substance of the decision had not been challenged, but the short time given to the applicants for comment on proposals was one of the procedural questions raised. 'Public concern' and 'public confidence in the regulatory system' were said to be relevant to the *urgency* with which a decision is taken, 'quite apart from the actual risk'.[85] Public concern is recognised as a factor that exists independently of 'actual risk', but does not have a decisive effect.

The role of 'public concern' in decision making has emerged for more detailed judicial consideration in a number of planning law disputes (Hilson 2004: 1638), most recently in respect of efforts to site mobile telephone masts.[86] The science suggests that the masts are 'safe'; the local community fears otherwise. The vital question has been whether public concern must have an objective basis in order to constitute a material consideration in planning law. While the Court of

82 DEFRA, above, note 4.

83 *R v Secretary of State for the Home Department, ex parte Venables, ex parte Thompson* [1998] AC 407 involved Secretary of State powers to set sentence 'tariffs' for a child convicted of murder: general considerations of public confidence in the administration of justice may be relevant, but public petitions, public opinion as expressed in the media and public protests would be irrelevant.

84 *R (on the application of Amvac Chemical UK Limited) v Secretary of State for Environment, Food and Rural Affairs, Secretary of State for Transport, Local Government and the Regions, Food Standards Agency* [2001] EWHC Admin 1011.

85 *Ibid.*, para 59.

86 *T-Mobile (UK) Ltd* v *First Secretary of State* [2004] EWCA Civ 1763; *Phillips v First Secretary of State* [2003] EWHC 2415; *Trevett v Secretary of State for Transport, Local Government and the Regions* [2003] Env LR D10.

Appeal has not been entirely consistent on this point, it seems most recently to have been accepted that public concern about safety is a material consideration, independently of scientific evidence on danger. *T-Mobile* is an interesting example of the way the courts approach public concern.[87] All parties to the litigation had accepted 'that actual health risk and perceived health risk or public concern about health, were both distinct matters treated as relevant considerations to the planning decision falling to be made and were so treated by [the relevant policy guidance]'.[88] The planning inspector in this case had rejected the appeal against refusal of planning permission, in spite of the fact that all safety standards were met, on the grounds that 'insufficient reassurance had been given to the public of health implications'. According to the Court, 'there is [. . .] nothing [. . .] to show why, on the facts of this particular case, compliance with the ICNIRP [International Commission on Non-Ionising Radiation Protection] guidelines was insufficient to allay perceived fears about health issues.'[89] This case illustrates how even accepting that public concern is legitimate, it is countered in law (if not in fact) by referring the public back to the 'official' scientific position.

This familiar ambivalence, recognising public concern, but then responding through science as if the concern were based on simple ignorance, is also apparent in the response to a number of factors emerging from the public debate on GMOs, as discussed above.[90] The 'deficit model', the idea that public concern is about public misunderstanding, and can be resolved by ever better explanation of science and education of the public, is rarely now openly expressed,[91] but does seem to be buried deep in decision-making instincts and legal structures. Again, the argument is not that government should simply allow public opinion its way every time (even if that were possible, given diverging views). If the concern does turn out to be based on ignorance, then education is indeed the correct response; otherwise, something more far reaching would be required.

Decision making, however, takes place in a very specific policy and statutory context, and the planning decisions (which at least recognise the relevance of public views) cannot simply be carried across to GMOs. In the case of mobile phone technology, there had been detailed planning policy guidance issued by central government on how decisions should be approached; *T-Mobile* turned largely on the interpretation of this policy. The legitimate purposes that may be pursued by decisions on GMOs are set out in the relevant legislation, which reflects the EU legislation. The legislation is framed around science and safety; the purpose of Part VI of the Environmental Protection Act 1990 is to ensure

> that all appropriate measures are taken to avoid damage to the environment which may arise from escape or release from human control of genetically modified organisms;[92]

87 *T-Mobile, ibid.*
88 *Ibid.*, para 13.
89 *Ibid.*, para 21.
90 See especially the response to the first six factors pulled out of *GM Nation?*. See text, above, note 77.
91 For the 'official' discrediting of this approach, see House of Lords, above, note 3.
92 Environmental Protection Act 1990, section 106(1), as amended by Genetically Modified Organisms (Deliberate Release) Regulations 2002, regulation 3(2).

human health is a consideration through the definition of 'damage to the environment'.[93]

The Court of Appeal decision in *ex parte Watson*[94] is the only decision of a higher court on the regulation of GMOs, and although it deals with the 'old' legislation, it illustrates the point. The applicant was an organic farmer, who was concerned his crop would be cross-pollinated by the GM maize being grown as part of a trial on a neighbouring farm, threatening his organic status. The applicant was successful in arguing that the application for the GM trial had not been properly made. The Court of Appeal, however, concluded that the Minister had no power to order the destruction of the crop: 'the only power the Minister has to require destruction of the crop before flowering is that provided by section 111(10). But that power can only be properly exercised in pursuance of the 1990 Act purposes – ie with regard to considerations of health and safety and the protection of the environment. Those considerations have already been fully taken into account and were not found sufficient to justify the defloration of the trial plants'.[95] It is not difficult to see how this approach could constrain the reliance on broader questions of public concern to justify particular decisions.

This very narrow legal framework is, however, now subject to some expansion at EU level, although how this will operate is still to be worked through. The Food and Feed Regulation explicitly provides that 'other legitimate factors' than risk assessment may be 'relevant to the matter under consideration',[96] and that 'in some cases, scientific risk assessment alone cannot provide all the information on which a risk management decision should be based'.[97] This formula (applying only to GMOs for food or feed) seems to allow considerable room for the incorporation into decisions of values and concern that go well beyond technical and scientific issues. Its ability to compete effectively with the appearance of objectivity and neutrality provided by science, however, must be open to doubt, at least in the short term.[98] The qualities ascribed to scientific information are politically appealing in any event, especially in highly controversial areas, but the legal context in which decisions are made enhances this appeal. So, decision makers may anticipate the possibility of being required to justify their position in the context of WTO dispute settlement;[99] and ECJ jurisprudence also tends to reinforce the role of scientific evidence in decision making; albeit so far in the context of legislation that does not contain the 'other legitimate factors' formula.[100] Given that the UK does not make autonomous decisions on GMOs, but contributes to EU level decisions, which in turn are subject

93 Section 107(2), (3) and (6) as amended by Genetically Modified Organisms (Deliberate Release) Regulations 2002, regulation 4. Human health receives separate consideration in respect of food through Regulation 1829/2003, above, note 8.

94 *R v Secretary of State for the Environment and MAFF, ex parte Watson* [1999] Env LR 310.

95 *Ibid.*, p. 319.

96 Regulation (EC) No. 1829/2003, above, note 8, Article 7(1).

97 Regulation (EC) No. 1829/2003, above, note 8, Recital 32.

98 See the discussion in Lee 2005: Chapter 9.

99 The preference for science as a basis for decision making is classically illustrated by the Appellate Body's approach in *European Communities – Measures Concerning Meat and Meat Products (Hormones)*, 16 January 1998, WT/DS26/AB/R, WT/DS48/AB/R.

100 See especially Case T-13/99 *Pfizer Animal Health SA v Council* [2002] ECR II-3305.

to WTO disciplines, the UK's ability to respond fully to the views of its publics is subject to certain constraints.

6 CONCLUSIONS

It is too soon to reach firm conclusions on the response of the UK government to GMOs; we are still at the beginning of the story. The UK, as other governments, remains subject to competing political, commercial and legal imperatives. Government policy still contains room for manoeuvre, and individual decisions are sometimes ambiguous. The official position is that no commercial cultivation is likely until 2008 at the very earliest (because of the time taken for authorisations, and sowing seasons). The UK is, however, voting in favour of authorisation at EU level in some cases.

GMOs have provided the context for an extraordinary consultation process, 'unthinkable in policy circles a decade ago'.[101] At the very least, the consultation was open, and it did not attempt to exclude any group or any perspective on the 'problem'. Emerging as it has in a context of wider governmental recognition of the importance of 'public participation', decision making on GMOs potentially has a great deal to say about how we make decisions on controversial developments more generally. Given especially this broader significance, the exploration of novel approaches is encouraging, even if the complexity of the process suggests that this extensive approach will be rare. Moreover, public participation and deliberation have been only one part of an enormous process, and it would be premature to suggest that we have a new 'participative' approach to decision making.

None of the material that emerges from the consultation process presents a straightforward picture for the regulator; accordingly, it is not easy to say which information is more influential. What is *said* by government on the way the material is considered is highly reflective of the academic debate on decision making. There is certainly an awareness that the co-opting of debate by science or economics would be unsatisfactory. However, when decisions are finally made and explained, refuge does seem to be sought in science and elite 'informed' opinion, including here the views of non-scientific bodies like the Nuffield Council. While the structures were provided for the full range of debate on GMOs, there are a number of barriers to the effective incorporation of 'other', that is, non-technical, issues. Most formally, the purposes of the legislation suggest that public concern will at most have a supporting role; a legal limitation compounded at the EU level of decision making, albeit with the recent relaxation of 'other legitimate factors'. And of course, the UK government does not have independent decision-making powers on this issue. Public opinion is complex and nuanced, and the economics and the science are not in the least straightforward. The reflection of such subtleties through the risk assessment or comitology processes at EU level is at best problematic, and certainly very far from transparent to national publics. This is a matter of much broader concern, going to the heart of the proper role of national or local democratic processes in EU, and indeed WTO, decision making. It may also be the case that the

101 Understanding Risk Team, above, note 19, p. 7.

intensity and the polarisation of the public debate make scientific justifications for decisions more politically attractive, not less. While it is very likely that UK delay on GMOs is actually prompted by the politics of the question, especially public concern, the decisions are justified on the basis of science; raising yet more questions of transparency.

The difficulty of getting robust 'other' information in place alongside technical information is perhaps the most interesting element of the whole experiment. The quality of the information from the public debate is already controversial and likely to be further disputed as new and changing information is provided. Even if the information were beyond dispute, there is nevertheless a clear difficulty with the level of genuine communication between the different aspects of the debate: here the scientific, economic and 'public' elements.[102] I do not wish to suggest that government necessarily has cynical motives. It may simply be that the practical arrangements for meaningful public participation, and the incorporation of its outcomes into decisions, are set to be at least as problematic as was gaining acceptance for the principle of public participation.

102 *Ibid.* See also Black 1998, on the 'integrating' role of the regulator.

BIBLIOGRAPHY

ACRE (2004a) *Advice on the implications of the farm-scale evaluations of genetically modified herbicide tolerant crops*, 13 January 2004, available at: <http://www.defra.gov.uk/environment/acre/pubs.htm>.

ACRE (2004b) *Response to Open Letter from AEBC on the Wider Issues Raised by the Farm Scale Evaluations*, available at: <http://www.defra.gov.uk/environment/acre/advice/pdf/acre_advice57.pdf>.

AEBC (2001) *Crops on Trial*, available at: <http://www.aebc.gov.uk>.

AEBC (2005) *Members' Reaction to the Review and the Future of the AEBC*, 18 January 2005, available at: <http://www.aebc.gov.uk/aebc/reports/members_response_aebc_review.pdf>.

Bayer CropScience (2004) *Press Release*, 31 March 2004, available at: <http://www.bcsbioscience.co.uk/documents.asp?sec=3&con=31&section=4>.

Beckett, M. (2004) *Statement on GM Policy*, 9 March 2004, available at: <http://www.defra.gov.uk/corporate/ministers/statements/mb040309.htm>.

Black, J. (1998) 'Regulation as facilitation: negotiating the genetic revolution', *Modern Law Review* 61: 621–60.

Department of the Environment, Food and Rural Affairs (DEFRA) (2003) *Government Response to the Environmental Audit Committee Report: GM Foods – Evaluating the Farm Scale Trials*, Second Report, Session 2003–04.

Department of the Environment, Food and Rural Affairs (DEFRA) (2004a) *The GM Dialogue: Government Response*, 9 March 2004, available at: <http://www.defra.gov.uk/environment/gm/debate/pdf/gmdialogue-response.pdf>.

Department of the Environment, Food and Rural Affairs (DEFRA) (2004b) *Guidelines for Environmental Risk Assessment and Management*, available at: <http://www.defra.gov.uk/environment/risk>.

Department of Trade and Industry (2005) *Government Response to the Review of the Agriculture and Environment Biotechnology Commission*, April 2005, available at: <http://www.ost.gov.uk/policy/bodies/aebc_review_apr05.pdf>.

Dobson, A. (2003) *Citizenship and the Environment*, Oxford: Oxford University Press.

Environment, Food and Rural Affair Select Committee (2004) 18th Report *Conduct of the GM Public Debate*, Session 2002–03, HC 1220.

Environmental Audit Committee (2004) *GM Foods – Evaluating the Farm Scale Trials*, 2003–04 Second Report, Volume 1, HC 90-I.

Environmental Audit Committee (1999) 1998–99 Fifth Report, *Genetically Modified Organisms and the Environment: Coordination of Government Policy*, HC 384-I.

Friends of the Earth (1999) *Press Release – Government Advisors split on Frankenstein Crop Approval*, available at: <http://www.foe.co.uk/resource/press_releases/19990120000147.html>.

GM Science Panel (2004) *Second Report: An Open Review of the Science Relevant to GM crops and Food based on Interests and Concerns of the Public*, available at <http://www.gmsciencedebate.org.uk>.

GM Science Panel (2003) *First Report: An Open Review of the Science Relevant to GM Crops and Food Based on the Interests and Concerns of the Public*, available at: <http://www.gmsciencedebate.org.uk>.

Heller, R. (2003) *GM Nation? The Findings of a Public Debate*, available at: <http://www.gmnation.org>.

Hilson, C. (2004) 'Planning law and public perceptions of risk: evidence of concern or concern based on evidence?', *Journal of Planning Law*, 1638–48.

Horlick-Jones, T., Walls, J., Rowe, G., Pedgeon, N., Poortinga, W., O'Riordan, T., Murdoch, G. Tait, J. and Bruce, A. (2004) *A deliberative future? An independent evaluation of the GM nation? Public debate about the possible commercialisation of transgenic crops in Britain*, Understanding Risk Working Paper 04–02, Norwich: School of Environmental Sciences, University of East Anglia.

House of Lords Select Committee on Science and Technology (2000) *Third Report: Science and Society*, Session 1999–2000, HL38, London: The Stationery Office.

Lee, M. (2005) *EU Environmental Law: Challenges, Change and Decision-Making*, Oxford: Hart Publishing.

Levidow, L. and Tait, J. (1993) 'Advice on biotechnology regulation', *Science and Public Policy* 20: 193–209.

Little, G. (2001) 'BSE and the regulation of risk', *Modern Law Review* 64: 730–56.

Nuffield Council on Bioethics (1999) *Genetically Modified Crops: the Ethical and Social Issues*, available at: <http://www.nuffieldbioethics.org/go/print/ourwork/gmcrops/introduction>.

Royal Commission on Environmental Pollution (1998) 21st Report, *Setting Environmental Standards*, CM 4053.

Steele, J. (2001) 'Participation and deliberation in environmental law: exploring a problem-solving approach', *Oxford Journal of Legal Studies* 21: 415–22.

Welsh Department for Environment, Planning and Countryside on GMOs (2000), *Genetically Modified Organisms (GMOs)*, available at: <http://www.countryside.wales.gov.uk/fe/master.asp?n1=4&n2=152>.

Williams, N. (2004) *Organisational and Performance Review of the Agriculture and Environment Biotechnology Commission*, available at: <http://www.ost.gov.uk/policy/bodies/review.html>.

Wynne, B. (1992) 'Uncertainty and environmental learning: reconceiving science and policy in the preventive paradigm', *Global Environmental Change*, 111–27.

Chapter 10

GMO regulation in the Netherlands: a story of hope, fear and the limits of 'poldering'

*Han Somsen**

1 INTRODUCTION

Global, regional, and national regulatory debates about the implications of modern agricultural biotechnology and genetically modified organisms (GMOs) are predominantly couched in the language of risk. Risks associated with GMOs remain uncertain to a considerable extent, so that debate has in turn inevitably become politicised. The formidable challenge facing any regulatory regime addressing research, patenting or trade involving GMOs is to accommodate, and to some extent pacify, opposing views that are entertained by different actors. As this chapter will show, this is a tall order for even a small and homogeneous country as the Netherlands, but may prove virtually impossible for a European Union (EU) of 27 that spans from the deserts of southern Spain to the most northerly tip of Finland.

In the EU, this balancing act finds expression in a body of directives and regulations that represent an ambition to achieve a high degree of harmonisation of the (commercial) use of GMOs. Harmonisation is informed, first and foremost, by the Union's trade paradigm, but also seeks to answer environmental and consumer imperatives, which over the past three decades have also matured into robust EU policies in their own right.

As a result of this intricate system of European Community (EC) law, Dutch GMO legislation is necessarily shadowing secondary EC law. Nonetheless, as is illustrated most powerfully by the thorny issue of coexistence, EC law on GMOs does not exhaustively regulate this policy field. As a starting point, in section 2 we shall therefore examine the residual powers Member States may exercise to pursue a discrete national policy on GMOs.

In section 3, we turn to Dutch policy on GMOs. The Netherlands has a longstanding tradition as a liberal trading nation, where innovative technology and applied research are regarded as crucial for sustainable economic prosperity. In line with this tradition, Dutch policy on GMOs from the 1980s onwards has been informed by the belief that the opportunities offered by modern biotechnology far outweigh its risks. Only for outsiders, who may have faint memories of the

* The author wishes to express his gratitude to Floor Fleurke, of the Centre of Environmental Law in Amsterdam, who assisted throughout the process of writing this chapter. Responsibility for any errors are exclusively the author's.

Netherlands as an environmental first mover, may it come as a surprise that the Netherlands did not support the *de facto* moratorium imposed on GM products in 1998.

The liberal perspective driving Dutch GMO policy is all too evident in the Dutch legal framework and in the numerous policy documents that underpin it. The precautionary principle, which provides the scaffolding for Directive 2001/18/EC on the Deliberate Release into the Environment of Genetically Modified Organisms (Deliberate Release Directive),[1] is only implicitly accommodated in the Dutch Decree on Genetically Modified Organisms that implements the Directive through a prior-approval system.[2]

In order to obtain proper insights into Dutch policy on GMOs, the legal framework governing decision making on GMOs is first discussed. Second, the role of science and expertise in this process is explored. This is followed by a discussion of the role of public information and participation in the Dutch decision-making process. We will then briefly discuss the current Dutch position on coexistence.

Contemporary developments in Dutch policy of GMOs will be evaluated in section 4, and give rise to some general concluding remarks in section 5.

2 EUROPEAN LEGAL FRAMEWORK AND THE DIVISION OF POWERS

From the early 1990s onwards, the Community legislature has pursued what is essentially a horizontal approach to the regulation of GMOs. National provisions that concern GMOs and genetically modified (GM) micro-organisms were harmonised so as to ensure the objective of the free circulation of goods produced with or from them in the internal market, while simultaneously aiming for a high level of health and environmental protection.

The Community legislator has set out to harmonise nearly all aspects of GMOs and GM products, irrespective of whether these are intended for deliberate release into the environment, for contained experimental purposes, or for use in food or feed. The basic pieces of Community legislation are:

- the Deliberate Release Directive;[3]
- Directive 98/81/EC amending Directive 90/219/EEC on the Contained Use of Genetically Modified Micro-Organisms (Contained Use Directive);[4]

1 Directive 2001/18/EC of the European Parliament and of the Council of 12 March 2001 on the Deliberate Release into the Environment of Genetically Modified Organisms, [2001] *OJ* L106/1 (hereafter: 'Deliberate Release Directive').

2 *Besluit genetisch gemodificeerde organismen Wet milieugevaarlijke stoffen* (Genetically Modified Organisms Decree, Environmentally Hazardous Substances Act), 25 January 1990, last amended at 1 July 2005, *Stb* 2005, 320.

3 Above, note 1.

4 Council Directive 98/81/EC of 26 October 1998 amending Directive 90/219/EEC on the contained use of genetically modified micro-organisms, [1998] *OJ* L330/13.

- Regulation (EC) No. 178/2002 Laying Down the General Principles and Requirements of Food Law, Establishing the European Food Safety Authority and Laying Down Procedures in Matters of Food Safety (General Food Regulation);[5]
- Regulation (EC) No. 258/97 Concerning Novel Foods and Novel Food Ingredients (Regulation on Novel Foods);[6]
- Regulation (EC) No. 1829/2003 on Genetically Modified Food and Feed (Regulation on GM Food and Feed);[7]
- Regulation (EC) No. 1830/2003 Concerning the Traceability and Labelling of Genetically Modified Organisms and the Traceability of Food and Feed Products from Genetically Modified Organisms and Amending Directive 2001/18/EC (Regulation on Traceability and Labelling).[8]

The Deliberate Release Directive is the central piece of EC legislation in the area of GMOs. It is a framework Directive that informs the way in which EU policy on GMOs operates in practice. Thus, concerning the environmental risk assessment for part C (explained further below), risk management, labelling, monitoring, information to the public and safeguard clause, the Deliberate Release Directive is a point of reference for GMOs as or in products authorised by other Community legislation. These should therefore provide for a specific environmental risk assessment, to be carried out in accordance with the principles set out in Annex II of the Deliberate Release Directive and on the basis of information specified in Annex III. This is without prejudice to additional requirements laid down by the Community legislation mentioned above, and for requirements as regards risk management, labelling, monitoring as appropriate, information to the public and safeguard clause at least equivalent to that laid down in the Deliberate Release Directive (Article 5).[9]

The basic tenet of the EU regulatory framework is deceptively simple and revolves around the requirement that any person must, before undertaking a deliberate release of a GMO or of a combination of GMOs, submit a notification to the competent authority of the Member State within whose territory the release is to take place, and obtain a subsequent authorisation (Article 6 for Part B releases; Articles 13–15 for Part C releases).

However, the functioning of this system in practice has proved exceedingly complex. In good part this is because, as will be explained below, the authorisation

5 Regulation (EC) No. 2002/178 of the European Parliament and of the Council of 28 January 2002 laying down the general principles and requirements of food law, establishing the European Food Safety Authority and laying down procedures in matters of food safety, [2002] *OJ* L31/1, as amended by Regulation 2003/1643/EC of the European Parliament and of the Council of 22 July 2003, [2003] *OJ* L245/4.

6 Regulation (EC) No. 258/97 of the European Parliament and of the Council of 27 January 1997 concerning novel foods and novel food ingredients, [1997] *OJ* L43/1.

7 Regulation (EC) No. 1829/2003 of the European Parliament and of the Council of 22 September 2003 on genetically modified food and feed, [2003] *OJ* L268/1.

8 Regulation (EC) No. 1830/2003 of the European Parliament and of the Council of 22 September 2003 concerning the traceability and labelling of genetically modified organisms and the traceability of food and feed products from genetically modified organisms and amending Directive 2001/18/EC, [2003] *OJ* L268/24.

9 Deliberate Release Directive, above, note 1.

system for Part C releases involves multiple levels of governance (involving different actors at local, national and European levels), as well as multiple actors (in that it establishes a role for political and scientific institutions) (Scott 2004). In systems of multi-level governance, the question of balance of power between Community authorities and Member States is as fundamental as it is muddled (Hervey 2001). Reserved powers of Member States concern the contained use of GMOs, authorisation and coexistence of experimental field trials, the way in which applications for granting a marketing authorisation of GMOs are administered and processed, issues of environmental liability, choosing the modalities for consultation, scientific research, monitoring and inspection, ethical issues, and the decision to adopt national safeguard measures.

A discussion of the Dutch regulatory regime pertaining to GMOs requires a brief, and by necessity incomplete, analysis of some of the most important powers left to Member States to take action concerning GMOs that exist within their territories. The focus will be on the two central instruments of the EC authorisation system: the Deliberate Release Directive[10] and the Regulation on GM Food and Feed. These two Community instruments will be subject to separate analyses, as the Regulation is based on a broader range of EC Treaty provisions, and the structure of decision making contained therein is also fundamentally different.[11]

2.1 The Deliberate Release Directive

The Deliberate Release Directive distinguishes releases of GMOs for any other purpose than for placing on the market (part B releases) and the placing of GMOs on the market as or in products (part C). In the first case, the release is normally for experimental purposes: it takes place within the territory of a single Member State, and the effects of any authorisation are confined to a single territory. In the case of the placing of GMOs on the market, products benefit from free circulation in the internal market, and its possible implications automatically transcend the territory of a single Member State. Whereas coordination needs are therefore limited in the first case, with regard to the placing on the market this issue becomes vitally important, opening up considerable potential for disagreement and conflict.

2.2 Part B releases

In respect of part B releases, the national authority that has received a notification plays a pivotal role in the decision-making process. It is responsible for examining the documents submitted by the notifier, the risk assessment, and the final decision to grant or refuse authorisation.[12] It is also responsible for managing the authorisation once it has been granted.[13] The national authority is obliged to send the Commis-

10 The results of our analysis of the Deliberate Release Directive will also apply to the Regulation on Novel Foods and the Regulation on Traceability and Labelling. They are all based on Article 95 EC, have similar structures, and pursue equivalent degrees of harmonisation, see Christoforou 2004: 670.

11 *Ibid.*

12 Deliberate Release Directive, above, note 1, Article 6(5).

13 *Ibid.*, Articles 10 and 8(2).

sion a summary that should 'adequately reflect' the information submitted by the notifier.[14] At its request, any Member State is permitted to receive a copy of the full notification from the competent authority of the Member State that received the notification.[15] The Commission immediately transmits this summary or the copy to other Member States, which have 30 days to ask for complementary information or make observations, either directly or through the Commission. Furthermore, the competent authority is obliged to inform other Member States and the Commission of its reasoned final decision.[16] In addition, a list of GMOs which have been released or rejected on their territory also has to be sent. These provisions merely oblige the Member State to *inform* other Member States and the Commission. The fact that they do not circumscribe the competence of the national authority any further is justified by virtue of the fact that the authorisation does not affect the free movement of GMOs.

2.3 Part C releases

In contrast to part B releases, part C releases affect the whole of the Community territory, which calls for a radically different approach. The Deliberate Release Directive provides that, before a GMO or a combination of GMOs as or in products is placed on the market, a notification must be submitted to the competent authority of the Member State where such a GMO is to be placed on the market for the first time.[17] If the competent national authority gives a favourable opinion on the marketing of the GMO concerned, this Member State informs the other Member States via the Commission. The other Member States are given the opportunity to make comments and reasoned objections within 60 days.[18] In respect of part C releases, national authorities of other Member States are thus fully involved in the consultation process. If there are no objections raised by other Member States or the Commission, the competent authority that carried out the original evaluation can grant consent for placing the product on the market.[19]

Several provisions in the Deliberate Release Directive allow Member States to 'make comments' or raise 'reasoned objections' during the evaluation and authorisation procedure.[20] These 'comments' or 'objections' concerning risk to human health or the environment must be submitted to the relevant scientific committee advising the Commission, in accordance with the comitology procedure.[21] If 'reasoned objections' are raised and maintained, a decision has to be taken pursuant to the regulatory Committee procedure of Article 5 of Council

14 Within 30 days of receiving the information.
15 Deliberate Release Directive, above, note 1, Article 11(2).
16 *Ibid.*, Articles 9 and 11(3).
17 *Ibid.*, Article 13.
18 *Ibid.*, Article 15.
19 *Ibid.*, Articles 15(1) and (3).
20 *Ibid.*, Articles 7(4), 15, 17 and 20.
21 *Ibid.*, Article 28.

Decision 1999/468/EC,[22] which has in practice meant that the Commission ultimately decides.[23]

2.4 Assessment by the competent authority

Recital 47 of the preamble of the Directive explains that 'the competent authority should give its consent only after it has been satisfied that the release will be safe for human health and the environment'. Article 4(1) of the Directive requires Member States to ensure that 'all appropriate measures are taken to avoid adverse effects on human health and the environment which might arise from the deliberate release or the placing on the market of GMOs'. The environmental risk assessment also takes account of 'potential long-term effects associated with the interaction with other organisms and the environment'. The responsible authorities are free to exercise their discretion in determining the appropriate level of protection, can ask for additional information, and can refuse or grant use of a GMO. At this stage of the authorisation procedure, the national authorities thus hold genuine power as they filter notifications: a national authority must first grant its approval, before authorisation on the market becomes possible. If the assessment is favourable, the procedure continues; if the notification is rejected, the procedure ends (Brosset 2004: 565). In the Preamble the Directive explicitly states that forum shopping is allowed.[24]

Once authorisation has been granted, the national authority is still important in identifying and transmitting new information. Notifiers must submit information to the competent authority on relevant methods to facilitate post-marketing control. Information on all GMOs released for research purposes must be registered, and details made available to the public.[25] Member States must also keep publicly available registers for GMOs intended for placing on the market. The location of commercial releases must be made known to the public in a manner deemed appropriate by national competent authorities.[26] In addition, there is the possibility to have recourse to the safeguard clause of Article 23, which permits the adoption of provisional measures if the national authority finds that the GMO presents a risk to human health or the environment. In that case 'new or additional information since the date of consent' has to be made available.

By way of interim conclusion, it may be said that the system in the Deliberate Release Directive for part C releases was designed as a decentralised authorisation system in which Member States and European institutions are assigned distinctive roles. In particular, Member States carry out the risk assessment following harmonised Community standards and thereby act as agents for the Community. Once a

22 Council Decision 1999/468/EC of 28 June 1999 laying down the procedures for the exercise of implementing powers conferred on the Commission, [1999] *OJ* L184/23.

23 Article 18. This is unless an agreement between the respective national authorities has been reached in the meantime, Article 15(1), above, note 1.

24 Recitals 36, 38 of the Preamble of the Deliberate Release Directive, above, note 1. This implies that rejection of a GMO by one national authority is without prejudice to any future decision about this GMO by another competent authority.

25 Deliberate Release Directive, above, note 1, Article 20.

26 *Ibid.*, Article 31(2).

product is approved in one Member State, other Member States can exert control only by raising objections or invoking the safeguard clause, possibilities that were intended to be used only in exceptional cases. Deep-rooted disagreements about both qualitative and quantitative aspects of risks posed by GMOs have corrupted this system, however. In practice, this means that by virtue of the comitology procedure it is ultimately for the Commission to take a final decision, which tends to be positive. For as long as this remains the case, the actual discretion of Member States will be limited.

Member State authorisation powers in the context of part B releases, in contrast, is almost exclusive. To gain a better understanding of the Dutch attitude and policy on GMOs, it is therefore most productive to examine national authorisations of experimental release of GMOs into the environment, as well as national authorisations for contained use.

2.5 The Regulation on GM Food and Feed

The Regulation on GM Food and Feed simultaneously pursues multiple objectives. Besides the establishment and maintenance of the internal market in GM food and feed, it is concerned with the protection of human life and health, as well as with environmental protection, animal health and welfare, and consumer interests.[27]

The Regulation concerns the placing on the market of GMOs for food and feed use, or food and feed containing GMOs that consist of such organisms or are produced from GMOs.[28] In contrast to the Deliberate Release Directive, it puts in place a centralised and uniform EU procedure for all applicants intending to place GM food and feed on the market, which covers both the GMO itself and the food and feed products derived therefrom. An indication of the intention of the Community legislator to minimise disparities between Member States is already provided by the choice of a regulation, rather than a directive. This conclusion also follows from a substantive analysis of the Regulation on GM Food and Feed. In particular, no authorisation may be granted or refused on grounds other than those set out in the Regulation.[29] The authorisation is subject to a single risk assessment process under the responsibility of the European Food and Safety Authority (ESFA), and a single risk management process involving the Commission and the Member States through a regulatory committee procedure. In contemporary EU jargon, a 'one door – one key' procedure for the scientific assessment and authorisation of GMOs and GM food is introduced, in which responsibilities are shared between Member States and the Community. The scope for public participation in the authorisation process is modest: the public may furnish comments to the Commission on the EFSA opinion. No further provision is made as to the manner in which these comments are to be

27 Above, note 7, Article 1.

28 *Ibid.*, Article 3.

29 *Ibid.*, Article 4(5).

taken into account. As a form of public participation, these provisions are weak (Scott 2004).

3 DUTCH LEGAL FRAMEWORK AND DECISION MAKING ON GMOs

In a wide range of policy documents, consecutive Dutch governments have stressed the opportunities provided by modern biotechnology.[30] The 'New Jerusalem' is anticipated to come in the form of sustainable farming, cleaner production methods, better health care, and a cleaner environment. At the same time, it is acknowledged that, 'their use should be accompanied by optimum safeguards to ensure safety, transparency of decision making, freedom of choice for the individual and ethical acceptability'.[31] There exists a significant public expertise infrastructure for biotechnology in the Netherlands, in part precisely because of government support since the early 1980s. Biotechnology accounts for little over 5 per cent of university research.[32] However, the high standard of Dutch biotechnology research has been insufficiently translated into innovative potential, a concern which current and future Dutch policy is aiming to address.[33] An important pillar of this policy consists of simplifying and streamlining the regulatory framework, which is regarded as too cumbersome and sometimes overly stringent as compared with other jurisdictions. The Ministry of Economic Affairs, in association with the Dutch Biotechnology Association (NIABA), is systematically keeping track of life-science companies that relocate abroad, and investigates which regulatory burdens have played a role in such decisions. There thus exists some empirical evidence that regulatory competition within Europe in this harmonised policy field remains a reality, at the very least in those areas where Member States have retained discretionary powers. Where Member States enjoy no such discretionary powers, the administrative operationalisation of the notification, authorisation and monitoring systems still offers scope for simplification and institutional coordination or, to use popular parlance, 'cutting red tape'.

30 *Beleidsnota Biotechnologie* (White Paper on Biotechnology) *Kamerstukken II* 2000–2001, 27 428, No. 2; *Beslissen over Biotechnologie* (Deciding on Biotechnology, government's standpoint on report of Scientific Council for Governments policy) *Kamerstukken II* 2002–2003, 27 428, No. 40; *Verantwoord en zorgvuldig toetsen, Een integraal toetsingskader voor biotechnologische ontwikkelingen* (Prudence and Care, A review of the integrated system for vetting biotechnology developments in the Netherlands) *Kamerstukken II* 2002–2003, 27 428, No. 39; *Kabinetsreactie op de Trendanalyse Biotechnologie 2004* (Government's standpoint on Trend Analysis Biotechnology 2004), *Kamerstukken II* 2004–2005, 27 428, No. 57.

31 Ministerie van VROM, *Integrale Nota Biotechnologie* (Integrated White Paper on Biotechnology). Den Haag: Ministerie van Volkshuisvesting, Ruimtelijke Ordening en Milieubeheer (*Kamerstukken II* 2000–2001, 27 428), p. 7.

32 *Ibid.*, at 11.

33 *Kamerstukken II* 2000–2001, 27 428, No. 2.

3.1 Legal framework

Under the Genetically Modified Organisms Decree,[34] a licence is required for the genetic modification of plants and micro-organisms.[35] This Decree implements the Deliberate Release Directive and the Contained Use Directive.[36] In accordance with the Deliberate Release Directive, the Decree provides that any person, before undertaking a deliberate release, must submit an application to the competent authority. After the competent authority has been satisfied that the deliberate release is safe from environmental and human health perspectives, it may give its consent by granting a permit. The competent Dutch authority is the Minister of Environment, who may seek advice from the expert Commission on Genetic Manipulation (COGEM). As has been seen, the Deliberate Release Directive leaves the choice of competent authorities to the Member States. In practice, the choice of competent authority has profound ramifications for the way in which the Deliberate Release Directive is applied. It is well known that the Ministry of Housing, Spatial Planning and the Environment (VROM) traditionally entertains more reservations towards GMOs than, in particular, the Ministries of Agriculture (LNV) and Economic Affairs (EZ), a fact that has given rise to bitter political infighting during the drafting of the Integrale Nota Biotechnologie.[37]

Dutch governments have underlined the importance of building expertise in biotechnology and the development of new applications within a framework of criteria pertaining to safety and acceptability. The regulatory framework that has come to embody that ambition is the Dutch GMO Decree, which in turn is to be applied in a way that reflects the precautionary principle. For an interpretation of the precautionary principle, guidance is sought in the Communication of the Commission on the Precautionary Principle.[38] According to this document, the Precautionary Principle has relevance mainly to risk management, in cases where a risk assessment has shown grounds for uncertainty about unacceptable risks.

Licences are prepared by the GMO Bureau of the Ministry of Housing, Spatial Planning and the Environment (VROM). Inspection and enforcement tasks have been assigned to the Environment Inspectorate.

Various licences may be granted under the GMO Decree, depending on the type of activity intended. Procedures with plants and micro-organisms can be divided into roughly three categories: contained use, field trials and market introduction. Contained use concerns biotechnological activities in confined institutions such as laboratories, glasshouses, factories and breeding cells. Confined institutions must

34 1990, pursuant to the Chemicals Substances Act, last amended on 1 July 2005, *Stcr.* 2005, 320. The Deliberate Release Directive, above, note 1, is also implemented in the Regulation on Genetically Modified Organisms, last amended 1 July, *Stcr.* 2005, 117. Implementation was only completed in 2004, while by October 2002 this Directive had to be transposed into national legislation. Several Member States, including the Netherlands had failed to do so by that date. Consequently, in June 2003, the European Commission referred these Member States to the European Court of Justice.

35 Articles 8 sub 1, 10 sub 1 and 11 sub 1 of *Besluit genetisch gemodificeerde organismen Wet milieugevaarlijke stoffen* (Genetically Modified Organisms Decree, Environmentally Hazardous Substances Act).

36 Above, note 4.

37 Above, note 31.

38 European Commission, *Communication on the precautionary principle*, COM(2000) 1, 2 February 2000, Brussels.

be licensed under the *Wet Milieubeheer* (Environmental Management Act). It is the municipalities, at local level, that are responsible for ensuring that licensees comply with structural requirements pertaining to the institution. The comprehensive public preparatory procedure contained in the *Algemene Wet Bestuursrecht* (General Administrative Act) is applicable to the licensing procedure.

VROM assesses applications for a licence on the basis of the GMO Decree. It assesses risks to human health and the environment, and decides what level of containment is necessary to address these risks. The GMO Decree contains a scheme which, for most examples of contained use, details the containment level required. If the scheme does not offer guidance for a particular activity for which a licence is sought, the expert body COGEM will be asked for advice.

If activities involving GMOs are not covered by the definition of contained use, they are covered by the legal regime concerning their introduction into the environment. This may be in the form of a field trial, or market introduction. In order to carry out a field trial, a VROM licence is required pursuant to the GMO Decree. The comprehensive public preparatory procedure under the General Administrative Act is applicable for the licensing procedures for field trials. Risk assessment of GMO field trials takes place on a 'case-by-case' basis and in accordance with the 'step-by-step' principle. The former means that every individual use of GMOs contained in a permit application is judged separately, so that the risk assessment is always geared to the specific nature of any particular use of GMOs. It also means that a permit application must be accompanied by a detailed profile of the GMO, together with a detailed description of the circumstances under which the application will be used. As for the step-by-step principle, this implies that the containment of GMOs is reduced and the scale of release increased gradually, step-by-step, but only if evaluation of the earlier steps in terms of protection of human health and the environment indicates that the next step can be taken.

The first stage of the risk assessment process consists of identifying potentially harmful effects on human health and the environment resulting from the genetic properties introduced, the organism used, its specific application, and the circumstances under which the trial will be carried out. Harmful consequences for humans and the environment also encompass effects on ecosystems and the safety of animal feed. The second stage aims to quantify the probability that such effects will occur, a process characterised by high degrees of scientific uncertainty.[39]

Decisions on applications are made in tandem with the Minister of Agriculture in so far as they concern aspects of environmental protection.[40] If the application is related to aspects of public health, the Minister of Public Health, Welfare and Sports (VWS) must be consulted.[41]

The resulting draft decision is available for inspection for a period of four weeks, during which interested parties may submit their observations. After a definitive decision has been taken by VROM, those who submitted observations may lodge an

39 On 'risk', 'uncertainty' and 'ignorance' and the problem of inconsumerability, see Stirling 1999.

40 Article 23(10) sub a of *Besluit genetisch gemodificeerde organismen Wet milieugevaarlijke stoffen* (Genetically Modified Organisms Decree, Environmentally Hazardous Substances Act).

41 Article 23(10) sub b of *Besluit genetisch gemodificeerde organismen Wet milieugevaarlijke stoffen* (Genetically Modified Organisms Decree, Environmentally Hazardous Substances Act).

appeal with the highest administrative court, the *Raad van State* (Council of State), where a preliminary injunction may be requested.[42] Social and political unrest concerning the deliberate release of GMOs has given rise to considerable delays in licensing procedures for field trials, and ultimately to a tightening up of field trial policy. Each permit for field trials with GM crops almost invariably triggered an appeal with the Council of State. The administrative courts usually recognised that VROM had a certain freedom of judgement. VROM must be able to show that the scientific risk assessment has been as thorough as possible, and that conclusions are scientifically objective, so that measures can be said to have been based on sufficient knowledge (Schenkelaars 2004). As a result of a ruling by the Council of State, applicants are also obliged to provide detailed information regarding the intended location of the field trial.[43] Destruction of trial fields has accordingly, become a significant problem. The average time needed to obtain field trial licences in 2004 was 148 days.

In 2004, a *milieuveiligheidsfunctionaris* (environmental safety officer) was introduced, responsible for the supervision of all activities that relate to the deliberate release of GMOs into the environment.[44] This officer is appointed within the organisation that performs activities regarding GMOs. His or her chief responsibility is to supervise environmental safety, and at the same time to serve as contact person for the government as an external inspector.

3.2 Science and expertise

The Genetically Modified Organisms Decree foresees the existence of an advisory body, COGEM, for the provision of scientific advice on notifications for contained use and applications for deliberate release.[45] This statutory advisory body advises the Environment Minister at his or her request or at its own volition by assigning the production of and activities with GMOs to various risk categories. COGEM advice is not a compulsory part of the licensing procedure, however. On the basis of the latest scientific knowledge, COGEM quantifies risks to human health and the environment flowing from particular uses of GMOs, and determines the safety measures necessary. If the adverse effects for human health and the environment are acceptable, or can be sufficiently reduced by the adoption of safety measures, COGEM advises approval of licence applications.[46] COGEM has complained about occasions where the Minister overturns its advice without proper motivation. This occurs regularly, but remains unknown to original applicants. Disregard of

42 This is 'judicial review', rather than 'administrative review'.

43 Ruling by the Council of State dated 16 November 2000 (20002946/1).

44 The legal basis for this 'official' found in the Deliberate Release Directive, above, note 1, which instructs the appointment of a 'responsible scientist' for each permit-request for the release of a GMO, Annex 111A sub I (B); Annex IIIB sub A(2).

45 The statutory basis for COGEM was introduced in the Environmental Management Act in 1997 in Article 2.25 *et seq.*

46 The number of applications for advice for COGEM has decreased in the last years (although the number of applications for permits increased), showed an independent evaluation of COGEM, 24 November 2004, 34674/AHY/RGO, available at: <http://www.cogem.net>. No research has been undertaken to explore the reason for this decrease.

COGEM's advice is a source of frustration among COGEM scientists, who fear that such disregard for their scientific input will adversely impact on their personal and institutional credibility. There have been suggestions that some of the top specialists may no longer wish to be involved with COGEM for this reason.[47]

In 2000, the government embarked upon a policy to increase the transparency of the advisory process and to improve the input of ecological know-how within COGEM.[48] In addition, apart from COGEM's statutory task to provide technical and scientific advice, it was felt that it should also take into account the social and ethical developments in the field of genetic modification. COGEM is therefore not only expected to consider individual cases, but also periodically and proactively to report what future developments may be expected. To fulfil this task, COGEM has been expanded and several new members were appointed, including experts in the fields of ecology, ethics and the social sciences more generally. In order to improve its transparency, COGEM periodically explains various aspects of its work at a higher level of abstraction. This includes such issues as how it conducts risk assessments in social contexts with specific attention to scientific uncertainty and ignorance.

These additional tasks of COGEM invite questions about the role of expert advice. According to COGEM, the aim of general recommendations on social-ethical issues is to inform the public about the values that play a role in science and to furnish the political sphere with relevant arguments for policy making. In this novel setting, it is still possible for scientists to offer advice and for regulators to decide.[49] However, while it is commonly understood that expert advice should remain unaffected by politics, COGEM's expanded mandate threatens that this separation between risk assessment and risk management will become increasingly blurred. Indeed, the majority of COGEM staff is confused about the socio-ethical 'role' that they have been assigned.[50] Although they appreciate the importance of the socio-ethical aspects of any policy on GMOs, they find it hard to reconcile this new paradigm with the technical and scientific part of their task.

It is appropriate to recall the Communication on the Precautionary Principle at this point, in which the Commission argues for a functional separation between risk assessment and risk management. According to the Commission, scientific advice should be kept separate from policy considerations. Indeed, the EC counterpart of COGEM, EFSA issues advice on a purely scientific basis.[51]

Although these socio-ethical recommendations are thus controversial, this did not stop COGEM from presenting an unsolicited study on an Integrated Socio-Ethical Evaluation Framework (ISEEF) to serve transparent, consistent and accountable decision making on different applications of biotechnology.[52] According to this study, it is necessary explicitly to provide opportunity for reflection on and expression of different views, followed by a phase of determining, through

47 *Ibid.*

48 In response to public unrest, the *de facto* moratorium, and acknowledgement of scientific uncertainty.

49 Social-ethical considerations are not taken into account in deciding individual permit applications.

50 Independent evaluation of COGEM, 24 November 2004, 34674/AHY/RGO, available at: <http://www.cogem.net>.

51 Above, note 5.

52 COGEM, 'Towards an Integral Societal-Ethical Evaluation Framework', CGM/03061802, 24 June 2003, available at: <http://www.cogem.net>.

democratic decision making by the parliament, the priorities of certain interests and values. A five-step procedure is proposed for the socio-ethical evaluation of individual cases. COGEM acknowledges that the precautionary principle should play a fundamental role in the decision-making process. In its recommendations to VROM, COGEM stresses that an integrated socio-ethical evaluation should not be restricted to weighing economic usefulness against scientific and technical risks. The category 'risk' should be extended so as to come to mean 'affected value', while 'usefulness' should also encompass 'societal usefulness'. Interestingly, COGEM urged for in-house expertise on ethical and social issues at VROM. COGEM also recommended explicitly applying the principle of proportionality in all legislative frameworks concerning biotechnology. These last two recommendations were rejected by the Junior Minister of VROM; with regard to the other recommendations, he likewise referred to the White Paper 'Prudence and Care', in which a review framework for biotechnological developments had already been set out.[53]

3.3 Information and participation

Until the mid-1990s, debates on the risks of GM crops were isolated and confined to a relatively small epistemic elite such as VROM, COGEM, life science companies, and occasionally Non-governmental Organisations (NGOs). This changed after the first imports of GM soy from North America into the Netherlands in 1996, which triggered the interest of Ministries, operators in the agro-food chain, and public interest groups. The issue of GM food, which had suddenly become controversial, all at once appeared high on the agenda of mainstream political parties and the mass media. In this climate, in June 1999 Parliament adopted a resolution, urging the government to organise a broad public debate on GMOs and food. For this purpose, the Minister of Agriculture installed the Commission for Biotechnology and Food (CBF). Indicative of the degree of public anxiety in the Netherlands is the fact that this stakeholder debate, a perfect example of Dutch obsession with consensual politics (domestically referred to as the 'polder model'), utterly failed to defuse public distrust. In almost any sense, the debate was a fiasco.

While information and public participation are compulsory elements of the Community regulatory framework, their practical organisation is left to Member States, leaving them with considerable discretionary powers. In this regard, there are recent developments suggesting that Dutch policy on information and participation is shifting.[54]

As for the current position, it has been observed that GOGEM has acquired information responsibilities in this respect, and has developed a vision where, even if it is believed that public perceptions of risks are irrational, it may still be necessary to take these perceptions into account.

The rationale underpinning the ideal of public participation and access to justice in respect of legislative measures and public decision making is closely linked with

53 *Kamerstukken II* 2003–2004, 27 428 and White Paper: 'Prudence and Care', A review of the integrated system for vetting biotechnology developments in the Netherlands, *Kamerstukken II* 2002–2003, 27 428, No. 39.

54 Further discussed in section 4, below.

political ideals of democracy, constitutional government, and good governance. In the absence of scientific certainty, decisions have to be taken under conditions of scientific uncertainty or ignorance. Under such circumstances of scientific uncertainty and ignorance, it is impossible to avoid recourse to extra-scientific and hence socio-political judgement. This amounts to a powerful argument for public participation in what is essentially political decision making about the direction of a technology for which regulatory bodies can no longer justify a retreat behind a screen of scientific pseudo-certainties (de Sadeleer 1999, Löfstedt and Frewer 1998).

The requirements regarding public information and participation contained in the Deliberate Release Directive, in as far as they relate to experimental purposes, have been transposed into administrative legislation.[55] The Minister of the Environment informs the public about any application for authorisation of releases for purposes not related to placing on the market by placing a notice in the official government gazette, national, regional and local newspapers, and on its website. The information which is accessible includes general descriptions of GMOs, the name and address of applicants, the purpose of the release, location(s) of site(s) where releases will take place, the intended use of GMOs, a description of potential effects on human health and the environment, a description of measures to limit adverse effects, a description of plans for monitoring effects, description of measures to treat GMO waste of releases, a description of emergency response plans, reports and advice issued by advisory committees, and a non-technical summary.[56] All documents relevant to the release of GMOs, such as environmental permits, are published on the website of VROM.

The public participation procedures allow the public to submit comments within four weeks and to appeal against the decision within six weeks. This gives rise to a period of 120 days between receipt of the notification and VROM's decision. This is 30 days in excess of the time limit mentioned in Article 6(5) of the Deliberate Release Directive, which is just within the limits of Article 6(6)b, which allows the 90-day period to be prolonged by a maximum of 30 days for the purposes of public participation.

The text of the final decision indicates how account has been taken of the outcome of public participation, and is publicly accessible through the VROM website and made available in government libraries. If an NGO or individual considers that the outcome of the public participation procedure has not been taken account of in the final decision, judicial review before a court of law is available. NGOs and individuals have made use of the legal provisions concerning public information and participation, which has resulted in clarification of the law, enhanced motivation for decisions, amendment of provisions in permits and in-depth political discussion on specific issues, such as herbicide-resistance breeding, feed use, organic farming and liability (Schenkelaars 2002). The main critique of

55 With regard to public information and participation on deliberate release of GMOs for the purpose of placing on the market, Community law requires that each notification must be submitted to the public twice; first in the national phase and second in the Community phase. Publication is carried out by the Joint Research Centre (JRC), the research institute of the European Commission and available at: <http://gmoinfo.jrc.it>.

56 Article 14 of *Besluit genetisch gemodificeerde organismen Wet milieugevaarlijke stoffen* (Genetically Modified Organisms Decree, Environmentally Hazardous Substances Act).

the public participation procedure, apart from the fact that it is so time-consuming, is that review by the Council of State is confined to the correct application of administrative rules by the competent authority. Scientific and technical controversies about risk assessment fall outside the remit of the judicial review.

3.4 Dutch coexistence policy

Coexistence in agriculture refers to the possibility of cultivating GM crops alongside conventional and organic farming without one excluding the other. Co-existence has been one of the flash points in debates on GMOs. The cultivation of GMOs in the EU is likely to have implications for the organisation of agricultural production. The possibility of adventitious (unintended) presence of GM crops in biological and traditional crops, and vice versa, raises the question as to how producer and consumer choice for the different production types can be ensured.

Member States are allowed to adopt measures to avoid the unintended presence of GMOs in other products.[57] The Commission issued a Recommendation on Guidelines for the Development of National Strategies and Best Practices to Ensure Coexistence of Genetically Modified Crops with Conventional and Organic Farming (Recommendation on Co-existence).[58] The Recommendation on Co-existence essentially leaves it to Member States to implement national coexistence measures, with the proviso that such measures concern economic aspects of admixture of GM and non-GM crops (Poli 2006).

The issue of coexistence features high on the Dutch political agenda, and the issue of 'safe' isolation distances between GM and traditional crops is frequently raised in appeals at the Council of State. The Minister of Agriculture wrote a letter to Parliament in October 2002, indicating that stakeholders had been given until April 2004 to establish a coexistence arrangement based on consensus. For that purpose, a Commission on Coexistence has been set up.[59] Stakeholders encountered difficulties in finding consensus that could form the basis for a self-regulatory regime. Organic farmers, in particular, maintained their position of 'zero-tolerance' of GM contamination of their products.

In 2003, COGEM issued a report on coexistence in which it concluded that knowledge gaps persist on the flow patterns of (trans)genes.[60] In its report, COGEM points out that, in order to prevent reciprocal liability claims and guarantee coexistence and consumer choice, agreements must be reached about measures and separation criteria to be applied. COGEM urged the undertaking of further scientific research on threshold values aiming to establish crop-specific criteria for

57 The Deliberate Release Directive, above, note 1, was amended for this purpose; measures were previously only allowed in the interest of the protection of human health and the environment.

58 Commission Recommendation 2003/556/EC, [2003] *OJ* L189/86.

59 *Kamerstukken II* 2003–2004, 29404, No. 2.

60 Although coexistence is not an environmental safety problem and therefore strictly speaking not part of COGEM's remit, COGEM's commission decided, in view of COGEM's expertise and the controversies surrounding this subject, to issue a further report about the technical aspects of cultivation, as announced in a previously (2003) published monitoring report on coexistence, 'Co-existentie in landbouw. Vermenging, uitkruising en isolatiegronden', No. 041013-01, 13 October 2004, available at: <http://www.cogem.net>.

coexistence, isolation distances between GM and traditional crop cultivation and chain segregation measures. By providing insights into the effects of cultivation measures on admixture, COGEM hoped to contribute to the formation of consensus. In its report, COGEM distinguishes four cultivation stages that are important for the issue of admixture. The measures needed to limit admixture will have to be examined for each stage and crop.

The Commission on Coexistence, in which all stakeholders were represented, continued their deliberations, which resulted in a report issued in 2004.[61] The parties had reached agreement on measures to prevent unintended admixture of GM and traditional crops. Moreover, they arranged for the setting up of a compensation fund for reimbursement for crop damage.[62] As regards liability, the question of how liability can be established for damage as a consequence of admixture of crops proved to be a tricky one.[63] The Commission on Coexistence agreed that compliance with the agreement reached constituted a defence against liability claims. For this category of damage, parties agreed to set up a compensation fund. Any person who, through no fault of his own, suffers demonstrable damage qualifies for reimbursement of economic loss from the fund where no other liable person can be identified. The fund is set up per crop, in the sense that, depending on the crop, the relevant parties contribute to the fund.

4 CURRENT DEVELOPMENTS: SIMPLIFICATION AND DEREGULATION

According to NIABA, partly because of the deteriorating climate for research and development, seven biotech-companies have reduced or ceased activities in the Netherlands in recent years. As a result, the Netherlands risks becoming more dependent on research results and products generated elsewhere.

The Ministry of Economic Affairs, alarmed about this development, commissioned a 'first phase survey of bottlenecks as experienced by applicants in the implementation practices of legislation for biotechnology research in the Netherlands' (Kampmeijer, Van der Zenden, Biocollectief 2003). In the report, 'Workability Practices', experiences of business and research institutions with applications and public consultation procedures for licences in the Netherlands are detailed for the period 2002–03 (Kampmeijer, Van der Zenden, Biocollectief 2003). In general, the Dutch part B approval procedure does not seem to differ much from three other EU countries (France, Germany and the United Kingdom) in terms of transparency, overall effects and manageability. The complaints that were aired in the report concern the way in which the rules concerning licensing work in practice. Criticism focused on the time consultative bodies need to deal

61 'Coëxistentie Primaire Sector', Report of the temporary commission on coexistence chaired by J. van Dijk, Den Haag, 1 November 2004. Parties that formed the commission: Biologica, LTO Nederland, Plantum NL and Platform Aarde Boer Consument.

62 The Deliberative Body did look at other possibilities, like insurance, but regarded this an unsuitable instrument.

63 The Ministry of Legal Affairs also explored the possibilities for liability within the current legal framework of civil liability.

with applications, insufficient communication and coordination between different consultative bodies, poor communication with and information supply to applicants, and insufficient collaboration between the (evaluation) bodies and applicants.[64] The report argues for more transparent and predictable application procedures, the development of additional and targeted communication and educational activities, and closer cooperation between consultative bodies and applicants.

In the spirit of the conclusions of the report, government proposed amendments to the Genetically Modified Organisms Decree designed to reduce administrative burdens for biotechnology companies and research institutions. In justifying the proposal it stated that:

> The intended regulations on Biotechnology will – in so far as relevant – take more explicit account of the consequences of scientific research on the national position and the economy, incidentally without compromising the standards of due care or safety that are to be upheld. This is with the aim of creating a level playing field for Dutch biotechnology companies. Care will be taken to avoid creating unnecessarily complex assessments when drawing up new regulations.[65]

For contained use these changes involve:

- for licensing: recourse to the normal public preparatory procedure, instead of the comprehensive public preparatory procedure, shortening the procedure from 129 days to 45 days;
- scrapping the prior approval system in favour of a notification system;[66]
- adopting the possibility for installations to derogate from administrative requirements that are perceived too rigid subject to VROM approval;
- taking 'contained use activities' out of the definition of 'installation' as formulated in the Environment Management Act, so that no permit needs to be obtained for contained use;
- simplifying the different categories of contained use;
- investigating possibilities for exempting contained use for micro-organisms that are genetically modified by application of self-cloning of plants.

For the deliberate release of GMOs, a similar deregulation exercise is proposed:

- two types of permits are to be introduced: standard permits that will be subject to a fixed set of conditions. For this standard permit no case-by-case risk

64 *Verantwoord en zorgvuldig vereenvoudigen van het Besluit genetisch gemodificeerde organismen* (Memorandum on decreasing the burden of, streamlining and simplifying biotechnology legislation and regulations), *Kamerstukken II* 2005–2006, 27 428, No. 69.

65 *Ibid.*, at 18.

66 In the proposed text, no classifications of different types of risks are included, while the Contained Use Directive n. 4 above, requires in Article 10 sub 2 that: 'A class 3 or higher class contained use may not proceed without the prior consent of the competent authority . . .'. We assume that this distinction will be taken into account in the final draft of the proposed amendments.

assessment is required. The second type of permit will be for experimental uses where conditions can be differentiated and a separate risk assessment is still required;

- for licensing, recourse will be had to the normal public preparatory procedure, instead of the comprehensive public preparatory procedure;
- the concept of a 'minor change' in permits concerning the deliberate release of GMOs should become possible, without informing the public of such minor changes. No preparatory procedure will be required in those instances;
- the possibility to be exempted from the obligation to appoint an environmental safety officer.

From the logic that informs these proposed amendments, we may conclude that the Dutch are prepared to compromise the hitherto defining value of Dutch consensual policy making that comes in the form of public information and participation, for the greater good of acquiring a competitive edge on the global market for biotech products. Although, at first sight, this streamlining of Dutch regulations remains within the boundaries of EC GMO law, it represents a departure from the consensual, transparent and deliberative model of governance the poldering Dutch once prided themselves on.

5 CONCLUDING REMARKS

This brief overview suggests that public divides about GMOs resonates at all levels of the European and national regulatory spectrum, including within the Netherlands.

In part, this is because the EU regulatory regime itself is flawed, which of course translates into incoherency of the national policies that are designed to transpose it. The root of this problem may lie in the fact that the EU regime regulating GMOs was initially conceptualised as simply having to balance trade imperatives with environmental and health concerns. Indeed, this balance has successfully been struck on many occasions in the past, notably in the context of EC environmental policy. In reality, however, GMOs represent a completely different, and much more difficult challenge. Politically, economically and ethically charged as it is, the Community's democratic deficit and lack of transparency has funnelled an unprecedented challenge to Community competence for the regulation of GMOs, culminating in the *de facto* moratorium.

The system contained in the Deliberate Release Directive is a delicate one, involving a decentralised Community authorisation procedure and risk assessment. Although such a system has been operating relatively smoothly for movements of waste, for the reasons explained, this success could not be repeated for GMOs.

The decentralised authorisation system in practice turns out to be little more than a first formal stage that ultimately ends in a centralised Community decision of approval in the context of the regulatory procedure of comitology. In other words, although Member States may object to authorisations in response to local conditions or preference, this merely amounts to a stay of execution, as experience thus far suggests that the outcome of the regulatory procedure almost invariably is that the marketing of the contested GMO will be approved by the Commission. Of course, this also means that, while the Community can safely trumpet the virtues of public participation and transparency accommodated in national authorisation procedures, in the meantime, the inevitable reality of comitology decision making is rather different and particularly intransparent. National recourse to Article 95(5) EC offers Member States little by way of compensation, since the conditions always have been interpreted restrictively, something that no amount of controversy about GMOs is likely to change.

For Member States with governments that are genuinely committed to act to reflect national distaste about GMOs (Austria), this harsh reality may be unpalatable. It is difficult to escape the impression, however, that other governments are privately rather content to have recourse to the excuse that GMOs are being forced upon it by Brussels or the WTO, in order to pacify their bio-sceptical electorates. The Dutch Government fits this category. For one, it is a staunch believer in GMOs, and consistently opposed the moratorium. It should be recalled that it was earlier forced by the Dutch Parliament against its explicit own wish to challenge the validity of Directive 98/44/EC on the Patentability of Biotechnological Inventions before the European Court of Justice.[67] Mercifully perhaps, the case was lost.

Against this background it becomes less surprising that, although one of the architects of Article 95(5) EC when it was first introduced as Article 100a(4) in the Single European Act, the Dutch Government has never contemplated use of this derogation clause in relation to GMOs, nor has it relied on the safeguard clause of Article 23 in the Deliberate Release Directive. On the contrary, it is actively exploring any room that is left to Member States under the EC regime to ease the regulatory burden for the life-science industry.

Still, as has been seen, EC law does not provide an all-encompassing excuse behind which national governments can hide. If EC law has offered a politically opportune excuse to bypass public discontent about GMOs for the sake of Dutch economic policy, that refuge has not been available in fields where the Netherlands enjoy reserved powers. An analysis of the way in which the Netherlands have exercised those powers therefore offers a glimpse of what a truly 'Dutch' policy GMOs amounts to. A confusing picture has emerged.

We have found concerted efforts to deregulate and cut red tape so as to serve the biotech-industry, but at the same time we discerned moves that introduce politics in the realm of risk assessment that are almost certain to horrify proponents of biotechnology. On reflection, however, this policy is the product of conflicting interests, pursued by freely competing Government Departments and Ministries, and more accurately reflects Dutch public attitude towards GMOs than the distorted picture that emerges in the context of the implementation of the EU regime.

67 Directive 98/44/EC of the European Parliament and of the Council of 6 July 1998 on the legal protection of biotechnological inventions, [1998] *OJ* L213/13; Case C-377/98 *Netherlands v Parliament and Council* [2001] ECR I-7079.

BIBLIOGRAPHY

Brosset, E. (2004) 'The Prior Authorisation Procedure Adopted for the Deliberate Release into the Environment of Genetically Modified Organisms: the Complexities of Balancing Community and National Competences', *European Law Journal* 5(10): 555–79.

Christoforou, T. (2004) 'The Regulation of Genetically Modified Organisms in the European Union: the Interplay of Science, Law and Politics', *Common Market Law Review* 41(3): 637–709.

Hervey, T.K. (2001) 'Regulation of Genetically Modified Products in a Multi-Level System of Governance: Science or Citizens?', *Review of Community and International Environmental Law* 10: 321–8.

Kampmeijer, J., Van der Zenden, R., Biocollectief (2003) *International comparison of the 'workability' of existing legislation for biotechnical research and recommendations to Dutch authorities*, Study in order of the Ministry of Economic Affairs, 1–112.

Löfstedt, R. and Frewer, L. (1998) *Risk & Modern Society*, London: Earthscan Publications Ltd.

Poli, S. (2006) 'Restrictions on the Cultivation of Genetically Modified Organisms: Issues of EC Law', in H. Somsen (ed.), *The regulatory challenge of bio-technology: human genetics, food and patents*, Cheltenham: Edward Elgar, 156–73.

de Sadeleer, N. (1999) *Les principes du pollueur-payeur, de prévention et de precaution: essai sur la genèse et la portée juridique de quelques principes du droit de l'environnement*, Brussels: Bruylant.

Schenkelaars Biotechnology Consultancy (2004) *Precautionary Expertise for GM crops: National Report – The Netherlands*, available at: <http://www.sbcbiotech.nl>.

Schenkelaars Biotechnology Consultancy (2002) *Public Information and Participation in the context of EU Directives 90/220 and 2001/18/*, Report of a European workshop, available at: <http://www.sbcbiotech.nl>.

Scott, J. (2004) *European Regulation of GMOs: Thinking about 'Judicial Review' in the WTO*, Jean Monnet Working Paper 04/04, Professor J.H.H. Weiler European Union Jean Monnet Chair, NYU School of Law, 1–31.

Stirling, A. (1999) *On Science and Precaution in the Management of Technological Risk*, Final Report of a project for the EC Forward Studies Unit under the auspices of the ESTO Network, published at: <http://www.sussex.ac.uk/Units/gec/gecko/r9e-prc-htm>.

Chapter 11

The Polish regulatory system on GMOs: between EU influence and national nuances

*Patrycja Dąbrowska**

1 INTRODUCTION

Coping with the risks and uncertainties that pervade our lives has become an increasingly onerous challenge for regulators (Baldwin 1997; Joerges 2001: 1). In particular, the challenge engendered by modern biotechnology has triggered numerous regulatory responses and legal developments at the national, regional and international levels (Christoforou 2004: 640; Murphy 2001: 47; R. Mackenzie 2002: 97). Yet, regulatory approaches to genetic engineering vary significantly, especially between Europe and the US (Scott 2003; Pollack and Shaffer 2001; Vogel and Teel 2000: 649). The differences have led to the already famous dispute at the WTO where the United States challenged EU policy on transgenic products, including national safeguard measures (Scott 2004). So, opposites may oppose one another, but, of course, they may also learn from each other. This is why it is constructive to scrutinise different regulatory systems on genetically modified organisms (GMOs), which operate at separate governance levels, in order to provide useful comparative insights that can help to achieve better understandings of (common) problems and to overcome shared difficulties. Moreover, it is also instructive to investigate the development and features of regimes that are new members of regional organisations – more particularly, the Polish regime within the EU – in order to examine how they fit within and adapt to the supranational framework.

Accordingly, this chapter presents the Polish regulatory system for GM products. It focuses on the provisions applicable to GMO use and commercialisation, but does not specifically discuss product-related regulations on GM food or pharmaceuticals. The following sections examine, first, the development of the Polish legal system regulating contained use and deliberate release of GMOs from its early years to the recent developments (2005–07), and, second, the most important features of the regulatory framework. In the latter context, the institutional design of the system, the means furnished for public participation and the implementation of the precautionary principle are analysed in detail. A fourth section appraises the complexities of decision-making processes on GMO risks, detailing current

* I am grateful to Prof. G. de Búrca, Dr B. Iwańska and P. Quillack for helpful comments on a draft of this chapter, and to the practitioners interviewed. I am indebted to Mr. Justice J. Gudowski, the Judge of the Polish Supreme Court, for his invaluable assistance. All errors remain my sole responsibility.

shortcomings and suggesting various improvements. A final section concludes with an examination of the particular peculiarities of the Polish system of GMO risk regulation.[1]

2 THE DEVELOPMENT OF THE POLISH REGULATION ON AGRICULTURAL BIOTECHNOLOGY

2.1 The early years of the regulatory framework

The history of Polish legislation applicable to genetically modified organisms is relatively short (Kwapich and Twardowski 2003: 26). It all began in 1997, seven years after the first EU Directives on GMOs were adopted,[2] when the previously existing Polish Environmental Protection and Design Act of 1980 was amended and became applicable to the deliberate release of GMOs.[3] Article 37a was inserted into the Act, initiating a procedure whereby the consent of the Minister of the Environment, Natural Resources and Forestry would be required for any commercial or experimental release of GMOs into the environment. In 1999, the Minister issued an additional executive regulation to implement Article 37a, which provided the framework under which the authorisation procedures for deliberate releases would be implemented.[4] This regulation detailed the requirements applying to notifications seeking the deliberate release of GMOs into the environment, including monitoring provisions, testing and emergency plans, the application of the principle of risk assessment, and conditions for the labelling and packaging of products (Dalbiak 2003: 26). Even though Article 37a constituted a very basic and 'incomplete' regulatory framework for GMOs – it failed to address various crucial issues such as the contained use of GMOs, the nature of scientific advice, and various procedural matters that had already been regulated within EU Directives – it nonetheless introduced GMO control into the scope of the Polish legal system, which in itself was a vital step (Jendrośka 2001b: 63–4).

It should be noted that the primary impetus for the introduction of Article 37a was parliamentary concern about the then treatment of GMOs within Poland. Parliament's major concern related to the fact that prior to the 1997 amendment Polish law maintained no control whatsoever over genetic engineering (Jendrośka 2001b: 63–4). In the mid-1990s, there had been cases whereby GM products were released into the environment without any prior risk assessment or administrative consent. For example, in 1996, a Greenpeace Report detailed alarm about the confirmed presence of transgenic carp, treated with human growth hormones, within a pond maintained by one of the Polish scientific institutes (Hajduk *et al.*

1 The text aims to present the law as it stood on 1 January 2008.

2 Council Directive 90/220/EEC on the deliberate release into the environment of genetically modified organisms, [1990] *OJ* L117/15; since 17 October 2002 repealed by Directive 2001/18/EC of the European Parliament and of the Council of 12 March 2001 on the deliberate release into the environment of genetically modified organisms and repealing Council Directive 90/220/EEC, [2001] *OJ* L106/1. In parallel, the Council Directive 90/219/EEC of 23 April 1990 on the contained use of genetically modified organisms as amended by Directive 98/81/EC, [1990] *OJ* L117/1.

3 Codified version of the Polish Environmental Protection and Design Act, *Journal of Laws* 1994, No. 49, Item 196, with amendments.

4 Old Regulation on Genetically Modified Organisms, *Journal of Laws* 1999, No. 86, Item 962.

2001: 46). In addition, however, Parliament was also concerned about the maintenance of a clear and well-balanced division of administrative competences with regard to the control of GM products in the Polish regulatory system (Jendrośka 2001b: 63–4).

Before regulation of genetic engineering formally entered Polish law in 1997, initial organisational arrangements gave scientists specialising in biotechnology the predominant role within the national authorities responsible for GMO-related matters. Above all, scientists dominated the Consultation Team for GMOs appointed by the Minister of Agriculture and Food Economy in 1996, as well as the Commission for the Registration of Biological and Chemical Plant Protection Propagations and Transgenic Plants. As a consequence, the environmental protection (and other) experts were underrepresented within these bodies; a situation causing great concern among ecological and consumer organisations as well as Members of Parliament that protection of public health and the environment would be undermined in relation to biotechnological sciences (Jendrośka 2001b: 63–4). Accordingly, the 1997 amendment apportioned responsibility for the control of GMO use to the Minister of the Environment rather than the Minister of Science. Later changes in 2001 also granted sectoral competences for oversight of GM food to the Minister of Health and Chief Sanitary Inspectorate (which is now further responsible for cooperation with the European Food Safety Authority).[5]

Placing the initiation of a Polish GMO regulatory regime within a broader context, it should likewise be noted that discovery of uncontrolled GMO releases within Poland coincided with the establishment of ecological non-governmental organisations in the field of transgenic production. The Federation of Greens – the Cracow Group – issued a special report on GMOs (*Playing God. Genetically Manipulated Food in Central and Eastern Europe*) in order to stimulate the awareness of the topic among Polish consumers and a broader public (Kossobudzki 2003: 44). This report had a strong impact, helping to initiate a month-long media debate on the production and consumption of GM food (Hajduk *et al.* 2001: 36), and contributing to the further development of the legal system. In addition, however, private companies, who, in view of the strong resistance with which they had met in other EU states, were keen to test and commercialise GMOs in Eastern and Central Europe, also lobbied for the establishment of a regulatory framework: they hoped (incorrectly) that new legal rules would allow them to release GM products under less restrictive condition than then prevailed within the Community regulatory framework (Hajduk *et al.* 2001: 36).

The Polish GMO regime began to develop a European dimension following signature of the European Association Agreement in 1991 and finalisation of accession negotiations in 2002; one of the major conditions for Polish membership within the EU was the approximation of laws and the adoption of the Community legal order.[6] Since regulation of transgenic products was part of the *acquis communautaire* to be

5 See, eg, Articles 91–3, the Polish Food and Nutrition Security Act of 25 August 2006, *Journal of Laws* 2006, No. 171, Item 1225.

6 Articles 68 and 69 of the Europe Agreement establishing an association between the European Communities and their Member States, of the one part, and the Republic of Poland, on the other part, approved by the Decision of the Council and of the Commission 1993/743/EC of 13 December 1993, [1993] *OJ* L348/1. See generally Cremona 2003.

transposed into Polish environmental protection law (Arnold and Inglis 2002: 657), the fragmentary legal solutions which existed at the end of the 1990s in Poland had to be adjusted to European and international standards (Iwańska 2003: 354). Fortunately, in the process of negotiation with the EU, biotechnology did not constitute a bone of contention (Radziejewski 2001), and Polish regulation on GMOs was smoothly harmonised with EU law, both with regard to public environmental law as well as private standards, without the need for transitional arrangements (Inglis 2004: 141). In addition, Polish legislators preparing new GMO laws took care to incorporate the knowledge and experience of the existing EU Member States within their work, drawing heavily upon these longer traditions of the regulation of genetic engineering (Załęska 2000: 80).

In summary, early biotechnology legislation in Poland was rather basic, but importantly, regulatory control was in operation. Between 1999 and 2000, the Minister of the Environment issued over 20 consents for GMO experimental releases.[7] At the same time, however, a need remained for a far more comprehensive legal framework; a need argued for both by the governmental bodies and by interested stakeholders, as well as underlined by the prospect of membership within the EU. As a consequence, a legislative procedure was initiated in 1999 to prepare the first Polish Act on GMOs. The resultant law was adopted in 2001, becoming the core of the regulatory framework within Poland.

2.2 An overview of the present regime on GMOs

As the preceding section indicated, the current GMO legal system in Poland is the result of two parallel trends (internal-national and external-EU). The first was triggered by the internal necessity to respond to technological development once modern biotechnology and its products had appeared on the Polish market. The second was triggered by the Polish aspiration to become a Member State of the EU.

The following sections present the key components of the current regulatory framework on GMOs in Poland: (1) the core Act of 2001 on Genetically Modified Organisms and its implementing measures; (2) private standards. In addition, it should be noted that following Polish Accession to the EU on 1 May 2004, all directly effective and applicable European laws, and, in particular, EU Regulations were automatically converted into rules that can be invoked before Polish courts, and which in principle prevail over any conflicting Polish norm according to the principle of supremacy of Community law (Craig and de Búrca 2007). This is particularly relevant within the GMO field, which is largely subject to EU Regulations, especially with regard to the approval of GM food/feed and traceability and labelling.[8]

7 See website of the Ministry of the Environment, in Polish, available at: <http://gmo.mos.gov.pl/usage/register/index.php?site=search>, visited: 7 August 2007. It is not clear from this register whether these consents are still valid.

8 Regulation (EC) 1829/2003 of the European Parliament and of the Council of 22 September 2003 on genetically modified food and feed, [2003] *OJ* L268/1; Regulation (EC) 1830/2003 of the European Parliament and of the Council of 22 September 2003 on traceability and labelling of GMOs and the traceability of food and feed products produced from GMOs, [2003] *OJ* L268/24.

2.2.1 Act of 2001 on Genetically Modified Organisms

The first Polish law providing for comprehensive regulation of transgenic products – the Act on Genetically Modified Organisms (hereinafter 'the GMO Act') – was adopted by the Polish Parliament on 22 June 2001.[9] It became a part of the system of environmental protection law within Poland (Jendrośka 1998; Bepler 2003). The GMO Act harmonised Polish law in line with binding EU Directives, as well as with the preparatory documents then being prepared to amend them.[10]

In accordance with the Community's regulatory approach (Hervey 2001: 321), the GMO Act is a horizontal measure, which contains provisions on GMO-related processes, but excludes particular products like GM food or GM pharmaceuticals that are regulated by sectoral EU Regulations.[11] The GMO Act determines the legal bases for any potential using GMOs and regulates the competence of governmental authorities on GMOs, including scientific bodies (Iwańska 2003: 354–6). It introduces the authorisation procedures and requirements for prior risk assessment (Article 6) in the case of contained use (chapter 3), experimental deliberate release (chapter 4), commercial deliberate release (chapters 4 and 5), as well as regulation on the export and transit of GM products in line with the Cartagena Protocol on Biosafety (Jendrośka, Bar and Bukowski 2004) (chapter 6). Additionally, it contains provisions on public participation in decision-making processes and transparency (public registers), labelling, and post-market control of GMOs, as well as establishing civil and criminal liability. Finally, the GMO Act also contains numerous implementing measures in order to enable its effective implementation.[12]

Interestingly, various Polish measures seem to be slightly more restrictive than the relevant Community provisions, especially with regard to environmental aspects of the control of contained use. Thus, for example, consent for the contained use of GMOs is limited to five years (when it is indefinite in the EU Directive); meanwhile mandatory approval is a prerequisite for any contained use (EU regulation only requires notification in some cases). This was typical of Polish environmental law, which having had little experience in implementation and enforcement was designed to safeguard the desired level of protection through imposition of stricter rules (Jendrośka 2001b: 65): the assumption was that stricter standards would provide for better protection of the environment; though, initially, stricter standards probably resulted in less effective compliance since various GMO rules were found on paper rather than in practice.

2.2.2 Polish norms (private standards)

The picture of the current Polish regulatory system on GMOs would be incomplete without mention of private standards. In Poland, these take the form of so-called

9 See a codified version of the Act on Genetically Modified Organisms, *Journal of Laws* 2007, No. 36, Item 233.

10 Above, note 2, and Francescon 2001.

11 After enlargement, various sectoral regulations were superseded by directly applicable EU Regulations. See Iwańska 2000: 64.

12 For English versions see the website of the Polish Ministry of the Environment, available at: <http://gmo.mos.gov.pl/aktyk_en.html>, visited: 20 May 2007.

'Polish norms' which are applicable voluntarily and developed by the national standardisation body, the Polish Committee for Standardisation ('the PCS').[13] This system mirrors the EU procedure where private standards are developed by European standardisation bodies (the CEN – *Comité Européen de Normalisation* – and the CENLEC – *Comité Européen de Normalisation Electrotechnique*) with the assistance of stakeholders and national institutions (Clark 1996). The PCS celebrated its 80th anniversary last year, but it has only been a full member of CEN since 1 January 2004. As regards biotechnology, recent involvement of the PCS within the CEN and CENLEC has been beneficial: 80 per cent of CEN standards developed for biotechnology and GMOs had been into the Polish standardisation system as Polish norms by the end of 2002 (Tudek 2002: 239). All European norms on control of contained use (good laboratory practice) and deliberate release of GMOs (monitoring, sampling and testing, detection of GMOs) have now been transposed into Polish norms.

Obligatory transposition of European 'technical provisions and norms' into the Polish standardisation system, which began as part of a one-way approximation process of Polish laws with the *acquis* in line with the Europe Agreement (Rutkowska 2002: 162–4, Rotko 2000), now continues in a systematic and cooperative manner so that new EU standards are also incorporated within the Polish system. Moreover, Poland also plays its active part within the EU-wide systems of cooperation between laboratories, which also promotes the development of standards (for example, post-market monitoring of GMOs and validation of detection methods).[14]

2.3 Recent developments – the law in transition (2005–2007)

The most important recent development in the Polish biotechnology regime has been the Proposal for a new GMO Act published in January 2005.[15] Although adoption was planned for June 2005, parliamentary elections in late 2006, as well as continuing governmental discussions on substance of the measure have retarded the legislative procedure; meanwhile, the new right-conservative government – in particular, the Ministry of Agriculture – has developed an aspiration to maintain Poland and Polish farms GMO-free. Although a GMO-free Poland is unlikely to be realised due to the EU obligations, the proposed legislation is still subject to a host of political disagreements and is jammed within inter-ministerial consultations. As of July 2007, the new Act has not been passed yet and the content of provisions has been undergoing some modifications. Its final substance remains uncertain and the adoption of the new law for GMOs is delayed for the unforeseeable future.

The following focuses on the original proposal for reform (as of January 2005), which sought to facilitate final transposition of EU Directives on GMOs into Polish

13 Article 9, the Standardisation Act, *Journal of Laws* 2002, No.169, Item 1386.

14 See European Network of GMO Laboratories (2004) 'Activity Report 2002–2004', Luxembourg: Office for Official Publications of the European Communities.

15 Proposal of the Ministry of the Environment for the new Act on Genetically Modified Organisms; the modified version dated 2 February 2007 is available at: <http://gmo.mos.gov.pl/akty/Ustawa_Prawo_%20GMO_RM.pdf>, visited: 8 August 2007.

law (Woźniak, Dalbiak and Bałon 2004: 97–100). Although the Polish GMO regulatory regime had already harmonised with Community law, Poland did not at that time systematically participate within the relevant Community organs and institutions necessitating current efforts to amend administrative provisions in order to allow both for the effective operation of the two-tier Community-national procedure in the case of the deliberate release of GMOs and for enhanced cooperation between the Polish Ministry and the competent authorities of other Member States. In addition, the proposed Act also sought to implement measures flowing from the significant changes made within the EU regime. At the same time, the Proposal seeks to adopt various measures that are less restrictive solutions than those currently foreseen within the 2001 GMO Act (annulment of obligatory approval for any contained use of GMOs, annulment of a limited five-year consent for contained uses and experimental releases, and a reduction in current penal sanctions of 12 years of imprisonment in the case of endangering human health and the environment). Finally, the Proposal contains important new rules on the coexistence of GM and non-GM crops.

Admittedly, these proposed changes are necessary for the more accurate implementation of the EU legislation into the Polish framework; however, it may likewise – at least with regard to environmental aspects of GMOs that do not relate directly to the commercialisation of GMOs and do not hinder the free movement of goods – that maintenance of higher Polish standards can be justified in line with Article 95(4) or 176 of the European Treaty.[16] Accordingly, mere notification to the Commission is required to justify maintenance of more stringent rules on contained use of GMOs with the aim of protection of the environment (Article 176 being the legal basis for the Contained Use Directive). By contrast, derogations from the Directive on GMO deliberate release (Article 95) are more burdensome since Commission consent is required and given only when conditions stipulated in this are fulfilled (regulatory derogations listed in Article 30 of the Treaty, or relating to the protection of the environment or the working environment) (de Sadeleer 2003: 889). A recent decision refusing an Austrian request for consent for a derogation (Article 95(5)) suggests that the Commission is taking a strict approach to derogations[17] and is unlikely to alter its approach since the Austrian decision has now been approved by the Court of First Instance.[18] However, on 31 March 2005, the Polish authorities requested the introduction of a temporary two-year ban on the use and placing on the market of seed material from GM-corn MON 810

16 Depending on the legal basis of the Directive from which derogation will be sought, above, note 2. Generally, Vos 2001.

17 Commission Decision 2003/653/EC of 2 September 2003 relating to national provisions on banning the use of genetically modified organisms in the region of Upper Austria notified by the republic of Austria pursuant to Article 95(5) of the EC Treaty, [2003] *OJ* L230/34. See also Commission Decision 2008/62/EC of 12 October 2007 relating to Articles 111 and 172 of the Polish Draft Act on Genetically Modified Organisms, notified by the Republic of Poland pursuant to Article 95(5) of the EC Treaty as derogations from the provisions of Directive 2001/18/EC of the European Parliament and of the Council on the deliberate release into the environment of genetically modified organisms, [2008] *OJ* L16/17.

18 Judgment of 5 October 2005 in joined cases T-366/03 and T-235/04 *Land Oberösterreich and Austria v Commission* [2005] ECR II-4005, paras 61–9; the Austrian appeal is currently pending, see joined cases C-439/05 P and C-454/05 P.

varieties based on a safeguard clause in the seed Directive.[19] After the unanimous, favourable vote of the Member States in the regulatory committee, the Polish employment of safeguard clauses was accepted by the Commission.[20]

A second interesting development within the Polish GMO regulatory framework is the planned establishment of the Polish Centre for Food Safety with powers most probably analogous to those of the EFSA (scientific opinions).[21] The Chief Sanitary Inspectorate has recently formed a team to work on the legal basis for such establishment. It is also considering establishment of a Scientific Team within the Centre to be responsible for risk assessment of all applications for commercial GMOs, including assessments of applications for the marketing of non-food products, which is currently the exclusive responsibility of the Minister of the Environment. The potential institutional tensions that such a move might give rise to may explain why the Office for European Integration has expressed reservations about the project. A final decision has yet to be taken; in any case, it has been suggested that responsibility for coordination ought to devolve to the Ministry of Health (and Chief Sanitary Inspectorate therein). In this regard, it is interesting to note that original efforts to draft the 2001 GMO Act included preliminary arrangements to establish a 'horizontal' Office within the Inspectorate for GMO Affairs, which would have been subordinate to the Minister of the Environment, but appointed in cooperation with several other Ministers (Agriculture and Health), or, alternatively, have been established outside the ministerial structure. Although this idea was abandoned (Jendrośka 2001b: 67), the proposed creation of the Polish Centre for Food Safety might justify its re-evaluation since this form of horizontal body might play a necessary role in fostering coordination and in streamlining any potential division of powers between ministries.

In summary, recent developments within the Polish regulatory system on GMOs are a consequence of Polish EU membership and have generally been influenced by EU concepts of governance. Although the final substance of proposed changes to the law cannot be fully anticipated, the following analysis considers all changes which might have a significant impact on the current features of the regulatory framework.[22]

19 Article 16(2), Council Directive 2002/53/EC of 13 June 2002 on the common catalogue of varieties of agricultural plant species, [2002] *OJ* L193/1. These varieties were inscribed in the Common Community Catalogue of agricultural plant species on 17 September 2004.

20 See Summary Record of the Meeting of the Standing Committee on Seeds and Propagating Material for Agriculture, Horticulture and Forestry, 9 March 2004 and Commission Decision 2006/335/EC of 8 May 2006 authorising the Republic of Poland to prohibit on its territory the use of 16 genetically modified varieties of maize with the genetic modification MON 810 listed in the Common catalogue of varieties of agricultural plant species, pursuant to Council Directive 2002/53/EC, [2006] *OJ* L124/26; Commission Decision 2006/338/EC of 8 May 2006 authorising the Republic of Poland to prohibit on its territory the use of certain varieties of maize listed in the Common catalogue of varieties of agricultural plant species, pursuant to Council Directive 2002/53/EC, [2006] *OJ* L125/31.

21 Official Response from Chief Sanitary Inspectorate dated 19 July 2005, GIS-HŻ-420-EFSA-26/PW /MJ/05.

22 Yet, it should also be noted that the recent governmental attempts to keep Poland absolutely GMO-free have been perceived by the Commission as incompatible with the EU laws, see eg C-165/08 *Commission v Republic of Poland*, pending.

3 FEATURES OF THE REGULATORY APPROACH

Following a review of the establishment of the Polish regulatory regime on GMOs, it is now appropriate to turn to the examination of each of the particular features of the regulatory approach: institutions responsible for assessing and managing GMO risks, the participation of the public in decision making, and, finally, the precautionary principle.

3.1 National institutions responsible for GMOs

The list of Polish national authorities competent for the pre- and post-market control of GMOs is very long. In consequence, a detailed description of their organisation and competences is beyond the scope of this chapter. As indicated above, the analysis concentrates on the authorities that participate within horizontal authorisation procedures applying when consent is sought for contained use and deliberate release of GMOs (sectoral provisions are excluded from the analysis[23]).

3.1.1 The competent authorities

Pursuant to Article 9 of the GMO Act (Article 19 of the Proposal for the new GMO Act), the Minister of the Environment is the governmental administrative authority competent for GMOs. It appoints an internal unit responsible for these matters – the GMO Team within the Nature Protection Department of the Ministry of the Environment assists the Minister in exercising his competences. At the same time, under the influence of the EU regime, sectoral competences for GM food devolved to the Chief Sanitary Inspectorate established within the Ministry of Health, while competences for GM seeds passed to the Minister of Agriculture.

In accordance with EU Directives, the Minister of the Environment is the designated national competent authority for the authorisation of the GMO activities.[24] National approval procedures, reproducing the EU regime, are detailed in the 2001 GMO Act.[25] Ministerial powers include granting of consent for the contained use and deliberate release of GMOs, granting of GMOs marketing permits and for export and transit, coordination of the control and the monitoring of activities regulated by the Act, and coordination of collection and exchange of information on human and environmental security. In addition, compliance with the GMO Act is overseen by the administrative bodies, or inspectorates, assigned an oversight role in relation to various industrial sectors.[26] Finally, reference laboratories were established to carry out tests on GMO products and issue scientific opinions (Article 15);

23 See also Articles 20–2 of the proposal for the new GMO Act.

24 Article 11(1), Directive 90/219, above, note 1, and Article 4(4), Directive 2001/18, above, note 2.

25 I omit here the Community comitology procedure in case of objections. See the judgment in case C-6/99 *Association Greenpeace France and Others v Ministère de l'Agriculture et de la Pêche and Others* [2000] ECR I-1651, paras 35–9.

26 Those include: State Sanitary Inspectorate, Plant Protection and Seed Service, Environmental Protection Inspectorate, Veterinary Inspectorate, Trade Inspectorate, State Labour Inspectorate, customs administrative authorities with regard to control of legal trading of GMOs, Inspectorate of Trade Quality of Foodstuffs.

laboratories were established in an effort to improve the effectiveness of post-market control.[27]

National procedures for GMO authorisation typically reproduced the national administrative system and are governed by the Code of Administrative Procedure.[28] The procedure results in an individual administrative decision issued by the Minister of the Environment after obligatory consultations (Article 29, Articles 192–4 of the Proposal for the new GMO Act). Before the decision is taken, the Minister seeks the advice of the GMO Commission and the public. In addition, when issuing consent for GMO operations the Minister of the Environment takes the precautionary principle into account.

3.1.2 The GMO Commission – from a multi-stakeholder body to an expert-political hybrid

According to the GMO Act, the Commission on Genetically Modified Organisms ('the GMO Commission') has been established as an opinion-making and advisory body to the Minister of the Environment (Soveroski 2004: 132). Its primary task is the preparation of opinions on the granting of consent or permits referring to any activity relating to GMOs for which an application is made, matters submitted by the minister within the scope of his competences under the GMO Act, legal acts related to GMOs and biological safety, and, finally, state policy recommendations on GMO applications and biological safety. In consequence, any application for the use of transgenic material must be addressed by an opinion of the GMO Commission, which is issued to the Minister in the form of a Resolution (positive or negative recommendation). The principal role of the Commission is to verify the accuracy of the data furnished by the notifier in any application for GMO use provided and to carry out an environmental risk assessment, taking into account the possible adverse effects for public health and the environment. The scope of the risk assessment is not explicitly regulated in the GMO Act, but it can be systematically constructed with reference to applicable legal rules. In particularly complicated cases, the Presidium of the GMO Commission may appoint outside reviewers and *ad hoc* experts in order to provide for a broader scientific discussion. According to the ministerial regulation, resolutions regarding the authorisation of any GMO uses are adopted in an open vote and by an absolute majority of votes, with at least half the Commission present. An examination of various records shows that Commission has occasionally resorted to the voting procedure, where there were clear divisions among scientists on the final recommendation (for example, on marketing of products), but has more generally sought consensual decision making in less contentious cases concerning contained use.

An equally interesting issue, however, is the composition of the Commission, which at first glance appears to be a 'purely' scientific body. Pursuant to the GMO Act, the Commission consists of 19 members appointed by the Minister for four

27 Currently there are three laboratories established by the Minister of the Environment, available at: <http://gmo.mos.gov.pl/laboratoria.html>, visited: 20 October 2006, see also Article 9 of the proposal for the new GMO Act.

28 Code of Administrative Procedure, *Journal of Laws* 2000, No. 98, Item 1071.

years. The members of the Commission include seven representatives from scientific circles with renowned authority and competence in environmental protection, health care, biological safety, biotechnology, plant breeding, and ethics; but also seven representatives who are selected by the individual ministries (public health, agriculture, national defence, economy, transport, science and the environment). In practice, many of the ministerial representatives have a scientific background. Five further members sitting in the Commission include a representative of the President of the Office for Competition and Consumer Protection, a representative of biotechnology entrepreneurs, two representatives of non-governmental environmental organisations, and one consumer representative (Article 19).

The composition of the GMO Commission thus suggests that it constitutes a forum to facilitate the representation of different interest groups, rather than a mere body of experts which delivers scientific opinions: in effect, mandatory consultation within the GMO Commission ensures a multi-stakeholder debate during the course of approval procedures. It has been suggested that the current character of GMO Commission derives from and reflects initial proposals for a national authority competent for GMOs, which would have been an interdisciplinary organ independent from the ministerial structure (see above). Yet, multi-stakeholders do not necessarily have a determinative say in discussions, since each member has one vote, so that scientists and politicians can form a majority; a structure given clear priority within the consultation procedure (see below).

The Proposal for the new GMO Act foresees some substantial modifications in the composition and competences of the GMO Commission.[29] Representatives of non-governmental organisations, business circles and the Office for Competition and Consumer Protection will no longer participate within this body; but the number of ministerial representatives remains at the level of eight members, nominated by the ministries for the environment, health, agriculture, defence, home affairs, science, and the Chief Sanitary Inspectorate. The number of scientific experts is planned to be raised to 16. The competences of the GMO Commission are also limited; it will no longer give its opinions on legal acts and declarations of state policy relating to GMOs.

As a result of these changes, the interdisciplinary nature of the GMO Commission, which allowed for the multi-stakeholder discussions, will come to an end. Instead, the Commission will become an expert-political hybrid with no clear status or authority. Clearly, political representatives are included by virtue of sensitivity about GMO matters; however, political concerns might likewise be most clearly enunciated during mandatory consultations at the ministerial level. Needless to say, this change is strongly criticised by environmental NGOs, who argue that this reform will eliminate effective public participation in decision-making processes on the environment and public health under the pretext of adjusting Polish law to the EU regime (Kędra 2004: 4). And indeed, the EU regime does form the formal basis for reform; yet, change seems also to have been prompted by intense disagreements between 'green' and 'expert' members of the GMO Commission over the content of final opinions, which have not been readily welcomed.

29 Articles 25–8, the Proposal for the new GMO Act.

Generally, the Polish implementation of GMO approval procedures and a complementary institutional structure has been accurate. Yet, there are some outstanding matters requiring clarification within the new GMO Act. Thus, for example, the current GMO Act has not yet identified all the necessary measures to ensure effective operation of the procedure at the Community level and stable cooperation with the other Member States. Nonetheless, proposed changes also aim to ensure systematic prior public consultation decision making on GMO activities (Articles 192–6 of the Proposal for the new GMO Act). The current nature of public participation is discussed below.

3.2 Public participation

By now, it is well established that public oversight over biotechnology is usually secured through a variety of means: access to information (transparency), consumer choice facilitated by labelling, and direct participation in decision-making processes (Bush, Jasanoff and Wayne 2004: 17). The opportunity for direct participation under the Polish GMO Act is of particular interest within the present analysis. According to the current GMO Act, two legal instruments exist to ensure public participation within risk-related decision making (Bar and Jendrośka 2004: 47). First, ecological, consumer and non-governmental organisations are represented within the GMO Commission. Although this mode of participation may soon be abandoned, a second mode of securing public comment is found within the approval procedures for any activity falling under the scope of the GMO Act, which call for so-called 'environmental proceedings' with public participation. The Act refers to Articles 31 to 39 of the Environmental Protection Law Act of 27 April 2001 (EPLA) that initiate 'horizontal procedural regulation', including a degree of public participation within proceedings on any matters concerning environmental protection, and including individual decisions on GMOs (Iwańska 2003: 367).[30] The key elements within this public participation procedure, which the authorities must implement, are: publication of all relevant information within the public register; provision of information to the public on initiation of proceedings and the mode of accessing documentation and submitting comments and recommendations (the later to be made within 21 days of the date indicated by the authority); granting of open access to applications; taking all comments and recommendations into consideration; providing information about the final decision, including its factual and legal grounds; ensuring that public hearings can be held (Bar and Jendrośka 2004: 55–6 ff). It should also be noted that the competent authority is obliged to provide information about the way the submissions presented were taken into consideration in the grounds for its final decision (Iwańska 2003: 367). However, authorities do not respond to the comments individually (Bar and Jendrośka 2004: 60). The aim of these instruments is to enable the public to present comments and recommendations prior to the granting of the consent for a GMO operation, and to guarantee that those comments are taken into account by the competent authority that issues the final decision.

30 Environmental Protection Law Act – codified version, *Journal of Laws* 2006, No. 129, Item 902.

The participatory rights described above can be conferred on any person. Additionally, Article 33 of EPLA provides for a very specific form of public participation within environmental protection proceedings, which is granted to any ecological organisation that chooses to participate 'as a party' (Iwańska 2003: 368; Bar and Jendrośka 2004: 61–9). An 'ecological organisation' is defined as a non-governmental organisation whose statutory objective is the protection of the environment (EPLA, Article 3(16)). Admittance to the procedure requires prior notification of the Minister of the Environment, which is competent to verify whether an ecological NGO can justify its participation with reference to the territory in which it operates.[31] This form of public participation has a great deal of impact since, once admitted as a party, the ecological NGO enjoys the possibility of involvement as a party at each stage of the proceedings as defined in the Code of Administrative Procedure (Bar and Jendrośka 2004: 69). The NGO might, accordingly, file applications, take part in hearings, lodge appeals and engage in judicial review of the adopted decision. However, parties do not enjoy material rights, such as an automatic request to demand withdrawal of an application for the consent for GMO activity (Iwańska 2003: 368).[32]

3.3 Implementation of the precautionary principle

On the one hand, it is often argued that the precautionary principle has long been acknowledged by Polish environmental law, with, for example, precaution having been one of the reasons why nuclear power stations were prohibited within the country (Jendrośka 2001a: 26). On the other hand, the principle has only recently been given a firm statutory basis being first codified in 2001 within the EPLA and subsequently included in the Polish Food and Nutrition Security Act. Even though the wording of the first codification seems to combine (or confuse?) precaution and prevention and it, surprisingly, makes no mention of decision making under conditions of scientific uncertainty it does belong to the catalogue of 'general principles' environmental protection law (Górski 2001; Radziszewski 2003)). Article 6(2) EPLA reads as follows: '[w]hoever undertakes an activity, whose negative impacts on the environment has not been fully recognised yet, shall, while applying precaution, undertake all possible preventive measures' (Jendrośka 2001a).

Accordingly, the Minister of the Environment (when granting permits for the use of GMOs) must respect the precautionary principle as a general principle of Polish environmental protection law, and, arguably, as a principle of EU law.[33] In addition, however, although not explicitly mentioned, the entire structure of the GMO Act appears to be subordinated to the precautionary principle. Thus, the GMO Act contains specific norms allowing for the exercise of precaution. First, as indicated above, the Act provides for the initial and ongoing oversight over every intended operation involving GMOs with the aim of responding immediately to any unforeseeable risk to human health or the environment (Iwańska 2003: 355 ff; Matthee

31 Article 33, EPLA in conjunction with Article 31, Code of Administrative Procedure.

32 See also Case C-6/99 *Greenpeace France v Ministère de l'Agriculture et de la Pêche* [2000] ECR I-1651.

33 C-236/01 *Monsanto Agricoltura Italiana SpA and Others v Presidenza del Consiglio dei Ministri and Others* [2003] ECR I-08105, para 133. Generally Macrory *et al.* 2004.

and Vermersch 2001: 183). Second, the GMO Act emphasises a case-by-case approach to risk assessment and demands, dependent upon the results of assessment, an adequate implementation of measures designed to preclude possible risks.[34] By the same token, the Minister must revoke consent for the GMO activity, where: the GMO user has violated the provisions of the GMO Act; there are justified reasons to believe that the safety measures will not be sufficient to avoid severe or irreparable damage; or where risk exceeds permissible risk limits (Article 28). Consent can also be revoked or amended if new information important in an assessment of hazards to human health or the environment comes to light (Article 39 and 49, see Articles 151–4 of the proposal for the new GMO Act). Additionally, the precautionary principle is further implemented by a specific safeguard clause allowing for mandatory termination of the marketing of GM products (Article 48, see Article 155 of the proposal for the new GMO Act), whereby the Minister of the Environment might temporarily prohibit or restrict the trading of GM products if there are reasons to believe that these endanger human health or the environment.[35] Finally, some authors consider that precaution is given a further firm implementation basis in Article 25, which states that: '[i]n the sake of the public interest, which is of particular importance with regard to the protection of human health and the environment and the specific risk of environmental deterioration, consent (. . .) shall establish the security of claims that result from potential damages' (Schweiger *et al.* 2003: 9). The security may take the form of a deposit, a bank guarantee or an insurance policy (Article 25, see Article 42 of the Proposal for the new GMO Act).

Once again, the regulation of the precautionary principle in the manner described above is typical of Polish environmental law. The precautionary principle is consequently rarely mentioned *expressis verbis* within legal texts, but is instead reflected within the construction of norms (Jendrośka 2001a: 26–7). Such specific precaution implementing measures allow for effective application of the principle on a case-by-case basis, but, at the same time, the lack of a tradition recording individual application of the principle, and above all, the lack of any jurisprudence on the principle, might well imply the existence of a degree of reluctance directly to employ the principle in decision making on GMOs. The almost total lack of written administrative decisions, policy document or judicial pronouncements on the issue make it difficult to analyse whether this reluctance exists in practice; by contrast, the Ministry of the Environment unambiguously declares that the precautionary principle is applied when necessary on a case-by-case basis in the course of enforcement of the provisions of the GMO Act.

34 One might further claim as well that the far-reaching precautionary approach is demonstrated by the new draft provisions on the coexistence of GM with non-GM plants inserted in the new proposal. They require an administrative consent of the competent authorities to establish a special zone where GMOs can be grown, otherwise it is not allowed, see Articles 172 ff of the proposal for the new GMO Act. In this context, it should be recalled that under Article 26a, Directive 2001/18, above, note 2, regulating 'co-existence' is the matter left for the Member States; see also Commission Recommendation 2003/556/EC of 23 July 2003 on guidelines for the development of national strategies and best practices to ensure the coexistence of genetically modified crops with conventional and organic farming, [2003] *OJ* L189/36.

35 See also C-6/99 *Greenpeace*, above, note 32, para 44; and C-236/01 *Monsanto*, above, note 33, para 110.

4 COMPLEXITIES OF RISK DECISION MAKING ON GMOs

The preceding sections provided some insights into the Polish regulatory framework, which, at least on a formal level, appears to have evolved plausible legal guarantees for GMO decision making. In summary, institutional structures are solid and participatory rights are extended to the public. The Minister of the Environment is a responsible national authority, which issues consent for GMO use after consulting the GMO Commission, which furnishes a risk assessment. In addition, the regime is based on the precautionary principle. However, things are unlikely ever to be this simple with regard to GMOs. Decision making on transgenic products always creates its own specific difficulties, demanding that a delicate path be woven between law, politics and science and that a subtle balance be struck between these different interests. The situation in Poland is no exception. Various problems have already been hinted at; some of them merit closer analysis.

Ironically, the first problem is posed in relation to the character of the primary player in GMO regulation, the GMO Commission. It is not entirely clear what the functional nature of this organ is. Currently, it is said to constitute the interdisciplinary body where various interests, including those of the public, are represented. Thus, it seems to provide a valuable forum for deliberation and discussion on risk assessment. On the other hand, it is dominated by scientists who are closely connected with a technological GMO debate and are not overeager to concern themselves with the valid arguments presented by ecological or consumer NGOs. Thus, although the Commission may deliver high-quality and comprehensive opinions assessing risks, at the same time, such opinions may likewise by over-influenced by technological viewpoints, industrial interests and political considerations. Likewise, even the scientific competence of the Commission might be doubted since political representatives play a part in its deliberations. The law should provide better guarantees for the functional and institutional separation of scientists and politicians who are responsible for final decisions. The current proposal for a change in the composition of the GMO Commission could have aimed at remedying this situation in line with EU governance concepts, but it does so only to a limited extent. As mentioned above, although the proposed new Act extends significantly the number of scientists with differing backgrounds, including ecology, in the Commission, eight ministerial representatives remain in place and retain voting rights.

This situation could be remedied as follows. The GMO Commission should be purged of its political representatives, or at the least, they should not have the right to vote and should participate solely as observers. Another important guarantee of the quality of the expertise would be the introduction of the requirement that members of the GMO Commission make a declaration of their interests. Furthermore, the political considerations, always an issue in an area as sensitive as biotechnology, should be addressed within inter-ministerial consultations following the initial risk assessment. Additionally, both a better separation of functions and the better coordination of the competences for all GM products (foodstuffs, seeds and pharmaceutical goods) could be assured by the establishment of additional consultation procedures between the Ministries of Health, Agriculture and the Environment currently responsible for the various sectors of GMO regulation. In addition, the establishment of the Polish Centre for Food Safety with a competence to issue scientific advice on all GMOs could perhaps further resolve these problems.

An additional desirable change would be the establishment of a socio-ethical advisory body, which would allow for the better institutionalised participation of ecological and consumers' representatives within the GMO decision-making process and remedy the current lack of ethical consultation within these processes in line with EU policy. The absence of any ethical considerations is a serious deficiency within the Polish system. The sole provision of the current GMO Act that tackles this issue is the requirement that at least one of the scientists within the GMO Commission must have an ethical background; and even this modest measure is abandoned within the proposed new legislation.

A further concern arising in relation to the GMO Commission is the lack of clarity within rules on accountability. In practice, its opinions have a decisive influence on GMO authorisations. There has not been a single case when the Minister did not follow the opinion of the GMO Commission, even though *de iure* it does not have any binding force. Formally, however, the Minister alone is responsible under law for decisions taken, since scientific opinions are not legally reviewable acts. Accordingly, the question arises as to whether members of the Commission should be made more accountable, both politically and legally. Political accountability for scientists is difficult to conceive of *in abstracto*; by contrast, judicial review of a ministerial decision could also extend to a review of the scientific advice given (including the summary records and opinions of rapporteurs appointed in each case). Nonetheless, the latter form of review cannot extend to an examination of the Commission's general mode of operation or its composition.

A second problem within the Polish environmental regime is that of the facilitation of public participation; a problem that is of particular importance since participation was previously unknown within this system. At present, the formal legal guarantees for public participation are formidable. Access to information on GMOs is also exemplary: the website of the Ministry of the Environment provides much data. Yet, the practice of public participation is still far from perfect since citizens are often not aware of their environmental rights. For example, virtually no public comments are submitted during authorisation procedures. Seen in this light, the new proposal on the composition of the GMO Commission, excluding representatives of the ecological and consumer organisations from its work, cannot be welcomed very warmly. Some commentators claim that the proposal will deprive civil society of its opportunities to exercise efficient social participation decision-making processes concerning the influence of GMOs on the environment and human health (Kędra 2004: 5). The provisions allowing ecological organisations to be admitted to the GMO procedure as parties might prove to be an effective substitute; to date, however, such an opportunity has yet to be exercised by environmental NGO in the GMOs, while consumer organisations are wholly excluded from the proceedings. Furthermore, and given the relative youth of the regime, there is a strong need for better risk communication and an increased public awareness about GMOs and environmental concerns generally.[36] The proposed socio-ethical

36 According to the survey conducted by the Public Opinion Research Centre (CBOS) in 2001 in Poland, 15 per cent of respondents do not know anything about GMOs, almost 60 per cent are not aware that

advisory body might, accordingly, also provide for the institutionalised exercise of public participation within public decision making on risk.

The third issue raising concerns within the Polish regulatory regime is the problematic application of the precautionary principle. As noted above, systematic investigation of this issue is hampered by the lack of documentary evidence and the scarce tradition of application of the principle within individual decision making. In this context, official guidance on the implementation and application of the precautionary principle by the competent authorities in individual decision making would be highly desirable (Jendrośka 2001a: 27), with guidelines substituting for the lack of case law or administrative records on the use and the content of the precautionary principle. Further, guidelines also appear apposite since, although Polish jurisprudence has tackled issues of scientific uncertainty, it has largely done so only within civil and criminal actions, which do not involve application of the precautionary principle: the administrative jurisdiction remains underdeveloped (Turek 2003; Wójcikiewicz 2000). The principal rules of evidence state that the judge has discretion in the assessment of the evidence submitted, including any scientific proof and its credibility and, in general, the jurisdiction seems to be quite open to any new scientific evidence and methods; albeit that limits to the use of scientific evidence are also recommended. According to Polish civil procedure, the judge may ask for scientific expertise from a scientific institute if the complexities of the case so require; but the Polish Supreme Court has likewise decided that this should be the exception rather than the rule (Gudowski 2004).[37] Certainly, in cases when the scientific expertise is inconclusive, the judge may use his discretion in individual cases and will probably recognise the competence of public authorities to evoke the precautionary principle. However, the further development of a more detailed case law on the questions of scientific evidence, scientific uncertainty, and the precautionary principle would be highly desirable since it would facilitate the application of the precautionary principle by the administrative authorities in individual cases.

In final summary, the above appraisal and suggestions do not mean to suggest that the Polish system on GMOs is unsafe. However, recognition of these comments and further changes would substantially contribute to the improvement of accurate risk decision making on GMOs.

5 CONCLUDING REMARKS

The Polish regulatory regime on GMOs is relatively new and has evolved under strong influence from EU governance models and standards. Paradoxically, at the outset, this influence led to the establishment of a more restrictive regime, which – once again under EU influence – will now be liberalised upon final passage of

such products are already available on the Polish market, and almost 70 per cent trust state institutions. At the same time, the agricultural lobby is raising concern about GMOs, 'First GMO-free zones declared in Poland', International Coalition to Protect the Polish Countryside, Poland, available at: <www.genet-info.org>, 3 August 2004.

37 Article 290 § 1, Code of Civil Procedure, *Journal of Laws* 1964, No. 43, Item 296 with amendments.

the new GMO Act. EU influence remains strong within Poland and is further demonstrated by the fact (not tackled in depth in this chapter) that all bodies within the Polish administration that are responsible for GMO oversight participate actively within the EU structures which operate in the field of transgenic products.

Generally speaking, the Polish regime for control and oversight of GMOs is robust and fit for purpose.[38] Nonetheless, a few areas remain in which improvement could be made within the system. More particularly, reform measures should now focus on the de-politicisation of the GMO Commission, the introduction of processes of ethical consultation into the decision-making process, raising of public awareness about environmental rights, and the establishment of clear criteria for the application of the precautionary principle in individual decision making where development within case law would be very helpful.

38 Moreover, the recent (2007–08) and very radical anti-GMO tendency among Polish authorities has blurred the picture of the Polish regulatory framework on GMOs. The efforts of Polish authorities have become inconsistent – on the one hand, attempts are made to block GM products with legal solutions contrary to the EU legislation and, on the other hand, the work upon the new GMO Act which would finalise the process of implementation of the detailed EU provisions, is continuously delayed (Dąbrowska 2007).

BIBLIOGRAPHY

Arnold, R. and Inglis, K. (2002) 'Approximation of laws', in A. Ott and K. Inglis (eds), *Handbook on European Enlargement – A Commentary on the Enlargement Process*, The Hague: T.M.C. Asser Press, 641–77.

Baldwin, R. (ed.) (1997) *Law and Uncertainty Risks and Legal Processes*, London: Kluwer Law International.

Bar, M. and Jendrośka, J. (2004) 'Udział społeczeństwa w podejmowaniu decyzji dotyczących organizmów genetycznie zmodyfikowanych', in Z. Bukowski (ed.) *Księga Pamiatkowa Profesora Ryszarda Paczuskiego*, Toruń: Tnoik.

Bepler, C. (2003) *Natur- und Gebietschutzrecht in Polen*, Baden-Baden: Nomos.

Busch, L., Jasanoff, S. and Wayne, B. *et al.* (2004) '*Amicus curiae brief submitted to the dispute settlement panel of the WTO in the case of EC: measures affecting the approval and marketing of biotech products*', Dispute Settlement Panel, World Trade Organization.

Christoforou, T. (2004) 'The regulation of genetically modified organisms in the European Union: the interplay of science, law and politics', *CM L Rev.* 41: 637–709.

Clark, P. (1996) 'European standardization in biotechnology' *BioSafety*, Volume 2, Paper 2 (BY96002) 22 May 1996, Online Journal, available at: <http://www.bdt.org.br/bioline/by>, visited: 6 August 2007.

Craig, P. and de Búrca, G. (2007) *EU Law: Text, Cases, and Materials*, Oxford: Oxford University Press.

Cremona, M. (ed.) (2003) *The Enlargement of the European Union*, Oxford/New York: Oxford University Press.

Dalbiak, A. (2003) 'Polskie regulacje ustawowe dotyczace organizmów modyfikowanych genetycznie', in A. Kędra (ed.), *GMO Poznajmy Swoje Poglądy*, Warsaw: Publication of the Conference of the Institute for Sustainable Development.

Dąbrowska, P. (2007) 'Compatibility of Polish laws with GMO regulations in the EU – the outline of problems', *Yearbook of Polish European Studies*, 10: 171–80.

Francescon, S. (2001) 'The new Directive 2001/18/EC on the deliberate release of genetically modified organisms into the environment: changes and perspectives', *RECIEL* 10(3): 309–20.

Górski, M. (2001) 'Przepisy ogólne ustawy Prawo ochrony środowiska', in T. Walkowicz and I. Mleczko (eds), *Prawo Ochrony środowiska*, Kraków, Oświęcim: Fundacja Wspierania Inicjatyw Ekologicznych Towarzystwo na Rzecz Ziemi.

Gudowski, J. (2004) *KPC Tekst Orzecznictwo Piśmiennictwo*, Warszawa: LexisNexis.

Hajduk, E., Slellwanowicz, E., Metera, D. and Kruszewska, I. (2001) 'Non-governmental organizations on GMOs', in *Genetically Modified Organisms: Who is Right?*, Warsaw: Publication of the Foundation for the Development of Polish Agriculture and Institute for Sustainable Development.

Hervey, T.K. (2001) 'Regulation of genetically modified products in a multi-level system of governance: science or citizens?', *RECIEL* 10(3): 321–33.

Inglis, K. (2004) 'Enlargement and the Environment Acquis', *RECIEL* 13(2): 135–51.

Iwańska, B. (2003) 'Co-operation in GMO-Matters in Polish Law', in L. Krämer (ed.), *Recht und Umwelt*, Groningen: Europa Law Publishing, 351–72.

Iwańska, B. (2000) 'Prawo techniki genetycznej – koncepcja horyzontalna a koncepcja wertyklana – wybór metody regulacji', *Prawo i Środowisko* 1(21): 64–72.

Jendrośka, J. (2001a) 'Report on Poland', in European Eco Forum, *Implementing Rio Principles in Europe Participation and Precaution*, published by European Eco-Forum, available at: <http://www.eco-forum.org/>, accessible at: <http://www.participate.org/index.php?option=comdocman&task=cat_view&gid=18&dir=DESC&order=name&limit=5&limit start=10>, visited: 6 August 2007.

Jendrośka, J. (2001b) *'Legal aspects of GMOs control', in Genetically Modified Organisms: Who is Right?*, Publication of the Foundation for the Development of Polish Agriculture and Institute for Sustainable Development.

Jendrośka, J. (1998) 'Environmental law in Poland', in D. Cole and J. Clark (eds), *Environmental Protection in Transition: Economic, Legal and Socio-political Perspectives on Poland*, Aldershot: Ashgate.

Jendrośka, J., Bar, M. and Bukowski, Z. (2004) *Protokół Kartageński o Bezpieczeństwie Biologicznym do Konwencji o Różnorodności Biologicznej Komentarz*, Wrocław: Centrum Prawa Ekologicznego; Radzików: Instytut Hodowli i Aklimatyzacji Roślin.

Joerges, C. (2001) 'Law, science and the management of risks to health at the national, European and international level – stories on baby dummies, mad cows and hormones in beef', *Columbia Journal of European Law* 7(1): 1–20.

Kędra, A. (2004), 'GMO', in *Observatory of 100 Days in the European Union*, A report by agricultural-, environmental- and consumer-based NGOs.

Kossobudzki, P. (2003) 'Polskie organizacje pozarzadowe a organizmy modyfikowane genetycznie', in A. Kędra, A (ed.), *GMO Poznajmy Swoje Poglądy*, Warsaw: Publication of the Conference of the Institute for Sustainable Development.

Kwapich, E. and Twardowski, T. (2003) *Biotechnologia a Prawo Zbiór przepisów*, Poznań Wyd: Agencja Edytor.

Mackenzie, R. (2002) 'The international regulation of modern biotechnology', *YIEL* 13: 97–163.

Macrory, R., Purdy, R. and Havercroft, I. (eds) (2004) *Principles of European Environmental Law*, Groningen: Europa Law Publishing.

Matthee, M. and Vermersch, D. (2001) 'The International Integration of European Precautionary Measures on Biosafety', *EE L Rev.*, 183–93.

Murphy, S.D. (2001) 'Biotechnology and international law', *Harvard International Law Journal* 42(1): 47–140.

Pollack, M.A. and Shaffer, G.C. (eds) (2001) *Transatlantic Governance in the Global Economy*, Lanham, MD: Rowman & Littlefield.

Radziejewski, J. (2001) 'Problemy przejęcia przez Polskę standardów UE w zakresie ochrony środowiska', in Z. Czahór (ed.), *Standardy Europejskie*, Wrocław: ATLA 2.

Radziszewski, E. (2003) *Prawo Ochrony środowiska: Przepisy i Komentarz*, Warszawa: LexisNexis.

Rotko, J. (2000) *Normy Techniczne w Prawie Ochrony środowiska*, Wrocław: PKW.

Rutkowska, H. (2002) 'Rola harmonizacji w UE', in E. Nitecka and M. Obiedziński (eds), *Prawo żywnościowe UE*, FAPA Fundacja Programów Pomocy dla Rolnictwa.

de Sadeleer, N. (2003) 'Procedures for derogations from the principle of approximation of laws under article 95 EC', *CMLRev.* 40: 889–915.

Schweiger, T., Kruszewska, I. and Ritse, G. (2003) *Will Enlargement Weaken EU Policy on GMOs? EU enlargement – GMO through the backdoor of EU accession?* Report prepared for ANPED, The Northern Alliance for Sustainability and Friends of the Earth Europe, Ljubljana: Umanotera, The Slovenian Foundation for Sustainable Development.

Scott, J. (2004) *European regulation of GMOs: thinking about 'Judicial Review' in the WTO*, 4 *Jean Monnet Working Paper.*

Scott, J. (2003) 'European regulation of GMOs and the WTO', *Columbia Journal of European Law* 9: 213–39.

Soveroski, M. (2004) 'EC enlargement and the development of the European environmental policy: parallel histories, divergent paths?', *RECIEL* 12(3): 127–34.

Tudek, B. (2002) 'Zastosowanie genetycznie zmodyfikowanych organizmów a działania Unii Europejskiej i Polski dla zachowania bezpieczeństwa biologicznego', *Biotechnologia* 4: 239–45.

Turek, J. (2003) *Czynności Dowodowe w Procesie Cywilnym*, Kraków: Zakamycze.

Vogel, D. and Teel, J. (2000) 'Regulating genetically modified products and processes: an overview of approaches', *NYUELJ* 8: 649–703.

Vos, E. (2001) 'Differentiation, harmonisation and governance', in B. de Witte, D. Hanf and E. Vos (eds), *The Many Faces of Differentiation in EU Law*, Antwerp: Intersentia, 145–80.

Wójcikiewicz, J. (2000) *Dowód Naukowy w Procesie Sadowym*, Kraków: Instytut Ekspertyz Sadowych.

Woźniak, M., Dalbiak, A. and Bałon, K. (2004) 'Organizmy genetycznie zmodyfikowane – Założenia do nowelizacji ustawy z 22 czerwca 2001 r. o organizmach genetycznie zmodyfikowanych', *Prawo i Środowisko* 2: 97–100.

Załęska, M. (2000) 'Projekt ustawy o organizmach zmodyfikowanych genetycznie (GMO)', *Prawo i Środowisko* 4: 80–5.

Chapter 12

The regulation of environmental risks of GMOs in the United States

*Michael Rodemeyer, J.D.**

In theory, if not in practice, the US approach to the regulation of environmental risks of genetically modified organisms (GMOs) is straightforward. According to a set of policy principles developed in the mid-1980s that continue to guide US regulatory policy today, products developed through biotechnology are subject to the same regulatory scrutiny as comparable products produced through conventional means. In other words, regulation is based on the risk characteristics of the product, not the process by which the product was made. Consequently, the degree to which a product is subject to regulatory scrutiny for environmental risks depends on the nature and the intended use of the product itself. While this policy principle continues to be cited by US policy makers, however, in actual practice the distinction is not as clearly applied as is generally presumed.

Unlike other jurisdictions, the United States has no laws that apply specifically to products developed through biotechnology. Instead, existing laws are used to regulate products developed through biotechnology. In most cases, however, these laws predate the development of modern biotechnology, and applying these laws to products of biotechnology has required a good deal of administrative creativity. Further, since these laws were passed at different times to respond to different problems, they vary considerably in their regulatory approach. To make matters even more complex, the laws are implemented through regulations issued by three executive branch agencies, each of which has a distinct set of priorities, cultures and constituencies.

As a consequence, it is difficult to generalise about the regulation of environmental risks of GMOs in the United States. Instead, it is necessary to look at specific products that may be produced through biotechnology and to look at the specific environmental laws and regulations that apply to such products. The policy goal in the United States is not to make environmental regulation consistent across all GM products, but instead to make environmental regulation consistent across comparable products, regardless of their method of production. As regulatory practice has evolved, however, agencies have in fact developed procedures that require different regulatory scrutiny for products produced through biotechnology.

* The author acknowledges the assistance of his colleagues at the Pew Initiative on Food and Biotechnology (PIFB) and the authors who contributed to PIFB publications noted in references below, from which this chapter draws heavily. PIFB is a non-profit research and education project of the University of Richmond supported by a grant from the Pew Charitable Trusts.

The application of existing laws to genetically modified plants has been the most well developed area of environmental regulation. The regulatory approach for genetically modified animals and insects is much less well developed.

It is important to note at the outset that although questions can be raised about the legal authority of US regulatory agencies to oversee environmental risk assessment of some types of GMOs, in practice developers seem to be complying with agency regulations and requests. To date, the authority of US agencies to regulate genetically modified organisms has not been challenged in court, and no instances have been reported in which a developer has brought a product to market without going through the appropriate regulatory agency review.

This chapter discusses how existing environmental laws have been applied in the United States to genetically modified organisms, identifies a number of questions that have been raised about the adequacy of the environmental regulation, discusses the role of scientific advice and public participation in environmental decisions, and identifies several issues relating to precautionary regulatory approaches.

I US POLICY FOR THE REGULATION OF GMOs: THE COORDINATED FRAMEWORK FOR THE REGULATION OF BIOTECHNOLOGY

In the mid-1980s, as the first products of biotechnology designed for release into the environment began to approach commercial reality, the Reagan administration began to develop a set of policy principles to guide the regulation of biotechnology products. In 1984, the Office of Science and Technology Policy within the Executive Office of the White House proposed policy guidance for the regulation of biotechnology products under existing laws (OSTP 1984). Final proposals were issued in 1986 (OSTP 1986) and further elaborated in later years (OSTP 1990; 1992). Together, these policy guidelines are collectively referred to as the Coordinated Framework for the Regulation of Biotechnology ('Coordinated Framework').

The major principles established in the Coordinated Framework are straightforward. The initial key principle is that the process of biotechnology does not in and of itself pose any unique risks. From that principle it follows that the fact that a product is developed through biotechnology does not change the fundamental risk characteristics of that product. Instead, regulation should be based on the risk characteristics of a product, rather than the process by which the product was made. Regulation should be process neutral.

The Coordinated Framework also established the principle that existing laws were adequate to regulate products developed through biotechnology. The Coordinated Framework published a matrix that showed how different biotechnology products would fall under the jurisdiction of different regulatory agencies using their existing authorities. The primary agencies involved were the Food and Drug Administration (FDA), the Department of Agriculture (USDA), and the Environmental Protection Agency (EPA). At that time, OSTP concluded that existing laws would be sufficient to cover any of the GMOs being contemplated, although it noted that this determination would need to be revisited as the technology continue to develop.

As a result, there is no single law that applies to the regulation of products developed through biotechnology processes. Instead, biotechnology products are regulated under any number of major laws that were intended to regulate other products. These laws vary significantly in their regulatory approaches. Under some laws, certain products or conduct are presumed to involve risk and therefore must be reviewed for safety and in some instances approved by a regulatory agency before they can be marketed. Products that are presumed to pose some environmental risk are generally subject to some pre-market regulatory review. On the other hand, most products enter into commerce without any prior agency review in large part because they are presumed not to pose environmental risks based on prior experience with comparable products. In such cases, agencies generally rely on their post-market authority to respond to any unanticipated problems that may arise. However, the post-market legal authority of the agencies varies widely by specific statute, and the ability of the agencies to monitor post-market conditions is frequently restricted by a lack of resources and dependence on the willingness of state level agencies to shoulder monitoring and enforcement responsibilities.

In the sections that follow, this chapter will examine the major categories of GMOs and the regulation of potential environmental risks. The chapter does not discuss the regulation of food safety issues posed by GMOs. A summary of the types of GMOs that are subject to US regulation is set out in Table 12.1.

2 LEGAL AUTHORITY FOR THE ENVIRONMENTAL REGULATION OF GMOs UNDER EXISTING US LAWS

2.1 Genetically modified plants

Two agencies share responsibility for reviewing the environmental risks of genetically modified plants. The EPA has primary responsibility for reviewing and approving the modification of plants intended to produce pesticidal proteins in plant tissues; the so-called Plant-Incorporated Protectants (PIPs). The Animal and Plant Health Inspection Service (APHIS) of USDA has the responsibility to review all genetically modified plants for potential environmental impacts.

The EPA regulates PIPs under its authority to regulate chemical and biological pesticides. The USDA regulates GM plants under its authority to control and prevent the introduction and spread of agricultural pests. The agencies operate under different statutory authority and under regulatory approaches that differ quite significantly.

GM plants raise a number of environmental concerns (NRC 1987; 2000; 2002b; 2004). Each agency looks at those sets of environmental concerns that fall under its authority. In a number of areas, there is overlap and both agencies are involved in environmental risk assessment and management activities.

2.1.1 EPA and PIPs

EPA regulates pesticides under the authority of the Federal Insecticide, Fungicide and Rodenticide Act (FIFRA). In general, FIFRA requires that no person may

Table 12.1 Comparison of environmental regulation of GM products in the United States

Selected GM Products	*Legal Category*	*Mandatory Pre-Market Notification*	*Mandatory Pre-Market Approval*	*Legal Standard*	*Burden of Proof*	*Post-Market Use Restrictions*	*Post-Market Monitoring and Reporting*
Pesticidal substances added to food crops through genetic engineering	Plant-incorporated protectant (pesticide)	Yes	Yes	No unreasonable adverse effects on environment	Developer (for approval)	Yes	Yes
Livestock and fish	New animal drug	Yes	Yes	Safe and effective	Developer (for approval)	Yes	Yes
Plants, animals and micro-organisms under APHIS permit	Plant pest	Yes	Yes[1]	May injure, damage or cause disease in any plant or plant product	Developer (for approval)	Yes	Yes
'De-regulation' of plants, animals and micro-organisms	None; not regulated	n/a	n/a	No greater plant pest risk than conventional counterpart	Developer (for deregulation[2]	No	No
Micro-organisms	New chemical substance	Yes	No[3]	No unreasonable risk to human health or environment	EPA[3]	Yes	Yes

Source: PIFB, Issues in the Regulation of Genetically Engineered Plants and Animals, Washington DC: PIFB 2004.

Notes:

1 In some cases, it may be possible to commercialise a GE plant under a field trial notification process that does not involve a formal agency approval.

2 In an enforcement proceeding, however, the burden would be on USDA to show that the organism is a plant pest.

3 Pre-market notification is mandatory under Section 5 of TSCA, but the burden is on EPA to find that a product poses an unreasonable risk to keep it from going to market.

distribute or sell any pesticide that is not 'registered', ie, approved by EPA.[1] Before the EPA grants the registration of the pesticide, the applicant must show through data that the pesticide 'when used in accordance with widespread commonly recognized practice [. . .] will not generally cause unreasonable adverse effects on the environment'.[2] The act further defines 'unreasonable adverse effects on the environment' to mean, in part, 'any unreasonable risk to man or the environment, taking into account the economic, social, and environmental costs and benefits of the use of any pesticide'[3] (EPA is also responsible under the Food, Drug and Cosmetic Act (FDCA) for establishing pesticide residues in food, which are then enforced by the FDA).

EPA requires applicants to generate significant environmental data according to EPA guidelines. EPA then reviews the pesticide for a wide variety of environmental risks, including its potential to cause adverse effects on humans, wildlife, fish and plants, including endangered species and non-target organisms. In making its risk management decision, however, EPA must weigh potential environmental, social and economic benefits of the pesticide against any potential environmental harm. The legal standard of 'unreasonable adverse effects on the environment' provides EPA with broad discretion to consider a wide range of non-environmental factors in approving a pesticide.

In 1994, EPA proposed regulations under FIFRA to cover genetically modified plants that produce pesticidal proteins in plant tissues (EPA 1994). In the regulations, EPA took the position that the genetic construct and its expressed proteins both constituted a 'pesticide' as defined in FIFRA, which includes, among other things, 'any substance [. . .] intended for preventing, destroying, repelling, or mitigating any pest'.[4] EPA has no regulatory authority over a 'living plant' under FIFRA; consequently, neither the seeds nor the plants are considered 'pesticides' under FIFRA.

EPA approves field trials as well as the commercial production of plants modified to contain 'plant-incorporated protectants' (PIPs). Developers who want to conduct field trials must obtain an 'experimental use permit' from the EPA. To commercialise a crop containing PIPs, developers are required to obtain a formal 'registration' from the EPA.

In permitting a field trial or in granting a registration, EPA may impose extensive use restrictions and post-approval monitoring requirements. Registrants are required to report any adverse effects possibly associated with their products. As with conventional pesticides, EPA can suspend or cancel the use of the pesticide if subsequent information shows that there is an unacceptable environmental or human health risk. EPA's original registrations of several *Bt* corn varieties were limited to five years, in order to give the agency an opportunity to review any environmental issues after several years' experience of planting. In 2000, following the publication of an article in *Nature* that suggested that monarch butterfly larvae could be harmed by *Bt* corn pollen, EPA used its authority under FIFRA to require a

1 7 U.S.C. § 136a(a).
2 7 U.S.C. § 136a(c)(5).
3 7 U.S.C. § 136(b)(b).
4 7 U.S.C. § 136(u).

data 'call in'. EPA was able to require the companies to submit additional data in order to determine whether there was a risk to monarch butterflies (PIFB 2002).

EPA's broad legal authority to impose use restrictions and to require post-approval monitoring and reporting is limited in practice by resource constraints. In many instances, enforcement of pesticide laws has been delegated to state environmental agencies, which carry the initial responsibility for monitoring and enforcement (Taylor *et al.* 2004). In addition, EPA is dependent on industry self-reporting, particularly in the case of PIPS. Because neither the seeds nor the GM plants are legally 'pesticides', EPA has no direct legal authority to require farmers to comply with planting restrictions intended to prevent the development of resistance to *Bt.* Instead, EPA requires the seed companies to monitor farmer compliance as a condition of registration (Taylor 2003).

2.1.2 USDA and GM plants

In contrast to EPA's authority over GM plants, which is narrowly limited to modifications involving proteins that have pesticidal properties, USDA's authority is quite broad. USDA regulates genetically modified plants through regulations issued under its legal authority to control and prevent the introduction and spread of agricultural pests. USDA's Animal and Plant Health Inspection Service (APHIS) has long had legal authority to control the importation and interstate transportation of agricultural pests, such as insects, diseased plants and other biological threats to agriculture. The Plant Protection Act, passed in 2000, consolidated a number of older plant pest statutes and authorities.[5] Among other things, these laws gave APHIS the power to impose quarantines to prevent the spread of agricultural pests. In January 2004, APHIS published a notice of its intent to revise its regulations for GM plants under the new consolidated Plant Protection Act (APHIS 2004a).

In 1987, APHIS issued regulations under its then-existing plant pest authority that established a new category of 'regulated articles' that could not be transported or released into the environment (ie, grown in a field trial) without either prior notification to APHIS or, in some cases, a permit. 'Regulated article' is defined to mean 'any organism which has been altered or produced through genetic engineering if the donor organism, recipient organism or vector or vector agent' is a known plant pest or a potential plant pest.[6] Since the transformation of many GM plants involves the use of DNA sequences from the cauliflower mosaic virus, a defined plant pest, this definition captured any plants using that common transformation technique – including perennials like grasses, ornamental plants, shrubs and trees. In essence, USDA's regulatory system makes the presumption that virtually all genetically altered plants have the potential to be a 'plant pest' because of the manner in which they were produced, and therefore should be subject to regulatory scrutiny before being allowed to be released into the environment.

Notification is a streamlined procedure intended to allow field trials of low-risk GM plants under circumstances intended to ensure the plants' containment and destruction. USDA review is largely limited to determining whether the particular

5 7 U.S.C. § 7701 *et seq.*
6 7 C.F.R. Part 340.1.

GM plant meets the criteria for the notification process. The overwhelming majority – over 90 per cent – of all field tests, importations and interstate movements of GM plants have been performed under the notification process.

APHIS requires permits for the importation, movement or field trials for GM plants which are not eligible for the notification process. APHIS grants a permit under conditions (such as setback or other management practices), which it believes are necessary to prevent the GM plant from becoming a plant pest.

A developer, who wishes to grow GM plants on a commercial scale, may request that APHIS 'deregulate' the plant. To grant a 'petition for non-regulation', APHIS must find from studies and data that the GM plant, if commercialised, would not pose a greater plant pest risk than the unmodified organism from which it was derived. By granting the non-regulated status petition, APHIS in effect finds that the GM plant is not a 'plant pest' within the meaning of the law and that APHIS therefore has no authority to impose further requirements. As a result, once a plant has been 'deregulated', APHIS has no clear legal basis to impose additional monitoring or reporting requirements. APHIS can use its permit authority to impose conditions and reporting only on those plants that are considered to be 'plant pests'.

The laws under which APHIS regulates plant pests are not environmental statutes; they do not include an explicit environmental standard for decision making or require a balancing of risks or benefits. Instead, APHIS is required to work within the 'plant pest' framework. The definition of a plant pest is a functional one. In order to be a plant pest, an organism must have a capacity to injure or cause damage to a plant or a plant product.[7] As a result, the relevant regulatory inquiry is whether a GM plant is, in fact, a plant pest – which is determined by reference to the plant pest characteristics of the unmodified organism. In other words, if the genetic modification does not increase the plant pest characteristics of the original organism, it will be released from further regulation. While the definition of a plant pest certainly includes consideration of many important environmental risks, it does not necessarily cover all the relevant environmental risks. For example, it is not clear that potential impacts on wildlife or non-target organisms would be covered unless the case can be made that there is an indirect adverse effect on plants.

Despite this limitation, in practice, APHIS considers a broad range of information about potential environmental risks in making permitting and deregulation decisions. APHIS indicates that it looks at such risks as (1) exposing other plants to pathogens; (2) harming other organisms, including agriculturally beneficial organisms, threatened and endangered species, and non-target organisms; (3) increasing weediness in another species with which it might cross; (4) having an adverse effect on the handling, processing or storage of commodities; or (5) threatening biodiversity. To date, however, APHIS has not issued any decisions denying a permit or a petition for deregulation that would clarify at what point such factors would make a plant a 'plant pest'.

While the plant pest laws are not environmental statutes, APHIS, like other federal agencies, must comply with the National Environmental Policy Act (NEPA)[8] in

7 7 C.F.R. Part 340.1.

8 42 U.S.C. § 4332.

making regulatory decisions (EPA is exempt from complying with the procedural requirements of NEPA since its actions are considered to be functionally equivalent to compliance). NEPA applies to 'major federal actions significantly affecting the quality of the human environment'. Agencies proposing to take some regulatory action, such as issuing a permit or licence, must first determine through an environmental assessment whether a proposed action would have a significant impact on the environment. If the agency finds it would not, the agency may proceed with its proposed regulatory action accompanied by a 'Finding of No Significant Impact'. Alternatively, an agency would be required to issue 'environmental impact statement' (EIS), a time-consuming and often expensive assessment of the environmental impact of the proposed action as well as possible alternative actions. By law, public comment is required on a draft EIS before it is made final.

Agencies may also 'categorically exclude' a certain class of activities from NEPA on the basis that such activities would not have a significant impact on the environment. APHIS has determined that a broad category of notifications and confined field trials would pose no significant impact on the environment, and, therefore, do not require individual environmental assessments. APHIS may require an environmental assessment or an EIS for a field release if it has the potential to have a significant environmental impact, as in a case where it involves 'new species or organisms' or 'novel modifications that raised new issues'.[9] APHIS requires an EA for deregulation petitions and provides for a public comment period of at least 30 days. In 2004, APHIS announced its first ever EIS requirement for the field trial of a genetically modified plant, a bentgrass that had been modified to be resistant to Monsanto's Round-Up herbicide (USDA APHIS 2004b). Two lower court decisions have recently found fault with APHIS's policies on environmental assessments and NEPA compliance.[10]

NEPA, however, is a procedural statute, not a substantive one. As a legal matter, an agency would be free under NEPA to proceed with a regulatory action likely to cause a significant impact on the environment. NEPA does not provide agencies with additional statutory authority. As a practical matter, however, APHIS uses the threat of the EIS requirement to negotiate environmental mitigation requirements with developers.

2.2 Genetically modified micro-organisms

In the early 1980s, prior to the Coordinated Framework, EPA asserted its authority to regulate environmental releases of GMOs under the Toxic Substances Control Act (TSCA) in the case of a strain of modified bacteria known as 'ice minus'. Later, the Coordinated Framework envisioned TSCA as the 'gap-filler': the law that would cover any GMOs not covered by other laws. As it has developed, however, TSCA has played a minor role in the regulation of GMOs in the United States.

9 7 C.F.R. § 372.5(d)(4).

10 *Geertson Seed Farms v Johanns*, No. C 06–01075 CRD, 2007 U.S. Dist. LEXIS 14533 (N.D.Cal. Feb. 13, 2007); *Int'l Center for Technology Assessment v Johanns*, Civil Action 03–00020 HHK, 2007 U.S. Dist. LEXIS 7773 (D.D.C. Feb. 5, 2007).

TSCA provides EPA with the authority to regulate certain 'chemical substances' that may present an 'unreasonable risk to human health or the environment' during manufacture, processing, distribution in commerce, use or disposal[11] (in general, substances that are regulated under other laws, such as food, drugs, pesticides, cosmetics, firearms and tobacco, are exempted from TSCA). The term 'unreasonable risk' is not further defined in the law, although it is clear that EPA is required to weigh both the benefits and risks of a product in making its determination about reasonableness.

Section 5 of TSCA requires companies that intend to manufacture or import a new commercial chemical substance to submit a 'premanufacturing notice' to the agency at least 90 days prior to the manufacturer or import of the substance. If the EPA takes no action within 90 days, the company can legally take the product to market. To block the product from going to market, the burden is on the EPA to demonstrate that the new chemical substance would pose an unreasonable risk to human health or the environment.[12]

EPA has interpreted the definition of 'chemical substance' in TSCA to cover transgenic micro-organisms, and has issued rules requiring developers to notify EPA 90 days before a GM micro-organism is used in commerce, and requiring permits for experimental environmental releases.[13]

2.3 Genetically modified animals

The regulatory frameworks for GM plants and GM micro-organisms are relatively well developed and include published regulations by EPA and USDA. In contrast, the regulatory framework for GM animals remains uncertain and continues to evolve. To date, no federal agency has clearly asserted jurisdiction over genetically modified animals or provided formal guidance on how it intends to regulate. However, a number of existing laws could theoretically apply to some of the environmental risk posed by GM animals (Table 12.2).

As the National Academy of Sciences concluded in a recent report, genetically modified animals can pose environmental concerns (NRC 2002a). Animals that are highly mobile and that easily become feral are of particular concern because of the potential to spread a transgene to wild populations and disrupt ecological systems.

The FDA has informally stated that a genetic construct inserted into an animal, as well as its expressed proteins, meet the legal definition of an 'animal drug' under the federal Food, Drug and Cosmetic Act (FDCA) (CEQ and OSTP 2001). Under the FDCA, a 'drug' is defined in part as 'any article' intended 'to affect the structure or function of the body of man or animal'.[14] A 'new' animal drug may not be marketed without prior approval by FDA. As a result of FDA's interpretation, it would appear that no transgenic animal could be brought to market unless FDA has found that the modification is both 'safe' and 'effective'.[15] To date, however, the

11 15 U.S.C. § 2605.

12 15 U.S.C. § 2604.

13 40 C.F.R. Parts 700, 720, 721, 723 and 725.

14 21 U.S.C. § 321(g)(1)(C).

15 21 U.S.C. § 321(u); 21 U.S.C. § 360b(d)(3).

Table 12.2 Potential regulatory authorities for GM animals in the United States

Agency	*Legal Authority*	*Scope of GM Animals Covered*	*Pre-Market Approval*	*Risks Considered*
FDA	General food safety authority under the Food, Drug and Cosmetic Act (FDCA)	Only those entering the food or feed supplies	No, unless food additive	Food safety
FDA	New animal drug approval authority under the FDCA	All	Yes	Food safety; animal safety; effectiveness; indirect human or animal health impacts
APHIS	The Animal Health Protection Act	Livestock only; scope uncertain, but probably very limited	Yes	Animal health; other environmental issues uncertain
APHIS	The Animal Welfare Act	Research animals only	N/A	Animal welfare
APHIS	The Plant Protection Act	Potentially broad	Yes	Injury to plants; limited for environmental risks
APHIS	The Animal Damage Control Act	Limited	No	Injury to agriculture and other interests

Source: PIFB, *Issues in the Regulation of Genetically Engineered Plants and Animals*, Washington DC: PIFB 2004.

FDA has issued no regulations or guidelines indicating whether or how the Act would apply. At least one company developing a transgenic salmon has publicly acknowledged that it is seeking approval from the FDA to market its product.

Additional confusion about the FDA's intention to apply the new animal drug laws to genetically modified animals followed from its decision in late 2004 that it would not regulate the Glofish, an ornamental zebra fish modified to luminesce. The FDA issued a short statement that the Glofish would not be regulated because it would not enter the food supply and did not appear to pose any environmental risks greater than that of its conventional counterparts. The FDA found 'no reason' to regulate the Glofish 'in the absence of a clear risk to the public health' (FDA 2003). The FDA's statement implied that it would assert jurisdiction over genetically modified animals only to the extent that they were intended to enter the food supply, or pose an environmental threat. However, this begs the question of how FDA would know that an animal did not pose an environmental threat unless it had been subjected to some scrutiny. Furthermore, it is inconsistent with the position that any genetic construct meets the definition of a new animal drug and therefore must be approved by FDA before marketing. FDA's argument that its decision not to regulate Glofish was properly within its discretion was affirmed in a court challenge.[16]

The FDCA is not an environmental statute and contains no environmental decision standard. Under the FDCA, FDA's decision is limited to a finding that a new animal drug is both safe and effective. The FDA has taken the position that its authority to consider safety encompasses environmental impacts that directly or indirectly pose risks to the health of animals or humans.

The scope of this authority is quite uncertain and untested. However, FDA has itself acknowledged that it does not have authority over non-health-related environmental impacts, which could have potential impacts on biodiversity and ecosystem functioning.

In any event, it is unclear what legal standard FDA would apply in judging the environmental risks that may be posed by GM animals. Like USDA, FDA is required to comply with the NEPA and therefore must determine whether granting an approval of a new animal drug would have a significant impact on the environment. Under NEPA, FDA can therefore request environmental impact information from the applicant and is reportedly doing so with respect to the transgenic salmon application it is currently considering. However, since NEPA is primarily a procedural statute, it does not give FDA additional authority to reject a new drug application on environmental grounds. Instead, it would simply require FDA to conduct an environmental impact statement. Ironically, FDA has acknowledged that NEPA's requirement for a public comment on an EIS appears to be in conflict with the FDCA's prohibition on disclosure of information in a new animal drug application.

FDA's policy in this area continues to evolve. It is possible that in the future FDA will limit its consideration only to animals intended for the human food supply. If that were to be the case, it is unclear what agency, if any, would have authority to look at the environmental risks of GM animals not intended for the food supply.

One possibility is the Animal Health Protection Act (AHPA) administered by the USDA's APHIS.[17] Like the plant pest quarantine acts which USDA has used as authority for regulating GM plants, AHPA provides USDA with broad authority to control and eradicate contagious and communicable diseases and pests of livestock and poultry. These quarantine laws and the regulations were established to protect the economic interests of US agriculture and have not historically been used to address other concerns, such as food safety or environmental issues. Furthermore, AHPA would appear to provide APHIS with only limited authority to look at the full range of environmental risks associated with all GM animals. AHPA is focused on livestock; further, it lacks both the broad grant of environmental protection authority and a specific standard under which any environmental review would be assessed and enforced. Nevertheless, it is conceivable that AHPA could provide some legal authority for APHIS to establish an approval process for some GM animals. To date, however, USDA has not indicated whether it intends to use the authority under this act to regulate genetically modified animals.

16 *International Center for Technology Assessment* v *Thompson*, 421 F.Supp. 2d 1 (D.D.C. March 8, 2006).
17 7 U.S.C. § 8301 *et seq.*

Insects provide a particular challenge for the US regulatory system (PIFB 2004b). Scientists are working on insects that have been genetically modified for a number of purposes. To date, no agency has indicated whether it will assert jurisdiction over insects that have been genetically modified (transgenic varieties of insects that are already considered 'plant pests' would be covered by APHIS's existing regulations, which are not limited to plants). This is of particular concern because, unlike all other GM animals, some public health and agricultural applications of GM insects require that the transgenic variety spread and replace the natural insect population, rather than be confined. This clearly raises environmental issues (NRC 2002a; 2004).

3 PRECAUTIONARY APPROACHES IN US ENVIRONMENTAL REGULATION OF GMOs

As noted previously, US policy presumes that the process of biotechnology poses no unique risk. Instead, US policy is based on the risk characteristics of the product itself, regardless of its method of production.

The several laws under which biotechnology products are evaluated for environmental risks reflect different regulatory approaches with respect to precaution. However, each of the laws addresses products which are assumed to contain an element of risk: pesticides, new animal drugs, new chemical substances and plant pests. As a result, each of these laws places restrictions on the introduction of these products into commerce without a prior agency review and, in some cases, approval. In this respect, the environmental laws differ from US food safety laws (PIFB 2004a).

In the case of pesticides, the burden is clearly on the applicant to prove that the pesticide, when used in accordance with instructions, would pose 'no unreasonable adverse effects on the environment'. A pesticide may not be marketed until the EPA has determined that the product meets the standard and establishes the existence of any food tolerances (ie, allowable pesticide residues in the food) for the pesticide. The legislative history of the pesticide laws shows increasing concern about the adverse environmental impacts of pesticides and the regulatory approach clearly places emphasis on the prevention of harm.

The new animal drug approval process is similarly quite strict. In enacting the new animal drug approval process of the FDCA, Congress was concerned about the potential impacts of animal drugs that were unsafe and that could create a food safety risk for humans who consume them as residues in food. As with pesticides, Congress adopted a precautionary approach that placed the burden on the applicant to prove that the new animal drug was both safe and effective before it could be marketed.

The regulatory approach to new chemical substances in TSCA is somewhat different. Again, Congress was concerned about the introduction into commerce of new toxic chemicals that could have lasting environmental and public health impacts. At the same time, however, Congress did not want to unduly interfere with the introduction of the hundreds of new chemical substances. As a consequence, the approach to new chemical substances in TSCA effectively places the burden on

EPA to prove that a new chemical substance would pose 'unreasonable environmental or public health risk' within a limited amount of time in order to prevent it from being introduced into the market. EPA often lacks adequate information to make such a finding, and has only limited authority to require additional testing.

The weaknesses in TSCA, combined with court decisions that have undercut EPA's ability to regulate existing chemicals, have led most environmental organisations to conclude that TSCA is a failed law. Since EPA has taken so few actions under TSCA, there has been little administrative or judicial guidance on the meaning of 'unreasonable risk'. In the *Corrosion Proof Fittings* case, which invalidated EPA's rule making to ban asbestos, the 5th Circuit Court of Appeals stated that 'the requirement that the risk be "unreasonable" necessarily involves a balancing test like that familiar in tort law: the regulation may issue if the severity of the injury that may result from the product, factored by the likelihood of the injury, offsets the harm the regulation itself imposes upon manufacturers and consumers'.[18]

The intent of the animal and plant quarantine laws is to prevent the importation and spread of economically damaging diseases and organisms to agriculturally valuable crops and livestock. The primary regulatory tool in these acts is the ability to control the movement of organisms through permits and quarantines. Plant and animal pests are therefore subject to a high degree of regulatory control. At the same time, Congress did not intend to impede commerce and transportation in seeds, plants, livestock and other agricultural organisms that were not plant or animal pests. As a result, the key regulatory decision is whether or not an organism is a plant or animal pest. Regulatory controls are quite precautionary for plant pests, since the intention is to prevent the establishment of plant pest that could prove difficult if not impossible to eradicate.

The decision to apply the plant pest rubric to GM plants raises some interesting questions. In effect, the regulations presume that any plant developed through genetic engineering is a potential plant pest, and places the burden on the developer to prove that the plants are not a plant pest. On its face, this approach appears to be inconsistent with the 'process neutral' policy outlined in the Coordinated Framework. Instead, there appears to be a presumption that the process by which a plant is produced increases its potential to be a plant pest. As a result, plants developed through biotechnology are in fact subjected to a higher degree of regulatory scrutiny than plants with similar traits developed through conventional breeding.

A similar question can be raised about the application of the pesticides laws and the FDCA to GM organisms. For example, EPA's regulations on PIPs exempt plants with enhanced pesticidal properties created through sexual reproduction.[19] Again, it could be argued that EPA is placing a higher regulatory burden on PIPs simply because of the process by which a trait was introduced into a plant. Animals with novel traits created through conventional breeding are not subject to any pre-market regulatory review. Only traits introduced through recombinant DNA techniques are subject to the 'new animal drug' approval process.

18 *Corrosion Proof Fittings v EPA*, 947 F2d 1201 (5th Cir. 1991).

19 40 C.F.R. § 174.25.

These observations underscore the difficulty of applying the 'product versus process' distinction in US policy. The reality is that process matters, not because the process itself is inherently risky, but because the process enables the creation of organisms with novel traits not possible to achieve through conventional breeding and with which there may be little prior experience to confidently predict environmental impacts. As a practical matter, the US regulatory system has evolved into a system that requires at least some agency review prior to the environmental release of a GM plant, and appears to be moving toward a similar approach for GM animals.

4 SCIENCE, TRANSPARENCY, PUBLIC PARTICIPATION AND LABELLING

4.1 Scientific advice

Each of the federal regulatory agencies discussed in this chapter – EPA, FDA and APHIS – employ career staff with scientific and technical training. Whether the scientific capabilities of the agencies are sufficient is difficult to judge. While FDA has significant expertise in animal health and safety, for example, it has relatively little expertise in areas such as aquatic ecology and fish population dynamics with which to assess potential environmental impact of escaped transgenic fish. In 2000, the National Research Council of the National Academy of Sciences released a report critical in some respects of the scientific quality of the environmental risk assessments conducted by APHIS, and recommended that it seek additional external scientific advice (NRC 2000). Since then, APHIS has moved to shore up its scientific and technical staff.

Both EPA and FDA have a tradition of using external scientific advisory panels to provide it with independent peer review of its scientific decisions. EPA has a standing scientific advisory committee to which it often refers scientific controversies; it has been active on a number of GM crop issues. Scientific advisory committees must comply with requirements of the Federal Advisory Committee Act, which, among other things, requires advisory panels to be balanced and that all meetings be held in public.[20] Agencies also use public workshops and conferences to obtain external scientific input as well as the views of industry, public interest groups, academics and others.

Congress and the Executive Branch agencies can also request the National Academy of Sciences to undertake a review of scientific issues or even to conduct an external peer review of an agency's scientific and technical programmes. The NAS is a government-chartered organisation, but it operates essentially as an independent contractor; in general, agencies pay the NAS for the Academy's studies. While the NAS is exempt from some aspects of the Federal Advisory Committee Act, it attempts to achieve balance in the panels it assembles to produce reports. In the late years of the Clinton Administration, EPA, USDA and FDA requested the NAS to review a number of key biotechnology scientific issues and to review existing regulatory programmes. From 2000 to 2004, the National Research Council, the NAS's

20 5 U.S.C. Appendix 2.

research arm, released four major studies dealing with environmental issues of GMOs and their regulation (NRC 2000; 2002a; 2002b; 2004). The reports contained a number of recommendations for improving agency science and regulation but found no serious flaws in the agencies' work.

4.2 Public information disclosure and public participation

The US regulatory system has long had a tradition of transparency, openness and public participation. In general, the idea is that government – including the government delegated to administrative agencies – should operate in the open. Agencies should be required to explain and justify what they are doing, make available the basis and data upon which they are making a decision, and allow the public an opportunity to comment before a final decision is adopted. By forcing agencies to explain and defend their positions, and to listen to public comment, the goal is to establish accountability, to reduce back-room deal making and private influence, and to improve decisions by bringing information to the agencies' attention.

In general, agencies are required, on request, to make information public unless it is specifically exempt from disclosure under the Freedom of Information Act.[21] One category of information that is exempt from public disclosure includes trade secrets and confidential business information.[22] Typically, when a GMO developer submits information in support of an application or permit to an agency, it may claim a great deal of that information to be exempt from disclosure as confidential business information. While agencies are bound by law to protect trade secrets and confidential business information, they can also seek to increase the amount of information publicly available by requiring the developer to show that the information is truly entitled to protection (NRC 2000). In some cases, FOIA is supplemented by specific provisions in laws relating to particular products or agencies. For example, the pesticide laws explicitly limit confidentiality protection for safety and efficacy data.[23]

The opportunity for public comment on a regulatory decision also varies considerably. The Administrative Procedures Act, which sets out the general framework for most US regulatory agencies, typically requires a public comment period on any rule or other action that has general applicability.[24] Depending on the scope and interest in the rule, public comment may range from a 30-day 'notice and comment' period to more extended public outreach that may include public hearings around the nation. Some agency rule proposals can be quite controversial and generate significant public comment, often through 'postcard' campaigns organised by interest groups. Most rule making generates only a modest number of comments, and relatively few from the general public. Since rule making of this sort has broad application, it is thought that a more 'legislative' approach, which involves public participation, is appropriate.

21 FOIA; 5 U.S.C. § 552 *et seq.*
22 5 U.S.C. § 552(b)(4).
23 7 U.S.C. § 136(h).
24 5 U.S.C. § 553.

In contrast, public participation opportunities are typically much less generous when it comes to agency actions involving a single product or individual, such as the granting of a permit or licence. Such agency actions are less legislative in nature and typically affect the rights or a single applicant. While an agency may provide public notice of its action, it often does so without a prior opportunity to comment. The new drug approval provisions of the FDCA go even further, prohibiting not only the disclosure of any information in the application, but also the fact that an application has even been filed.[25] However, NEPA's requirements for public comment on an EIS apply to granting of permits, licences and product approvals as well as general rules.

It is interesting to note that even scientific risk assessments and other technical information relied upon by an agency in issuing a rule of general applicability are subject to public comment. Frequently, the data, analysis and assumptions used by an agency in conducting a risk assessment to support a general rule are subjected to substantial criticism and comment by various interested parties, and it is not surprising to see some of the same arguments surface in subsequent court challenges to the final agency action. In some cases, the comments may bring to the agency's attention new data or flaws in its interpretation that will lead it to modify its original analysis.

4.3 Labelling requirements

Labelling is another policy tool that contributes to market efficiencies and transparency. In the GMO debate, much of the labelling debate has focused on food safety. However, labelling can also be a helpful tool for managing environmental risks. Labelling and tracking can help prevent unauthorised environmental releases and can help growers manage unwanted gene flow to wild relatives or to non-GM or organic crops and to implement management practices to reduce pesticide use and the development of *Bt* resistance in crop pests.

There is no general consumer 'right to know' in US law. Instead, labelling and consumer disclosures are required only in specific situations under specific laws. For example, provisions in the FDCA prohibiting the misbranding of food would require a label disclosure if a food has been materially altered to prevent consumer deception.[26] In the case of food derived from GM plants, however, FDA has determined that most foods are likely to be 'substantially equivalent' to their conventional counterparts and therefore have not been changed in any material way that would require disclosure. In any event, the information to be disclosed is the material change, not the process by which it was achieved. So, for example, if a potato developed through biotechnology had significantly lower levels of a nutrient than would be found in a conventional potato, that fact would need to be disclosed – but not that the food was derived from a GM process (FDA 2001). One state law which required labelling of milk treated with rBST was challenged in court and invalidated on constitutional grounds, having been found to be a violation of commercial free speech in the absence of evidence of adverse health effects.[27]

25 21 U.S.C. § 331(j).

26 21 U.S.C. § 343.

27 *International Dairy Foods Ass'n v Amestoy*, 92 F.3d 67 (2nd Cir., 1996).

The US government also often provides support to voluntary certification systems and marketing standards intended to help marketers non-deceptively communicate salient characteristics of their products to the marketplace. For example, USDA's organic certification programme provides a consistent definition of the term 'organic' and sets up a voluntary certification programme to ensure that marketers are using the label appropriately.[28] At the present time, however, there is no generally agreed-upon standard for the meaning of 'GM-free' and, as a result, producers marketing food with such a claim may face the risk of FDA action for deceptive marketing (FDA 2001).

While several individual states have expressed interest in requiring labelling of GM seeds to prevent unintended mixing with non-GM or organic seeds, there is no federal requirement for GM seed sellers to label seeds or to follow standards intended to prevent unintentional mixing. Seed producers, of course, have a strong commercial interest in ensuring that those who buy their seeds pay technology fees. While farmers know what they are growing on their own fields, there is no way for them to know what the neighbouring farmers are growing.

EPA and FDA have the authority to require labelling disclosures on pesticides and drugs, respectively, to prevent mishandling of the materials that could cause environmental or human health risk. EPA typically prescribes a label with use restrictions for conventional chemical pesticides, and the use of the pesticide in a manner inconsistent with the label is considered a violation of the law. However, because EPA does not regulate GM seeds or plants directly, but only the genetic construct and the expressed pesticidal protein, there is nothing on which to affix a label. As a result, EPA depends on the seed manufacturer to provide information and handling instructions to farmers. For the FDA, using the authority of the new animal drug approval provisions of the FDCA could enable it to require post-approval labelling and handling to prevent potentially harmful environmental releases.

Market demands for GM-free commodity crops have also led to voluntary agreements, enforced through contracts, between buyers and sellers setting requirements for GM content. These agreements, although pervasive in US agriculture, provide little information for consumers since the information on GM content is not passed on by major food manufacturers in retail products.

5 CONCLUSION

The US regulatory system for environmental risks of GMOs is complex and continues to evolve. Because the US regulates GMOs on a statute-by-statute basis, the regulatory approach, standards of decision making, burden of proof, and risk assessment methodologies vary depending on which law applies to the specific GMO and which agency is assessing the GMO. While some of the approaches taken by US regulatory agencies seem to raise questions about scope and authority, there is no evidence to suggest that developers are failing to comply with agency regulations and requests for review and information. Nor is there any evidence to suggest that GM organisms are being released into the environment without at least some

28 7 C.F.R. Part 205.

prior agency notification or review. However, the continuing lack of clarity on the regulation of GM animals and insects does raise concerns that developers could move into field trials or commercialisation without prior regulatory review.

BIBLIOGRAPHY

Animal and Plant Health Inspection Service, US Dept. of Agriculture (APHIS, USDA) (2004a) 'Environmental impact statement: introduction of genetically engineered organisms', *Federal Register* 69: 3271–2.

Animal and Plant Health Inspection Service (APHIS) (2004b) 'Environmental impact statement: petition for deregulation of genetically engineered glyphosate tolerant creeping bentgrass, *Federal Register* 69: 57257–60.

Council on Environmental Quality and Office of Science and Technology Policy, the White House (CEQ and OSTP) (2001) *CEQ and OSTP Assessment: Case Studies of Environmental Regulations for Biotechnology*, Washington DC: OSTP.

Environmental Protection Agency (EPA) (1994) 'Plant pesticides subject to the Federal Insecticide, Fungicide, and Rodenticide Act and the Federal Food, Drug, and Cosmetic Act: proposed policy', *Federal Register* 59: 60496–547.

Food and Drug Administration (FDA) (2003) *FDA statement regarding Glofish*, 9 December, In Rockville, MD: FDA, available at: <http://www/fda/gov/bbs/topics/news/2003/new00994.html>.

Food and Drug Administration (FDA) (2001) 'Guidance for industry: voluntary labelling indicating whether foods have or have not been developed using bioengineering: availability', *Federal Register* 66: 4839–42.

National Research Council, National Academy of Sciences (NRC) (2004) *Biological Confinement of Genetically Engineered Organisms*, Washington DC: National Academy Press.

National Research Council (NRC) (2000) *Genetically Modified Pest-protected Plants: Science and Regulation*, Washington DC: National Academy Press.

National Research Council (NRC) (2002a) *Animal Biotechnology: Science Based Concerns*, Washington DC: National Academy Press.

National Research Council (NRC) (2002b) *Environmental Effects of Transgenic Plants: the Scope and Adequacy of Regulation*, Washington DC: National Academy Press.

National Research Council (NRC) (1987) *Introduction of Recombinant DNA-engineered Organisms into the Environment: Key Issues*, Washington DC: National Academy Press.

Office of Science and Technology Policy, the White House (OSTP) (1992) 'Announcement of policy: exercise of federal oversight within scope of statutory authority: planned introductions of biotechnology products into the environment', *Federal Register* 57: 6753–62.

Office of Science and Technology Policy, the White House (OSTP) (1990) 'Announcement of policy: exercise of federal oversight within the scope of statutory authority: planned introductions of biotechnology products into the environment', *Federal Register* 55: 31118.

Office of Science and Technology Policy, the White House (OSTP) (1986) 'Announcement of policy and notice for public comment: coordinated framework for regulation of biotechnology', *Federal Register* 51: 23302–50.

Office of Science and Technology Policy, the White House (OSTP) (1984) 'Proposed coordinated framework for regulation of biotechnology', *Federal Register* 49: 50858–907.

Pew Initiative on Food and Biotechnology (PIFB) (2004a) *Issues in the Regulation of Genetically Engineered Plants and Animals*, Washington DC: PIFB.

Pew Initiative on Food and Biotechnology (PIFB) (2004b) *Bugs in the System? Issues in Science and Regulation of Genetically Modified Insects*, Washington DC: PIFB.

Pew Initiative on Food and Biotechnology (PIFB) (2003) *Future Fish? Issues in Science and Regulation of Transgenic Fish*, Washington DC: PIFB.

Pew Initiative on Food and Biotechnology (PIFB) (2002) *Three Years Later: Genetically Engineered Corn and the Monarch Butterfly Controversy*, Washington DC: PIFB.

Taylor, M.R. and Tick, J.S. (2003) *Post Market and Oversight Biotech Foods: is the System Prepared?*, Washington DC: Pew Initiative on Food and Biotechnology and Resources for the Future.

Taylor, M.R., Tick, J.S. and Sherman, D.M. (2004) *Tending the Fields: State and Federal Roles in the Oversight of GM Crops*, Washington DC: Pew Initiative on Foods and Biotechnology.

Part III

EU and international models

Chapter 13

The EU regulatory system on food safety: between trust and safety

*Ellen Vos**

I INTRODUCTION

Food is the key to good health and well-being since it supplies essential nutrients which 'feed' the individual's needs. In addition to being a means of survival for human beings, it is also an expression of cultural habits and traditions. Moreover, food is an important economic good; with an annual turnover of almost €800 billion, the food and drink industry is one of the most important industrial sectors of the European Union and a major employer and exporter.[1] The assurance of food safety and quality is therefore of high importance to consumers, producers and public authorities. The 1996 BSE crisis demonstrated severe shortcomings in this assurance. Accused of having given less consideration to health and safety protection than to the trading of beef,[2] the European Commission declared in the aftermath of the BSE crisis to have food safety as its prime interest.[3]

Food safety regulation has therefore become of pivotal importance for the European authorities. This means that in pursuing its objectives of the internal market, industrial and agricultural policy as well as of human health and safety protection, the EU is also increasingly faced with the concerns of today's 'risk society'. In this, the EU authorities are faced with the need to deal with 'uncertain risks', ie those risks that concern situations of suspected, possible hazards, which are usually associated with complex causalities, large-scale, long-term and trans-border processes, and which are generally difficult to control and also transcend human sensory capacities.[4] Moreover, food safety regulation must accommodate both economic interests and health and consumer protection, while also taking account of cultural differences and ethical concerns.

Unsurprisingly, this complex area of regulation has turned out to be a classical example of what may be called 'contested governance' (Ansell and Vogel 2006: 10–11); it is an area which illustrates the particular intense and broad conflict about its foundational assumptions and institutional frameworks. What, where and how food safety should be regulated and the basis for institutional arrangements become compelling questions. The BSE crisis put the spotlight on a series of severe

* I would like to thank Joanne Scott for her comments on an earlier version of this chapter.

1 Eurostat, 2006: 39–63, Chapter 2: Food, beverages and tobacco.

2 *European Parliament Final BSE Inquiry Report*, Rapporteur Manuel Medina Ortega, A4–0020/97/A, 1997.

3 European Commission, *White Paper on Food Safety*, COM(99) 719 final, 12 January 2000, Brussels.

4 Van Asselt, Vos and Rooijackers in this volume.

shortcomings in the institutional structures of EU food and other policies on risk-related matters. These same shortcomings have led some to conclude that there existed an 'organised irresponsibility', in the words of the German sociologist Ulrich Beck,[5] as it was hard to determine which actor was exactly 'to blame' for the BSE crisis. Was it the experts who for many years told the public that meat was safe? Was it the meat industry that, in order to increase profit, took too many risks? Was it the politicians not wanting to acknowledge the problem? Or could the consumers be blamed for preferring to buy low-priced meat (see Hajer and Schwarz 2001: 7)? Predictably, this crisis led to a crisis of confidence in both the EU authorities and other public authorities, their science-based decisions, and their established institutional structures.

This decline in trust underlies some of the most pressing tensions in the contested governance of food safety, namely: increasing divergence between scientific and public opinion, conflicting scientific opinions of Community, national and international bodies and, closely linked to this, the increasingly differentiated positions of Member State and Community authorities. It therefore comes as no surprise that the reform undertaken in the aftermath of the BSE crisis tries to tackle these tensions and revisit the existing institutional arrangements aiming at restoring the trust of consumers and regulators. This chapter will examine the reforms made to the EU's regulatory system on food safety aimed at (re-)establishing trust and ensuring food safety.

2 IN THE UNION WE TRUST?[6]

2.1 Decline in trust of both citizens and national authorities

The decline in trust of both citizens and regulators in the EU institutions and their regulatory decisions is considered to be one of the EU's most vital problems (see Majone 2000: 273–302). In its White Paper on European Governance of 2000, the Commission expressed its concern that 'people increasingly distrust institutions and politics or are simply not interested in them', and that this problem 'is particularly acute at the EU level'. The Paper also noted that 'many people are losing

5 Although food scares, such as the BSE scare, are repeatedly presented as extraordinary events, according to Beck, they all are normal accidents inherently linked to technological development. Beck's theory argues that modern society is no longer so much preoccupied with the distribution of wealth, and the division of society along class lines, but is increasingly concerned with the distribution of risk. Modern society has thus transformed into a 'risk society'. Questions of responsibility arise in the case of catastrophes, as well as who should participate in decision making about levels of exposure. As a result, the main focus of the society shifts from the distribution of the rewards of modernisation, to – as Beck puts it – 'the distribution of the bads'. Since it is unclear who is ultimately responsible, Beck speaks of an 'organized irresponsibility'. Thus, Beck indicates that the existing rules on liability and responsibility are failing. In his opinion, the traditional decision-making processes, management strategies and production methods (in the administration of justice, science, industry and politics) bring about both the material destruction of nature, as well as its symbolic normalisation (see Beck 1986 and Beck 2001: 92).

6 See title of Lenaerts' article (Lenaerts 2004: 317–43).

confidence in a poorly understood and complex system'.[7] The Commission partly blamed public dissatisfaction with EU policies and institutions on the perceived inability of the EU to act effectively during food scares.[8] This comes as no surprise in view of the inadequacies of EU activities during and before the 1996 BSE crisis uncovered in the 1997 Report by the EU Inquiry Committee into BSE (Medina Ortega Report).[9]

General public unease about food safety regulatory institutions has been confirmed by European opinion polls.[10] Clearly, the distrust towards EU public authorities is also a reflection of more general concerns as to the legitimacy and accountability of the EU and its law-making powers, due to the pervasiveness of EU integration in many fields (Wincott and Arnull 2002; Lenaerts and Desomer 2002: 1217–53). These concerns relate to a sense of a lack of involvement in major decisions, a low level of understanding of how the EU functions and a weak acceptance of the system as a whole.

Not only citizens, but also Member States have voiced explicit distrust towards the European Union and appear increasingly willing to ignore or to disagree openly with EU legislation. Member States increasingly rely on the opt-out provisions of the Community's harmonisation measures or the safeguard clauses laid down in the relevant directives in the field of health and safety and environmental protection and set higher levels of protection for their own citizens (for an analysis, see de Sadeleer 2003: 889–915; Zander 2004: 65–79). Examples include the French refusal to implement the Commission's decision of 1999 to lift the embargo on the export of British beef,[11] the Italian refusal to allow GM maize into its market notwithstanding its authorisation by the Commission,[12] and the Austrian prohibition of GMO material in its province of Upper Austria, thereby derogating from the general authorisation scheme on GMOs laid down in the GMO Directive 2001/18.[13]

2.2 The concept of trust and how to regain it

The question of how to regain the trust of citizens and the national authorities is therefore compelling. Therefore the issue of trust is often emphasised in European regulatory provisions and policy documents. Significantly, trust is nowhere defined. Yet, when determining the measures that are necessary to regain trust, it seems logical first to identify 'trust'. 'Trust' is not a uniform concept and in a recent overview of its meaning at least 16 definitions were identified (see also Kasperson,

7 European Commission, *European Governance: A White Paper*, COM(2001) 428 final, 25 July 2001, Brussels, p. 3.

8 *Ibid.*

9 Above, note 2.

10 See Eurobarometer No. 49, *Les Européens et la sécurité des produits alimentaires*, 1998, available at: <http://www.ec.europa.eu/public_opinion/archives/ebs/ebs_120_fr.pdf> and Eurobarometer, No. 58, *Europeans and Biotechnology*, 2nd edition, March 2003, available at: <http://europa.eu.int/comm/public_opinion/archives/ebs/ebs_177_en.pdf>.

11 Case C-1/00 *Commission v France* [2001] ECR I-9989.

12 Case C-236/01 *Monsanto Agricoltura Italia SpA and Others v Presidenza del Consiglio dei Ministri and Others* [2003] ECR I-08105, para 114.

13 See joined Cases T-366/03 and T-035/04 *Austria v Commission* [2005] ECR II-4005. The appeal against this judgment is still pending: see Cases C-439/05 P and C-454/05 P.

Golding and Kasperson 2005: 181–201). The definition given by Anthony Giddens seems particularly useful since it concerns decision making about risks and uncertainty. He views trust as meaning confidence in the reliability of a person or a system regarding a given set of outcomes or events. Thus, confidence would express a faith in the probity or love of another or the correctness of abstract and technical principles (Giddens 1990: 34). Ragnar Löfstedt refines this definition to the 'acceptance of the constituents without questioning the rationale behind them' (Löfstedt 2005: 6). Viewed thus, decision makers, in particular EU institutions, have an incentive to strive to regain the trust of citizens in their policies and institutional arrangements and so to restore the credibility of their regulatory actions. In order to ensure that the right instruments are used, we need first to understand the criteria used by the public and stakeholders in trusting some measures and/or authorities rather than others.

Two factors are important here: impartiality/fairness and competence.[14] First, trust depends on whether a decision has been brought about in a fair and impartial manner. This concerns both the decision-making process itself (who has participated?) and its outcome (have all interests been weighed?). In cases where regulators are not seen as impartial or fair, deliberation with the public and/or stakeholders may be necessary to gain trust. Second, the competence of authorities to act is viewed as essential for gaining trust. If authorities do not have the necessary scientific and technical background to deal with the issue at stake, they should rely on external additional expertise, for example, on scientific advisory boards (Löfstedt 2005).

Returning now to the issue of reforms made by the EU in the area of food safety, we see that they are foremost concentrated on these two factors of trust: impartiality/fairness and competence, focusing on transparency and increased participation of stakeholders and/or citizens in the decision-making process and resorting more to independent scientific experts. In the aftermath of the 1996 BSE crisis, both the EU Inquiry Committee into the BSE and the UK Inquiry Committee into BSE[15] indicated clearly that special attention needed to be paid to the 'trust-enhancing' (Lenaerts 2004: 317–43) principles of transparency and participation in risk assessment and risk management (see Vos 2000: 227–55). Following this advice, the European Commission pleaded for a more transparent and inclusive decision making.[16]

The new provisions on food safety therefore aim to introduce more transparency and participation as well as to enhance the expertise and the independence of scientific advice.[17] We will now examine how the new European regime on food

14 A third factor efficiency would also play a role according to Löfstedt and is employed to see how taxpayers' money is used in the regulatory process. Yet, relating efficiency to trust in still underdeveloped and will not be discussed here.

15 BSE Inquiry Report, 2000, available at: <http://www.bseinquiry.gov.uk/report/index.htm>.

16 Above, note 7.

17 European Commission, *Green Paper: the general principles of food law in the European Union*, COM(1997) 176 final, 30 April 1997, Brussels; *White Paper on Food Safety*, above, note 3 and Regulation (EC) No. 178/2002 of the European Parliament and of the Council of 28 January 2002 laying down the general principles and requirements of food law, establishing the European Food Safety Authority and laying down procedures in matters of food safety, [2002] *OJ* L31/1, as amended by Regulation (EC) No. 1642/2003 of the European Parliament and of the Council of 22 July 2003, [2003] *OJ* L245/4.

safety shapes these elements of trust and the problems encountered by this regime (see sections 4 and 5). First an overview of the main provisions of the new food safety regime is given.

3 EU FOOD SAFETY REGULATION: NEW PROVISIONS

As set forth above, the BSE crisis was instructive because it revealed an 'organised irresponsibility' within policy making by the Community institutions in the years before the outbreak of the crisis and the secretive manner of decision making. The EU BSE Inquiry Committee attributed a large part of the responsibility for the crisis to the system of comitology because of its complexity, obscurity and undemocratic character.[18] This made it, so the Committee argued, even more difficult to allocate responsibilities to the various institutions and committees and had allowed institutions to shift the burden of both political and administrative responsibilities onto one another. It viewed that:

> By virtue of the opaqueness, complexity and anti-democratic nature of its workings, the existing system of comitology seems to be totally exempt from any supervision, thereby enabling national and/or industrial interests to infiltrate the Community decision-making process. Although the powers of the Standing Veterinary Committee were delegated by the Council, it is the Commission that exerts control over it. However, the committee's work is based on the opinions of the Scientific Veterinary Committee, and it is clear that the UK was able to control this latter committee through the convening of the meetings, the agendas and attendance, and the drafting of minutes.[19]

It is this 'organised irresponsibility' that the new food safety regime tries to tackle by allocating more clearly the various responsibilities. At the same time, it clearly addresses the trust problem concentrating on the two elements mentioned above, impartiality and competence, by introducing more transparency and participation, while looking for ways to enhance scientific competence.

European Parliament and Council Regulation 178/2002, also known as the General Food Law,[20] aims to overcome the trust problem in particular by setting up an independent agency which replaces the existing scientific committees and by severing risk assessment and risk management. The establishment of the European Food Safety Authority (EFSA) by the General Food Law was, in the words of former Commissioner David Byrne, '[. . .] central to our plans to improve food safety and restore consumer confidence'.[21]

The General Food Law sets out the contours of EU risk regulation in matters of food safety, as outlined in the new 'From the Farm to the Fork' policy. It considers that harmonisation of national legislation is necessary in order to achieve the free

18 Above, note 2.

19 *Ibid.*

20 Regulation 178/2002, above, note 17.

21 Former Commissioner David Byrne: Key Issues, available at: <http://ec.europa.eu/archives/commission_1999_2004/byrne/key-issues_en.htm>.

movement of foodstuffs. It lays down common principles, procedures and responsibilities with regard to foodstuffs,[22] 'whilst ensuring the effective functioning of the internal market'.[23] It aims to provide a high level of protection of both health and consumers' interests, including protection against fraudulent practices, adulteration of food and other misleading practices. It also requires account to be taken, where appropriate, of fair trade, animal health and welfare, plant health and the environment.[24] The establishment of an independent agency, the EFSA, has resulted in a factual separation of responsibilities for legislation/risk management and scientific advice. It has a central position in the food safety policy (see section 5).

The General Food Law labels the precautionary principle as a general principle of food safety. The precautionary principle is one of the principles by means of which the Community attempts to equip itself for the challenges of the risk society, by enabling the authorities to adopt protective measures in situations of scientific uncertainty. This principle is also seen to enhance public trust (Lenaerts 2004). Although there is no uniform definition of this principle, most authors view scientific uncertainty as its core element (eg Cameron 2001: 113–42),[25] and European courts view its application 'by definition' to coincide with a situation in which there is scientific uncertainty.[26] The General Food Law codifies and defines the precautionary principle in its Article 7, and also coins 'scientific uncertainty' as a central element of the precautionary principle.[27] Importantly, it does not specify any degree of scientific uncertainty, while it requires measures based on the precautionary principle to be of a provisional character.

Other important pillars of the new food safety policy include the principle of transparency, participation, the duty of information, rapid alert system, crisis

22 Article 2 of Regulation (EC) No. 178/2002 of the European Parliament and of the Council of 28 January 2002 ([2002] L31/1) defines first of all the notion of 'food' or 'foodstuff'. This covers any substance or product, whether processed, partially processed or unprocessed, intended to be, or reasonably expected to be, ingested by humans. The notion includes drink, chewing gum and any substance, including water, intentionally incorporated into the food during its manufacture, preparation or treatment. It further covers water after the point of compliance, as defined in Article 6 of Directive 98/83/EC and without prejudice to the requirements of Directives 80/778/EEC and 98/83/EC. Excluded from the definition are feed, live animals unless they are prepared for placing on the market for human consumption, plants prior to harvesting, medicinal products and cosmetics, tobacco and tobacco products, as well as narcotic and psychotropic substances.

23 Article 1, Regulation 178/2002, above, note 17.

24 Article 8, Regulation 178/2002, above, note 17.

25 See for a survey of the legal opinion: Faure and Vos 2003.

26 Eg Case T-13/99 *Pfizer Animal Health SA* v. *Council* [2002] ECR II-3305; Case T-70/99 *Alpharma v Council* [2002] ECR II-3495.

27 Article 7 reads as follows: '1. In specific circumstances where, following an assessment of available information, the possibility of harmful effects on health is identified but scientific uncertainty persists, provisional risk management measures necessary to ensure the high level of health protection chosen in the Community may be adopted, pending further scientific information for a more comprehensive risk assessment. 2. Measures adopted on the basis of paragraph 1 shall be proportionate and no more restrictive of trade than is required to achieve the high level of health protection chosen in the Community, regard being had to technical and economic feasibility and other factors regarded as legitimate in the matter under consideration. The measures shall be reviewed within a reasonable period of time, depending on the nature of the risk to life or health identified and the type of scientific information needed to clarify the scientific uncertainty and to conduct a more comprehensive risk assessment.'

management and emergencies and surveillance.[28] Risk analysis is, according to the General Food Law, the basis for food policy.[29] Risk analysis consists of risk assessment, risk management and risk communication.[30] Here the General Food Law links up with the general definition of risk analysis as determined by the WHO and Codex Alimentarius.[31] Risk assessment is based on the available scientific data and is carried out in an independent, objective and transparent way. It is a scientifically based process consisting of four steps: hazard identification, hazard characterisation, exposure assessment, and risk characterisation.[32] Risk management is the process of weighing policy alternatives in consultation with interested parties.[33] It takes into account the result of risk assessment,[34] other legitimate factors, and the precautionary principle.[35] These legitimate factors include social, economic, traditional, ethical and environmental factors as well as the feasibility of control.[36] Risk communication means the interactive exchange of information and opinions throughout the risk analysis process (as regards hazards and risks, risk-related factors and risk perceptions) among risk assessors, risk managers, consumers, feed and food businesses, the academic community and other interested parties.[37]

Allocating responsibilities to the various actors forms an important element in the shaping of the new food policy. The primary responsibility for food safety lies with the food and feed business operators: '[f]ood shall not be placed on the market if it is unsafe'.[38] Operators must see to it that products at all stages of production, processing and distribution within the businesses under their control fulfil and meet the requirements of food law.[39] Furthermore, they are obliged to withdraw products from the market when they suspect that these products do not satisfy the safety requirements.[40] The general implementation of procedures based on the Hazard Analysis and Critical Control Points (HACCP) principles, together with the application of good hygiene practice, is meant to reinforce food business operators' responsibility.[41] Moreover, the General Food Law defines the tasks of the Community and national actors in regulating food safety. The national and EU

28 See for a further discussion Vos 2004.

29 Article 6, Regulation 178/2002, above, note 17.

30 Article 3(10), Regulation 178/2002, above, note 17.

31 See 'Application of Risk Analysis to Food Standards Issues', a Joint FAO/WHO Expert Consultation, Geneva, Switzerland, 13–17 March 1995, available at: <http://www.who.int/foodsafety/publications/micro/en/march1995.pdf>. See, for an overview of the risk analysis framework: <http://www.who.int/foodsafety/micro/riskanalysis/en/>. See also Codex Alimentarius Commission, Working Principles 1997, Procedural Manual of 2003, 42–8.

32 Article 3(11), Regulation 178/2002, above, note 17.

33 Article 3(13), Regulation 178/2002, above, note 17.

34 In particular the advice of the European Food Safety Authority.

35 Article 6(3), Regulation 178/2002, above, note 17.

36 Para 19 of the Preamble, Regulation 178/2002, above, note 17.

37 Article 3(13), Regulation 178/2002, above, note 17.

38 Article 14(1) and for feed a similar requirement has been laid down in Article 15, Regulation 178/2002, above, note 17.

39 Article 17, Regulation 178/2002, above, note 17.

40 Articles 18 and 19, Regulation 178/2002, above, note 17.

41 Regulation (EC) No. 852/2004 of the European Parliament and of the Council on the hygiene of foodstuffs, [2004] *OJ* L139/1. A discussion as to how far this means a shift from public to private governance is beyond the scope of this chapter.

authorities must exercise careful supervision and ensure enforcement. These principles are further developed in the official food and feed regulation.[42]

4 TRUST AND IMPARTIALITY: THE PRINCIPLES OF TRANSPARENCY AND PARTICIPATION

Increased transparency and participation have generally been indicated as means to enhance citizens' trust (see Löfstedt and Frewer 1998). The Medina Ortega Report was particularly instructive where it unveiled the political character of the European way of science making. This generated a call for more transparency and democratisation of EU policy making. Unsurprisingly, the Commission stressed in its White Paper on Food Safety that, in order to restore consumers' confidence in EU science-based food legislation, scientific advice should be of the highest standards of independence, excellence and transparency.[43] The Commission's White Paper on European Governance of July 2001 also expressed its desire to tackle public distrust in the European institutions.[44] It did this with recourse to greater openness, accountability and responsibility, better involvement and more effectiveness and coherence in the European policy-making process.

4.1 Transparency

'Transparency is essential for citizens to monitor the exercise of powers by the Community institutions'[45] and to 'strengthen the democratic character of the institutions and the trust of the public in the administration'.[46] These observations of the Court of First Instance express the importance of transparent decision making to enhance trust of citizens in the administrations. European institutions had to open up their decision-making processes on food safety, after being criticised in the Medina Ortega Report for being obscure and non-independent, and greater transparency at all levels of food safety policy was therefore the 'golden thread' running through all levels of food safety policy, thus 'contribut[ing] fundamentally to enhancing consumer confidence'.[47] To restore confidence of both consumers and trading partners, the General Food Law, under the heading of transparency, stipulates that the public has to be consulted during the preparation, evaluation and revision of food laws.[48] In this manner, it highlights one element of the range of values covered by the concept of transparency, such as access to documents,

42 Regulation (EC) No. 882/2004 of the European Parliament and of the Council of 29 April 2004 on official controls performed to ensure the verification of compliance with feed and food law, animal health and animal welfare rules, [2004] *OJ* L165/1.

43 Above, note 3.

44 Above, note 7.

45 See, *inter alia, Interporc Im- und Export GmbH v Commission* ('Interporc II') [1999] ECR II-3521, para 39.

46 See, *inter alia, Svenska Journalistförbundet v Council* [1998] ECR II-02289, para 66 and Case T-14/98 *Heidi Hautala v Council* [1999] ECR II-02489, para 83 (see also Lenaerts 2004: 317–43).

47 Above, note 3, para 117 (see Vos and Wendler 2006: 102).

48 Article 9, Regulation 178/2002, above, note 17.

responsibility for decision making, how decisions are made and the duty to state reasons (O'Neill 1998: 403).

These other elements of transparency are covered by the general rules applicable for the Community institutions (such as access to documents), or are separately laid down for the specific phases of decision making.

4.1.1 Risk assessment

For risk assessment, the General Food Law requires that EFSA carries out its activities with a high level of transparency,[49] both with regard to the outcomes of its work and the processes leading up to them,[50] thereby ensuring the widest possible access to the documents it holds, receives or has drawn up, with the exception of commercially sensitive information.[51] EFSA has been active in developing and spelling out the application of this principle, detailing the information that is displayed to the public or kept concealed, for example, in the interests of commercial confidentiality.[52] It has *inter alia* on its own initiative – and in contrast to the practice followed by other agencies – opened up its Management Board meetings through live webstream and placed draft opinions on various issues on its website to be commented on by interested parties. In addition, its Advisory Forum is currently reflecting on how to introduce more transparency in risk assessment, importantly, also by revealing uncertainty information.[53]

While showing willingness to open up its opinions and other documents, EFSA has demonstrated reluctance to open up the debates leading to its scientific opinions. Contrary to the practice of the American 'sunshine committees',[54] EFSA's Scientific Committee or Panels do not generally meet in public. This remains a sensitive issue. Allowing access to meetings of scientific bodies is considered by some authors to be particularly troublesome, as this could lead to the political pressuring of scientists and hence to a further politicisation of science, risking paralysis of the process (Bal, Bijker and Hendriks 2002: 315). Yet, it is also recognised that leaving the construction of sound science only to certified experts may lead again to the technocratic approach one would wish to avoid (Bal, Bijker and Hendriks 2002: 315). Indeed, EFSA keeps such internal discussions confidential so that participants feel able to discuss issues freely and thereby achieve high-quality opinions,[55] which seems on the face of it in apparent contradiction to its claimed commitment to transparency. Should EFSA allow for more transparency as regards the meetings of the scientists?

49 Article 38, Regulation 178/2002, above, note 17.

50 Article 43, Regulation 178/2002, above, note 17.

51 See, in more detail, Vos and Wendler 2006: 102–5. The General Food Law makes explicit reference to scientific opinions, stating that conclusions of scientific panel opinions should 'on no account' be kept confidential, Article 39(3).

52 See, eg, the decision of the Management Board concerning implementing measures of transparency and confidentiality requirements, MB 10.03.2005 – 10.

53 AF 08.04.2005 – 5, point 1.

54 See the US Freedom of Information Act ('FOIA'), 5 U.S.C. § 552; the Federal Advisory Committee Act (FACA), 5 U.S.C. app. II and the Government in the Sunshine Act, codified in 5 U.S.C. section 552b.

55 MB 16.09.2003 – adopted; Decision concerning access to documents, Article 7(i).

To answer this question and to understand what EFSA is doing, it is helpful to look at insights from science and technology studies, in particular the work by Hilgartner, an expert in social dimensions and the politics of contemporary and emerging science and technology. He has introduced the metaphor of a theatre play to describe the role of scientific bodies. Applying this metaphor, the work within EFSA's Scientific Committee and Panels can be analysed as a backstage production of an onstage performance. And, just like in the theatre, the activities that take place backstage cannot be displayed without radically changing the meaning of the performance onstage (Hilgartner 2000).[56] EFSA thus seems to distinguish between procedural and substantive transparency. Bal, Bijker and Hendriks argue that scientific bodies rightly limit their procedural transparency to access to documents, keeping meetings closed in order to increase their substantive transparency (Bal, Bijker and Hendriks, 2004: 1339–41). As regards the Dutch Health Council, they conclude that 'although the existence of a "back region" seems to contradict the notion of transparency, it is central to the Council's functioning as a scientific advisory body' (Bal, Bijker and Hendriks 2004: 1339–41). They stress that opening up meetings could lead to the situation in which political and interest lobby groups put committee members under strong pressure.[57] Given that this was exactly what happened with the scientists in the Scientific Veterinary Committee during the BSE crisis, it seems undesirable to open up meetings. In relation to risk assessment, therefore, transparency should not be about getting rid of the difference between what is happening backstage and onstage, but about creating public spheres in which differences in opinion can be ventilated and viewpoints can be exchanged and discussed.[58] For example, we could then conceive of a situation whereby the drafting of the 'terms of reference' in which the Commission defines the problem that EFSA must answer, should be opened up to the public.

4.1.2 Risk management

Where the General Food Law has interpreted transparency as public consultation and information, the Commission has initiated a number of consultation procedures on food safety, with the objective of applying the principles of openness and transparency. For instance, stakeholders have been given the opportunity to comment on the evaluation of Regulation 258/97 on novel foods.[59] Furthermore, it has developed a system of online consultation (see section 4.2). According its minimum standards for the participation of civil society,[60] the Commission must report on the results of consultation.

56 See as regards an analysis of the Dutch Health Council, Bal, Bijker and Hendriks 2002: 318. See also Bal, Bijker and Hendriks 2004.

57 See the example given by Bal, Bijker and Hendriks about the American situation.

58 See in the context of the Gezondheidsraad, Bal, Bijker and Hendriks 2002: 318.

59 See: <http://europa.eu.int/comm/food/consultations/index_en.htm>.

60 European Commission, *Communication from the Commission toward a reinforced culture of consultation and dialogue – General principles and minimum standards for consultation of interested parties by the Commission*, COM(2002) 704 final, 11 December 2002, Brussels. See <http://europa.eu.int/eur-lex/en/com/cnc/2002/com2002_0704en01.pdf>.

It was foremost the Commission's interaction with the national representatives within the framework of comitology that was criticised by the Medina Ortega Report for being obscure, complex and undemocratic.[61] In an attempt to simplify the fragmented system of multiple standing committees, first various standing committees, such as the Standing Committee on Foodstuffs, were absorbed into one committee: the Standing Committee on the Food Chain and Animal Health (SCFCAH). Following the new 1999 Comitology decision, comitology became much more visible. Committees are, for instance, required to adopt their own rules of procedure and follow the Community's policy of open access to their own documentation.[62] Moreover, the Commission is obliged to inform the Parliament of the committee agendas, the draft decisions that the Commission sends to the committees, the voting results, to make a summary of the meetings and to issue annual reports on committee activities. However, in practice, many stakeholders still complain about the obscurity surrounding the refurbished SCFCAH, in particular the problematic access to information on this Committee (Vos and Wendler 2006: 129). This is confirmed in the recent debate on the GM approval procedure, where Member States have clearly voiced their discontent with the transparency of the procedure and the operation of this Committee.[63] Does this mean that comitology meetings too must be opened up? Here, too, the theatre metaphor may be used and a similar argument presented for the closure of meetings of risk assessors within EFSA could be developed for the transparency of activities of comitology in risk management, thus 'protecting' national representatives from the public eye and their Member States' eye, allowing them at times to have a freer, deliberative discussion.

4.2 Participation

4.2.1 Risk assessment

Participation in both decision making and science as a means to regain trust is promoted in several studies and documents.[64] Opening up the traditionally closed circles of science, by allowing interested parties to participate is, nevertheless, still quite revolutionary, even in national contexts (Bal, Bijker and Hendriks 2002: 312). Moreover, active participation in decision making raises problematic issues, such as, who should participate (stakeholders, civil society and/or the general public), how those participating should be defined and what degree of

61 Above, note 2.

62 See, already, *Rothmans* case and implicitly Regulation (EC) No. 1049/2001 of the European Parliament and of the Council of 30 May 2001 regarding public access to European Parliament, Commission and Council documents, [2001] *OJ* L145/43.

63 EU Food Law Weekly, No. 247, 10 March 2006, p. 4.

64 See, *inter alia*, Report of the Working Group 'Democratising expertise and establishing scientific reference systems' (Group 1b) (rapporteur Liberatore), European Commission, 2001, available at: <http://europa.eu.int/comm/governance/areas/group2/report_en.pdf> and the Conclusions of the Conference 'Science and Governance in a Knowledge Society: the Challenge for Europe', organised by DG Joint Research Centre and DG Research, Brussels, 16–17 October 2000, p. 2, available at: <http://europa.eu.int/comm/governance/areas/group2/contribution_en.pdf>.

representativeness they should have (see, for example, OECD 2001). The question therefore arises whether, when and how one should allow participation in deciding upon food safety issues. The book *Late Lessons from Early Warnings*, drawing on 14 case studies, which include BSE, benzene, hormones and asbestos, concludes that several benefits flow from involving a wide range of stakeholders, and taking account of their values and interests at the earliest stage of regulatory appraisal and choice of technological and social options brings several benefits. First, this would augment the information available for policy making. Second, this may also improve public trust in society's capacity to control hazards, without necessarily stifling innovation or compromising science. Moreover, it may also make better science (Harremoës *et al.* 2002: 216–17). Stirling makes a conceptual distinction between three very different rationales and imperatives for participatory engagement: *normative democratic* ('because it is the right thing to do'); *substantive* ('because it leads to better decisions') and *instrumental* ('because it facilitates particular favoured decisions') (Stirling 2003: 381–401). This conceptual distinction helps to define the need for participatory processes in particular contexts.

Although it is neither necessary nor desirable to open meetings of risk assessors to the general public (see above), the substantive rationale of participation pleads for some form of participation by stakeholders in science making so that knowledge can be transferred to the risk assessors, leading to better scientific opinions. The need for a dialogue with stakeholders is indeed recognised by EFSA. First, it is expressed in the composition of its Management Board, in which four members are represented with background in organisations representing consumers and other interests in the food chain. Furthermore, EFSA is committed by law to open up its work to public scrutiny and to maintain 'efficient' contacts with its stakeholders.[65] This obligation and the pressure from stakeholders has led EFSA in 2005 to institutionalise stakeholder participation by way of the creation of a Consultative Stakeholder Platform and to organise public hearings on significant scientific issues.[66] In practitioners' eyes, EFSA's Stakeholder Platform was created to exchange information and discuss science with the stakeholders in a two-way learning process, in which EFSA would be able to obtain information from the stakeholders and also learn from them how EFSA can best serve their interests (Vos and Wendler 2006: 124). Whether this works well remains to be seen.

4.2.2 Risk management

As regards risk management, it is clear that the Commission carefully learned its BSE lessons and takes participation more seriously. It thus promised to engage in broad consultation processes to regain trust in food safety regulation. It first made use of green and white papers, while also using seemingly new instruments like

65 Article 42, Regulation 178/2002, above, note 17.

66 EFSA Press Release of 3 December 2003, 'EFSA plans greater public involvement in its work', available at: <http://www.efsa.eu.int/pdf/pressrel_mb011_final_en.pdf>. See activities of EFSA's Advisory Forum.

reflection papers and discussion papers.[67] In addition, as set forth above, it has developed an online consultation, 'Your Voice in Europe'.[68] Within this framework, the Commission has launched several consultation procedures relating to food safety.[69] Whether such initiatives are really meaningful depends partly on the rationales of such participatory processes and what the Commission will do with the outcomes. Where increased consultation and deliberation are used for mere trust-enhancing purposes, hence relating more to the instrumental rationale of participation, such dialogue initiatives might soon become an exercise in 'empty proceduralism' (Chalmers 2003: 552). Therefore, to avoid these consultation procedures and dialogue initiatives becoming mere 'public relation' actions (Frewer 2004) paying mere lip-service to participation,[70] these participatory processes must also fulfil the substantive rationale and serve to enhance the quality of the decision making. So, where the current practice of the Commission relates simply to access for people to comment on its initiatives and/or concrete proposals, giving little and only very general feedback, this is unlikely to lead to more trust.

The same applies to the initiatives of the Commission to institutionalise stakeholder participation. With the creation of the Advisory Group on the Food Chain and Animal Health,[71] the Commission aims to set up an effective ongoing consultation system involving consultation of citizens through bodies representing interests related to the food chain and animal and plant health at European level. This Group revives and replaces the former Advisory Committee on Foodstuffs[72] and various other advisory committees.[73] The change in name from 'Committee' to 'Group' seems to emphasise a more informal setting than within a 'committee' while also indicating that it makes a new start, especially in view of the long period of inactivity of the former Advisory Committee on Foodstuffs. Within this setting, consumers, industry, retailers' and farmers' organisations are consulted and informed. The Advisory Group will be made up of a maximum of 45 members from EU level organisations representing stakeholders' interests.[74] Here, at least on paper, the Commission seems more interested in quality consultation rather than mere instrumentalisation of participation. In view of the unsuccessful practice of the former Advisory Committee on Foodstuffs, it remains to be seen how effective this transformation will be.

67 With these new expressions, the Commission seemingly wants to suggest that these papers are truly meant for discussion. In contrast to the Green and White Papers, these documents are not official COM documents. See for an example of a discussion paper: Directorate General Health and Consumer Protection (SANCO D4), 'Discussion Paper on the Implementation of Regulation (EC) No. 258/97 of the European Parliament and of the Council of 27 January 1997 concerning novel foods and novel food ingredients', July 2002, available at: <http://europa.eu.int/comm/food/fs/novel_food/discussion_en.pdf>.

68 See <http://europa.eu.int/yourvoice/index_en.htm>.

69 See <http://europa.eu.int/comm/food/consultations/index_en.htm>.

70 See Somsen in this volume.

71 Commission Decision 2004/613/EC of 6 August 2004 concerning the creation of an advisory group on the food chain and animal and plant health, [2004] *OJ* L275/17.

72 See Commission Decision 75/420/EEC of 26 June 1975 setting up an Advisory Committee on Foodstuffs, [1975] *OJ* L182/35.

73 Commission Decision 98/235/EC of 11 March 1998 on the advisory committees dealing with matters covered by the common agricultural policy, [1998] *OJ* L88/59.

74 Above, note 71, Article 3(1).

5 TRUST AND COMPETENCE: THE PRINCIPLES OF QUALITY AND INDEPENDENCE

The problematic relationship between excellence and independence of scientists is well-known and again appeared on the political agenda in the BSE aftermath. Prior to the BSE crisis, the Commission had worked with scientific committees (already established since the late 1960s) to provide it with scientific advice. Yet, the independence of members of these committees already appeared problematic for a number of reasons. First, scientists on these committees were very much linked to Member States (one scientist per Member State, with the bigger Member States having two scientists). This situation meant that scientists could be put under political pressure, as was apparent in the BSE crisis. In addition, they received very little financial compensation for their committee work, which made it difficult to attract excellent scientists. Moreover, individual Directorates-General of the Commission were responsible for the administration of the relevant committees, which led to an intertwining of interests (for example, Directorate-general Agriculture being responsible for health).[75]

The Medina Ortega report issued a number of recommendations to improve the functioning of scientists: the introduction of a Member State independent nomination procedure for the scientists, the introduction of guarantees to safeguard the independence of the scientists on the committees, the recording of minority views of scientists in the scientific opinions; the establishment of a procedure for reimbursement for travel and subsistence costs and the establishment of monetary remuneration.[76]

As Byrne indicated, the creation of a clearly visible agency, EFSA, outside – at 'arm's length' – the Commission, serves several purposes. First, EFSA is aimed to address the problem of confidence by guaranteeing more independence and excellence and greater transparency as well as strengthening the scientific basis for food safety regulation.[77] Second, the establishment of an independent agency with its own scientific staff that can collect data and prepare opinions, also tackles the problems that arose in practice in relation to the EU system of scientific advisory committees coordinated by DG SANCO. In the past years, that system had come under ever-growing strain because of the increased need for quick, reliable and scientifically sound advice in the field of food safety. In view of the limited ability of the committees to carry out both a safety evaluation of scientific files and an evaluation of issues of public health in general, in practice it proved impossible for the system to continue.[78] Moreover, by combining the existing scientific committees and the Scientific Steering Committee under the umbrella of EFSA it addresses the problem of fragmentation and creates a more coherent approach to several topics

75 Above, note 2.

76 See also the attempts by the Commission to set criteria for science making, *Communication from the Commission on the collection and use of expertise by the Commission: principles and guidelines – 'Improving the knowledge base for better policies'*, COM(2002) 0713 final, Brussels.

77 See, eg, Speech of former Commissioner Byrne 2000.

78 See, for instance, testimonies of the members of the scientific steering group in: *Joint Conference on the EU and Food Security: Lessons to be learned from the BSE crisis* (Brussels, 30 November and 1 December 1998), available at: <http://www.europarl.eu.int/conferences/bse/cre-toc_en.htm>.

of food safety. Ultimately, the creation of EFSA can be understood as yet another step towards the Europeanisation of science and the scientification of European food safety regulation.

The aim to achieve better quality of science is reflected in the General Food Law's requirement for EFSA to provide 'the best possible' independent scientific opinions on all matters that directly or indirectly influence food safety.[79] EFSA is the main actor responsible for risk assessment at the EU level, giving advice to the Commission, Parliament and Member States. It is also required to communicate risks to the public. Importantly, the Commission still needs to consult EFSA on all matters involving the public health. EFSA has, for example, to give its opinion on pre-market approval procedures including GM food and feed, pesticide residues and novel food. The quality of its opinions is augmented by abolishing criteria for membership based on nationality and introducing strict selection criteria for scientists. The Panels comprise leading independent scientists for a three-year period, which is renewable twice. They are appointed by the Management Board, acting on a proposal from the Executive Director, after publication of an open competition in the Official Journal and leading scientific publications.[80] The composition of the Panels requires coverage of a broad range of scientific competence and expertise and geographical representation.[81] The latter requirement seems nevertheless to be led by political rather than quality considerations.

With a daily remuneration of €300, the Community tries to ensure the independence and excellence of panel members and to loosen links with industry and authorities. Yet, the issue of EFSA independence remains a contentious one. The General Food Law indicates only generally that members of the Scientific Committee and the Scientific Panels shall 'undertake to act independently of any external influence'.[82] A close scrutiny of its practice shows that EFSA can be considered to be both independent from the Commission and the Member States, albeit not completely. Unlike other European agencies, Member States have less of a grip on this agency as they are not members of EFSA's Management Board, yet representatives of national competent authorities continue to play an important role through its Advisory Forum. However, the link between members of the Scientific Committee and Panels and Member States has been removed through changes in the selection criteria. As regards the Commission, it is notable that EFSA is placed at a distance from the Commission and has administrative independence, whereas previously the Commission was in charge of all administrative support of scientific committees. However, there still exists a 'grey zone' of close cooperation and deliberation between EFSA and the Commission in practice (Vos and Wendler 2006), which nonetheless does not necessarily impinge on EFSA's independence (see Jasanoff 1990). It is clear that EFSA, as a Community agency, is not, and should not be, completely independent of the public authorities: EFSA is subjected to the

79 Article 22 (2); 23(a), Regulation 178/2002, above, note 17.

80 Article 28(5), Regulation 178/2002, above, note 17. See for the appointment of the members of the Committee and the Panels: <http://www.efsa.eu.int/pdf/sci_panels_list_en.pdf>.

81 MB 17.10.2002 – 3, Article 4(2). For a breakdown of the Scientific Panels into the nationality of the Members, see Annex.

82 Article 37(2), Regulation 178/2002, above, note 17.

supervision of the European Parliament since it is, currently at least,[83] financed wholly out of the European budget.[84]

Acknowledging that scientists and other members of EFSA cannot be completely 'interest-free', members of the Management Board and the Advisory Forum and the Executive Director must commit themselves to act 'in the public interest'[85] or, as regards the Scientific Committee and Panels, act 'independently of any external influence'.[86] They must declare any interests which could be considered prejudicial to their independence and links with industry should be disclosed. In practice, however, the rules on interest declaration still appear to be vague as regards how and what interests precisely need to be declared. Furthermore, it is also not clear what is done with declarations and how far panel members, who declare to have an interest, are excluded from the science-making process. For example, in 2004, Friends of the Earth Europe accused the scientists in EFSA's GMO Panel of not being independent and not declaring all relevant conflicting interests, being biased towards industry.[87] While EFSA reacted to this by explicitly denying a financial clash of interests among its scientists, it is clear that this situation is in urgent need of clarification. Moreover, national authorities have questioned some of EFSA's positive assessments in the context of GM food authorisation procedures. In particular, they criticised EFSA for not taking due account of the objections raised by Member States and for failing to resolve diverging scientific opinions within the context of the authorisation procedures of GMOs.[88]

6 CONCLUDING REMARKS

I would like to make a few concluding remarks. The BSE crisis has caused numerous reforms in EU food safety regulation. These reform initiatives were foremost led by the desire of the European institutions to regain trust in their science-based decision making, while also ensuring food safety. The new EU policy and rules have become more transparent and allow for greater participation, which are important elements in the EU's efforts to regain public trust. An increasing number of documents are being put on the Internet which make the activities of EFSA, the Commission and comitology more visible. Yet, stakeholders still complain that this transparency is insufficient to give them a true picture of what is happening in the decision-making process. They argue that transparency is only applicable for those who actively look on the Internet and that documents are being disclosed with

83 There has been an ongoing discussion about whether European Food Safety Authority (EFSA) could levy fees, for example for conducting risk assessments in the context of authorisation procedures. See <http://europa.eu.int/comm/food/committees/advisory/summary_05072005.pdf>.

84 EFSA annual financial report 2003, available at: <http://www.efsa.eu.int/about_efsa/efsa_funding/catindex_en.html>.

85 Article 4, Regulation 178/2002, above, note 17.

86 Article 37, Regulation 178/2002, above, note 17.

87 Throwing caution to the wind, Friends of the Earth Europe, November 2004.

88 See EU Food Law Weekly, No. 247, 10 March 2006, p. 4. See also Van Asselt, Vos and Rooijmakers in this volume.

much delay. Moreover, the question of access to comitology meetings and EFSA panels need to be opened up remains disputed.

In relation to this, the question of whether the inherent political character of scientific advice should also be subject to external political supervising seems especially problematic. Insights from social studies of science could provide guidance for establishing the level of transparency and, closely linked to this, participation in science making and to some extent policy making. Recognition that EFSA's process of science making is divided into a 'frontstage' and a 'backstage', would initially lead to a plea for the blurring of these different stages and to shed more light on what happens 'backstage'. Yet, various social studies of science tell us that it is important that stakeholders should not have too big a role in EFSA's science making, as this would affect its position as an independent agency (Bal, Bijker and Hendriks 2002). The latter is, of course, essential for the trust issue. This would lead us to suggest that both transparency and participation as regards risk assessment should be about creating public spheres for exchange of opinions and discussion.[89] In addition to the instrumental rationale of participation, such an approach is ultimately likely to contribute to the quality of the science making. To a large extent, this seems to be precisely what EFSA is doing with the establishment of its Stakeholder Platform. Moreover, with regard to the currently closed interface between EFSA and the Commission, one should envisage access (both in terms of transparency and participation) for stakeholders to the process of drafting of the 'terms of reference' in which the Commission defines the problem that EFSA needs to answer (Dreyer *et al.* 2006). The conceptualisation of participation by Stirling into normative democrative, substantive and instrumental, is particularly helpful to identify situations in which participation of stakeholders should be allowed in science making, namely where this serves the substantive rationale of participation and thus where more input by stakeholders is required to enhance the quality of science making.

Similar reasoning as regards transparency and participation applies within the comitology setting.

It is in any case important to observe that, when upholding the separation between what is happening onstage and backstage, EFSA and the Commission (comitology) should not be secretive about what is happening 'backstage'. This, as the BSE crisis taught us, would be disastrous for the trust of regulators, stakeholders and citizens. Instead, transparency about the arguments used and the procedure followed should guarantee that no capricious horsetrading takes place. Taken together these suggestions would not only augment the trust in, but also the quality of European science-based decision making and therefore also food safety more generally.

89 See also Van Asselt, Vos and Rooijackers in this volume.

BIBLIOGRAPHY

Ansell, C.K. and Vogel, D. (2006) *What's the Beef? The Contested Governance of European Food Safety*, Cambridge, MA: MIT Press.

Bal, R., Bijker, W. and Hendriks, R. (2004) 'Democratisation of scientific advice', *BMJ* 329: 1339–41.

Bal, R., Bijker, W. and Hendriks, R. (2002) *Paradox van wetenschappelijk gezag: over de maatschappelijke invloed van adviezen van de Gezondheidsraad, 1985–2001,* Den Haag: Gezondheidsraad.

Beck, U. (2001) 'Wereldrisicomaatschappij en de toekomst van de ecologische politiek', in U. Beck, *De wereld als risicomaatschappij,* Amsterdam: De Balie, 92–7.

Beck, U. (1986) *Risikogesellschaft. Auf dem Weg in eine andere Moderne,* Frankfurt am Main: Suhrkamp Verlag.

Byrne, D. (2000) 'Food safety a top priority in the EU', Informal Agricultural Council, Biarritz, 5 September 2000, available at: <http://europa.eu.int/comm/dgs/health_consumer/library/speeches/speech54_en.html>.

Cameron, J. (2001) 'The precautionary principle in international law', in T. O'Riordan, J. Cameron and A. Jordan (eds), *Reinterpreting the Precautionary Principle,* London: Cameron May, 113–42.

Chalmers, D. (2003) ' "Food for thought": Reconciling European risks and traditional ways of life', *The Modern Law Review* 66(4): 532–62.

Dreyer, M. *et al.* (2006) 'Institutional re-arrangements in European food safety governance: a comparative analysis', in E. Vos and F. Wendler (eds), *Food Safety Regulation in Europe,* Antwerp: Intersentia, 9–64.

European Parliament (1997) *Final BSE Inquiry Report,* Rapporteur Manuel Medina Ortega, A4–0020/97/A.

Eurostat (2006) *European Business – 2006 Edition,* Brussels: Eurostat.

Faure, M. and Vos, E. (eds) (2003) *Juridische afbakening van het voorzorgsbeginsel: mogelijkheden en grenzen,* The Hague: Health Council, available at <http://www.gr.nl/pdf.php?ID=723>.

Frewer, L. (2004) *Consumers, Food, Trust and Safety – The Need for Collaboration between the Social and Natural Sciences,* Wageningen: WUR Publications.

Giddens, A. (1990) *The Consequences of Modernity,* Cambridge: Polity Press.

Hajer, M. and Schwarz, M. (2001) 'Inleiding. Contouren van de risicomaatschappij', in U. Beck, *De wereld als risicomaatschappij,* Amsterdam: De Balie, 7–22.

Harremoës, P. *et al.* (eds) (2002) *The Precautionary Principle in the 20th Century: Late Lessons from Early Warnings,* London: Earthscan.

Hilgartner, S. (2000) *Science on Stage: Expert Advice as Public Drama,* Stanford USA: Stanford University Press.

James, P., Kemper, F. and Pascal, G. (1999) *A European Food and Public Health Authority: The Future of Scientific Advice in the EU,* Brussels: European Commission, available at: <http://europa.eu.int/comm/food/fs/sc/future_food_en.pdf>.

Jasanoff, S. (1990) *The Fifth Branch: Science Advisors as Policy Makers,* Cambridge MA: Harvard University Press.

Kasperson, R.E., Golding, D. and Kasperson, J.X. (2005) 'Risk, Trust and Democratic Theory', in J.X. Kasperson and R.E. Kasperson (eds), *The Social Contours of Risk. Vol. I: Publics, Risk Communication & Social Amplification of Risk,* London: Earthscan, 181–201.

Lenaerts, K. (2004) ' "In the Union we trust": Trust-enhancing principles of Community law', *Common Market Law Review* 41(2), 317–43.

Lenaerts, K. and Desomer, M. (2002) 'New models of constitution-making in Europe: the quest for legitimacy', *Common Market Law Review* 39(6), 1217–53.

Löfstedt, R.A. (2005) *Risk Management in Post-Trust Societies,* Hampshire: Palgrave Macmillan.

Löfstedt, R. and Frewer, L. (eds) (1998) *Risk and Modern Society,* London: Earthscan Publications.

Majone, G. (2000) 'The Credibility Crisis of Community Regulation', *Journal of Common Market Studies* 38(2), 273–302.

OECD (2001) *Citizens as Partners. Information, Consultation and Public Participation in Policy-making,* Paris: OECD.

O'Neill, M. (1998) 'The right to access to Community held documentation as a general principle of EC law', *EPL,* 403–32.

Randall, E. (2001) *The Plan for a European Food Authority and the Politics of Risk in the Union*, Working Paper Policy library, available at: <http://www.policylibrary.com/Essays/RandallEFARisk/EFARisk1.htm>.

de Sadeleer, N. (2003) 'Procedures for derogations from the principle of approximation of laws under Article 95 EC', *Common Market Law Review* 40(4), 889–915.

Stirling, A. (2003) 'Beyond public perceptions of gene technology: Community participation', in H. Dietrich and R. Schibeci (eds), *Public Understanding of Science* 12(4): 381–401.

Vos, E. (2004) *Overcoming the Crisis of Confidence: Risk Regulation in an Enlarged European Union*, Universiteit Maastricht: Unigraphic.

Vos, E. (2000) 'EU Food Safety Regulation in the aftermath of the BSE crisis', *Journal of Consumer Policy* 23(3): 227–55.

Vos, E. and Wendler, F. (2006) 'Food Safety Regulation at the EU level', in E. Vos and F. Wendler (eds), *Food Safety Regulation in Europe*, Antwerp: Intersentia, 65–138.

Wincott, D. and Arnull, A.M. (eds) (2002) *Accountability and Legitimacy in the European Union*, Oxford: Oxford University Press.

Zander, J. (2004) 'The Green Guarantee in the EC Treaty: Two recent cases', *Journal of Environmental Law* 16(1): 65–79.

Chapter 14

The EU regulatory system for GMOs

Gregory C. Shaffer and Mark A. Pollack

The regulation of genetically modified (GM) foods and seeds in the European Union (EU) exemplifies the challenge of European multilevel governance in the area of risk regulation, an area which covers multiple policy domains, ranging from internal market and external trade promotion, science, research and development coordination, to environmental and consumer protection. On the one hand, regulatory power in this area has become increasingly centralised at the EU level. On the other hand, the European Commission's authority has constantly been challenged within the EU and abroad, respectively by the EU Member States and their constituents, as well as the United States and a number of other agricultural exporting nations, using the rules of the World Trade Organization (WTO) as leverage. Such pressures have called into question the legitimacy of EU policy making itself in this area.

This chapter examines the historical development of GMO regulation in the European Union in five parts. Part 1 provides historical background, examining the interactions of EU institutions, Member States and private actors in the creation of EU regulations and directives concerning GMOs, and laying out the provisions of the EU's landmark 1990 Directive on the deliberate release of genetically modified foods and crops into the environment[1] and its 1997 'novel foods regulation'.[2] In part 2, we examine the substantial challenges of implementing the Union's early regulations because of a revolt among member governments that invoked safeguard clauses against GM varieties that had been approved, and that imposed a *de facto* moratorium on the approval of new ones. Faced with widespread governmental and public challenges, the Union responded with a major reform of EU policies to provide for a stricter and more comprehensive regulatory approach. Examined in part 3, this reform included the substantial revision of the 1990 Directive as well as new regulations establishing a European Food Safety

* This chapter draws upon our analysis of the EU regulatory system for GMOs in Wallace, Wallace and Pollack 2005 and in our book *When Cooperation Fails* (2009). The authors would like to thank Timo Weishaupt, Geoff Seufert and Andrew Hinkel for their invaluable research assistance, and the Center for World Affairs and the Global Economy at the University of Wisconsin-Madison for financial support.

1 Council Directive 90/220/EEC of 23 April 1990 on the deliberate release into the environment of genetically modified organisms, [1990] *OJ* L117/15.

2 Regulation (EC) No. 258/97 of the European Parliament and of the Council of 27 January 1997 on novel foods and novel foods ingredients, [1997] *OJ* L43/1.

Authority[3] and setting out rules regarding the labelling of GM foods and the traceability of GM crops 'from the farm to the fork'.

The EU's regulatory approach, however, cannot be understood without placing it in a global context. In part 4, we examine the relationship between EU regulations and international trade and environmental rules. As we shall see, the law and jurisprudence of international institutions such as the WTO have shaped EU regulations, focusing these on the use of individualised scientific risk assessment as the basis for biotechnology regulation, while the EU has simultaneously sought to export its domestic regulatory principles, including its version of the 'precautionary principle', to the international arena. The final section concludes with regard to the manner in which EU biotechnology policy has been shaped by sustained, simultaneous and countervailing challenges to the legitimacy of EU decision making from above (the WTO) and from below (the EU Member States and their constituents).

I HISTORICAL ORIGINS OF EU BIOTECH POLICY

The 1957 Treaty of Rome Establishing the European Community made no explicit mention of an EU policy for agricultural biotechnology, or even for the closely related areas of environmental protection and food safety, which remained primarily a national responsibility within each of the Community's Member States. Over time, however, the Community developed a *de facto* policy on biotechnology, eventually including the regulation of the approval, content and labelling of GM foods and crops. This regulation, however, has been difficult to formulate and implement, as it has pursued two complementary and conflicting objectives, with competing actors attempting to push one over the other – internal market and technology promotion, on the one hand, and environmental and consumer protection, on the other.

Much EU regulation in this domain resulted, in large part, from 'spillover' from EU internal market policy. Disparate Member State regulation obstructs the free movement of goods. European authorities sought to ensure free movement of biotech products throughout the European market by creating a new EU regulatory framework which would foster trade and investment and, as a result, the increased international competitiveness of the European biotechnology industry. However, in attempting to remove Member State obstacles, EU authorities pursued environmental and consumer protection objectives as well. On the one hand, social protection and internal market objectives are complementary, since a single regulatory framework removes Member State regulatory barriers to trade. On the other hand, stringent regulation at the EU level can create substantial commercial obstacles for the marketing of GM products.

Genetic engineering first emerged as a concern for national and international regulators in the 1970s, as biological scientists began making fundamental advances

3 Regulation (EC) No. 178/2002 of the European Parliament and of the Council of 28 January 2002 laying down the general principles and requirements of food law, establishing the European Food Safety Authority and laying down procedures in matters of food safety, [2002] *OJ* L31/1.

in rDNA research (Patterson 2000: 319–32; Cantley 1995). During this early period, from the 1970s through the mid-1980s, the development and marketing of GM foods and crops lay in the distant future, and regulators in Europe and elsewhere focused primarily on issues relating to laboratory research and to the development of a competitive biotechnology industry. In 1978, the Commission Directorate-General for Science, Research and Development (then DG XII) proposed a Community R&D programme in molecular biology, together with a draft Directive requiring notification and prior authorisation by national authorities for all biotechnology research.[4] This latter proposal was withdrawn by the Commission in 1980, in favour of a non-binding 1982 Council of Europe resolution calling for notification of rDNA research to national authorities.[5] Commission concerns about the competitiveness of the EU's biotechnology industry remained, however, and in 1983 the Commission incorporated biotechnology into its multi-annual Framework Programme for research and technological development.

By the mid-1980s, a number of EU Member States were regulating biotechnology in response to developments in genetic engineering technology. The Commission reacted by more actively exploring the adoption of a Community framework for biotechnology regulation. The Commission created several inter-departmental coordinating bodies, most notably the Biotechnology Steering Committee (1984) and the Biotechnology Regulation Inter-service Committee (1985) (Patterson 2000: 324–32). Within these groupings, policy leadership shifted gradually away from the DG XII (Science, Research and Development), which had taken the leading role during the early years,[6] and increasingly towards other DGs and in particularly DG XI (Environment). DG Environment became increasingly involved during the late 1980s as biotechnology began to move out of the laboratory and toward deliberate releases into the environment and the eventual marketing of GM foods and crops.

With DG Environment taking the lead, the Commission released a new Communication in 1986, 'A Community Framework for the Regulation of Biotechnology.'[7] The Commission noted that the European Parliament had already called (in 1987) for Community-level regulation, and that a number of Member States had already moved to adopt a range of national measures.[8] 'The internal market arguments for Community-wide regulation of biotechnology are clear,' it argued. 'Microorganisms are no respecters of national frontiers, and nothing short of

4 European Commission, *Proposal for a Council Directive establishing safety measures against the conjectural risks associated with recombinant DNA work*, [1978] *OJ* C301/5.

5 Council of Europe, *Thirty-Third Ordinary Session of the Parliamentary Assembly*, Recommendation 934 (1982), on Genetic Engineering (text adopted by the Assembly on 26 January 1982 (22nd sitting)).

6 Prior to 1983, Cantley 1995: 535 notes, 'the other DGs . . . saw the mysteries of biotechnology as still playthings of DG XII and the scientific community . . .'. Hence, '[t]he Commission communications on biotechnology, although presenting a strategic approach, were in practice largely drafted by the research service, DG XII, with marginal additions by the other services' (Cantley 1995: 543).

7 European Commission, *A Community Framework for the Regulation of Biotechnology, Communication from the Commission to the Council*, COM(1986) 573 final, 4 November 1986, Brussels.

8 As noted in the Commission's 1988 proposal, Member State approaches included: (a) a ban on deliberate release (subject to exceptions) in Denmark and Germany; (b) a case-by-case approach to the release of individual GMOs in a number of Member States (UK, France, Belgium, Netherlands and Luxembourg); and (c) an absence of legislation in other Member States (Ireland, Greece, Italy, Spain and Portugal): Council Directive 90/220/EEC of 23 April 1990, [1990] *OJ* L117/15.

Community-wide regulation can offer the necessary consumer and environmental protection.'[9] The Commission therefore indicated its intention to come forward with concrete regulatory proposals covering both laboratory use and deliberate release into the environment of genetically modified organisms.

2 DIRECTIVE 90/220 ON THE DELIBERATE RELEASE OF GMOs INTO THE ENVIRONMENT AND THE NOVEL FOODS REGULATION

In 1990, the EU finally enacted Directive 90/220 on the Deliberate Release into the Environment of Genetically Modified Organisms (GMOs), which laid out a complicated, multi-level approval process for the release and marketing of GM foods and crops.[10] Under the Directive, a manufacturer or importer seeking to market a GMO or release it into the environment had to first submit an application to the national competent authority of an EU Member State, including an extensive scientific risk assessment for the GMO in question. The Member State to which the application was submitted then examined the dossier, and either rejected the application or accepted it. In the case of a favourable opinion, the dossier was forwarded to the European Commission and to the other member governments, each of which had a right to raise objections. If no objections were raised, then the Member State carrying out the original evaluation formally approved the product, which could be marketed throughout the European Union.

If one or more Member States raised an objection, however, a decision had to be taken at the EU level. The Commission, acting on the basis of an opinion from its scientific committees, adopted a draft decision. This draft decision was forwarded to a committee of Member State representatives, who could approve the decision by a qualified majority vote. If the regulatory committee did not approve the decision, however, it was to be sent to the Council of Ministers, which could approve the Commission decision by qualified majority or reject it by a *unanimous* vote. If the Council failed to act within three months, the directive provided that 'the proposed measures shall be adopted by the Commission' (Article 21). Finally – and significantly, in light of later developments – a Member State could, on the basis of new evidence about risks to human health or the environment, 'provisionally restrict or prohibit the use and/or sale of that product on its territory'. The Member State in question would be required to inform the Commission, which would approve or reject the Member State measures in cooperation with the regulatory committee mentioned above.

In 1997, the regulatory structure of Directive 90/220 was supplemented by Regulation 258/97, the so-called Novel Foods Regulation.[11] According to the terms

9 European Commission, *A Community Framework for the Regulation of Biotechnology: Communication from the Commission to the Council*, COM(1986) 573 final, 4 November 1986, Brussels, quoted in Cantley 1995: 553.

10 Above, note 1.

11 Above, note 2. For excellent analyses of the regulation, see Hunter 1999: 217–25 and European Commission, *Novel Foods and Novel Food Ingredients*, available at: <http://europa/eu.int/scadplus/leg/en/lvb/I21119.htm>.

Box 14.1 Key events in EU biotechnology regulation

1975	Asilomar conference on biohazards posed by GMOs
1978	Commission proposes Directive requiring prior notification and authorisation of GM research (withdrawn 1980)
1983	Biotechnology included in EU Framework R&D Programme
1984	Commission forms Biotech Steering Committee
1986 (Nov)	Commission report, 'A Community Framework for the Regulation of Biotechnology'
1988	Commission proposes twin Directives on contained use and deliberate release of GMOs
1990	Council adopts Directives 90/219 and 90/220
1996 (March)	Start of BSE crisis, questioning of EU food safety regulation
1997 (Jan)	Council adopts Novel Foods Regulation
1997 (Jan)	Commission approves sale of GM maize; three Member States invoke safeguard clause
1998 (Oct)	Start of *de facto* moratorium on approval of new GM varieties
1999 (June)	Declaration of moratorium on GM approvals by five Member States
2000 (Jan)	White Paper on Food Safety
2000 (Jan)	White Paper on the Precautionary Principle
2000 (Jan)	Cartagena Protocol on Biosafety Adopted
2001 (March)	Council and EP adopt Directive 2001/18, replacing 90/220, on deliberate release of GMOs
2002 (Jan)	Establishment of European Food Safety Authority
2003 (May)	US launches WTO complaint over EU regulation of GMOs
2003 (Sept)	Council and EP adopt Regulation 1830/2003 on Traceability and Labelling of GMOs
2003 (Sept)	Council and EP adopt Regulation 1829/2003 on Genetically Modified Food and Feed
2004 (Apr)	Entry into force of Regulations 1829/2003 and 1830/2003
2004 (May)	Commission ends moratorium with approval of Bt-11 sweet maize

of the regulation, 'novel foods' were defined as all foods and food ingredients that had 'not hitherto been used for human consumption to a significant degree within the Community' and included both foods that had been genetically modified as well as foods produced from, but not containing GMOs (for example, oils processed from genetically modified crops but no longer containing any traces of GM material).[12] The regulation imposed an authorisation procedure for novel foods, which was similar to the procedure under Directive 90/220 described above. Significantly, however, the regulation provided a simplified regulatory approval procedure for foods derived from, but no longer containing, GMOs, provided that those foods remained 'substantially equivalent' to existing foods in terms of 'their composition, nutritional value, metabolism, intended use and the level of undesirable substances contained therein' (Article 3). This determination would be made by the competent authority in the Member State receiving the application, and would be notified to the Commission, which would in turn notify the other Member States. This provision would prove to be significant in the coming years, as individual Member States would approve a number of products as being 'substantially equivalent' to their conventional counterparts.[13] Finally, and again significantly in terms of later developments, the regulation (like the earlier Directive 90/220) contained a safeguard clause allowing Member States, 'as a result of new information or a reassessment of existing information', to 'temporarily restrict or suspend the trade in and use of the food or food ingredient in question in its territory' (Article 12).

3 THE PROBLEMS OF IMPLEMENTING EU POLICY: MEMBER STATE REVOLT AND INTERNATIONAL REACTION

The enactment of the EU legislation was soon followed by Member State revolt, undermining its implementation and resulting in a complete breakdown of normal EU decision making that has yet to be resolved. To understand the difficulties of implementation, we need to place this regulation in the context of a series of developments in the mid-1990s and, in particular, the BSE food-safety scandal that struck in 1996. In March 1996, the British Government of Prime Minister John Major revealed a possible connection between Creutzfeldt-Jakob disease, a fatal disease for humans, and bovine spongiform encephalopathy (BSE), a disease spread among cattle through their consumption of contaminated feed, popularly known as 'mad cow disease'. The BSE disease infected some 150,000 cattle in the UK, triggering a wide-scale slaughter of cattle, a Union ban on the export of British beef, a plummet in beef sales throughout Europe, and a loss of consumer confidence in regulatory officials. Perhaps most importantly for our purposes, the BSE scandal raised the question of risk regulation 'to the level of high politics, and indeed of constitutional significance' (Chalmers 2003: 534–8), generating

12 The regulation would not apply to food additives, flavourings or extraction solvents, governed by other EU legislation (Article 2).

13 By contrast, no products consisting of or containing live GMOs were authorised under the terms of the Novel Foods Regulation, above, note 2. See European Commission, *Question and Answers on the Regulation of GMOs in the EU*, MEMO/02/160-REV, 4 March 2003.

extraordinary public awareness of food safety issues and widespread public distrust of regulators and scientific assessments.[14]

It was in this political context that genetically modified crops were first commercially introduced in the United States and Europe. In April 1996, within a month of the ban on British beef, the Commission approved the sale of genetically modified soy products over Member State objections.[15] In November 1996, GM soy was imported from the United States to the EU, spurring widespread protest by Greenpeace and other groups. Soy is used in animal feed, stoking activist groups' concerns that GM soy would replace feed that had been banned in response to the BSE crisis.[16] In short, widespread media coverage and public debate about GM foods began just as the BSE food crisis struck. News reports about genetic modification often mentioned the BSE crisis, helping link the two issues before the European public (Ansell *et al.* 2006).[17]

Two other events occurred in late 1996 that add important context to the contestation that was to engulf EU decision making over GMOs. In December 1996, a Scottish scientist announced to the world the first successful reproduction of a cloned mammal, a sheep named 'Dolly', suggesting that the cloning of humans could follow shortly. The announcement spurred ethical challenges to biotechnological research. Also in December, the United States and Canada lodged complaints before the World Trade Organisation challenging the EU's ban on hormone-treated beef on the grounds that the EU ban constituted a disguised barrier to trade and was not justified on the basis of a scientific risk assessment.[18] The WTO judicial bodies subsequently held against the EU, and, when the EU failed to comply with the ruling, authorised the United States and Canada to retaliate by withdrawing trade concessions in an amount equivalent to their trading losses. Both countries did so, imposing trade sanctions worth US$116.8 million and CAN$1.3 million per year. The WTO case further rallied a federation of smaller French farm producers, which was a fervent opponent of GMOs, the *Confédération*

14 A study showed that only around 12 per cent of Europeans stated that they trusted national regulators, whereas 90 per cent of US citizens believed the US Department of Agriculture's statements on biotechnology. See Vogel 2003, citing Enriquez, J. and Goldberg, R.A. (2000) 'Transforming Life, Transforming Business: The Life Science Revolution', *Harvard Business Review*, available at <http://www.hbsp.harvard.edu/products/hbr/marapr00/R00203.html>. Vogel notes that, in the BSE scandal, 'the European Commission had relied on the advice of the Scientific Veterinary Committee, which was chaired by a British scientist and primarily reflected the thinking of the British Ministry of Agriculture, Fisheries and Food – advice which subsequently proved flawed.' *Ibid.*, at 27.

15 See Commission Decision 96/281/EC of 3 April 1996 concerning the placing on the market of genetically modified soya beans, [1996] *OJ* L107/10.

16 Soya beans also are ingredients in more than half of processed foods, and the US shipped between 25 and 40 per cent of its soya beans to the EU (Vogel 2003: 10).

17 To give just one example of this pattern, the *European Voice* published two half-page articles under the topic 'Survey: Consumer Protection' in its weekly edition of 13 April 2000. The article on the top half of the page is entitled 'Spate of health scares pushes food safety to top of the EU agenda', while that on the bottom half is entitled 'Union faces dilemmas as it debates new GMO rules'. See *European Voice*, 13–19 April 2000, p. 15.

18 WTO Appellate Body Report, *European Communities – Measures Concerning Meat and Meat Products (Hormones)*, 16 January 1998, WT/DS26/AB.

Paysanne, led by Jose Bové.[19] Bové quickly became a symbol for anti-globalisation and anti-WTO movements worldwide, and a French national hero, at one time embraced by the leaders of each major French political party (Henley 1999: 14).

The close succession of these events illustrates how the popular understanding of GM products in Europe became associated with consumer anxieties related to food safety crises, distrust of regulators and scientific assessments, disquiet over corporate control of agricultural production, ethical unease over genetic modification techniques, environmental concerns, and anger over the use by the United States of international trade rules to attempt to force GM foods on Europeans. A widespread cross-sectoral movement was organised to oppose GMOs in Europe, bringing together environmentalists, consumers and small farmers. The movement operated at multiple levels, working the media and local and national political processes, coordinating transnationally, and lobbying the Commission and EP (Ansell *et al.* 2006). Negative European attitudes towards GM crops and foods rose rapidly. In early 1996, 46 per cent of the French were against GMOs, a figure that rose to 65 per cent in 1999, and 75 per cent in 2002.[20] Similarly, over 80 per cent of Germans expressed negative opinions about GMOs by late 1998 (Gaskell, Allum and Stares 2003).

In the midst of the fray, the Commission approved the sale of another GM food crop (Bt-maize) in January 1997, over the objection or abstention of all but one of the 15 Member States.[21] The Commission was able to do so because of the approval procedure set forth in Directive 90/220, which allows a single Member State (in this case France) to block amendment of the Commission's proposal before the Council. Even though 14 Member States refused to support the Commission, the approval went forward.

The Member States did not simply accept the Commission's decision. They undermined its implementation, invoking the safeguard clause of Directive 90/220 which permitted a Member State to prohibit an approved GM variety in its territory if it had 'justifiable reasons to consider that [the] product . . . constitutes a risk to human health or the environment'. As Member State deployment of safeguard bans grew, they undermined the central purpose of Directive 90/220 to create a single market for GM crops under a harmonised regulatory system. By January 2004, nine Member State safeguards, applied by Austria, France, Greece, Germany, Luxembourg and the United Kingdom, were in effect (European Commission 2004b). Italy also invoked an analogous safeguard procedure under Article 12 of the Novel Foods Regulation to ban the sale of food products containing ingredients from four varieties of GM maize.[22] The Commission forwarded to the regulatory

19 'The CP is a farmers' union styled as an alternative to the large mainstream union . . . [It] expands agriculture into a social issue, directly opposing the industrial farming supported by FNSEA and advocating sustainable farming practices and various other social causes', see Ansell, Rahsaan and Sicurelli 2006.

20 Compare, for example, Eurobarometer on Biotechnology, 1997, based on Oct.–Nov. 1996 data, indicating that those optimistic about genetic engineered outweighed pessimists by 43 per cent to 22 per cent.

21 See Commission Decision 97/98/EC of 23 January 1997 concerning the placing on the market of genetically modified maize, [1997] *OJ* L031/69. The vote in the regulatory committee in April 1996 showed four Member States opposed and four abstaining. See Bradley 1998 for an excellent review of this case.

22 European Commission, *Information note concerning forthcoming decisions on GMOs and GM food, feed and seed*, SEC(2003) 1131, available at: <http://register.consilium.eu.int/pdf/en/03/st13/st13733.en03.pdf>.

committee a proposal to initiate a legal challenge against these Member State bans, but proceeded no further when the committee refused to support it. The Commission decided to bide its time while it proposed new legislation governing GM crops and foods.

Opponents of GMOs worked not only the political process, they took their battle to the marketplace as well. Under pressure from potential consumer boycotts of their foods, many large European retailers refused to buy or sell GM foods (Vogel 2003: 10). Thus, although GM soy and maize varieties had been legally authorised for marketing throughout the EU and validated by risk assessments conducted by EU scientific committees, they were subject to Member State bans and were barely commercialised at all (Vogel 2003: 11). In short, the scientific committee recommendations were simply ignored.[23]

Responding to the popular backlash against GMOs, a group of Member States pronounced in June 1999 the need to impose a moratorium on approvals of GM products.[24] Since the earlier date of October 1998 (when two GM varieties of carnations were approved), no GM varieties had been authorised for sale in the EU market, the only exception being for foods derived from GM varieties deemed 'equivalent' to traditional foods under the Novel Foods Regulation.[25] For all these reasons, any account of EU policy making in the sphere of biotechnology must address not only the *legislative* politics of adopting EU Regulations and Directives, but also the subsequent and equally acrimonious politics of *implementation*.

The Commission was in a particularly delicate situation at the time. In February 1997, the European Parliament adopted the Medina report that criticised the Commission for its handling of the BSE issue and threatened censure.[26] Parliament's concern over the Commission's handling of EU finances eventually led to a highly critical report from five independent experts in March 1999 that triggered the resignation of the Santer Commission.[27] Under the circumstances, the Commission did not wish to provoke further the Member States and Parliament by using its powers under existing regulatory procedures to approve GM crops over their objections.

The Commission, nonetheless, was caught in a vice, as it faced determined opposition to the moratorium from the United States. US regulatory policy tends to treat GM crops and foods as 'substantially equivalent' to non-GM varieties, and, in consequence, relies largely on industry self-regulation (Pollack and Shaffer 2009;

23 The Scientific Committee on Plants issued 16 favourable opinions on applications for placing GM plant varieties on the market under Directive 90/220/EEC, above, note 1, and only one unfavourable opinion 'due to an insufficient risk assessment', resulting in the withdrawal of the application. See European Commission, MEMO/02/160, 15 October 2002 (questions and answers on the regulation of GMOs in the EU).

24 Council of Ministers, 2194 the Council Meeting-Environment-Luxembourg, 24–25 June 1999, Press 203-Nr 9406/99.

25 This exception, however, was closed under new directives adopted in 2003, as discussed below.

26 European Parliament, *Report on alleged contraventions or maladministration in the implementation of Community law in relation to BSE, without prejudice to the jurisdiction of the Community and national courts*, Rapporteur Manuel Medina Ortega, 1997, available at: <http://www.europarl.eu.int/conferences/bse/a4002097_en.htm>.

27 Committee of Independent Experts, *First Report on Allegations Regarding Fraud, Mismanagement and Nepotism in the European Commission*, 15 March 1999.

Shaffer and Pollack 2005). By the end of 2003, around 81 per cent of soybeans, 73 per cent of cotton and 40 per cent of corn grown in the United States were genetically modified varieties, and these figures were rising annually.[28] US farm and industry trade associations pressured US authorities to challenge European trade restrictions bilaterally and under WTO rules. GMO regulation in the Union faced not only the challenge of multi-sectoral coordination, but also a multi-level one.

4 THE REFORM OF EU POLICY SINCE JANUARY 2000

Facing pressure on multiple fronts, the Commission looked for a way to resume approvals of genetically modified varieties, free up commerce in the internal market, thwart a potential WTO challenge, assuage Member States and their constituents that adequate controls were in place, implement an EU-wide labelling regime, and restrict Member State opt-out rights under 'safeguard' provisions. It was not an easy task, leading to considerable frustration within the Commission. The Commission hoped that the problem of the moratorium on GM approvals could be addressed through new legislation that would replace or complement Directive 90/220 and the Novel Foods Regulation. In 1997–98, the Commission adopted several measures toughening the labelling requirements for GMO-produced foods.[29] Although US farmers and grain traders vociferously objected to the labelling requirements, the internal pressure on the Commission to propose more stringent regulations continued.

In response to challenges to the legitimacy of European GMO regulations from above and below, the Commission in 1998 proposed a new directive to govern the deliberate release of GMOs into the environment and the placing of GM food products on the market, replacing Directive 90/220. Both the European Parliament and Council pressed the Commission for further regulatory controls. The majority of the European Parliament, however, insisted on tighter restrictions regarding labelling requirements and thresholds pursuant to which products that contain traces of GMOs could still be sold in the EU.[30] The Member States were mixed in their views, with some appearing to do everything possible to ensure that no GM crops would be grown in their territories (such as Austria and Luxembourg), and others being torn between the demands of GM opponents and those of the biotech

28 Pew Initiative on Food and Biotechnology, *Issues in the Regulation of Genetically Engineered Plants and Animals'*, available at: <http://pewagbiotech.org/research/regulation/Regulation.pdf>, accessed on 12 June 2004, p. 3 (citing figures for 2001–2003).

29 See Commission Directive 97/35/EC of 18 June 1997 adapting to technical progress for the second time Council Directive 90/220/EEC on the deliberate release into the environment of genetically modified organisms, [1997] *OJ* L169/72. See also Commission Regulation (EC) 1813/97 of 19 September 1997 ([1997] *OJ* L257/07), which specifically required labelling of foods produced from the approved GM soy and maize varieties, even though they were approved prior to the Novel Foods Regulation, above, note 2, having taken effect. See also Council Regulation 1139/98 of 26 May 1998 concerning compulsory indication on the labelling of certain foodstuffs produced from genetically modified organisms, of particulars other than those provided for in Directive 79/112/EEC, [1998] *OJ* L159/4.

30 'Genetic Engineering: European Parliament's Vote on GMOs Described as a Step Backwards,' *European Report*, 15 April 2000.

sector (such as Germany and the United Kingdom). The resulting legislation, Directive 2001/18, was finally adopted in March 2001 by co-decision between the Council and European Parliament.[31] Once more, the need to assuage those Member States that desired stringent regulation of GMOs had led to a ratcheting up of EU regulatory requirements for GMOs so as to facilitate the free circulation of agricultural and food products in a single EU market (Young 2003). The directive's central objective was to protect the environment and human health when GMOs are released into the environment and placed on the market 'as or in products', '[i]n accordance with the precautionary principle'.[32]

Although touted by the EP's rapporteur David Bowe as 'the toughest laws on GMOs in the whole world',[33] the adoption of Directive 2001/18 did not satisfy a core of Member States (in particular Austria, Denmark, France, Greece, Italy and Luxembourg), which continued to insist on the moratorium's continuation and on the need to impose national safeguard bans in the absence of still more stringent EU regulations.[34] Unable to obtain the regulatory committee's approval of a legal challenge against these bans, the Commission worked toward passage of yet further EU legislation governing the authorisation, labelling and traceability of GM products. For this reason, only the directive's provisions governing the release of GMOs into the environment remain in effect,[35] while its provisions governing the marketing of GMOs used for commercial crops were replaced within a mere 18 months by two new EU regulations regarding the labelling and traceability of GM foods and their use in food and feed, respectively.

These new regulations for labelling and traceability were finally adopted in September 2003, once again after drawn-out bargaining among the Commission, Council and European Parliament.[36] As we will see, it has again been difficult to

31 Directive 2001/18 of the European Parliament and of the Council of 12 March 2001 on the deliberate release into the environment of genetically modified organisms and repealing Council Directive 90/220, [2001] *OJ* L106/1. For good accounts of the conciliation process, and the key issues separating the EP and Council delegations, see 'Genetic Engineering: Key Issues in GMO Conciliation Become Clearer,' *European Report*, 1 November 2000; and 'Biotechnology: Conciliation Talks Move Towards Agreement on GMOs,' *European Report*, 13 December 2000.

32 The precautionary principle is noted in Articles 1 and 4 and paragraph 8 of the preamble.

33 Quoted in Blake Evans-Pritchard, 'Vote on GMO Legislation Today,' *euobserver.com*, 14 February 2001, accessed on 6 June 2003.

34 In a joint statement, France, Italy, Austria, Denmark, Greece and Luxembourg 'reaffirm[ed] their intention [...] of ensuring that the new authorizations for cultivating and marketing GMOs are suspended pending the adoption' of new provisions on traceability, labelling and environmental liability. Quoted in Mann, M. (2001) 'Six EU States Refuse to Lift Block on New Modified Crops', *Financial Times*, 16 February 2001, p. 8.

35 Part B of the directive covers the 'deliberate release of GMOs for any other purpose than for placing on the market' that go beyond the 'contained use' of GMOs (ie it addresses the testing of GMOs in pilot plots). Council Directive 90/219/EEC of 23 April 1990 on the contained use of genetically modified organisms, [1990] *OJ* L117/1, continues to govern the contained use of GMOs. As amended by Council Directive 98/81/EC of 26 October 1998, [1998] *OJ* L330/13.

36 The Commission initiated its original proposals in 2001. See European Commission, *Proposal for a Regulation of the European Parliament and the Council on Genetically Modified Food and Feed*, COM(2001) 425 final, 25 July 2001, Brussels; European Commission, *Proposal for a Regulation of the European Parliament and the Council Concerning Traceability and Labelling of Genetically Modified Organisms and Traceability of Food and Feed Products Produced from Genetically Modified Organisms and Amending Directive 2001/18/EC*, COM(2001) 182 final, 25 July 2001, Brussels. For the Commission's amended proposal, see COM(2002) 559 final.

implement them. Both legislative instruments took the form of regulations, and not directives, placing authority predominantly in the hands of Community institutions. Regulation 1829/2003, regarding the authorisation of GMOs in food and feed, replaced the provisions of Directive 2001/18 governing the authorisation for marketing of GMOs as or in products, and the labelling provisions of the Novel Foods Regulation. Regulation 1830/2003, in turn, created new rules on the traceability of GM products throughout the production and distribution process.[37] (The revised EU regulatory scheme is summarised in Box 14.2.)

The regulations tightened EU requirements in a number of respects. Regulation 1829/2003 broadened the definition of legitimate objectives that may be pursued in determining whether to approve or reject a GM food or feed variety. The objectives now include not only the protection of the environment and of human life and health (as under the 2001 deliberate release directive), but also the rather vague criterion of 'consumer interest in relation to genetically modified food or

Box 14.2 EU legislation governing GMOs and GM products as of May 2004

Step-by-step Activities in the Production Process	*Applicable EU Legislation*
GMO research in laboratories	Contained Use Directive 90/219
All GMO experimental releases (trials)	Directive 2001/18
GMO environmental releases and marketing authorisations for non-food or feed seeds and crops (such as flowers)	Directive 2001/18
GMO environmental releases and marketing authorisations for seeds and crops for food or feed	Regulation 1829/2003 and Directive 98/95/EC (common seed catalogue)
Authorisation for marketing of GM food and feed	Regulation 1829/2003
Labelling of GM food and feed	Regulation 1829/2003
Traceability and labelling of GM food and feed products	Regulation 1830/2003

37 Regulation 1829/2003 of the European Parliament and of the Council of 22 September 2003 on genetically modified food and feed, [2003] *OJ* L268/1; Regulation 1830/2003 of the European Parliament and of the Council of 22 September 2003 concerning the traceability and labelling of genetically modified organisms and the traceability of food and feed products produced from genetically modified organisms and amending Directive 2001/18/EC, [2003] *OJ* L268/24 (hereinafter Regulation 1830/2003). Since Regulation 1829/2003 involved authorisations for both food and feed, its legal basis (which the Member States contested) rested on three separate Treaty provisions: Article 37 (common agricultural policy), Article 95 (internal market), and Article 152(4)(b) (public health). Both regulations became effective on 18 April 2004.

feed.'[38] Moreover, in preparing its draft decision over the authorisation of a GM variety, the Commission is to take into account not only EFSA's scientific opinion, but also 'other legitimate factors relevant to the matter under consideration'.[39] The regulation also broadened the scope of product coverage. The regulation's authorisation and labelling requirements cover GM animal feed for the first time, and covers food and feed that do not contain or consist of GMOs, but nonetheless are 'derived, in whole or in part, from GMOs' or contain ingredients that are 'derived, in whole or in part, from GMOs'.[40]

One of the most controversial elements of the new regulation was the establishment of a set of thresholds for permitted traces of genetically modified ingredients, provided their presence is 'adventitious'. Recognising that it is practically impossible to ensure that any shipment is entirely free of GM material because of the way crops are threshed, stored and transported, the Commission initially proposed a threshold of 1 per cent GM material, below which any crop would not have to be labelled as containing GM foods. Opposition came from environmental and consumer groups, as well as the European Parliament and some Member States, that the threshold was too high, while biotech companies and the United States Government criticised it as too low. The final regulation represents a compromise, setting two different thresholds and exempting some products produced with the aid of GMOs, with thresholds varying from 0.5 per cent to 0.9 per cent, and with the possibility of their being lowered.[41]

Although the approval procedure for GM products remains somewhat similar to that provided under Directives 90/220 and 2001/18, it became even more centralised. First, EFSA, a centralised EU agency, oversees the application file and works in conjunction with Member State competent authorities and a Community reference laboratory to conduct risk assessments and product evaluations.[42] Second, the regulation further restricts the grounds on which Member States may ban GMOs unilaterally as a 'safeguard' measure. A Member State may adopt 'interim protective measures . . . where it is evident that products authorized . . . are likely to constitute a serious risk to human health, animal health or the environment', provided that it first informs the Commission of the 'emergency' situation and the Commission does not act.[43] The Commission's original proposal provided for no Member State

38 Compare Article 1 of Regulation 1829/2003, above, note 37, with Article 1 of Directive 2001/18, above, note 37.

39 Regulation 1829/2003, Article 7(1), above, note 37.

40 See Regulation 1829/2003, Articles 2(10) and 3(1) (defining the scope of coverage), above, note 37.

41 First, it provides that food products will not violate its labelling requirements if they contain material consisting of or produced from EU-approved GMOs 'in a proportion no higher than 0.9% of the food ingredients considered individually [. . .] provided that this presence is adventitious or technically unavoidable.' Second, however, the regulation establishes a stricter threshold of 0.5 per cent for GMOs not yet approved for environmental release in the EU, provided that they have received a favourable EU scientific risk assessment. It also establishes a three-year window after which no residues of such non-approved GMOs will be allowed in food or feed product unless new regulations are enacted. The regulation provides that the Commission may further lower these thresholds over time.

42 Compare Articles 4–6 of the Novel Foods Regulation, above, note 2, and Article 13 of Directive 2001/18, above, note 37 (where the Member State competent authority conducted the initial risk assessment and made the initial authorisation decision).

43 Article 34 of the directive provides that Articles 53 and 54 of Regulation (EC) No. 178/2002, above, note 3 (that established EFSA) will apply in such a situation. Compare Article 16 of Directive 90/220, above, note 1 and Article 23 of Directive 2001/18, above, note 37.

safeguard powers, but the Parliament and Council succeeded in including this clause, although the Parliament preferred to grant greater autonomy to Member State authorities (Scott 2003: 224).

The application process still begins when an operator submits an application and dossier to the competent authority of one of the Member States. That Member State authority, however, now immediately provides the file to the new European Food Safety Authority, which, in turn, provides a copy to the other Member States and the Commission, and makes a summary of the file publicly available. EFSA is to issue its opinion, based on risk assessments, within six months from its receipt of the file, subject to extensions if further information is needed. EFSA submits its opinion to the Commission, the Member States, and the applicant, and, after the deletion of any confidential information, makes it publicly available. The Commission is then to issue a draft decision, which may vary from EFSA's opinion. The Commission's draft decision is again provided to the regulatory committee consisting of Member State representatives. If the committee supports the Commission's proposed decision by a qualified majority vote, then the decision is approved. If the committee fails to approve it by a qualified majority, then the Commission must submit its proposal to the Council. Unless the Council, in turn, opposes the Commission's proposal by a qualified majority vote, then the proposed decision 'shall be adopted by the Commission', unless of course the Commission independently withdraws its proposal.[44] These voting rules represent a change compared to those applicable under Directive 90/220, under which the Member States could only overturn a Commission decision by a unanimous vote.

Regulation 1830/2003 complemented the new authorisation and labelling rules with a more centralised framework for tracing genetically modified products, as Directive 2001/18 had left this responsibility to the Member States. The new regulations required the Commission to establish a system of unique identifiers for each genetically modified organism in order 'to trace GMOs and products produced from GMOs at all stages of their placing on the market through the production and distribution chain'. The regulation requires producers to collect and retain for five years data regarding the GM content of foods and crops one step backward and one step forward in the distribution chain. These strict traceability requirements have been bitterly criticised by many US producers (whose commodity system does not require and is not designed for tracing GMOs through the distribution chain), as well as by some European producers, but has been justified by the Commission as vital to the EU labelling system as well as for any future recalls of GM foods or crops.

The Commission and biotech companies tried to step up enforcement against Member State non-compliance with some EU regulatory requirements in 2003, although they have not been nearly aggressive as they could be.[45] In April of that year, the Commission issued a 'letter of formal notice' to 12 Member States that had failed to implement Directive 2001/18, as required (Kirwin 2003). It initiated a

44 See Articles 7, 19 and 35 of Regulation 1829/2003, above, note 37, which, in turn, refer to the operation of the Standing Committee on the Food Chain and Animal Health, pursuant to Article 5 of Council Decision 1999/468/EC of 28 June 1999 laying down the procedures for the exercise of implementing powers conferred on the Commission, [1999] *OJ* L184/23 (known as the 'Comitology Decision').

45 As Scott (2004) writes, the Commission's reticence to use the law 'has served to allow the law to stand aside, pending political resolution'.

Box 14.3 Authorisation process for GM food and feed under Regulation 1829/2003

Operator	An operator submits an application to the competent authority from one of the Member States.
Member State	The Member State provides the file to the new European Food Safety Authority (EFSA).
EFSA	The EFSA provides a copy to the other Member States and the Commission, and makes a summary of the file publicly available.
EFSA	Within six months, the EFSA submits its opinion, based on risk assessments, to the Commission, the Member States, and the applicant, and, after the deletion of any confidential information, makes it publicly available.
Commission	The Commission is then to issue a draft decision, which may vary from EFSA's opinion, to the regulatory committee consisting of Member State representatives.
Regulatory Committee Council Commission	The regulatory committee is to deliver its opinion on the Commission's draft decision. If the committee does not support the proposal by a qualified majority, the Commission must submit its proposal to the Council. If the Council does not oppose the Commission's proposal by a qualified majority vote, then the proposed decision 'shall be adopted by the Commission'.

lawsuit against 11 of them in July. When Austria proposed to make the region of Upper Austria a GM-free zone in March 2003, the Commission (following an opinion from EFSA)[46] ruled that Austria's general ban would be illegal since GMO restrictions should be based on attributes of specific GMOs.[47] Concurrently, three biotechnology companies (Monsanto, Syngenta and Pioneer) challenged Italy's ban of food products containing authorised GM maize before the Italian courts. In September 2003, following an Italian court referral to it, the European Court of Justice ruled that Italy must conduct 'a risk assessment which is complete as possible . . . from which it is apparent that, in light of the precautionary principle, the implementation of such measure is necessary in order to ensure that novel foods do not present a danger', which Italy had so far failed to show.[48]

Finally, the EU tentatively resumed approvals of a few GM varieties in 2004 and 2005. By early 2004, the Commission had received 22 notifications for approvals of

46 See the EFSA Journal 2003 (opinion of 4 July 2003).

47 See, eg, Andrew Osborn, 'Brussels blocks Austrian attempt to create GM-free zone,' *The Guardian*, 3 September 2003.

48 The matter then returned to the Italian courts to apply the ruling based on Italy's presentation of any studies supporting its restrictions. See Judgement of the Court, Case C-236/01 *Monsanto Agricoltura Italia SpA and Others v Presidenza del Consiglio dei Ministri and Others* [2003] ECR I-8105 (reference for a preliminary ruling from the Tribunale amminstrativo regionale del Lazio).

genetically modified varieties – 11 involving import processing only, and 11 for cultivation (Commission 2004b). With the completion of the new regulatory framework, the Commission moved to resume approvals of new GM varieties. In November 2003, it proposed to approve the importation of a variety of GM maize (Bt-11 sweet corn), for which EFSA had delivered a favourable opinion. This was the first time that the Commission had initiated a GM approval since 1998. The regulatory committee, however, again refused to approve the Commission's proposal so that the matter was referred to the Council, which was given until the end of April to act.[49] On 26 April, a divided Agriculture Council failed to reach agreement on the Commission's proposal.[50] In the absence of a decision by the Council, the Commission was free to adopt the proposal – the first new approval of a GM variety in nearly six years.[51] Despite this apparent breakthrough, US officials noted that the Commission's decision – greeted by a chorus of condemnation among European environmentalists and consumer groups – was taken over the objections of a block of implacably hostile member governments, with no guarantee that additional approvals were to follow or that EU risk managers would continue to be guided by the scientific risk assessments carried out by the EFSA.[52] Under the circumstances, Syngenta, the crop's manufacturer, indicated that it had no immediate intention of marketing Bt-11 sweet corn in Europe (European Report 2004).

Subsequent approval procedures appeared to support this cautious interpretation of the 'end' of the moratorium. One month following the approval of Bt-11 sweet maize, a regulatory committee of Member-State representatives from the now-enlarged EU failed to agree on the Commission's proposed approval of a genetically modified rapeseed (or canola). Significantly, six of the ten new Member States (Cyprus, Estonia, Hungary, Malta, Lithuania and Poland) joined six existing members (Austria, Denmark, Greece, Italy, Luxembourg and the UK) in voting against the approval, which was then scheduled for decision by the Council of Ministers.[53] A similar pattern emerged later that month when the Environment Council met to consider the Commission's recommendation to approve another Monsanto variety, the NK603 genetically modified corn. Here again, the Council was divided.[54] Still another new variety, a Monsanto corn modified to resist rootworms (MON863), was submitted for importation as animal feed and was approved by the EFSA, but also encountered a deadlocked Regulatory Committee when it was submitted for a vote

49 See Bridges BioRes, 'European Food Committee Fails to End de facto Biotech Moratorium,' Vol. 3, No. 22, 15 December 2003, available at: <http://www.ictsd.org/biores/03-12-15/story1.htm>.

50 European Commission 2004c: 4.

51 Commission Decision 2004/657/EC of 19 May 2004 authorising the placing on the market of sweetcorn from genetically modified maize line Bt11 as a novel food or a novel food ingredient under Regulation (EC) No. 258/97 of the European Parliament and of the Council, [2004] *OJ* L300/48.

52 As one US official put it, '[t]he approval of a single product is not evidence that applications are moving routinely through the approval process in an objective, predictable manner based on science and EU law, rather than political factors', quoted in Anthony Browne, 'Protests after Europe Ends GM Food Freeze,' *The Times*, 20 May 2004, p. 18.

53 For good accounts of the debate over the approval of the GT73 rapeseed, see 'Biotechnology: EU Member States Fail to Agree on GM-Rape GT-73', *European Report*, 19 June 2004; and Andrew Beatty, 'Majority of New EU States Block GMO Approval,' *euobserver.com*, 21 June 2004.

54 Nine Member States (including four of the new members) reportedly voted against, nine in favour, and seven abstained. See EurActiv News Release, *Member States still divided over new GM products*, 29 June 2004, available at: <http://www.euractiv.com/Article?tcmuri=tcm:29-118076-16&type=News>.

in May 2005.[55] Once again, Member States simply ignored the agency recommendations backed by scientific assessments from the European Food Safety Authority. Significantly, these three cases also seemed to dispel some initial concerns that the new Member States – most of which were already engaged in the cultivation of GM crops, often without adequate controls – might serve as a 'Trojan horse' for the United States and the biotech industry.[56]

In May 2005, the new Barroso Commission held an 'orientation debate' on GMOs, examining past Commission policy and laying down guidelines for future Commission action to implement the EU's legislative framework for GM foods and crops.[57] In preparation for this meeting, an inter-service group of Commissioners prepared an internal communication to the College of Commissioners, which is remarkable for the candour with which it describes the state of affairs, and is worth citing at length. The Communication (European Commission 2005) begins by noting that the completion of the EU's strict regulatory framework had not succeeded in overcoming resistance to GMOs among the public or among the representatives of the Member States. With regard to the latter, the Commissioners noted the difficulty of resuming approvals and of overturning the Member State bans in the face of Member State opposition:

> In spite of the application of the new regulatory framework, so far it has proven impossible to obtain support of a majority of Member States when it comes to implementation, namely the adoption of decisions on specific products. However, the legislation itself is not contested.
>
> At the current time, only a few Member States tend to vote consistently in favour while several Member States tend to vote consistently against and many abstain. Other Member States' position varies; some of them consistently follow the advice of their own scientific bodies which sometimes diverge from the European Food Safety Authority (EFSA) assessments.
>
> Against this background, it will be difficult if not impossible to obtain a qualified majority either in favour or against the approval of the pending decisions in either the Regulatory Committee or the Council.
>
> In view of the above, it is expected that, in accordance with the legislation, **the Commission will** have to continue to take ultimate responsibility **for adoption of pending decisions for the placing on the market of new GMO products** at least for the immediate future (European Commission 2005: 3, bold in original).

In light of this situation, the Communication laid out a plan of specific actions, including the final approval of the GT73 oilseed rape, the submission of a draft

55 'EU Again Fails to Break Deadlock on GMO Foods', *Reuters*, 20 May 2005.

56 On the new members as a 'Trojan horse', see Paul Brown, 'EU Races to Thwart Influx of GM Food from East', *The Guardian*, 14 February 2004. A more detailed but equally critical study is Thomas Schweiger, 'EU Enlargement: The Introduction of GMOs by the Backdoor of EU Accession?', *Northern Alliance for Sustainability and Friends of the Earth Europe*, May 2003.

57 The Prodi Commission had held a similar orientation debate in January 2004, focusing on the completion of the legislative framework, the issue of coexistence of GM and conventional crops, and the resumption of approvals. For a good discussion, see 'EU Commission Pushes for GMO "Green Light" ', available at: <http://www.eurunion.org/news/press/2004/20040010.htm>, accessed on 17 July 2005.

approval of MON863 corn to the Council, and the continued submission to the Regulatory Committee and the Council of draft approvals for all new GM varieties 'if there are no risks to human health and to the environment based on scientific information' (European Commission 2005: 7).

In addition, the Commission indicated that it would pursue its challenge to the eight national bans that had persisted under the safeguard clause. Relying on the safeguard clauses of Directive 90/220 and 2001/18, five Member States had adopted temporary bans on eight different GM varieties, which were claimed to be unsafe to put on the market.[58] The European Food Safety Authority, however, had concluded that none of these bans was justified in scientific terms, and in November 2004 the Commission proposed to the Regulatory Committee that these bans be overturned, but the committee once again deadlocked, returning the question to the Commission. Following the 22 March meeting, the Commission resolved to forward the eight draft decisions to the Council of Ministers, which it hoped would vote to overturn the bans, a hope that was soon dashed.

Perhaps most strikingly, the Commission commented on the role of the member governments in the Regulatory Committee and the Council as follows. 'So far,' it noted, '**every single one of the 13 Commission's proposals failed to get the required qualified majority**, even for those GMOs not intended for cultivation, but for import and processing only' (European Commission 2005: 6, bold in original). It continued with an explicit challenge to the member governments:

> Both the Commission and the Member States have a role to play in implementing this legislation. However, so far, some Member States have tended to avoid taking a position in the Regulatory Committee and in the Council. Member States should be called upon to participate effectively in the process with a view to reaching clear positions.
>
> In the current legal context, when submitting proposals following an inconclusive opinion of the Regulatory Committee, **the concerned Councils should be requested to hold a thorough debate** in order to avoid adoption by abstention and to openly discuss the reasons for their reluctance to support the authorization of specific products which the Commission considers to be in compliance with the EU regulatory framework (Commission 2004: 7, bold in original).

The Commission meeting itself revealed some differences among the various Commissioners in their attitudes toward GM foods and crops, and the full Commission reportedly decided to delete in full the previously cited paragraph calling on the Council to have a thorough debate; but the meeting backed the substance of the communication, including the decision to proceed with new approvals and with the proposed overturning of the national safeguard bans.[59]

58 Corn varieties T25 and MON810 were banned in Austria; Bt-176 maize was banned in Austria, Germany and Luxembourg; oilseed rape MS1×RF1 was banned in France; and oilseed rape Topas 19/2 was banned in France and Greece. See 'GMOs: Commission Pushes on with Proposal to Lift National GMO Bans', *European Report*, 30 April 2005.

59 'Genetic Engineering: Commissioners Debate EU Policy and Say They Will Push Ahead with GM Approvals', *European Report*, 22 March 2005.

The Commission's new strategy met with a number of immediate setbacks. On 22 March, the day of its GMO debate, the Commission was notified by the Swiss agribusiness firm Syngenta of an accidental release of the experimental Bt-10 corn, an estimated 1,000 tons of which has been distributed in the United States along with the well-established Bt-11 corn. Bt-11 corn had been approved in both the United States and the EU, but Bt-10 had yet to be submitted for approval in either jurisdiction. Within the United States, the Environmental Protection Agency and the US Department of Agriculture investigated the accidental release and the properties of the experimental corn, eventually ruling that Bt-10 posed no threat to humans, plants or animals.[60] Syngenta was accordingly fined some $375,000 by the USDA, but was not required to issue a recall of the previously distributed corn. By contrast, the European Commission, under pressure from public opinion and facing the prospect that some of the unauthorised corn might have entered the EU among US imports, issued a statement 'deploring' the import of an experimental and unauthorised GM crop.[61] In April, the Commission went further, requiring all imports of corn gluten feed and brewers' grain from the United States to be certified as free from Bt-10.[62] The European Food Safety Authority later issued a report agreeing that Bt-10 was 'as safe as conventional maize', but the EU certification system remained in place, and a US corn-gluten shipment was turned away from an Irish port in May after traces of Bt-10 were discovered.[63]

The most serious setback to the Commission's plan, however, occurred on 22 June 2005, when the Environment Council met to consider two sets of proposals from the Commission. First, the Commission issued a draft decision approving for the market Monsanto's MON863 maize, which had been approved by the EFSA only to meet a deadlocked regulatory committee the previous month.[64] In this case, as in previous votes, the Council was unable to secure a qualified majority vote either for or against the approval, and the file was therefore returned to the Commission for a final decision. Second, and more significantly, the Commission submitted to the Council a series of eight draft decisions which would overturn the eight national bans on GM varieties that had been declared safe by the EFSA. By contrast with the pattern of deadlocks over the approval of specific GM varieties, on this issue the Council was able to summon lopsided majorities of 22 Member States voting *against* the Commission proposals – and therefore in favour of the continuation of the Member State bans.[65] Luxembourg Environment Minister Lucien Lux, who chaired

60 Bt-10 does have an antibiotic resistance marker gene, which had been the subject of controversy in early reports, but this marker is not active in the plant and therefore had no impact on the safety of the corn.

61 'EU/US: Commission "Deplores" Unauthorised Imports of Bt-10 Maize into EU', *European Report*, 2 April 2005.

62 European Commission, *Bt10: Commission requires certification of US exports to stop unauthorized GMO entering the EU*, RAPID press release, IP/05/437, 15 April 2005.

63 'EFSA Says Bt-10 Variety "As Safe as Conventional Maize" ', *European Report*, 21 May 2005; 'EU Says Ireland Intercepted Illegal US Biotech Corn', *The Associated Press*, 25 May 2005.

64 'EU Again Fails to Break Deadlock on GMO Foods', *Reuters*, 20 May 2005.

65 According to *European Report*, only the British delegation voted in favour of the Commission's eight proposals to overturn the Member State bans, with Sweden and Finland abstaining and with the Czech Republic and Portugal each voting to overturn a single ban (on T25 maize and MON810 maize, respectively). 'Genetic Engineering: Commission Faces Stinging About-Turn in Council on GMO Bans', *European Report*, 29 June 2005.

the meeting during the Luxembourg Presidency of the Council, expressed his 'great satisfaction' at the outcome, noting pointedly that, 'We were able to give a clear message to the European Commission.'[66] Following the vote, the Commission retained the option of submitting new or amended proposals to the Council, but its reaction indicated that it had little interest in openly defying the Member States on such a politically charged issue. Following the vote, Environment Commissioner Stavros Dimas called on his colleagues in the Commission to discuss the 'political significance' of the vote, and to consider how to proceed regarding both the pending approval of new varieties as well as the national safeguard bans.[67] The US response was predictably critical, suggesting that the '... decision is further evidence that the EU's legal structure for regulating biotechnical products is badly broken and driven much more by politics than by science'.[68]

The continuing approval of new GM varieties – and, even more so, the cultivation and marketing of these varieties within the Union – thus remains in doubt. The Commission has stated that the 'completion' of the EU regulatory framework and the resumption of approvals are major steps forward. Yet a careful examination of the approval process reveals continuing opposition to GMOs among EU member governments as well as in the European Parliament and in European public opinion. Member States continue to demand restrictions in the face of new perceived threats, including a proposed liability regime and rules on the coexistence of GM and non-GM crops.[69] GMOs continue to generate public controversy.[70]

The Commission thus remains concerned about Europe's loss of competitiveness in the agricultural biotech sector. A 2004 Communication from Romano Prodi, the Commission's President, noted the 'exodus of researchers and rapid decline in GMO field research in the EU and the consequent negative repercussions in innovation and competitiveness'.[71] Prodi similarly remarked in 2002 that Europe's biotech industry lagged 'four or five years' behind and was worth 'roughly one-third as much as its US counterpart' (Skogstad 2003: 336). The Commission's 6th Framework Programme for research, technological development and demonstration activities proposed that the area of life sciences and biotechnology was its 'first priority' (European Commission 2002). In light of the European public's continued scepticism, however, the EU's promotion of this technology continues to face considerable obstacles.

66 Honor Mahoney, 'Member States Rebuff Commission in GM Vote', *eu.observer.com*, 27 June 2005.

67 For a good discussion of internal Commission discussions following the vote, see 'Biotech Crop Policy in EU Gets Rethink after Rebuff', *Reuters*, 30 June 2005.

68 USTR spokesman Richard Mills, quoted in 'US Slams EU Ban on Biotech Foods', *Agence France-Presse*, 24 June 2004. These problems, Mills continued, 'are at the crux of what we have argued in our WTO case'.

69 See Commission Recommendation of 23 July 2003 on guidelines for the development of national strategies and best practices to ensure the coexistence of genetically modified crops with conventional and organic farming, [2003] *OJ* L189, pp. 0036–0047 (para 1.3, noting discussion with 'a range of stakeholders representing the farming sector, industry, NGOs, consumers and other players').

70 See Paul Brown, 'Weed discovery brings calls for GM ban', *The Guardian*, 26 July 2005.

71 European Commission (2004).

5 THE INTERNATIONAL CONTEXT

As we have noted, EU regulatory policy for GMOs faces external challenges as well, and in particular from the United States, which has pressured the EU in light of the rules of the World Trade Organization. The Commission must thus respond not only to EU Member State and constituent pressure, but to US bilateral demands and international legal constraints as well. The WTO Agreement on Sanitary and Phytosanitary Measures (SPS Agreement) places the onus on the EU to demonstrate that its regulatory measures pertaining to GM products are based on scientific risk assessments and are not otherwise disguised restrictions on trade.[72] In the earlier US-EU dispute over the EU's ban on hormone-treated beef, the WTO Appellate Body held that the EU had violated the SPS because it had failed to base its ban on a scientific risk assessment. When the EU did not comply with the ruling, the WTO Dispute Settlement Body authorised the United States and Canada to prescribe retaliatory tariffs against EU products, which they continued to apply in early 2006.[73]

Starting in 1997–98, when the EU tightened labelling requirements for GM foods, stopped approving new GM varieties, and effectively shut down the marketing of varieties that had been approved, the United States threatened to bring a complaint before the WTO. It nonetheless hesitated to initiate legal proceedings for years (Pollack and Shaffer 2009; Shaffer and Pollack 2005). In part, the United States was preoccupied with the EU's ability to retaliate against the United States' non-compliance with other WTO rulings.[74] In part, it was concerned with larger systemic challenges to the international trade regime that such a controversial case could trigger. In part, it hoped that the dispute would subside once Europeans learned to accept genetically modified products under a reformed European food safety regime. Yet, because the EU moratorium continued and because affected US commercial interests became increasingly frustrated, the United States finally stepped up the pressure by filing a WTO complaint in May 2003 against the EU moratorium, EU decisions over specific GM varieties, and the Member State 'safeguard' bans.[75] On 23 February 2004, the United States, Argentina and Canada asked the WTO Director-General to appoint a panel to rule on their complaint, which was formed in March. In September 2006, after much delay, the WTO panel found that the EU's moratorium and a number of EU decisions on specific GM varieties violated provisions of the SPS agreement, and, in particular, the requirement of Article 8 and Annex C which provides that 'Members shall ensure, with

72 Agreement on the Application of Sanitary and Phytosanitary Measures, 15 April 1994, WTO Agreement, Annex 1A, available at: <http://www.wto.org>.

73 The EU, however, filed a complaint in the WTO against the legality of these retaliatory tariffs, claiming that the EU had since complied with the ruling in light of new scientific assessments. Appellate Body Report, *United States – Continued Suspension of Obligations in the EC – Hormones Dispute*, 23 January 2006, WT/DS320/9.

74 See Dan Pruzin (2002) 'WTO Gives EU Green Light in Sanctions against United States over FSCs,' 19 *International Trade Reporter (BNA)* 1484, 2002; and 'European Commission News Release on Request to WTO Compliance Panel for Imposition of Sanctions in US, FSC Dispute, with Indicative Product List,' *International Trade Reporter (BNA)* 17, 23 November 2000, p. 1792.

75 Argentina, Canada and Egypt simultaneously filed complaints against the EU.

respect to any procedure to check and ensure the fulfilment of sanitary or phytosanitary measures, that: (a) such procedures are undertaken and completed without undue delay . . .' The panel likewise found that the Member State bans were in violation of SPS requirements.[76] The biotech industry has pressed the complainants to challenge as well the EU labelling rules under the SPS agreement and the WTO Agreement on Technical Barriers to Trade.[77]

WTO rules, and the threat of an adverse WTO judicial ruling, have influenced EU decision making in two primary ways. First, EU authorities would like to tailor the EU's regulatory regime in a manner that will survive a challenge under WTO rules. In order to fend off a US challenge, European public officials have been pressed to set up a system where they do not simply ban GMOs without justification and without examining regulatory alternatives.[78] They rather must conduct risk assessments on a case-by-case basis, explicitly justify their decisions on the basis of these assessments, and take account of alternative measures that could accomplish the same regulatory goals in a less trade-restrictive manner. Second, many European constituents, and, in particular, the European biotechnology sector, favour a more flexible European legal regime toward GMOs. They have allies at different levels of government who wish to facilitate the EU's development of this technology. WTO rules offer these advocates a further rationale to press for a more conducive EU agricultural biotech legal regime.

The EU has not accepted passively the influence of WTO rules on its regulatory system, however. Instead, the EU has sought actively to export its precautionary approach to the international trade, environmental and food safety regimes, and thus help shield the EU from a WTO legal challenge (Skogstad 2001). During the late 1990s, the EU worked with other countries to press for a new international environmental treaty governing genetically modified organisms. The treaty was eventually signed in January 2000 as a protocol to the 1992 Convention on Biodiversity, after the United States failed to block it. The protocol, known as the 'Biosafety Protocol' or 'Cartagena Protocol', entered into force in June 2003.[79] The Biosafety Protocol expressly incorporates the precautionary principle, providing that a country may reject the importation of a GMO for release into the environment where there is 'lack of scientific certainty regarding the extent of the potential adverse effects ... on biological diversity in the Party of import, taking also into account risks to human health' (Article 10). The EU can now cite the protocol as evidence of international consensus (involving over 130 signatory countries)

76 See Panel Report, *European Communities – Measures Affecting the Approval and Marketing of Biotech Products*, 29 September 2006, WT/DS291/R.

77 See, eg, Gary Yerkey, 'US Firms Urge Administration to Move against EU in WTO over new Labelling Rules,' 20: 48 *International Trade Reporter (BNA)* 1991 (4 December 2003); and 'Argentina Seeks US Help in Challenging EU's Labelling, Traceability Rules for GMOs,' 21: 2 *International Trade Reporter (BNA)* 61 (8 January 2004). For an analysis of WTO claims, see Howse and Mavroidis 2000; and Macmillan and Blakeney 2001.

78 See Scott 2003: 223 (concerning the impact of WTO rules and decisions on the Commission and Court of First Instance concerning the application of the precautionary principle); and Young and Holmes 2006.

79 Cartagena Protocol on Biosafety to the Convention on Biological Diversity, 29 January 2000, 29 I.L.M. 1027. See the Protocol website at: <http://www.biodiv.org/biosafety/>.

regarding the application of the precautionary principle. No such treaty could be cited in the earlier WTO meat-hormones case.

By internationalising its precautionary approach to GMOs through the Biosafety Protocol, the EU has helped shield itself from attack under international trade law disciplines. In modifying the international environmental and food safety legal regimes, the EU hoped to influence the WTO dispute settlement panels' interpretation of WTO rules. Indeed, the Appellate Body already had exhibited a trend toward providing more policy space for WTO members' domestic regulations (Young and Holmes 2006). Significantly, in the GMO case, while the WTO panel found that the EU failed to comply with the SPS agreement on account of 'undue delay' in decision making, it refrained from finding that the EU failed to comply with other requirements, such as the requirement to base its decisions on a risk assessment under Article 5.1. In other words, the panel refrained from substantively determining whether the products posed (or did not pose) a risk that would authorise (or not authorise) EU restrictions. The EU has similarly hoped to affect how foreign (and particularly US) producers and distributors operate, so that they segregate and label genetically modified products for export markets.[80] If commercial enterprises adapt to the EU's regime, they will be less likely to press their governments to initiate legal challenges under WTO rules.

This internationalisation of GM regulation also represents a further centralisation of powers within the Commission, which is responsible for coordinating Member State positions in these fora, and, as regards the WTO and now the Codex Alimentarius Commission (the international body for the setting of food standards), formally speaking and voting on behalf of the Member States. In November 2003, the EU acceded to the Codex Alimentarius Commission so as to ensure the coherence between EU and Member State biotech regulations and the EU's and Member States' international obligations.[81] The Commission now speaks and votes on behalf of the EU 'where an agenda item deals with matters of exclusive Community competence'.[82]

Overall, in light of the multi-sectoral, multi-level nature of GM risk regulation, international rules have both constrained and offered opportunities for EU authorities. The Commission, in particular, can refer to WTO rules to further its policy goals in EU internal debates so as to end Member State safeguard bans and the moratorium on new approvals of genetically modified products. It will undoubtedly use the WTO panel decision against the 'undue delay' in EU decision making on GM varieties as leverage against recalcitrant Member States. The Commission has also acted as an international policy entrepreneur by working to export the EU's precautionary regulatory approach for GM products to the world. Once the Biosafety Protocol was adopted, the Commission then incorporated these international environmental obligations into the EU's internal legislation governing GMOs.[83]

80 Young (2003: 468–9) explains how the US grain industries have worked to segregate crops.

81 See Council Decision 2003/822/EC of 17 November 2003 on the accession of the European Community to the Codex Alimentarius Commission, [2003] *OJ* L309/14.

82 *Ibid.*, Annex III, Agreement between the Council and the Commission regarding preparation for Codex Alimentarius meetings and statements and exercise of voting rights.

83 See, eg, Article 44 of Regulation 1829/2003, above, note 37, and Article 32 of Directive 2001/18, above, note 37.

6 CONCLUSIONS

The regulation of biotechnology has presented the Union with a number of challenges. Many of these challenges are common to all EU regulations, but others relate specifically to the nature of biotechnology as a highly politicised case of risk regulation, a multi-sectoral challenge requiring cross-sectoral coordination, and a multi-level concern in which EU regulations must respond to both national fears and international disciplines.

Although the EU has been a pioneer and a laboratory for international regulatory harmonisation, it is joined in this endeavour by other international organisations, such as the WTO, to the disciplines of which EU regulation is increasingly subject. Indeed, a central lesson of the biotech case is that EU policy making is no longer simply above the nation-state, but instead lies *between* the nation-state and the growing imperatives of global governance. Paradoxically, the Commission's perception of a need to manage challenges to the legitimacy of EU decision making both from above and from below over the perceived risks of GMOs has led to greater centralisation of EU policy making in this domain, further raising the stakes for EU authorities.

Most importantly, the case of agricultural biotech regulation in the EU points to the limitations of EU supranational policy making when regulatory issues become highly politicised. Neither the adoption of a more centralised regulatory model, nor attempts to complement it with transgovernmental and stakeholder modes of policy making (Shaffer and Pollack 2005; Pollack and Shaffer 2009), have shielded EU risk-management decisions on GMO approvals from public challenge. In the area of GMOs, Member State politicians, reacting to their public's lack of acceptance of EU decision making, have thwarted numerous attempts to implement a harmonised EU approach, and, in the process, ratcheted up the stringency of EU-level requirements. The Commission itself must take heed of European public opinion if its regulatory decisions are to have any legitimacy or authority. This dynamic between Member State publics, their national representatives, and EU authorities appears to best explain the gap to date between the Union's law-in-the-books for GMOs and its law-in-action. Disputes over risk regulation in this domain have become disputes over the legitimacy of EU law itself.

BIBLIOGRAPHY

Ansell, C., Rahsaan, M. and Sicurelli, D. (2006) 'Protesting food: NGOs and political mobilization in Europe', in C. Ansell and D. Vogel (eds), *Why the Beef? The Contested Governance of European Food Safety*, Cambridge: MIT Press, 97–122.

Ansell, C. and Vogel, D. (eds) (2006) *Why the Beef? The Contested Governance of European Food Safety*, Cambridge: MIT Press.

Bradley, K.St.C. (1998) 'The GMO-committee on transgenic maize: alien corn, or the transgenic procedural maize', in M.P.C.M. van Schendelen (ed.), *EU Committees as Influential Policymakers*, Aldershot: Ashgate, 207–22.

Cantley, M. (1995) 'The regulation of modern biotechnology: a historical and European perspective: a case study in how societies cope with new knowledge in the last quarter of the twentieth century', in H.J. Rehm and G. Reed (eds) in cooperation with A. Pühler and

P. Stadler, *Biotechnology, Volume 12: Legal, Economic and Ethical Dimensions*, Weinheim: VCH, 503–681.

Chalmers, D. (2003) 'Food for thought: reconciling European risks and traditional ways of life', *Modern Law Review* 66(4): 532–64.

European Commission (2005) *Communication to the Commission (from the President in association with Mrs Fischer Boel, Mr Dimas, Mr Kyprianou, Mr Mandelson, Mr Verheugen and Mr Potocnik) – For an orientation debate on Genetically Modified Organisms*, SEC (2005) 396/3 of 21 March 2005.

European Commission (2004) *Communication to the Commission (from the President in association with Mrs Wallstrom, Mr Byrne, Mr Fischer, Mr Lamy, Mr Liikanen and Mr Busquin) – For an orientation debate on Genetically Modified Organisms and related issues*, IP-04-118, 28 January 2004, available at: <http://www.eurunion.org/news/press/2004/20040010.htm>.

European Commission (2002) *Communication from the Commission to the European Parliament, the Council, the Economic and Social Committee and the Committee of the Regions, Life Sciences and Biotechnology – A Strategy for Europe*, COM(2002) 27 final, Luxembourg: Office for Official Publications of the European Communities.

European Commission (2000) *Commission Communication on the Precautionary Principle*, COM(2000) 1 final, 2 February 2000, Brussels.

European Commission (1996) *Report on Directive 90/220/EEC on Genetically Modified Organisms*, ip/96/1148, 10 December 1996, Brussels.

European Commission (1994) *White Paper – Growth, Competitiveness, Employment: The Challenges and Ways Forward into the 21st Century*, COM(93) 700 final, 5 December 1993, Brussels.

European Commission (1988) *Proposal for a Council Directive on the Deliberate Release to the Environment of Genetically Modified Organisms*, COM(88) 160 final, 4 May 1988, Brussels.

European Parliament (1990) *Recommendation of the Committee on the Environment, Public Health and Consumer Protection on the COMMON POSITION of the Council for a directive on the deliberate release to the environment of genetically modified organisms (C3-228/89)*, Doc A3-0049/90 of 23 February 1990. Rapporteur: Mr Gerhard Schmid.

European Parliament (1989) *Report drawn up on behalf of the Committee on the Environment, Public Health, and Consumer Protection on the proposal from the Commission to the Council*, COM(88)160 final – Doc C 2-73/88 for a directive on the deliberate release to the environment of genetically modified organisms, PE Doc A 2-142/89. Rapporteur: Mr Gerhard Schmid.

European Report (2004) 'Biotechnology: contrasting reactions to authorisation for Bt11 transgenic corn', *European Report*, 29 May 2004.

Gaskell, G., Allum, N. and Stares, S. (2003) 'Eurobarometer 58.0: a report to the EC Directorate General for Research from the project "Life Sciences in European Society" ', QLG7-CT-1999-00286.

Henley, J. (1999) 'McDonald's campaign spawns French hero: political activist turned French peasant has fast food on the run,' *The Guardian*, 11 September, p. 14.

Howse, R. and Mavroidis, P. (2000) 'Europe's evolving regulatory strategy for GMOs – The issue of consistency with WTO law: of kind and brine,' *Fordham International Law Journal* 24: 317–70.

Hunter, R. (1999) 'European regulation of genetically modified organisms,' in J. Morris and R. Bate (eds), *Fearing Food: Risk, Health, and Environment*, Oxford: Butterworth Heinemann, 189–230.

Kirwin, J. (2003) *EU Formally Warns 12 States for Failing to Conform to GMO Licensing Directive*, 20:16 International Trade Reporter (BNA) 671 (17 April 2003).

Macmillan, F. and Blakeney, M. (2001) 'Genetically modified organisms and the World Trade Organization', *Tulane Journal of Technology and Intellectual Property* 3: 93–116.

Meller, P. and Pollack, A. (2004) 'Europeans appear ready to approve a biotech corn', *The New York Times*, 15 May, B1, B3.

National Corn Growers Association (2003) 'USGC pleased US pursuing case against EU moratorium (press release). 13 May', available at: <http://www.ncga.com/news/releases/2003/may/news051303.htm>.

Patterson, L.A. (2000) 'Biotechnology policy: regulating risks and risking regulation', in H. Wallace and W. Wallace (eds), *Policy-Making in the European Union,* Oxford: Oxford University Press, 317–44.

Patterson, L.A. and Josling, T. (2002) 'Regulating biotechnology: comparing EU and US approaches', available at: <http://www.agtrade.org/consumer_issues/research.htm>.

Pollack, A. (2004) 'Narrow path for new biotech food crops', *The New York Times,* 20 May, C1, C3.

Pollack, M. and Shaffer, G.C. (2009) *When Cooperation Fails: The International Law and Politics of Genetically Modified Foods,* Oxford: Oxford University Press.

Scott, J. (2004) 'European regulation of GMOs: thinking about judicial review in the WTO', Jean Monnet Papers 04/04, New York University School of Law.

Scott, J. (2003) 'European regulation of GMOs and the WTO', *Columbia Journal of European Law* 9: 213–39.

Shaffer, G. and Pollack, M. (2005) 'Dealing with regulatory differences: global markets, international institutions and the dispute over agricultural biotechnology', in M. Pollack, G. Shaffer, H. Wallace and D. Andrews (eds), *The Future of Transatlantic Economic Relations: Continuity Amid Discord,* Florence: European University Institute, available at: <http://www.iue.it/RSCAS/e-texts/Future_Transat_EconRelations.pdf>.

Skogstad, G. (2006) 'Regulating food safety risks in the European Union: a comparative perspective', in C. Ansell and D. Vogel (eds), *Why the Beef? The Contested Governance of European Food Safety,* Cambridge: MIT Press, 213–36.

Skogstad, G. (2003) 'Legitimacy and/or policy effectiveness? Network governance and GMO regulation in the European Union', *Journal of European Public Policy* 10(3): 321–38.

Skogstad, G. (2001) 'The WTO and food safety regulatory policy innovation in the European Union', *Journal of Common Market Studies* 39(3): 485–505.

Tiberghien, Y. and Starrs, S. (2004) 'The EU as global trouble-maker in chief: a political analysis of EU regulations and EU global leadership in the field of genetically modified organisms', paper presented at 2004 Conference of Europeanists, Chicago.

Vogel, D. (2003) 'The politics of risk regulation in Europe and the US', *The Yearbook of European Environmental Law* 3, 1–42.

Wallace, H., Wallace, W. and Pollack, M. (eds) (2005) *Policy-making in the European Union,* 5th edn, Oxford: Oxford University Press.

Young, A.R. (2003) 'Political transfer and "trading up"? Transatlantic trade in genetically modified food and US politics', *World Politics* 55: 457–84.

Young, A.R. and Holmes, P. (2006) 'Protection or protectionism? EU food safety rules and the WTO', in C. Ansell and D. Vogel (eds), *Why the Beef? The Contested Governance of European Food Safety,* Cambridge: MIT Press, 281–306.

Chapter 15

European regulation of GMOs: thinking about 'judicial review' in the WTO*

Joanne Scott

1 EUROPEAN REGULATION OF GMOs

The European approach to the regulation of genetically modified organisms (GMOs) is predicated upon the concept of prior approval. The legal framework for prior approval is finally in place. Amidst a mass of legislation, two instruments stand out as central, *viz.* the 2001 Deliberate Release Directive[1] and the 2003 GM Food and Feed Regulation.[2] As may be exemplified by specific reference to the latter, European Union law performs a three-fold function in relation to the prior approval of GMOs.

First, European Union law identifies the objectives which may legitimately be pursued by the system of prior approval. The range of objectives is somewhat expanded in the GM Food and Feed Regulation. Alongside the critical internal market objective, this is concerned not only with the protection of human life/health and the environment, but also with animal health and welfare and 'consumer interests in relation to genetically modified food or feed'.[3] Though expanded, the range of underlying objectives nonetheless remains finite. No authorisation shall be granted or refused other than on the grounds set out in the Regulation.[4] The paradigm for prior approval is fixed and closed. Viewpoints which cannot be accommodated within this paradigm will be excluded, and voices which do not resonate within this paradigm will not be heard. To take an example, there is provision in the GM Food and Feed Regulation for consultation with the European

* An earlier version of this chapter appeared in *2004 Current Legal Problems* (OUP 2005), pp. 117–47.

1 Directive 2001/18/EC of the European Parliament and of the Council of 12 March 2001 on the deliberate release into the environment of genetically modified organisms, [2001] *OJ* L106/1. By way of background reading see Hervey 2001: 321; Spaangard 2003: 79; Howse and Mavroidis 2000; Scott 2003: 213. For a more complete bibliography see: <http://www.law.georgetown.edu/iiel/current/gmos/gmos_bib.html>.

2 Regulation 1829/2003 of the European Parliament and of the Council of 22 September 2003 on genetically modified food and feed, [2003] *OJ* L268/1.

3 Above, note 2, Article 1. This contrasts with Article 1 of the deliberate release directive which is concerned only with the protection of human health and the environment. It is interesting to observe that neither the environment nor the consumer protection legal bases were included among those upon which the 2003 Regulation rests. Given the centrality of these objectives to the regime established this seems strange. One explanation might lie in the fact that the Regulation seeks to achieve exhaustive harmonisation which would not be in keeping with the minimum harmonisation approach laid down in the areas of environment and consumer protection.

4 Above, note 2, Article 4(5).

Group on Ethics in Science and New Technologies.[5] Yet, other than to the extent that ethical concerns may be packaged as integral to the attainment of the above objectives, their place in prior approval is not clear. Similarly, it is for the European Commission to draw up a draft of the authorisation decision in respect of GM food or feed. In so doing, it shall take account not only of the opinion of the European Food Safety Authority (EFSA), but also of 'other legitimate factors relevant to the matter under consideration'.[6] In view of the strictures above – requiring that no authorisation be granted or refused other than on the grounds set out in the Regulation – the place of 'legitimate factors not integrally connected to the closed list of stated objectives' remains, at best, uncertain.

The second function performed by EU law in relation to GMOs is to structure the governance arrangements according to which prior authorisation will proceed. The arrangements are elaborate. Every detail was contested in the course of legislative enactment. The system is:

1 *multi-level*, involving actors across different levels of government, from the local to the European. In a multi-level system of governance, the question of balance of power is all-important. All participate but all are not equal. In the GM Food and Feed Regulation, as noted, it falls to the Commission to draw up a draft of the authorisation decision. The final decision will be taken in accordance with a regulatory committee procedure, implying an overall supervisory function for the Member States, via their representatives in the Standing Committee on the Food Chain and Animal Health,[7] and ultimately via their representatives in Council.[8] In this way, power does not accrue exclusively to any one level of governance, but is shared across the different levels. Significant too, in assessing power relations between the different levels, is the question of the residual autonomy enjoyed by Member States, or by regions, following the conclusion of a Europe-wide position on authorisation. This autonomy may flow from the EC Treaty – by way of the Article 95 'environmental guarantee' for example.[9] It may flow also from the text of the governing legislation, and in particular by virtue of the inclusion therein of a safeguard clause conferring emergency

5 Above, note 2, Article 33.

6 Above, note 2, Article 7(1).

7 Above, note 2, Article 35(2).

8 See generally, above, note 2, Article 7. Note that the new regulatory committee with scrutiny procedure introduced in 2006, conferring veto powers on the European Parliament in comitology, will not apply to authorisation decisions under this regulation. See Council Decision 2006/512 of 17 July 2006 amending the 1999 comitology decision ([2006] *OJ* L200), by adding this new option to the range of available procedures.

9 For an example of the Commission denying the lawfulness of recourse to Article 95(5) in respect of GMOs, see Commission Decision 2003/653 *OJ* [2003] *OJ* L230/34. This concerned a notification put forward by Austria concerning a blanket ban on GMOs in North Austria. The Decision was subject to unsuccessful judicial review by Austria (joined cases T-366/03 and T-235/04, and is currently pending on appeal before the ECJ. AG Sharpston delivered an unfavourable opinion on 15 May 2007 (see joined cases C-439/05 P and C-454/05 P). See also Commission Decision 2006/215 of 15 March 2006 ([2006] *OJ* L80) declaring a notification under Article 95(5) by Cyprus inadmissible for lack of necessary information. This concerned a Cypriot rule requiring that GM food be placed on separate supermarket shelves.

powers. It is notable that the safeguard powers of the Member States have been significantly curtailed in the 2003 GM Food and Feed regime, relative to earlier measures.[10]

2 *multi-actor*, in that it establishes a role for political and expert actors. The expert dimension has been given a glossy new exterior with the establishment of EFSA.[11] This is to operate in accordance with certain foundational values; notably independence, scientific excellence, transparency and diligence.[12] This new agency is charged with issuing an opinion on any application for the authorisation of GM Food or Feed. It shall give reasons for this opinion and include information upon which it is based.[13] Responsibility for the provision of this opinion will rest with the EFSA scientific panel on genetically modified organisms.[14] Where the Commission's decision is not in accordance with this opinion, it must provide 'an explanation for the differences'.[15] It is at least arguable, on the basis of the case law, that any such explanation must give reasons for departure which operate at a 'scientific level at least commensurate' with that of the EFSA opinion.[16] The role for public opinion in the GM Food and Feed authorisation process is small. The public may make comments to the Commission on the EFSA opinion.[17] No further provision is made as to the manner in which these comments are to be taken into account. As a form of public participation, these provisions are notably weak. They stand in contrast to more ambitious experiments in public participation in EU environmental law more generally.[18]

The third function of European law in relation to GMOs is a disciplinary one. It serves as a basis to discipline the recalcitrant, be they Member States or Community institutions. This discipline may seek to prise open the markets of reluctant Member States. It may serve to ensure compliance with established procedures for the authorisation of GMOs. Conceivably at least, it could serve also to question the adequacy of the level of protection pursued.[19]

10 See above, note 2, Article 34 which is parasitic upon the emergency measures laid down in the Regulation laying down the general principles and requirements of food law, and establishing the European Food Safety Authority. Regulation 178/2002 of the European Parliament and of the Council of 28 January 2002, [2002] *OJ* L31/1. See specifically Articles 53 and 54. The bottom line here is that Member States may only make autonomous recourse to emergency measures where the Commission has not acted, and even then only for a period of 10 days within which time the matter must go to the Standing Committee on the Food Chain and Animal Health for extension, amendment or abrogation.

11 *Ibid.*, Regulation 178/2002.

12 Above, note 2, Article 22(7). This speaks of the 'scientific and technical quality of the opinions which it issues' for which I have substituted 'excellence' above. This language of excellence derives from the case law of the CFI. See Case T-13/99 *Pfizer* [2002] ECR II-3305.

13 Above, note 10, Regulation 178/2002, Article 6(6).

14 This is a standing panel, the membership of which is listed on the web.

15 Above, note 10, Regulation 178/2002, Article 7(1).

16 Above, note 12, *Pfizer.*

17 Above, note 10, Regulation 178/2002, Article 6(7).

18 The example of environmental impact assessment is exemplary in this respect. See, especially Directive 2003/35 of the European Parliament and of the Council of 26 May 2003, [2003] *OJ* L156/17 and especially Article 3.

19 See Case C-236/01 *Monsanto* [2003] ECR I-8105, judgment of 13 March 2003.

Until recently, this disciplinary dimension has taken a back seat. This is surprising in view of the fact that the entire system for the authorisation of GMOs ground to a halt in 1998.[20] Neither the Commission, nor private companies, exploited the legal avenues open to them in a bid to kick-start the system on the books. The Commission long desisted from deploying Article 226 in mounting actions against recalcitrant Member States, seeking instead to engage in a constructive exercise in regime building, hoping to buy the trust and support of the Member States through the elaboration of a new framework for authorisation. The reticence of the Commission in deploying legal enforcement tools was made possible by virtue of its unfettered discretion in respect of Article 226 EC. The Commission may decide to proceed against an allegedly offending Member State. Or it may decide not to. The existence of such discretion has often provoked the fury of environmentalists. On this occasion, though, for a time, it served them well by allowing the Commission to stand back in the face of blatant and repeated illegality. It served to allow the law to stand aside, pending political resolution.

The new framework is now in place and still a number of Member States are refusing to step into line. The Commission's patience finally ran out and in 2003 it initiated proceedings against 14 Member States for their failure to implement the 2001 Deliberate Release Directive.[21] The Commission has approved several applications for GM food, but only in the face of divisions between the Member States which were such as to preclude a decision in Council.[22] Other applications are proceeding slowly – very slowly! As far as Member State safeguards are concerned things are even worse. Nine safeguard measures remain in place, introduced by six Member States, Hungary the most recent among them.[23] Most worryingly for the Commission, despite contrary advice from the EFSA GM panel, Member States in Council have voted against Commission proposals to revoke them.[24] Still, politics and science appear to be pulling in different directions, the tension as yet unresolved and producing conflicting results.

Before turning to the WTO, it is important to be aware of the very great activity of the European courts in the area of risk regulation. While, bar *Monsanto*,[25] the case law is not specifically concerned with the issue of GMOs, the findings of the courts

20 See the Institute of International Economic Law at Georgetown site for an excellent overview of developments in the EU and in the WTO as regards GMOs, available at: <http://www.law.georgetown.edu/iiel/current/gmos/>.

21 Bulletin EU-11 (2002), available at: <http://europa.eu.int/abc/doc/off/bull/en/200211/p109001.htm>. See, for example, Case C-422/03 finding against the Netherlands. The Commission is currently requesting the imposition of fines against Italy and France.

22 For an update of applications approved or rejected, and applications pending, see the annex to: <http://europa.eu/rapid/pressReleasesAction.do?reference=MEMO/07/117&format=HTML&aged=0%3Cuage=EN&guiLanguage=en>. The ability of the Commission to decide in favour reflects the fact that if the comitology committee and the Council fail to take a decision one way or another by the requisite qualified majority of votes, the Commission is empowered to enact its original proposal. For an excellent internet resource bringing you up-to-date on developments see: <http://www.foodlaw.rdg.ac.uk/>.

23 See: <http://ec.europa.eu/environment/biotechnology/safeguard_clauses.htm>. Additional safeguards are in place for GM seed varieties.

24 See: <http://europa.eu/rapid/pressReleasesAction.do?reference=IP/05/793&format=HTML&aged=1&language=EN&guiLanguage=en> 24 May 2005. This concerned eight of the nine safeguard measures. A similar decision regarding the Hungarian ban has also been taken.

25 Above, note 19.

nonetheless bear directly upon this question. Notable in this respect are the pronouncements of the courts on the so-called precautionary principle.[26] These have served to delineate, in some detail, the circumstances in which Community institutions (or Member States) may enact protective measures to guard against risk. Two aspects are particularly striking. While the courts grant a wide margin of discretion to the political branch, this discretion is made contingent in two important respects. First, and in language strikingly resonant of the WTO Appellate Body, 'a preventive measure cannot properly be based on a purely hypothetical approach to risk, founded on mere conjecture which has not been scientifically verified'.[27] 'The precautionary principle can therefore apply only in situations in which there is a risk, notably to human health, which, although it is not founded on mere hypotheses that have not been scientifically confirmed, has not yet been fully demonstrated.'[28] Second, legality will be assessed having regard to a wide range of procedural criteria. For example, a scientific risk assessment must be carried out which is based on the principles of excellence, transparency and independence.[29] While, for reasons of 'democratic legitimacy' the decision maker may disregard scientific advice, it must give specific reasons for so doing, and the statement of reasons must be 'of a scientific level at least commensurate with that of the opinion in question'.[30] It must fight science with science.

As noted, the language of the Court of First Instance is strongly resonant of that of the WTO Appellate Body, notably in the *Hormones* case.[31] Here, it lays emphasis upon the fact that 'theoretical uncertainty' of the kind that arises 'since science can *never* provide *absolute* certainty that a given substance will not *ever* have adverse health effects' is not the kind of risk which can ground protective measures under Article 5.1 of the Agreement on Sanitary and Phytosanitary Measures (SPS Agreement).[32] The WTO Agreement does not have direct effect in Community law, but it does enjoy indirect – or interpretative – effect.[33] The evolving understanding of the precautionary principle in Community law represents a single and striking example of this. The salience of this extends beyond the sphere of risk regulation. It is of constitutional importance. Direct effect was denied on the basis of a need to preserve the autonomy of the political and legislative branches, notably in view of the room for manoeuvre which they enjoy under the WTO Dispute Settlement Understanding. In the event that WTO 'recommendations and rulings' are not implemented within 'a reasonable period of time', 'compensation and the

26 See Article 174 EC. For a discussion of the recent case law see Scott, 2004.

27 *Pfizer*, above, note 12, para 143.

28 *Pfizer*, above, note 12, para 146.

29 *Pfizer*, above, note 12, para 172.

30 *Pfizer*, above, note 12, para 199. On the democratic legitimacy point, see para 210, where the CFI observes that '[t]hat finding can also be justified on grounds of principle relating to the political responsibilities and democratic legitimacy of the Commission. While the Commission's exercise of public authority is rendered legitimate, pursuant to Article 155 of the EC Treaty [. . .] by the European Parliament's political control, the members of SCAN [Scientific Committee on Animal Nutrition], although they have scientific legitimacy, have neither democratic legitimacy nor political responsibilities. Scientific legitimacy is not a sufficient basis for the exercise of public authority'.

31 *EC-Hormones* (WT/DS26/AB/R).

32 *Ibid*, para 187.

33 Case C-149/96 *Portugal v Council* [1999] ECR I-8395.

suspension of concessions or other obligations are temporary measures available' as alternatives.[34] Yet, this room for manoeuvre may be just as effectively – if frequently less visibly – undermined by way of interpretative fidelity to the WTO.

2 EUROPEAN REGULATION OF GMOs AND THE WTO[35]

This takes us on to the WTO. In this domain we do not find any bespoke regime devoted to the regulation of GMOs. There is no WTO side agreement on GMOs. Instead, what we find is a series of agreements containing broad and open-ended obligations; obligations which are characterised by the kind of deep ambiguity which is often the hallmark of consensus-based drafting. It may be, nonetheless, that the same tripartite division of functions outlined above will serve us also in the case of WTO law.

The WTO Agreement serves to identify the objectives which may be legitimately pursued by the Member States. Article XX GATT, for example, lays down a series of general exceptions. These relate, for example, to the protection of human, animal or plant life or health, and the conservation of exhaustible natural resources. The SPS Agreement represents an elaboration of GATT, Article XX(b) and is concerned only with measures which are applied to protect human, animal or plant life or health.[36] The Technical Barriers to Trade is more open-ended. Here, Member States may adopt measures which are necessary to fulfil a legitimate objective.[37] While the agreement identifies some such objectives, the list is not exhaustive.

It is clear that the nature of the objective pursued will have a bearing upon the legal framework according to which an assessment of conformity will proceed. Thus, for example, an SPS measure is functionally (as well as territorially) defined.[38] These are measures which are applied with a view to protecting human, animal or plant health from certain specified risks. These include risks to human or animal life or health arising from additives, contaminants, toxins or disease-causing organisms in foods, beverages or feedstuffs. The nature of the objective pursued is thus critical in classifying a measure as an SPS measure.

In the recent *EC-Biotech* report, the panel interpreted the scope of the SPS Agreement very widely. At each turn, it injected breadth, stressing the textually unqualified nature of the language and its comprehensive scope. The measures challenged pursued a wide range of environmental and public health objectives. Yet

34 Article 22, WTO Understanding on the Settlement of Disputes.

35 By way of background reading, and for some of the articles which have informed my attitude to the issues under discussion (see Howse 2000a: 2329–57; Howse 2000b; Sykes 2002; Dunoff 2001. See, more specifically Covelli and Hohots 2003: 773.

36 See recital 2 of the preamble to this agreement and Article 2.1. See also Annex A for a long and convoluted definition of what constitutes an SPS measure. This is defined not only in terms of the objectives being pursued but also on the basis of the nature of the risk which the Member State is seeking to guard against. It also has a territorial dimension in that a measure will only be classified as an SPS measure if it seeks to protect the objective in question within the territory of the regulating state.

37 Article 2.2 TBT.

38 Annex A(1) SPS.

only in so far as the regime established labelling requirements to prevent consumers from being misled, or to protect them from nutritional disadvantage, was it deemed to fall outside of the SPS Agreement.[39] It is notable also that the panel was prepared to accept that a single measure might be capable, at one and the same time, of being both a TBT and an SPS measure due to the multiplicity of its underlying objectives.[40]

Moving on to the second function of WTO law, the WTO Agreement may also be conceived as shaping governance arrangements with respect to the regulation of GMOs. Thus, as will be discussed further below, the various agreements establish a variety of procedural obligations relating to governance. To take a single example for now, the TBT Agreement contains quite detailed notification and consultation requirements. Member States must publish a notice of proposed technical regulations and notify other Members of their scope, objective and rationale. They must, further, allow a reasonable time for other Members to make written comments on these proposed measures, and take these written comments (and the results of any discussions about them) into account.[41]

Finally, there can be no doubt that the WTO Agreement serves to discipline recalcitrant states. Leaving aside issues of practical compliance, Members must bring their measures into conformity with WTO rulings within a reasonable period of time. Where they fail to do so, they must, if requested, enter into negotiations with a view to developing mutually satisfactory compensation. If this is not agreed, the complaining party may request permission to suspend concessions or other obligations under the covered agreement.[42] As noted previously, neither compensation nor suspension of concessions is to be preferred to full implementation. This disciplinary dimension has recently come to the fore. As is well known, the United States, Argentina and Canada initiated dispute settlement proceedings against the EU in the WTO in the area of GMOs.[43] This was directed against the EU's so-called moratorium on GMOs, whereby applications for authorisation are allegedly not being processed even in accordance with the demands of the EU's own regime. It was also directed at the actions of the Member States in respect of their widespread recourse to safeguard powers established under the relevant legislation.[44]

Even if – as suggested – this same tripartite division of functions may assist in understanding the role of the WTO in relation to the regulation of GMOs, one crucial difference at least may be identified. This relates to the relative prominence

39 For an overview see Scott 2007 and the contributions to July 2007: 6 *World Trade Review* examining in detail different aspects of the *Biotech* case.

40 See the discussion at paras 7.172–7.173, also identifying the conditions in which this may occur.

41 See in particular Article 2.9–2.12 and Article 10 TBT.

42 Article 23 DSU.

43 See WTO Panel Report, *European Communities – Measures Affecting the Approval and Marketing of Biotech Products*, 8 August 2003 WT/DS291/23. Note that the complaint was also directed at the actions of the Member States which 'maintain a number of national marketing and import bans on biotech products even though those products have already been approved by the EC for import and marketing in the EC'. This refers to Member State recourse to their safeguard powers, especially under the (1990) deliberate release directive. As the EC has exclusive competence in trade in goods, it has responsibility regardless of the identity of the state actor said to be committing a breach.

44 The EC has exclusive competence in the area of trade in goods. Hence, the action is taken in the name of the EC even where the wrong-doing is perpetrated by the EC Member States.

of the role of the 'judicial branch' in the WTO, as compared to the EU. The EU's GM regime has been painstakingly constructed over many years. It establishes a legislative framework which is specific to GM and mind-boggling (or mind-numbing) in its detail and complexity. Its elaboration followed long and fierce debates between the different political branches at EU level and between the different Member States (and their constituents including sub-state actors). Of course, interpretative questions remain. Some have already been alluded to, such as the scope and role of 'other legitimate factors' in the course of prior approval. Though ambiguities remain it would, however, be foolish to deny the additional degree of interpretative discretion enjoyed by the WTO's judicial branch in this sphere. As already observed, the lawfulness of the EU's regime will, from the perspective of the WTO, be assessed in the light of a series of supremely open-ended pronouncements. In so far as it falls for consideration under the SPS Agreement, these bodies will be charged with assessing whether the contested measure is supported by sufficient scientific evidence, or whether it is based upon a risk assessment.[45] To the extent that it falls within the ambit of the TBT Agreement, the 'judicial organs' will be required to ascertain whether the contested measure is necessary to secure fulfilment of a legitimate objective.[46] As regards the application of the GATT, these bodies may be required to develop and apply criteria on the basis of which the 'likeness' of GM and conventional products may be assessed.[47] At the level of the WTO there is no elaborate legislative regime, painstakingly constructed over the course of several decades. At the level of the WTO – a commitment to textual fidelity notwithstanding – the answers will not leap forth from the text, but will flow from the judgement of those charged with its elucidation. In the WTO, the role of the judicial branch is key.

The WTO dispute settlement bodies are called upon the perform a judicial review type function *vis-à-vis* decisions of the Member States.[48] This function is performed by a WTO panel, subject to the possibility to appeal on points of law to the Appellate Body (AB). Contrary to the situation under the GATT, the adoption of panel and AB reports by the inter-governmental Dispute Settlement Body is virtually automatic, requiring consensus against in order to prevent this.

This judicial review function may be performed in respect of executive or

45 Articles 2.2 and 5.1 SPS. Subject, of course, to the possibility of adopting provisional measures on the basis of Article 5.7 SPS where there is an insufficiency of scientific evidence.

46 Article 2.2 TBT.

47 Article III.4 GATT.

48 The WTO dispute settlement bodies – the panels and the Appellate Body – may be conceived of performing a judicial review type function. Their role is to assess the compatibility of measures adopted by WTO Members with the terms of the WTO Agreement. While the dispute settlement bodies do not annul measures which are incompatible, '[p]rompt compliance with recommendations or rulings of the DSB [Dispute Settlement Body] is essential in order to ensure effective resolution of disputes to the benefit of all Members': Article 21.1 DSU. It is true that compensation and suspension of concessions are available as alternatives to compliance. These are, however, explicitly stated to be 'temporary measures', and neither is to be 'preferred to full implementation of a recommendation to bring a measure into conformity with the covered agreements': Article 22.1 DSU. For a recent discussion of the relationship between these alternatives see Jackson 2004: 109. While this issue concerning the obligations of parties found to be in breach of the WTO Agreement is of great importance, and should be constantly borne in mind, it does not form the subject matter of discussion in this chapter.

administrative acts, but it bites also in respect of legislative acts, including those adopted by democratically elected parliaments within the Member States. In performing this task the AB enjoys extensive interpretative room for manoeuvre. It is called upon to exercise judgement. This fact of judicial review at the level of the WTO presents a profound challenge to the legitimacy of this organisation from the perspective of democracy. The challenge is not unique to the WTO. It inheres in the institution of judicial review more generally. For this reason, it may be useful in contemplating the challenge to consider the reactions which it has provoked in domestic debates.

It was Alexander Bickel who coined the – by now almost hackneyed – phrase 'the counter-majoritarian difficulty' (Bickel 1986: 16).[49] Alluding to the power of 'a handful of unelected and unaccountable judges to strike down laws passed by a representative legislature' (Waldron 1999: 286), this difficulty casts doubt upon the compatibility with democracy of judicial review of legislation. It casts doubt upon the very idea of 'constitutional democracy', in so far as it is judges who are charged with interpreting and applying the constitution, and with upholding the rights which it is deemed to protect. Different strategies have been developed to attempt extrapolation from the counter-majoritarian difficulty.

Some seek to disparage the democratic credentials of the legislative branch:

> It is surely the case that the assumption that legislatures have a lock on democratic legitimacy is seriously flawed. First, legislative outcomes are not majoritarian: legislative outcomes do not truly manifest majoritarian will and consequently their later setting-aside by courts, whatever it might do, does not upset decisions made by a majority. Individual legislators rarely claim to vote in line with the preferences of their constituents and, when they function as a group, there is no evidence to suggest that the outcome on any particular issue will coincide with majoritarianism. (Hutchinson 1999: 206)

Christopher Eisgruber agrees. 'Electorates and legislatures will distort the judgments of the people in predictable ways', due in part to the incentives faced by voters and legislators 'to make political decisions on the basis of self-interest' (Eisgruber 2002a: 15).[50] Even if the legislative will could be regarded as representative of the majority, still – for some – it should not be equated with democracy. Thus for Eisgruber, for example, majority rule 'cedes government to a mere fraction of the people', whereas democracy demands 'government by the whole people' (Eisgruber 2002b: 7–8).

Many, often building on this, seek to defend the democratic credentials of judicial review. There are versions of this approach galore.[51] The nuance of the argument need not detain us here. Suffice it to note the existence of two broad schools.

49 See the insightful work of Jeffrey Dunoff in developing related ideas (Dunoff 1999).

50 For a fuller exposition see Eisgruber 2002b.

51 For a discussion and references to the broad literature see Waldron, chapter 13. Waldron is, of course, the best known and most convincing of the 'judicial review skeptics', at least in the context of constitutional review of primary legislation. The best-known and enduring example is the seminal work by Ely 1980.

For some, the democratic credentials of judicial review lie in its capacity to constitute and perfect the political process, rendering it more authentically democratic. Within this group, some will place emphasis upon the protection of procedural rights (as opposed to substantive values) – and in particular upon 'the right of rights', participation (Waldron 1999: chapter 11 and p. 283), notably on the part of minorities whose interests may tend to be swamped by open majoritarian processes.[52] Others within this group may go further, conceiving democracy as more than a merely procedural ideal, and as demanding more than actual and equal participation. For them, democracy is said to encompass a substantive dimension which represents 'conditions for the legitimacy or moral respectability of democratic decision-making' (Waldron 1999: 283). 'Democratic procedures cannot remain democratic unless they are utilised by people who share some basic equality and liberty' (Hutchinson 1999: 206).

A second, distinct approach places emphasis not so much upon the instrumental capacity of judges to contribute to improved legislative democracy, as upon the free-standing democratic credentials of the judiciary in the performance of its review function. Such arguments may rest upon the 'democratic pedigree' of judges (Eisgruber 2002b: 29),[53] or upon the mode of reasoning which they deploy. As to the latter, the emphasis may be placed upon the moral integrity of judges, or their disinterestedness, or upon their heightened capacity for moral reason or (moral) deliberation.

It is with the thinking of the first of these two groups that this chapter is concerned, and specifically with those who conceive the role of the judiciary in terms of its capacity to enhance – through recourse to procedural precepts – the democratic nature of the political process; legislative and executive. Even so, this discussion may, at first sight, seem a long way from the WTO. It may, moreover, seem counter-intuitive as a starting point given that that organisation comprises members which are democracies and members which are not. Nonetheless, it is possible to argue that this 'democracy-reinforcing' conception of judicial review has something to offer us in contemplating the activities of the AB in the WTO.

The role of judicial review in constituting or re-enforcing democracy will vary according to context. It will vary according to the origins of the decision under review and according to the dangers or deficiencies which characterise the decision-making process in question. Of course, the judicial conception of these dangers or deficiencies will depend ultimately upon their underlying conception of democracy. Thus, to give a straightforward example, the relationship between democracy and judicial review will vary according to the identity of the body promulgating the contested act. The approach will be different in the case of the review of primary legislation as compared to the review of a regulatory act. Further, taking the latter, the court's approach will vary according to whether, for example, it

52 See Ely, above, note 51. Ely places emphasis upon the role of courts in 'clearing the channels of political change' in order to ensure an open and effective democratic process. This leads him to charge the courts with the protection of free speech and voting rights, and with the enforcement of the non-delegation doctrine. As noted, a second strand to his theory charges the courts with re-enforcing the representation of minorities within a participatory political process.

53 Eisgruber points out that (in the US) judges have a democratic pedigree by virtue of their being political appointees, nominated and confirmed by elected officials.

adopts a 'transmission belt' or 'deliberative' perspective on democracy. Whereas the former is 'backwards-looking', placing emphasis upon the limited scope of the delegated powers conferred, and upon the democratic authority of the conferring authority, the latter looks forwards to the processes according to which the delegated act was adopted and justified.

The WTO may be thought to operate against the backdrop of a particular kind of democracy deficit; a deficit which arises as a result of the disjuncture which has grown up between 'jurisdiction' and 'impact' (Keohane 2003).[54] It is a truism to say that decisions adopted within a given polity frequently spill over beyond the boundaries of that polity and affect people – often profoundly – who do not form part of the relevant demos. Those so affected cannot be said to be truly self-governing if their fate is determined in (large) part by decision makers who are not only not representative of them, but who are not in any sense accountable to them. Thus, as Robert Keohane has pointed out, this gap between jurisdiction and impact generates an all-important 'external accountability gap' (Keohane 2003); external accountability being defined as 'accountability to people outside of the acting entity, whose lives are affected by it' (Keohane 2003: 141). Keohane argues that this external accountability deficit represents one of the most pressing normative problems of our time, particularly in so far as powerful states are concerned, immune as they are from established mechanisms of accountability, reputational, economic and so on. For Keohane, organisations such as the WTO represent rare pockets of institutionalized external accountability and it would, he argues, 'be tragic if the "anti-globalization" movement succeeded in demolishing or diminishing the institutions and networks developed to cope with globalization, without putting comparable institutions in their place' (Keohane 2003: 151). For Keohane, from the perspective of external accountability, these organisations represent a 'glimmer of hope' (Keohane 2003: 150).

Viewed from this perspective, it may be interesting to ask whether judicial review in the WTO may be conceived as a tool to mitigate this all-important external accountability gap, and hence to re-enforce democracy in an age when the concept of statehood no longer captures all dimensions of power.[55] The concept of accountability is a multi-faceted and evolving one. It is subject to continuous transformation as it tries to keep up with the challenges posed by the emergence of dramatically new forms of (transnational) governance. This is reflected in the multiplicity of forms and mechanisms for accountability highlighted by Keohane in his work; electoral, legal, reputational, economic and so on. At the core, however, for

54 See also Raustiala 2004 for a parallel discussion as regards the arguably sovereignty strengthening impact of international economic law.

55 The suggestion here is not that accountability and democracy are synonymous. Indeed, the relationship between these two concepts is complex and contested and is worthy of exploration. For now though, the argument of this paper rests upon the premise that there is a relationship between external accountability and democracy, and that accountability is a necessary though not a sufficient condition for democracy. The point is not that external accountability in the kinds of forms under discussion here could ever 'close' the democracy gap, but merely that it can make some contribution in giving voice to 'outsiders' in the adoption of decisions which impact upon them, but in respect of which they are normally wholly excluded.

Keohane accountability, in its many guises, comprises two elements, *viz.* a requirement on the part of those reaching decisions to report to the individual or group to which they are accountable (a transparency dimension), and the ability of that individual or group to sanction the decision maker (Keohane 2003: 139). Thus, accountability is viewed as a relationship between actors. One rationale for the constitution of accountability relationships is defined in terms of 'impact', whereby those who are ' "choice determining" for some people [should be] fully accountable for their actions to those people'.[56]

Turning first to the obligation to report: this may be weak or strong in form. It may, at minimum, imply an obligation to inform those affected of the existence and content of the decision in question. As we move down the continuum from weak to strong, there may arise also an obligation to explain the basis of the decision adopted; to give reasons for it and to make available the information upon which it is said to be based. The obligation to report may be more than one way; active on the side of the decision maker but passive on the side of the recipient. It may necessitate more active engagement on the basis of consultation or dialogue. Any explanation proffered may be required to address the specific concerns raised by the notified parties. Conceivably, participation opportunities may be provided to such parties through, for example, a right to a hearing.

Expressed in this way, it is not hard to see that there may be seeds of an external accountability-based approach inherent in the activities of the WTO. As noted previously, the WTO Agreement contains a multitude of notification and consultation obligations, whereby members proposing to introduce restrictive measures are required to notify other members of their decisions and to receive and discuss comments put forward by them. Regular fora for consultations are established in the form of committees, and such committees are to encourage consultations or negotiations between states.[57] Transparency, reason giving, and consultation and dialogue emerge as treaty-based instruments of external accountability.

Notable also are the conclusions of the AB in the recent *EC Tariff Preferences* report.[58] Here the AB was called upon to examine the compatibility with the 'Enabling Clause' of one aspect of the European Union's Generalised System of Preferences (GSP).[59] It was specifically concerned with the Drug Arrangements inherent in this, which operate to grant additional tariff preferences to certain specified developing country members. The current practice of the EC is to concede concessions to 12 beneficiary countries (but not to India, the complaining state). The AB, like the panel, found that the Drug Arrangements operate in a manner which is not consistent with the non-discrimination requirement inherent in Article 2(a) of the Enabling Clause. Unlike the panel, it did so while keeping open the possibility of differentiation as between developing countries in the

56 Keohane 2003: 141, citing the work of David Held.

57 See, eg, Article 12 SPS Agreement. Dunoff (2007) has undertaken work on the crucial role of the SPS Committee. See also Scott 2007: chapter 2.

58 WTO Appellate Body Report, *EC – Conditions for the Granting of Tariff Preferences in Developing Countries*, 20 April 2004, WT/DS246/AB/R.

59 Council Regulation 2501/2001 of 10 December 2001, [2001] *OJ* L346/1.

operation of preferential trading regimes. The conclusions of the AB on the discrimination point were premised upon two key considerations.

First, and procedurally, the EU regime was found to be deficient in that it did not provide any mechanism according to which the list of beneficiaries could be supplemented or amended. Subject to the possibility of amending the primary legislation, the list of beneficiaries was 'closed'. As such, the tariff preferences available under the Drugs Arrangements could not be regarded as 'available to all GSP beneficiaries suffering from illicit drug production and trafficking'.[60]

Second, the AB laid emphasis upon the absence of 'criteria or standards to provide a basis for distinguishing beneficiaries under the Drug Arrangements from other GSP beneficiaries'.[61]

> [B]ecause the [GSP] Regulation does not defined the criteria or standards that a developing country must meet to qualify for preferences under the Drug Arrangements, there is no basis to determine whether those criteria or standards are discriminatory or not.[62]

The approach of the AB in GSP is noteworthy from the perspective of external accountability. It concedes considerable flexibility to the regulating Member State in terms of the choice of objective which it wishes to pursue, and to this end is willing to permit reasoned differentiation as between individual developing countries. Nonetheless, it places heavy emphasis upon transparency on the one hand, and upon procedural propriety on the other. If special benefits are to be made available to third countries, this must be on the basis of criteria which are transparent and which reflect the development, financial or trade need to which the differential treatment is intended to respond. The preferences must be available to all GSP beneficiaries similarly affected by the problem at hand. In the case of the EU Drug Arrangements, there was 'no indication as to how the beneficiaries . . . were chosen or what kind of considerations would or could be used to determine the effect of the "drug problem" on a particular requirement'.[63] Related to this is the requirement that procedures must be put in place which render the policy responsive to change; such that the special preferences may over time be extended to similarly situated states, or withdrawn from those which are no longer capable of being regarded as similarly situated. For the AB differentiation is one thing, discrimination another. Absent clear criteria, applied consistently and in a manner which is responsive to change, it is not possible to guarantee that differentiation will not serve to mask discrimination.

Yet more telling, perhaps, though not dissimilar in some ways, are the decisions of the AB in *Shrimp-Turtle*.[64] Here the AB may be thought to be striving after external accountability. The AB focused upon the manner in which the US restriction in question has been *applied*. In condemning the United States, the AB laid emphasis,

60 Above, note 58, para 187.
61 Above, note 58, para 188.
62 Above, note 58, para 188.
63 Above, note 58, para 183.
64 WTO Panel Report, *US – Prohibition on the Import of Shrimp and Shrimp Products*, WT/DS58/WT/R, and for the Article 21.5 DSU AB report see WT/DS58/WT/RW.

inter alia, upon its failure – prior to the enactment of the unilateral measures – to engage in serious, across-the-board and good-faith negotiations with the third countries affected,[65] with a view to reaching multilateral or bilateral agreements with them on the protection and conservation of sea turtles. It laid emphasis too upon the abject failure of the United States to respect the fundamental requirements of basic fairness and due process in the operation of its import certification scheme. This scheme was condemned as operating in a manner which was singularly informal and casual, requiring no reason giving, no transparency, and providing no right to a hearing at any stage.

In *Shrimp-Turtle*, famously, the AB did not second-guess the policy objectives of the United States. On the contrary, it adopted a permissive stance . . . Emphasis was laid upon the manner in which the United States had behaved *vis-à-vis* its trading partners in the operationalisation of its sea turtle conservation regime. It might be thought that the United States was condemned for being insufficiently 'other-regarding' in its attitude to those situated outside of the polity, but affected by decisions adopted within it. If, as Keohane argues and I accept, external accountability is a key requirement of democratic legitimacy in a globalised order, the decisions of the AB may be thought to have rendered a positive service to democracy; to have re-enforced rather than to have undermined it.

It is also important to note that an emphasis upon external accountability may frequently serve to dissipate conflict. Evidence from the SPS Committee would seem to bear this out (Dunoff 2007). The specific facts of *Shrimp-Turtle* may also attest to this. Here, where the United States had tried to negotiate, this had led to the conclusion of the inter-American Convention for the Protection and Conservation of Sea Turtles. This required the parties to put in place regulations providing for the use of such turtle exclusion devices in shrimp fishing, such as were 'jointly determined to be suitable for a particular party's maritime area'. This, as is evident from the discussion above, stands in stark contrast to the unilateral rules applied by the United States in the absence of any such agreement.

There is much in the recent *Biotech* report which resonates with the discussion above. This is a long and complex report and this is not the place for full analysis.[66] Suffice it for now to observe that the approach of the panel is predominantly a procedural one. This is most evident in the panel's analysis of the EU's handling of specific applications for authorisation. This centred upon the obligation in the SPS Agreement to undertake and complete control, inspection and approval procedures without undue delay.[67] The central purpose of this, according to the panel, is to prevent members from avoiding or evading substantive disciplines by simply failing to reach decisions on applications. It is treated as a 'good faith' requirement,[68] obliging members to come to a decision with no unjustifiable loss

65 But contrast with *US – Gambling* (7 April 2005, WT/DS285/AB/R) where the AB eschews a prior negotiations obligation, where the objective being pursued was one where unilateral action could suffice.

66 Above, note 43.

67 Annex C(1)(a).

68 Above, note 43, paras 7.1498–7.1499.

of time, or as soon as possible under the circumstances. What this means in practice will vary according to context. The length of the delay is not the key, but rather than the question of whether there is a legitimate reason or justification for it. Rhetorically, the panel is reticent about defining in the abstract what is to count as a good or bad reason for delay.[69] This is in keeping with the emphasis upon context. The panel is decidedly less reticent in determining which reasons are good reasons in the context of this specific case. Thus a failure on the part of the applicant to provide additional requested information may pass muster, so long as such requests are not a mere pretext to delay the completion of the procedure.[70] On the contrary, the fact of scientific uncertainty, or the existence of shortcomings in the existing regulatory framework, are not such as to justify delay. In essence, the panel put itself in the position of evaluating putative justifications put forward by the EU, insisting not merely on reason giving, but on the availability of reasons which it deems to be consistent with the overall objective of the agreement. In so doing it is seeking to ensure that members cannot hide behind a failure to decide, making the published regulatory framework effectively inoperative, and undermining the legitimate expectations of applicants based upon this. Annex C explicitly instils a due process requirement, demanding that the standard processing procedure for applications be published or communicated to the applicant on request, and that there be a procedure to review complaints concerning the operation of this procedure. The panel reinforces this due process dimension by virtue of its willingness to demand reasoned justification for delay and to determine, contextually, and in the light of the object and purpose of the agreement, on what basis delay may be reasonably necessary for members to determine with adequate confidence that their WTO-consistent SPS measures are fulfilled.

Also worthy of note in *EC-Biotech* is the emphasis placed by the panel upon the risk assessment obligation in Article 5.1 SPS. While there is no independent procedural requirement for a member to carry out its own risk assessment,[71] the member must ensure that it has at its disposal information satisfying each of the separate components of what amounts to a risk assessment as defined in Annex A(1). For example, under the first definition, a member must ensure that there is an evaluation of the likelihood of entry or spread of a pest or a disease. Where, as with the Austrian safeguard measure on T25 maize, the studies at the disposal of the regulating member do not indicate relative probability of the potential risks, or even establish an inability to determine probability, this will not meet the requirements of the agreement.[72] The panel is very strict in policing member compliance with the informational demands implied by the concept of risk assessment. As such it is able to conclude that none of the EU Member States relying on the safeguard clause had put forward risk assessments, independent from that of the EU, which were such as to satisfy the demands of the agreement. Thus, other than to the extent that they were seeking to rely on the EU's own risk assessment, the Member States

69 Above, note 43, para 7.1523.
70 Above, note 43, para 7.1522.
71 Above, note 31, para 196.
72 Above, note 43, para 7.2044.

fell at the first hurdle. They had not accumulated the information which they are obliged to accumulate before enacting a trade-restrictive measure of this kind.[73]

In contemplating these aspects of the *Biotech* case from an accountability perspective, it is important to bear in mind that the EU regulator was not processing applications in accordance with the procedures and values established by the EU legislature. Likewise, the EU was not policing recourse to the safeguard clause by the Member States on the basis of the established conditions for their use. Such wilful non-application of established rules not only threatens external accountability but also internal accountability within the EU system. Even on the basis of a quite traditional, hierarchical, conception of accountability, it is clear that the agent (the executive) was acting in a way which was out of keeping with the demands laid down by the principal (the legislature).

If the proceduralism inherent in these various cases may be cited to support the perspective that the activities of the WTO might serve to enhance rather than undermine accountability, this tentative conclusion should be viewed in the light of two cautionary remarks.

First, and at some length, any relief that this approach might offer to the dispute settlement bodies would surely be short-lived. With the new legislative package in place, it seems only a matter of time before the premises underpinning that package come directly to form the subject of scrutiny in the WTO. In evaluating the WTO-compatibility of eventual, actual authorisation decisions, it seems unlikely that the AB will adopt an approach which is purely procedural. In many cases – *Shrimp-Turtle* and *GSP* included – the dispute settlement bodies have self-evidently moved beyond a mere focus on the procedural dimension. In these cases, the basis for their evaluation lies in substantive, not procedural, norms. These substantive benchmarks vary widely in nature and intensity. In *GSP* non-discrimination formed the substantive focus for analysis. In *Shrimp-Turtle*, the AB focused not merely upon the due process failure of the United States, but also upon the substantive nature of its certification regime. It focused in particular upon the 'rigid' and 'unbending' nature of the US rules, such that other WTO members were obliged to adopt 'essentially the same policies and enforcement measures' as the United States, regardless of the conditions prevailing within these states. Standards which were different, but comparable in their effectiveness, would not be such as to meet the requirements of the US regime. Thus, an additional benchmark against which the legality of the US measures was assessed was that of *flexibility*. '[A] measure should be designed in such a manner that there is sufficient flexibility to take into account the specific conditions prevailing in *any* exporting Member.'[74] This demand for flexibility may be viewed through the lens of external accountability. Accountability to peoples situated outside of the regulating state may be thought to demand that where states seek to protect their vital interests, they should do so in a

73 Note, though, that before being able to conclude that Article 5.1 applied, as opposed to the less demanding Article 5.7, the panel was required to find that there was indeed sufficient scientific evidence to permit a risk assessment. It regarded the concept of sufficiency as an objective one, and was prepared to substitute its judgement for that of the EU on this point. Again see Scott 2007: Chapter 5 for a fuller analysis.

74 Article 21.5, para 149.

manner which generates the least possible negative external effects. It would not be appropriately other-regarding for states to impose costs *needlessly* upon their trading partners. Protective measures which, though not identical, are equivalent in the level of protection which they offer must be recognised in order that *unnecessary* costs can be avoided.

Though substantive in nature, flexibility (and equivalence) and non-discrimination fall on the weak side of the substantive continuum. They acknowledge the autonomy of members in setting their own standard of protection, placing demands only in relation to the manner in which these standards are to be attained. Other substantive benchmarks would go further. These might demand, for example, not merely that members report as to the content of their measures, and as to the epistemic basis upon which they rest, but also that there be a 'rational' or 'objective' relationship between the premises said to underpin the measure and the measure itself. As is well known, such a requirement is imposed in respect of sanitary and phytosanitary measures, whereby protective measures must be reasonably or rationally sustained by the results of a risk assessment.[75]

This rationality requirement may be differently construed, and even more intensive in the scrutiny which it implies. It may be deemed, for example, to encompass a proportionality dimension. This dimension might extend beyond the least restrictive means test already inherent in the concept of flexibility discussed above. It might, in addition, imply a balancing of costs and benefits, such that the negative consequences associated with restrictions on trade must be justified having regard to the scale of the positive benefits said to ensue.[76] A weaker reading of the rationality requirement is evident in both *Hormones* and in *EC-Biotech* (Scott 2007: 104–10). Here, rationality was deemed to demand objective relationship between the risk assessment and the measure.[77] This was deemed to leave room for members to base their measures on minority scientific opinion.[78] A single risk assessment may justify different policy responses, and where there are factors affecting scientists' level of confidence in a risk assessment, precautionary measures might well be justified.[79] Here, in a more gentle reading of the rationality requirement, the *Biotech* panel merely insisted that absent any explanation, an unequivocally positive risk assessment will in general not be able to serve as a rational basis for a categorical prohibition.

As we move from the procedural to the substantive and from the weak substantive to the strong, it might be thought that the WTO comes to present a challenge to our conception of judicial review as democracy re-enforcing. Whatever the external accountability gains may be, substantive discipline of this kind may be thought to pose a threat to the internal accountability of states. According to Keohane, internal accountability is owed by rulers to those who authorise the regime in question, and

75 See Articles 2.2 and 5.1 of the SPS Agreement and *EC-Hormones*, above, note 31.

76 There are signs of this in *Japan – Apples* (10 December 2003, WT/DS245/AB/R) where it was found that the multi-faceted Japanese regulatory measure was clearly disproportionate relative to the negligible risk which had been established. See *Japan – Apples* (Panel), para 8.181 and Scott 2007: 86–90. See, in the context of the GATT, Article XX, *Korea Beef* (11 December 2000, WT/DS161 and 169/AB/R).

77 Above, note 31, para 189.

78 Above, note 31, para 194.

79 Above, note 43, paras 7.3064 and 7.3065–7.3066.

to those who support it, notably through taxation (Keohane 2003: 140). Keohane seems relatively untroubled by any such threat to internal accountability. 'Globalization', he asserts, 'may weaken internal accountability within democracies, but is political institutionalization is a condition for external accountability' (Keohane 2003: 151). He conceives of a competition between internal and external accountability claims, implying a clear recognition that one may be gained at the expense of the other (Keohane 2003: 146).

This vision of an external/internal accountability trade-off may be too absolute in the case of the WTO. We saw previously that existing WTO jurisprudence may be thought to serve internal accountability by enhancing fidelity to established procedures and values, and by virtue of the introduction of good governance precepts such as reason giving and transparency requirements. Nonetheless, the tension remains; particularly but not only in respect of the review of legislative acts. And the more intrusive the judicial review tools, and the more intensive the standard of review, the more clearly this tension will come to the fore. This may be a dilemma which the dispute settlement bodies may succeed in dodging as regards the moratorium. It is, however, not one which they can dodge indefinitely.

The second cautionary observation may be more succinctly put. It is not entirely unrelated in the dilemma which it throws up. Put simply, it is important to recall the backdrop to the EC moratorium. This came into being by virtue of the reluctance of a majority of Member States to play any constructive role in the established system for prior authorisation. Over time the Commission bowed to this concerted campaign of disobedience, and began to desist from even submitting applications received to the relevant committee, comprising representatives of the Member States. At least on one reading, this Member State defiance was a result of strong public antipathy to the use of GM technology in agriculture. It was born of responsiveness to European-wide public opinion.[80]

Whatever the truth of this as regards the EC moratorium, it might seem a poor excuse for behaviour which is non-transparent and inadequately reasoned, as well as out of synch with the EC's established normative framework. However, it does bring to the fore a fundamental issue of immense importance; namely the place of public opinion in the regulation of GMOs. Within the framework of this discussion, this question has two dimensions. The first relates to the place of public opinion within the evolving European framework for the regulation of GMOs. The second is concerned to ascertain the extent to which responsiveness to public opinion is, or ought to be, relevant to an assessment of the WTO-compatibility of Member State protective measures.

As noted at the start of this chapter, the 2003 GM Food and Feed Regulation is notably reticent in reaching out to involve the public in governance. Admittedly, the public may make comments to the Commission following the publication of EFSA's opinion.[81] Neither the scope nor the salience of such comments is

80 For evidence from the UK, following an innovative experiment in public consultation, see the results of 'GM Nation', available at: <http://www.gmnation.org.uk/>. Eurobarometer surveys offer an insight into public attitudes to biotechnology in respect to agriculture and other matters. See, for example, <http://www.vib.be/TechTransfer/EN/Flanders+Assets/Public+opinion/> and <http://europa.eu.int/comm/research/press/2001/pr2312en.html>.

81 Above, note 2, Article 6(7).

outlined.[82] The public is nowhere defined, and there is a conspicuous absence of accountability mechanisms such that might induce these comments to resonate within the decision-making process. The Commission is not specifically mandated to take these into account. Though it incurs a general obligation to give reasons, and must explain any departure from the EFSA opinion, the Commission is not required to justify its stance with specific reference to the content of the public comments received. In drafting its approval (or non-approval) decision, the Commission is required to take account of the EFSA opinion, together with 'any relevant provisions of Community law and other legitimate factors relevant to the matter under consideration'.[83] The place of public opinion under these headings would be a matter for legitimate debate. The concept of relevant, legitimate factors is not defined in the 2003 Regulation. To the extent that this concept is parasitic upon the broader normative framework for the regulation of food safety constituted by the EFSA Regulation, it might be thought to extend to those factors identified in the preamble thereto. These are said to 'include' 'societal, economic, traditional, ethical and environmental factors and the feasibility of control'.[84] Though this list may properly be regarded as indicative rather than exhaustive, public opinion is not singled out.

The 2003 Regulation, developed against the backdrop of the alleged moratorium, does not seem to be fundamentally concerned with eliciting public participation. Its transparency requirements make much of the relevant information available to the public, and the labelling requirements may be thought to empower the public in its marketplace activities. But still the Regulation is strikingly weak in the public participation for which it provides.

A further question arises in examining the place of public opinion in the European system for the approval of GM food. This may be posed as a negative. Are there, as a matter of Community law, limitations upon the extent to which decision makers may have regard to public opinion in reaching their approval decisions? This speaks not to any positive requirement to have regard to public opinion, but to the legal limitations in their entitlement to do so.

Here it is important to recall that approval decisions are to be granted or refused only on the grounds set out in the GM Food and Feed Regulation. It is not precisely clear to what the concept of 'grounds' refers, but it would seem to suggest that such decisions must be in the service of the 'requirements' laid down, whereby the food or feed must not have adverse effects on human or animal health or the environment, mislead the consumer, or differ from the food which it is intended to replace to such an extent that its normal consumption would be nutritionally disadvantageous for the consumer.[85] The Regulation is intended to serve certain specified ends.[86] Responsiveness to public opinion or the mitigation of public fears are not in

82 Contrast usefully with the EU's new chemicals regime REACH (Regulation 1907/2006 of the European Parliament and of the Council of 18 December 2006, [2006] *OJ* L396/1), where the role of interested parties is enhanced in the authorisation process especially under Article 60(2) as compared to Article 60(4) as is the duty of the various actors to take these into account.

83 Above, note 2, Article 7(1).

84 Maria Lee makes this point in her forthcoming book on environmental law and risk regulation in the EU. See above, note 11, recital 19 EFSA Regulation.

85 Above, note 2, Article 4(5).

86 See also *ibid.*, Article 1.

themselves included among these ends. Any decision premised principally upon these latter concerns, disassociated from the specific objectives explicitly laid down, would seem vulnerable to challenge as a misuse of powers.[87]

Equally, it is necessary to recall the recent and repeated insistence of the European courts that 'a preventive measure cannot properly be based on a purely hypothetical approach to risk, founded on mere conjecture which has not been scientifically verified'.[88] This statement seems uncompromising and the threshold which it establishes absolute. Absent specific evidence of risk, such that transcends this 'merely hypothetical' threshold, it is not open to the relevant institution to act, regardless of the manner in which the public views that hypothetical risk, and regardless of the intensity of the public fears which the existence of the 'merely' hypothetical risk provokes.

By contrast, while above this threshold the autonomy of the political branch is preserved,[89] it remains subject to over-arching principles of Community law. Among the most important is the principle of proportionality which, in the sphere of risk regulation, also encompasses a requirement to engage in cost-benefit balancing.[90] Ambiguity persists as to the extent to which public attitudes to risk may properly be reflected in decision making and relevant from the perspective of proportionality. Even if public opinion is to be regarded as a factor which may legitimately be taken into account, it is critical also that it be allowed to resonate within the framework of a proportionality analysis.

Turning now, and in a manner which is necessarily speculative, to the place that public opinion could (and to some extent does) play in the WTO. The issue here is to ascertain the extent to which WTO law might accommodate Member State responsiveness to public opinion. Three modes of accommodation may be contemplated.

First, the capacity of Member States to respond to public opinion in regulation will depend upon the stringency or the intensity of the WTO benchmarks for review. To the extent that these are construed and applied in an expansive manner, they will be capable of accommodating diverse responses and diverse conceptions of appropriateness in terms of regulatory response. This will remain true regardless of the motivations which underpin that regulatory response, in so far as these benchmarks are not concerned with subjective intent. Thus, for example, we saw above that the rationality requirement which underpins the

87 This is defined by the European Court in the following terms: '[. . .] misuse of powers is defined by settled case law as the adoption by a Community institution of a measure with the exclusive or main purpose of achieving an end other than that stated or evading a procedure specifically prescribed by the Treaty for dealing with the circumstances of the case'. See Case C-180/96 *United Kingdom v Commission* [1996] ECR I-3903, para 64. See also Case T-13/99 *Pfizer v Council*, above, note 12, where the CFI finds that 'where the measure at issue is a measure taken for the purpose of protecting public health [. . .] the findings made by the institutions, which differ from those set out in the SCAN opinion must be founded on that purpose alone' and rejecting the argument that the Council had allowed itself 'to be influenced, as regards the risk assessment, by concerns expressed in the media' (paras 203 and 207). It is, however, important to recall once more than the regulatory regime at stake in *Pfizer* did not specify the relevance of 'other legitimate factors' in the authorisation process.

88 *Pfizer* above, note 12, para 143. See also *Monsanto*, above, note 19.

89 See *Pfizer*, above, note 12, para 201.

90 Above, note 12.

risk assessment requirement in SPS is sufficiently open-ended to permit the adoption of measures to protect public health even in the face of scientific disagreement as to the nature and magnitude of the risk. The limits to this lie in the requirement that there be positive evidence of the existence of a risk, rather than merely the kind of 'theoretical' presupposition of risk which flows from the impossibility of securing absolute, enduring, scientific certainty. In the regulatory space above that threshold, Member States remain free to be more or less responsive to public opinion, on the basis of their own precepts as to the processes – democratic or otherwise – according to which regulatory outcomes ought to be determined. In this sense, it will be apparent that the salience of the issue of public opinion will increase, along with the intensity or intrusiveness of the 'normal' benchmarks for review.

Second, it is possible to contemplate circumstances in which the relevant benchmarks for review will themselves be infused with a sensitivity to public opinion; in which their very construction will serve to accommodate this dimension. Three concrete examples may be given by way of illustration.

In the context of the SPS Agreement, Article 5.1, the AB drew up its substantive benchmark for review in the light of what 'responsible and *representative* [my emphasis]' governments sometimes do (namely act on the basis of divergent scientific opinion). The parameters of what is to be considered as reasonable in this setting appear to be shaped by the AB's understanding of the way in which representative governments operate. Here, what democratic governments in fact do is allowed to infuse the AB's normative conception of what such governments ought to be allowed to do.

In the context of the application of the 'national treatment' principle in GATT, Article III, the question of 'like' products is critical. To the extent that products are not alike, they may be treated differently, without this differentiation amounting to discrimination. The AB has accepted that 'consumers' tastes and habits', as expressed on the marketplace, are one relevant criterion in the analysis of likeness.[91] Though the weight of this criterion, and its relationship with other relevant criteria, remains uncertain, public opinion as mediated through marketplace behaviour is accepted as playing a role in the construction of the national treatment principle, by virtue of its role in an assessment of likeness.

Article 5.5 SPS lays down a 'consistency' requirement, whereby Members may not institute arbitrary or unjustifiable distinctions in the level of SPS protection sought as between different risk situations, where these distinctions result in discrimination or a disguised restriction on trade. There remains considerable uncertainty as to the kinds of reasons which might be accepted as rendering distinctions non-arbitrary or justifiable.[92] In *Hormones* the AB stated that Article 5.5 does not impose an absolute consistency requirement; this by virtue of the fact that governments 'establish their appropriate levels of protection frequently on an *ad hoc* basis and over time, as different risks present themselves at different times'.[93] Yet the connotations of this

91 WTO Appellate Body Report, *EC-Asbestos*, 12 March 2001, WT/DS135/AB/R. For a discussion of the ambiguity inherent in this report see Regan 2002.

92 See the discussion in Scott 2007: chapter 4.

93 Above, note 31, para 214.

remain unclear. The extent to which differences in the public perception of risk may serve to justify distinctions in the level of protection is of critical importance, but as yet unsettled.

One area where this issue of the relevance of public opinion may come to the fore is in respect of the labelling of GM food. As noted above, the 2003 Regulation instantiates a broad and demanding labelling regime. This encompasses a public health dimension, but extends well beyond it. It is premised more generally upon the assertion of 'the right of consumers to information' in the interests of their being able to make an 'informed choice'.[94] It operates in the interests of market transparency, to use the language of the AB in the *Sardines* case.[95] While at first sight it might seem hard to quibble with information-based demands of this sort, as many have observed labelling regimes raise a host of difficult trade related questions.[96] As the European Court has implied, labelling may serve to facilitate consumers' indulgence of their irrational prejudices.[97] Also, conceptually, there is almost no limit to the kinds of information which members might demand by way of labelling requirements. These could range from the palpably reasonable (the presence of nuts for example, or the presence of extraneous DNA which might raise religious concerns) to the palpably absurd (the colour of the uniforms worn by those in the factory in which the product was manufactured). Yet, in terms of market transparency, the basis for distinguishing between these is not clear. Significantly, one factor to which the EU turns in a bid to justify its labelling regime is public opinion. The Preamble to the 2003 Regulation provides:

> The labelling should include objective information to the effect that a food or feed consists of, contains or is produced from GMOs. Clear labelling, irrespective of the detectability of DNA or protein resulting from the genetic modification in the final product, *meets the demands expressed in numerous surveys by a large majority of consumers* [my emphasis], facilitates informed choice and precludes potential misleading of consumers as regards methods or manufacture or production.[98]

Thus, in seeking to distinguish the reasonable from the absurd the EU cites, among other things, the existence of a prior public demand to know. The strength of public feeling is such that labelling may be viewed as responding to public concerns. It may be, as an empirical matter, that labelling will further stoke these concerns, but still it is responding to prior concerns. It might be argued that this fact of responsiveness to public opinion might serve to nudge the regime in the direction of the reasonable as opposed to the absurd.

All of this is well and good. It contemplates public opinion as an element in the application of the rules. In view of the open-endedness of the text of the WTO Agreement this route offers considerable potential in injecting sensitivity to

94 Above, note 2, recital 17.

95 WTO Appellate Body Report, *EC-Sardines*, 23 October 2002, WT/DS231/AB/R.

96 For an example in the area of GMOs, see Appleton 2000.

97 Case C 207/83 *Commission v United Kingdom* [1985] ECR 1201.

98 Above, note 2, recital 21.

public opinion into the terms of the agreement. It might be that it is a sensible place to stop!

Yet a third mode of accommodation may be contemplated in respect of public opinion in the WTO; one which is more direct and more extreme. According to this third mode, the WTO might recognise a specific and explicit public opinion style defence. That is to say that, subject no doubt to safeguards, it would (according to this mode of accommodation) be open to members to justify restrictions on the basis that the protective measures in question are necessary precisely, and conceivably exclusively, because the public considers them to be so. The objections to any such suggestion spring readily to mind. The objections are so numerous and so intense that it may be misconceived to even contemplate travelling down this road. Public opinion is harder to ascertain than it is to manipulate. Adept at the strategic framing of issues, members may contrive to achieve results which merely shroud their choices in the garb of democracy. Public opinion is rarely uniform and less often static. Even where policies do, unequivocally, command public support, these policies may rest upon assumptions which are ignorant and prejudiced. To this list, one must add arguments about the nature of a properly functioning democracy. Even for those for whom democracy is essentially a procedural ideal, the ideal tends to add up to more than the mere, uncritical, aggregation of ill-informed public preferences.

The work of Cass Sunstein stands as a powerful reminder of the limits of populism in thinking about risk. He celebrates the 'centrality of science and expertise to the law of risk', defending an approach which is explicitly 'technocratic' and 'sharply sceptical of populism' (Sunstein 2003: 294).[99] Sunstein examines and explains the mistakes that people make in evaluating risk. He argues that these flow, on the whole, from the mental shortcuts – or heuristic devices – upon which we rely, from the social pressures or influences to which we are exposed, and from our tendency to neglect 'trade-offs' according to which protective measures generate their own, different – invisible or unanticipated – risks (Sunstein 2006: 55). Sunstein's many examples are compelling and his insights of crucial importance.

Even Sunstein, though, feels compelled to qualify his celebration of technocracy. His qualifications flow in part from a form of reasoning which is consequentialist. He points to the negative consequences which may flow from the failure of the state to respond to public perceptions of risk. 'A sensible approach to risk will attempt to reduce public fear even if it is baseless' (Sunstein 2003b: 45). 'Public alarm, even if ill-formed, is itself a harm, and is likely to lead to additional harms, perhaps in the form of large scale "ripple effects" (Sunstein 2003b: 45). Similarly, "technocrats tend to ignore the fact that to work well, a regulatory system needs one thing above all – public support and confidence". This is so whether or not a lack of confidence is fully rational' (Sunstein 2003a: 294).

Sunstein's qualifications are, however, not only rooted in consequentialism. They are rooted also in his conception of democracy; deliberative democracy. He is not a

99 Eisgruber's study also provides a particularly good account of why democracy should not be equated with majoritarianism. He focuses upon the incentives which bear upon both legislatures and voters to act out of self-interest, rather than on the basis of moral judgement. See also the excellent exchange between Sunstein and critical commentators (Sunstein 2006).

populist but he is a democrat. Whereas it is not appropriate for governments to capitulate in the face of vociferous but wrong-headed public demands, it is appropriate for governments to respond to people's values, at least where these values 'can survive a process of reflection' according to the precepts of deliberative democracy (Sunstein 2003a: 65).

This tension between technocracy and democracy is one which Sunstein approaches constructively, or positively. He seeks to outline the contours of a solution such that governments may do better in regulating risk. For the WTO, the challenge is somewhat different. The dispute settlement bodies will be called upon to delimit, in a manner which may be universally applied – in states which are (deliberative) democracies and in states which are not – the circumstances in which additional latitude is to be granted to members to respond to public opinion, even when in so doing the member in question will fall foul of the 'normal' benchmarks for review. What Sunstein's position does reveal, however, is that even those who are in general technocratic in their leanings, are willing to admit of circumstances in which 'right answers' must acknowledge public opinion and respond to the fears and the values which underpin it. It cautions as much against complacent and uncompromising disregard for public opinion as it does against complacent and uncompromising acceptance of it.[100]

The issue of the role of public opinion presents a audacious challenge for the WTO, especially in the context of this third form of more direct accommodation. It is in part a textual challenge. In certain respects the text of the Agreement would seem to be permissive. A free-standing public opinion style defence could be integrated into the range of legitimate objectives contemplated by TBT, Article 2.2. In other respects the Agreement seems less open. The introduction of a defence of this kind would be more difficult to secure in the context of the GATT, where the list of Article XX exceptions is deemed exhaustive.

Though the textual challenge is important, especially in view of the AB's literal approach to interpretation, it is, however, the normative challenge which is most daunting; even for those who accept that governments do, and indeed sometimes ought to, take steps to respond to 'irrational' public opinion. This is a challenge which has received little attention in the WTO, due no doubt to the multiplicity and the intensity of the objections which spring so readily to mind. But given that even commentators such as Sunstein desist from an uncompromising disavowal of the relevance of public opinion, we should perhaps be modest in acknowledging and confronting this dilemma.

In reflecting upon this issue, we should recall the AB case law discussed above. This reminds us that, in its articulation and application of core concepts, the AB has devised a range of devices which allow it to be permissive of state autonomy, but not uncompromisingly or uncritically so. In *Shrimp-Turtle*, it opens the door of the environmental exception to measures concerned with production process standards. Yet flexibility (in the sense of openness to equivalence), due process and a

100 Likewise Eisgruber observes: 'I do not, however, suggest that it would be acceptable if the Supreme Court (or any other aspect of democratic government) were unresponsive to public deliberation. On the contrary, I insist that democratic institutions, including courts, must be sensitive to public deliberation about justice'. See Eisgruber 2002a: 58.

commitment to multilateral cooperation intervene to guard against abuse. In *GSP* the AB proves more forgiving than the panel of differential tariff treatment of developing countries. But safeguards are introduced to guard against abuse. Such differentiation must be based on objective criteria relating to the development, financial or trade needs of similarly situated developing countries, and the scheme in question must be sufficiently transparent and adaptable in its mode of operation to connect authentically to the objective pursued.

Perhaps then the challenge for the WTO in relation to public opinion is not to exclude it as uncompromisingly irrelevant, but to instantiate with care the conditions according to which its entry into the justification equation may be mediated. Such conditions must be such that the WTO neither foists internal democracy on reluctant Member States, nor undermines its wide variety of prevailing guises. Most obviously, any such conditions would be concerned with the nature of the evidence required to substantiate claims relating to public opinion. Equally though, additional safeguards could be introduced. These might relate to transparency, both in terms of the fact of reliance upon public opinion as an element in the defence, and in terms of the evidential record upon which this element rests. Any such safeguards might, moreover, acknowledge the peculiarly volatile and contingent nature of public opinion. Thus, measures which purport to rest upon this, might reasonably be required to be regarded as provisional, to be re-visited on a regular basis in order to verify the continuing validity of their evidential base. Additional positive obligations could be incurred by states as preconditions for recourse to a public-opinion style defence. To re-iterate, the language of the TBT Agreement, with its focus upon necessity in the fulfilment of legitimate objectives, is highly permissive in this regard. Such preconditions might oblige states to explore and to communicate, proactively and vigorously, the costs and benefits of its regulatory stance rooted in public opinion. Awareness of costs should extend not only to those endured within the territory of the regulating state, but also to external costs and to the manner and consequences of their distribution. To the extent that members choose to fall back on arguments from public opinion to justify their regulatory choices, such members might reasonably be expected to incur a duty to seek to stimulate informed and critical reflection on the part of the fearful or objecting public. To the extent that members are passive in the face of public opinion which is not demonstrated to be rooted in those forms of rationality which resonate in the WTO, the 'necessity' of their measures may be open to doubt.

The salience of this discussion may be exemplified by reference to recent experience in the United Kingdom. Here, as noted previously, the government instituted an ambitious and self-consciously deliberative 'public debate' on genetic modification in agriculture.[101] The message was clear. 'People are generally uneasy about GM.' 'The more people engage in GM issues, the harder their attitudes and the more intense their concerns.' 'The debate was welcomed and valued.' However 'there was a widespread suspicion that the debate's results would be ignored by government'. It would be a brave government which would set in motion a far-reaching experiment in public deliberation of this kind, were its hands tied at the

101 See the contribution by Maria Lee in this volume.

outset by the WTO. And it would be a diminished WTO which would act as deterrent to such public deliberation.

If the challenge posed by public opinion is complex, it is not one which can or should be avoided. There are problems on both sides of the line. Problems confront those who favour responsiveness (the institution of a dangerously limitless loophole) and those who do not (the severing of connection between governors and governed). This is an issue which has received surprisingly little attention to date, and these last remarks should be regarded as nothing more than an invitation for further reflection on a topic of immense and, in the context of the GM debate, pressing importance.

BIBLIOGRAPHY

Appleton, A.E. (2000) 'The labeling of GMO products pursuant to international trade rules', *NYU Envtl LJ* 8: 566–78.

Bickel, A. (1986) *The Least Dangerous Branch: The Supreme Court at the Bar of Politics*, 2nd edn, New Haven, CT: Yale UP.

Covelli, N. and Hohots, V. (2003) 'The health regulation of biotech foods under the WTO agreement', *Journal of International Economic Law* 6(4): 773–95.

Dunoff, J. (2007) 'Lotus eaters: reflections on the *varietals* dispute, the SPS Agreement and WTO Dispute Resolution', in G. Bermann and P. Mavroidis (eds), *WTO Law and Developing Countries*, New York, NY: CUP, 283–91.

Dunoff, J. (2001) 'The WTO in transition: of constituents, competence and coherence', *Geo. Wash. Int'l L Rev* 33: 979–1013.

Dunoff, J. (1999) 'Death of the trade regime', *European Journal of International Law* 10: 733–62.

Eisgruber, C.L. (2002a) 'Constitutional self-government and judicial review: a reply to five critics', *San Francisco Law Review* 37(1): 115–90.

Eisgruber, C.L. (2002b) *Constitutional Self-Government*, Cambridge, MA: Harvard University Press.

Ely, J.H. (1980) *Democracy and Distrust: A Theory of Judicial Review*, Cambridge, MA: Harvard University Press.

Hervey, T. (2001) 'Regulation of genetically modified products in a multi-level system of governance: science or citizens?', *RECIEL* 10(3): 321–33.

Howse, R. (2000a) 'Democracy, science, and free trade: risk regulation on trial at the World Trade Organization', *Mich. L Rev* 98(7): 2329–57.

Howse, R. (2000b) 'Adjudicative legitimacy and treaty interpretation in international trade law: the early years of WTO jurisprudence' in J.H.H. Weiler (ed.), *The EU, the WTO, and the NAFTA: Towards a Common Law of International Trade?*, Oxford: Oxford University Press, 35–69.

Howse, R. and Mavroidis, P. (2000) 'Europe's evolving regulatory strategy for GMOs: the issue of consistency with WTO law of Kine and Brine', *Fordham International Law Journal* 24: 317–70.

Hutchinson, A. (1999) 'The rule of law revisited: democracy and courts' in D. Dyzenhaus, *Recrafting the Rule of Law*, Oxford: Hart Publishing.

Jackson, J.H. (2004) 'International law status of WTO dispute settlement reports: obligation to comply or option to "buy out" ', *American Journal International Law* 98(1): 109–25.

Keohane, R. (2003) 'Global governance and democratic accountability' in D. Held and M. Koenig-Archibugi, *Taming Globalization: Frontiers of Governance*, Cambridge: Polity, 130–59.

Lee, M. (2008) *EU Regulation of GMOs: Law, Decision-making and New Technology*, Cheltenham: Edward Elgar (forthcoming).

Lee, M. (2005) *EU Environmental Law: Challenges, Change and Decision-Making*, Oxford: Hart Publishing.

Raustiala, K. (2004) 'Rethinking the sovereignty debate in international economic law', *Journal International Economic Law*, 841–78.

Regan, D. (2002) 'Regulatory Purpose and "Like Products" in Article III.4 of the GATT (with Additional Remarks on Article III.2)', *JWT*, 443–78.

Scott, J. (2007) *The Sanitary and Phytosanitary Measures Agreement: A Commentary*, Oxford: Oxford University Press.

Scott, J. (2004) 'The precautionary principle before the European Courts', in R. Macrory, *Principles in European Environmental Law*, Groningen: Europa Law Publishing.

Scott, J. (2003) 'European regulation of GMOs and the WTO', *Columbia Journal of European Law* 9(2): 213–39.

Spaangard, T. (2003) 'The marketing of GMOs: a supra-national battle over science and precaution', in *Yearbook of European Environmental Law* Vol. 3, Oxford: Oxford University Press.

Sunstein, C.R. (2006) 'Misfearing: a reply', *Harvard Law Review* 119, 1110–25.

Sunstein, C.R. (2003a) *Risk and Reason: Safety, Law and the Environment*, Cambridge: CUP.

Sunstein, C.R. (2003b) 'Beyond the precautionary principle', University of Chicago Public Law and Legal Theory Working Paper No. 38. See: <http://www.law.uchicago.edu/academics/publiclaw/>.

Sykes, A. (2002) 'Domestic regulation, sovereignty, and scientific evidence requirements: a pessimistic view', *Chi. J. Int'l L.* 3: 353.

Waldron, J. (1999) *Law and Disagreement*, Oxford: Oxford University Press.

Chapter 16

The Codex Alimentarius Commission and its food safety measures in the light of their new status*

Marielle D. Matthee

1 INTRODUCTION

At an international level, various international institutions work in the field of food safety and biotechnology. The most important food safety standard setting body is the Codex Alimentarius Commission.[1]

Established in 1962 by the decision-making organs of the Food and Agriculture Organization (FAO) and the World Health Organization (WHO), the Codex Alimentarius Commission has been attributed with the task of implementing the Joint FAO/WHO Food Standards Programme, including the task of adopting the Codex Alimentarius, a collection of international food standards and other measures. The establishment of the Codex was an answer to the expanding international food market after the Second World War and the need to create an international forum to coordinate national food regulations. As a forum with international membership, it built upon the model of already existing regional initiatives (the Codex Alimentarius Europaeus and the Latin American Food Code). In addition, the Codex Alimentarius Commission was given the task of coordinating other international food standards initiatives then being undertaken by the OECD, the UNECE and the International Dairy Federation (IDF). It was decided that the Codex Alimentarius Commission was to function under the auspices of the FAO and the WHO. As a consequence, the Codex Alimentarius Commission cannot be classified as an independent organisation, but is a subsidiary body of these organisations. Accordingly, its competences are delegated to it by its parent organisations, rather than being directly attributed to it by its member countries.

During its first 10–15 years, several scholars undertook legal analysis of the Codex Alimentarius Commission and its work (Dobbert 1969: 677–717; Alexandrowicz 1973; Leive 1976). However, and largely due to the lack of binding force attributed to the measures adopted by the Codex Alimentarius Commission, international scholars lost interest. Nonetheless, during the last decade, the Codex Alimentarius Commission has received increased attention from scholars and governmental and

* This chapter is based on research conducted in the context of a dissertation. Issues raised in this chapter are more thoroughly discussed in Masson-Matthee 2007.

1 Other institutions include the Organisation for Economic Cooperation and Development (OECD) and the United Nations Economic Commission for Europe (UNECE).

non-governmental organisations.[2] The primary reason for renewed attention are references to the work of international standard-setting bodies within the *SPS Agreement* and the *TBT Agreement*[3] and European legislation.[4] These references have given international standards, including Codex standards and recommended codes of practice and guidelines (Bossis 2005: 121–2; Muñoz 2003: 463), increased stature.

This increased status has led to a new discussion on the legitimacy of the international standard-setting bodies generally, with particular attention being focused on the Codex Alimentarius Commission due to its success in finalising and adopting a large number of standards during its 46 years of existence. This chapter therefore first examines the augmented status of Codex measures as a result of the adoption of the WTO Agreement, concentrating on the SPS Agreement and its importance in relation to food safety and/or biotechnology measures. Additionally, increased use of the Codex food safety measures by European Community institutions is considered and contributes towards a final discussion of the various legitimacy concerns arising as a result of the increased authority of the Codex Alimentarius Commission.

2 INCREASED STATUS FOR THE CODEX ALIMENTARIUS THROUGH THE SPS AGREEMENT AND EC SECONDARY LEGISLATION FOR FOOD

2.1 The Codex Alimentarius and the SPS Agreement

Measures adopted by the Codex Alimentarius Commission aim to achieve two objectives: the protection of public health and the promotion of fair practices in food trade. Codex food safety measures, the particular focus of this chapter, account for the majority of its measures aiming to protect public health.[5] Several WTO Agreements use international standards or other decisions taken by 'outside' international institutions as instruments to promote harmonisation for the purposes of the elimination of trade barriers, eg the SPS Agreement, the TBT Agreement, TRIPs, the Agreement on Preshipment Inspection and GATS. It is in the context of the SPS Agreement, however, that Codex food safety measures serve as a harmonisation tool.[6] In fact, the SPS Agreement explicitly mentions the Codex Alimentarius

2 For instance, the reaction of the European Parliament to the decision of the WTO Panel in *EC-Hormones*, EP resolution, [1997] *OJ* C222/53 (Avery, Drake and Lang 1993; Suppan 2005; Bizet 2000; Victor 2000, 118–69; Bossis 2005; Makatsch 2004; Sander 2000; Veggeland and Borgen 2005: 675–708).

3 Both agreements are annexed agreements to the WTO Agreement and entered into force in 1995.

4 In particular, as a result of the adoption of the European Parliament and Council Regulation 178/2002/EC of the European Parliament and of the Council of 28 January 2002 laying down the general principles and requirements of food law, establishing the European Food Safety Authority and laying down procedures in matters of food safety, [2002] L31/1.

5 Other measures aiming to protect public health that cannot be classified as food safety measures are, for example, Codex measures that deal with nutrition issues.

6 Under the TBT Agreement, Codex measures also serve as a harmonisation tool. However, the scope of the TBT Agreement is restricted by the scope of the SPS Agreement. This means that only technical regulations and conformity assessment procedures that are not covered by the scope of the SPS Agreement are examined under the TBT Agreement.

Commission as the international standard-setting body in the area of food safety standards *par excellence*.[7]

The SPS Agreement aims to eliminate trade barriers through harmonisation. References to international standards as harmonisation tools are found in several SPS provisions. Article 3.1 SPS Agreement lays down an obligation for WTO Members to use international standards as a basis for their national regulations. Article 3.2 contains a presumption that national regulations that are in conformity with international standards are necessary barriers to trade. Furthermore, Article 3.1 in conjunction with Article 3.3 SPS Agreement allows WTO Members to deviate from international standards. This right is, however, not unlimited but restricted by two conditions as laid down in Article 3.3 SPS.

Although most scholars agree that references within the SPS Agreement necessarily promote the status of Codex measures (Bossis 2005: 121–2; Muñoz 2003: 463), there is no agreement on what this increased status consists of. Opinions vary: on the one hand, Codex standards are viewed as benchmarks (Prévost and Van den Bossche 2005: 269), on the other, as 'safe harbour' standards (Roberts 1998: 379). However, authors generally reject the notion that Codex standards are legally binding (Scott 2004: 330; Bossis 2005: 130; Quick and Blunther 1999: 613). Several findings of the Panel and Appellate Body in *EC-Hormones* seem to support this conclusion: the explicit rejection by the Appellate Body of the argument that international standards should have binding force;[8] the Appellate Body's finding that the right to determine a higher level of protection than that laid down in international standards is an autonomous right of WTO Members instead of an exception to the obligation to apply international standards;[9] the Panel's conclusion that whatever the two conditions laid down in Article 3.3 for justifying sanitary measures aiming for a higher level of protection may mean, such measures will in any case have to be in consistency with the requirements under Article 5.[10] Despite these findings, however, the following discussion illustrates that the *de facto* binding force of Codex measures (or, at least, some of their elements) under the SPS Agreement should not be too rapidly rejected.

2.1.1 The Appellate Body's rejection of the binding force of Codex standards

The Panel in *EC-Hormones* held that the obligation to base measures on international standards means that measures of WTO Members must be in conformity

7 Annex A, provision 3(a) and 3(d): *International standards, guidelines and recommendations*. In contrast, the TBT Agreement does not explicitly mention the Codex Alimentarius Commission. However, in *EC-Sardines* (26 September 2002, WT/DS231/AB/R) the Panel and the Appellate Body concluded that the Codex Alimentarius Commission was an international standard-setting body in the context of the TBT Agreement.

8 Report of the Appellate Body, *European Communities-Measures Concerning Meat and Meat Products (Hormones)*, 16 January 1998, WT/DS26/AB/R, paras 162–5.

9 *Ibid.*, para 172.

10 Report of the WTO Panel, *EC-Measures Concerning Meat and Meat Products (Hormones)*, Complaint by the United States, 18 August 1997, WT/DS26/R/USA, para 8.83. Report of the WTO Panel, *EC-Measures Concerning Meat and Meat Products (Hormones)*, Complaint by Canada, 18 August 1997, WT/DS48/R/CAN, para 9.86. Report of the Appellate Body, *EC-Measures Concerning Meat and Meat Products (Hormones)*, 16 January 1998, WT/DS26/AB, paras 176–7.

with international standards.[11] However, the Appellate Body subsequently rejected the Panel's interpretation.[12] It held that the use of different wordings in the different provisions (Article 3.1 ('based on') versus Article 3.2 ('conformity with') SPS Agreement) is not deliberate, but the meaning of the wordings is distinct.[13] According to the Appellate Body a measure that is in conformity with a Codex standard is equally based on that same standard. However, the contrary is not necessarily the case as a measure based on a Codex standard may incorporate *only some and not all elements* of the standard.[14] The Appellate Body further states that a measure that is in conformity with an international standard would amount to the complete embodiment of that standard within the sanitary measure and, thus, for practical purposes converts it into a municipal standard. However, a measure is based on an international standard if it *stands or is founded or is built* on the standard. In rejecting the Panel's interpretation that 'based on' equals 'conformity with', the Appellate Body explicitly rejects the binding force of international standards.[15]

The Appellate Body's rejection of the binding force of the international standards is nonetheless unconvincing. For example, the deduction that the wording 'conformity with' entails binding force, whereas the wording 'based on' does not, is a rather hasty decision. Norms that must be used as a basis can still have binding force, although not necessarily with regard to all their elements. To take EC secondary legislation as an example, directives are only binding as regards the results to be achieved. The difference in wording is instead an indication of the harmonisation method to be used. For instance, the wording 'conformity with' indicates the use of the method of full harmonisation (total national conformity), whereas the wording 'based on' may indicate that partial harmonisation is acceptable. Unfortunately, the Appellate Body in *EC-Hormones* neglected this possibility and it is accordingly to be regretted that the Appellate Body was not more specific as to which of the elements found in international standards must be incorporated within the national measure.

2.1.2 The autonomous right to determine a higher level of protection

A second element that may undermine the status of the international standards under the SPS Agreement is the conclusion of the Appellate Body in *EC-Hormones* that the right to deviate from international standards (Article 3.3 of the SPS Agreement) is an autonomous right and not an exception to the obligation under Article 3.1 of the SPS Agreement.[16] This finding of the Appellate Body has led several scholars to conclude that the SPS Agreement does not oblige WTO

11 Report of the WTO Panel, *EC-Measures Concerning Meat and Meat Products (Hormones)*, Complaint by the United States, 18 August 1997, WT/DS26/R/USA, para 8.72. Report of the WTO Panel, *EC-Measures Concerning Meat and Meat Products (Hormones)*, Complaint by Canada, 18 August 1997, WT/DS48/R/CAN, para 9.75.

12 Report of the Appellate Body, *EC-Measures Concerning Meat and Meat Products (Hormones)*, 16 January 1998, WT/DS26/AB, paras 162–5.

13 *Ibid.*, para 164.

14 *Ibid.*, para 163.

15 *Ibid.*, para 165.

16 *Ibid.*, para 172.

Members to use international standards (Prévost and Van den Bossche 2005: 266). Instead, the SPS Agreement would merely 'encourage' their use (Button 2004: 62), such that the binding force that some elements of the international standards may have under Article 3.1 of the SPS Agreement does not apply. Furthermore, the conclusion of the Appellate Body determines that the burden of proof does not shift to the defendant party as the relationship between Article 3.1 and Article 3.3 is not one of rule-exception. Consequently, the complainant party must establish a *prima facie* case of inconsistency of the measures with Article 3.3 of the SPS Agreement. As a consequence, it may be easier for WTO Members who wish to depart from international standards to justify these deviations.

However, the Appellate Body has not concluded that Article 3.1 of the SPS Agreement has become obsolete as a result of the autonomous character of the right to deviate. It concludes that 'Article 3.1 of the SPS Agreement simply *excludes from its scope of application* the kinds of situations covered by Article 3.3 of that Agreement'.[17] Consequently, the scope of application of Article 3.1 is not empty, but depends on the consistency of the sanitary measures with the requirements of Article 3.3. As regards the burden of proof, its reversal does not necessarily amount to imposition of a heavier burden of proof upon the complainant party seeking to establish a *prima facie* case.[18]

2.1.3 The application of Article 5 SPS Agreement and the role of international standards therein

The third element that may affect the status of international standards is the reference to Article 5 contained in the conditions for justification of sanitary measures aiming at a higher level of protection as laid down in Article 3.3. Under Article 3.3, WTO Members are allowed to promulgate measures which result in a higher level of protection than the one that would be achieved by measures based on international standards alone. However, this right is not unlimited. It is conditioned by two criteria, of which at least one must be fulfilled: it must either be demonstrated, on the basis of the evaluation of available scientific information in conformity with the relevant provisions of the SPS Agreement, that international standards are not sufficient to achieve the appropriate level of protection; alternatively, an appropriate level of protection must be established by the WTO Member in accordance with Article 5.[19] Both the Panel and Appellate Body in *EC-Hormones* concluded that measures must, at the very least, be consistent with the requirements of Article 5 of

17 *Ibid.*, para 104 (emphasis added).

18 See on the reverse of the burden of proof under the TBT Agreement and a similar provision on the right to deviate from international standards, Horn and Weiler 2005: 273. They conclude that the evidentiary weight required is so minimal that it *de facto* nullifies the consequences of the reverse of the burden of proof. Under the SPS Agreement, the reverse of the burden of proof results in the requirement for the complainant party to establish a *prima facie* case of inconsistency with Article 5. Also in this case, it is questionable whether the reverse of the burden of proof *de facto* places a greater burden on the complainant. In *EC-Hormones*, the reference to the international scientific risk assessments on which the international standards are based sufficed to establish a *prima facie* case as regards inconsistency with Article 5.1 (Roberts 1998: 388).

19 Article 3.3 in conjunction with footnote 2 to the SPS Agreement.

the SPS Agreement in order to be considered justified under Article 3.3.[20] Article 5, however, which obliges WTO Members to base their sanitary measures on a risk assessment, also applies in cases where no international standard exists. Following the Panel's decision, some have argued that Article 3.1 simply supports WTO Members who wish to use international standards as a basis for their sanitary measures and is not, in itself, an independent obligation (Pauwlyn 1999: 656; Scott 2004: 327), determining that WTO Members are in no worse a position if they deviate from international standards than they would be were no relevant international standards to exist (such that Article 3 does not apply) (Button 2004: 62). Clearly, this would greatly diminish the status of international standards. However, these conclusions cannot be built on the Panel's interpretation of Article 3.3 alone. These conclusions are only sound if international standards do not have any bearing on the examination of the national measures' conformity with Article 5. However, the contrary is the case.

Article 5 details the obligation of WTO Members to base their measures on a scientific justification. Article 5 makes barely a mention of international standards, determining only that Members must take the risk assessment techniques of international standardising bodies into account when basing their measures on a risk assessment. The wording 'taking into account' indicates that this obligation is less stringent than obligation arising out of the wording 'based on'.[21] Furthermore, the obligation only concerns risk assessment techniques and not necessarily the regulatory outcome. However, in spite of this lack of explicit reference to international standards, other provisions of the SPS Agreement on harmonisation (in particularly Article 3.1 and 3.2) have their own influence. The presumption of consistency afforded measures that are in conformity with international norms (Article 3.2) determines that these international norms are presumed to be 'necessary' trade barriers in the context of the SPS Agreement. This has an influence on the consideration of international standards under Article 5. For instance, Article 5.1 places an obligation on WTO Members to base their measures on risk assessments. Risk assessments conducted by relevant international organisations, such as the Codex Alimentarius Commission, on which relevant international standards are based will play an important role in the examination of consistency with Article 5.1. They represent a scientific justification which the WTO is willing automatically to accept (Abdel Motaal, D. 2004: 858). The examination of the Panel in *EC-Hormones* of the EC measures' consistency with Article 5.1 demonstrates that the scientific reports brought forward by the EC are compared to these risk assessments to see whether they invalidate or contradict the latter.[22] This renders the justification of measures

20 Report of the WTO Panel, *EC-Measures Concerning Meat and Meat Products (Hormones)*, Complaint by the United States, 18 August 1997, WT/DS26/R/USA, para 8.83. Report of the WTO Panel, *EC-Measures Concerning Meat and Meat Products (Hormones)*, Complaint by Canada, 18 August 1997, WT/DS48/R/CAN, para 9.86. Report of the Appellate Body, *EC-Measures Concerning Meat and Meat Products (Hormones)*, 16 January 1998, WT/DS26/AB, paras 176–7.

21 See, eg, Report of the WTO Panel, *Japan-Measures Affecting the Importation of Apples*, 15 July 2003, WT/DS245/R, para 8.241.

22 Report of the WTO Panel, *EC-Measures Concerning Meat and Meat Products (Hormones)*, Complaint by the United States, 18 August 1997, WT/DS26/R/USA, paras 8.128 and 8.132. Report of the WTO Panel, *EC-Measures Concerning Meat and Meat Products (Hormones)*, Complaint by Canada, 18 August 1997, WT/DS48/R/CAN, paras 9.131 and 9.135. See also Roberts 1998: 393.

based on different risk assessments highly difficult; a difficulty that only increases in view of the fact that experts consulted by the Panel had also served as members of international standardisation risk assessment bodies.

International standards also play a role in the context of Article 5.6, which prohibits WTO Members from adopting measures more restrictive of trade than is necessary to achieve the appropriate level of protection. As a result of the presumption of consistency contained in Article 3.2, international standards are also considered to be 'acceptable' restrictive measures in the context of Article 5.6. This is clearly reflected in the wording 'without prejudice to paragraph 2 of Article 3' at the beginning of Article 5.6. This means that more restrictive measures will again be compared with international standards.[23] The discussion on whether a more restrictive measure is justified will concentrate on: the technical and economic feasibility of the international norm to be applied at a national level; the ability of the international norm to achieve the appropriate level of protection, and; the question of whether the national measure is significantly more restrictive.

2.2 The Codex Alimentarius and EC law on food

With the adoption of Regulation 178/2002 the Codex Alimentarius also gained in status within EC food legislation.[24] Prior to its adoption, Codex measures were only used on an *ad hoc* basis.[25] Although they had played their useful part in the initial integration phase of the EC food market,[26] the increased powers afforded to Community institutions to adopt secondary legislation on the establishment of the internal market, led to a decline in use of Codex measures; a decline that was only halted on adoption of the WTO Agreements.[27] The preliminary report of the Panel in *EC-Hormones*, in particular, highlighted the increased importance of

23 In *EC-Hormones*, the Panel did not examine Article 5.6 due to judicial economy. However, the Panel in *Australia-Salmon* (12 June 1998, WT/DS18/R) was confronted with international standards as adopted by the International Office of Epizootics (OIE). It concluded that, given the repeated reference made in the SPS Agreement to international standards, appropriate weight should be given to the relevant international standard in the context of Article 5.6 (Report of the WTO Panel, *Australia-Measures Affecting Importation of Salmon*, 12 June 1998, WT/DS18/R, para 8.180). The fact that the international standard in question (the OIE Code) played a rather limited role is due to the agreement of both the complainant and defendant party and the consulted experts that the option of evisceration proposed by the OIE Code would not be effective to achieve the appropriate level of protection as sought by Australia (see footnote 465 to paragraph 8.180 of the Panel Report).

24 Regulation (EC) No. 2002/178 of the European Parliament and of the Council of 28 January 2002 laying down the general principles and requirements of food law, establishing the European Food Safety Authority and laying down procedures in matters of food safety of 22 July 2003, [2003] *OJ* L3245/4, Article 5(3).

25 For example, Council Regulation (EEC) No. 2377/90 of 26 June 1990 laying down a Community procedure for the establishment of maximum residue limits of veterinary medicinal products in foodstuffs of animal origin of 18 August 1990, [1990] *OJ* L224/1.

26 During the 1960s and 1970s, the Codex Alimentarius Commission was more productive in establishing food standards than the institutions of the European Communities. This may be explained by the fact that, in contrast with EC secondary law, Codex standards did not have binding force without the explicit consent of its members.

27 During the negotiations preceding the adoption of the WTO Agreements, questions were asked about the possible consequences that the adoption would have on the EC food policy. See questions by Llewellyn Smith No. 1644/92, 1645/92, 1646/92, 1649/92 and 1650/92, C 333/2, 8.12.93.

the Codex Alimentarius for the EC within the context of application of the SPS Agreement,[28] and may have been the prime reason why a provision referring to international standards was inserted in Regulation 178/2002.

Under its Article 5(3), Community institutions are now obliged to take international standards into consideration when developing or adopting food law.[29] This formulation is nearly a combination of the wordings of Articles 3.1 and 3.3 of the SPS Agreement together with Article 2.4 of the TBT Agreement (an obligation similar to that of Article 3.1 SPS Agreement). Despite this resemblance, there is one fundamental difference. In contrast to the WTO provisions, Article 5(3) does not oblige the Community institutions *to base* food law on international standards. It merely obliges them *to take* the standards *into consideration*. The obligation resulting from Article 5(3) seems to be restricted to a procedural approach, instead of a substantive approach. In other words, although Codex standards must be taken into account during the legislative process, this need not necessarily be reflected in the outcome: the adopted EC food measure. Nevertheless, since the adoption of Regulation 178/2002, an increasing number of EC regulations and directives state that Codex measures have been taken into account.[30] In some cases, the consideration of Codex measures has even resulted in adjustment of EC provisions. For instance, Directive 2002/63/EC mentions in its preamble (4) that existing EC methods for sampling to control pesticides residues in and on products of plant and animal origin have been replaced by ones established by the Codex Alimentarius Commission.[31] It is not yet clear, however, whether this is primarily the result of the adoption of Regulation 178/2002, or whether it is mainly court-driven, in the sense that the mention of Codex measures aims to anticipate and avoid problems that might be faced in the context of the dispute settlement mechanism of the WTO.

2.3 The change in status of Codex measures

With EC Regulation 178/2002 and, in particular, the SPS Agreement, food safety standards adopted by the Codex Alimentarius Commission have gained a legal

28 Resolution of the European Parliament on the conclusions of the World Trade Organization Hormones Panel of 21 July 1997, [1997] *OJ* C222/53.

29 Article 5(3): 'where international standards exist or their completion is imminent, they shall be taken into consideration in the development or adaptation of food law, except where such standards or relevant parts would be an ineffective or inappropriate means for the fulfilment of the legitimate objectives of food law or where there is a scientific justification, or where they would result in a different level of protection from the one determined as appropriate in the Community'.

30 Common Position (EC) No 1/2004 of 24 February 2004 adopted by the Council with a view to adopting a regulation of the European Parliament and the Council on the hygiene of foodstuffs, [2004] *OJ* C48E/1. Commission Directive 2004/2/EC of 9 January 2004 amending Council Directives 86/362/EEC, 86/363/EEC and 90/642/EEC as regards maximum residue levels of fenamipos, [2004] *OJ* L14/15. Commission Directive 2003/113/EC of 3 December 2003 amending the Annexes to Council Directives 86/362/EEC, 86/363/EEC and 90/642/EEC as regards the fixing of maximum levels for certain pesticide residues in and on cereals, foodstuffs of animal origin and certain products of plant origin, including fruit and vegetables, [2003] *OJ* L324/24.

31 Commission Directive 2002/63/EC of 11 July 2002 repealing Directive 79/700/EC, [2002] *OJ* L187/30. Another example (although not a food safety measure) is Commission Regulation 1988/2002 of 7 November 2003 amending Regulation 2568/91 on the characteristics of olive oil and olive-pomace oil and on the relevant methods of analysis, [2003] *OJ* L295/57.

stature that was not foreseen at the inception of the Codex Alimentarius Commission. The exact measure of this change is demonstrated by comparison with the original status accorded to food standards by the Codex Alimentarius Commission. Prior to 1994 Codex standards did not have binding force unless a country had given its consent through the Codex acceptance procedure. The original acceptance procedure, abolished by the Codex Commission in 2005, foresaw three acceptance modes.[32] The first was the method of 'full acceptance', which meant that the country accepted the Codex standard in its entirety.[33] Acceptance with specific deviations further allowed countries to accept Codex standards while making reservations as regards some provisions. A third mode of acceptance was the declaration of free distribution, meaning that food products that complied with Codex standards could freely circulate on a national territory. No Codex member was obliged to accept Codex standards in any of these ways. Furthermore, only Codex standards were subject to acceptance procedure, leaving recommended codes of practice and guidelines voluntary in nature. Flexibility determined that binding acceptance of Codex standards was entirely in the hands of the Codex members, who might equally unilaterally withdraw from their given acceptance. The reluctance to accord binding force to Codex standards is demonstrated by the fact that the acceptance procedure never really functioned. Nevertheless, the existence of the procedure for 40 years allowed several developments to take place. For example, flexible procedure served to promote wide agreement on detailed norms:[34] Codex members were allowed to adapt standards to their particular circumstances, obviating the need for 'safeguard clauses' in the standards themselves, with the consequence that Codex norms are often very detailed in nature. Furthermore, Codex standards (in contrast to codes of practice and guidelines) use wordings expressing the mandatory nature of the provisions, such as the frequent use of the wording 'shall'. In total the Codex Alimentarius now consists of 216 standards, 47 codes of practice, 40 guidelines, maximum residue levels (MRLs) foresticide residues for over 360 commodities and MRLs for 47 different veterinary drugs, and seven other measures.[35]

Under the SPS Agreement, by contrast, the status of Codex standards no longer depends on national consent, but results from the mere fact that Codex standards have been adopted as a result of the Codex standard-setting procedure.[36]

32 Report of the 28th Session of the Codex Alimentarius Commission, Rome, 4–9 July 2005, ALINORM 05/28/41, para 36. Reasons for the abolition were the fact that the acceptance procedure never really worked and that it was no longer relevant in the framework of the WTO SPS and TBT Agreement (Report of the 22nd Session of the Codex Committee on General Principles, Paris, 11–15 April 2005, ALINORM 05/28/33A, paras 77 and 80).

33 Provisions 4, 5 and 6 of the 'General Principles of the Codex Alimentarius', *Procedural Manual*, 14th Edition, 2004, 31–5. Also non-Codex members could accept Codex standards provided that they were members of FAO or WHO; see Dobbert 1969: 692; Alexandrowicz 1973: 78, footnote 10.

34 See, for discussion, Report of the 5th Session of the Codex Alimentarius Commission, Rome, 20 February–1 March 1968, ALINORM 68/35, para 14.

35 The collection of Codex norms is called the Codex Alimentarius.

36 In *EC-Hormones*, in response to the issue raised by the EC that the Codex MRLs had not been adopted by consensus, the Panel decided that there are no conditions imposed by the SPS Agreement on the relevance of international standards for the purposes of Article 3. The relevance for Article 3 resulted from the fact that they existed. Report of the WTO Panel, *EC-Measures Concerning Meat and Meat Products*

Furthermore, the SPS Agreement does not differentiate between Codex standards and other Codex norms such as codes of practice and guidelines, which means that the latter will most likely have the same status under the SPS Agreement as Codex standards.[37]

3 QUESTIONS OF LEGITIMACY

Legitimacy is a prerequisite for the effective operation of an international organisation. International organisations depend on member countries for the attribution of their powers, such that Member State acceptance of the legitimacy of the organisation is essential for its continued existence. When the Codex Alimentarius Commission was established in 1962, its legitimacy was based on the need for international cooperation to adopt food standards in the light of the internationalisation of the food market and the need for the coordination of food standards activities undertaken elsewhere. The Codex Alimentarius Commission accordingly acquired a mandate to develop, adopt and publish food standards aiming to protect human health and to ensure fair practices in food trade.[38] The Codex Commission's competences, however, remain restricted since, as it is a subsidiary organ of the FAO and the WHO, it is financially dependent on its parents, its Secretariat are FAO staff and it lacks the ability to enter into agreements with other international organisations.[39] Yet, notwithstanding its subsidiary position, it has been given certain significant independent competences, the most important of which is an autonomous normative power to prepare, adopt and publish food standards without reference to its parent organisations.[40] Furthermore, the Codex Alimentarius Commission has the power to establish and amend its own standard-setting procedure and to establish subsidiary bodies.[41] It has adopted an eight-step procedure that consists of two readings and it has established an extensive

(Hormones), Complaint by the United States, 18 August 1997, WT/DS26/R/USA, para 8.69. Report of the WTO Panel, *EC-Measures Concerning Meat and Meat Products (Hormones)*, Complaint by Canada, 18 August 1997, WT/DS48/R/CAN, para 9.72. A similar issue was raised in *EC-Sardines* as regards the TBT Agreement. In this case, the Panel decided explicitly that the acceptance procedure had no relevance under the TBT Agreement. Report of the WTO Panel, *EC-Trade Descriptions of Sardines*, 29 May 2002, WT/DS231/R, para 6.5.

37 On the fact that the SPS Agreement does not differentiate between the different types of Codex measures, see response of the SPS Committee to the Codex Alimentarius Commission, G/SPS/W/86 and G/SPS/W/86/Rev. 1. See also Prévost and Van den Bossche 2005: 270.

38 See Report of the Joint FAO/WHO Conference on Food Standards, Geneva 1–5 October 1962, ALINORM 62/8.

39 Other elements that reflect the subsidiary position of the Codex Alimentarius Commission are, for example, the fact that the Statutes (the constitutional document of the Codex Alimentarius Commission) can only be amended with the approval of the FAO Conference and the WHO Health Assembly. Also the Codex Alimentarius Commission's Strategic Vision and Medium-Term Plan can only be adopted by these two governing bodies. Furthermore, the Director-Generals of the FAO and the WHO have far-reaching powers in the establishment of the agenda of the Codex Alimentarius Commission's meetings.

40 Article 1(c), (d) and (e) of the Statutes.

41 Article XI.1 of the Rules of Procedure of the Codex Alimentarius Commission. Article 7 of the Statutes of the Codex Alimentarius Commission and Article X of the Rules of Procedure.

institutional framework of subsidiary bodies involved in the standard-setting procedure. Both the adoption of the standard-setting procedure and the establishment of numerous subsidiary bodies have enabled the Codex Commission to give content, or *ratione materiae*, to its mandate. During its first 30 years, its legitimacy was hardly questioned.

Increasing status for Codex norms has strengthened the practical authority of the Codex Commission, but has likewise led numerous scholars to question the legitimacy of the Codex Alimentarius Commission to adopt such standards (Horn and Weiler 2005: 255; Romi 2001: 201–13; Shapiro 2002: 451–3; Bodansky 1999: 596–624). Similarly, the FAO and WHO have commissioned an evaluation of the Joint FAO/WHO Food Standards Programme to improve its operation. The following examines the institutional and procedural framework of the Codex Alimentarius Commission, in order to investigate its legitimacy.

3.1 The institutional structure and delegation of powers

The Codex Alimentarius Commission is assisted in standard-setting by various other bodies and institutions. It has delegated powers to prepare standards to three types of bodies: subsidiary codex bodies; other international institutions; and expert bodies. Its relations with each type of body differ, leading to distinct concerns raised as regards the delegation of powers.

3.1.1 Subsidiary Codex bodies

The Codex Alimentarius Commission is assisted by a Secretariat responsible for day-to-day work and an Executive Committee which acts as the executive organ of the Commission between sessions. The Executive Committee was named in the first version of the Codex Statutes: it was accordingly established at the explicit command of the FAO and the WHO. Secretariat members are FAO staff and the secretariat is financially dependent on this latter parent organisation. Alongside these two subsidiary bodies, Article 7 of the Codex Statutes allow the Codex Commission to establish other subsidiary bodies, as it deems necessary to accomplish its tasks and subject to the availability of funds. The Codex Alimentarius Commission has used this competence, strengthening its position as an international standard-setting body, using the 'host country' construction to circumvent its financial dependence on its parent organisations and the need for their approval for the establishment of these bodies. The 'host country' construction means that one Codex member is responsible for financing, administering and organising the meetings of a particular subsidiary body. In return, the Codex member is granted with the Chair of the subsidiary body in question, an advantage that has not been neglected by Codex members (Lu 1970: 202). The host country construction has provided a solid basis for the operation of Codex Committees. It has ensured their continuity. In total, the Codex Alimentarius Commission is currently assisted by 22 subsidiary bodies (nine general Codex Committees responsible for preparation of 'horizontal' provisions applicable to more than one commodity, six commodity Codex Committees preparing food standards for one commodity, one *ad hoc* Task Force and six Codex Coordinating Committees[42]).

Codex Committees play an important part in the standard-setting procedure. They are responsible for the preparation of draft (proposed) standards (step 4 and/or step 7 of the Codex standard-setting procedure) to be submitted for approval by the Codex Alimentarius Commission (step 5 and/or step 8). Furthermore, Codex Committees, in particular general Codex Committees, consist of members with a high level of expertise since Rule X.4 of the Codex Rules of Procedure requires that committee members must be specialists in the relevant field. Likewise, they maintain contact with consulted expert bodies. However, this delegation of tasks to strong, competent and independent bodies has also led to a 'de-centralisation' of the standard-setting process. The broadly defined terms of reference of the Codex Committees and their competence to propose new work may impede the coherent operation of the Codex Alimentarius Commission and its subsidiary bodies if not carefully supervised and coordinated.[43]

The Codex Alimentarius Commission may intervene to supervise and coordinate committee activities at three points during the standard-setting procedure: at step 1 (the approval of new work), at step 5 (during the first reading of the draft proposed standards), and at step 8 (during the second final reading). The Codex Alimentarius Commission is assisted in this task by the Executive Committee, which, in line with the new Rules of Procedure (2004), must critically review the proposals for new activity and give its advisory opinion to the Commission. Proposals for new activity must be accompanied by a 'project document', satisfy several criteria laid down in the 'Criteria for establishing work priorities', and must also be relevant to the Codex strategic objectives.[44] The latter requirements aim to ensure that proposed new activity is in line with the overall activities undertaken by the Codex Alimentarius Commission in order to avoid fragmentation. This new obligation may strengthen Commission oversight over Codex Committees; nonetheless, initiation or revision of MRLs for pesticides, veterinary drugs and food additives and the maximum levels (MLs) for contaminants is excluded from the scope of this obligation. Furthermore, the Codex Procedural Manual does not comprehensively regulate division of

42 Task Forces differ from Codex Committees as they are automatically dissolved once they have finished their task. Codex coordinating committees are responsible for the preparation of regional Codex standards (regional standards are adopted less and less) and the exchange of information between the members of a particular region.

43 See *Terms of Reference of the Codex Committees as contained in the Procedural Manual*, 15th Edition, 2005: 122–43. The general terms of reference of Codex Committees (Guidelines for Codex Committees) include the task to establish their own working priorities (*Working Principles for Risk Analysis for Application in the Framework of the Codex Alimentarius, Procedural Manual*, 15th edition, 2005: 49). The majority of proposals to initiate the preparation of a standard occur at Committee level and are submitted for approval to the Codex Alimentarius Commission. During the 20th Session of the Codex Alimentarius Commission, the idea was raised that the Codex Alimentarius Commission should play a greater role in the supervision of new work as proposed by the Codex Committees (Report of the 20th Session of the Joint FAO/WHO Codex Alimentarius Commission, Geneva, 28 June–7 July 1993 ALINORM 93/40, para 75). Also the overlap of activities undertaken by the Committees was a topic of concern (Report of the evaluation of the Codex Alimentarius and other FAO and WHO food standards work, ALINORM 03/25/3, para 116).

44 Provisions 2 and 3 of Part 2 of the *Working Principles for Risk Analysis for Application in the Framework of the Codex Alimentarius, Procedural Manual*, 15th edition, 2005: 21.

activities between Codex Committees, detailing relations to be maintained between General Codex Committees and Commodity Codex Committees, but remaining silent on the relationships established between the different General Codex Committees.

3.1.2 Other international organisations

The Codex Alimentarius Commission also delegates the preparation of draft proposed standards to other international organisations, which are themselves standard-setting bodies. For example, the 'Procedures for the Elaboration of Codex standards and related texts' state that recommendations of the International Dairy Federation (IDF), an international standard-setting body for dairy products, shall be distributed during step 2 of the elaboration of Codex measures related to milk and milk products (preparation of the proposed draft standard and the consultation of expert bodies). Likewise, a provision contained in the terms of reference of the Codex Committee on Fresh Fruits and Vegetables (a Codex commodity Committee) states that the Committee is to cooperate with a working party of the United Nations Economic Commission for Europe (UNECE) working on the standardisation of Perishable Products. As the Codex Alimentarius Commission does not have the competence to enter into agreements with other international organisations, the delegation of tasks during the standard-setting procedure is a useful instrument to establish strong relations with these organisations. However, these organisations are not bound by the internal rules of the Codex Alimentarius Commission. They have different aims and priorities, a different membership, and different working procedures. For instance, the IDF is a non-governmental organisation composed of representatives of the dairy industry. Likewise, the membership of the UNECE is limited to the European Members of the United Nations, the US, Canada, Switzerland and Israel.[45]

In 2005, the Codex Alimentarius Commission adopted 'Guidelines on co-operation with other international intergovernmental organisations',[46] stating that the Codex Alimentarius Commission, or a subsidiary body, may entrust the initial drafting of a proposed draft standard to other intergovernmental organisations and explicitly referring to the international organisations as mentioned in Annex A of the SPS Agreement: the Office of Epizootics (OIE) and the international organisation operating in the framework of the International Plant Protection Convention (IPPC). They require, however, that these international organisations must have the same principles of membership (membership must be open to members of the FAO and the WHO) and the same standard-setting principles as the Codex. These guidelines, however, only apply to cooperation with international *governmental* organisations and do not cover cooperation with the non-governmental IDF or the UNECE, both of whom still perform material functions within Codex Alimentarius activities. Consequently, the guidelines only respond partly to the need to adequately regulate cooperation with other organisations. Equally, the relationship of the guidelines

45 Terms of Reference of the Economic Commission for Europe, United Nations, E/ECE/778/Rev. 3.

46 Report of the 28th Session of the Codex Alimentarius Commission, Rome 4–9 July 2005, ALINORM 05/28/41, paras 43–4 and Appendix IV.

vis-à-vis explicit references to other international organisations elsewhere in the Codex Procedural Manual remains unclear and potentially contradictory: UNECE, for example, does not have the same principles of membership as the Codex Alimentarius Commission.

3.1.3 Expert bodies

The third category of bodies involved in the Codex standard-setting procedure are expert bodies. The relationship maintained between these expert bodies, on the one hand, and the Codex Commission and its subsidiary bodies, on the other, is classified as one of risk assessors versus risk managers.[47] The separation between the risk assessors and the risk managers is effected by virtue of the fact that expert bodies are not subsidiary bodies of the Codex Alimentarius Commission, but fall under the direct responsibility of the FAO and the WHO. The most frequently consulted expert bodies are the Joint FAO/WHO Expert Committee on Food Additives (JECFA), the Joint FAO/WHO Meeting on Pesticide Residues (JMPR), and the Joint FAO/WHO Expert Meetings on Microbiological Risk Assessment (JEMRA). The expert bodies have an advisory role and, in the context of the standard-setting procedure, they work at the request of the Codex Alimentarius Commission and its subsidiary bodies.[48]

Codex food safety provisions, however, are often trans-scientific in nature, covering issues and dealing with questions that cannot be addressed by scientists alone. In order to arrive at conclusions useful for risk management purposes, risk assessments are based on certain assumptions and decisions that are often political in nature. In the context of the Codex Alimentarius Commission, the definition of these assumptions and decisions is referred to as 'risk assessment policy'. The 'Definitions for the purposes of the Codex Alimentarius' defines risk assessment policy as 'documented guidelines for scientific judgement and policy choices to be applied at appropriate decision points during risk assessment'.[49] In the past several concerns have been expressed as regards the danger that expert bodies or members of the expert bodies may exceed their competences as scientific advisors and that the scientific integrity of their work might be doubted. For example, the mandate given to expert bodies has not always been clearly defined by the Codex Committee in its capacity as risk manager.[50] In several cases, this has resulted in the blurring of scientific and political considerations.[51] As a

47 Consideration 3 of the *Working Principles for Risk Analysis for Application in the Framework of the Codex Alimentarius, Procedural Manual*, 15th Edition, 2005: 101.

48 In addition to their consultations for the Codex Alimentarius Commission, these expert bodies may also undertake activities at the request of the FAO and the WHO or their member countries.

49 *Working Principles for Risk Analysis for Application in the Framework of the Codex Alimentarius, Procedural Manual*, 15th Edition, 2005: 45.

50 See Consultant's report, Review of the Working Procedures of the Joint FAO/WHO Meeting on Pesticide Residues (JMPR), 2002: 38. The lack of procedural rules to ensure independence of expert members has led to difficulties when ensuring the scientific integrity of risk assessment procedures. Working procedures have been adopted by the FAO and the WHO to respond to this concern.

51 See Consultant's report, Review of the Working Procedures of the Joint FAO/WHO Meeting on Pesticide Residues (JMPR), 2002: 38.

consequence, the expert bodies have often been left to take political decisions by themselves.[52] The 'Working Principles for Risk Analysis for Application in the Framework of the Codex Alimentarius' adopted during the Alimentarius Commission of 2003, address this concern by clearly defining the responsibilities of expert bodies as risk assessors and those of the Codex Committees as risk managers. The Principles explicitly state that definition of the risk assessment policy is the responsibility of the risk manager.[53] However, despite this codification of responsibilities, practical interaction between expert bodies and the Codex Committees is still not satisfactory.[54] A more direct degree of interaction between expert bodies and the responsible Codex Committees could be achieved through joint sessions attended by both organs in order to discuss the preliminary reports of the expert bodies.

3.2 The standard-setting procedure

As noted, Codex members are no longer free to choose to accept Codex standards following their adoption and are consequently far more eager to ensure that the standard to be adopted fully corresponds with their particular concerns during the standard-setting procedure. Accordingly, a question now arises as to whether the Codex standard-setting procedure is adequate to ensure that all concerns are taken into consideration. Three particular procedural elements, which prove to be determinative in relation to enhanced Codex member input, are considered in this section: decision making by consensus, impartial participation, and transparency.

3.2.1 Consensus

It has always been common practice for the Codex Alimentarius Commission to adopt standards and other related texts by consensus. However, the adoption of the WTO Agreements and the increased status of Codex standards have led to a 'politicisation' of the Codex standard-setting procedure and consensus has become harder to achieve.[55] On several occasions, the Codex Alimentarius Commission has proceeded to a vote in order to overcome the impasse.[56] After numerous Codex members expressed their resentment about this mode of adopting standards, the Rules of Procedure of the Codex Alimentarius Commission were amended to emphasise the

52 See Consultant's report, Review of the Working Procedures of the Joint FAO/WHO Meeting on Pesticide Residues (JMPR), 2002: 38.

53 Consideration 13, *Working Principles for Risk Analysis for Application in the Framework of the Codex Alimentarius, Procedural Manual*, 15th Edition, 2005: 102.

54 Report of the FAO/WHO electronic forum on the provision of scientific advice to Codex and Member countries, February 2004: 18–19 and 38. Report of a Joint FAO/WHO Workshop, 'Provision of Scientific Advice to Codex and Member countries', WHO Headquarters, Geneva, 27–29 January 2004: 20.

55 On the politicisation of the Codex standard-setting procedure, see Roberts, Orden and Josling 2004: 341; Poli 2004: 613–30; Braithwaite and Drahos 2000: 403; Veggeland and Borgen 2005: 675–708; Cosbey 2000: 9.

56 The adoption of the MRLs for five growth hormones (the subject of *EC-Hormones*) occurred by vote and were adopted by a small majority of 33 votes in favour, 29 votes against and seven abstentions (Report of the 21st Session of the Joint FAO/WHO Codex Alimentarius Commission, Rome, 3–8 July 1995, ALINORM 95/37, para 45).

importance of taking decisions by consensus and to discourage voting.[57] However, under the amended Rules of Procedure, decision making by vote is still possible. Although the menace of a voting procedure is not in itself a negative aspect and may contribute to the overcoming of deadlock, the Rules of Procedure fail to indicate when efforts to reach consensus have failed and when the Codex Alimentarius Commission must proceed to a vote: there is no definition of consensus and no general agreement on what consensus means. Equally, other problems arise: for example, in the case of a vote final decisions are taken by simple majority, rather than by, say, a two-thirds majority, which might be considered more appropriate to a transition from consensus to vote, and which is a voting method already in use within the Codex procedures (for amendment of the Agenda of Codex Alimentarius Commission meetings' two-thirds majority[58]). Likewise, under the current rules, final decision making by vote could, in principle, be triggered at the request of only one Codex member;[59] a provision that is potentially further destructive of consensus.

3.2.2 Participation

The adoption of the WTO Agreements has also led to an increased number both of Codex members and of state representatives per delegation attending the Codex meetings (Veggeland and Borgen 2005: 687–8). Likewise, the number of non-governmental organisations attending the meetings has equally increased (Spencer 1998: 179). However, attention has likewise been drawn to the dominant influence of developed Codex members and industry-interest groups *vis-à-vis* developing Codex members and public-interests or NGOs (Avery, Drake and Lang 1993: 1; Spencer 1998: 179; Salter 1988: 70–1 and 74; Rosman 1993: 346; Leive 1976: 435–6; Victor 1997: 198–201; McCrea 2000: 155; Suppan 2005).

Developing Codex members often lack the financial resources to attend all relevant Codex meetings.[60] However, even when they do attend, some developing Codex members lack the necessary experience and expertise to participate effectively. In the absence of a modern domestic institutional and legal infrastructure, it is hard for national representatives to assess whether the standard under preparation is appropriate to their circumstances.[61] Furthermore, although *de jure* all Codex members have equal participation rights, the allocation of tasks among Codex members during the standard-setting procedure illustrates that the *de facto* participation opportunities are not evenly balanced. For example, preparation of

57 Report of the 23rd Session of the Joint FAO/WHO Codex Alimentarius Commission, Rome 28 June–3 July 1999, ALINORM 99/37, paras 61–2. The new Rule XII.2 of the Rules of Procedure states: '[t]he Commission shall make every effort to reach agreement on the adoption or amendment of standards by consensus. Decisions to adopt or amend standards may be taken by voting only if such efforts to reach consensus have failed' (*Procedural Manual*, 15th Edition, 2005: 16).

58 Rule VII.6 of the Rules of Procedure, *Procedural Manual*, 15th Edition, 2005: 11.

59 The voting procedure of the Draft Revised Standard on Mineral Waters illustrates that this has happened in practice.

60 Given the high number of subsidiary bodies, the number of meetings taking place during one year is large.

61 Marovatsanga 2000: 138: '[u]nfortunately, many developing countries with economies in transition lack the necessary food control infrastructure to implement both strategy and programs to protect their consumers and to overcome their disadvantaged status in the international trade in food'.

discussion papers or the drafting of proposed standards is more frequently attributed to developed Codex members (during step 2 of the procedure). Likewise, the host-country construction puts developed Codex members in an advantageous position as most subsidiary Codex bodies are financed and hosted by developed Codex members and their meetings take place in Europe and North America. This not only means that these subsidiary bodies are chaired by representatives from developed Codex members, but also that developing Codex members have higher travel costs.

Several efforts have been made to stimulate the active participation of developing Codex members. For instance, some developed Codex members responsible for the hosting of Codex Committee meetings have organised the co-chairing of these meetings by developing Codex members. In other words, while the developed Codex member still provides financial resources, the meeting takes place in the country of the developing Codex member.[62] Furthermore, the FAO and the WHO have launched the 'Trust Fund for the participation of developing countries and countries in transition in the work of the Codex Alimentarius Commission'. The trust fund aims to assist developing Codex members to attend and actively participate in the Codex meetings by contributing to their travel costs and by the development of capacity-building activities designed to enhance the scientific and technical expertise of the participants.

Equally, however, industry INGOs find themselves in a more advantageous position than public-interest INGOs, largely by virtue of their different backgrounds and circumstances. As promoters of food production technology, industry INGOs possess a high level of expertise in the area and can draw on plentiful information sources. Consequently, they are considered useful advisors and contributors to the standard-setting procedure. Furthermore, industry INGOs often have the financial resources that allow them to attend the relevant Codex meetings and to lobby actively. Public-interests INGOs, on the other hand, may lack expertise and/or sufficient funding to participate in the Codex meetings effectively (Van der Tweel 1993: 39; Avery, Drake and Lang 1993: 5; McCrea 2000: 153). From the beginning of the 1990s, the Codex Alimentarius Commission has highlighted the importance of increasing the degree of participation of consumer organisations in the Codex with the consequence that the position of the public-interests INGOs has improved slightly (Van der Tweel 1993: 38–9; Victor 1997: 201). However, the main responsibility to increase the participation of public-interests groups is placed upon Codex members[63] who have been encouraged to establish national Codex consultative committees, within which views of interested parties integrated within national positions.[64] The Codex Alimentarius Commission is first and foremost concerned with

62 Examples are the meeting of the Codex Committee for Food Additives and Contaminants in China (2000) and in Tanzania (2003), the Codex Committee on Food Hygiene in Thailand (2001), the Codex Committee for Residues of Veterinary Drugs in Foods (CCRVDF) in Mexico (2006) and the Codex Committee on Pesticide Residues in India (2004) and Brazil (2006).

63 See, Report of the 20th Session of the Joint FAO/WHO Codex Alimentarius Commission, Geneva, 28 June–7 July 1993 ALINORM 93/40, para 52.

64 Report of the 21st Session of the Joint FAO/WHO Codex Alimentarius Commission, Rome, 3–8 July 1995, ALINORM 95/37, para 90. This was also recommended during the 1991 FAO/WHO Conference on Food Standards, Chemicals in Food and Food Trade. See Avery, Drake and Lang 1993: 38.

promoting the active participation of all its members within its procedures. Only then is it concerned with improving participation for observers, clearly reflecting the state-oriented character of the institution.

3.2.3 Transparency

Transparency is an important instrument to optimise stakeholder participation. During the 1990s, the Secretariat of the Codex Alimentarius Commission undertook important steps to ensure access to Codex documents through publication on their internet-site (McCrea 2000: 151). Nevertheless, several concerns as regards transparency have arisen. First, a discussion on the improvement of the structure and the presentation of the Procedural Manual is now taking place.[65] The Procedural Manual, a codification of most of the internal rules of the Codex, is designed to assist member governments to participate effectively in the work of the Codex Alimentarius Commission.[66] The current version of the Procedural Manual, however, clearly reflects the *ad hoc* nature of the codification of different practices and agreements over the years. Several parts have become incomplete, obsolete, or are even inconsistent.

Second, not all bodies involved in the standard-setting procedure are open to (all) Codex members and questions of transparency accordingly arisen in relation to certain of the expert bodies.[67] The need for clear and transparent reporting has been emphasised.[68] Equally, the degree of openness of the Executive Committee has been doubted since it currently only includes a limited number of Codex members. However, since it is now restricted to advisory tasks,[69] transparency has not been sought through enlarged membership but through other means, such as webcasting of its meetings or the establishment of listening rooms.[70] Third, preparatory documents for subsidiary Codex committee meetings have sometimes not been circulated prior to meetings, or have been circulated too late,[71] leaving Codex members with little time for reflection. Furthermore, the late distribution of documents makes it difficult for the delegations to discuss the issues with interest groups

65 Report of the 22nd Session of the Codex Committee on General Principles, Paris, 11–15 April 2005, ALINORM 05/28/33A, paras 98–105.

66 See consideration 1 of the Introduction to *Working Principles for Risk Analysis for Application in the Framework of the Codex Alimentarius, Procedural Manual*, 15th Edition, 2005: 1.

67 Report of the Eleventh Session of the Codex Committee on General Principles, ALINORM 95/33, 1994, para 35: '[t]he Committee proposed that the Commission should advise FAO and WHO of the desire of this Committee that a greater transparency should be incorporated into the working procedures of expert groups . . .' Report of the evaluation of the Codex Alimentarius and other FAO and WHO food standards work, ALINORM 03/25/3, paras 193–4.

68 Considerations 4 and 6 of the *Working Principles for Risk Analysis for Application in the Framework of the Codex Alimentarius, Procedural Manual*, 15th Edition, 2005: 101.

69 Prior to 2004, the Executive Committee could take decisions as regards the initiation of standards and advancing standards beyond step 5 of the procedure.

70 Report of the 19th (Extraordinary) Session of the Codex Committee on General Principles, Paris, 17–21 November 2003, ALINORM 04/27/33, paras 40–5.

71 See for example, the explanations with regard to the proposed draft guidelines for evaluating acceptable methods of analysis as contained in paragraph 20 of the Report of the 24th Session of CCMAS, ALINORM 03/23, 2002 or Report of the 25th Session of the CCMAS, ALINORM 04/27/23, 2004, para 8. See also McCrea 2000: 165.

at a national level (McCrea 2000: 165). Fourth, complaints are sometimes heard about late distribution of translated documents and the quality of translation. As a large number of developing Codex members do not have English as first language this is a serious concern.[72]

4 CONCLUSIONS

The reference to Codex measures contained in Article 3 of the SPS Agreement has greatly augmented their status. This chapter argues that Codex measures can be classified as *de facto* legally binding. This conclusion is based on the mode in which WTO dispute Panels apply standards within the ambit of Articles 3 and 5 SPS. This binding force, however, is limited only to various elements within the standards and does not apply to the standards as a whole. Unfortunately, the WTO Appellate Body has failed clearly to define which elements of international standards must form the basis for national standards leaving us with a considerable degree of legal uncertainty. Given the restricted objective of the SPS Agreement (trade liberalisation) *vis-à-vis* the Codex standards themselves (food safety protection and trade liberalisation), it would be logical that the references to standards made in the SPS Agreement primarily concern those elements within the standards which aim to ensure that trade is restricted by sanitary concerns as little as is possible.

The increased status of Codex measures, both in the SPS Agreement, as well as within EC regulation, represents a considerable departure to that prior to 1994, when standards became binding on individual member governments only in the light of their explicit acceptance. Codex members were afforded a large degree of discretion and might adapt international standards freely to suit their own circumstances. Since the introduction of the SPS regime, Codex members no longer have a say in whether measures will have binding force; instead, binding force now results from the adoption of Codex measures by the Codex Alimentarius Commission.

The increased importance of Codex measures has likewise augmented the authority of the Codex Alimentarius Commission. However, until very recently the Codex Alimentarius Commission still functioned on the basis of its old institutional and procedural structure. As a result, scholars and INGOs have questioned its legitimacy at a number of levels: the delegation of powers to subsidiary bodies could, in the absence of effective supervision, lead to inconsistency in the functioning of the Codex; the delegation of tasks to 'external' international standard-setting institutions, who are not bound by the internal rules of the Codex Alimentarius Commission, raises various concerns; mandates for expert body scientific are not always clearly defined; final decision making within the Codex Alimentarius Commission is not always perceived to be legitimate, especially in the light of recent strains on the long-standing consensus procedure; developed member countries and industry INGOs are felt to dominate the standard-setting procedure at

72 Report of the 22nd Session of the Joint FAO/WHO Codex Alimentarius Commission, Geneva, 23–28 June 1997, ALINORM 97/37, para 193. See also McCrea 2000: 165: '[e]ven providing adequate translations in Spanish, an official Codex language, was a problem at the 1998 session [of the CCHFSDU], and thereby excluded effective participation from Spanish-speaking delegations'.

the expense of developing countries and public interest groups; finally, transparency of the standard-setting procedure and access to relevant documents is not always adequately ensured.

Recent developments, including the evaluation of the Codex Alimentarius Commission conducted by its parent organisations, have addressed these concerns. As a result, considerable improvements have been made: a trust fund seeking to enhance the participation of developing Codex members, the codification a principle of consensual decision making, the codification of the responsibilities of risk assessors (expert bodies) and risk managers (subsidiary Codex bodies) and the imposition of a duty upon the Executive Committee to review critically work undertaken by Codex bodies.

Nonetheless, recent reform efforts may also be criticised at a fundamental level. Reforms are based on an 'issue-oriented' approach, addressing specific concerns in the short run, but not guaranteeing the long-term legitimacy of the Codex Alimentarius Commission. A more structural approach is required which would pay greater attention to the functioning of the fundamental mechanisms that ensure operation of the Codex Alimentarius Commission: the Procedural Manual (codified internal rules) and a Codex standard-setting procedure that is based on two readings of the proposed standards. As codification of internal rules, the Procedural Manual is a crucial instrument to ensure the internal and external transparency of the Codex Alimentarius Commission and its standard-setting procedure and to foster trust in its operation. However, it is not one of the best examples of clarity. The *ad hoc* codification of internal rules over the years, and the various modifications made to them, have left parts of it incoherent, obsolete or incomplete. Even recent reform-oriented modifications have only added to fragmentation. Clearly, thorough revision of the Procedural Manual is a top priority on the road to legitimacy. Likewise, a clearer definition of the two readings of the standard-setting procedure, and the role of the Codex Alimentarius Commission within them, might optimise the structure of accountability of subsidiary and external bodies *vis-à-vis* the Codex Alimentarius Commission.

BIBLIOGRAPHY

Abdel Motaal, D. (2004) 'The "multilateral scientific consensus" and the World Trade Organization', *Journal of World Trade* 38(5): 855–76.

Alexandrowicz, C.H. (1973) *The Law-Making Functions of the Specialised Agencies of the United Nations*, Sydney: Angus and Robertson.

Avery, N., Drake, M. and Lang, T. (1993) *Cracking the Codex*, London: National Food Alliance (a study undertaken for Consumers International).

Bizet, J. (2000) 'Sécurité alimentaire: le Codex Alimentarius', *Les Rapports du Sénat* 1999–2000 – No. 450.

Bodansky, D. (1999) 'The legitimacy of international governance: a coming challenge for international environmental law?', *The American Journal of International Law* 93(3): 596–624.

Bossis, G. (2005) *La sécurité sanitaire des aliments en droit international et communautaire. Rapports croisés et perspectives d'harmonisation*, Bruxelles: Bruylant.

Braithwaite, J. and Drahos, P. (2000) *Global Business Regulation*, Cambridge: Cambridge University Press.

Button, C. (2004) *The Power to Protect. Trade, Health and Uncertainty in the WTO*, Oxford: Hart Publishing.

Codex Alimentarius Commission (2005) *Working Principles for Risk Analysis for Application in the Framework of the Codex Alimentarius, Procedural Manual*, 15th Edition.

Cosbey, A. (2000) *A Force Evolution? The Codex Alimentarius Commission, Scientific Uncertainty and the Precautionary Principle*, Canada: International Institute for Sustainable Development.

Dobbert, J.P. (1969) 'Le Codex Alimentarius vers une nouvelle méthode de réglementation internationale', *XV Annuaire Français de Droit International* 15: 677–717.

Dobbert, J.P. (1971) 'Decisions of international organizations-effectiveness in Member States. Some aspects of the law and practice of FAO', in S.M. Schwebel (ed.), *The Effectiveness of International Decisions 1971 – Papers of a conference of The American Society of International Law and the Proceedings of the conference*, Leyden: A.W. Sijthoff, 206–76.

Horn, H. and Weiler, J.H.H. (2005) 'European Communities – trade description of sardines: textualism and its discontent', in H. Horn and P. Mavroidis (eds), *The WTO Case Law of 2002*, Cambridge: Cambridge University Press, 248–75.

Leive, D.L. (1976) *International Regulatory Regimes*, Lexington: Lexington Books.

Lu, F.C. (1970) 'The joint FAO/WHO food standards programme and the Codex Alimentarius', *WHO Chronicle* 24(5): 198–205.

Makatsch, T. (2004) *Gesundheitsschutz im Recht der Welthandelsorganisation (WTO). Die WTO und das SPS-Ubereinkommen im lichte von Wissenschaftlichkeit, Verrechtlichung und Harmonisierung*, Berlin: Duncker & Humblot.

Marovatsanga, L.T. (2000) 'The Need for Developing Countries to Improve National Infrastructure to Contribute to International Standards', in N. Rees and D. Watson (eds.), *International Standards for Food Safety*, Gaithersburg, Maryland: Aspen Publishers, 137–48.

Masson-Matthee, M. (2007), *The Codex Alimentarius Commission and its Standards*, The Hague: T.M.C. Asser Press.

McCrea, D. (2000) 'A view from Consumers', in N. Rees and D. Watson (eds), *International Standards for Food Safety*, Gaithersburg, Maryland: Aspen Publishers, 149–68.

Muñoz, R. (2003) 'La Communauté entre les mains des normes internationales: les conséquences de la décision "Sardines" au sein de l'OMC', *Revue du Droit de l'Union Européenne* 2: 457–84.

Pauwlyn, J. (1999) 'The WTO Agreement on Sanitary and Phytosanitary (SPS) Measures as applied in the first three SPS disputes. EC-Hormones, Australia-Salmon and Japan-Varietals', *Journal of International Economic Law*, 641–4.

Poli, S. (2004) 'The European Community and the Adoption of International Food Standards within the Codex Alimentarius Commission', *European Law Journal* 10(5): 613–30.

Prévost, D. and Bossche, P. Van den (2005) 'The agreement on sanitary and phytosanitary measures', in P.F.J. Macrory, A.E. Appleton and M.G. Plummer (eds), *The World Trade Organization: legal, economic and political analysis, Vol I*, New York: Springer, 231–370.

Quick, R. and Blunther, A. (1999) 'Has the Appellate Body erred? An appraisal and criticism of the ruling in the WTO hormones case', *Journal of International Economic Law*, 603–39.

Roberts, D. (1998) 'Preliminary assessment of the effects of the WTO Agreement on Sanitary and Phytosanitary Trade Regulations', *Journal of International Economic Law* 1: 377–405.

Roberts, D., Orden, D. and Josling, T. (2004) 'Sanitary and phytosanitary barriers to agricultural trade: progress, prospects, and implications for developing countries', in M. Ingco and A. Winters (eds), *Agriculture and the New Trade Agenda*, Cambridge: Cambridge University Press, 329–58.

Romi, R. (2001) 'Codex Alimentarius: de l'ambivalence à l'ambiguité', *Revue Juridique de l'Environnement* 2: 201–13.

Rosman, L. (1993) 'Public participation in international pesticide regulation: when the Codex Commission decides, who will listen?', *Virginia Environmental Law Journal* 12: 329–65.

Salter, L. (1988) *Mandated Science, Science and Scientists in the Making of Standards*, Dordrecht: Kluwer Academic Publishers.

Sander, G. (2000) 'Gesundheitsschutz in der WTO – eine neue Bedeutung des Codex Alimentarius im Lebensmittelrecht?', *Zeitschrift für Europarechtliche Studien* 3(3): 335–75.

Scott, J. (2004) 'International trade and environmental governance: relating rules (and standards) in the EU and the WTO', *European Journal of International Law* 15(2): 307–54.

Shapiro, S.A. (2002) 'International Trade Agreements, Regulatory Protection, and Public Accountability', *Administrative Law Review* 54: 451–3.

Shubber, S. (1972) 'The Codex Alimentarius Commission under international law', *International and Comparative Law Quarterly* 21: 631–55.

Spencer, G.E., Jahncke, M.L. and Cole, E.A. (1998) 'Effects of Codex and GATT', *Food Control* 9(2–3): 177–82.

Suppan, S. (2005) *Governance in the Codex Alimentarius Commission*, London: Consumers International.

Tweel, C.C. van der (1993) *Een nieuw GATT-Verdrag en de Codex Alimentarius. Een bestuurskundig onderzoek naar internationale beleidsvorming en nationale beleidsruimte*, Leiden: Rijksuniversiteit Leiden.

Veggeland, F. and Borgen, S.O. (2005) 'Negotiating international food standards: the World Trade Organization's impact on the Codex Alimentarius Commission', *Governance: An International Journal of Policy, Administration, and Institutions* 18(4): 675–708.

Victor, D.G. (2000) 'Risk management and the world trading system: regulating international trade distortions caused by national sanitary and phytosanitary policies', in National Research Council (ed.), *Incorporating Science, Economics, and Sociology in Developing Sanitary and Phytosanitary Standards in International Trade: Proceedings of a Conference*, Washington DC: National Academies Press, 118–69.

Victor, D.G. (1997) *Effective Multilateral Regulation of Industrial Activity: Institutions for Policing and Adjusting Binding and Nonbinding Legal Commitments*, PhD Thesis, Harvard University: Massachusetts Institute of Technology.

Part IV

Improving the legitimacy and credibility of risk regulation: science, procedures, participation and deliberation

Chapter 17

Three intimate tales of law and science: hope, despair and transcendence

Michelle Everson

1 INTRODUCTION

Forms of scientific uncertainty, and especially those forms of uncertainty manifest within supranational and international regimes of risk governance, have resulted in much and urgent academic questioning of the appropriate relationship that should now be maintained between law and science. Within post-national polities, generally characterised by normative constraints on action,[1] a lack of daily political direction, and a consequent degree of reliance upon material (or factual) proof-bases for decision making, science necessarily becomes a vital informative element within legal process: either proving determinative within jurisprudential appreciation of material fact; or, by contrast, being recognised as a privileged actor within a technocratic executive, which demands a special degree of protection for itself within legal schemes of institutional design. However, such science-based or science-shaped governance regimes are also highly vulnerable when, to use the vernacular, 'the science runs out'.[2] The law of governance is faced with a similar challenge: if, under conditions of scientific uncertainty, material fact can no longer be ascertained, which if any role does scientific rationality still have to play within legal governance; more cogently, if scientific rationality is no longer available to law as a convincing tool of or for governance, and direct political legitimation for law also remains weak, what if anything can justify continuous legal authority?

Scientific uncertainty within supranational or international regimes of risk governance is a modern phenomenon, presenting us with a unique complex of troublesome issues. First, uncertainty itself is just as surely an indication of increasing scientific sophistication as it is one of the existence of scientific limitations: the very notion of scientific uncertainty represents a quantum shift in scientific aspirations; aspirations which now no longer restrict themselves to interrogation of the simple progression from cause to effect, but which seek instead to measure – and, vitally, to admit of the lack of possible measurement within – complex, multi-causal chains of harm production.[3] Second, increasingly sophisticated notions of appropriate scientific method are themselves also a reflection of a societal

1 Or, a higher legal commitment of the polity to apolitical goals, such as market deregulation.
2 See Van Asselt, Vos and Rooijackers in this volume, for discussion on the nature of scientific uncertainty.
3 See Van Asselt, Vos and Rooijackers in this volume; see also, Van Asselt 2005.

willingness to submit national economies to post-industrial models of global, market-driven wealth production; models which, by their very nature, constantly present us with new and unforeseen patterns of risk. Finally, post-national risk governance regimes are, at one and the same time, a modern normative commitment to the establishment of a global economy, with all the risks that that entails, as well as a manifestation of an unprecedented global ambition to control or govern that same risk.

Seen in this light, the complexity that characterises the current relationship between science and law might be considered a uniquely modern phenomenon, not only by virtue of increasing scientific and market sophistication, but also with regard to the unmatched faith that is now placed in the ability of law to govern beyond national boundaries. Nonetheless, encounters between law and science are not new, and, in seeking to address the appropriate place of law and science within modern risk governance regimes, this chapter reaches back to tell two stories of the intimate relationship that has been established between law and science within government. Sketching out one initially optimistic and one perennially pessimistic vision of the place of science within legal government, the chapter hopes to learn 'deep' historical lessons with the aim of establishing a third tale of legal-scientific interaction; one which is appropriate to the context of modern scientific uncertainty.

2 OVERCOMING THE PARADOX OF LAW: SCIENCE AS SAVIOUR

A firm post-war belief in the powers of juridification, or the ability of a global economic community to order its affairs under the protective regulative umbrella of an international (and supranational) law, is perhaps all the more surprising since the first half of the 20th century was characterised by an unprecedented crisis within law. The advent of modernity, to the exact extent that it was founded within reinforced belief in the sovereignty of man and the rationality of human governance, had likewise exposed the 'illogical' genesis of the natural law of the *ancien régime*. Stripped of its transcendental legal authority, law found itself in the uncomfortable place of the emperor, whose carefully tailored clothes, or old theologies of natural justice, might be dismissed as a miasma, a fog of quasi-logical obfuscation, concealing the simple fact that the God of all of its authority was undeniably dead.

In the face of such a calamitous unmasking of its own internal discourse of justification, the first plank within the modern resurrection of legal authority was a shameless adoption and adaptation of the language and mores of modernity. The story is well known, but bears brief repetition. Theology and science would no longer stand in opposition to one another; rather, the theology of legal language would be reborn as modern scientific method. New gods of law would be found within a material world; initially within retrospective (Kantian) appeals to Platonic forms of (natural) justice that might be derived from (material) human rationality, and subsequently within a more prosaic subordination of law to the god of national (democratic) sovereignty. Legal positivism was established as – with the passing of the legal torch of modernist rebirth from (in German legal theory) Savigny to von

Jhering, and finally to Kelsen[4] – the new legal god or *Grundnorm* of human political sovereignty was deemed to be best served by the establishment of a subordinated but closed legal methodology, which, just like science, would identify its own truths, not with reference to the potential 'value irrationalism' of external social or moral beliefs, but rather in the light of its own internal premises, logics and modes of deduction.[5]

If truth be told, the daily mechanics of positivist legal application at least appear to be very similar to those of an older legal theology; each are thus supremely indifferent to those ideas and concepts which have no nominated value within a closed system of argumentation. Nonetheless, the modern positivist legal debt to science betrays an often overlooked intimacy in the relationship between the two: scientists might and can demure (see below, section 3); yet, in aping abstract forms of scientific deduction, positivist law, or legal *science*, laid and continues to lay renewed claim to a legal ability to identify 'truths' within a material world. Or does it? Doubts inexorably remain: within the 20th century and within legal discourse itself, the abstractions of positivism, though deemed to be vital for purposes of *internal* legal legitimation, were thus likewise to come to be regarded as a barrier to the establishment of a legal authority that would always be recognised by actors *outside* the law. With this a second chapter was also opened in the optimistic entwinement of law and science, with law not merely being reinvented as science, but also moving to adopt non-legal science as a tool of legal legitimation within the material (non-legal) world.

The impetus for the establishment of a dual relationship between law and science was best described in the 1930s by the political theorist Harald Laski. With his observation that the 'juristic philosopher' was faced with a primary demand to validate 'his purely formal analysis of categories for the actual world around us' (Laski 1993), Laski not only gave voice to a growing legal theory concern that the reinvention of law as science had inured lawyers to justice demands for necessary social readjustments in a law-external world. Instead, and quite paradoxically, he not only re-iterated the vital importance of the maintenance of scientific method within law; instead, and at the same time, he also began to sketch out a manner in which law might deploy science 'proper' in the effort to overcome the *lacunae* in its own modes of social recognition.

With the rebirth of law as scientific method, an uncomfortable paradox had arisen. Law remained servitor of its social context, and, to that end, had sought to give itself new legitimacy as a neutral (asocial and apolitical) tool of government through adoption of its own closed premises and logically coherent chains of reasoning. By the same token, however, the 'seamless web of law' thus created was no longer responsive to changing social conditions, such as, say, the growing imbalance in bargaining power between employees and employers, which had negated one of

4 Savigny's efforts to furnish a 'legitimate' scheme of interpretation of the Napoleonic *Code Civil* – a mode of interpretation which sought to safeguard the political antecedents of the code through strict limitation of the forms of reasoning which lawyers might apply (literal, grammatical, schematic) – finally resolving itself, within the positivistic theory of Kelsen, in the statement that the legitimacy of law is assured by its subordination an external sovereign (political authors of the code and constitutions).

5 The justification for closed formal reasoning being most powerfully stressed by Weber (1969), who argued that only a process of formal closure could protect law from contamination by 'value irrationalism'.

the primary reasoning premises of formal law, freedom of contract (Sinzheimer 1977). A closed legal system had lost any degree of immediate contact with prevailing social conditions and was no longer capable of recognising or satisfying emerging demands for social justice, especially among a growing class of legally disenfranchised industrial employees. Law might well have been mandated by a political sovereign; yet, in its practice, it was blind to social reality and thus in urgent need of its own immanent window on the world. It required the services of other disciplines and other methodologies, which could reveal and explain the external world to the law.

In Laski's own time, social science was the obvious source upon which law could call, in order to ameliorate its own formal application. Law was still science: the guiding feature of a socially responsive law remained its mechanical or 'scientific' character. 'The mechanism for the discovery of necessary legal change' was thus not one that might be 'discrete or casual'; instead, legal change, the adaptation of abstract categories of law to social reality, should be 'organised and continuous in nature' (Laski 1958). Increased social responsiveness within law undoubtedly demanded the socialisation of lawyers themselves, or the development of a 'moral insight into the law', which might allow them to ameliorate its external consequences (Laski 1958: 571). Nonetheless, such moral insight was also to be organised with reference to scientific principles, with lawyers being required to develop an 'intimate acquaintance' with the notion of 'political economy', as well as with a 'critical jurisprudence', which would not only furnish them with a 'healthy scepticism' of the instrument of formal law, but which might likewise give 'the law its insight into the environment of which it is the expression' (Laski 1958: 26–7).

As we know, and with time, law's window on the world has grown beyond the social sciences to encompass 'hard science', with, in particular, technical, biological and chemical sciences playing their vital role, not only in providing an evidential basis for supranational and international jurisprudence and regulation (see Everson and Eisner 2007, chapter 2; Everson and Joerges 2007; and Joerges in this volume), but also, in furnishing a law weak in political legitimation with a mechanism with which it might delimit and justify its formal jurisprudence (Everson and Eisner 2007, chapter 2). The latter point is determinative for law: yet, at the same time, requires us more closely to examine the exact logic that underpins a scientific and scientifically justified law; an examination which also begins to reveal the specific difficulties that haunt this peculiarly optimistic tale of law and science.

3 UNDERMINING THE RULE OF LAW: SCIENCE AS DEMON

As noted, notions of science have played a vital role within legal efforts to overcome a fundamental paradox within law: in order to maintain its authority law must remain distinct from, yet responsive to the social context which it regulates. To this end, adoption of scientific method *within* law (formal jurisprudence) is argued to maintain legal apartness; meanwhile, deployment of science *beyond* law is said to justify its (post-political) re-engagement with the social (material justice), or the promotion by law of particular social policies, values or interests. Nonetheless, paradoxes are not generally easily dissolved, and, in this case, the presented paradigm of reflexive, yet insulated, law may be doubted on several interrelated counts: first, can law ever be termed a true science; second, can law ever fully appreciate or understand the method of science proper; and finally, which particular dangers might the modern reliance of law upon science pose to 'good' governance?

Returning to the reinvention of law as science, an initial doubt must thus arise with regard to the character of 'scientific' legal method: to what degree is law science and to what degree does it remain a theology? Positivist law, it should be recalled, was a creature of necessity, serving a primary goal of the internal legitimation of law. The methodological premises of law are necessarily closed, not simply in order to insulate law from the contamination of socially derived value irrationalism, but rather also in order to maintain the transcendence of law within a society, which it must govern authoritatively. At a methodological level, the distinction is slight but meaningful: legal methodological closure serves two potentially contradictory masters. For law, the preservation of legal authority is paramount, dictating that, in formal mode, law may sometimes appear to external observers to succumb to its own form of value irrationalism. Moving on to the interrelated question of whether social or hard science can or will be allowed to act as law's window on the world, a degree of legal irrationalism thus becomes readily visible (at least in the eyes of science) as scientific proofs are occasionally rebutted and not deemed worthy of designation as legal proofs. Most famously apparent in the reluctance of competition law jurisdictions to accept economic proofs of business malpractice,[6] legal blindness to the (equally closed) methodological premises of hard science has found its most startling exemplar within the intermittent judicial demands, made, among others, by the European Court of Justice, that science must prove a negative.[7]

For scientists, the legal translation of the methodological proof statement 'there is no evidence that harm will result, therefore the product is safe' into a legal stipulation that 'a product is safe only if it can be proven that is causes no harm',[8] thus reveals legal science to be a chimera. Law demands impossible proofs and unmasks itself as a Galileo-denying theology, as an irredeemably transcendental institution that is disregarding of scientifically constructed proofs, and as just one more actor behaving irrationally within the governance context. For lawyers, of course, and by stark contrast, the importation of the principle of 'precaution' into the normative framework of law can and does legitimate legal foreclosure of scientific method;[9] at the same time, however, the particular legal interpretation afforded the principle of precaution in any one instance – in this case, an absolute, if potentially irrational,

6 Judges prefer, rightly or wrongly, to interrogate market actors within the courtroom, in order to gain a picture of 'what went on' (see Everson and Eisner 2007, chapter 4).

7 The most extraordinary example of this legal tendency being the case of *Pfizer*, Case T-13/99 *Pfizer* [2002] ECR-II 03305, where European judges applied the precautionary principle as an absolute standard of 'no possible harm'. See, for exhaustive consideration, Van Asselt 2005 and Everson 2004.

8 See, again, the formulations deployed by judges in *Pfizer*, Case T-13/99 *Pfizer* [2002] ECR-II 03305. Contrast this, however, with *Monsanto*, Case C-236/01 *Monsanto v Italy* [2003] ECR I-8105, wherein a European precautionary principle appeared to be deemed to be commensurate with scientific methodology, or the notion that a product is only harmful if science says that it is. See, for exhaustive consideration, Everson and Joerges 2007, and Joerges in this volume.

9 See *Pfizer*, Case T-13/99 *Pfizer* [2002] ECR-II 03305.

standard of *no* evidential harm – also represents a legal choice to privilege *particular* social concerns and interests, and it is exactly at this point of legal choice that the paradox of formal versus material justice (or openness versus closure) inexorably returns to haunt the law.

Between application of its own science of formal closure and application of the science proper that bears with it the potential to reveal the externalities to the world of law, the governing legal system is inexorably drawn into the making of value judgments. Even within Harald Laski's analysis, scientifically constructed modes of legal reality recognition continue to revolve around the non-quantifiable legal quality of 'moral insight'. Alternatively, legal principles, such as precaution, being an integral part of the formal complex of legal analysis, but likewise being open to differential interpretation, form a highly nebulous reasoning fulcrum within which law may assess and adjust its own methodology of application, not simply in view of scientific fact, but also in the light of wider normative concerns or moralities. Certainly, lawyers might have an intimate acquaintance with the methodologies of political economy and even of hard science. Nonetheless, at the point of decision, assessment of the effects of legal application will and does entail qualitative decision making.

Lawyers as 'judge-kings', acting outside the direct control of social and political forces:[10] for Max Weber, the exercise of moral insight within law was anathema, an assault upon the vital neutrality of legal authority and a opening of the law up to particularist assault by the plural interests and ideologies, which characterise each and every society, and yet, which also have the potential to tear each and every society apart (see Weber 1969). Arguing in the face of the pluralist dissolution, which foreshadowed collapse in the coherence of the Weimar Republic, Weber asserted the immutable nature of the paradox of law. Formal justice could never be safely ameliorated by virtue of judicial promotion of substantive justice or material consideration by law of fact. Instead, such attempted amelioration would also inexorably entail socially derived value irrationalism and the undermining of the vitally impartial authority of law.

And yet, the potential tragedy inherent to the failure to unlock the paradox of law was also present within Weber's work and, in the context of this chapter, begins to hint at a second highly uncomfortable intimacy within the relationship established between science and law. For all that Weber promoted formal rationality within law, he also raised concerns about the potential inhumanity of a wider 'bureaucratic' rationality, thus foreshadowing post-modern concerns about the threat posed to human governance by the concept of modernity itself.[11]

At this level of high theory, fears about the relationship established between law and science within an executive governance power, are of an existential nature, are questioning of the concept of modernity itself, and derive directly from continuing disquiet about the implications of the Enlightenment endeavour to rid human schemes of government of all notions of God-given order. Alternatively, the brave efforts of modernity to re-root its post-revolutionary government and its positive law within an objective sphere of human organisation are argued to pose dangers of

10 The notion is taken from the work of the founding father of German legal sociology, Ehrlich 1987.

11 See, for an overview, and for the curious parallelity, if not congruence, of critical theory and modern theology, Milbank 2007.

their own. Drawing upon the existence of innate 'humanity', which is given material legal recognition through notions of citizenship, the government of modernity is thus anchored within a conception of human sovereignty, within which the unitary sovereign comprises the body of citizens and is reciprocally shaped by and shaping of its own sovereign and positive law. In this manner, government is shielded from the damning critique that it is transcendental rather than real in nature. At the same time, however, material modernity is necessarily and forever haunted by the spectre of its own dissolution.

To give effect to the objective government and positive law of humanity, a single and despotic sovereign must be created through which the (self-establishing) will of the citizenry might be channelled. A paradox is then at once created: objective human organisation is necessarily undermined by its own sovereign, and more particularly so by the institutional execution of sovereign power by an executive tyrant, which is conditioned by its own despotic nature to disregard the very human wellspring from which it sprang. Translating in the modern hands of Carl Schmitt into a notion of 'technicity',[12] which gives monstrous (Behemothic) form to Max Weber's vaguely stated concerns about the 'inhumanity' of rational bureaucratic process, the paradox of sovereignty versus humanity therefore present us with a *fait accompli* vision of a dark hour of the executive, whereby humanity itself is undermined by its own struggle to identify an appropriate channel of executive expression (see Milbank 2007).

Such high theoretical concerns are apocalyptic in nature, as are the more radical modes of their possible correction; in particular, Carl Schmitt's consequent denial and destruction of Enlightenment ideals. Nonetheless, they remain eternally current both in critical theory and in governance practice, and although we might doubt and decry any connection between the establishment of global risk regimes governance and the emergence of a de-humanising global executive (as well as a totalitarian backlash against that executive), the notion of the dark hour of the executive nevertheless poses fundamental questions about the roles of science and law within modern governance in two particular and interrelated ways.

First, and recalling the de-humanising potential of formal law, or its self-closure to external social and political influence, the reinvention of law as science within modernity has undoubtedly given rise to its own 'human' victims; stretching from the industrial workers denied their collective rights of association within the first years of the 20th century, to entire generations of women, typically excluded from employment by virtue of legal blindness to gender imbalance in the language of positivism, and, most shockingly, including the victims of totalitarian but 'legal' regimes.[13] By the same token, of course, scientists whose proofs might have been ignored within the courtroom, might also feel themselves to be very human victims of law; and yet, opening up of law to science and their entwinement within technocratic regimes of post-national governance may also have its own de-humanising impact.

Thus, second, and staying firmly within technocratic parameters of regulation, the dedication of global and supranational executive governance to wholly

12 The notion of technicity is ascribed to Schmitt's musings by McCormick 1999.

13 The subject of the famous debate between Lon Fuller and H.L.A. Hart (1958a, 1958b).

technical models of implementation and oversight also has as its potential corollary the 'scientification' of large areas of human activity (Everson and Joerges 2007). Alternatively, be the efficiency criteria against which appropriate technical governance must be measured economic or scientific in nature, technocratic and scientific governance bears with it its own dehumanising potential as the citizenry and its tangible environment are logically reduced to units of economic production, or, possibly far worse, scientifically distilled down to their genetic components in, say, GMO or genetic technology regulatory regimes;[14] a process which now give immediate corporeal form to Michel Foucault's once very esoteric theoretical concerns about the spread of 'bio-power' – or the innate tendency of the executive to assert its sovereign power over the very definition of the notion of humanity (Milbank 2007). Alternatively, the rule of law, the greatest achievement of modernity is negated as it cannibalises itself, destroying the humanistic genesis within which it was born.

4 PROCEDURAL TRANSCENDENCE: THE NECESSARY MODESTY OF SCIENCE AND LAW

Despair indeed: in the critical analysis power is not congruent with intent, such that the exercise of bio-power cannot be traced back to a single human source, but must instead be accepted as a systemic demon, as an inevitable spectre haunting modernity; the *Ungeheuer*, which lies behind all of our very human aspirations to govern a material world justly. Seen in this light, we might thus correctly invert the old adage to declare that 'just because no one is out to get us that is no reason not to be paranoid'. Within modernity, paranoia is no bad thing, and, for all the threats posed to a global polity by the threat of pluralist dissolution, the low-level re-politicisation that we observe within supranational and global governance regimes must also be applauded as an effort to re-assert humanity above Behemoth. Less prosaically, the existence of bio-power *necessarily* prompts corrective and evasive action within a public sphere. Alternatively, just as surely as technocratic governance weaves its efficient web across the whole of a regulatory regime, it quite properly gives rise to demands for the re-assertion of humanity over the executive, with, for example, individual lawyers playing their humanistic part within the irrational definition and redefinition of precaution and social interest groups making renewed calls for the global consumer to be re-categorised as an ethical being concerned with the maintenance of a socially just and ethical sphere of consumption (Everson and Joerges 2007).

Paranoia, value-irrationalism, sceptical and moral insight, as well as the positive promotion of the politics of social interest: a final intimacy is established within the relationship between law and science as each discipline is confronted within supranational and international governance regimes with the very emotions of humanity, which both are conditioned to ignore and which both view as a threat to their own methodological coherence. With human paranoia only heightened by the existence of scientific uncertainty, or the necessary admission that neither science, nor science

14 See Joerges in this volume.

entwined with law, can assert material truth even within their own methodologies, both would thus seem to be enjoined (however antagonistically) within a death waltz of social irrelevance and diminished authority.

The interim conclusion that must thus be drawn in relation to global risk governance regimes is, therefore, the highly inconvenient one that they must be constituted by politics rather than by law. Value-irrationalism, as well the pluralism that haunts it, can only be mediated within political process, whereby interests are assuaged, irrationalities given voice or overcome, and guiding moralities asserted in contentious social interaction. The paradigm of modern global governance relies heavily upon the authority of law and technical rationality; yet, it has likewise only emphasised and heightened the paradox inherent to the law of modernity, or to executive rationality in general, resulting in methodological paralysis and the establishment of a threat to its own coherence, as the authority of law and scientific rationality are inevitably undermined. The historic paradigm shift[15] from national to global government, from the politics of interest conflict to the governance of rationality, has ended in a paralysis all of its own, an essential and immutable conflict between humanity (paranoia) and rationality, such that, in the absence of the establishment of a global political community,[16] advance out of paralysis is only possible through a final act of transcendence, or an act of 'morphogenesis', which releases both law and science from the impossible task of identifying material truth in an authoritative manner and refocuses them upon the ongoing, open-ended task of providing authoritative support for emerging political contention.[17]

Alternatively, historic tales of legal-scientific intimacy teach us that the search for material fact within closed methodological disciplines also remains a dangerous chimera: the allure of constructed truth, however it is ameliorated and however much it is claimed to be based within material fact, only fades as it disenfranchises individuals, groups and humanity as a whole. If a global governance regime is to remain stable, politics must be re-admitted within its executive structures, with law, and or with science, seeking not to neutralise social value-irrationalism, but, rather, to give it an appropriate means of expression.

Within a modern scientific idiom, the critical theory demand for methodological transcendence is particularly troublesome, seemingly reproducing, in relativistic rather than theological terms, the myriad and increasingly violent pre-modern assaults now being made on scientific rationality by the surprisingly reinvigorated forces of theology and/or social ideology. Nevertheless, the very admission of scientific uncertainty, of the limits to science, is also indicative of a natural or inherent modesty within scientific method, which, although necessarily committed to its own rationality, is thus likewise made aware of the need to relativise, at least the reach of scientific truths in the light of other social and political forces, no matter how irrational such forces might appear to be. In this regard, then, a modern exhortation to law in its dealings with science might usefully be one to cease to

15 The famous paradigm shift having being introduced by Kuhn (see Kuhn 1970).

16 Or, the lack of one single, authoritative, global political sovereign.

17 The concept of morphogenesis was developed by Whitehead and Russel in order to allow for escape from paradoxical paradigms. Importantly, for the purposes of this study, morphogenesis does not entail the establishment of a new paradigm in a process of shift, but rather entails open-ended processes of escape from any one world view. See, for exhaustive consideration, Teubner 2005.

deploy science to bolster its own authority, to cease to use science as its own, always very opaque, window on the world and, instead, to subject science to its own very real legal talents of forensic examination. In other words, lawyers should be skilled in the arts of scientific method, not in the hope that this will qualify them to identify material reality, but rather as a part of their general procedural goal of ensuring open and transparent confrontation between the plural forces of global contestation.

Alternatively, the precautionary principle must be re-conceptualised. Given systemic incoherence between science and law, or the impossibility of coherent translation of material fact from scientific into legal method, the principle is inexorably emptied of all authority as a determinative normative governing principle, being simply undermined by the personalised moral pronouncements of the judge-king. Rather, the principle must now be opened up as a site of political contestation, within which legal authority is no longer derived from moral insights that are veiled by simple assertion of legal positivism,[18] nor distilled from judicial assertion of scientific truths that are only ever seen by law through a glass darkly.[19] Instead, legal authority within political contention must now be created by legal disavowal of substantive decision making, and the consequent dedication of law to procedural and forensic investigation of the robustness of social-political interaction and conflict within governance.

In final conclusion, then, vital legal authority within risk governance regimes must be sought, not in the empty proceduralism, say, of the WTO Panel on GMOs, which (in bio-power mode) obscures its garbled assertion of the authority of scientific rationality over human affairs through appeal to the procedural let-out clause of 'individual administrative expectations',[20] but rather in its exact opposite. If the adjudicative measure of this Decision is to be found in its use of ancient legal mantras, its setting aside of the legitimacy of a robust European process of political debate with the argument that its very lengthiness had impinged upon individual commercial rights and expectations, then the moral authority of global law is dead. The concept of legal proceduralism must be radicalised. In an emergent global risk polity, the structures of political interaction and contestation are not clear. Given these circumstances, the law of global risk governance may not hide behind the constituting procedures and principles of the new *ancien regime*. Instead, it must act with forensic immediacy, investigating the scientific and economic rationalities that are presented to it, both in terms of their proper (internal) identification of their own limits, and with regard to whether or not they have been properly exposed to relativising political and social contestation, in whichever institutional or informal

18 Alternatively, the *Pfizer* 'solution', Case T-13/99 *Pfizer* [2002] ECR-II 03305.

19 In essence, the approach adopted by the ECJ in *Monsanto*, Case C-236/01 *Monsanto v Italy* [2003] ECR I-8105. The most important point to note here being the fact that the Court's judgment cannot recognise scientific uncertainty. The judgment simply reverses the illogical nature of *Pfizer*, asserting that scientific uncertainty can be treated in a scientific manner. See, for extensive consideration, Joerges in this volume.

20 See WTO Panel Report, *European Communities – Measures Affecting the Approval and Marketing of Biotech Products*, 13 October 2006, WT/DS291/Interim, WT/DS292/Interim, WT/DS293 (complaints by United States, Canada and Argentina respectively), available at: <http://www.wto.org/english/news_e/news06_e/291r_e.htm>. See, for consideration of the case, Everson and Joerges 2007 and Joerges in this volume.

form it is evolving.[21] Certainly, pluralist dissolution will continue to haunt any global risk governance regime. That, however, is surely a more appealing prospect than legal acquiescence in the cannibalisation of humanity.

21 See Joerges in this volume. Since an evolving global polity is still developing its institutions of political contestation, law cannot work with any pre-conceived notion of 'legitimate' sites for political contestation, but must instead be prepared to evaluate existing sites of contestation for their inclusiveness and robustness, wherever they appear – at national, supranational or global level.

BIBLIOGRAPHY

Van Asselt, M.B.A. (2005) 'The complex significance of uncertainty in a risk era: Logics, manners and strategies in use', *International Journal for Risk Assessment and Management* (special issue on uncertainty) 5(2/3/4): 125–58.

Ehrlich, E. (1987) *Freie Rechtsfindung und freie Rechtswissenschaft* (reprint from 1903), Aalen: Scientia.

Everson, M. (2004) 'Solidarity with Strangers in the Transnational Republic? A Comment on Eriksen & Fossum, "Europe at a Crossroads: Government or Transnational Governance?" ', in Ch. Joerges (ed.), *Good Governance in the Transnational Order*, Oxford: Hart Publishing.

Everson, M. and Eisner, J. (2007) *The Making of a European Constitution*, London: Glasshouse-Routledge.

Everson, M. and Joerges, Ch. (2007) 'Consumer Citizenship in Postnational Constellations?', in K. Soper and F. Trentmann (eds), *Citizenship and Consumption*, New York: Palgrave Macmillan.

Hart, H.L.A. (1958a) 'Positivism and the Separation of Law and Morals', *Harvard Law Review*, 593–629.

Hart, H.L.A. (1958b) 'Positivism and Fidelity to Law – A reply to Prof. Hart', *Harvard Law Review*, 630–72.

Kuhn, T.S. (1970) *The Structure of Scientific Revolutions*, Chicago: University of Chicago Press.

Laski, H. (1993) 'Law and the State' (*Studies in Law and Politics* 1935), reproduced in P. Hirst, *The Pluralist Theory of the State*, London: Routledge.

Laski, H. (1958) *A Grammar of Politics*, 4th edn, London: Allen & Unwin.

McCormick, J. (1999) *Carl Schmitt's Critique of Liberalism: Against Politics as Technology*, Cambridge: Cambridge University Press.

Milbank, J. (2007) *Paul against Biopolitics*, available at: <http://www.theologyphilosophycentre.co.uk/papers.php#milbank>.

Teubner, G. (2005) 'Dealing with Paradoxes of Law: Derrida, Luhmann, Wiethölter', in O. Perez and G. Teubner (eds), *On Paradoxes and Inconsistencies in the Law*, Oxford: Hart Publishing.

Sinzheimer, H. (1977) *Ein Arbeitstarifgesetz – Die Idee der sozialen Selbstbestimmung im Recht*, Berlin: Duncker & Humblot.

Weber, M. (1969) 'Economy and sociology: An outline of interpretative sociology', in G. Roth and C. Wittig (eds), *Economy and Sociology*, vol. 2, Berkeley: University of Berkeley Press.

Chapter 18

Science, knowledge and uncertainty in EU risk regulation

Marjolein B.A. van Asselt, Ellen Vos and Bram Rooijackers

1 INTRODUCTION

The sociologist Beck (Beck 1986; 1997) is famous and much cited for his convincing appeal for critical reflection on the modern risk society.[1] A key question that can be derived from his agenda-setting critique and provoking notion of 'organised irresponsibility' is one of how to deal responsibly with situations in which there are suspicions that hazards may exist, although (sufficient) scientific or historical evidence for them is lacking, ie situations entailing 'uncertain risks'. This question has acted as a stimulus for an extensive interdisciplinary research agenda, which has only just begun to be defined.

This chapter aims to understand the role of science and knowledge in uncertain risk regulation by examining how various actors deal with science, knowledge and uncertainty in the field of EU risk regulation. Our analysis may help to identify the difficulties of dealing with uncertain risks and to discern some ways to address these problems. These uncertain risks concern situations of suspected, possible hazards, which are usually associated with complex causalities, large-scale, long-term and trans-border processes, and which are generally difficult to control and also transcend human sensory capacities. In such situations, since scientific knowledge is perceived or portrayed to be limited, experts, stakeholders or the public have or create doubts about the possibility or severity of hazards (Van Asselt 2005). At the same time, regulators habitually turn to science and experts in these cases in order to justify their decisions (Hilgartner 2000; Jasanoff and Wynne 1998; Ravetz 1990; Van Asselt 2005; Van Asselt *et al.* 2007). This situation, which we term the 'uncertainty paradox' (Van Asselt and Vos 2005; 2006), raises important questions about the role of science, knowledge and experts in the regulation of uncertain risks. To date, attention paid to this issue has been scant: even legal literature on the precautionary principle, legitimating decisions and actions in situations characterised by uncertainty (Faure and Vos 2003), often treats science and expertise as unproblematic in nature.

For the purpose of this chapter, we identify the following actors who participate within the regulatory process (in accordance with Ravetz 2001):

1 Beck's sociological conclusions are mirrored by risk scholars (Wynne 1982; Ravetz 1996; Jasanoff 1993; Jasanoff 2005, Löfstedt 2005; Hajer 1995; Klinke and Renn 2002).

- *risk producers:* technologists, companies or organisations who pursue potentially hazardous technologies or activities and, indirectly, consumers and other parties using these technologies or associated products;
- *risk assessors:* scientific experts in relevant fields who seek to consider and analyse risks;
- *risk managers:* the civil servants and institutions charged with controlling and deciding on risks, who are usually a part of, or strongly affiliated with, governments;
- *risk protesters:* the persons and organisations who object to particular technologies, activities or modes of life because of negative impacts attributed to them, usually in the name of (potential) risk victims, such as the public in general or NGOs aiming to protect the environment.

The case of EU risk regulation is of exemplary importance for a variety of reasons. First, the EU currently plays a leading role in addressing uncertain risks usually associated with long-term, large-scale and trans-border hazards. Second, it has a leading role in advancing the precautionary principle, which can be interpreted as an explicit attempt to legitimate decision making on, and regulation of, uncertain risks (Petersen and Van der Zwaan 2003; Van Asselt 2004; Van Asselt and Vos 2005; Klinke and Renn 2002). In particular, EU regulation on genetically modified organisms (GMOs) furnishes us with an exemplary case study on the risk society (Borrás 2006; Jasanoff 2005), because of its particular complexity with regard to the number of actors involved in decision making, as well as the controversies that are manifest in this field. In addition to risk assessors (EFSA) and risk managers (the European Commission and Member States), risk producers (Monsanto) and risk protestors (Greenpeace, Friends of the Earth) are also actively engaged in the regulatory process.

Before entering into the specifics of GMO regulation, however, this chapter will first clarify the notion of 'uncertain risks', a potentially ambiguous concept since, traditionally, a distinction is drawn between risk and uncertainty. Subsequently, we will introduce the 'uncertainty paradox' (Van Asselt and Vos 2005; 2006): uncertainty is acknowledged, but the role of science and experts is consistently phrased in terms of providing certainty on uncertain risks. Manifestation and propagation of this uncertainty paradox may result in regulatory complexities, as we argue with reference to EU GMO regulation. In conclusion, some suggestions are advanced on the best manner of dealing with the difficulties thus revealed.

2 REGULATING UNCERTAIN RISKS

2.1 Contesting the risk-uncertainty dichotomy

Traditionally, risk is used to refer to hazards which are known and calculable from previous experience. As early as 1921, the economist Knight argued that it is necessary to distinguish uncertainty from risk (Knight 1921). This risk-uncertainty dichotomy is still the dominant way of looking at risk. In this framework, 'risk' refers to hazards that are considered real, because of previous experience. This paradigm gave rise to the famous formula of risk as a function of probability (the chance that something happens) and effect (the associated damage). The most common version is simply: RISK = probability × effect.

Both probability and effect are derived from statistical data on past occurrences. For example, the risk of flooding is derived from records on past floods. How often have floods occurred? How severe were these floods? And what damage did they cause? The probability of flooding (1:250, or, on average, one flood in 250 years) and the effect of flooding (usually in terms of costs) are derived from such statistics.

In Knightian thinking, also referred to as the positivistic risk paradigm (Krayer von Kraus *et al.* 2005; Van Asselt 2000), risks are viewed as calculable, hence controllable, islands in the sea of uncertainty (Nowotny *et al.* 2001; see also Jasanoff 1993 and Klinke and Renn 2002). Uncertainty accordingly refers to cases in which probability and/or effect are not 'known'. Within Knightian logic, 'uncertain risk' is a nonsensical notion, since it entails the unacceptable collapsing of categories. If a risk is uncertain, it is not a risk, but uncertainty. Uncertainty denotes hazards that are difficult or impossible to calculate or new hazards, where no statistics on previous occurrences are available.

However, these categories often collapse, as neither the likelihood of occurrence nor the harmful consequences can be estimated or established. Risks are uncertain, because they are associated with new technologies, new developments or the long-term consequences of past or present acts (RMNO 2004). Examples include the introduction of a new (chemical or genetically modified) substance, the extensive application of a new technology and unprecedented human intervention within the environment, such as CO_2 emissions. Vercelli (1995) explicitly questions the risk-uncertainty dichotomy:

> The terminology and foundations suggested by Knight and followers must be considered unacceptable. Uncertainty refers to the impossibility of exact predictions. Risk refers to the possible negative consequences of uncertainty. Any kind of uncertainty [. . .] implies risks whose modalities crucially depend on those of the underlying uncertainty. Therefore, a distinction between uncertainty without risk, and risk without uncertainty, is highly confusing.

On the basis of their analysis of 14 situations of risks, ranging from radiation, benzene, asbestos and PCBs to chemical contamination of lakes, hormones as growth promoter and BSE, Harremoës *et al.* (2001) argue that conclusive evidence ('certainty') on risks only becomes available after the harm has been done. The old dichotomy even appears to be inadequate in the case of simple flood risks. Vrijling (2004) reveals that most of the effect estimates in flood risk calculations in the Netherlands are fairly inconclusive ('uncertain'). For example, estimates of economic impact are based mainly on the 1953 disaster and recent minor damage due to high water in the Meuse delta. However, the economic value of buildings and infrastructure has increased greatly over the last 50 years. As a consequence, the economic effects of flooding in the Netherlands are actually much more uncertain than figures used in risk calculations suggest. The same is true of the flooding probability estimates. Climate scientists (Intergovernmental Panel on Climate Change (IPCC)) agree that a different climate will impact on river run-off patterns and that it may yield a rise in sea level. Both river run-off and sea level rise are important phenomena in view of flood risks, especially in the world's deltas.

Different climate change scenarios have been developed which enable experts to think about possible changes in flood regimes in an exploratory manner (Middelkoop *et al.* 2001; 2002). However, these scenarios do not provide a basis to determine the possibilities of flooding in a particular region. This example illustrates that, in practice, experts are confronted with uncertain risks, ie hazards that should be considered but which cannot be calculated in Knightian terms.

In societal debates, incalculability and hence uncontrollability (uncertainty categories in Knightian terms) are attributed to risk. Uncertain hazards, such as waste disposal, health effects of air pollution, genetically modified organisms and climate change, are still talked about in terms of risk, both by experts, the public and politicians. Notwithstanding these uncertainties, instances of genetic modification are subjected to risk assessment. In the EU, the European Food Safety Authority (EFSA) performs such risk assessments. We note that where risks are uncertain, experts (EFSA and its GMO Panel), citizens, stakeholders, decision makers and regulators alike, still consider them to be risks and treat them accordingly. Accordingly, the distinction made between uncertainty and risk is not only confusing, but may be equally damaging if we aim to deal with risk in a responsible manner.

Many uncertain risks transcend our sensory capacities: we cannot hear, smell, see or feel them. As a consequence, two shifts can be observed in thinking about risk assessment. First, science is increasingly needed to make these risks 'visible'. Theories, models and sophisticated measurements are needed where our senses fall short. Accordingly, the role of science has partly shifted from calculating hazards faced by people to assessing potential dangers that we do not experience. Second, current risk assessment is increasingly future-oriented. The main question has shifted from one of 'what has happened in the past' (probability) as a basis for risk assessment to one of 'what may happen in the future' (possibility).[2] Accordingly, risk assessment is increasingly affected by all kinds of uncertainties pertaining to future developments that cannot be ignored.

Hence, although we necessarily may concede that many risks are calculable and fall within the category of risks as described by Knight, we nonetheless argue that a group of risks exist that involve complex causalities, large-scale, long-term and transborder processes, and which are generally difficult to control and transcend the sensory capacities. These risks remain uncertain, notwithstanding the claimed theoretical impossibility by Knight and followers. Blurring of Knight's categories is not an anomaly, but is, instead, the order of the day within risk assessment and management and in societal debates about risk. The calculable-non-calculable, and the knowing-not knowing distinctions invoked by them cannot be retained. Scholars in the field of Science and Technology Studies (STS)[3] convincingly argue that these dichotomies are fundamentally flawed. 'Purification' of categories is no longer an option, but is, instead, a simple case of cherishing illusions.

Importantly, however, notwithstanding our criticism of the Knightian risk-uncertainty dichotomy and our deliberate blurring of his categories, we do not argue

2 This move is often an unconscious one: risk assessors and managers still use probability language; however, they are concerned with possibilities.

3 See Jasanoff *et al.* 1995; Hess 1999; Biagioli 1999.

that risk and uncertainty are synonyms. 'Uncertain risks' should be distinguished from 'safe uncertainties', as uncertain risks pertain to those uncertain situations that may result in effects valued negatively or which are considered unacceptable by at least one, but possibly more, societal actors. The notion of risk thus restricts in a normative sense: it refers to damage, loss, calamities, disasters or even catastrophes. In other words, risk refers to 'bad chances' (RIVM 2003) and 'bad effects' (RMNO 2004). Uncertainty is a broader category and a more 'neutral' notion.

2.2 Defining uncertain risks

The notion of uncertain risks[4] allows us to indicate a particular kind of situation that matters to decision making, in which there are suspicions of hazard, although scientific or historical evidence is lacking. These situations are politically relevant, because societal actors or the public at large may worry about these hazards and consider these uncertain risks to be unacceptable threats. In such situations, experts, stakeholders or the general public have or create doubts about the possibility or severity of hazards; a situation made possible since scientific knowledge is perceived to be or portrayed as limited (Van Asselt 2005). At the same time, such doubts cannot be negated on scientific grounds: risks are uncertain, because the dangers can neither be verified nor refuted. Accordingly, societal actors and/or members of the public usually turn to political actors, with the consequence that uncertain risks also entail situations in which the realm of decision making and regulation and the realm of science and expertise interact, or even intersect. Because of the complexity involved, science and experts are needed to make the risks 'visible'.[5] Notwithstanding the inability to provide certainty about the articulated hazards (whether positive or negative), science and expertise are not irrelevant in situations of uncertain risks. In accordance with Jasanoff (1990), we are convinced that scientific expertise can 'inject much needed competence and critical intelligence into a regulatory system that otherwise seems all too vulnerable to the demands of politics'. Yet, exactly how experts' competence and intelligence should be mobilised and their scientific knowledge and expertise should be used by decision makers in situations shrouded in scientific uncertainty is still open to question.

Uncertainty is not simply the absence of knowledge (Van Asselt 2005). Some uncertainties can even be estimated quantitatively, for example in the form of a range. But, more importantly, experts do possess (though often tacitly) knowledge about:

- uncertainties that do play a role;
- reasons why something is uncertain (ie the underlying sources of uncertainty);
- the significance of particular uncertainties for the societal/policy problem at issue;
- an idea of reducibility: is it possible to reduce or even eradicate uncertainty, and if so how?

4 Other scholars, among them lawyers and risk experts, also use the notion: de Sadeleer 1999; de Sadeleer 2002; Löfstedt 2005, Tickner and Gouveia-Vigeant 2005.

5 Mourik (2004) illustrates the vital role played by experts in 'seeing' risks.

- an estimate of the interpretative flexibility of uncertainty (Pinch and Bijker 1987): which interpretations of uncertainty are deemed valid and which interpretations do definitely contrast with the current state of scientific knowledge?

It is, therefore, necessary to collect this knowledge and to gather information about uncertainty. This 'uncertainty information' comprises the full range of answers and insights that experts can provide on the above issues. Experts can be invited or even challenged to make such uncertainty information available (RMNO 2003), but they cannot provide certainty about uncertain risks. In other words, experts can share what they know about particular uncertain risks with decision makers, stakeholders and the public, but they cannot provide a definite answer on the issue of whether something constitutes a real hazard and what risk it entails. In the context of uncertain risks, risk assessment has, or should have, a different meaning: delineating uncertainty information seems an important challenge, which will be further substantiated in this chapter.

2.3 The uncertainty paradox

The so-called *Pfizer* case (European Court of First Instance 2002; Van Asselt and Vos 2005; 2006; Vos 2004) proves illustrative within this analysis, first, since the precautionary principle was explicitly relied upon by EU regulators as a means to legitimise decision making, and, second, since it is exemplary of the 'uncertainty paradox':[6] although uncertainty was acknowledged, the role of science and experts was always falsely framed in terms of the provision of certainty about uncertain risks. Although, on the one hand, it is generally recognised that science cannot provide decisive evidence on uncertain risks, on the other, policy makers and judicial authorities are increasingly resorting to science for a greater degree of certainty and conclusive evidence (Weingart 1999). *Pfizer* was an equally paradoxical case, being marked both by the existence of deep scepticism about what science *can* deliver, and by extraordinary optimism about what it *should* be able to deliver (Forrester 2006).

Pfizer concerned regulation of feed additives and the use of the antibiotic virginiamycin as growth promoter under the relevant EU regulatory regime. Referring to a Danish National Veterinary Laboratory analysis, Denmark notified the Commission in January 1998 that it had banned the use of virginiamycin by virtue of risk of transferral of resistance to that antibiotic from animals to humans. The Commission submitted this report to the Scientific Committee on Animal Nutrition (SCAN) for advice. SCAN (1998) concluded that use of virginiamycin did not constitute an immediate risk to public health in Denmark. Nevertheless, the Commission proposed a ban and submitted its proposal to the Standing Committee on Feedingstuffs (StCFe) for approval. This precautionary proposal was so heavily contested that the committee was unable to reach an opinion. In accordance with the relevant provisions (regulatory, *contre-filet* procedure), the Commission subsequently sent its proposal to the Council, who confirmed the Commission's position and adopted a

6 Case T-13/99 *Pfizer Animal Health SA v Council of the European Union* [2002] ECR II-03305.

ban on the use of virginiamycin as a feed additive.[7] Pfizer, the producer of virginiamycin, immediately challenged this decision before the Court of First Instance (CFI);[8] the Court upheld the Council's decision.

'Uncertainty' played its key role within Pfizer, allowing regulators to legitimate a highly controversial course of action (Forrester and Hanekamp 2006). Risk managers (the Commission) initially asked risk assessors (SCAN) for a decisive answer to the question of whether the risk was a hazard. The experts attempted to comply furnishing a 'plausibility proof' or a decisive statement on whether 'real' risk existed. They, nonetheless, concluded that there was 'no immediate risk';[9] rather than follow this conclusion of no immediate risk, however, risk managers focused on the uncertainty information that had crept into SCAN's advice to develop their own line of reasoning that uncertainty existed, mobilising this information as justification for application of the precautionary principle and a ban on virginiamycin.

With time, however, judicial authorities also lost their way in the scientific complexities of the case, but were required to reach a decision: Pfizer evoked legal notions of 'manifest error' in relation to the risk assessment and misapplication of the precautionary principle, forcing the Court to examine the scientific arguments involved, even though the latter repeatedly asserted that only a limited review was within its material competences.[10] We argued that the whole regulatory endeavour propagated the uncertainty paradox, with as a consequence that the Court was forced to evaluate scientific claims. The Court attempted to overcome deadlock through construction of a situation of scientific uncertainty, treating scientific evidence brought before it by both the Commission and Pfizer as being manifest of uncertainty in order to justify application of the precautionary principle and the Council's ban. The Court spent all its efforts on constructing itself scientific uncertainty in order to escape the deadlock, thus preventing complete stagnation of the regulatory process (Van Asselt *et al.* 2007; Van Asselt and Vos 2005).

3 EVADING UNCERTAINTY: EU REGULATION OF GMOs

The uncertainty paradox is disruptive of regulatory and judicial processes alike, a situation further exemplified with regard to the EU GMO regulatory regime.

3.1 GMOs as uncertain risks

GMOs are natural life forms whose DNA is altered through insertion of DNAs from other organisms in the effort to improve the qualities, characteristics and functioning of the original organism. Within the EU legislative framework, GMOs,

7 Council Regulation 2821/98/EC amending, as regards withdrawal of the authorisation of certain antibiotics, Directive 70/524/EEC concerning additives in feedingstuffs [1998] *OJ* L351/4.

8 Case T-13/99 *Pfizer Animal Health SA v Council of the European Union* [2002] ECR II-03305.

9 Scientific Committee on Animal Nutrition (1998), Conclusion 1.

10 Above, note 6.

excepting human organisms, are organisms whose genetic material has been altered in a mode not occurring naturally (through reproduction and/or natural recombination),[11] while GM food contains, consists of, or is produced from GMOs.[12] The following analyses three different GMOs and their regulatory regime: NK 603 maize, hybrid maize MON 863 × MON 810 and GT 73 oilseed rape. NK 603 maize is genetically modified maize, designed as to be resistant to the herbicide glyphosate, and was created by insertion of a gene from bacterium into natural maize (EFSA 2003). MON 863 × MON 810 maize is modified to resist corn root-worm and particular pests and is a hybrid of MON 863, a GM maize resistant to the corn rootworm, and MON 810, a maize made resistant to insects through insertion of an insecticidal protein gene (EFSA 2004a). MON 810 was deemed safe in 1998 by the Scientific Committee on Plants,[13] while MON 863 was not tested (EFSA 2004a). GT 73 oilseed rape is also designed to be resistant to the herbicide glyphosate through insertion of two genes encoding proteins (EFSA 2004b).

Genetic modification was first undertaken in the early 1970s (Jelsma 1999) and is claimed by its proponents to entail great benefits such as better taste and freshness, higher yields, higher vermin and herbicide resistance and lower water requirements, as well as the potential to solve world hunger. As with any new technology, genetic modification is associated with uncertain risks; however, uncertainties about the safety of GMO crops have a very high profile in public debate (Van Asselt 2004). Kuiper (in this volume) attributes this to uncertainty about the biological significance of observed changes as well as fundamental ignorance about underlying processes and complex multi-causal relationships. Because of limited experience of GMO technology no definite conclusions can be drawn on risks, such as the threat to traditional agriculture, with the result that public debate on GMO regulation is a politically highly relevant case of uncertain risks (Wynne 2001).

3.2 Case studies

The same agricultural company, Monsanto, requested authorisation for all three products. All three cases are noteworthy by virtue of the complexity of the regulatory procedure encompassing three different regimes (GMO Directive 2001/18; Novel Food Regulation 258/97 and GM Food and Feed Regulation 1829/2003[14]), controversy around the decision-making process, with the Commission requesting scientific opinions from EFSA on the food safety aspects of GM Maize NK603 and MON863 × MON810 and the environmental effects of GT 73 oilseed rape. The following examines how the risk producer, Monsanto, the main EU risk assessor

11 Directive 2001/18/EC of the European Parliament and of the Council of 12 March 2001 on the deliberate release into the environment of genetically modified organisms and repealing Council Directive 90/220/EEC – Commission Declaration, [2001] *OJ* L106/1, Article 2(b).

12 Regulation (EC) No. 1829/2003 of the European Parliament and of the Council of 22 September 2003 on genetically modified food and feed, [2003] *OJ* L268/1, Article 2(6).

13 Scientific Committee on Plants, *Opinion of the Scientific Committee on plants regarding the genetically modified, insect resistant maize lines notified by the Monsanto Company*, Notification C/F/95/12/02, 10 February 1998, Brussels: European Commission.

14 Directive 2001/18, above, note 11, Regulation (EC) No. 258/97 of the European Parliament and of the Council of 27 January 1997 concerning novel foods and novel food ingredients, [1997] *OJ* L43/1 and Regulation 1829/2003, above, note 12.

(EFSA) and risk managers (Member States and the Commission), as well as risk protestors (Greenpeace and Friends of the Earth) deal with uncertain risks and mobilise science and expertise.

3.3 Risk producers: Monsanto

Monsanto promotes agricultural application of biotechnology. Its website (<www.monsanto.com>) states that the company is concerned about the safety of its products ('The safety of our employers, the communities where we operate, our customers, consumers and the environment will be our highest priority') and that it is part of its business ethics to be transparent and honest. Although legally required to do so,[15] Monsanto seeks to suggest that it performs safety assessments on its own initiative. Reports describing the assessments on NK 603 and GT 73 are freely available on Monsanto's website, although there is no assessment on MON 810 × MON 863, but rather only on the parent GMO maizes (MON 810 and MON 863), further suggesting that Monsanto assumes that safety of the parent guarantees safety of the hybrid. The language and tone in Monsanto's assessment reports vary from highly technical to overtly promotional. Analysis and advertising intertwine. Informed by its own assessments, Monsanto has concluded that all three products are safe.

3.3.1 Constructing safety: a detailed analysis of Monsanto's NK 603 assessment

Monsanto generally follows similar risk assessment procedures, and, by way of initial example, we provide detailed analysis of how Monsanto constructs the safety of NK 603 (Monsanto 2002b). NK 603 assessment involved six different analyses. First, detailed characterisation of the molecular structure of the new NK 603 maize was carried out to show the stability of the new genetic structure and examine the concentration of the new proteins. Second, analysis focused on the safety of these new proteins. Safety issues were examined in several ways. Potential toxicity was investigated on the basis of tests conducted with mice: Monsanto researchers found that the new proteins do not raise allergenic concerns, since they share no traits with currently known allergens. The third analysis involved a compositional analysis of the corn grain itself to find out whether or not the GM maize is markedly different from those already available on the market. According to the Monsanto report, it performed a comparative analysis of the presence of 51 different components present in the maize, such as minerals, fibres, vitamins, acids and fats. Monsanto experts did not find any significant difference between the NK 603 maize and its organic counterpart. The next analysis focused on the question of whether the GM maize has the same nutritional value as regular maize. To that end, two studies were carried out: one with rats over a period of 90 days and a second with chickens over a 42-day period. One group of animals was fed the NK 603 maize while the control group received regular corn. The animals' weights and sizes were compared with regular growth patterns. According to Monsanto, both studies

15 According to Directive 2001/18; Regulation 258/97 and 1829/2003, above, note 14.

confirm comparability between NK 603 maize and its organic counterparts. Moreover, on average, the chickens fed NK 603 maize were reported to be '2.3%' larger than those in the control group. The fifth analysis deals with the environment: Monsanto experts compared the agronomic characteristics of the modified maize with that of normal maize. The growth rates, harvest yields and plant counts of the newly modified maize were measured and then compared with regular variants. Finally, Monsanto tested interaction of NK 603 maize with pests and diseases through observation of GM maize in the field. Again, no negative results were reported. In addition, Monsanto claimed that NK 603 maize did not have any negative impact on biodiversity. Based on their assessment, Monsanto concluded that their product does not adversely affect non-target organisms (humans, animals and beneficial insects) and that it is just as safe as regular, organic variants of maize.

3.3.2 Uncertainty intolerance: the rat study affair

As the exemplary case of NK 603 maize testing demonstrates, Monsanto assessments are detailed and might be argued to be comprehensive. Nonetheless, certain doubts do arise and have arisen, in particular with regard to testing of MON 863: following discussion with the UK environment minister, the UK *Guardian*[16] reported that Monsanto had not immediately and voluntarily shared existing test results indicating that MON 863 caused unexplained kidney damage to rats. Consequently, upon a Greenpeace action to gain access to the document (Greenpeace 2005), a German court in Münster ordered Monsanto (20 June 2005) to disclose the suppressed report. The full rat study report (Burns 2002) (1,100 pages), as well as a summary document (Lemen *et al.* 2002), were then made available on Monsanto's website. Interestingly, although the MON 863 assessment was released in August 2003, it made no reference to the rat study results, which were dated December 2002, and was constructed as if these tests had never been performed and no anomalous results had been found. Despite its claimed openness, it appears that Monsanto had tried to hide information that indicated uncertainty about safety and risk.

A further interesting feature of the 'rat affair' is the grounds argued by Monsanto for its dismissal of the rat study report. The report stated that tested rats had less mineralised kidney tubules than average. According to Monsanto, this finding was of 'no biological significance' and was consequently dismissed as irrelevant to the assessment (Lemen *et al.* 2002: 11). As Van Asselt has argued (Van Asselt 2005), claims of irrelevance allow experts to claim certainty in uncertain situations. Equally, Monsanto also stated that the effect could not be considered 'test-related' (Lemen *et al.* 2002: 11); a highly puzzling statement, especially in view of the fact that no indication was given of alternative causes for the altered kidneys within the control study group. What, if not intake of GM maize, caused these alterations? Given the fact that a report that claimed effects negative were 'irrelevant' and 'unrelated' was suppressed, it is difficult to avoid the impression that Monsanto is highly 'uncertainty intolerant'.

16 Although it did not specify its sources.

3.3.3 *Monsanto and uncertain risks*

How did Monsanto, the risk producer, deal with risk and how did it perceive of risk? The focus that the risk producer places on its own responsibility for safety indicates that this actor recognises, and is forced by regulators to recognise, that the products it develops are risk-sensitive. Stakeholders and the public do have concerns about risks associated with Monsanto's GMO products. All assessments and conclusions, however, are phrased in terms of 'safety', with the risk producer appearing deliberately to avoid the vocabulary of risk and uncertainty. The report on NK 603 does not mention uncertainty, while 'risk' is only used in contexts not directly related to NK 603, or in favourable comparison with the 'risks' posed by conventional maize, implying that NK 603 is as safe or even safer. Generally speaking, Monsanto appears to be dedicated to proving that there are zero adverse effects, and, thereby is implicitly attuning its assessment to the famous formula of risk = probability × effect, with zero effect meaning zero risk. As the degree of uncertainty intolerance evinced in the rat study affair appears to demonstrate, risk producers fear uncertainty as it threatens safety. In sum, Monsanto's safety assessments might be argued to be deliberate efforts to transform any uncertainty about risk into absolute certainty about safety: avoiding mention of uncertainty, defining it away, or even suppressing reports that suggest its existence, Monsanto positively advances the positivistic risk paradigm, not just blurring categories, but redefining uncertainty as, and equating it with, risk.

3.4 Risk assessors: EFSA

Following the BSE crisis (Vos 1999; Vos 2000; Vos and Wendler 2006), the European Food Safety Authority (EFSA) was founded to provide independent scientific advice on food safety,[17] beginning its remit in May 2003, first in Brussels. EFSA has since assessed each of the GMOs.

3.4.1 *NK 603 maize*

In January 2001 Monsanto requested permission from Spanish authorities to import and process NK 603 maize in Spain under Directive 2001/18 and made a similar request to the Dutch authorities in April 2001 under the Novel Food Regulation 258/97. Both countries carried out an initial risk assessment, concluding that foods and food ingredients derived from NK 603 were as safe as those derived from conventional maize and could be used in the same manner. These assessments were subsequently sent to the European Commission, who forwarded them to the other Member States. Various countries, including Italy, Belgium and Austria, rejected the Dutch and Spanish assessments, arguing that important data (on the levels of chloroplast in NK 603 and the allergenic qualities of the new maize) were lacking.

17 Regulation (EC) No. 2002/178 of the European Parliament and of the Council of 28 January 2002 laying down the general principles and requirements of food law, establishing the European Food Safety Authority and laying down procedures in matters of food safety, [2002] *OJ* L31/1, as amended by Regulation 2003/1643/EC of the European Parliament and of the Council of 22 July 2003, [2003] *OJ* L245/4.

Following these objections, the Commission requested EFSA's GMO Panel[18] to study the safety of food and food ingredients derived from NK 603 maize and to provide a scientific opinion as to 'whether there is any scientific reason to believe that the placing on the market of NK603 maize [. . .] is likely to cause any adverse effect on human health or on the environment' (in the context of Directive 2001/18) and to specify 'whether the authorisation of foods and food ingredients derived from NK 603 is likely to have an effect on public health' (in the context of Reg. 258/97) (EFSA 2003: 1).

The GMO Panel's risk assessment consisted mainly of review of data provided by Monsanto. These assessments were first tested for their accuracy; thereafter, the Panel assessed whether toxicity levels were in accordance with EU regulations (Chalmers 2004: 10). At one level, Monsanto's own assessment was more extensive than that of the GMO Panel, which did not assess the environmental effects of NK 603, since Monsanto wished only to market and not to grow NK 603 maize in Europe, raising the presumption that the maize would not intrude European ecosystems (EFSA 2003: 7–8). At another level, however, and under pressure to respond to concerns raised by Belgium and Italy, for instance, the GMO Panel conducted a more extensive assessment, checking levels of chloroplast in NK 603 maize (Chalmers 2004: 9). The Member States had asked the Panel for additional experimental data. The Panel, however, invoked only one study on chloroplast in tobacco and referred to scientific literature in general. Based on Monsanto's assessment and on this single study on chloroplast in tobacco, the Panel simply concluded that 'insertion of the chloroplast fragment in NK 603 does not constitute a risk' (EFSA 2003: 6).

As regards the allergenic qualities of the protein CP4 EPSPS, the Panel concluded it was safe on the basis of earlier risk assessments carried out by EC Scientific Committees and national authorities. Curiously, however, the Panel did not refer to these assessments themselves, but instead referred only to scientific literature providing guidelines for assessment. The Panel stated that the CP4 EPSPS protein was safe since it was not aware of any new information on allergenicity that would require the Panel to change its mind (EFSA 2003: 9). Austria's concerns about the potential for increased allergenicity posed by the NK 603 maize organism in its entirety was likewise dismissed as irrelevant: maize is not considered to be allergenic; adding elements likewise not known to be allergenic is unlikely to make it more so as a result of some unintended side-effect of the genetic recombination (EFSA 2003: 10). In this assessment, EFSA implicitly relied on Monsanto's conclusions, as it employed the same logic.

Two further issues raised by the Member States might have forced the Panel to go beyond a mere evaluation of Monsanto's assessment. The first concerned the need for monitoring of the GM maize once it had been released onto the market. Several Member States asserted that Monsanto should be obliged to monitor effects and report on it every six months. The Panel refused to examine this matter as it considered this to be a 'non-scientific' (quote from the preamble of the EFSA 2003 report) issue (Chalmers 2004: 9–10). Second, Member States raised concern

18 The Joint Research Centre of the European Union is also involved in the risk assessment as a Community Reference laboratory and approved Monsanto's methods. See Vos and Wendler 2006 for details.

about cross-contamination of regular maize. The GMO panel considered this issue to be outside its jurisdiction. Furthermore, it explicitly stated that cross-contamination was the responsibility of risk managers: '[t]he Panel is not in a position to evaluate co-existence issues which relate to risk management and not risk assessment' (EFSA 2003: 8). The Panel reiterated its view that since authorisation was required only for import and processing purposes, there was no need for scientific additional data on environmental effects associated with NK 603 maize cultivation. Furthermore, EFSA argued that since no wild maize can exist outside areas of human cultivation maize, the dangers of self-establishment of NK 603 were non-existent, a finding backed up with reference to anonymous European studies indicating that the modified maize does not exhibit enhanced 'weediness'. Interestingly, and even though it is an 'irrelevant' matter, 'outside its jurisdiction', EFSA thus chose explicitly to argue that the likelihood of unintended environmental effects is no larger than would be the case for conventional maize. The use of probabilistic vocabulary ('likelihood'), however, is revealing as it indicates that potential environmental effects cannot be fully ruled out. This rare example within the risk assessment of an implicit acknowledgement of the existence of uncertainty is, however, mirrored by the Panel's explicit choice to 'agree' with conclusions advanced by other risk assessors (EFSA 2003: 7): the notion of agreement might thus be argued to be an (unconscious) admission by EFSA that its own risk assessment entails a social process of deliberation, rather than finding of absolute proof, and might be subject to disagreement. Uncertainty had thus crept into a certainty-oriented discourse, even though it was never explicitly mentioned.

Taken together, the GMO Panel's conclusions on contamination are revealing. Where Chalmers (2004: 10) asserted that the NK 603 Panel interpreted its role in the narrowest and most formal sense, justifying a minimal risk assessment, we argue that more can be said: where mere import 'negates' the potential for environmental interference or EU-wide cross-contamination, the entire issue has been redefined as a 'non-risk' such that it is not necessary to engage in any 'boundary work'. 'Boundary work' is a notion coined by Gieryn (Gieryn 1983; 1995): it is a strategic and purposeful act in which boundaries are drawn between realms, for example, between science and non-science and between science and politics. Boundary work involves the building and/or (re)drawing of contrasts through selective attributions, which effectively demarcate spheres in order to construct 'self-evident justification' and 'superiority in designated terrains' (Gieryn 1999). The strategic and intentional tactical elements within boundary work are powerful: it has been convincingly demonstrated that boundary work extends beyond the attribution of formal responsibilities, entailing, instead, an ongoing negotiation process on roles and the manner in which these are portrayed to other actors. The GMO Panel was thus actively engaged in the drawing of the boundaries of its own jurisdiction and between risk assessment and management and science and non-science; in the latter case notably arguing that it had only been asked to consider the scientific objections of the Member States (EFSA 2003: 4). Constructed boundaries were deployed to ease the Panel's task in relation to uncertainties about environmental interference and cross-contamination, minimising the scope of the risk assessment. Constructed boundaries legitimise the GMO Panel's reluctance to deal with particular national concerns, disqualifying and dismissing those concerns as 'non-scientific' and 'issues of risk management'.

Boundary work made possible the evasion of uncertainty, which enabled EFSA's GMO Panel to declare NK 603 to be safe (EFSA 2003). Although the Panel was asked by the Commission to explore 'whether there are any scientific reasons to believe', the GMO Panel refused this invitation systematically to discuss the uncertainties involved and instead gave a clear answer: NK603 'is as safe as conventional maize and therefore the placing on the market [. . .] is unlikely to have an adverse effect on human and animal health and [. . .] the environment' (EFSA 2003: 11). In the classical risk perspective guiding the Panel, 'unlikely' can be read as 'low risk'. Read in combination with the claim that modified maize is 'as safe as' conventional maize, it might therefore be argued that the Panel had sought to provide a 'plausibility proof', even though the Commission had requested no such 'non-risk' conclusion. EFSA's GMO Panel did not actively seek to identify uncertainties overlooked by the risk producer, Monsanto, and proved itself to be just as uncertainty intolerant.

3.4.2 GT 73 oilseed rape

GT 73 oilseed rape had already received EU market approval in 1996 (as food and feed additives) and 1997 (as food).[19] Monsanto applied to the Dutch Government for authorisation for import into the Netherlands in July 1998. The assessment carried by the Dutch authorities was completed in 2003 (!), on which basis the Dutch Government concluded that there were no reasons to withhold authorisation. Five years later, however, the previous GMO regime was replaced by the new EU Directive 2001/18, which required Dutch authorities to notify the Commission following initial assessment. Again Member States raised objections. In response, the Commission similarly asked EFSA to consider 'whether there is any scientific reason to believe that the placing on the market of GT 73 oilseed rape, for import and processing, is likely to cause any adverse effects on human health and the environment within the scope of Directive 2001/18' (EFSA 2004b: 1).

Again, national concerns forced EFSA's GMO panel to go beyond mere review of the risk producer's assessment, doubting: the manner in which Monsanto had prepared its data concerning the molecular characterisation of the GMO and the methodologies used for molecular detection; the adequacy of information on potential allergenic risks; the significance of rat tests indicating increased liver weights; and the adequacy of potential cross-contamination monitoring plans (EFSA 2004b). Once again, however, national doubts were circumvented.

Opening their argument, the Panel engaged in explicit boundary work: 'EFSA was not requested to give an opinion on the non-scientific objections' (EFSA 2004b: 4). Drawing this boundary between science and non-science, EFSA mobilised its subsequent authority to evade the uncertainties embedded within Member States' concerns. The Panel addressed the concern about the manner in which Monsanto had prepared its data, simply by expressing its satisfaction with additional data

19 Under Council Directive 89/107/EEC of 21 December 1988 on the approximation of the laws of the Member States concerning food additives authorised for use in foodstuffs intended for human consumption, [1989] *OJ* L40/27 and Regulation (EC) No. 258/97 of the European Parliament and of the Council of 27 January 1997 concerning novel foods and novel food ingredients, [1997] *OJ* L43/1, Article 5 respectively.

provided by Monsanto. Furthermore, the issue of molecular characterisation and detection was again addressed through boundary work: EFSA stated that these issues were 'presently not within the scope of the GMO Panel remit' (EFSA 2004b: 4). The Panel then investigated the potential allergenic qualities of the modified CP4 EPSPS and GOXv247 proteins (EFSA 2004b: 9), appearing to conclude in relation to the first protein that Monsanto analysis sufficed and sharing its conclusion that the protein is non-allergenic (EFSA 2004b: 9). This finding was bolstered by reference to the previous Panel assessment for NK 603 (EFSA 2004b: 9). Nonetheless, as noted above, this assessment was itself based upon the earlier findings of national authorities and EC Scientific Committees, which were not reviewed. Again, the Panel explicitly stated that new information on allergenicity would be required in order to change its opinion (EFSA 2004b: 9). A strategic authority claim was accordingly constructed to satisfy concerns about the non-allergenicity of the protein.

Responding to national concern about a 1995 rat study, EFSA drew on other rat studies and, in particular, one dating from 1994 that also indicated increased liver weights, but was likewise characterised by obvious flaws in the testing procedure. Even though Member States did not refer to the 1994 study, EFSA seems to have used it to create the impression that increased liver weights may be artificial. In addition, EFSA completed its smoke-screen by deploying a second study, which it qualified as 'comprehensive':

> The study did not reveal any significant difference in weight gain, feed intake or organ (liver, kidney) weights between rats fed GT 73 and the parental Westar line and the commercial lines. Closer examination of the data indicated that liver weights varied considerably between replicates and between control groups fed different varieties of non-transgenic oilseed rape. The liver weights of the GT 73 replicate groups fell well within the range of the responses for the different controls including Westar (EFSA 2004b: 10).

EFSA reviewed similar studies on animals (rainbow trout, quail, chickens and lamb (EFSA 2004b: 11)), seemingly furnished by Monsanto (p. 13), thus casting the 1995 study into the background: its 'anomalous' results were not used to explore uncertainty or to open up discussion on whether and how rat liver-weight might result from GMO oilseed rape; instead, 'normal' findings in the other studies were used to argue that GT 73 was safe.

Although the adequacy of cross-contamination monitoring plans was only dealt with briefly, the Panel did comment on cross-contamination issues it had previously deemed to lie beyond its jurisdiction (see above). Illustrating the flexibility of boundaries drawn between risk assessment and risk management, the Panel reasoned that spillage could only reasonably occur at seaports of import, which are normally located in industrial areas, making contact with regular plants and gene transfer highly unlikely (EFSA 2004b: 14). Monsanto argued that, since gene-transfer as a result of spillage would be highly unlikely, a more advanced monitoring plan was unnecessary (EFSA 2004b: 14). EFSA mobilised this agreement with the risk producer's experts in order to construct a close-to-zero risk.

In sum, the Panel concluded that the GT 73 oilseed rape is as safe and wholesome as its organically grown counterparts (EFSA 2004b: 15). Although it conducted a wider-ranging assessment than for NK 603 maize, once again illustrating the strategic dynamics within boundary work, EFSA evaded the uncertainties noticeable in Member States' concerns.

3.4.3 MON 810 × MON 863 hybrid maize

MON 863 × MON 810 hybrid maize entered the EU consciousness following a successful marketing application made in Germany, which was subsequently contested by other Member States. The Commission accordingly turned to EFSA, who requested the GMO Panel 'to consider whether there is any scientific reason to believe that the placing on the market of MON 863 and MON 863 × MON 810 maize, for import and processing, is likely to cause any adverse effects on human health and the environment' (EFSA 2004a: 1). Identical phrasing was used in the Commission's evaluation request for NK 603 and GT 73.

Matters of molecular characterisation, comparative analysis and food safety were addressed in much the same ways as before. However, in this case, EFSA failed to close the file: following assessment of both parents and hybrid, the Panel decided that only MON 863 and MON 810, and *not* the hybrid, could be deemed safe (EFSA 2004a: 19–20). Two particular controversies played their part: doubts on the methodology used to assess hybrid genes and concerns about MON 863 toxicity, following liver-damage in test-rats (Chalmers 2004: 14). Although the Panel initially hypothesised that since MON 863 and MON 810 were both deemed safe, it would be 'scientifically valid' to assume that the conventionally created cross hybrid is as safe as either of the individual parents (EFSA 2004a), the Panel remained divided on the need for additional data to confirm this assumption, with some members calling for a 90-day rat study to test the hybrid maize. No clear decision was reached on the safety of the MON 863 × MON 810 maize: the report stated simply that agreement could not be reached (EFSA 2004a: 19).

Persistent disagreement in the GMO panel forced EFSA to highlight methodological uncertainties, as well as uncertainty relating to the limits of available data. Nonetheless, EFSA did not systematically explore underlying sources of uncertainty, neither did it discuss the issue of (ir)reducibility or interpretative flexibility of uncertainties, let alone the decisional consequences of uncertainty. It instead portrayed these uncertainties as obstacles to consensus. 'The need for confirmatory data' (EFSA 2004a: 2) took precedence over discussion on the specific uncertainties relating to MON 863 × MON 810, once again delegating the problem to the future.

Here EFSA requested an additional rat study from Monsanto, 'in order to allow the Panel to finalise its evaluation' (EFSA 2005), which was provided in April 2005. Meanwhile EU legislation changed and Monsanto applied for permission for use of MON 863 × MON 810 for food and feed purposes. EFSA requested its GMO Panel 'to conclude its risk assessment', thus presenting earlier disagreement as a mere lack of data, which could be resolved in the future, and a final opinion on MON 863 × MON 810 was forthcoming two months later, which can be read as a postscript to EFSA's previous opinion. Despite some anomalous results showing that rats fed hybrid maize were of statistically significantly lower weight, these results were immediately dismissed with the unsubstantiated assertion that 'this difference did not exhibit a dose-response relationship', and the Panel concluded that there are no safety concerns (EFSA 2005). This was a further example of EFSA's use of authority claims to evade uncertainty.

3.4.4 EFSA and uncertain risks

On the basis of the three case studies, it seems that where EFSA cannot furnish a yes-or-no answer, it lacks alternative modes of informing risk regulation. The three GMO cases demonstrate that EFSA feels that a risk assessment should provide a plausibility proof. *Pfizer* was a case in which risk managers sought to force experts to provide certainty about uncertain risk. In the case of EFSA, we see that experts are also inclined to view their role as one of providing a plausibility proof. Even if unconsciously so, risk assessors are likewise active propagators of the uncertainty paradox, with the consequence that where they are unable to evade uncertainty, they cannot act.

A further interesting feature of the case studies is the degree of flexibility inherent in the GMO Panel's boundary work. Chalmers recognises that the GMO panel 'drew a new boundary between risk assessment and risk management' (2004: 14–15) in relation to MON 810 × MON 863. Whereas the Panel refused to investigate wider issues of environmental interference and cross-contamination in relation to GT 73 and NK603, emphasising the contrast between risk assessment and risk management, it chose to comment on environmental safety, despite the fact that MON 810 × MON 863 maize was for import and processing only. Arguing, first, that cross-contamination was unlikely since maize had never transplanted itself beyond cultivated areas in Europe, and, second, that the proteins providing the hybrid with insecticidal qualities degrade rapidly as a result of digestion (or within microbial processes in manure) and are thus unlikely to threaten non-target insects (EFSA 2004a: 18–19), EFSA does provide us with an insight on the uncertainties that play a role in decision making. It further shares with us its reasoning about the importance of the uncertainties involved, no longer reasoning that there is no risk involved, but instead implicitly arguing that there are no scientific reasons to believe that cross-contamination is very likely or hazardous. The boundaries between risk assessment and risk management are dynamic: for NK 603, cross-contamination issues were deemed to be a matter for risk management and, therefore, irrelevant; for MON 810 × MON 863, cross-contamination was discussed in the context of risk assessment, albeit that uncertainty was likewise diffused with the 'highly unlikely' formula.

EFSA's risk assessments in all three case studies entail review of the risk producer's safety assessment in response to specific national concerns. The GMO panel works under severe time constraints (six months[20]) and, as a consequence, cannot carry out independent research, but relies on external studies, whether carried out by risk producers themselves or other researchers, and may likewise feel unable to request additional information (Chalmers 2004). Similarly, GMO-Panel members are not full-time EFSA employees, but are recruited on a part-time basis: Panel members receive a (small) fee in order to ensure their independence (Vos and Wendler 2006). Such constraints notwithstanding, particular troublesome features and consequences of EFSA's approach to risk assessment should be highlighted.

In practice, the GMO Panel's reliance on the risk producer's safety assessment

20 Above, note 12, Article 6(1).

entails practical delegation of risk assessment and associated testing to risk producers, such as Monsanto, who become *de facto* risk assessors. Accordingly, assessment becomes dependent on the applicant's willingness to disclose all relevant information. Monsanto's uncertainty-intolerant behaviour with regard to adverse effects tests demonstrates that dependency is not a theoretical issue, but a practical difficulty. EFSA's independence is thus compromised by its reliance on Monsanto's problem-framing, tests and willingness to disclose uncertainty and adverse results.

Chalmers (2004: 12) characterises EFSA's style of reasoning as providing 'its own corpus of proof' to find no evidence of risk: the GMO Panel seeks to construct of yes-no answers to questions that can by contrast being read as tolerant of uncertainty. The Commission asked EFSA to 'consider whether there is any scientific reason to believe' that the placing of GMOs on the market 'is likely to cause any adverse effects on human health and the environment' (EFSA 2003; 2004a; 2004b), an open formulation, which contrasts starkly with the closed question (ie whether or not the activity constitutes a risk) it asked of SCAN in *Pfizer*. Arguably, in the former case, the Commission is uncertainty tolerant: rather than request positive proof that the hazard is a risk, it is open to indications of adverse effects; rather than refer to science as a source of absolute truth and certainty, the Commission's use of the 'to believe' notion demonstrates its awareness that science cannot provide certainty about uncertain risks.

Rather than accept this invitation to provide uncertainty information, however, the GMO Panel successfully constructed plausibility proofs for NK 603, GT 73 and MON 863 × MON 810. Comparing GMOs with *Pfizer*, a paradox is apparent: in *Pfizer*, risk managers requested a plausibility proof, which they received, but then reconstructed as uncertainty in order to legitimise a position in opposition to risk assessors; in the GMO cases, risk managers arguably phrased their request in an uncertainty tolerant manner, but EFSA's GMO Panel sought to provide plausibility proofs instead.

In common with the risk producer, the Panel is uncertainty intolerant: risks exist or they do not. Does EFSA's GMO Panel likewise conflate uncertainty with risk? Risk research (Frewer *et al.* 2003) indicates that many risk experts are convinced that information about uncertainty will increase public distrust, as well as cause panic, since they are convinced that 'uncertainty' is interpreted as meaning more risk and more danger. Accordingly, it is conceivable that the GMO Panel's reluctance to disclose uncertainty information derives from their fear that uncertainty and risk will be conflated, the one with the other, *by others*.

This analysis demonstrates EFSA's use of dynamic boundary work to assert irrelevance and the authority of its own claims in order to construct safety findings. Jasanoff (2005) refers to this behaviour as 'less transparent', but politically significant, boundary work: 'believe the experts' is the implicit message within the Panel's often un-explained and un-referenced mobilisation of 'the scientific literature'. The authoritative voice, which EFSA thereby establishes for itself, allows it to evade uncertainty. EFSA is seemingly as uncertainty intolerant and safety-oriented as Monsanto, and, although we must emphasise that EFSA never deliberately promotes Monsanto's interests (similarity is the *effect* of EFSA's attitude towards uncertainty, and not its point of departure), the uncertainty intolerance shared by the two parties determines that their reasoning modes are mutually supportive. Once again, mutual uncertainty intolerance impacts to propagate the uncertainty paradox, regardless of the greater openness displayed by risk managers. The lesson to be learnt is that EFSA will only enhance its independence and enrich its role as risk assessor when it dares to be more uncertainty tolerant and risk oriented.

3.5 Risk managers: Member States and the Commission

The European Commission and Member States act as risk managers. In addition, Member States, such as Spain, the Netherlands and Germany acted as initial risk assessors upon receipt of Monsanto's authorisation requests. Whenever Member States object to national risk assessments, or authorisation requests concerning GM food or feed under Regulation 1829/2003, a Community authorisation procedure must be followed: the Commission takes a decision in accordance with the 'regulatory committee procedure', based on an EFSA opinion. Prior to adopting a decision, the Commission must consult the Standing Committee on the Food Chain and Animal Health (SCFCAH)[21] or the Standing Committee on Release of GMOs into the Environment:[22] each adopts its opinion by qualified majority.[23] If it is in accordance with the Committee's opinion, the Commission adopts its draft decision. Where Committee and Commission opinions diverge, however, or no opinion is delivered, the Commission refers to the Council, which decides by qualified majority within a period laid down in the relevant directive or regulation (maximum of three months). Where the Council objects to the proposal made, the Commission must re-examine it, and then either submit an amended proposal, re-submit its proposal to the Council or present a legislative proposal on the basis of the Treaty. If the Council fails to act, or to indicate opposition, the Commission adopts its proposed measure.[24]

This centralised 'one-door-one-key' approach has often been characterised by problems at Standing Committee level. In our case studies, decision making was tortuous: heated debate within the Standing Committee failed to produce an opinion on NK 603, and the Commission's authorisation proposal (in line with EFSA's opinion) failed to receive support from Denmark, Greece, Luxembourg, Austria and Portugal, with Germany and Spain abstaining. Surprisingly, Italy, known for its scepticism about GMOs, voted in favour. National resistance forced the Commission to submit the issue to the Council, who also failed to reach agreement.[25] The Standing Committee also failed to give an opinion in the two maize cases.

In practice, 'the extraordinary procedure' has become the norm in GMO regulation. Equally, since Commission decisions are based on EFSA advice, the advisory institution is the *de facto* decision maker. Since democratic deliberation by the Member States is overruled by expert opinion, we argue that this is a typical case of technocratic decision making. Notwithstanding rhetoric and institutional reform following BSE, which conferred decisional responsibility on the Commission, our

21 Above, note 12.

22 Above, note 10.

23 Council Decision 1999/468 of 28 June 1999 laying down the procedures for the exercise of implementing powers conferred on the Commission, [1999] *OJ* L184/23.

24 Above, note 23, Article 5.

25 Explanatory Memorandum, COM(2004) 439 final 2.

analysis shows that scientific experts continue to play the central, undisputed role in EU GMO regulation (Borrás 2006). Despite national resistance, the Commission authorised the marketing of NK 603[26] and GT 73 oilseed[27] under Directive 2001/18, taking EFSA's opinion as its justification. The decision-making process was more complex for MON 810 × MON 863 due to disagreement within EFSA's GMO Panel. In 2004, Member States failed to reach a majority in favour or against authorisation, but since the Commission could not rely on a plausibility proof, the decision-making process temporarily evaporated. Following changes to the regulatory regime, and the issuance of a new EFSA opinion, the Commission presented a new proposal to the Standing Committee in 2005, but again the Member States failed to establish a majority. The matter was referred to the Council, who failed to react within the time period, with the consequence that the Commission was also able to authorise the European marketing of MON 863 × MON 810 in this case.[28]

One Commission official's depiction of the relationship between the Commission and EFSA as being one of a blind driver and a passenger, with EFSA acting as the directions-giving passenger (Vos and Wendler 2006), is remarkably apt: all three cases are marked by technocracy and uncritical Commission compliance with EFSA scientific assessments. EFSA is the *de facto* risk manager. Blind Commission compliance further reifies the uncertainty paradox: risks are uncertain, but experts respond with constructed plausibility proofs. In view of these attempts by risk assessors to evade uncertainties, disagreement nonetheless (and unsurprisingly so) reigns among risk managers (Member States and Council). Accordingly, the technocratic risk manager (the Commission) once again turns to experts for certainty, justifying its decision with the contested risk assessment and new plausibility proof. Löfstedt (2005) argues that the technocracy implies systematic underestimation of uncertainty information, a conclusion supported by our case studies.

As the 'blind-driver' image indicates, Commission compliance with EFSA opinions seems to be founded on an established pattern of trust, which corresponds with patterns described by Thompson and Bloom (2000) and Löfstedt (2005): risk managers largely trust risk assessors. Risk managers believe that risk assessors are efficient and comprehensive in their approach and consequently assume that their analyses and assumptions are valid. As a consequence, and despite certain anomalies found, say, in *Pfizer*, risk managers readily accept the plausibility proofs constructed by risk assessors.

Nonetheless, and seemingly paradoxically so, Thompson and Bloom (2000) also

26 Commission Decision 200/448/EC of 3 March 2005 authorising the placing on the market of foods and food ingredients derived from genetically modified maize line NK 603 as novel foods or novel food ingredients under Regulation (EC) No. 258/97 of the European Parliament and of the Council, [2005] *OJ* L158/20.

27 Commission Decision 2005/635/EC of 31 August 2005 concerning the placing on the market, in accordance with Directive 2001/19/EC of the European Parliament and of the Council, of an oilseed rape product (Brassica napus L., GT73 line) genetically modified for tolerance to the herbicide glyphosate, [2005] *OJ* L228/11.

28 Commission Decision 2006/47/EC of 16 January 2006 concerning the placing on the market, in accordance with Directive 2001/18/EC of the European Parliament and of the Council, of a maize product (Zea mays L., hybrid MON 863 × MON 810) genetically modified for resistance to corn rootworm and certain lepidopteran pests of maize, [2006] *OJ* L26/17.

note that risk managers often crave greater information about the implications of uncertainty. On the one hand, the 'open' questions posed by the Commission in GMO cases (is there any scientific reason to believe) reflect this craving; on the other, however, its uncritical acceptance of EFSA plausibility proofs becomes difficult to understand. EU risk regulation demonstrated that 'risk managers' are a heterogeneous group of actors: a stark distinction should be made between the Commission and the Member States. Some Member States contested EFSA's plausibility proofs, highlighting uncertainties they considered relevant to decision making. It might be argued that such States are risk managers who are prepared to consider uncertainties, although, at the same time, it is impossible to determine whether such concern is motivated by an interest in human health and the environment, or whether economic protectionism is the driving force, since objections about genetic modification can be used to block US imports into the European agricultural sector (Fitzgerald 2003). If the latter is a motivation, it is likewise an example of the 'politicisation' of uncertainty that many risk experts fear. Politicians, stakeholders, special interests groups and/or the public may act opportunistically highlighting, amplifying or attenuating uncertainties in order to serve other hidden interests (Funtowicz and Ravetz 1990; Pollack 2003; Smithson 1993; Stocking and Holstein 1993; Wells Bedsworth *et al.* 2004). Since our data neither proves nor disproves whether Member States are, 'correctly' so, more uncertainty-tolerant (having justified interest in uncertainty information) and have left the positivistic risk paradigm behind, or whether they merely use uncertainty as a political resource, neither option can be discounted.

Finally, however, all three products are legally permitted to circulate within the EU. Luxembourg, Austria, Germany, France and Greece continue to resist GMO products for environmental reasons (Brown 2005), but have offered no 'new' scientific evidence, determining that the Commission may chose to enforce its decisions; an option it has yet to use. The Commission's decision to authorise the marketing of these GM products can also be qualified as a 'non-decision'. This equally suggests that the technocratic approach fails short in the case of uncertain risks, which is, instead, a highly delicate, political matter.

3.6 Risk protestors: Greenpeace and Friends of the Earth

The main risk protestors active in our study are the environmental NGOs, Greenpeace and Friends of the Earth. Although comprehensive scrutiny of protest is beyond our scope, Greenpeace critiques of GT 73 assessments (Greenpeace 2004), and Friends of the Earth's disquiet about the workings of EFSA's GMO Panel (Friends of the Earth Europe 2004), provide a preliminary insight into the approach adopted by risk protestors towards uncertain risks. Shortly after EFSA's opinion on GT 73 became public, Greenpeace published a brief critique on the assessment methods used. For example, Greenpeace concluded that irregularities in the molecular characterisation of GT 73 oilseed rape had not been investigated satisfactorily (Greenpeace 2004: 2). EFSA's report indicated that, in addition to genes added by Monsanto, GT 73 contained a small DNA fragment not found in its unmodified counterpart, and also lacked some DNA usually found in oilseed rape

(EFSA 2004b: 5). Greenpeace argued that the Panel should have investigated further, believing that insufficient molecular characterisation implies uncertainty, which denotes risk. Greenpeace did not consider the possibility these uncertainties could also be 'safe uncertainties' (RMNO 2004; Van Asselt 2004), revealing a tendency on the part of risk protestors to equate uncertainty with risk, a strategy also applied by Monsanto, although with radically different intentions. Monsanto avoids uncertainty in order to demonstrate safety; Greenpeace highlights uncertainty in order to demonstrate risk.

Friends of the Earth, by contrast, argue that the Commission mobilises EFSA in order to advance stealth marketing of GMO products. This conspiracy is constructed in reference to the Commission's reliance on EFSA opinions above those of the Member States on the safety of NK 603: 'the Commission decided to rely solely upon the EFSA point of view to license this product' (Friends of the Earth Europe 2004: 6). The NGO is explicitly critical of EFSA's handling of uncertainty: '[b]y failing to frame its opinion within the context of continuing scientific debate and uncertainty about fundamental issues relating to its conclusions, the Panel has failed to provide decision makers with an adequate analysis of scientific uncertainty' (Friends of the Earth Europe 2004: 15–16). Risk protestors differ in their expectation of risk assessors. Rather than expect a plausibility proof, risk protestors demand systematic analysis of scientific uncertainty:

> The GMO Panel disregards statistically significant differences between GM and their non-GM counterparts, instead agreeing with the industry that the results of such tests are not biologically relevant or treatment related. In addition the Panel ignores EU requirements to identify the level of uncertainty in its assumptions, and fails to take in legal requirements that regard is given to the long term effects of eating or growing GM foods. (Friends of the Earth Europe 2004: 17)

This is not an unreasonable expectation: an (unintended) consequence of EFSA's evasion of uncertainty is increased distrust among risk protestors. It is grist to their mill and further underlines the vulnerability of uncertainty-intolerant, technocratic approaches to uncertain risks. Although it is argued that persistent risk protestors will always find something to complain about, and it must be equally underlined that conspiracy theories fail to understand that concordance between Monsanto and EFSA assessments derives from their mutually supportive uncertainty intolerance, rather than from commercial-political strategy, protestors surely also make in this case a valid point. A more uncertainty-tolerant approach, encompassing systematic efforts to furnish uncertainty information and serious discussion on uncertainties and their consequences, would allow risk assessors and managers to be more critical of risk producers and would make it harder for risk protestors simply to equate uncertainty with risk. At the least, it would pre-empt conspiracy theories: EFSA is currently seeking to insert greater transparency within its risk assessments and, in this context, has suggested that risk assessments should also describe underlying assumptions and uncertainties.[29]

29 EFSA-Q-2005-050, Transparency in Risk Assessment, development of comprehensive guidance.

4 CONCLUSIONS

Our three case studies of EU decision making on GMO risks scrutinised how the risk producers, assessors and managers struggle with uncertain risks. The following conclusions with regard to the mechanisms, patterns, tendencies and strategies deployed in practice:

- In these cases, the risk producer is the *de facto* risk assessor.
- Both the risk producer and risk assessor exhibit uncertainty-intolerant behaviour, evading and defining away uncertainty. Furthermore, uncertainty intolerance among the risk assessor is reflected in the politically significant mobilisation of boundary work.
- The risk producer and risk protestors both seek to equate uncertainty with risk, though with radically different goals. Where decision-regulation is technocratic and dominated by uncertainty intolerance, this theoretically troublesome equation is not challenged and is successful in practice.
- Plausibility proofs are constructed through irrelevance and authority claims and dynamic boundary work. However, this approach to risk assessment may create political paralysis (non-decisions), and is vulnerable to the meaningful critique of risk protestors.
- Exceptional decision-making procedures have become the *de facto* norm: the Commission decides in cases where no qualified majority can be built among the Member States in Council. This creates a political deficit and technocratic and science-led risk management as the Commission blindly follows EFSA opinions. Significantly, this practice also undermines post BSE crisis political efforts to create a clear division of responsibilities between expert advice and political legitimacy; the *raison d'être* for establishment of EFSA.

The uncertainty paradox is clearly manifest within EU GMO regulation. Risk producers, assessors and managers spent most of their way out of the deadlocks caused by the propagation of the uncertainty paradox, and failed to make full use of the critical intelligence and uncertainty information that experts can inject into the political system. The uncertainty paradox derives from interplay between uncertainty intolerance, conflation of risk and uncertainty, boundary work and technocracy.

Risk producer and risk assessor evasion of uncertainty is typical of this uncertainty paradox. Even though risk managers may not request plausibility proofs, while risk protestors highlight the need for uncertainty information, risk producers and assessors seem, by contrast, to be driven to construct plausibility proofs. Are producers and assessors dedicated to the production of certainty, whereas societal actors wish to learn more about uncertainty? The failure of the GMO Panel to reach agreement on MON 810 × MON 863 left EFSA without plausibility proofs. Risk managers proved themselves unable to deal with this situation, even though their open formulation of the regulatory question had left the experts room to discern uncertainty. Risk managers also appear to need plausibility proofs, indicating that evasion of uncertainty is not internally driven, but rather systematic within the decisional infrastructure of which EFSA is a part.

Our findings allow us to put national discontent about authorisation procedures in context. In March 2006, in heated exchanges in an Environmental Council, several national environment ministers voiced dissatisfaction about the manner in which their concerns about GMOs are addressed by EFSA and the Commission. EFSA was roundly criticised for failing to tackle national objections and resolve divergence between scientific opinions. Austria, one of the fiercest GMO opponents, expressed its desire to re-open discussion on EFSA safety findings, since some Member States felt it had approved products without adequate research.[30] Denmark argued that justified scientific objections should be better addressed, while Italy and Germany demanded greater consultation with national authorities in the increasing number of cases of diverging scientific views (in particular, between EFSA and national authorities), in order to lessen the danger that assessments would subsequently be challenged. Italy further highlighted political implications, noting that consumers are very worried about GMOs. Both Hungary and Belgium doubted EFSA's science, the latter arguing that the GMO panel did not have suitable qualified experts to assess environmental risks: 'we do not think that this [environmental risk assessment] takes place at the moment'.[31] Slovenia noted that data from applicant companies for the GMO authorisations should be independently verified. Demands were also made for a change in comitology procedures, such that the Commission would no longer be able to approve GMOs where the majority of Member States do not favour authorisation.[32] In April 2006, even the EU Environment Commissioner, Dimas, openly questioned the quality of EFSA's scientific opinions,[33] noting that EFSA relied too heavily on industry data, concentrating on short-term effects, and consequently failed to give sound advice on long-term effects.[34] Dimas has also argued that although EFSA is still young, its risk assessments should be made as comprehensive and transparent as possible, in order to augment trust and diminish organisational reliance on comitology decisional procedures.[35]

At first glance, our findings surely coincide with national critiques of EFSA: EFSA's boundary work has allowed it to disregard national claims rather than welcome concerns within systematic discussion of uncertainty; equally, Belgian doubts find some support in our finding that risk producers may act as *de facto* risk assessors, a problem that has practical implications, as the rat-study affair demonstrates. Nonetheless, it is also apparent that criticism of EFSA is also indelibly caught within the uncertainty paradox: many Member States, as well as the environmental Commissioner, continue to frame EFSA's role in terms of providing certainty about uncertain risks. EFSA is expected to resolve scientific divergence and to conduct research in order to provide conclusive evidence. Various risk managers do appear to be more uncertainty tolerant. At the same time, however, the uncertainty paradox is further reified. Regulatory reform that still propagates the uncertainty paradox is doomed to fail.

30 See <http://www.euractiv.com/EN/biotech>.

31 *EU Food Law Weekly*, No. 247, 10 March 2006, p. 4.

32 *Ibid.*

33 See <http://today.reuters.com/news/newsArticle.aspx?type=scienceNews&storyID=2006-04-05T105928Z_01_L05651737_RTRUKOC_0_US-FOOD-EU-GMO.xml&archived=False>.

34 *Ibid.*

35 Above, note 31, p. 5.

Subtle differences may be noted in the *Pfizer* case, but both it and EU GMO regulation demonstrate that the uncertainty paradox is reified and prolonged by risk producers, risk assessors and risk managers. More innovative regulatory reform will be needed if we are ever to escape its paralysing clutches. In particular, reform must seek to tackle uncertainty head-on.

- Panels, such as the GMO Panel, should not only be made up of experts on specific uncertain risks, but should also welcome uncertainty-tolerant experts, who might better organise resistance to institutionalised production of plausibility proofs. Such experts might also help to frame and phrase EFSA's opinions in a manner understandable to a lay audience.
- Forums should be created within which risk producers, risk assessors and risk managers might meet and develop exchanges beyond indirect communication through formal reports. Such forums might promote new discussions on uncertainties and allow risk managers to gain better understanding of what science can and cannot provide.
- Where expert bodies, such as EFSA, evade uncertainties, technocratic loopholes should be closed and political and democratic decision making enhanced. The responsibility and accountability of politicians must also be rethought: politicians and other decision makers should not be allowed to hide behind experts.
- Politicians should assume a responsibility to guard against definition of problems by risk producers. This point is of vital significance: currently Monsanto sets the agenda, defines problems and frames issues through its safety assessments; EFSA can only assess products within frameworks of meaning conjured up by Monsanto.
- Likewise, EFSA should be given a budget-independent verificatory research. Even though independent research might never furnish conclusive evidence and might even increase problems of paralysis, for carrying out second opinion research, even though it cannot yield conclusive evidence and it might increase the risk of 'analysis paralysis', comparative research might also aid experts more critically to identify and examine the uncertainties in industry assessments. Experts can also produce uncertainty information (Krayer von Kraus 2005; Petersen *et al.* 2003) and EFSA is currently reflecting on ways to provide uncertainty information.[36]
- Although dependency on the risk producer as risk assessor can and should be lessened, it is doubtful that EU bodies will ever be able to reproduce the comprehensive testing conducted by risk producers. It necessarily remains a matter of trust; yet, trust should never be naively or blindly given. Failure to respect the atmosphere of mutual trust should, at the very least, have negative consequences for the risk producer. As it currently stands, Monsanto's marketing efforts have not been affected by the infamous 'rat-study affair'. Whether suppression of data derived from lack of due diligence, or was a deliberate attempt to hide uncertainty information, risk managers remained sanguine. How can we expect trustworthy behaviour when abuse is tolerated?

36 EFSA-Q-2005-050, Transparency in Risk Assessment, development of comprehensive guidance.

BIBLIOGRAPHY

Van Asselt, M.B.A. (2005) 'The complex significance of uncertainty in a risk era: Logics, manners and strategies in use', *Int. J. for Risk Assessment and Management* 5(2/3/4): 125–58.

Van Asselt, M.B.A. (2004) 'Onzekere risico's en riskante onzekerheden', in G. van Calster and E. Vos (eds), *Risico en voorzorg in de rechtsmaatschappij*, Antwerp: Intersentia, 1–16.

Van Asselt, M.B.A. (2000) *Perspectives on Uncertainty and Risk: The PRIMA Approach to Decision Support*, Dordrecht: Kluwer Academic Publishers.

Van Asselt, M.B.A., Mesman, J. and Van 't Klooster, S.A. (2007) 'Dealing with prognostic uncertainty', *Futures* 39(6), 669–84.

Van Asselt, M.B.A. and Vos, E. (2006) 'Precautionary principle and the uncertainty paradox', *Journal of Risk Research* 9(4), 313–36.

Van Asselt, M.B.A. and Vos, E. (2005) 'The precautionary principle in times of intermingled uncertainty and risk: Some regulatory complexities', *Water, Science and Technology* 52(6), 35–41.

Bal, R., Bijker, W.E. and Hendriks, R. (2002) *Paradox van wetenschappelijk gezeg: over de maatschappelijke invloed van adviezen van de Gezondheidsraad*, Den Haag: Gezondheidsraad.

Beck, U. (1997) *The World as Risk-society: Essays on the Ecological Crisis and the Politics of Progress* (in Dutch), I van der Aart, Translator, Amsterdam: De Balie.

Beck, U. (1986) *Risk Society: Towards a New Modernity*, London: Sage.

Biagioli, M. (1999) *The Science Studies Reader*, New York/London: Routledge.

Borrás, S. (2006) 'Legitimate governance of risk at the EU level? The case of genetically modified organisms', *Technological forecasting and social change* 73(1): 61–75.

Brown, P. (2005) 'EU votes to continue ban on GM crops', *The Guardian*, 25 June 2005, available at: <http://environment.guardian.co.uk/food/story/0,,1849225,00.html>, accessed 29 January 2006.

Burns, J.M. (2002) *13 week dietary subschronic comparison study with MON 863 Corn in rats preceded by a 1-week baseline food consumption determination with PMI certified rodent diet #5008*, St. Louis: Monsanto Company.

Chalmers, D. (2004) Risk, Anxiety and the European Mediation of the Politics of Life: The European Food Safety Authority and the Government of Biotechnology, available at: <http://www.law.harvard.edu/programs/elrc/events/2004-2005/socialregulation.pdf>, accessed July 2005.

Dunsby, J. (2004) 'Measuring environmental health risks: the negotiation of a public right-to-know law', *Science, Technology & Human Values* 29(3): 269–90.

Edwards, A. (1999) 'Scientific expertise and policy-making: the intermediary role of the public sphere', *Science and Public Policy* 26(3): 163–70.

EFSA (2005) 'Opinion of the Scientific Panel on Genetically Modified Organisms on a request from the Commission related to the Notification (Reference C/DE/02/9) for the placing on the market of insect-protected genetically modified maize MON 863 × MON 810, for import and processing, under Part C of Directive 2001/18/EC from Monsanto', *The EFSA Journal* 251: 1–22.

EFSA (2004a) 'Opinion of the Scientific Panel on Genetically Modified Organisms on a request from the Commission related to the Notification (Reference C/DE/02/9) for the placing on the market of insect protected genetically modified maize MON 863 and MON 863 × MON 810, for import and processing, under Part C of Directive 2001/18/EC from Monsanto', *The EFSA Journal* 49: 1–25.

EFSA (2004b) 'Opinion of the Scientific Panel on Genetically Modified Organisms on a request from the Commission related to the Notification (Reference C/NL/98/11) for the placing on the market of glyphosatetolerant oilseed rape event GT73, for import and processing, under Part C of Directive 2001/18/EC from Monsanto', *The EFSA Journal* 29: 1–19.

EFSA (2003) 'Opinion of the Scientific Panel on Genetically Modified Organisms on a request from the Commission related to the safety of foods and food ingredients derived from herbicide-tolerant genetically modified maize NK603, for which a request for placing on the market was submitted under Article 4 of the Novel Food Regulation (EC) No. 258/97 by Monsanto', *The EFSA Journal* 9: 1–14.

European Court of First Instance (2002 (brought to CFI in 1999)) 'Judgment Case T-13/99 *Pfizer Animal Health SA v Council of the European Union* [2002] ECR II-03305'.

Faure, M.G. and Vos, E. (2003) *Juridische afbakening van het voorzorgsbeginsel: Mogelijkheden en grenzen*, Den Haag: Gezondheidsraad.

Friends of the Earth Europe (2004) 'Throwing Caution to the Wind. A review on the European Food Safety Authority and its work on genetically modified foods and crops', available at: <http://www.foeeurope.org/GMOs/publications/EFSAreport.pdf>, accessed 14 July 2006.

Fitzgerald, S.J. (2003) 'Putting the EU in Its Place: Why Filing a GMO Case with the WTO Is Crucial', Executive Memorandum, The Heritage Foundation, available at: <http://www.heritage.org/Research/Europe/em855.cfm>, accessed 27 November 2007.

Forrester, I. and Hanekamp, J.C. (2006) 'Precaution, Science and Jurisprudence: a Test Case', *Journal of Risk Research* 9(4): 297–311.

Frewer, L.J., Hunt, S., Brennan, M., Kuznesof, S., Ness, M. and Ritson, C. (2003) 'The views of scientific experts on how the public conceptualize uncertainty', *Journal of Risk Research* 2(6): 75–85.

Funtowicz, S.O. and Ravetz, J.R. (1994) 'The worth of a songbird: ecological economics as a post-normal science', *Ecological Economics* 10: 197–207.

Funtowicz, S.O. and Ravetz, J.R. (1993a) 'The emergence of post-normal science', in R. von Schomberg (ed.), *Science, Politics and Morality: Scientific Uncertainty and Decision-making*, Dordrecht: Kluwer Academic Publishers, 85–123.

Funtowicz, S.O. and Ravetz, J.R. (1993b) 'Science for the post-normal age', *Futures* 25(7): 739–55.

Funtowicz, S.O. and Ravetz, J.R. (1990) *Uncertainty and Quality in Science for Policy*, Dordrecht: Kluwer.

Gezondheidsraad (1996) *Risk is More than Just a Number* (in Dutch) *1996/03*, The Hague: Health Council of the Netherlands: Committee on risk measures and risk assessment.

Gezondheidsraad (1995) *Not All Risks are Equal* (in Dutch) *1995/06*, The Hague: Health Council of the Netherlands: Committee on risk measures and risk assessment.

Gieryn, T.F. (1999) *Cultural Boundaries of Science: Credibility on the Line*, Chicago: University of Chicago Press.

Gieryn, T.F. (1995) 'Boundaries of science', in S. Jasanoff, G.E. Markle, R.E. Petersen and T. Pinch (eds), *Handbook of Science and Technology Studies*, London: Sage.

Gieryn, T.F. (1983) 'Boundary-work and the demarcation of science from non-science: Strains and interests in professional ideologies of scientists', *American Sociological Review* 48: 781–95.

Greenpeace (2005) 'Monsanto ordered to make secret study public', available at: <http://eu.greenpeace.org/downloads/gmo/MON863GermanCourt050620.pdf>, accessed 1 July 2005.

Greenpeace (2004) 'Greenpeace critique of Monsanto's Roundup Ready Oilseed Rape, GT73', available at: <http://eu.greenpeace.org/downloads/gmo/GPTechCritiqueOfEFSAOpinion.pdf>, accessed 1 July 2005.

Hajer, M. (1995) *The Politics of Environmental Discourse: Ecological Modernization and the Policy Process*, Oxford: Clarendon Press.

Halffman, W. (2003) *Boundaries of Regulatory Science: Eco/toxicology and Aquatic Hazards of Chemicals in the US, England, and the Netherlands, 1970–1995*, Amsterdam: University of Amsterdam.

Halffman, W. and Hoppe, R. (2004) 'Science/policy boundaries: a changing division of labour in Dutch expert policy advice', in S. Maasse and P. Weingart (eds), *Scientific Expertise and Political Decision Making*, Dordrecht: Kluwer, 135–52.

Harremoës, P., Gee, D., MacGarvin, M., Stirling, A., Keys, J., Wynne, B. and Guedes Vaz, S. (2002) *The Precautionary Principle in the 20th Century: Late Lessons from Early Warnings*, London: Earthscan.

Harremoës, P., Gee, D., MacGarvin, M., Stirling, A., Keys, J., Wynne, B., and Guedes Vaz, S. (2001) *Late Lessons from Early Warnings: The Precautionary Principle 1896–2000*, Copenhagen: European Environment Agency.

Hess, D.J. (1999) *Science Studies: An advanced introduction*, New York: New York University Press.

Hilgartner, S. (2000) *Science on stage: Expert advice as public drama*, Stanford: Stanford University Press.

Hoppe, R. and Huijs, S. (2002) *Grenzenwerk tussen wetenschap en beleid: Paradoxen en dilemma's*, Den Haag: RMNO.

Jasanoff, S. (2005) *Designs on Nature: Science and democracy in Europe and the United States*, Princeton: Princeton University Press.

Jasanoff, S. (1993) 'Bridging the two cultures of risk analysis', *Risk Analysis* 13(2): 123–9.

Jasanoff, S. (1990). *The Fifth Branch: Science Advisers as Policy-makers*, Cambridge: Harvard University Press.

Jasanoff, S., Markle, G.E., Petersen, J.C. and Pinch, T. (1995) *Handbook of Science and Technology Studies*, Thousands Oaks: SAGE Publications.

Jasanoff, S. and Wynne, B. (1998) 'Science and decision-making', in S. Rayner and E.L. Malone (eds), *Human Choice and Climate Change*, Washington DC: Battelle Press, 1–87.

Jelsma, J. (1999) *Van onhandelbaar naar onderhandelbaar risico? De introductie van gemodificeerde organismen in het milieu*, Den Haag: Rathenau instituut.

Klinke, A. and Renn, O. (2002) 'A new approach to risk evaluation and management: Risk-based, precaution-based, and discourse-based strategies', *Risk Analysis* 22(6): 1071–94.

Knight, F.H. (1921) *Risk, Uncertainty and Profit*, Boston: Houghton Mifflin.

Krayer von Kraus, M.P. (2005) *Uncertainty in Policy Relevant Sciences*, Copenhagen: Technical University of Denmark.

Krayer von Kraus, M.P., Van Asselt, M.B.A., Henze, M., Ravetz, J. and Beck, M.B. (2005) 'Uncertainty and precaution in environmental management', *Water, Science and Technology* 52(6): 1–9.

Kuhn, T.S. (1970) *The Structure of Scientific Revolutions*, Chicago: University of Chicago Press.

Kuiper, H. (2008) 'The Role of Scientific Experts in Risk Regulation of Foods', in this volume.

Lahsen, M. (2005) 'Technocracy, democracy and U.S. climate politics: the need for demarcations', *Science, Technology & Human Values* 30(1): 137–69.

Lassen, J. and Jamison, A. (2006) 'Genetic technologies meet the public: The discourses of concern', *Science, Technology & Human Values* 31(1): 8–28.

Lemen, J.K., Hammond, B.G., Riordan, S.G., Jiang, Ch. and Nemeth, M. (2002) *Toxicology Summary Report: Summary of study CV-2000-260: 13-week dietary subschronic comparison study with MON 863 Corn in rats preceded by a 1-week baseline food consumption determination with PMI certified rodent diet #5008*, St. Louis: Monsanto Company.

Löfstedt, R.E. (2005) *Risk Management in Post-trust Societies*, Hampshire/New York: Palgrave Macmillan.

Marchant, G.E. and Mosman, K.L. (2004) *Arbitrary and Capricious: The Precautionary Principle in the European Courts*, Washington DC: AEI Press.

Martin, B. and Richard, E. (1995) 'Scientific knowledge, controversy and public decision making', in S. Jasanoff, G.E. Markle, J.C. Petersen and T. Pinch (eds), *Handbook of Science and Technology Studies – Revised edition*, Thousand Oaks: SAGE, 506–26.

Mayo, D.G. and Hollander, R.D. (1991) *Acceptable Evidence: Science and Values in Risk Management*, New York: Oxford University Press.

Middelkoop, H., Kwadijk, J.C.J., Van Deursen, W.P.A. and Van Asselt, M.B.A. (2002) 'Scenario analyses in global change assessment for water management in the lower Rhine delta', in M. Beniston (ed.), *Climatic Change: Implications for the Hydrological Cycle and for Water Management. Advances in Global Change Research*, Dordrecht: Kluwer, 445–63.

Middelkoop, H., Daamen, K., Gellens, D., Grabs, W., Kwadijk, J.C.J., Lang, H., Parmet, B.W.A.H., Schädler, B., Schulla, J. and Wilke, K. (2001) 'Impact of climate change on hydrological regimes and water resources management in the Rhine basin', *Climatic Change* 49: 105–28.

Monsanto (2003) 'Safety Assessment of YieldGard Rootworm – Corn', available at: <http://www.monsanto.com/monsanto/content/products/technicalAndSafety/yieldgard_rw/pss.pdf>, accessed 14 July 2005.

Monsanto (2002a) 'Safety Assessment of Roundup Ready Canola Event GT73', available at: <http://www.monsanto.com/monsanto/content/sci_tech/prod_safety/roundup_canola/pss.pdf>, accessed 14 July 2005.

Monsanto (2002b) 'Safety Assessment of Roundup Ready Corn Event NK603', available at: <http://www.monsanto.com/monsanto/content/products/technicalAndSafety/roundup_corn/pss_NK603.pdf>, accessed 14 July 2005.

Monsanto (2002c) 'Safety Assessment of YieldGard Insect-Protected Corn Event MON 810', available at: <http://www.monsanto.com/monsanto/content/products/technicalAndSafety/yieldgard_corn/pss.pdf>, accessed 14 July 2005.

Mourik, R. (2004) *Did Water Kill the Cows? The Distribution and Democratisation of Risk, Responsibility and Liability in a Dutch Agricultural Controversy on Water Pollution and Cattle Sickness*, Amsterdam: Pallas Publications.

Nowotny, H., Scott, P. and Gibbons, M. (2001) *Re-Thinking Science: Knowledge and the public in an age of uncertainty*, Cambridge: Polity Press in association with Blackwell Publishers.

Petersen, A.C., Janssen, P.H.M., Van der Sluijs, J.P., Risbey, J.S. and Ravetz, J.R. (2003) *Mini-checklist & Quickscan Questionnaire*, Bilthoven: RIVM.

Petersen, A.C. and Van der Zwaan, B.C.C. (2003) 'The precautionary principle: (Un)certainties about species loss', in B.C.C. van der Zwaan and A.C. Petersen (eds), *Sharing the Planet: Population – Consumption – Species. Science and Ethics for a Sustainable and Equitable World*, Delft: Eburon Academic Publishers.

Pinch, T.J. and Bijker, W.E. (1987) 'The social construction of facts and artifacts: Or how the sociology of science and the sociology of technology might benefit each other', in W.E. Bijker, T.P. Hughes and T.J. Pinch (eds), *The Social Construction of Technological Systems*, Cambridge: MIT Press, 17–50.

Pollack, H.N. (2003) *Uncertain Science . . . Uncertain World*, Cambridge: Cambridge University Press.

Ravetz, J.R. (2001) 'Models of risk: an exploration', in M. Hisschemöller, R. Hoppe, W.N. Dunn and J.R. Ravetz (eds), *Knowledge, Power and Participation in Environmental Policy Analysis*, New Brunswick, USA/London, UK: Transaction Books, 471–92.

Ravetz, J.R. (1996) *Scientific Knowledge and its Social Problems*, New Brunswick, USA/London, UK: Transaction Publishers.

Ravetz, J.R. (1990) *The Merger of Knowledge with Power*, London: Mansell.

RIVM (2003) *Nuchter omgaan met risico's*, 251701047/2003, Bilthoven.

RMNO (2004) *Spotting New Risks?* (in Dutch), The Hague: Lemma.

RMNO (2003) *Niet bang voor onzekerheid*, Den Haag: Lemma.

de Sadeleer, N. (2002) *Environmental Principles*, Oxford: Oxford University Press.

de Sadeleer, N. (1999) 'Het voorzorgsbeginsel: een stille revolutie', *TMR* 8: 82–99.

Scientific Committee on Animal Nutrition (1998) 'Opinion of the SCAN on the immediate and longer-term risk to the value of Streptogramins in Human Medicine posed by the use of Virginiamycin as an animal growth promoter', <http://europa.eu.int/comm/food/fs/sc/scan/out14_en.html>.

Scientific Committee on Plants (1998) 'Opinion of the Scientific Committee on Plants

Regarding the Genetically Modified, Insect Resistant Maize Lines Notified by the Monsanto Company', Notification C/F/95/12/02, 10 February 1998, Brussels: European Commission.

Smithson, M. (1993) 'Ignorance and science: Dilemmas, perspectives, and prospects', *Knowledge: Creation, Diffusion, Utilization* 15(2): 133–56.

Stocking, S.H. and Holstein, L.W. (1993) 'Constructing and reconstructing scientific ignorance: Ignorance claims in science and journalism', *Knowledge: Creation, Diffusion, Utilization* 15(2): 186–210.

Thompson, K.M. and Bloom, D.L. (2000) 'Communication of risk assessment information to risk managers', *Journal of Risk Research* 3(4): 333–52.

Tickner, J. and Gouveia-Vigeant, T. (2005) 'The 1991 Cholera Epidemic in Peru: Not a case of precaution gone awry', *Risk Analysis* 25(3): 495–502.

Uggla, Y. (2004) 'Risk and safety analysis in long-term perspective', *Futures* 36(5): 549–64.

Uggla, Y. (2002) *Environmental Politics and the Enchantment of Modernity: Mercury and Radioactive Waste Disposal in Sweden*, Örebro: Örebro University.

Vercelli, A. (1995) 'From soft uncertainty to hard environmental uncertainty', *Economie appliquée* 48(2), 251–69.

Vos, E. (2004) 'Antibiotics, the precautionary principle and the Court of First Instance', *MJ*, 187–200.

Vos, E. (2000) 'EU food safety regulation in the aftermath of the BSE crisis', *Journal of Consumer Policy* 23, 227–55.

Vos, E. (1999) Institutional Frameworks of Community Health and Safety Regulation: Committees, Agencies and Private Bodies, Oxford/Portland Oregon: Hart Publishing.

Vos, E. and Wendler, F. (eds) (2006) *Food Safety Regulation in Europe. A Comparative Institutional Analysis*, Antwerp: Intersentia.

Vrijling, H. (2004) 'Vroegtijdige detectie van milieurisico's – transitie "Verhoogde dijken" ', in M. van Asselt (ed.), *Nieuwe risico's in 't vizier?*, Den Haag: RMNO & Lemma, 62–7.

Weingart, P. (1999) 'Scientific expertise and political accountability: Paradoxes of science in politics', *Science and Public Policy* 26(3): 151–61.

Wells Bedsworth, L., Lowenthal, M.D. and Kastenberg, W.E. (2004) 'Uncertainty and regulation: The rhetoric of risk in the California low-level radioactive waste debate', *Science, Technology & Human Values* 29(3): 406–27.

Wynne, B. (2001) 'Creating public alienation: expert cultures of risk and ethics on GMOs', *Science as Culture* 10(4): 445–81.

Wynne, B. (1982) *Rationality and Ritual: The Windscale Inquiry and Nuclear Decisions in Britain*, Chalfont St. Giles: British Society for the History of Science.

Chapter 19

The role of scientific experts in risk regulation of foods

Harry A. Kuiper

1 BROADER FRAMEWORK FOR RISK ANALYSIS OF FOODS

Food safety incidents in Europe like BSE, dioxins and outbreaks of *E. coli* 0157 have shown considerable gaps in knowledge of the seriousness of effects that scientific uncertainty can produce, the degree of magnification and spreading of risks, as well as of failures in adequate risk management strategies. Globalisation of trade and transboundary movements of raw and intermediate materials for food production demand specific measures regarding traceability and quality control in order to guarantee a safe and healthy food supply which may not always be transparent and trustworthy for the consumer. Moreover, the introduction of new food production technologies such as modern biotechnology and the application of nanotechnology in food production apparently evoke specific questions regarding the potential impact on the safety and health of humans, animals and the environment, in particular, with regard to the potential existence of long-term and irreversible adverse harm.

These examples indicate why the confidence and trust of the European consumer in the safety and wholesomeness of the European food supply is relatively low. Moreover, analysis of food safety risks and their management has to date largely been the exclusive domain of scientific experts and professional risk managers, while input from other interested parties, such as consumer and environmental organisations, within this process has been generally low.

Risks are not just expressions of the various chances that harmful effects might occur: instead, their seriousness and impact on other non-scientific interests should also be taken into account when decisions are made on the acceptability of identified risks. Risks may be perceived of and experienced as being 'dreadful' and imposed in the absence of voluntary agreement, and may likewise give rise to uncertain 'feelings' as regards their longer-term negative impacts. Moreover, consumers' concern about risks may also arise on the basis of concerns and interests that are utterly alien to the considerations that scientists bring to bear when engaging in a risk assessment.

Current procedures for decision making on risks (defined as risk analysis) are composed of risk assessment, management, monitoring and review of decisions (EU Scientific Steering Committee 2000; 2003a; Figure 19.1; FAO/WHO 1997). The risk analysis process within this framework is iterative: it is continuously

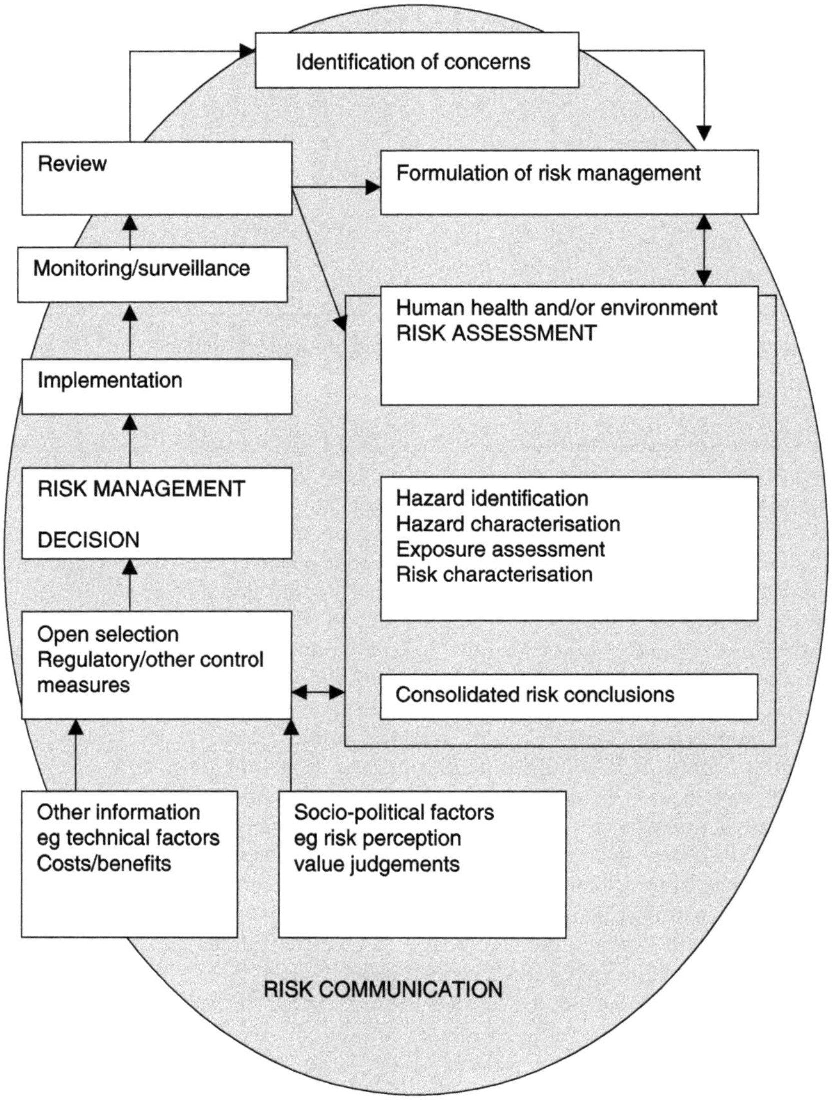

Figure 19.1 The Risk Cycle: components of risk analysis.

Figure taken from EU Scientific Steering Committee 2000, p. 24.

reviewed and adapted if needed, based on the monitoring and surveillance of implemented measures and on new information emerging. New technological needs, new exposures, new toxicological or microbiological data might be gathered that in turn gives rise to demands for adjustments or wholesale re-evaluations within risk assessments and for new risk management strategies.

In addition, the EU Scientific Steering Committee has identified other values, the so-called Quality-of-Life values, which currently are *not* incorporated within the formal risk assessment process, but which should be taken into account. At general level, these parameters include: (i) animal welfare, (ii) sustainability, (iii) human 'Quality-of-Life' parameters, (iv) risk perception, (v) ethics, and (vi) social and economical benefits. The Scientific Steering Committee has proposed a general schedule for risk analysis, which will take account of the assessment of these Quality-of-Life parameters (EU Scientific Steering Committee 2003a, Figure 19.2). According to this proposal, the specific Quality-of-Life parameters that should now be assessed to assuage lack of consumer and public confidence include adverse effects within humans, nutritional efficacy within humans, health protective/promotional effects in humans, environmental impact, ecological impact (farming, fishery, industry), occupational health issues in farming and industry, associated animal welfare issues, local and global sustainability issues, economical impact assessments, ethical issues and consumer perception issues.

The Integrated European Project SAFE FOODS (www.safefoods.nl) attempts to design a new model for risk analysis (risk governance) of foods, whereby classical technical risk assessment techniques will be integrated with social and economical considerations about identified risks, in order to identify and select appropriate options for risk management. The model under construction is based on models as established by FAO/WHO (1997), EU Scientific Steering Committee (2000; 2003a) and by the International Risk Governance Council (IRGC) (2005). In order to develop a new model for the governance of foods produced by different agricultural and industrial methods and practices, the SAFE FOODS consortium is developing improved solutions with regard to five aspects of food safety governance: (i) the development of new analytic tools by means of the adaptation of modern profiling technologies for use on foods; (ii) the improvement of models for the understanding of health impacts upon the general population, taking into effect the combined exposures of that population to beneficial nutrients and natural and chemical toxicants; (iii) the design of new working procedures for the early identification of emerging microbial and chemical risks in trans-national food production chains; (iv) analysis of consumer confidence in risk analysis procedures for foods; and (v) investigation of the role of the very diverse EU institutions that are involved in the governance of food safety.

2 ROLE OF TECHNICAL-SCIENTIFIC EXPERTS

The technical risk assessment of food safety issues, as developed and agreed upon at the international level, consists of: (i) hazard identification, (ii) hazard characterisation, (iii) exposure assessment and (iv) risk characterisation (EU Scientific Steering Committee 2000; 2003a; FOSIE, EU Concerted Action on Food Safety in Europe: Risk Assessment in Chemicals, see <http://europe.ilsi.org/activities/ecprojects/FOSIE/overview.htm>; ENTRANSFOOD 2004). The role of the technical-scientific expert within the broader context of risk analysis remains focused on: (i) identification of (new) emerging hazards appearing in food production chains as early as is practicably possible; (ii) assessment of the identified hazards with respect to estimated frequency of occurrence and severity of potential

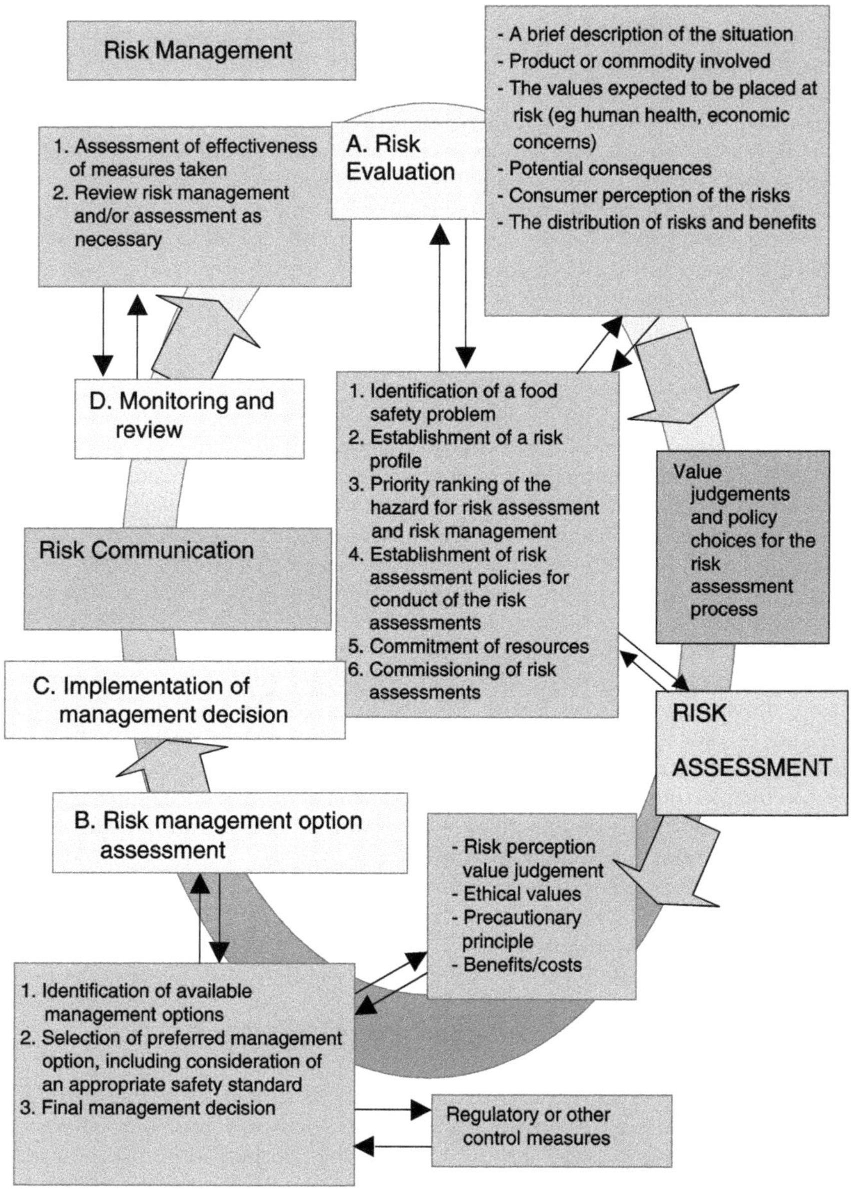

Figure 19.2 General schedule of the risk analysis.

Figure taken from EU Scientific Steering Committee 2003a, p. 33.

adverse effects; and (iii) formulating options for the risk manager regarding mitigation of identified risks for human/animal health and the environment.

2.1 Uncertainty analysis

When characterising identified risks and evaluating their possible impact upon human/animal health and the environment, experts should describe and where possible quantify *uncertainties* inherent to the models and procedures applied for risk assessment. Many factors determine the extent of uncertainties, for example:

- variability in measurements in data points (systematic and random errors);
- significance and predictivity of test parameters;
- methodological uncertainties in the models applied and presumptions made;
- assumptions for extrapolation (metabolic and sensitivity differences between humans and animals, genetically predisposed and sensitive subgroups in the human population, short-term versus long-term exposure);
- biological significance of observed changes;
- complexity of identified problems;
- fundamental ignorance of how systems work.

It is the task of the risk assessor to highlight and describe the *unknowns* in risk assessment and to indicate the degree to which these uncertainties should, for example, influence for the determination of acceptable safety limits, by means of the choice of safety or extrapolation default mechanism. Where necessary, the risk assessor should indicate that a risk assessment *cannot* be completed because of the poor quality of data or even the lack of essential data.

Alongside risks, the potential *benefits* of various identified factors or new technological developments should be taken into account during the risk analysis process. This is particularly relevant, for example, during the evaluation of genetically modified food crops or other novel foods that make specific nutritional or health beneficial claims. The challenge here is one of the balancing or 'weighting' of potentially adverse and beneficial aspects, without ever compromising a 'safety-first' approach.

The final risk characterisation should result in informed guidance for risk managers, and most preferably in a series of 'options', designed to secure an acceptable level of risk mitigation. In this regard, the assessment should also pay due regard to the feasibility of the proposed post-market surveillance and monitoring mechanism that may be required in order to validate the results of the risk assessment and to identify potential adverse effects, which were 'missed' during the pre-market assessment.

In summary, the primary role of the scientific expert is one of a technical risk assessor, who should describe the type and severity of identified risks, where possible quantify them and indicate who is at risk. Furthermore, any inherent uncertainties identified during the risk assessment should be made explicit, in order to facilitate the act of risk management, when final decisions on risk acceptability and mitigation are made. An increasingly important aspect of the scientific expert's work is the notion of 'communication'; more particularly, communication of information about the social impact of the technical risk assessment, an aspect of work which demands that the technical scientific expert also plays an important role as a scientific advisor, facilitator and mediator.

3 ROLE OF THE EUROPEAN FOOD SAFETY AUTHORITY IN RISK ANALYSIS OF FOODS

The General Food Law (Regulation (EC) 178/2002)[1] provides for an integrated approach to ensure food safety across the EU Member States and across the human food and animal feed sectors. The new law clarifies the particular accountability of all legal entities involved in food production and regulation in the EU by imposing requirements on both relevant Member State agencies and on food companies. The law also provides a legal basis for an EU-wide rapid alert and crisis management system network, made up of national institutes and authorities, within which the European Commission Directorate General for Health and Consumer Protection (DG SANCO) plays a central role. The general principles of EU food law are applicable to all products necessitating EU-level regulatory action, such as food additives, novel foods and foods derived from genetically modified organisms. Generally, the EU framework requires that risk analyses for foodstuffs should be based upon processes of scientific risk evaluation undertaken by the European Food Safety Authority (EFSA).

EFSA's primary objectives are to improve the quality of risk assessment with regard to food safety related issues, to further develop the science of risk assessment, and to be engaged in risk communication. In practice, if not under formal law (final risk management decisions must be taken by the Commission), EFSA has been established as an 'independent' agency: it is not a part of the institutional structures of the European Commission, nor is it answerable to it with regard to the quality of its scientific advice. Instead, it is overseen by a Management Board, whose members are charged with acting in an independent capacity, and not as representatives of the Member States (<www.efsa.eu.int>).

The Agency responds to questions raised by the Commission, the European Parliament, or Member States, or it may address scientific issues on its own initiative. EFSA aims to furnish greater transparency within the process of risk assessment, providing a greater degree of efficiency in relation to assessment timeframes, and fostering better liaison with and between Member States and stakeholders. EFSA comprises a Scientific Committee and eight Panels made up of leading European experts, active in the various areas of food and feed production. To date, EFSA Panels and the Scientific Committee have produced more than 300 Scientific Opinions on a wide range of food safety issues, as well as various Guidance Documents, which provide advice on the performance of appropriate science-based risk assessments. Generally speaking, these documents are well received and appreciated by the 'outside' world.

Since EFSA and the European Commission share responsibility for processes

1 Regulation (EC) No. 178/2002 of the European Parliament and the Council of 28 January 2002 laying down the general principles and requirements of food law, establishing the European Food Safety Authority and laying down procedures in matters of food safety, [2002] *OJ* L31/1.

of risk communication, doubts can be raised about the degree of coordination established between these bodies and the extent to which they simply reproduce communication strategies; a problem that is particularly acute given EFSA's physical separation from the European Commission (EFSA is located in Parma). Above all, a particular degree of cooperation is necessary between the two bodies when the evaluation of results of the technical scientific risk assessments is combined with an evaluation of the social and economic impact of the risks identified.

4 ROLE OF PRECAUTION WITHIN RISK ANALYSIS

As the problems posed by risk grow ever more complex, we can surely reckon with an increase in the degree of scientific uncertainty about possible impacts of new production methods on human and animal health and on the environment. In practice, scientists take a highly conservative approach to risk analysis by means of application of relatively expansive safety or uncertainty factors. This approach has worked particularly well in the relatively simple areas of the evaluation of pesticide residues and the presence of animal drugs or food additives within foodstuffs. However, in complex examples, such as the spread of the avian influenza virus, BSE or the introduction of new food production/processing technologies, standard procedures for risk estimation and application of uncertainty factors have yet to evolve. Accordingly, and as a matter of some urgency, efforts should now be made to identify areas in which we have a 'fundamental' lack of knowledge about the functioning of biological systems, and to model the consequences of system derailments (type/severity of effects, magnification, reversibility/irreversibility, possibilities of risk handling and control).

Accordingly, risk assessors are surely charged with being both critical and transparent with respect to the evaluation of available data, and should in particular identify the unknowns of the systems under study, indicating how uncertainty is 'judged' or treated during the final part of the risk assessment: the risk characterisation. The risk characterisation is based on agreed scientific principles in order to exclude 'personal' risk perceptions, and to ensure that advice and guidance to risk managers are always qualitative and where possible or appropriate quantitative in nature.

The conservative (that is, precautionary) approach taken by technical risk assessors is distinct from the procedure of application of the precautionary principle. Where scientific information is insufficient, inconclusive or uncertain, or where there are indications that the possible effects on the environment, or human or plant health, may be potentially dangerous and inconsistent with the chosen level of protection, the precautionary principle may be invoked (EC 2000). Application of the precautionary approach is the responsibility of the risk manager and not of the technical risk assessor. Risk assessors and risk managers should work closely together, but within their own responsibilities, in order to arrive at final conclusions on the basis of which decisions can be made.

5 STAKEHOLDER INVOLVEMENT IN RISK ASSESSMENT AND RISK MANAGEMENT

Food production, processing and preparation entail a complicated (chain) process which involves many steps and many professional organisations (breeders, industries, retailers, etc). Moreover, quality and safety assessment and assurance require the application of specific expertise during the production sector and within the activities of regulatory authorities. Last but not least consumers, and consumer and environmental organisations have an interest in the risk-benefit analysis of foodstuffs and the general regulation of food. Stakeholder participation within the risk analysis process is of particular importance in the case of the assessment of generic risk-benefit issues and of the introduction of new food producing technologies and new foods.

Active stakeholder participation within the risk analysis process can be imagined at a number of levels: (i) during the process of problem identification; (ii) during the organisation of the risk analysis process, and above all decisions about who should participate within that process; (iii) in relation to the identification of the relevant technical, social and economical parameters that should be applied during risk analysis; (iv) with regard to the establishment of judgement values on the acceptance and mitigation of identified and characterised risks; and (v) with regard to the measures to be taken to monitor and control risk factors that have already been released into the environment.

Naturally, stakeholder participation must also occur within its own limits and with due regard for further guarantees for the legitimacy of the regulatory process, such as the notion of scientific expertise. Thus, technical-scientific evaluation of risk-benefit issues demands a high level of expertise and must be carried out initially by professionals who are free from the influence of non-scientific interests. Nonetheless, technical-scientific assessment should also be subject to broader public scrutiny prior to their scrutiny and use by risk managers. Equally, stakeholder participation should be differentiated in line with the functional nature of the problem posed. Relatively simple problems can and should be dealt with by scientific experts acting alone where routine assessment procedures are available and generally accepted and where constant referral to the public would surely only result in risk fatigue. In the case of more complex problems, however, participation of the various stakeholders should be secured by means of public hearings, consultations and workshops. Above all, stakeholder participation is crucial at the level of the initial definition of the particular risk-benefit problem at issue and of the process of risk analysis (risk governance) that will as a consequence be applied. Thus, for example, should GMO products be evaluated with reference to foodstuffs produced by industrial farming? Alternatively, should their potential benefits be tested against the far higher criterion of organic foodstuffs? It is at this level that broad public consensus must be secured, and SAFE FOODS is further dedicated to an exploration of the opportunities for inclusion of stakeholders within all stages of the risk governance procedure for foods.

6 CONCLUSIONS

1 Current procedures for risk analysis of foods are based on risk assessment, management, monitoring and review of decisions. In addition, however, other values, which currently are *not* incorporated in the formal risk assessment process, should now be taken into account: (i) animal welfare, (ii) sustainability, (iii) human Quality-of-Life parameters, (iv) risk perception, (v) ethics, and (vi) social and economical benefits.

2 The Integrated European Project SAFE FOODS is seeking to design a new model for risk analysis of foodstuffs, whereby classical technical risk assessment procedures will be integrated with social and economical considerations about risks identified, in order to identify and select appropriate options for risk management. Furthermore, the active involvement of stakeholders in the various stages of the risk analysis procedure will be promoted.

3 The primary role of the scientific expert is that of a technical risk assessor, who should describe the type and severity of identified risks, where possible quantify them and indicate who is at risk. Furthermore, inherent uncertainties identified during the risk assessment should be made explicit, in order to facilitate risk management regarding risk acceptability and risk mitigation. The technical scientific expert has also a role to play as scientific advisor, facilitator and mediator.

4 The European Food Safety Authority (EFSA), active since 2002 and responsible for risk assessment of food safety and risk communication, has produced a large number of 'well-received' Scientific Opinions on a wide range of food safety issues, as well as various Guidance Documents. Since EFSA and the European Commission share responsibility for risk communication, however, more intense cooperation and better streamlining of procedures should be considered.

5 The conservative (precautionary) approach taken by technical risk assessors is distinct from the procedure of application of the precautionary principle. Where scientific information is insufficient, inconclusive or uncertain, or where there are indications that the possible effects on the environment, or human or plant health may be adverse and inconsistent with the chosen level of protection, the precautionary principle may be invoked. Application of the precautionary approach is the responsibility of the risk manager and not of the technical risk assessor.

6 Active stakeholder participation within the risk analysis process can be envisaged at the level of problem identification, organisation of the risk analysis process and establishment of judgement values regarding acceptance/mitigation of identified and characterised risks.

7 The technical-scientific evaluation of risk-benefit issues demands a high level of expertise and must be carried out by experts acting alone. However, the results of the technical-scientific assessment should be subject to broader public scrutiny prior to any final decision on risk management.

8 The nature of stakeholder participation should be differentiated according to the nature of the identified risk problem. Involvement of different stakeholders in the framing of the risk-benefit problem and of the risk analysis (risk governance) process is essential in order to ensure broad public consensus.

BIBLIOGRAPHY

Barlow, S., Dybing, E., Edler, L., Eisenbrand, G., Kroes, R. and Van den Brandt, P. (Guest eds) (2002) Food Safety in Europe (FOSIE): 'Risk Assessment of Chemicals in Food and Diet', *Food and Chemical Toxicology* 40(2/3): 139–427.

EU Scientific Steering Committee (2003a) *Report on Setting the Scientific Frame for the Inclusion of New Quality of Life Concerns in the Risk Assessment Process*, 10–11 April 2003, European Commission (DG SANCO), available at: <http://ec.europa.eu/food/fs/sc/ssc/out362_en.pdf>.

EU Scientific Steering Committee (2003b) *First and Second Report on the Harmonisation of Risk Assessment Procedures, Part 1 and 2*, available at: <http://ec.europa.eu/food/fs/sc/ssc/outcome_en.html>.

EU Scientific Steering Committee (2000) *The First Report on the Harmonisation of Risk Assessment Procedures*, adopted by the Scientific Steering Committee at its meeting of 26–27 October 2000, see <http://ec.europa.eu/food/fs/sc/ssc/out83_en.pdf>.

ENTRANSFOOD (2004) Genetically modified crops in the EU: food safety assessment, regulation, and public concerns. Overarching report Entransfood, the European network on safety assessment of genetically modified food crops, European Commission, Luxembourg, 2004, <www.entransfood.com>.

European Commission (2000) *Communication from the Commission on the Precautionary Principle*, COM(2000) 1 final, 2 February 2000, Brussels.

FAO/WHO (2003) *Working Principles for Risk Analysis for Application in the Framework of the Codex Alimentarius*, Appendix IV, Alinorm 03/41. Report of the Codex Alimentarius Commission 26th Session, 2003.

FAO/WHO (1997) *Expert Consultations 1995*, Geneva: WHO.

International Risk Governance Council (2005) *White Paper on Risk Governance: Towards an Integrated Framework*, Genf: IRGC.

Kuiper, H.A., Kleter, G.A., König, A., Hammes, W.P. and I. Knudsen (Guest eds) (2004) 'Safety Assessment, Detection and Traceability, and Societal Aspects of Genetically Modified Foods, European Network on Safety Assessment of Genetically Modified Food Crops (ENTRANSFOOD)', *Food and Chemical Toxicology* 42(7): 1195–202.

Chapter 20

Inclusive risk governance through discourse, deliberation and participation

Andreas Klinke

1 INTRODUCTION

Contemporary societies are challenged by risks that entail high degrees of complexity, uncertainty and ambiguity – for example, SARS, avian flu, human-induced climate change, diminished genetic diversity, release of persistent toxic substances and terrorism – which cannot be tackled by means of unilateral or simple governmental action. Complex risk issues are further characterised by functional and structural interdependencies between human societies and natural, technological, economic, political, social and cultural systems. They are often a product of profound and rapid technological, economic, social and/or environmental change. Such risks confound traditional political institutions and create unanswered challenges for policy makers within national governments and international bodies. Their negative effects are often pervasive, impacting upon areas well beyond the obvious primary issue areas. Nor do they respect physical boundaries, disciplinary bonds, territorial statehood or political spheres of influence. In many cases, it is a difficult task to detect and to measure the cause–effect relationships inherent to risks and damage. Even experts are uncertain whether a specific set of potential risk candidates will trigger specific adverse effects. There might be other factors, or more likely, an unclear variety of different and uncertain variables, which reduce confidence in the estimated cause and effect chain. Hence, ambiguous evaluations and interpretations emerge, even though based on identical observations or data assessments, and accordingly give rise to scientific and political controversy.

The complex, uncertain and ambiguous character of these risks reveals that there is an apparent need for something beyond the traditional, hierarchical approach found in national risk regulation. The frequency, level and scope of their occurrence instead require coordination and harmonisation of different risk policies and politics throughout Europe and within international governance. Within these governance frameworks, shifting patterns of authority are now observable: that is, we are witnessing a transformation from interventionist (inter)governmental regulation to the inclusion of civil-societal and economic stakeholders within regulatory structures and the emergence of new and innovative forms and arrangements of governance. The debate within political science and social scientific risk research focuses on the question of the adequacy of different governance approaches; a debate within which the model of deliberative governance has increasingly gained attention (see, for example, Klinke 2006; Renn 2005; Schmalz-Bruns 1999). Several systematic arguments may be made in favour of public discourse, deliberation and participation as an appropriate model for inclusive risk governance within multi-level systems, namely its role in overcoming the tension between input-oriented legitimacy and output-oriented effectiveness; its reference to functionally defined risk policy making rather than interventionist national risk politics; as well as its horizontal, dialogue-oriented forms of communication and interaction between state and non-state actors.

This chapter develops a deliberative approach, which can be argued to be relevant both as a normative and a practically adaptive model for risk policy making. The model will be illustrated with reference to the North American Great Lakes Regime, which entails an exceptional quality of deliberative governance across national borders, and from which lessons can be drawn on how best to organise inclusive risk governance. First, the three properties of complexity, uncertainty and ambiguity, which challenge risk governance, will be elaborated. Following this, three discourse types, namely an epistemological, a reflective and a participatory discourse, will be sequentially arranged in order systematically to integrate those stakeholders who can contribute to tackling risk properties within the debate. Particular attention will then be paid to the changing role of state authority within risk policy making and the connectivity of new governance forms and arrangements within the European and international context. An innovative and promising form of deliberative risk policy making will subsequently be designed as a three-dimensional model. The Great Lakes Regime then acts as an exemplary case, successfully implementing discourse, deliberation and public participation within inclusive risk governance. Finally, some conclusions can and will be drawn on the prerequisites for the organisation of inclusive risk governance through discourse, deliberation and participation in similar risk areas.

2 CHALLENGES FOR RISK GOVERNANCE

The following example of human-induced climate change illustrates that the crucial factors distinguishing specific transboundary risk issues from other 'conventional' perils are common properties of high complexity, uncertainty and/or ambiguity. In particular, worldwide emissions of CO_2, through production of energy and manufacturing, car traffic and heating, as well as the release of methane in the agricultural sector, result in man-made climate change. Significant indications of an increasing worldwide temperature due to climate change are the reduction of the Arctic ice thickness by two metres in the last three decades (Johannessen *et al.* 1999) and the decline of the Alpine glaciers by 50 per cent (Lozán *et al.* 1998). Furthermore, global warming causes extreme weather events such as floods, droughts, heavy rain and thunderstorms, which give rise to human casualties as well as economic and ecological damage. Climate change can probably also be linked to an increase in hurricanes: global warming raises the temperature of the oceans, which is the triggering factor for hurricanes. Even though a direct parallel might not be drawn with the proverbial beating of a butterfly's wing, the various factors that contribute to an increase in hurricanes, as well as to climate change as a whole, are characterised by complex interdependencies and scientific uncertainties. Whereas the scientific deliberations within the Intergovernmental Panel on Climate Change (IPCC) have certainly generated shared 'causal beliefs' on global warming and its impacts, the potential for the emergence of an effective international governance system will remain poor for as long as the United States (the state responsible for the highest carbon emissions worldwide) still continues to emphasise the ambiguity within current data assessments and observations.

The potential negative physical impacts of specific risks, which are sometimes immediate and obvious, but are more often subtle, latent and delayed, distinguish risks such as climate change, loss of biological diversity, pandemics and terrorism from other threats. When such risks manifest themselves as 'harm', the resulting effects can cause a dramatic sequence of secondary and tertiary impacts. These may be felt in a wide range of seemingly divergent social systems, from the economy to the health sector, inflicting damage in realms far beyond their own. Against this background, the major properties of these risks, namely complexity, uncertainty and ambiguity (Klinke and Renn 2002; cf. also Renn 1999a), need further explanation.

Complexity refers to the difficulty of identifying and quantifying causal links between a multitude of potential risk candidates and specific adverse effects (Schellnhuber 1999; WBGU 2000). The nature of this difficulty may be traced back to interactive effects among risk candidates (synergism and antagonisms), long delay periods between cause and effect, inter-individual variation, and intervening variables. It is precisely this degree of complexity that makes sophisticated scientific investigations necessary since the dose-effect relationship is neither obvious nor directly observable. Non-linear responses may also result from feedback loops that constitute a complex web of intervening variables. Complexity therefore requires sensitivity towards non-linear transitions, as well as to scale (on different levels). It also demands attention to a multitude of exposure pathways and the composite effects of other agents that are present in the exposure situation. Under these conditions, scientific models of risk assessment (including hazard identification, exposure characterisation, risk characterisation and risk quantification) are the most appropriate instruments to gain a better (but never complete) picture of the relative risks associated with these complex causal chains. In the case of highly non-linear or even chaotic relationships, which cannot be adequately addressed within probability models, complexity turns into indeterminacy, which is a component of uncertainty. In this case, the limits of analytical modelling are reached. The same is true, of course, for the component of ignorance, which also describes an element of uncertainty.

Uncertainty is different from complexity. It comprises different and distinct components. These components can be classified as follows (cf. also Van Asselt 2000):

- *Variability* defines the observed or predicted variation of individual responses to an identical stimulus among the individual targets within a relevant population, such as humans, animals, plants, landscapes and so forth. Within the process of risk management, the notion of 'safety factor' is used to capture this form of variability within risk management models.
- *Systematic and random measurement errors* encompass the imprecision or imperfection of measurement, the problems associated with drawing inferences

from small statistical samples, extrapolation from animal data, bio-surveys or other experimental data on humans, uncertainties of modelling, including the choice of functional relationships for extrapolating from large to small doses. All of these difficulties are usually expressed through statistical confidence intervals.

- *Indeterminacy* results from a genuine stochastic relationship between cause and effect(s), apparently non-causal or non-cyclical random events, or badly understood non-linear, chaotic relationships.
- *Lack of knowledge* results from ignorance, from the deliberate definition of system boundaries and hence from the exclusion of external influences, measurement impossibilities and others factors.

These components are often highly correlated. In many instances, however, the four components may produce quite different results. All components have one feature in common, however: uncertainty reduces strength of confidence in the estimated cause and effect chain. If complexity cannot be resolved by means of recourse to scientific methods, uncertainty increases. Even simple relationships, however, may be associated with high degrees of uncertainty if either the knowledge base is missing or the effect is stochastic by virtue of its own nature. Under these circumstances, strategies based on precautionary or resilience management are required. Precaution is therefore a response to high degrees of uncertainty, and, in particular, to indeterminacy and ignorance.

The third challenge is *ambiguity*. This term denotes the variability of (legitimate) interpretations based on identical observations or data assessments. Most of the scientific disputes in the fields of risk analysis and management do not refer to differences in methodology, measurements or dose-response functions, but to the question of what all this means for human health and environmental protection, and management requirements (Harrison and Hoberg 1994: 20 ff). Variability of interpretation, however, is not restricted to expert dissent. Lay people's perception of risk often differs from expert judgements because it is also a response to qualitative risk characteristics, such as familiarity, personal or institutional control and trust and assignment of blame. Moreover, in contemporary pluralist societies, diversity of risk perspectives within and between social groups is generally also fostered by divergent value preferences, variations in interests and the existence of very few, if any, universally applicable moral principles; a degree of diversity that only increases where problems are complex and uncertain. Ambiguity may lead to social mobilisation and conflict. This may derive from conflicting moral perspectives or from conflicting views on what constitutes a fair distribution of risks and benefits. Again, emergence of ambiguity is favoured by high degrees of complexity and uncertainty. Nonetheless, even quite simple issues may also cause controversy and thus increase social and political ambiguity.

It is important to note that the challenges of complexity and the lack of certainty and ambiguity are inexorably intertwined. The answers to these individual challenges, which must be found within risk governance arrangements, must accordingly be conceived of as being interrelated and supplementary. By the same token, the following proposed discourses are each an attempt to cope with these interrelating challenges.

3 EPISTEMOLOGICAL, REFLECTIVE AND PARTICIPATORY DISCOURSE[1]

Dealing with 'conventional' risks requires hardly any changes to the traditional decision-making framework within risk regulation processes. Necessary decisional data is provided by statistical analysis, law or statutory requirements determine the regulative goals; meanwhile, the role of risk management is to ensure that all risk reduction measures are implemented and enforced. Traditional risk-benefit analyses combined with cost-effectiveness are the instruments of choice for finding the right balance between under- and over-protection of the public. In addition, monitoring the risk situation is important in order to ensure that no unexpected consequences may occur. For this reason, 'conventional' risks must be addressed by means of an instrumental discourse among agency staff and enforcement personnel. The objective here is to find the most cost-effective method for a desired risk reduction level. If necessary, stakeholders may be included in the deliberations as they have information and know-how that may provide useful efficiency hints.

Resolving complexity requires deliberation among experts. This sequence is designated as *epistemological discourse*. Within an *epistemological discourse* experts (not exclusively scientists) argue over the factual assessment and the best estimation for characterising the risks under consideration. The objective of such a discourse is the identification of the most adequate description of or explanation for a phenomenon (that is, the question of which physical impacts are to be expected in the case of the emission of specific substances). The more complex, the more multidisciplinary and the more uncertain a phenomenon appears to be, the more necessary is a communicative exchange of arguments among experts. The goal is to achieve a homogeneous and consistent definition of and explanation for the phenomenon in question, as well as a clarification of dissenting views. The discourse produces a concrete profile of the risk with reference to selected criteria. Second, however, an *epistemological discourse* may also reveal that there is more uncertainty and ambiguity hidden in the case than the initial appraisers had anticipated. If the discourse includes both social as well as natural scientists, future controversies and risk debates may be anticipated. Where *epistemological discourse* also encompasses consideration of individual or group perceptions and processes of social mobilisation, the resulting appraisements may serve as early warning systems for controversies to come.

If risks are associated with a high degree of uncertainty, scientific evaluation is only the first step within a more complex evaluation procedure. It is still essential to compile the relevant data and the various arguments, justifying the positions taken by different science camps. Procedures, such as the 'Pedigree Scheme' suggested by Funtowicz and Ravetz (1990), are an aid in the matter of the organisation and classification of existing knowledge. In a second step, however, information about the different types of uncertainties must be collected and be brought into a deliberative arena. The players within this arena extend beyond scientists to include directly affected stakeholders and public interest groups (Yosie and Herbst 1998).

1 With regard to the following classification of discourse types cf. also Klinke and Renn 2002; Klinke *et al.* 2006 and Renn 1999b.

The objective here is to find the right balance between too little and too much precaution. There is no scientific answer to this question and even economic balancing procedures are of limited value, since the stakes are uncertain. This type of deliberation will be denoted *reflective discourse. Reflective discourses* deal with the clarification of knowledge (similar to the epistemological) and the assessment of trade-offs between the competing extremes of over- and under-protection. They are mainly appropriate as a means to decide on the appropriateness of risk-averse or risk-prone approaches to action. This discourse provides answers to the question of how much uncertainty we are willing to accept in the hope of future benefit. Is taking the risk worth the potential benefit? The classic question of 'how safe is safe enough' is also an integral part of this type of discourse. Policy makers, representatives of major stakeholder groups and scientists should all be included within *reflective discourses.* Political or economic advising committees, who propose or evaluate political options, could also be established in an effort to advise this core group. Special procedures, such as negotiated rule making, mediation and round tables, are the most appropriate for reaching the desired purpose of *reflective discourses* (Fiorino 1995). Value-tree analysis and other decision-aiding tools (Renn *et al.* 1993) can and should be used as structuring instruments within this discourse.

The last type of discourse, which is called *participatory discourse,* focuses on resolving ambiguities and differences about values. Established legal decision-making procedures, but also novel procedures, such as citizen advisory panels and citizen juries, belong within this category. *Participatory discourses* are mainly appropriate as means to search for solutions that are compatible with the interests and values of the people affected and to resolve conflicts among them. This discourse involves the subjective weighting of evaluation criteria and an interpretation of the results. Issues of fairness and environmental justice, visions on future technological developments and societal change, and preferences about desirable lifestyles and community life play a major role within these debates (Webler 1999). At regional and local level, citizen panels or juries (randomly selected), and voluntary public advisory committees might be appropriate participative procedures. At national and multinational level, the Danish model of consensus conferences, as well as other participatory techniques, might prove their worth in the effort to resolve ambiguities and norm and value conflicts (Schneider *et al.* 1998).

4 RISK GOVERNANCE

Procedurally and substantively adequate strategies, tools and measurements to handle and to manage risks are in the spotlight of current discussions within the social scientific field of risk research that aims to establish appropriate risk governance. A large part of the literature deals with the management of locally, regionally and nationally limited risk issues, such as, for example, nuclear plants, waste disposal, mobile telephone systems and threshold setting for pollutant emissions. However, an increasing number of studies are now focusing on risk management beyond national regulations, and also seek to compare different national and European risk regulation approaches (Hood *et al.* 2001; Linneroth-Bayer *et al.* 2001; Löfstedt and Vogel 2001).

In the past years, the term 'governance' has enjoyed immense popularity within political science and within the social scientific field of risk research. The remarkable upswing in use of the term has led to fruitful, if contested, discussion (cf. eg, Kennedy *et al.* 2002; Renn 2005; Wilkinson and Hughes 2002; Zürn and Joerges 2004). In contrast to the hierarchical enforceability structures found within traditional 'government', the notion of governance embodies a horizontally organised structure of functional self-regulation, which encompasses both state and non-state actors, and which identifies collectively binding risk decisions even absent a superior authority (cf. eg, Mayer *et al.* 1993; Wolf 1999). The degree of institutionalisation of functional self-regulation, as well as interaction between and coordination of different institutions and heterogeneous actors, define governance: that is, actors involved in governance govern themselves by means of institutional arrangements. Increasingly, risk governance at national, European and international level is characterised by a shift from state-driven risk regulation and intergovernmental cooperation to the inclusion of economic (businesses, industry, corporations) and civil-societal actors (science, non-governmental organisations (NGOs), epistemic communities), and the emergence of new forms and arrangements of governance. Non-state actors are playing an increasingly important role since they have decisive information and resource advantages compared to states (Cutler *et al.* 1999; Reinicke 1998). Although governmental agencies still retain the authority to collect and appraise the data and information used in risk assessments, in some areas industry is the true source and producer of the necessary data and information (for example, in the food, chemical and pharmaceutical sectors). Accordingly, the central role of states has diminished and new, more inclusive forms of governance have emerged as public-private cooperation has weakened the hierarchical relationship once maintained between state and non-state actors.

Risk governance occurs within multilevel structures and networks of public and private actors. In this manner, risk policy making has been disentangled from traditional political institutions within and beyond the state and new forms and arrangements of risk governance are emerging. The classical vertical process of the generation of risk regulation is being increasingly replaced by a horizontally organised and dialogue-oriented process among governmental, corporate economic and civil-societal actors. All this still presupposes that the state is a necessary actor; at the same time, however, governance entails a changed division of roles and tasks among public and private actors. The symbiosis of different institutional arrangements ensuring democratically legitimate and effective risk problem solving capability aims to create 'good' risk governance.[2] The appearance of these new governance forms nonetheless poses challenging research questions. First, the normative criteria underlying traditional political structures lose relevance in relation to new governance forms: the structures of the forms of interaction witnessed in and the division of functions within 'governance' have yet to be fully understood, while systematic normative appraisal categories have yet to be elaborated. Second, the legitimacy and effectiveness of emerging non-state authorities can be questioned: how might we best legitimise and ensure the effectiveness of risk governance

2 European Commission, *European Governance: A White Paper*, COM(2001) 428 final, 25 July 2001, Brussels.

institutions, which include stakeholders representing economic and civil societal interests alongside governmental actors?

The governance perspective disturbs the dualism of hierarchically organised domestic states and a horizontally structured international system by accentuating the multilevel and network characteristics of modern regulatory action. State action has been transferred to different territorial levels and increasingly relies on corporative societal actors and public-private cooperation for its effectiveness. Thus, a conceptual conjunction of domestic, European and international risk governance is required. I pursue a multi-disciplinary approach, which incorporates various controversial theories, allowing for a higher level of abstraction than is the norm within individual disciplines (cf. Dogan and Phare 1990). The effort to establish an inclusive perspective on risk governance benefits greatly from a broader research perspective, which combines political science research on governance and deliberative and participatory democracy, with insights drawn from the social scientific field of risk research.

5 A DELIBERATIVE MODEL FOR RISK POLICY MAKING

In the following section, the notion of public deliberation will be conceptually developed in an effort to provide a normative as well as practically adaptive model for risk governance. Subsequently, this model will be used to appraise the factual deliberative quality of the Great Lakes Regime.[3] This model of public deliberation does not rely on a territorially defined political space; instead, it refers to functionally differentiated governance. The model has four elements: the procedural realisation of an epistemological discourse suited to the resolution of complexity; the establishment of a reflexive discourse designed to overcome uncertainty; and finally, the creation of a participatory discourse, which can furnish clarity in ambiguous cases. This deliberative model does not fall victim to over-expectation as regards the discursive rationality of procedures and their rationalising effect (cf. Bohman 1996; 1998); instead, it attempts to reconcile different demands with reference to notions of procedural fairness and cognitive validity. Accordingly, public deliberation is understood as a dialogue-oriented process, within which participants seek a 'rationally acceptable' risk policy. Such a process is characterised by argumentative procedures, which are accessible to lay persons, and within which 'arguing' takes on the role of the identification of appropriate and common-good-oriented risk management strategies. The deliberative model is founded upon three constitutive criteria.

5.1 Fair access to risk policy making

Deliberation is underpinned by the institutionalisation of fair access to risk policy making for governmental, civil-societal and economic actors (cf. Bohman 1999; Knight and Johnson 1997). This criterion raises procedural issues and questions of

3 For the detailed development of the pragmatic model of deliberative governance see Klinke 2006.

inclusion, such as the role of the gatekeeper, representation of interests, and the forms of direct participation to be established for affected or interested people (for example, public hearings, consensus conferences, mediation, round tables, public advisory councils, citizen panels or juries and negotiated rule making and so forth). Which non-state actors will be selected for participation, and how? Who plays the role of the gatekeeper? Who concedes to whom, when and on which level, access to the risk policy-making process? When and how will external experts, civil-societal and economic stakeholders, affected groups, and representatives of the public be directly involved? When will their interests be represented? All direct participation procedures have their advantages, but all also have disadvantages: there is no single procedure which fulfils all deliberative requirements with regard to inclusion, interest representation, exchange of arguments and problem-solving capability.

Conceptually speaking, deliberative risk policy making ranges from the inclusion of 'all' affected and interested actors to the indirect representation of civil-societal and economic interests through stakeholders. While the inclusion of 'all' becomes implausible as soon as the appropriate definition of what we mean by 'all' is called into question (Offe and Preuss 1991: 418), the representation of interests raises the problem of which interests must be included or excluded. A feasible deliberative approach in risk policy making need not depend on making every decision the product of deliberation by 'all' (Bohman 1998: 418). Fair access to risk policy making might be realised through an institutionalised participatory process that directly involves affected and interested citizens in argumentative procedures. Concretisation of participation has (at least partially) proven to be successful in the context of alternative dispute resolution procedures as regularly applied within the US and Canada. Within Europe, however, such procedures have been used only rarely (Weidner 1998). Against this background, and the fact that citizens have few possibilities directly to engage within cross-border risk governance, the role of NGOs (as representatives of civil society and public interests) has become more important. While NGOs exert significant influence in the generation and implementation of risk policies, they only play a subordinate role within the formal decision-making processes on risk regulation.

Alongside the anecdotal knowledge brought to the debate by a lay public, systematic input of scientific knowledge remains essential. A maximum of cognitive reliability must be ensured in the efforts to address risks characterised by high complexity, uncertainty and/or ambiguity: political risk decision makers and citizens may be unable to tackle scientific challenges of highly complex, uncertain and ambiguous risks; scientific expertise, nonetheless, has the potential to provide the necessary cognitive reliability. Scientists provide valid causal knowledge allowing for the rationalisation and categorisation of different risk perceptions. Furthermore, scientific knowledge provides us with a cognitive constant, with regard to which we can agree on a common risk definition, evaluate risk consequences and find common-good-oriented risk management policies. Accordingly, risk governance must be conceived of as entailing a cognitive division of labour between lay people and experts.

5.2 Horizontal and dialogue-oriented communication and interaction

The deliberative model likewise draws on horizontal and discursive forms of communication and interaction between governmental policy makers, civil-societal and economic stakeholders and directly affected people, which are concretised within argumentative procedures. The quality of communication and interaction can range from moderate strategic action dominated by both bargaining and arguing, in order to achieve mutual acceptable compromises over argumentative action (Zangl and Zürn 1996), to the Habermasian ideal of communicative action (1984), which creates an ideal speech situation without any constraints. Deliberative risk policy making is successful if argumentative action prevails. Although less ambitious with regard to discursive and procedural rationality than communicative action, it nonetheless facilitates common preference formation at cognitive level. The aim of argumentative procedures is the generation of a commonly accepted risk definition, the evaluation of risk consequences on the basis of recognised criteria, and the factual adequacy and common good orientation of the risk policy.

5.3 Effective risk management

Finally, the deliberative model must also address the question of how effective risk management strategies and measures might be established, which are respected by all persons affected by decision making. The specific potential to formulate the 'right' risk decisions emanates from the argumentative procedures. This potential is more than the lowest common denominator of preferences: a directly affected public and addressees of risk regulations should approve the decision as the appropriate risk policy in two regards. First, the risk management policy adopted must be a substantially adequate mechanism to prevent, mitigate or control the risk. Second, the risk management options should take into account the common good of the affected people in the risk issue area and must not promote particular interests. The common-good-orientation of risk management strategies raises the question of inclusion or exclusion, whose good ought to be taken into account and what, substantively spoken, is the common good (Dahl 1989: 306). The common good reference becomes valid and publicly accountable, if the relevant framework of action is specified politically, socially and/or territorially. Since the substantial dimension of the common good can cover prosperity, full employment, education, health, internal and international peace, social, military and civil security, sustainable use of natural resources, and sustainable growth, neither a hierarchy nor a charging for these units is possible (Offe 2001: 482). But it is possible to resort to the category of justice, even if it is a relational term and has to be defined as (for example) compensatory, distributional, intergenerational or procedural justice. Accordingly, the product of deliberative risk policy making does not rely on an independent standard; instead, it embodies the result of cognitive reflection and interpretation within argumentative procedures.

6 INCLUSIVE RISK GOVERNANCE WITHIN THE GREAT LAKES REGIME IN NORTH AMERICA

The Great Lakes Regime maintained between the United States and Canada represents a remarkable example of inclusive risk governance, from which lessons can be learnt. The political practice is based on a deliberative approach integrating public participation, argumentative procedures and effective risk management. A transnational network and multilevel risk governance system has been implemented, whose legal basis is found in the Boundary Waters Treaty (IJC 1909) and Water Quality Agreement (IJC 1989). In these treaties, the governments of the US and Canada have commonly agreed on democratic principles such as cooperation, publicity, public participation, transparency, accountability, and discursive dispute settlement. These accords also provide the constitutive prerequisites for the establishment of a competent and politically independent bilateral risk policy-making system, in which the International Joint Commission (IJC) is the political decision-making body. The system is composed of four major advisory boards (Water Quality Board, Science Advisory Board, Council of Great Lakes Research Managers and International Air Quality Advisory Board), and a further 14 boards responsible for observation, monitoring, inspection and control as well as a number of task forces, subcommittees and working groups. In addition to their scientific, technical, juridical and political-administrative competences, the four central advisory boards are in charge of organising and moderating different public participation procedures on different political-institutional levels. The boards aggregate the results of the participation procedures in their regular reports for the IJC. On the basis of the scientific and public input, the IJC compiles a biannual report for the two governments containing reports on the true state of the environment as well as policy recommendations setting priorities with regard to the successful implementation of the Water Quality Agreement.

Three types of public participation are implemented across the national boundaries (Klinke 2006): first, public hearings are declamatory procedures, at which all affected or interested people are entitled to be heard, even though a discursive exchange of arguments proves to be elusive. Such public hearings are organised at bi-national level at the end of each two-year working cycle. They are further accompanied by workshops and meetings, which deal with specific issues. Despite the shortcomings regarding discursive quality, the biennial public hearings provide one of the most important of forums for participation for an affected and interested public. The fact that such hearings are regularly attended by 400–500 attendees emphasises their central role.

The second form of public participation within this regime emphasises discursive procedures within problem-oriented meetings, workshops, round tables, focus groups and consultations, in which specific issues and questions are discussed. Such meetings are characterised by the discursive exchange of reasons, arguing, mutual understanding and learning. A major goal is to achieve a common understanding of risk, of the basis for the evaluation of consequences, and for the evolution of effective risk management options. Discursive procedures are the most frequently and most widespread used form of public participation within the Great Lakes Regime: subjects tackled vary from the identification of environmental and health risks through common ecological indicators to normative issues, such as the identification of the exact aims of the Water Quality Agreement.

The third type of participation within the regime is assured through the establishment of permanent public advisory bodies at the regional level of the Lakes and at local levels, identified as 'Areas of Concern', within which environmental, tribal, industrial, business, health and academic interests are represented. For three of the five lakes, bi-national public forums were constituted in order to develop and implement 'Lakewide Management Plans' in cooperation with the regional and sub-national governments of the US federal states and the Canadian provinces. At local level, Canada and the United States identified particular 'Areas of Concern' that were specifically troubled by contaminated sediment, wastewater, pollution or degraded habitats. Within these 'Areas of Concern' public advisory councils have been formed to generate and realise 'Remedial Action Plans' in cooperation with local governments. Public advisory councils are the conciliating link between the public and political decision makers in local governments. Both 'Lakewide Management Plans' and 'Remedial Action Plans' seek to identify long-term risk management strategies and measures designed to restore and maintain the integrity of the fresh water bodies and the environment.

In conclusion, the Great Lakes Regime represents an example of inclusive risk governance with a high quality of discourse, deliberation and participation across national borders. The cornerstone is the bilateral contract, in which the United States and Canada agree on shared normative principles to protect and restore the integrity of the environment of the fresh water system. The transboundary risk policy-making process is realised through a network and multilevel participation structure. The IJC and its advisory boards form a stable and enduring institutional governance arrangement that strengthens and consolidates the role and influence of the public in the risk policy-making process. The different procedural types of public participation institutionalised in the multilevel system have both merits and problems. In this account, the regime does not have one single participatory form, but is founded upon the functional and structural combination of different procedures that realise a successful system of inclusive risk governance, in which epistemic discourses to resolve complexity, reflective discourses to dissolve uncertainty and participatory discourses to account for mutual understanding and clarity are implemented within clear though diverse institutions.

7 CONCLUSIONS

The Great Lakes Regime is an exemplary case that allows us to draw conclusions on the institutional prerequisites for the concretisation of inclusive risk governance. The institutional implementation of inclusive risk governance through discourse, deliberation and participation emanates from a shared normative orientation on democratic principles such as cooperation, dialogue and public participation, which should be legally agreed by contract or treaty. The more these principles are specified through general and specific standards of action, the more likely it is that successful inclusive risk governance will evolve. Deliberative arenas primed with argumentative-oriented procedures, such as platforms of discourse, deliberation and public participation, must be established, in order to afford fair access to risk policy making for directly affected and interested people. An institutional structure consisting of an independent decision-making body and an advisory system might prove to be a useful contribution to risk governance. Only an institutionalised system with appropriate capacities and instruments has the ability to organise, moderate and coordinate different argumentative procedures on different political-institutional levels and to aggregate the outcomes of public opinion and will formation processes. The following combination of participative procedures reflects the strong points of the Great Lakes Regime and tries to avoid its shortcomings (Klinke 2006):

- In public, discursive-oriented hearings at the beginning of a working cycle, 'all' affected people would have access to the decision-making regime and be entitled to be heard within the overall effort to set an agenda and to determine topics and priorities for public discourse and participation in the forthcoming working cycle.
- In discursive procedures, specific problem-oriented, cognitive and/or normative issues, which were selected in the public hearings, are discussed and clarified. On the basis of expert and lay knowledge, the participants develop a common risk understanding, evaluate consequences and elaborate risk policies and general risk management strategies.
- In the implementation process public advisory bodies linked with citizen panels of affected people develop practicable risk management strategies at regional and local level. Participants should avail themselves of suggestions made within discursive procedures and tailor specific risk management strategies, measures and tools to their given situation.
- Within a multilevel system, the different deliberative arenas characterised by various participatory procedures are only loosely coupled with one another: that is, the opinion and will formation that takes place in one deliberative arena may not produce a mandatory decision for other deliberative arenas (cf. Benz 1998: 215). Thus, the important function of aggregation of public input and political decision making remains in the hands of the bilateral decision-making body and the advisory boards. The political influence of the public is based on the convincing power of reasons and proposals. The reasoning through publicly acceptable common good rationality is the political influence that motivates political bodies to take into account the publicly proposed risk management strategies. For the success of inclusive risk governance through discourse, deliberation and public participation it is vital that policy-making and advising bodies consider and condense unadulterated public input. In this manner, they might (re)gain credibility and trustworthiness.

BIBLIOGRAPHY

Benz, A. (1998) 'Postparlamentarische Demokratie? Demokratische Legitimation im kooperativen Staat', in M. Greven (ed.), *Demokratie – eine Kultur des Westens? 20. Wissenschaftlicher Kongreß der Deutschen Vereinigung für Politische Wissenschaft*, Opladen: Leske and Budrich, 201–22.

Bohman, J. (1999) 'International regimes and democratic governance: political equality and influence in global institutions', *International Affairs* 75(3): 499–513.

Bohman, J. (1998) 'Survey article: the coming of age of deliberative democracy', *The Journal of Political Philosophy* 6(4): 400–25.

Bohman, J. (1996) *Public Deliberation. Pluralism, Complexity, and Democracy*, Cambridge and London: MIT Press.

Cutler, A.C., Haufler, V. and Porter, T. (eds) (1999) *Private Authority and International Affairs*, Albany: State University of New York Press.

Dahl, R.A. (1989) *Democracy and Its Critics*, New Haven and London: Yale University Press.

Dogan, M. and Phare, R. (1990) *Creative Marginality. Innovation at the Intersections of Social Sciences*, Boulder: Westview Press.

European Commission (2001) *European Governance: A White Paper*, COM(2001) 428 final, 25 July 2001, Brussels.

Fiorino, D.J. (1995) 'Regulatory negotiation as a form of public participation', in O. Renn, T. Webler and P.M. Wiedemann (eds), *Fairness and Competence in Citizen Participation. Evaluating New Models for Environmental Discourse*, Dordrecht and Boston: Kluwer, 223–38.

Funtowicz, S.O. and Ravetz, J.R. (1990) *Uncertainty and Quality in Science for Policy*, Dordrecht: Kluwer.

Habermas, J. (1984) *The Theory of Communicative Action. Vol. 1. Reason and the Rationalization of Society*, London: Heinemann Education.

Harrison, K. and Hoberg, G. (1994) *Risk, Science, and Politics: Regulating Toxic Substances in Canada and the United States*, Montreal: McGill-Queen's University Press.

Hood, C., Rothstein, H. and Baldwin, R. (2001) *The Government of Risk. Understanding Risk Regulation Regimes*, Oxford: Oxford University Press.

International Joint Commission (ICJ) (1989) *Great Lakes Water Quality Agreement of 1978. Agreement, with Annexes and Terms of Reference, between the United States and Canada Signed at Ottawa November 22, 1978 and Phosphorus Load Reduction Supplement Signed October 16, 1983 as Amended by Protocol Signed November 18, 1987*, Ottawa: IJC.

International Joint Commission (IJC) (1909) *Treaty between the United States and Great Britain Relating to Boundary Waters, and Questions Arising Between the United States and Canada*, Washington.

Johannessen, O.M., Shalina, E.V. and Miles, M.W. (1999) 'Satellite evidence for an arctic sea ice cover in transformation', *Science* 3(286): 1937–9.

Kennedy, P., Messner, D. and Nuscheler, F. (eds) (2002) *Global Trends and Global Governance*, London: Pluto Press.

Klinke, A. (2006) *Demokratisches Regieren jenseits des Staates. Deliberative Politik im nordamerikanischen Grosse Seen-Regime*, Opladen: Barbara Budrich Publisher.

Klinke, A. and Renn, O. (2002) 'A new approach to risk evaluation and management: risk-based, precaution-based and discourse-based strategies', *Risk Analysis* 22(6): 1071–94.

Klinke, A., Dreyer, M., Renn, O., Stirling, A. and Van Zwanenberg, P. (2006) 'Precautionary Risk Regulation in European Governance', *Journal of Risk Research* 9(4): 373–92.

Knight, J. and Johnson, J. (1997) 'What sort of equality does deliberative democracy require?', in J. Bohman and W. Rehg (eds), *Deliberative Democracy. Essays on Reason and Politics*, Cambridge and London: MIT Press, 279–319.

Linneroth-Bayer, J., Löfstedt, R. and Sjöstedt, G. (eds) (2001) *Transboundary Risk Management*, London: Earthscan.

Löfstedt, R. and Vogel, D. (2001) 'The changing character of regulations: a comparison of Europe and the United States', *Risk Analysis* 21(3): 399–405.

Lozán, J.L., Graßl, H. and Hupfer, P. (eds) (1998) *Warnsignal Klima. Mehr Klimaschutz – weniger Risiken für die Zukunft*, Hamburg: Wissenschaftliche Auswertungen.

Mayer, P., Rittberger, V. and Zürn, M. (1993) 'Regime theory: state of the art and perspectives', in V. Rittberger (ed.), *Regime Theory and International Relations*, Oxford: Clarendon, 391–430.

Offe, C. (2001) 'Wessen Wohl ist das Gemeinwohl?', in L. Wingert and K. Günther (eds), *Die Öffentlichkeit der Vernunft und die Vernunft der Öffentlichkeit*, Frankfurt/M: Suhrkamp, 459–88.

Offe, C. and Preuss, U.K. (1991) 'Democratic institutions and moral resources', in D. Held (ed.), *Political Theory Today*, Cambridge: Polity Press, 143–71.

Reinicke, W.H. (1998) *Global Public Policy. Governing without Government?*, Washington: Brookings Institution Press.

Renn, O. (2005) *Risk Governance. Towards an Integrative Approach. White Paper No. 1 of the International Risk Governance Council*, Geneva: IRGC.

Renn, O. (1999a) 'Participative technology assessment: meeting the challenges of uncertainty and ambivalence', *Futures Research Quarterly* 15(3): 81–97.

Renn, O. (1999b) 'Diskursive Verfahren der Technikfolgenabschätzung', in T. Petermann and R. Coenen (eds), *Technikfolgenabschätzung in Deutschland. Bilanz und Perspektiven*, Frankfurt/M: Campus, 115–30.

Renn, O., Webler, T., Rakel, H., Dienel, P.C. and Johnson, B.B. (1993) 'Public participation in decision making: a three-step-procedure', *Policy Sciences* 26: 189–214.

Schellnhuber, H.-J. (1999) ' "Earth System" analysis and the second Copernican revolution', *Nature* 402: C19–C23.

Schmalz-Bruns, R. (1999) 'Deliberativer Supranationalismus. Demokratisches Regieren jenseits des Nationalstaats', *Zeitschrift für Internationale Beziehungen* 6(2): 185–244.

Schneider, E., Oppermann, B. and Renn, O. (1998) 'Implementing structured participation for regional level waste management planning', *Risk, Health, Safety and Environment* 9: 379–95.

Van Asselt, M.B.A. (2000) *Perspectives on Uncertainty and Risk: The PRIMA Approach to Decision Support*, Boston and Dordrecht: Kluwer.

Webler, T. (1999) 'The craft and theory of public participation: a dialectical process', *Journal of Risk Research* 2(1): 55–71.

WBGU, German Advisory Council on Global Change (2000) *World in Transition. Strategies for Managing Global Environmental Risks. Annual Report 1998*, Berlin *et al.*: Springer.

Weidner, H. (ed.) (1998) *Alternative Dispute Resolution in Environmental Conflicts. Experiences in 12 Countries*, Berlin: Sigma.

Wilkinson, R. and Hughes, S. (eds) (2002) *Global Governance. Critical Perspectives*, London: Routledge.

Wolf, K.D. (1999) 'The new raison d'état as a problem for democracy in world society', *European Journal of International Relations* 5(3): 333–63.

Yosie, T.F. and Herbst, T.D. (1998) 'Managing and communicating stakeholder-based decision making', *Human and Ecological Risk Assessment* 4: 643–6.

Zangl, B. and Zürn, M. (1996) 'Argumentatives Handeln bei internationalen Verhandlungen', *Zeitschrift für Internationale Beziehungen* 3(2): 341–66.

Zürn, M. and Joerges, C. (eds) (2004) *Governance and Law in Postnational Constellations. Compliance in Europe and Beyond*, Cambridge: Cambridge University Press.

Chapter 21

Sound science in the European and global market: Karl Polanyi in Geneva

Christian Joerges

1 THE EUROPEAN EXPERIENCE: THE UNFORESEEN OUTCOME OF MARKET BUILDING

We have heard and said it so often: European Market building was not about deregulation, but about modernisation, re-regulation and the re-embedding of the market within a European context once it had been disembedded from its national contexts.

1.1 What we have observed

The Delors Commission's 1985 *White Paper on Completion of the Internal Market*[1] is widely perceived as a turning point and a breakthrough in the integration process. Jacques Delors' initiative promised to overcome a long phase of stagnation; the means to this end was the strengthening of Europe's competitiveness. Economic rationality, rather than 'law', was, from now on, to be understood as Europe's orienting maxim, its first commitment and its regulative idea. In this sense, it seems justified to characterise Delors' programme as a deliberate move towards an institutionalisation of economic rationality. This appears to be even more plausible when we consider the two complementary institutional innovations accomplished through, and subsequent to, the Maastricht Treaty, namely, Monetary Union and the Stability Pact. Europe appeared then to be a market-embedded polity governed by an economic constitution, rather than by political rule.

This characterisation, however, soon proved to be too simplistic by far.[2] What had started out as an effort to strengthen Europe's competitiveness and to accomplish this objective through new (de-regulatory) strategies, soon led to the entanglement of the EU in ever more policy fields and the development of sophisticated regulatory machinery. It was, in particular, the concern of European legislation and the Commission with 'social regulation' (the health and safety of consumers and workers, and environmental protection), which served as irrefutable proof of this fact. The weight and dynamics of these policy fields had been thoroughly underestimated by the proponents of the 'economic constitution'. Equally important and

1 European Commission, *Commission White Paper to the European Council on Completion of the Internal Market*, COM(1985) 310 final, 14 June 1985, Brussels.

2 See, on the following, in more detail, Joerges 1994: 29–62.

equally unsurprising was the fact that the integration process deepened with the completion of the Internal Market and affected ever more policy fields. This was significant not so much in terms of its factual weight, but, rather, in view of Europe's 'social deficit', in terms of the new efforts consequently made to strengthen Europe's presence in the spheres of labour and social policy.

These tendencies became mainstream during the preparation of the Maastricht Treaty, which was adopted in 1992. This is why this amendment of the Treaty, officially presented as both a deepening and a consolidation of the integration project, met with fierce criticism. The most outspoken critique came not from the political left, but from the proponents of the new economic philosophy, and, in particular, from Germany's ordo-liberals (see Streit and Mussler 1995: 5–30). And, indeed, the Maastricht Treaty of 1992 can be read as a break with the ordo-liberal economic constitution. After the explicit recognition and strengthening of new policy competences, which was accomplished in Maastricht, it no longer seemed plausible simply to assign a constitutive function to the 'system of undistorted competition', because this very 'system' had now been downgraded to one among many others. In addition, the expansion of competences in labour law by the Social Protocol and Agreement on Social Policy of the Treaty blurred the formerly clear lines between Europe's (apolitical) economic constitution and the political responsibility that Member States had for social and labour policies.

1.2 Why did it happen?

A consensus on the interpretation of this new constellation has yet to emerge. Was this progression a result of contingent events and decisions? Was there a deeper 'logic' at work? Back in 1944, Karl Polanyi, in his seminal book, 'The Great Transformation', had argued that markets will always be 'socially embedded' (Polanyi 1992: 45–58, 71–80). He did not spell out the political and normative implications of his sociological observations, but the European experience seems, in principle, reconcilable with his messages. Once it is becoming apparent that markets could not be understood simply as being mechanisms that functioned perfectly and automatically to adjust supply and demand,

> [t]he critical question is no longer the quantitative issue of how much state or how much market, but rather the qualitative issue of how and for what ends should markets and states be combined and what are the structures and practices in civil society that will sustain a productive synergy of states and markets.[3]

This 'social embeddedness' thesis can help us to understand why Europe has developed an ever more sophisticated regulatory machinery entrusted with the management of the internal market. But, we need nonetheless to be careful. Polanyi neither attempted to predict the shape of social embeddedness; nor did he assure that it would be beneficial and unproblematic. What we must now be particularly aware of is the exposure of the socially embedded European to globalisation processes and their particular institutional forms.

3 See Block 2005: 3 and most recently Beckert 2007.

2 GLOBALISATION AS REGRESSION: THE WTO PANEL REPORT ON THE GMO DISPUTE

The international constellation is, quite clearly, very different. Even though we might expect a social-embeddedness imperative to operate at international level, here, its powers will clearly be of a very different kind. Of necessity, international contracting has created its own legal frameworks for international trade;[4] frameworks within which national and European efforts to defend the health and safety of citizens have already proven to be powerful irritants and transformative accelerants.

This trend is most visibly demonstrated in relation to the transformation of the old GATT trade regime into the new WTO legal system. The main objective of the General Agreement on Tariffs and Trade (GATT), concluded in 1947, was the phasing out of tariffs introduced by states in order to protect their national economies. Since the early 1970s, however, non-tariff barriers to free trade have become the main focus for attention. This shift was necessitated by the intensification of domestic economic regulation, especially in the fields of health and safety, consumer and environmental protection. In 1994, the international trade system adapted to this situation by transforming the GATT into the World Trade Organization (WTO). The most important reforms included an overhaul of its procedures of dispute settlement and the conclusion of special agreements concerning non-tariff barriers to free trade, such as the *Agreement on the Application of Sanitary and Phytosanitary Measures* (SPS) and the *Agreement on Technical Barriers to Trade* (TBT). These agreements aim at the balancing of their main economic objective, free trade, with the domestic regulatory concerns of WTO members.

There are obvious parallels to the European experience after the abolition of tariff barriers. But there are also important differences. The Members of the WTO did not confer 'positive' regulatory powers upon that organisation, although they agreed that WTO law should impose restraints on the exercise of their domestic regulatory powers. WTO law cannot simply copy the European turn to 'positive' integration via re-regulation. The co-originality of market and regulation, postulated by Polanyi, must find its expression within different mechanisms. Currently, the most important of these mechanisms that accompany the restraints imposed on domestic regulatory policies is an intense process of quasi-legal norm-production at the international level, organised by both non-governmental and governmental actors, and especially so in the field of product safety (see Joerges and Petersmann 2006).

2.1 The *GMO* case and its object

This chapter restricts its discussion on the impact of globalisation on the European market constellation to one single case, namely the dispute between the EU, the US, Canada and Argentina on the legitimate or otherwise use of genetically modified

4 See, recently, Gralff-Peter Calliess 2002: 185–216; 2006.

organisms (GMOs) in foodstuffs.[5] There are many reasons for this specific focus. Foodstuffs are highly politicised products; accordingly, no legal system has ever been able fully to dispense with more or less comprehensive or stringent regulatory supervision of them. GMOs represent the technologically most advanced and, at the same time, most controversial of all foodstuffs, if not of all consumer products. This is so for a broad range of reasons.[6] GMO production requires highly developed technologies, within which the US is the world's leader, but which have also been mastered to a greater or lesser degree by countries such as Argentina, Brazil and India. The socio-economic implications of new GMO technologies are necessarily ambivalent: India, for example, with a high percentage of its labour force occupied within the agrarian sector, is a scene of great conflict about GMOs as development imperatives clash with employment concerns (see Zarrilli 2006: 231–54). The most intensive controversy, however, focuses on the risks of GMOs. Sceptics and GMO promoters agree to a large degree that the 'safety' of genetically modified foodstuffs has not been 'positively' challenged (see van den Daele 2007). The main concern of the critics, however, is with the production process; the risks of contamination of non GMO-crops by GMOs released into the environment. The debate is also and, in an illuminating way, all about the importance of consumer anxieties and consumer choice. Do we have a 'right to know' what we are eating?[7] Are governments entitled to require the labelling of GMOs because a majority or significant minority of their constituency refuses to accept them?[8] The EU has accordingly 'perfected' its authorisation procedures by means of the establishment of an ethical advisory body (see Dabrowska 2006: 200 ff).

The GMO controversy has a long history (Shaffer and Pollack 2005: 167–229). The present legalised stage[9] began in the spring of 2003 with the request for formal dispute settlement consultations by the US, supported by Argentina and Canada. In that request the complainants argued that the EC had imposed a *de facto* moratorium on approvals of biotech products and 'national marketing and import bans on biotech products' issued by Member States of the EU and approved by it. Following the request, the panel was formed in March 2004. Its report was announced several times and then postponed. The conclusions of the Panel's preliminary report of 7 February 2006 were made public soon thereafter.[10] Having received the

5 See WTO Panel Report, *European Communities – Measures Affecting the Approval and Marketing of Biotech Products*, 13 October 2006, WT/DS291/Interim, WT/DS292/Interim, WT/DS293 (complaints by United States, Canada and Argentina respectively); available at: <http://www.wto.org/english/news_e/news06_e/291r_e.htm>; for the preliminary confidential report leaked by Friends of the Earth see: <http://www.foe.co.uk/resources/press_releases/leaked_wto_report_us_misle_28022006.html>.

6 For a summary cf the *amicus brief* submitted in the GMO dispute by Winickoff, Jasanoff, Busch, Grove-White and Wynne 2005: 81–125.

7 See, on this controversy, Sand 2006: 185–92.

8 See European Commission, *Europeans and Biotechnology in 2005: Patterns and trends, Eurobarometer* 64.3, May 2006; see also *GM Compass, June 22* 2006, available at: <http://www.gmcompass.org/pdf/documents/eurobarometer2006.pdf>.

9 See, for a detailed survey of the arguments brought forward, Petersmann 2006: 173–200.

10 The full preliminary report was made public by Friends of the Earth (see <http://www.foe.co.uk/resources/press_releases/leaked_wto_report_us_misle_28022006.html>), an indiscretion on which the final report, above, note 5, lamented upon at some length (see paras 1.124–1.137).

responses to its preliminary report, the WTO panel published its modified report on 29 September 2006. It now covers 1,087 pages and has 10 annexes.[11]

2.2 Three core issues

The reasoning in WTO reports is highly formalised. The reports reconstruct the arguments of the parties to the disputes, of all other participants and of the *amici curiae*; they document how they have replied to their adversaries – and then take great pains to furnish a *lege artis* interpretation of the agreements on which they must base their findings and conclusions. There is of course much more in the reports than can be addressed here – but not everything is important in the light of the leitmotif of this essay: what form of social embeddedness of the market for GMOs does WTO law, in the view of the panel report, seek to achieve?

The answers to this query seem surprisingly simple. We single out and differentiate between three aspects: (1) the authority of science; (2) the autonomy of politics; and (3) consumer choice.

2.2.1 *Supremacy of science*

The US and the EU differ in their regulatory approaches to GMOs significantly in two respects. The US focuses on the health risks posed by the food produced whereas the approach of the EU is much more comprehensive in that it places a much greater emphasis on environmental risks (see Shaffer and Pollack 2005: 169 ff). In their safety assessments, US authorities tend to approve products unless there is some scientific evidence confirming risk allegations, whereas the EU has committed itself to the 'precautionary principle'. That principle is of constitutional authority within the EU since the Maastricht Treaty of 1992;[12] each and every legislative, administrative and judicial act must respect it. The rules and principles governing the resolution of conflict between the two legal orders are to be found in the SPS Agreement. All of them point to the authority of science. That is by no means surprising.

As already underlined, the WTO does not have any 'positive' legislative competences, but recognises in principle the regulatory autonomy of WTO Members. In order to ensure the compatibility of regulatory policies with its commitment to free trade it makes use of underlying conflict of laws principles, asking Members to exercise some self-restraint in the interpretation and application of their domestic law and, where this does not suffice, seeking to resolve conflicts with the aid of a meta-rule to which all the parties can be expected to subscribe. As such, WTO law reproduces the old European model to overcoming national regulatory policies that created obstacles to trade. Classically, the European model identified

11 WTO Panel Report, *European Communities – Measures Affecting the Approval and Marketing of Biotech Products*, 13 October 2006, WT/DS291/Interim, WT/DS292/Interim, WT/DS293 (complaints by United States, Canada and Argentina respectively). Findings and conclusions: <http://www.wto.org/english/tratop_e/dispu_e/291r_conc_e.pdf>. Full panel report: <http://www.wto.org/english/news_e/news06_e/291r_e.htm>.

12 Now Article 174(2) EC Treaty.

legitimate policy objectives for national regulation (such as health, safety and environmental protection) and then required Member States to provide scientific evidence that these regulatory concerns were, in fact real (see Joerges 1997: 295–324). Through its resort to science, Europe invoked a non-partisan objective authority that national policy makers could accept. This is, of course, not to say that Europeans would not know that the assessment and risk management of risk involves political and policy questions such as the acceptability of risks and regulatory responses to them (cf. Gouldner 1957: 281–306, 1958: 444–80). And yet, the standards of science as well as the techniques of risk assessment can claim some meta-political validity. Where scientists cannot agree, they nonetheless continue to interpret their controversies as a scientific exercise and entrust the scientific community with the competence to assess their claims.

What has been practised with such remarkable success within the EU suggests itself equally as a conflict mediating strategy in international arenas. The acceptability of technically complex and potentially harmful products cannot be assessed without the help of pertinent expertise. And vice versa: where WTO Members raise objections against free access to their markets, they can be expected to provide scientific evidence supporting the legitimacy of their policies. This is exactly what the SPS Agreement provides for.[13]

Nonetheless, a question remains: what if science cannot help to resolve controversies because scientists agree that they are confronted with uncertainty they cannot hope to overcome? This need not be the end of methodologically disciplined discourses. Such discourses have, however, come to an end, where one party adopts a version of the precautionary principle in which the quest for scientific evidence is rejected *a priori*. The borderlines are by no means obvious as the efforts of European Courts document.[14] It would be too much to expect a WTO body to explain that its own mandate ends where science has no answers on offer. In the *Hormones* case[15] the WTO Appellate Body found that the '[precautionary] principle has not been written into the SPS Agreement as a ground for justifying SPS measures that are otherwise inconsistent with the obligations of Members set out in particular provisions of that Agreement'. The panel in the *GMO* case follows suit in a more elegant way: recalling 'that according to the Appellate Body, the precautionary principle has not been written into the *SPS Agreement* as a legitimate ground for justifying SPS

13 'Members shall ensure that any sanitary or phytosanitary measure is . . . based on scientific principles and is not maintained without sufficient scientific evidence . . . (Art. 2(2))'. 'Members may introduce or maintain . . . a higher level of sanitary or phytosanitary protection . . . if there is a scientific justification, . . .' (Art. 2(3). 'In the assessment of risks, Members shall take into account available scientific evidence . . .' (Art. 5(2)). 'In cases where relevant scientific evidence is insufficient, a Member may provisionally adopt sanitary or phytosanitary measures on the basis of available pertinent information, including that from the relevant international organisations as well as from sanitary or phytosanitary measures applied by other Members. In such circumstances, Members shall seek to obtain the additional information necessary for a more objective assessment of risk and review the sanitary or phytosanitary measure accordingly within a reasonable period of time' (Art. 5(7)).

14 Most prominently ECJ, Case C-236/01 *Monsanto v Italy* [2003] ECR I-8105. See also Cases T-13/99 *Pfizer* [2002] ECR-II 03305, and T-70/99 *Alpharma* [1990] ECR-II 2027.

15 WTO Appellate Body Report, *European Communities – Measures Concerning Meat and Meat Products (Hormones) (EC-Hormones)*, 13 February 1998, WT/DS26/AB/R and WT/DS48/AB/R.

measures';[16] the panel went on to explain that 'even if a Member follows a precautionary approach, its SPS measures need to be "based on" (ie "sufficiently warranted" or "reasonably supported" by) a risk assessment. Or, to put it another way, such an approach needs to be applied in a manner consistent with the requirements of Article 5(1).'

Alternatively, the WTO clearly feels entitled to impose the yardstick of science it finds in the SPS agreement regardless of the constitutional positions taken up and applied by its Member States.

2.2.2 *Distorting politics*

Resort to science in such trans-scientific matters is to invoke an emperor without clothes, one might object. If scientific uncertainty is a 'fact', the insistence on science as the legally prescribed arbiter of controversies does not make sense. A variety of alternatives are conceivable. The closest to the logic of the panel report is a broader understanding of 'science' and 'risk assessment'. In the pronouncements of the Appellate Body in the *Hormones* case just cited[17] the recognition of uncertainty resulting from incomplete knowledge and disputes between experts seems to mirror conservative interpretations of the precautionary principle. Thus, the ECJ in its most important judgment on the precautionary principle has explained that this principle must not be understood as legitimating 'a purely hypothetical approach to risk, founded on mere suppositions which are not yet scientifically verified';[18] it requires instead 'a risk assessment which is as complete as possible in the particular circumstances'.[19] A second alternative is the extension of risk assessments to production processes and/or to their use. Both alternatives, however, imply that non-scientific criteria will have an impact on risk evaluations (see Herwig 2006: 301–26). Once one becomes aware of this implication, it is difficult to explain why socio-economic considerations about the social costs and benefits of a new technology should be illegitimate *per se*. To rephrase this observation from a different perspective: since the legal system cannot refuse to take a decision simply because state-of-the-art expertise does not provide it with guidance, the resort to trans-scientific criteria must suggest itself. Socio-economic considerations concerning, for example, the impact of the introduction of new technologies on the agricultural sector are not simply irrational.[20]

Two further implications need to be underlined. First, where uncertainty prevails, diversity in the assessment of the given problem will be unavoidable. Second, such diversity needs a framework within which it can be managed. The EU seems particularly well equipped in that respect. The ECT explicitly recognises the right of Member States to move beyond the level of consumer protection foreseen in legislative acts (Article 95(5) ECT; Article 153 ECT) and its commitment to precaution

16 Para 7.0365, note 1905.

17 Above, note 15.

18 Case C-236/01 *Monsanto v Italy* [2003] ECR I-8105, para 106.

19 Case C-236/01 *Monsanto v Italy* [2003] ECR I-8105, para 107.

20 But of course hardly acceptable within systems building upon free trade as their *raison d'être*. For the WTO system cf Zarrilli 2006.

also suggests that in cases of scientific uncertainty the Member States should retain autonomy. Furthermore, each and every piece of pertinent secondary legislation contains safeguard clauses with exit options for Member States who find the majority response unacceptable (most significantly in the present context, the authorisation of genetically modified organisms).[21]

Diversity in a system understanding the establishment of a common market as its *raison d'être* is, however, apparently difficult to accept. Recourse to the safeguard identified by the ECJ is available only on the basis of 'evidence which indicates the existence of a specific risk' and not for reasons 'of a general nature'.[22] The search for uniform standards within the European market is clearly visible in such remarks.[23] The ECJ has confirmed that safeguard procedures must be understood in 'in the light of the precautionary principle' and may therefore justify a temporary derogation, but only, however, where 'it proves impossible to carry out as full a risk assessment as possible . . . because of the inadequate nature of the available scientific data'.[24]

And yet, what the European Court refused finally to do, was to subject European governments to an 'objective' standard, such as is advocated by the proponents of sound science. The WTO Panel, by contrast, was far less timid: notwithstanding doubts about the completeness of scientific evidence, the Panel insisted upon the exclusive validity of a yardstick, which, its indeterminacy notwithstanding, both overrules precautionary reservations in cases of uncertainty and de-legitimises political processes and solutions. If you cannot prove that GMOs are not safe, you have no reason to reject them.

This final tendency, the de-legitimisation of political process, is very clear in the Panel's treatment of European submissions. Europe's final regulatory regime for GMOs did not appear out of the blue. Rather, it was many years in the making. The first directive appeared in 1990 (see Dabrowska 2006, chapter 2.1: 43 ff); yet, in the light of ongoing political debates and discussions, many revisions were to be made, with the European Council of Environmental Ministers agreeing on a final common platform for a new framework only in June 1999.[25] By the same token, the final regulatory directive took longer to detail. Although the WTO panel report did not question the seriousness of such lengthy political processes directly, it nonetheless found a very convenient and indirect means of de-legitimatising them. Having once decided that the SPS agreement was applicable to the authorisation of GMOs, the panel could then point to Article 8 SPS Agreement in connection with Annex C 1(8a). These provisions require that applications must not be treated with 'undue delay'. The right of applicants seeking authorisation for their products trumps all other; it is irrelevant that time may be required to overcome internal political difficulties. The panel found that the completion of the approval process had been 'unduly delayed' in 24 cases. It therefore requested the EU to bring the measures

21 See, on the European authorisation procedures in detail, Dabrowska 2006: 177–372.

22 Case C-236/01 *Monsanto v Italy* [2003] ECR I-8105, para 109.

23 See the analysis of Corkin 2006, Section V 2 C: 504 ff. Cases T-366/03 and T-235704 *Land Oberösterreich and Austria v Commission of the EC* [2005] ECR-II 4005.

24 Case C-236/01 *Monsanto v Italy* [2003] ECR I-8105, para 109.

25 For instructive details cf van den Daele 2007.

'into conformity with its obligations under the SPS Agreement', effectively asking the EU to complete the approval process for the outstanding applications.

Equally indirect and effective was the panel's critique of the autonomy, which Member States of the EU feel entitled to claim when resorting to 'safeguard measures'. The national bans on the marketing and import of EU-approved biotech products imposed in France, Germany, Austria, Italy, Luxembourg and Greece were found to be incompatible with WTO law. This conclusion was based on the panel's understanding of a proper handling of these measures under European law. The panel did not question the approval procedures, which allow individual EU Member States to impose SPS measures that differ from EU-wide measures, but opined that, after the EU's scientific committee had already assessed the risks of the biotech products and judged them to be safe, the challenged EU Member States had not undertaken risk assessments in line with the requirements of the SPS Agreement that would 'reasonably support the prohibition'. WTO law as specified in the risk assessment provisions of the SPS Agreement governs. National bans can be accepted only if based on an SPS-compliant risk assessment.

2.2.3 *'Sound science and the market'*

The opening of national markets is dependent on the establishment of transnational regimes ensuring the trustworthiness of free trade with complex and potentially hazardous products. This observation remains valid. The WTO panel report can be read as explicitly confirming that the market will always be 'socially embedded'. The type of embeddedness the report advocates is, however, of a specific kind and the regulatory frameworks it is ready to endorse operate with a very limited mandate. The report recognises implicitly the right to introduce new technologies. It follows that reasons must be given for restricting their introduction. Safeguarding important private and public goods, such as the health of consumers, are unquestioned. The restrictions imposed, however, need an objective basis – and science rather than politics provides the grounds on which restrictions can be based. The consumer can feel safe. He is not actively contributing, however, to his regulatory environment: 'sound science' is now the consumer's guardian.

The epistemic community of WTO lawyers will read the report carefully and critically. The EU has decided not to appeal against the panel report – with Commission Trade spokesman Peter Power declaring '[t]he impact of that judgment is entirely of historical interest'.[26] Is the spokesman right? Karl Polanyi not only argued that the liberal project of a disembedded market is purely utopian; he also concluded that the disembedding of socially embedded markets cannot be successful.[27] What will happen next?

26 See <http://www.euractiv.com/en/trade/eu-accepts-trade-ruling-gmos/article-159918>.

27 This is at any rate how Fred Block interprets Polanyi's argument (1992: xxv–xxvii).

BIBLIOGRAPHY

Beckert, J. (2007) 'The Great Transformation of Embeddedness: Karl Polanyi and the New Economic Sociology', MPIfG Discussion Paper 07/1.

Block, F. (2005) 'Towards a New Understanding of Economic Modernity,' in Ch. Joerges, B. Stråth and P. Wagner (eds), *The economy as a polity. The political construction of modern capitalism – an interdisciplinary perspective*, London: UCL Press.

Calliess, Gralff-Peter (2006) *Grenzüberschreitende Verbraucherverträge, Rechtssicherheit und Gerechtigkeit auf dem elektronischen Weltmarktplatz*, Tübingen: Mohr/Siebeck.

Calliess, Gralff-Peter (2002) 'Reflexive transnational law. The privatisation of civil law and the civilisation of private law', *Zeitschrift für Rechtssoziologie* 23(2): 185–216.

Corkin, J. (2006) *A Manifesto for the European Court: Democracy, Decentred Governance and the Process-Perfecting Judicial Shadow*, Ph.D. Thesis EUI Florence.

Dabrowska, P. (2006) *Hybrid solution for Hybrid Products? EU Governance of GMOs*, Ph.D. Thesis EUI Florence.

van den Daele, W. (2007) 'Legal framework and political strategy in dealing with the risks of new technology – the two faces of the precautionary principle', in J. Somsen (ed.), *Regulating Biotechnology*, Cheltenham: Edward Elgar.

European Commission (2006) *Europeans and Biotechnology in 2005: Patterns and trends*, Eurobarometer 64.3.

Gouldner, A.W. (1958) 'Cosmopolitans and Locals: Towards an Analysis of Latent Social Roles', *Administrative Science Quarterly*, 444–80.

Gouldner, A.W. (1957) 'Cosmopolitans and Locals: Towards an Analysis of Latent Social Roles', *Administrative Science Quarterly*, 281–306.

Herwig, A. (2006) 'The Precautionary Principle in Support of Practical Reason: An Argument Against Formalistic Interpretations of the Precautionary Principle', in Ch. Joerges and E.-U. Petersmann (eds), *Constitutionalism, Multilevel Trade Governance and Social Regulation*, Oxford: Hart Publishing, 301–26.

Joerges, Ch. (1997) 'Scientific Expertise in Social Regulation and the European Court of Justice: Legal Frameworks for Denationalized Governance Structures', in Ch. Joerges, K.-H. Ladeur and E. Vos (eds), *Integrating Scientific Expertise into Regulatory Decision-Making. National Traditions and European Innovations*, Baden-Baden: Nomos, 295–324.

Joerges, Ch. (1994) 'Economic Law, the Nation-State and the Maastricht Treaty', in R. Dehousse (ed.), *Europe after Maastricht: an Ever Closer Union?*, Munich: C.H. Beck, 29–62.

Joerges, Ch. and Petersmann, E.-U. (eds) (2006) *Constitutionalism, Multilevel Trade Governance and Social Regulation*, Oxford: Hart Publishing.

Petersmann, E.-U. (2006) 'The WTO Dispute Over Genetically Modified Organisms: Interface Problems of International Trade Law, Environmental Law and Biotechnology Law', in F. Francioni and T. Scovazzi (eds), *Biotechnology and International Law*, Oxford: Hart Publishing, 173–200.

Polanyi, K. (1992) *The Great Transformation: The Political and Economic Origins of Our Time*, Boston: Bacon Press.

Sand, P.H. (2006) 'Labelling Genetically Modified Food: The Right to Know', *Review of European Community & International Environmental Law* 15(2): 185–92.

Shaffer, G.C. and Pollack, M.A. (2005) 'Reconciling (or Failing to Reconcile) Regulatory Differences: The Ongoing Transatlantic Dispute over the Regulation of Biotechnology', in D. Andrews, M.A. Pollack, G.C. Shaffer and H. Wallace (eds), *The New Transatlantic Agenda and the Future of Transatlantic Economic Governance*, Florence: European University Institute, 167–229.

Streit, M. and Mussler, W. (1995) 'The Economic Constitution of the European Community. From "Rome" to "Maastricht",' *European Law Journal* 1: 5–30.

Winickoff, D., Jasanoff, S., Busch, L., Grove-White, R. and Wynne, B. (2005) 'Adjudicating the

GM Food Wars: Science, Risk, and Democracy in World Trade Law', *Yale Journal of International Law* 30: 81–125.

Zarrilli, S. (2006) 'International trade in GMOs: Legal frameworks and Developing Country Concerns', in F. Francioni and T. Scovazzi (eds), *Biotechnology and International Law*, Oxford: Hart Publishing, 231–54.

Index

For Product Safety Concerns and Information please contact our EU
representative GPSR@taylorandfrancis.com
Taylor & Francis Verlag GmbH, Kaufingerstraße 24, 80331 München, Germany

www.ingramcontent.com/pod-product-compliance
Ingram Content Group UK Ltd.
Pitfield, Milton Keynes, MK11 3LW, UK
UKHW022006180926
475701UK00003B/228
* 9 7 8 0 4 1 5 5 4 2 5 2 4 *